Law

a modern introduction
4th edition

Paul Denham, BA, LLB, DMA,
Barrister of the Inner Temple
Senior Lecturer in Law
at The University of Central England
in Birmingham

B.

17 . .J20

WITHDR.

FROM ST

Hodder & Stoughton

A MEMBER OF THE HODDER HEADLINE GROUP

A catalogue record for this title is available from the British Library

ISBN 0 340 70481 0

First published 1983
Second Edition published 1989
Third Edition published 1994
Fourth Edition published 1999
Impression number   10 9 8 7 6 5 4 3 2 1
Year   2002 2001 2000 1999

Copyright © 1999 Paul Denham

All rights reserved. No part of this publication may be reproduced or transmitted in any form or by any means, electronic or mechanical, including photocopy, recording, or any information storage and retrieval system, without permission in writing from the publisher or under the licence from the Copyright Licensing Agency Limited. Further details of such licences (for reprographic reproduction) may be obtained from the Copyright Licensing Agency Limited, of 90 Tottenham Court Road, London W1P 9HE.

Typeset by Multiplex Techniques Ltd, Orpington, Kent.
Printed in Great Britain for Hodder & Stoughton Educational, a division of Hodder Headline Plc, 338 Euston Road, London NW1 3BH by Redwood Books, Trowbridge, Wilts.

CONTENTS

PREFACE TO THE FOURTH EDITION

The fourth edition of this basic legal text for A-level/early undergraduate students has seen its most major reorganisation since the first edition appeared in 1983. With the ever-expanding nature of the law, some sections (such as sexual offences under Crime) have now been dropped, but the essential core of the original text has been retained.

The book has been revised at a time of constitutional and legal change, since the dramatic result of the General Election in May 1997. The previous government did much to change the law, even towards the end of its lifetime at a relatively minor level, such as the establishment of the unified body, the Broadcasting Standards Commission under the Broadcasting Act 1996. But the new administration had soon published White Papers/Bills on devolution of power to Scotland and Wales, and the incorporation of the European Convention on Human Rights into British law; by any standards a radical departure from the past. On the other hand the new government will not change planned reforms to 'control' the escalating legal aid budget, as evidenced in the Lord Chancellor's consultative paper published in February 1998. Also in the earlier part of 1998, at the time of completing this fourth edition, the Government published proposals to reform the jury system in complex fraud trials, thus reviving the Roskill debate of 1986. Meanwhile another debate continues, on implementing the Woolf and Middleton reports, concerning access to justice, whilst the Bowman Report has been published on the organisation of the Court of Appeal.

In June 1998 the Glidewell Report on the CPS was published; in the same month the Court of Appeal made an important decision on occupiers' liability in the case of *Jolley* v. *London Borough of Sutton*. Note should also be made of *R* v. *Powell and English* (1997) 3 WLR 959 where the House of Lords laid down further rules about accessorial liability in crime; *Economides* v. *Commercial Union Assurance plc.* (1997) 3 WLR 1066 which concerned misrepresentation; *Hunter* v. *British Coal Corporation* (1998) 2 All ER 97, a case again illustrating the judicial problems surrounding nervous shock; and *Bolitho* v. *City and Hackney Health Authority* (1997) 3 WLR 1151, being an important House of Lords decision on medical negligence. At the time of completing this script (summer 1998) the Government had promised a substantial White Paper on legal reform (including legal aid) towards the end of the year. A full pardon for Derek Bentley came in 1998 – see *The Times*, 31 July 1998.

I am grateful for the academic assistance given by Jacqueline Martin and Robin Otter, from indeed the first edition onwards. Also, Phillip Charalambous has been of help on the organisation of the book.

The law is stated as at the end of September 1998.

Paul Denham
Cheltenham, December 1998.

ACKNOWLEDGEMENTS

The author and publishers would like to thank the following for permission to reproduce material in this volume.

The Director of Publications at The Stationery Office; The Modern Law Review; The Hansard Society for Parliamentary Government; The Guardian; Butterworths; The Financial Times; Century Hutchinson; and Oxford University Press.

1 One

THE NATURE OF LAW

1.1   Law and society

'If he only knew a little of law, he would know a little of everything.' So said that most quoted of persons – Anonymous. The law affects us all from the moment we are born. We may not like it, but for better or for worse, we live in a society that is bound by rules. Not all these rules are legal ones: many will simply be social conventions. For instance, it is a convention that a man will normally take his hat off in church. But it is a legal rule that one person shall not hit another.

Society, by one means or another, has developed a formal system of rules which are designed to be both observed and enforced. The police and the courts are the principal enforcement agencies. If an individual breaks a legal rule he will be penalised in some way. That is what the law is about: it consists of minimum standards of conduct which all members of society are expected to follow.

The most usual meaning of the phrase 'the law' is that of a legal rule: in other words we might ask 'what is the law concerning theft or trespass or immigration?' Legal rules influence many different aspects of life. Secondly, 'the law' is the complete body of all those individual rules that bind society together. Thirdly, the phrase may also mean the process by which rules are made and applied. The development, the content and the application of those rules add up to a *legal system*, complete with judges, courts, solicitors, barristers, police and indeed politicians in their role as law-makers (legislators).

For some people contact with the 'law' may have unfriendly overtones. At the worst it may mean prison. It might mean the expense of hiring a lawyer. It might mean the sheer frustration of trying to establish what a particular legal rule means in an everyday context, for legal language is often – if the pun can be excused – a 'law unto itself'. Law in that sense, it could be argued, needs to be avoided or at the very least kept at a distance.

In fact, far from being remote, the law, as indicated above, affects every citizen at many points in his life. We marry, we inherit property, we die with or without making a will. We make almost daily contracts or agreements, if only in the purchase of a minor item of food. We park on yellow lines. All these activities are subject to rules that society has intended to be legally binding.

But the law does not stand still. The public's attitudes and habits do change, human nature being an odd mixture of both the rational and the irrational, of both conservatism and radicalism. The legal system – including judicial outlook – has to accommodate itself to such shifts in the climate of opinions. This was clearly reflected, for example, in the changing nature of the law of contract and the law of tort from the late nineteenth century onwards (tort covers a range of civil wrongs – from defamation to negligence). Recent generations have come to expect a greater degree of governmental and parliamentary interference than our Victorian forefathers ever encountered. The era of economic free-wheeling as epitomised by the Industrial Revolution has probably gone for all time. Truism as it may sound, we live in a technological and complex society. Nowadays the emphasis is much more upon regulation and standardisation and upon fairness and equality of opportunity, or at least until the advent of Thatcherism. As P. S. Atiyah has put it in respect of the development of the law of contract, the eighteenth and nineteenth centuries were the heyday of the theories of natural law and the philosophy of laissez-faire – in short it was up to individuals to make what agreements they willed, it was a fundamental right so to do, the State had no place in commercial bargaining. In that period the judge merely acted as a kind of umpire, who would step into the breach when something went wrong. Not so today: the making of a contractual agreement is far more closely regulated. In a similar vein J. G. Fleming has noted that both Parliament and the judiciary were not enthusiastic about extending the boundaries of the law of tort, for fear of opening up a Pandora's box of litigation. Only in the twentieth century have certain tortious liabilities, such as negligent misstatements, been clearly established by the legislators and the courts.

In the last half century or so it is Parliament that has become the most important source of legal rules. And in an age of one person, one vote, in a time of almost total adult literacy, it can be argued that parliamentary law is shaped by public opinion, whether in a general sense or in the representative form of pressure groups and political parties. The public also plays its part in other areas of the law: for example it is the contemporary jury that can redefine the parameters of certain types of legal 'morality', whether in defamation cases or in cases brought under the Obscene Publications Act 1959 or in other matters, such as the *Gay News* trial in 1977, the first prosecution for blasphemous libel in fifty years.

The law, therefore, is by no means a static, rigid structure, despite having, on occasion, a popular image to that effect. On the contrary, the legal system is full of contrasting colours, many of them of a political hue. From time to time the law must embrace freshly defined values and codes of behaviour. Nonetheless the law may move slowly: change, whether societal or legal, is not necessarily rapid. The legal system is rooted in political compromise, at least where it attempts to pursue the twin yet contradictory goals of stability and change. In the end, of course, it is for Parliament (or rather the government's parliamentary majority) to decide where the balance, if any, should be struck.

1.2   The modern political
system

Without doubt the British parliamentary process is one of the most celebrated in the Western world, although whether that particular model sufficiently copes with today's economic problems is entirely another matter. However, it is *democratic* – the adult population over many decades has acquired the right to elect its representatives for a maximum period of five years at national level; governments may come and governments may go, but the democratic system continues. In the United Kingdom the basis of the system is a Parliament elected by those over eighteen years of age who turn out to vote (about 75 per cent). The party which wins the most seats, but not necessarily most votes (as in 1951 and February 1974), forms a government for up to five years until the next general election.

But while Parliament and the government remain the focal points of the British system, it is equally important to remember that like other states, especially in the Western world, Britain is a pluralistic society. Power is dispersed; it rests with the voter, with political activists, with people in positions of key influence – the so-called Establishment, with big business, with senior civil servants, trade unionists, as well as pressure groups and political parties, plus, of course, MPs and ministers. Moreover, other events, frequently external, will all combine to affect the workings of government, such as the devaluation of sterling in 1967, the crisis of oil prices in 1973 and 1979, the miners' strike of 1974, the industrial difficulties of 1978, the Falklands War in 1982, the Gulf War of 1990.

Politics, it is often thought, is about choices and the allocation of resources, and as Bismarck, the famous German leader in the nineteenth century, was reputed to have said, politics is the art of the possible. In the United Kingdom voters consider the success or failure, frequently in economic terms, of the government of the day and cast their votes accordingly at the next election. However, it should be recalled that it is by no means a majority of the voting electorate, let alone of the total electorate, which votes a government into or out of office; under the British electoral system it is quite likely that a government will be elected with a large majority of seats on a minority of the votes, as Mrs Thatcher's 'decisive' win in 1983 well illustrated, where the anti-government votes were almost equally divided between two principal Opposition groupings, and as did Mr Blair's 179 seat majority on 45 per cent of the popular vote in 1997.

Politics is about how people live and work together, and it is about the cohesion of a complicated, technological society. It is concerned with achieving agreed goals, agreeing on the route to realise those goals and, from time to time, reviewing objectives. Equally, political life is about disunity, disagreements, revolts, revolutions and the use of military force.

In the United Kingdom political activity is regulated by a law-making body. As long as there is free debate and a relatively open society, the laws that the representative body passes are usually expected to be obeyed. This poses a problem for those who violently disagree with a particular law, such as coal miners in respect of the laws on picketing during the 1984–85 miners' strike. Naturally, a very powerful government with no democratic base, could imprison its most trenchant critics; there are numerous examples, past and present, of dictatorships that do precisely that. In totalitarian systems there is far less open political activity: criticism of the government is regarded as anti-State behaviour and all opposition is, at worst, ruthlessly suppressed, or, at best, ignored.

In respect of disobeying the law, one former Prime Minister had this to say. On the *Panorama* programme on BBC1 in 1982, James Callaghan endorsed the TUC's day of illegal, secondary action in support of the National Health Service workers saying: 'If the law is a bad law, there is always a contingent right to take action that you would otherwise not take.' But 10 years before, in 1972, he had said in Parliament:

The rule of law is upheld and should be upheld by all political parties. Political parties in a democracy live and survive by the acceptance of the law by the nation as a whole. The advice . . . on bad laws is this: accept the law and change the Government, so that the law itself can be changed.

A further important point is that in a Western political system, such as Britain's, the concept of democracy is deeply embedded, and has been over the past hundred years or so, at many different levels in society. The most important element remains the election of a Parliament and drawn from that a government at national level, although as indicated above a government can often be elected on a minority of the votes. Voters are given some kind of choice and political parties compete for power. But elections also occur at local government level, primarily in counties and districts. And democracy operates in other areas of life, too, such as trade unions and local clubs or associations and at shareholders' meetings in companies; in these organisations it is not always a simple majority that is required. For example, in order to achieve change, such as a constitutional amendment, the rules of the body concerned may demand a weighted majority like two-thirds or three-quarters.

In an economically and socially complex country, such as the United Kingdom, densely populated with 55 million people, there can be no true or moral democracy. Democracy here is indirect, representatives are elected for one reason or another and each voter hopes the promises representatives make, and the way in which representatives use their discretion, will match the voter's own political aspirations. This, however, will never work out fully in practice. Given the size of the population, the difficulty of ascertaining majority opinion on all issues, the fact that governments are there to lead as well as to follow opinion, the problems of detailed technical issues and of unexpected events, such as a run on sterling, or a war, no voter will ever be completely satisfied. Democracy may be about fulfilling people's wishes, or at least the desires of the majority, but politics is concerned with compromise and achieving what appears to those elected to be sensible, just and proper, and in the case of the central government what is 'in the national interest'. Hence the moral dilemma that arises when the governing party in

Parliament passes laws which displease not only the minority but also elements of the majority. On the other hand, the government governs and currently Parliament legislates for all parts of the United Kingdom, including, since 1972, Northern Ireland. If there were not some degree of social unity and political consensus (if only about the rules of the game), the centralised state, even if the nation is geographically small, would be a political non-starter. Of course, the 'unitary' constitution has been under challenge, as the Kilbrandon Report on devolution in 1973 graphically illustrated, the issue on which James Callaghan's government fell in 1979, and an issue to which the new Labour government of 1997 has immediately returned.

Is it possible to satisfy the electoral minority? There are several considerations. Firstly, if special rules are made for minority rights, might not the minority become tyrannical in respect of the majority? Special provision, such as positive discrimination in law on behalf of racial minorities, might deprive the majority of its political wishes. Such positive discrimination in the broadest, American sense (for example legislating that the Metropolitan Police must have, say, a 15 per cent black quota) has never appeared on the political agenda, notwithstanding 'race' riots in Bristol (1980), London and Liverpool (1981) and Birmingham (1985) and a judicial inquiry into the London (Brixton) disturbances (Lord Scarman's Report). Equally, a majority can behave tyrannically towards a minority; history is littered with examples, such as the early settlers to America who were forced to emigrate because of religious persecution. These were problems that taxed, for example, the mind of the famous nineteenth-century philosopher, John Stuart Mill. Secondly, as stated above, governments in this country can easily be elected, given the nature of the British electoral system, by a minority of the total vote, let alone of the total electorate. Thirdly, majority public opinion is constantly shifting; it is not easy to identify, despite the frequent use of opinion polls. What may be a 'majority' at election time can, within months, become a clear minority, as far as support for the government and its policies (or lack of them) is concerned.

AN UNWRITTEN CONSTITUTION?

It is frequently claimed that the British constitution is unwritten. There are no codes, or sets of rules, as in the American case, no fundamental Bill of Rights to which the government is answerable, no Supreme Court, again as in the USA, which can strike down actions of the Executive. It is true that apart from Israel and to a more limited extent New Zealand we live, alone among the developed nations, by political custom and convention. But it is frequently forgotten that much has been written down; it is more accurate to say that the constitution is partly unwritten.

Vernon Bogdanor wrote in 1997:

the successful working of the British Constitution rested on contingent factors – it presupposes a deferential and homogeneous society divided by class. In such a society most voters will find themselves in

effect represented by just two parties, one broadly social democratic, the other broadly capitalist; and they will be happy for politicians to take decisions on their behalf. A society of this kind existed between the 1940s and the Seventies, but it has now passed away. Our political system thus needs to be refashioned to meet the needs of a new society. The point today is not to reinterpret the British Constitution, but to change it.

Even if a constitution is partly written, that may leave the political process in a rather uncertain condition. On the other hand, just because the political rules are neatly set out in a series of documents, it does not mean to say that political life becomes easier or more efficient. In the first place, those rules may be conveniently ignored by the governing power. In the second there is always the problem of interpretation, whether by the executive (government) or the judiciary or other institutions. Thirdly, a written constitution may over-formalise the political process; the British, it appears, are born pragmatists – it is best, they might say, to deal with problems as they arise, rather than develop a theoretical framework and adopt elaborate solutions for future difficulties that may never materialise.

The late Professor John P. Mackintosh has written:

It is often said that Britain has an unwritten Constitution, but this is true only in the sense that rules guiding the system are not set out in a single document with a special procedure required for amending these rules, as was done in the United States. But a great number of these rules are written and embodied in Acts of Parliament such as the Representation of the People Act [1983], which prescribes the arrangements for holding elections, or the Parliament Acts of 1911 and 1949 which set out some of the relations between the House of Lords and the House of Commons. Other aspects of the system which are not laws but are established practices (such as the convention to form a government) are written down in many books on British politics. It is not illegal to break these established practices but if a serious attempt to avoid them occurred, it would indicate that profound changes were taking place in the whole system. Again, there is another category of practices, examples being the way the Cabinet is organised or parliamentary candidates selected, which are neither law nor established conventions but are simple convenient methods of procedure whose change would involve no major shake-up in the process of government. It might even be some time before such changes were noticed.

The difficulty in producing an accurate and comprehensive account of these laws, conventions and practices is partly that they are scattered over the history of the country from the Habeas Corpus Act of 1679 which prevents people being held in prison without trial and the convention that the Queen will not veto legislation, which has been built up since 1708, to recent changes in parliamentary procedure dealing with the control of public expenditure. In part, the difficulty is that situations which call for the application of certain conventions may be few and far between. Thus how far a convention would apply today may not be absolutely clear while some conventions (such as 'the collective responsibility of ministers') may have changed their actual content or meaning though the words used remain the same. As a result, to try and describe the British Constitution is like trying to explain the working of an ancient university with its old statutes, more recent regulations, traditions begun for one purpose but still useful for another where new students and teachers are continually altering current practice.

It is because of the ancient origins of many of the laws and conventions of the Constitution that books on British government often start with an historical section. However, it is not essential to go back into history because most of the conventions, practices and maxims which have been inherited either date from the late nineteenth century or were in operation then. Also it is important not just to list the various acts or to describe how Parliament or the Civil Service developed, but to show their interconnections. Each part of the machinery of government can only be understood in terms of the other cogwheels with which it must intermesh and many of the maxims or descriptions are only meaningful if they can be seen in relation to the whole system in operation at the time when the conventions became established.

Certainly, as Mackintosh indicated, the modern British political process has developed over a long period of time; unlike many other systems, it is rooted in history. That makes an academic analysis or description difficult, since the nature of the British system, with its largely unwritten constitution, is circular – begin at one point and the reader may find he has to back-track.

In many ways the British electorate takes its system for granted. It is often assumed that Westminster is the mother of many parliaments; if it is, it has given birth to some rather embarrassing offspring. Also, to many British people, strangely, and rather cynically, politics is a dirty business. Politicians are assumed to be in the business only for their own profit. Conversely, the standards of public life seemed to be high, at least as far as the Salmon Report was concerned in 1976. But a rather different picture was painted by the first Nolan Report of 1995 on standards in public life (arising out of the 'cash for questions' saga at Westminster) and the second Nolan Report in 1996 on standards in local public spending bodies, as well as the Scott Report of 1996 (the arms-to-Iraq/Matrix Churchill public interest immunity inquiry). Corruption is not endemic as in many developing countries or certain totalitarian regimes, although one notorious corruption scandal at local level concerned West Wiltshire District Council in 1989-90 over the privatisation of its computer software group. The third Nolan Report in 1997, on misuse of public office, looked at corruption in local government. A new Code of Conduct for Members of Parliament was prepared following the first Nolan Report (the

Committee on Standards in Public Life) (see the report of the Select Committee on Standards and Privileges in 1996; for the work of select committees in general see the report of the House of Commons Liaison Committee in 1997).

That does not mean to say, however, that an 'old boy network', patronage and the Establishment, for want of better words, do not exist, or do not combine to exert powerful political influences. And if the popular perception is that politics is rather a grubby business, the law, in contrast, pure and simple, is relatively untainted. Judges (as opposed, perhaps, to solicitors) enjoy prestige – they, unlike politicians, appear to most people to be fair and scrupulous. Yet, paradoxically, judges frequently only apply the laws made by politicians. As already indicated, the most important source of law nowadays is parliamentary law – an Act of Parliament. Of course, some Acts are overtly political, like legislation which denationalises an industry. Other laws are lawyers' law, not politicians' law as such; a measure which reforms the systems of claims for personal injuries, for example, would not be the subject of bitter party dispute.

Hitherto the stability of the system and its seemingly endless capacity to cope with change in an orderly and gradual manner have been assumed. Such, it is popularly said, is the traditional and major selling-point of British politics. Indeed gradual change is very much the key phrase in the evolution of the Westminster Parliament itself, and although it would be futile to deny that there are other important political groups and institutions besides Parliament in a modern industrial society, nevertheless Westminster still plays a crucial part in decision-making. There remains an element of pride among the electorate in the fact that Parliament has survived so many crises in history.

PARLIAMENT AND GOVERNMENT

The distinguishing features of British politics are, then, a Parliament which legislates (or has legislated) for the whole of the United Kingdom, including Northern Ireland, whose domestic legislature, Stormont, was suspended in 1972. The British state is thus correctly described as a unitary or centralised one, yet it also possesses a formidable system of local government, although the latter's financial powers were curbed by Mrs Thatcher's Government.

There is little in the way of regional government, and little English demand for it. However, the question of domestic assemblies for Scotland and Wales – the 'devolution question' – was an important issue in the mid-1970s, although following public referenda in those two countries, the proposed bodies were aborted in 1979. But devolution of power away from Westminster, and towards Wales and Scotland in particular, is by no means off the political map, as evidenced by the work of the unofficial Scottish Convention, and its prominence as an issue in the 1992 and 1997 general elections. Northern Ireland, however, is a rather different case, with its own special problems since the partition of Ireland in 1922. Parts of the Irish community have never accepted a divided Ireland, and the relentless activity of the IRA from 1954-62 and then more particularly since 1969, and most notably in 1972, underlines that fact, notwithstanding the change in the political climate following the Downing Street Declaration in 1993 (between Mr John Major and Mr Albert Reynolds, the Republic's Taoiseach) and the Framework Document of 1995 after the IRA and paramilitary Unionists' 'ceasefires' of 1994.

The terms 'Parliament' and 'government' are frequently used in the same breath, since in Britain there is no true separation of powers as in the USA. The government is usually and largely formed from the leading figures of the majority party in the House of Commons. But it is the government which proposes and Parliament which disposes. Most of the legislation that Parliament passes is initiated by the government. Legislation is, however, the result of many influences (as discussed in Chapter 2).

Parliament is concerned not only with legislation, important though that function is: there is other business to accomplish, such as general debates. Moreover, while Parliament is supposedly supreme, and may achieve whatever it wishes to achieve, there are political limitations. Very often, Parliament allows ministers to fill in the fine print of legislation – ministers are given authority in certain instances to make their own rules (delegated or secondary legislation). Also, by convention Parliament has little say in the conduct of foreign affairs, the Saturday debate on the Falklands crisis in 1982 being a notable exception. Nor, by custom, does Parliament scrutinise in detail the operations of the secret intelligence services. However, whether day-to-day government should be more open is entirely another matter, as underlined by the Open Government White Paper in 1993.

Ministers are responsible to Parliament for their actions and those of their civil servants. But whether answerability entails resignation from office is very doubtful nowadays, examine the Crichel Down affair in 1954 (Sir Thomas Dugdale), the Falklands War in 1982 (Lord Carrington), the Maze Prison escape in Northern Ireland in 1983 (Mr James Prior) and the Westland affair in 1986 (Mr Michael Heseltine and Sir Leon Brittan). Ministers are also responsible to each other for the conduct of policy. This is collective or Cabinet responsibility. If a minister violently disagrees on an issue, then he should either 'shut up' or 'get out'. But the Cabinet is a leaky ship, and many leaks come from the Prime Minister's own Press Secretary, as seen during the Westland affair. The lobby system, whereby certain accredited journalists have rights of access to ministers and Downing Street, ensures that Cabinet government is never totally confidential: journalists once briefed, albeit off the record, are expected to 'leak' or report. There would not be much point to the lobby system if their lips remained permanently sealed.

'Cabinet government' is a phrase invariably associated with the British parliamentary process. Key decisions are taken in Cabinet, collectively, or more likely in a Cabinet committee (although not always even there, as shown in 1956 during Eden's conduct of the Suez crisis). But at times the image of government by the Cabinet appears to recede: a strong, or paranoiac, Prime Minister may become almost presidential in the conduct of affairs (such as Lloyd George in 1918–22, Harold Wilson in 1966–68 (although a more suspect example) or, more pertinently, Mrs Thatcher throughout her premiership, from 1979 to her political demise in 1990).

Further, it is not only Parliament and the executive whose powers and membership overlap. Parliament also overlaps with the judiciary, for the highest court in the land is the Appellate Committee of the House of Lords, the upper chamber of Parliament.

Moreover, while the Lords is the 'upper chamber' in terms of constitutional tradition, since the passage of the Parliament Acts 1911 and 1949 its powers are quite definitely subordinate to those of the Commons. That two-thirds of its membership are hereditary, a unique enough feature on any political landscape, does not, nowadays, imply that the Conservatives have a majority. Indeed, Conservative governments have on occasion found the House of Lords to be a thorn in the legislative side, as seen in 1980 in respect of the Housing Act, and more particularly in 1991 with the War Crimes Act which was passed only by utilising the mechanisms of the Parliament Acts 1911–49.

Three other points are worthy of note. Firstly, since the turn of the century, and in particular since 1945, there has developed the practice of government intervention in certain industries of key importance to the running of the economy. The public corporation is well known if not always well loved. But under Mrs Thatcher the 'frontiers of the State' were rolled back after 1979 and the government's interests in such familiar organisations as British Gas, British Airways, British Telecom, British Rail, the National Bus Company, the British Airports Authority, British Steel, Rolls-Royce, the electricity and water boards have been removed. On the other hand, the proportion of state spending, that is the proportion of the gross domestic product (GDP) committed to public expenditure, has not substantially altered since Mr Callaghan lost power.

Secondly, the United Kingdom likes to think of itself as a country of free speech, but whether the media are as free as their counterparts in the USA is doubtful. The laws of confidence, libel, contempt and official secrecy are powerful instruments that blunt the otherwise sharp cutting edge of the 'Fourth Estate'. The BBC prides itself on its independence, but being dependent upon the government to determine its income, via the licence fee, it sometimes runs into difficulties on self-censorship, as the row over a television film on Ulster in 1985 clearly demonstrated.

Thirdly, the British political system is based upon competitive party politics. But the electoral system is another issue. For some years the Liberals have been declaring themselves cheated; they accumulate lots of votes by coming second in a constituency, but under the 'first past the post' or 'winner takes all' method, they are denied, they claim, their true representation in Parliament. Proportional representation is now more actively and publicly discussed, but one electoral swallow does not make a political summer. It might need several 'hung' parliaments or lop-sided election results for a change in the voting system to come about, unless the issue is resolved by a national referendum as the new Labour Government appeared to promise in 1997.

1.3   Social change and the law

In terms of substantive law, as opposed to the general background of the legal system, this book is primarily concerned with four major branches – crime, tort, contract and civil liberties (political or constitutional law). All these areas, and others, have been shaped by historical developments. For example the rules governing industrial relations and trade unions have their roots in the campaigns for factory reform, free association and the extension of the right to vote. Sometimes 'advances' were made only after celebrated incidents, such as the Sheffield Outrages in 1866 which led to legislation recognising trade unions' right to exist and the right to strike. But the courts could also have their say – in 1901 the Taff Vale judgment by the House of Lords denied trade unions a right of immunity from being sued for loss of profits, a matter reversed by statute in 1906.

In other words, the economic success of the emergent industrialised state, together with the protection of land-owning and property interests, was paramount to those who wielded power and exercised influence. Such matters took priority over social reform, and Parliament and the courts reflected this attitude.

But with considerable leaps in technology and with the introduction of universal suffrage, the legislators and the judges have become progressively more 'enlightened'. Whilst it may still be difficult and expensive, for instance, to bring an action for civil negligence, it is certainly easier to persuade the courts nowadays than it was at the turn of the century. In the area of contract and consumer protection, the individual has enjoyed greater rights in the past few decades than at any time previously. In the province of crime, sentencing policies are more 'enlightened' than before, as perhaps seen in the Criminal Justice Act 1991, although some might argue too 'soft', as was evidenced by parliamentary criticism in 1987 when several thousand prisoners were granted early release by the Home Secretary in order to ease pressure on overcrowding, the prison population having reached some 51,000.

As economic conditions, with certain major exceptions, have largely improved throughout the twentieth century, so reform and protection of the individual have merited greater attention. For example the Health and Safety at Work Act 1974 imposed legal duties on not only employers, but also employees, manufacturers and subcontractors to use and maintain equipment with proper care; the 1974 Act also gave workers a legal right to participate in safety at work procedures. Housing is another good illustration. Partly because of abuse over the years, reflecting the shabbier side of the 'free market' or economic liberalism, private tenants, although now declining in numbers, have been given extensive rights of protection during the post-war period under the Housing and Rent Acts. 'Rachmanism' in the 1960s was a term of opprobrium in legal and social vocabulary; thus harassment of a tenant by a landlord is now a criminal offence. Landlords' 'rights' were further circumscribed under the Landlord and Tenant Act 1987 which enabled tenants to buy if a landlord decided to sell a block of flats and gave tenants additional rights over their landlords where the latter failed to discharge their responsibilities adequately, for example, over maintenance and insurance. Recently, a still more controversial piece of legislation was passed – the Leasehold Reform, Housing and Urban Development Act 1993.

Conversely, as reflected down the ages, the basic right to enjoy private property has not been disturbed by the courts or Parliament, as seen, for example, in the extensive statutory land reforms of 1925 and, more recently, taken a stage further in the 'right to buy' legislation of 1980 for tenants in the public sector. Moreover, some 50 per cent of the land is still owned by private individuals or organisations. Nationalisation of the land, an idea much discussed in Lloyd George's time, remains a remote concept. On the other hand, the law has changed in terms of planning controls – who builds what, where and when. It is true to say that the United Kingdom benefits from a strict planning regime, although it is equally true to observe that a decision by the Environment Secretary on a controversial planning application can lead to much hue and cry and accusations of manipulation by large commercial interests.

The Second World War had a remarkable impact on social attitudes. Not just in the fields of planning were laws radically changed, but, again, building upon legislation of the inter-war period, Parliament developed the Welfare State, based on the Beveridge scheme. Social security legislation has mushroomed and is now complex, but if individual property rights are sacrosanct, so the laws governing health and social welfare are dismantled at a government's peril. Equally, since the end of the war, society has come to expect companies and the City to behave responsibly, and company and financial services legislation, as reformed in the 1980s, is now wide-ranging, if not still sufficiently comprehensive for some critics, as seen in the Guinness and Maxwell scandals in 1991 and 1992.

And, of course, since 1945 society has also become much more technologically innovative and complicated. So, for example, the Computer Misuse Act 1990 deals with the problem of 'computer hacking' – by section 1 of the Act a person is guilty of an offence if he causes a computer to perform 'any function with intent to secure access to any program or data held in any computer [and] the access he intends to secure is unauthorised'.

It can be seen therefore that economic and political developments, within the capitalist structure, over the past 200 years or so, conditioned by the Industrial Revolution, political upheaval and two World Wars, have left profound marks on the legal condition of society.

CIVIL LAW AND CRIMINAL LAW

English law divides principally into two categories – criminal or public, and civil or private. Criminal law concerns matters deemed by society to be so serious that in the event of a person transgressing a legal rule it is society itself which must punish the wrongdoer. Thus a murderer will be *prosecuted* by the State, that is in the name of the Crown. The case will thus read *R* v. *Smith* (say), *R* standing for *Regina* or *Rex* – the Queen or the King.

Civil law is concerned with disputes between individuals or indeed groups of individuals such as public companies and corporations. Society will lay down the framework of legal rules within which such disputes must be settled. But society itself is not a party to any legal proceedings: it acts more as a referee. So a civil case will read, for example, *Brown* v. *Smith*. Indeed the object of civil law is to compensate the injured party, rather than to punish the 'wrongdoer'. One individual sues another. Farmers who know their law ought to display notices reading 'Trespassers will be sued' rather than 'Trespassers will be prosecuted'!

This appears to imply that in terms of society's morality and values civil matters are less serious or less weighty than criminal issues. And often that is the case: to be sent to prison or to pay a fine is more grave than to be ordered to compensate another person. Yet it need not always be so. Consider, for instance, the following two cases.

Firstly, in 1979 in *Lim Poh Choo* v. *Camden and Islington Area Health Authority* the plaintiff, that is the person aggrieved, was awarded record damages of £229,000 against the defendant (the Health Authority). The plaintiff was a Malaysian doctor who on account of clinical negligence in a minor operation had suffered irreversible brain damage. That was a civil case. At the end of 1985 the sum of £679,264 was awarded to a 16 year-old married woman who had suffered severe permanent brain damage as a result of admitted medical negligence (*Thomas* v. *Wignall*, 1987). Damages in negligence broke the £1 million mark in 1989 when £1.2 million was awarded in a High Court settlement for a university student injured in a car crash near Barnstaple in 1985.

Secondly, in 1982 in *R* v. *Danes* the defendant was prosecuted at Exeter Crown Court for the alleged theft of two pork pies from a Brixham supermarket where he had worked as a cleaner. The total value of the pies was 58p. The defendant was acquitted, but in his summing-up to the jury the judge was at pains to point out that the principle of theft was the same, no matter how great or how small the sum of money involved.

Which was the more 'grave' of the two cases, the civil one or the criminal one?

It should also be added here that there is nothing like unanimity about what activities in life should be subject to legal rules, especially criminal ones. The arguments in favour of the legalisation of cannabis are a familiar enough example. Any legal rule that appears to interfere with a personal freedom is bound to be controversial, but then, logically, all legal rules do precisely that. In July 1982 the former Secretary of State for Education and Science, Mr Mark Carlisle QC, was reported as saying that the introduction of the compulsory wearing of seat belts (under the Transport Act 1981) carried the limits of the criminal law beyond that to which they should be carried; in other words an individual should be free to risk his own personal injury.

It is possible to speak in terms of three branches of the law, the third being constitutional and administrative law. This area of legal rules covers such matters as the powers of Parliament and the government, the powers of the police and the administration of justice, personal freedoms including race relations and immigration, and the freedoms of expression and assembly. The greater part of such administrative law will fall under civil law in the broadest sense and the rest under criminal law. Other countries take a different approach, however. France has a highly developed system of administrative law, quite distinct from the civil and criminal processes. A French citizen who, for example, feels he has a grievance against a government department may take the complaint before a *tribunal administratif*, with a right of appeal to the highest administrative court – the *Conseil D'Etat*.

Many of these branches of the law will be examined in detail in later chapters. But if we think of the law as a mirror of society's values (the mirror might not always be true, though) and if we understand that legal rules do not remain unchanged, then the next obvious step is to look at the very sources of law. Law may reflect what society wishes, but can we pinpoint accurately its origins? That is the matter discussed in Chapters 2 and 3, and those sources, apart from the concept of natural justice, are common law and precedent, parliamentary law, as already alluded to above, equity, and last but not least the growing importance of European law. However, before passing on to those issues, it is also appropriate to look at the philosophy that underpins the law, including such critical concepts as justice, ethics and morality, and whether the writings of such leading academics in this area as Professors Ronald Dworkin and H. L. A. Hart have thrown fresh light on what otherwise may have been regarded as an obscure branch of legal studies.

1.4   Law, justice and morality

Lon Fuller, Harvard Professor of Law, has written in *Anatomy of the Law*:

> **For men to live together successfully they need rules that will keep peace among them, make them deal justly with one another, and enable them to collaborate effectively. Since men are likely to differ about what these rules should be, it is necessary to set up some procedure by which the rules may be authoritatively declared, for example, by enactment of a legislative assembly or by judgment of a court. . . Finally, some incentive to obey the rules must be provided. . . More commonly, the method of law is to impose some kind of unpleasantness on the rule-breaker, who may be fined or sentenced or have an award of damages assessed against him.**

People's behaviour is governed partly through custom, partly through habit, partly through defined values. Sometimes the Latin word 'mores' is used in its literal sense to describe customs and habits generally, and occasionally it is used to describe values too. In addition members of society may be influenced by religious morality, including the doctrines and teaching of the Church, and by ethical principles, such as a doctor pledging to keep his patient's medical confidences. All these things, customs, morality, religious teaching, ethics, habits and values, are up to a point reflected in the legal system.

Moreover, a legal system reflects what society understands to be collective norms – rules of behaviour backed by sanctions in the form of punishment, orders or threats. (Sanctions are often taken to mean punishment, although in a broader sense they might include orders and threats.) Much of a person's conduct will be normative, either socially or legally. An act may be punished by the rest of the community but the punishment is outside the province of the law; if it is 'serious' enough punishment or compensation may be ordered by the courts. Classifying a person's behaviour may not, however, be an easy task. If a young person gives up his seat to a senior citizen on a crowded bus, for instance, can the action be described as a custom or a habit or the manifestation of some kind of ethical principle? It is certainly not a normative rule, in the sense of belonging to a body of substantive law, for no-one could seriously suggest that the young person, on account of his remaining seated, should be prosecuted or sued before the courts. It is hardly likely to be a normative rule in the purely social sense either: he is not under threat of punishment if he keeps his place; he might not be regarded highly by other older passengers, but is hardly likely to be thrown off the bus. On the other hand he might be told to leave the bus if he refuses to take his feet off the opposite seat; and if he refuses to pay the fare, he might face legal action as well as being told to leave.

If he does give up the seat, the action could conceivably be seen in a religious context: acting as a good neighbour. It might even be seen as the carrying out of a moral or ethical principle or perhaps just as a custom in the broadest sense. Morality and ethics, however, usually operate at a different level from custom. It is immoral rather than uncustomary to lie. Telling 'white lies' may attract no sanction; it is not a normative act. But normally telling lies will be subject to a social penalty; indeed telling lies will sometimes make the action the subject of a legal rule – for example, perjury (false evidence given on oath) and fraud. And, of course, telling lies is irreligious.

In contrast, the use of foul language, for example, will probably offend against religious rules and rules of etiquette, but will have little to do with rules of morality, ethics or customs. Distinguishing between ethical and moral rules themselves is difficult. In one sense *ethics* is simply the scientific and academic study of morality, justice, customs and the like. *Ethical rules*, however, are often concerned with standards of conduct in professional life such as teaching, medicine and the law itself. In that sense ethics might be seen as a sub-division of morality. 'Standards of conduct' or 'conventions' are what might be regarded as terms generic to rules of morality, custom, ethics, religion and etiquette.

MORAL OBLIGATION

When considering customs, morality, religious and ethical principles, it is possible to think in terms of the potentiality of legal rules. Thus it is customary not to create nuisances (such as noise or bonfire smoke) that irritate your neighbour. But where the noise or smoke reaches an unreasonable level the social custom becomes a legal rule. While customs, laws and morality can exist independently of each other, they can also be seen as overlapping concepts. Professor Hart noted: 'In all communities there is a partial overlap in content between legal and moral obligation; though the requirements of legal rules are more specific and are hedged round with more detailed exceptions than their moral counterparts.' Samuel Stoljar has observed: 'Thus, contrary to what legal positivists often assert, morality is not just another so-called "source" of law, a source like statute or custom; over a large and central area law is in fact applied morality.' (Legal positivism is examined below.) And as Richard Card has commented, the criminal law is co-extensive with social morality up to a point, but many rules of social morality are not recognised by the criminal law and equally many rules of criminal law have little or nothing to do with social morality in its broadest context. After all, the criminal law means the whole of society – or the State in other words – ranged against the individual on account of his transgressions against that society. Indeed, viewed one way the law can be interpreted as a sub-system of a wider morality. An alternative view is to equate criminal law – as far as possible – with public morality, civil law with private morality since it is essentially concerned with disputes between individuals, and to regard constitutional law as falling outside morality altogether, with religious and ethical codes forming a non-legal, individual morality. But such roughly hewn distinctions leave much to be desired; for instance, judges themselves, the very people who have developed if not manufactured the common law, sometimes admit to being guided by religious principles.

Cutting across all this is the idea of justice – a legal system must both possess fair procedures and apply them equitably. Justice must be seen to be done. Moreover, laws in themselves should be just. But what of laws (Hitlerian or otherwise) that are thought by many or most to be palpably unjust? When can we rightly disobey the law? Such is a question that has exercised the minds of members of the Welsh Language Society, for example, in recent years, and it is an issue to which we shall return.

One person's moral meat may, indeed, be another's judicial or legal poison. The case of *Hurley* v. *Dyke* (1979) adequately illustrates this point. In 1971 a nine year-old three-wheeled Reliant car was purchased at an auction sale in Tewkesbury. The car was in a dangerous condition, but the successful bidder intended to cannibalise it for spares. After the auction a disappointed bidder offered the purchaser another £10 for the vehicle; the purchaser accepted the offer. The second purchaser, who unlike the original seller at auction, the proprietor of a small garage, had no specialist knowledge of cars, drove the Reliant away and was killed a few days later in an accident. His passenger, who now brought the action against the garage owner, Mr Dyke, was permanently maimed. The trial judge awarded Mr Hurley, the passenger, £46,000, but by a majority the Court of Appeal reversed that decision.

The House of Lords held, too, that the seller had not been legally obliged to warn the second purchaser of the car's dangerously defective state. Were moral, ethical or religious considerations an entirely separate issue? For it could conceivably be argued that it was the seller's Christian duty to inform the second purchaser of the relevant facts; or simply that it was immoral not to do so in terms of social standards, that is in terms of what was expected by others in the community; or that if it was not immoral at least it was unethical in terms of good business practice. As stated earlier the distinction between 'moral' and 'ethical' may be slight, but 'ethical' is often applied in a professional context – for example, the doctor–patient relationship. Did such principles lie at the heart of the legal rules the court considered? And as for justice, that had been executed in so far as the highest court in the land had fairly and carefully listened to all the evidence and arguments placed before it. Legal obligation, therefore, is by no means the same as moral obligation. As *Hurley* v. *Dyke* showed, the law, as opposed to morality, is not there to 'spoonfeed' the 'innocent' purchaser.

In *R* v. *Somerset County Council ex parte Fewings* (1995), the County Council had passed a resolution prohibiting stag hunting on certain land it owned. This ban was challenged by the Quantocks Staghounds with regard to the council's powers under s.120 of the Local Government Act 1972. Lord Justice Swinton Thomas made it clear that the morality of hunting was a matter for parliamentary legislation if need be.

At this point it may be appropriate to consider, briefly, what approach the leading figures in the world of legal philosophy – or jurisprudence – adopt in respect of broad concepts such as law, justice and morality.

ALLOTT'S VIEW OF LAW

Antony Allott takes law as that which is made by a political society. Legal rules are frequently made by people as a whole as represented in legislative assemblies. Law very often deals with external conduct, but the more laws are made to regulate thoughts and attitudes the closer will that society have moved towards a totalitarian system. Compliance with legal rules is at the very heart of any legal system; in Western societies non-compliance is dealt with by the courts. As for religion, Allott argues that that too is a normative system, like morality and mores, but also that it is something more than that. For religions, whether Buddhism, Christianity or Islam, usually share one thing in common – they try to account for the reality of the world in a total sense, that the world as we see it is linked to a spiritual world. That link may be symbolised by rituals and practices which go far beyond the mere wearing of robes and wigs by barristers and judges. Compliance may be more difficult to enforce in religion. Morality is a close relation, but can be a more generalised code of behaviour. It is a system for right living, that is frequently shared by an entire community. In that sense it sounds like a legal system; yet on the other hand it is much wider in application, particularly if morality is seen not so much as a community-based system as an individual code – in short a person's conscience. Thus every eventuality in life ought to be covered and compliance with conscience must, of necessity, be total. In contrast mores may simply mean local customs, folk-ways, rituals, etiquette and the like. Mores are almost norms in the purest sense, since they consist of codes of behaviour generally shared by one or more communities. Mores concern external behaviour rather than internal thoughts. Compliance is therefore much more likely to be optional.

THE HART–DEVLIN DEBATE

Of course, where morality and the law, or perhaps more accurately a system of legal rules, clash most frequently – or at least appear to – is in the area of sexual mores. Crime, sin and the law can appear to become hopelessly entangled, as the debate between Lord Devlin and Professor Hart in the 1960s well underlined. For Lord Devlin society required certain moral principles to be observed and therefore even if public opinion was slowly changing, the breach of those principles in the meantime was still an offence against society as a whole and not merely against the injured party. Professor Hart, however, argued strongly for a clearer separation of the law and private morality, morality in the sense that it is a matter for private judgement. Hart rested his case on the nineteenth-century philosophy of the utilitarians and Bentham as built upon by John Stuart Mill, to the effect that a free society is better than a disciplined one, for in the longer term that condition leads to a greater good for all.

The 'grey' areas of law and morality have usually centred around such matters as abortion, homosexuality, suicide, bigamy, drugs, pornography, incest and euthanasia. It is notable that in respect of the first three 'offences', total or partial decriminalisation has now taken place – in the liberal decade of the 1960s (under the Abortion Act 1967, the Sexual Offences Act 1967 and the Suicide Act 1961 respectively). Nonetheless Professor Hart conceded that in general terms a society could not exist without a form of morality which mirrored and supplemented the law's proscription of conduct injurious to others. Without that particular kind of morality society itself, Hart argued, would not survive. Morality in that context meant shared beliefs as to what was fundamentally right and wrong; thus murder would probably appear at the top of most people's list of proscribed behaviour. To preserve life would count as one of Hart's 'universal values'. Outside of those universal values individual diversity, as Mill recognised, might abound. But for Lord Devlin the greater emphasis was upon the use of the law to preserve and protect the moral essentials of society.

DEVLIN'S 'KEY' PRINCIPLES

Lord Devlin saw four key principles that legislators had to bear in mind when distinguishing between those moral offences which ought to be prohibited by law and those which ought not. The maximum individual freedom that was to be allowed must be consistent with the integrity of society. The limits of such toleration were not static. Privacy must be respected as far as possible. And the law was generally concerned with minimum rather than maximum standards of behaviour. Furthermore disgust, intolerance and indignation were all forces behind the moral law.

But this latter point raises a difficulty: who exactly is to express views about disgust and about what is tolerable and what is not? Here the reasonable, right-minded individual could be taken to exhibit higher or at least different intellectual standards compared with the average or common individual, with the person plucked at random from that notorious bus. The juror may well be the so-called average person on his or her way to Clapham, but equally the juror delivers a verdict only after due deliberation, argument and instruction. To place the decision as to what is moral virtue in the hands of right-minded or enlightened people smacks of Aristotle's autocratic society – a society ruled by wise men. The riddle is that the 'common man' must be wise himself in order to decide who constitutes a wise man. In any case enlightened people frequently end up disagreeing among themselves, not least in respect of formulating moral and ethical principles.

Enlightened people can be a mixture of conservatives and radicals as much as the rest of society, the conservatives being those who want to preserve all that is good in the law, the radicals being those who put a greater emphasis on moving the law to a new position. Was it then enlightened people in general or radicals alone who were instrumental in changing the law on such matters as the burning of witches at the stake and the hanging of murderers? Or, more crudely, was it simply that legislators enjoy a higher standard of education than the bulk of the population? Lord Devlin has hinted strongly that that is so; the educated man is not unrelated to the 'right-minded man.'

Nonetheless as Basil Mitchell has remarked, it is sensible not to discount the opinions of the ordinary man, pejorative as that phrase may be. Public opinion is – as indicated earlier – very relevant to the content of the law. For democratic reasons at least public opinion should be heeded and for pragmatic reasons the gap between the law and common morality should never become too large, otherwise the law, in short the legal rules of society, will not be truly effective if it either jumps too far ahead or lags too far behind the general state of public opinion. Legislators may lead in the process of law-giving and judicial figures may do likewise in the process of interpreting the rules, but in so doing both need on occasion to glance over their shoulder. Only in that way can legislation be formulated on the basis of rational political and moral arguments. Professor Hart would add that where 'moral offences', some of which may be religious in origin (for example artificial contraception, surrogate parenthood and test-tube fertilisation), cannot be given secular rationalisation or justification, because injury or suffering is not caused to others or some well-defined social aim (for example, rooting out bribery or corruption) is absent – in broad terms the utilitarian argument – then such offences cannot be given the backing of legal sanction. To do so would be to travel too far down the paternalistic path. In a modern legal system the pendulum would have swung too far from liberalism towards conservatism. Lord Devlin, on the other hand, would argue that law and public morality are too interdependent to be easily separated; unsupported by public morality the law would become inoperative and that in any case the law is allowed to preserve morality where it is essentially safeguarding the very existence of society. Indeed, as Basil Mitchell has noted, the Hart–Devlin arguments in many ways have centred around Mill's form of liberalism, in the sense that Mill argued that only in a free society could new discoveries be made in morals as in other spheres and could old truths be kept simultaneously and effectively alive. Certainly Mill's belief would be close to Professor Hart's position, even where Hart talked about the basic 'universal values' of each society, that is a clearly shared morality that binds society together. In part this relates to what Hart called 'the minimum content of Natural Law' – natural law is discussed below.

The difficulties in the relationship between law and morality in the context of the debate on abortion and euthanasia were examined in a recent work, *Life's Dominion*, by Professor Ronald Dworkin. Dworkin has argued that the conflict between the 'pro-life'/anti-abortion movement and the 'pro-choice' groups is not 'the clash of absolutes' as often portrayed. Dworkin, the liberal philosopher, claims that essentially we all share the same ideal, that human life is sacred, whether the sacredness comes from a Creator or is to be seen in art and human culture. Dworkin says that to keep a baby alive without a brain, or to ignore the wish to die of an old person racked with Alzheimer's disease, is in fact to deny the sacredness of life. There are, however, according to Dworkin, two conflicting positions, the 'goal of conformity' which attempts to compel individuals to 'obey rules and practices that the majority believes best express and protect the sanctity of life', and the 'goal of responsibility' that requires citizens to 'recognise that fundamental intrinsic values are at stake in such decisions and decide reflectively, not out of immediate convenience but out of examined conviction'. Dworkin, as the liberal, favours the second goal.

Similar issues arose in the case of *Airedale NHS Trust* v. *Bland* (1993). Here the patient, aged 17, was very seriously injured in the Sheffield Hillsborough football tragedy in 1989. His lungs were crushed and oxygen to his brain interrupted, with the result that he was left in a persistent vegetative state (PVS). The House of Lords upheld the decision of the High Court and Court of Appeal that it was lawful to discontinue life-sustaining treatment, including the termination of ventilation, nutrition and hydration by artificial means. In the Court of Appeal, Sir Thomas Bingham, the Master of the Rolls, observed:

> **The present appeal raises moral, legal and ethical questions of a profound and fundamental nature, questions literally of life and death. . . . Strong and sincerely held opinions have been expressed both in favour of the decision under appeal and against it. . . . [The case] is not about euthanasia, if by that it meant the taking of positive action to cause death. It is not about putting down the old and infirm, the mentally defective or the physically imperfect. It has nothing to do with the eugenic practices associated with fascist Germany. The issue is whether artificial feeding and antibiotic drugs may lawfully be**

withheld from an insensate patient with no hope of recovery when it is known that if that is done the patient will shortly thereafter die.

In the House of Lords, where Lord Browne-Wilkinson called upon Parliament to clarify the law, Lord Mustill concluded:

But even if *Bolam* is left aside, I still believe that the proposed conduct is ethically justified, since the continued treatment of Anthony Bland can no longer serve to maintain that combination of manifold characteristics which we call a personality. . . . In particular we cannot know whether [a spiritual essence] perishes with death or transcends it. Absent such knowledge we must measure up what we do know. So doing, I have no doubt that the best interests of Anthony Bland no longer demand the continuance of his present care and treatment. This is not at all to say that I would reach the same conclusion in less extreme cases, where the glimmerings of awareness may give the patient an interest which cannot be regarded as null. The issues, both legal and ethical, will then be altogether more difficult.

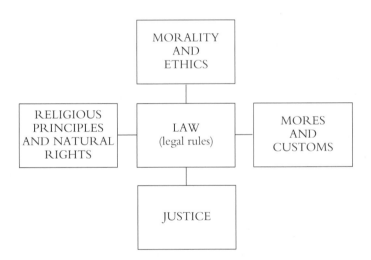

FIGURE 1 *Legal Concepts*

THE PURPOSES OF LAW

Perhaps, therefore, before turning to other jurisprudential concepts and to the thoughts of other legal philosophers, it might be useful to pause at this point and sum up what the main purposes and features of the law appear to be.

1   Law exists to enforce public order and to protect individuals and their property.

2   Law must protect the institutions of society, and not just the visible ones like Parliament itself, but invisible ones – like the institution of marriage.

3   Most laws (or legal rules) are today made by Parliament. But parliamentary law in turn reflects competing political philosophy, public opinion, the influences of pressure groups, the reports and recommendations of official committees, and established social conventions. Legislation is the result of such factors.

4   Established social conventions and norms are the reflection of religion, mores and morality and here the relationship between many normative rules and the law becomes difficult. Where such a convention or norm can be judged to be a 'universal value' then the law may protect it. Free speech is one such value although it is limited by certain rules such as defamation. As a result the law may be paternalistic on occasion (for instance, in respect of the race relations legislation and the obscenity laws).

5   Individual privacy and freedom should be both respected and upheld in any system of democratic law. This point was developed by Bentham and Mill and the utilitarian school of thought. For they emphasised the rational, secular approach to law-making: moral values could only be reflected in law where the individual was still able to enjoy maximum freedom. But such freedoms had to be compatible with the freedom of the majority; thus the doctrine of utility or utilitarianism meant that society's greatest good was the greatest happiness of the greatest number.

6   The law should nonetheless take account of the views of the minority; as Mill himself foresaw, a majority can still be tyrannical towards others.

7   Laws can only be effectively implemented where by and large they command the respect of most reasonable or right-thinking people. Otherwise the law will become an ass and fall into disrepute, a point made by the Vice-Chancellor (of the Chancery Division), Sir Nicolas Browne-Wilkinson, in the hearings on the 'Wright Case' in 1987, where the Government sought injunctions banning the publication of *Spycatcher*, the memoirs of a former MI5 officer now living in Australia.

8   Where the function of the law is to punish it should do so fairly and equitably.

An alternative formulation of the functions of law comes from Robert Summers, in *The Technique Element in Law*. He puts forward five functions: to remedy grievances; to prohibit and prosecute forbidden behaviour; to promote certain defined activities, such as marriage; to manage various governmental public benefits such as education and welfare; and to give effect to certain private arrangements between members of society. A less complimentary view was put forward by Karl Marx – the function of legal rules is primarily to reinforce the existing class structure by which the dominant class controls and manipulates the rest.

JUSTICE

The difficult relationship between law and morality, and to a lesser extent between law, mores and religion has been illustrated. But so far little has been said about the concept of justice. It is certainly not a simple concept. However, as has already been stated we can talk about justice in two main senses.

Firstly, justice is about the fair application of legal rules. When, for example, two parties are before a court, it is axiomatic to judicial proceedings that each must be given a fair hearing. And it would be wrong for one of those parties (whether two individuals or the State versus an individual) to act as a judge of his own cause. Both those principles belong to what is known as 'natural justice'. Moreover, the courts have over the years evolved their own rules of evidence to ensure that a fair trial takes place. For example, when a jury in a criminal case sits, the judge will invariably tell its members that it is the judge's job to interpret the law and that it is the jurors' job to decide upon the facts. If therefore an argument between counsel for the prosecution and defence develops over a point of law or a procedural difficulty, then the jury is sent out, for their minds should not be coloured by matters that are not directly their concern and which may involve frank exchanges between judge and counsel about witnesses and the defendants.

The type of justice that is concerned with settling disputes as fairly, equitably or reasonably as possible could be called *commutative justice*. Yet strictly speaking it would be accurate to think in terms of commutative justice as applying to civil law, in the sense that 'commutative' relates to changing the nature of obligations or at least changing the balance of those obligations in respect of the parties in dispute. For the object of civil law is rarely to punish, but to adjudicate between individuals within the framework of legal rules that society has formulated over a period of time. In contrast one object of criminal law is to punish the wrongdoer. In that sense the justice that is applied there may be termed punitive justice. However, 'punitive' in common parlance can mean 'excessive'; *retributive justice* is therefore a more satisfactory term.

Secondly, justice is concerned with content. Laws should be fair and reasonable in themselves, *per se*; it is not just a matter of applying rules reasonably, whatever those rules might be, it is also about making society a fairer and more reasonable place in which to live. Such justice may be called *distributive justice* since it is about the distribution of obligations and opportunities in society. Of course, this kind of debate takes us into the broader perspectives of social and political justice. This has been dwelt upon at some length by the American moral philosopher John Rawls, in his major work *A Theory of Justice*. There he has explored such matters as opportunity, wealth and poverty, political power, international relations and war.

It was also an issue which Aristotle considered at some length. In Book V of his *Ethics* he distinguished two senses of the term justice: a broader sense, in which it is equated simply to obedience to the law; and a narrower sense, in which it means fairness in the distribution of good things, and in the correction of wrongs done by one person to another. The first type of justice he called universal justice, 'laid down from the point of view of education for the common good'. The second he termed particular justice and divided into 'distributive' and 'remedial'; the former was 'manifested in the distribution of honours, wealth or whatever else is divisible among those who enjoy citizen rights and which can be held by men in unequal proportions'. The latter was 'manifested in the adjustment of balance in transactions between man and man'. Thus 'all that is unfair is unlawful', Aristotle claimed, 'but not all that is unlawful is unfair.'

> **Remedial justice is twofold, for transactions are a) voluntary [such as sale, purchase and loans] and b) involuntary, the latter being either (i) clandestine [such as theft and adultery] or (ii) violent [such as assault, imprisonment, murder, robbery with violence and insult].**

ETHICS

The reference here to social justice in the wider context raises a related point about the concept. Justice is not the monopoly of the courts and of rules that have been developed directly by Parliament and the common law. In the first place there is a form of quasi-justice which is to be found in administrative law (*administrative justice*). As we have seen earlier there are today a range of tribunals and 'ad hoc' bodies whose authority is to be found almost always in statutory law but whose disciplines are quite distinct and separate from the ordinary courts, such as the Employment Appeal Tribunal and the immigration tribunals.

Secondly, there is what may be called *ethical justice*, another form of quasi-justice. A number of professional bodies have their own codes of behaviour or ethics. For example, the General Medical Council (the GMC) has powers for striking errant doctors off the professional list, with all the consequences of disgrace and loss of job. This ethical code may be 'private'. If, for example, a male doctor has sex with his patient in the surgery, he may be struck off the list, but the law will not in that context be concerned, unless it is a case of assault or rape, or the patient is under 16, if female, or 18, if male. If, however, the doctor has revealed the nature of his discussions with his patient to a third person, the law of confidence may have something to say on the matter – the ethical code becomes 'public', in short a positive legal rule. The Football Association (the FA) has powers to fine or suspend soccer players for unseemly behaviour on the pitch. The Church of England has its own ecclesiastical courts for dealing with immoral clergymen.

Lastly, *justice must always be seen to be done* (see below, Chapter 2.4). Sometimes, however, the courts feel it is desirable to hold a hearing in secret; thus in 1984 the trial of an MI5 officer (*Attorney-General* v. *Bettaney*) was conducted largely *in camera* on account of the sensitive nature of the charges under the Official Secrets Act. In the Queen's Bench Division pre-trial hearings are conducted in private. So, too, are appeal applications to the Commercial Court in respect of arbitration awards. Secret trials and private hearings are the beginnings of a slippery slope to injustice: last century Jeremy Bentham remarked, 'Only in proportion as publicity has place can any of the checks applicable to judicial injustice operate. Where there is no publicity, there is no justice.' And Lord Scarman has commented, 'Justice is done in public so that it may be discussed and criticised in public. Moreover, trials will sometimes expose matters of public interest worthy of discussion other than the judicial task of doing justice between the parties in the particular case.'

DISSENSUS AND DISOBEDIENCE

If, however, justice is about the content of legal rules as well as the application of law, what happens when those rules are ostensibly unjust in themselves? Do we disobey? As law is man-made and secular nowadays and as the human species is not infallible, inevitably some laws will be unjust. Here we are back to immorality: injustice is another face of immorality. The easy way out is to say that an unjust law cannot be a law at all: *lex injusta non est lex*. St Augustine noted that without justice states were nothing but organised robber bands. He qualified his remarks, however, by saying that an unjust law would not *appear* to be law (*non videtur esse lex, quae justa non fuerit*). Other moral and legal philosophers of ancient times – Cicero, Plato and Aristotle – took much the same line. The famous medieval scholar, St Thomas Aquinas, was, though, more careful to avoid the issue.

The alternative argument is that law is law: this line of thought has owed much to the writings of A. V. Dicey at the end of the last century. Dicey was much concerned with the concept of the rule of law in a parliamentary democracy. However unpopular a certain law may be, for example, the Industrial Relations Act 1971 which was bitterly opposed by the trade union movement, and the Housing Finance Act 1972 which was resisted by a number of local councils, Dicey underlined the need to maintain stability in society by the rule of law – laws in a parliamentary democracy should be obeyed that more easily, for unpopular measures can always be reversed once the government is changed, usually following a general election. But under dictatorships or limited parliamentary regimes the position is far more difficult. Although a number of laws could be regarded as unjust and immoral, and as such permanently built into the system, judges in Nazi Germany nonetheless applied those laws since they were made by an apparently sovereign and competent body. Judges in pre-1990 South Africa took the same approach in respect of apartheid legislation.

It is unfortunate perhaps that of late the phrase 'the rule of law' has become almost synonymous with that of 'law and order'. If society is not ordered and policed, then, the argument runs, the kind of crime of which most fair-minded people disapprove would grow unchecked. The incidence of murder, muggings, rape, theft and burglary would increase until the point was reached where the agencies of law enforcement could no longer cope. The stability of a civilized society would crumble and a state of anarchy would result: it would be a matter not of 'law and order' but 'law and disorder'. The question of law and order is related to both the civil and criminal legal codes, but mostly to the latter. And just as the broader questions of social deviance and civil disobedience pervade all levels and all classes of society, so too does crime. Yet as Professor J. B. Mays has said, in a 'saner and more just society . . . the seeds of crime will find less nourishment.'

'LAW AND ORDER'

The term 'law and order' has been shot through with emotive overtones in the context of industrial unrest and the Northern Irish troubles. Nowadays 'law and order' can more closely imply privilege 'above the law' and direct disobedience, moral or otherwise, of the legal code, instead of meaning simply the keeping of order in a disciplined society. As one commentator, Robert Taylor, writing in 1979, has said in respect of the industrial situation, 'there is a widespread belief in Britain that the trade unions are now 'above the law', overmighty subjects with legal privileges that provide them with an irresponsible power to pursue their sectional interests'. In the opinion of Lord Denning, former Master of the Rolls and scourge of the unions in the Court of Appeal, Parliament had conferred more freedom from restraint on trade unions than had ever been known to the law before. 'All legal restraints have been lifted so that they can now do as they will.' But since 1980 a great deal of legislation has restricted trade union power.

Yet despite what Lord Denning has said, if Parliament in its legislative wisdom has decided, as it has, to give the trade union organisations various rights and duties, such as under the Trade Union and Labour Relations Act 1974, the Health and Safety at Work etc Act 1974 and the Trade Union and Labour Relations (Consolidation) Act 1992, then trade unions can hardly be said to be 'above the law', they are simply obeying the law as stated by statute, and parliamentary law, as already observed, is supreme. That, however, assumes that there is a political consensus about those statutory provisions in the first place, which in recent years has been questionable. If, though, that agreement is noticeably absent in the wider community outside Westminster, then disobedience may result and the law can truly become an ass. This was, in effect, the result of the Industrial Relations Act 1971; parts of that Act, in the face of strong and organised trade union opposition, became unworkable, just as senior civil servants had predicted to government ministers at the time the Bill was being drafted. The problem in framing contentious legislation is to know where to draw the line precisely and subtly enough to avoid dissensus and conflict. This point was well illustrated by the problems raised by the provisions of the Housing Finance Act 1972 which sought to extend the 'fair' market rent principle to council house tenancies. A number of local housing authorities put up stout resistance to the Act; however, it was the adamant refusal of Clay Cross Urban District Council in Derbyshire to comply with the terms of the Act which became the *cause célèbre*. In 1974 the new Labour Government repealed the Act, but the Clay Cross councillors had already been surcharged (fined) by the District Auditor. The Clay Cross Council was, in any case, about to disappear under the local government reorganisation of 1974. Furthermore, the councillors had already been disqualified from holding local office. The final result was that the Housing Finance (Special Provisions) Act

1975, while not giving retrospective amnesty to the actions, or rather omissions, of the Derbyshire councillors, did nonetheless strike out the possibility of any future prosecutions and surcharges in respect of the 1972 Act. Not surprisingly the Opposition charged the new Government with holding statutory law up to moral ridicule. In the late 1980s the 'poll tax' raised similar issues.

'EMERGENCY' LAWS

The phrase 'special' or 'emergency' or 'temporary provisions' has a familiar if ominous ring about it in the context of Ulster affairs. Under the Prevention of Terrorism (Temporary Provisions) Act 1989 suspected terrorists can be held without being charged for up to seven days. The Northern Ireland (Emergency Provisions) Act 1978 made special provision for the detention of suspected terrorists in Ulster itself, and for trial without a jury for serious offences within the province. The Northern Ireland (Emergency Provisions) Act 1987 amended and provided for the eventual repeal of the 1978 Act; the law, including Part VI of the 1989 Act, has been re-enacted under the Northern Ireland (Emergency Provisions) Act 1991, as amended by the Criminal Justice Act 1993 (now consolidated by the Northern Ireland (Emergency Provisions) Act 1996). (Part VI of the Criminal Justice and Public Order Act 1994 had also amended the terrorism laws.) But such legislative arrangements may not attract much support from a large part of the Irish community, nor indeed from the mainland British population, when it is shown that police interrogation techniques have been found badly wanting, as seen in the Bennett Report of 1979. As Gavin Drewry has said, 'There comes a point where the State must acknowledge that it has a war on its hands . . . and that the *political* issues underlying the conflict cannot simply be reduced to the dichotomy of 'right' versus 'wrong' which is implicit in the ordinary process of criminal trial.'

Drewry went on to emphasise the point made above, that if enough people disobey a particular law, that law will quickly become redundant. He observed that, in 1941, 1,000 miners at a Kent colliery were prosecuted for going on strike and thus breaching wartime regulations. Despite arrests the strike continued and the authorities were forced to climb down and release imprisoned men, unpaid fines being conveniently forgotten. 'Most people would agree, however, that disobedience of the law is not something to be used lightly. We all have a stake in an ordered society,' Drewry remarked. He claimed that it was no good an individual trying to pick out the bits of law that appeared more attractive and consequently to ignore those that were rather more unappealing; only anarchy would result in the longer term. The answer, compromise as it might sound, was, he said, to enforce laws 'rationally and with due regard to the interests of different groups in society . . . History will be the ultimate judge . . . of the law which [people] have elected to defy. And history can be a harsh judge.'

As the trial judge remarked in the prosecution of Peter Hain in 1972 for disrupting sporting fixtures with South Africa, 'the rule of law requires that all men should exercise their rights according to the law . . . No-one has the right to dispense with, suspend or opt out of a law with which he does not agree, or which he may find unacceptable.' However, it is true to say that in modern times defying the law has been concerned with a wide range of political problems – in the area of trade unionism, civil liberties, women's rights, racial equality, the Welsh language, nuclear disarmament and American involvement in Vietnam and Cambodia. All this led one writer, Geoffrey Marshall, to ask in 1973:

> **Ought it not now to be one of the main tasks of political philosophy to construct an unambiguous, plain man's guide to law-breaking? Unfortunately, although the study of civil disobedience is becoming a philosophical boom industry, very little that is both true and of any particular use has emerged from it. Plain men are left hovering between two rather general and noticeably inconsistent views about the moral right to disobey the law,**

in effect the view that there is no such right, that the law of a parliamentary democracy must always be obeyed, and the claim that breaking the law is all part of democracy *provided* that the person doing so sincerely and absolutely believes that a piece of legislation or governmental policy is in error. It becomes almost a matter of the 'party of law and order' versus the 'party of conscience'. Protest and civil disobedience may, of course, be directed towards public officials or the like who are themselves infringing the rules.

The argument thus comes to centre around the nature of a 'national contract': we all give up certain rights and freedoms in return for some kind of collective security. On the other hand none of us want to give up the sacrosanct right to protest, to say 'no' when our consciences prick us to do so. Frequently the latter desire becomes caught up with arguments about the subjection to moral and political tyranny, arguments which may well be only a few steps removed from breaches of either the criminal or civil code or both. In that sense it may be difficult to distinguish between rebellion and civil disobedience. We are then back to legal square one – by what means and in what circumstances can particular provision be made for the dissenting opinions of the minority, how can they in practice be accommodated, is there any real chance of a legal and political *modus vivendi*?

The overriding danger in any modern, complex society is that views which are not agreed with, and which have failed to achieve change by constitutional means, may be treated by the holders of those opinions – the dissidents – as views ignored or not heard. If that kind of situation develops, Geoffrey Marshall has argued, the chances are that peaceful protest will transform itself into 'violent dissent' – and there are many different forms of violence that the criminal law recognises other than that done to the human body. Thus judging what the majority opinion happens to be at any given moment is not, as members of the legal profession are only too aware, a simple matter of performing straightforward arithmetical calculations; it is also a case of calculating whether the strongly committed philosophies of those who fall outside the majority can be either legally permissible or morally tolerable. Marshall continued:

> Though there is nothing magic or morally conclusive about the
> boundary line between lawful and unlawful action, a persistent tenden-
> cy to devalue its significance ought, in a constitutional democracy, to
> put us on our guard. Because direct action of many kinds is being
> increasingly used, party politicians and political scientists (and even
> law professors) can now be heard discussing it as if it were just another
> form of political or group activity . . . Direct action has begun to enjoy
> a status that is on a par with free speech, lobbying and postal voting.

Such problems could be observed in the deep public disquiet about the 'poll tax'
or community charge, a policy that turned out to be exceptionally short-lived
(1989–93) and which contributed in no small measure towards Mrs Thatcher's
downfall as Prime Minister in 1990.

If, however, man-made law is on occasion palpably unjust are there certain fundamental rights and duties that can never be obliterated by the secular legislator,
whether parliamentary or dictatorial? Are there certain natural laws, divinely transmitted, which the secular law-makers ignore at their peril? This brings us on to a
brief consideration of natural law and positivism.

NATURAL LAW AND POSITIVISM

As Allott has clearly outlined, the history of natural law theories is not unlike that
of the Phoenix; such theories have attempted to pin down those principles of justice that create duties and rights outside of contemporary, secular law. One of the
greatest exponents of natural law was St Thomas Aquinas, whose views remained
influential until the eighteenth century. Aquinas believed that God had a master-
plan for the world – an *eternal law*. Some of this plan consisted of *divine law*, that
which God thought suitable to be revealed. The rest of God's laws could be discovered through rationality and reason on the part of humans – *natural law*. Hence
medieval kings 'discovered' God's law; they could not, at least theoretically, create
it. Humans also had both the right and ability to make their own rules – *human
law* or *positive law*, providing, of course, it did not conflict with natural and divinely revealed laws. As Theodore Benditt has put it, whatever did not comply with
natural law was, according to this philosophy, not law at all, since human law was
bound to comply with natural law. It is possible, therefore, to see natural law as
being a set of principles of practical reasonableness in ordering human life and the
human community. Natural law, in other words, was in essence a divinely
inspired moral code.

The philosophers of the nineteenth century by and large knocked the concept of
natural law on its head. They were led by the utilitarians – Jeremy Bentham and
John Stuart Mill, to whom reference has already been made. In the middle of that
century, Bentham's ideas were taken a stage further by John Austin. This was the
age when parliamentary democracy, and therefore parliamentary law-making,
began to come into its own right. Austin argued that a legal system embraced all

laws which were issued by one or more persons. Those laws only worked – in the sense of being obeyed – if they had been passed by a sovereign body, a king or a parliament, or strictly speaking in the United Kingdom the King in Parliament, for it is the Royal Assent that must be given to the Bills passed by both Houses of Parliament. Austin built upon Bentham's idea that sovereignty had little or nothing to do with morality or moral principles. Sovereignty existed because the habit of obedience was a social fact. Only the laws that were made in a positive, political manner – at a secular level – could be laws at all.

Kelsen and Weber

In more recent times Austin's theories have been extended and modified by others, perhaps most notably by Hans Kelsen who placed more stress than Austin on the efficacy of a legal system – that without a minimum degree of efficacy a legal system does not exist.

In contrast to Austin, Kelsen, with his emphasis upon normative behaviour, did not separate different types of rules, into a legal rule (a law) backed by another rule which might be described as socio-legal or normative in the sense of providing a sanction or punishment in respect of disobedience of the legal rule. For Kelsen only one sort mattered – that which imposed a duty on officials to punish others. In short a legal system meant one of coercive rules. Kelsen thought law was neither a static, ready-made set of rules, nor an instrument of political expediency, nor a near reflection of a natural or revealed moral code. It was, he said, a coercive order of rules arranged as a pyramid, constantly created and recreated at each level by legislators, officials, judges and even individual citizens acting within the limits and authority of the law.

Another writer to note here is Max Weber. Weber, writing in the early part of this century, outlined three types of authority in society. In the first place he spoke about technologically primitive societies: such displayed *traditional authority*. The elders made the laws and people obeyed because to do so was a traditional way of life; they knew no other. *Charismatic authority* was to be found when certain leaders who appeared specially inspired, such as Mohammed or Gandhi or Hitler or Peron, commanded automatic allegiance: their words were law. *Patrimonial authority* was a variation of traditional authority. Leaders might be chosen but would then be given full powers to make laws. They might be aided in their task by some kind of council of advisers, irrespective of whether they were chosen or whether they inherited their position. Yet if they overstepped the mark and crossed the boundaries of natural law, then they could be dismissed. Such was the position of medieval European monarchs; such is the position today of the chiefs of what tribes remain in Africa and Asia.

Finally, *rational–legal* authority was the modern form of the bureaucratic state. Citizens obeyed officials because the rules that those officials worked out related to other rules or laws passed by a recognised and properly constituted body. The office-holder ruled according to law, not according to patronage.

For Austin there was one considerable difficulty. If the only form of legal rules that counted as positive law was that made by Parliament, what was the position of common law? Common law had been evolved over many centuries by judges, not legislators in the purest sense. To some extent common law was based on local, regional and national customs, hence customary or common law, although there is something of a myth in that belief – very often judges simply made up the rules themselves. Similar cases led, usually, to similar decisions – law was made as a result of the cases brought before the courts (case-law). Hence, a decision in one case would lay down clear guidelines, that is create a precedent, for future cases with like circumstances.

Hart and positivism

For the leading figure of twentieth century positivists, H. L. A. Hart, this posed less of a problem. Parliament implicitly recognised the existence of common law; as it gradually legislated in more and more areas, common law would diminish in importance. Today we are a statute-orientated society. Nonetheless Hart's positivism was more complex than that of Austin. Hart belonged to a pluralistic world of developed political parties and pressure groups; Austin scarcely did.

Thus positivists argue that the authority of the law is owed either to a legislative body or to some other human source that determines what the law is. Outside of these boundaries law is not law and judges should not stray. Laws – the rules of society – can only be transgressed when to do so is prohibited (*mala prohibita*). In contrast, the naturalists argue that irrespective of legislative or similar sources there is an independent range of natural principles and human rights. To upset these are wrongs in themselves (*mala in se*). To ignore such natural rights is to abandon any attempt to build into society a sense of 'fairness'. Yet natural law and positive law need not be mutually exclusive. As Professor Ronald Dworkin has pointed out in his 'rights concept', the ground rules for basic individual rights, common to all, can be written down, in a kind of modern day version of Magna Carta – in short a Bill of Rights or an American-style written constitution, which even Parliament may be forbidden or discouraged to alter. On the other hand it can be argued that the American federal Supreme Court does have very wide interpretative powers. While the British Constitution is largely unwritten, it should be borne in mind that the United Kingdom is a party to various charters that have a natural law flavour – for example, the United Nations' Universal Declaration of Human Rights (1948) and the European Convention for Human Rights and Fundamental Freedoms (Council of Europe) (1950–51). Perhaps natural law was seen still to be alive most of all at the time of the Nuremberg war trials of Nazi leaders, in which Britain played such a leading part (1945–46), and which pioneered the prosecution of 'crimes against humanity' and 'crimes against peace'.

Hart himself recognised the continuity of natural law – in what he called the 'minimum content of Natural Law'. Any system of positive law must recognise that among other things all humans are roughly equal physically ('approximate equality') if less so intellectually. Each is vulnerable to attack by another. Further, human beings are neither totally selfish nor totally altruistic ('limited altruism').

They are also subject to limited resources in the world as they are to 'limited understanding and strength of will'. In other words men and women recognise that over-competition is self-destructive. Thus sanctions are required as a guarantee that those who are prepared to obey shall not be destroyed by those who are not: 'what reason demands is *voluntary* co-operation in a *coercive* system.'

Hart divided his system of positive law into primary and secondary rules. Essentially primary rules were pre-legal rules of the coercive type, the static duties, obligations and rights of society. Secondary rules consisted of three things – the rules of recognition, rules of change and rules of adjudication. The latter were principally rules about rules, in other words the rules that judges, civil servants, Government ministers and others must follow in applying and interpreting the law. Rules of change meant agreed rules that provided for making changes in the law as currently established. At the highest level electoral law, for instance, provides for parliamentary elections which may result in a different Parliament, a different government and a consequent change in primary law.

The rules of recognition have posed a greater philosophical problem. Nonetheless they are fundamental rules and are at the heart of the positivist school of thought. Law is only law if it is recognised as flowing from an accepted, established and recognisable source. A written constitution, as in the USA, is therefore a rule of recognition. As the United Kingdom enjoys a largely unwritten constitution, it is Parliament and the courts themselves which approximate to that rule. Society recognises the law as made by fellow human beings (primary positive law as opposed to natural law), but the way in which it is made has to be acceptable too – in today's case that means the parliamentary process (the secondary rule of recognition). Hart argued that it is only when there exists a real union of primary and secondary rules that a legal system can operate effectively. It is the primitive, traditional society which will lack a system of secondary rules. In those societies social rules become muddled up with or at least indistinguishable from what should be purely legal rules: there is no parliamentary process which separates them out. 'Wherever such a rule of recognition is accepted, both private persons and officials are provided with authoritative criteria for identifying primary rules of obligation.' As John Raz has summarised it, the rule of recognition is concerned with the activity of the legislative body as guided by normative considerations, that is by what people expect that body to do, on the basis, say, of a party election manifesto, and that it will be punished if it fails to deliver the electoral goods in some form or other. That the rule of recognition is a political fact, and that in effect one Parliament may bind its successors in all but name, was recognised by Lord Bridge in the *Factortame (No 2)* case.

Dworkin's criticisms

Although Professor Hart has dominated British legal philosophy in the twentieth century, his views and those of other positivists have been much criticised of late, notably by Ronald Dworkin, an American and Professor of Jurisprudence at Oxford University, in his book *Taking Rights Seriously*. Dworkin argues that no legislator can afford to ignore the public's views or sense of outrage, since public opinion, however fickle, will throw up boundaries around what Parliament and the Government can 'get away with'. Nevertheless, most conventional moral practices 'are more complex and more structured than [Lord Devlin] takes them to be . . . .' In other words, while legislators may be practising, and thus restricted by, what is the art of the possible, the role for the judiciary may be somewhat different – great dangers for society may lie ahead if judges attempt to travel too far in trying to establish what public opinion is according to their own *predetermined* values.

> **Hart may say that a social rule of recognition exists, but is nevertheless uncertain, when members of the community disagree about the proper application of that verbal formulation to particular cases. So the rule of recognition, that whatever Parliament does is law, exists as a social fact, but it is uncertain to the degree that judges disagree over particular cases . . . The matter would then be . . . left to their discretion.**

In that context Dworkin devotes a chapter in his critique of English law to 'hard cases', actions at law in which judges *appear* to push the legal boat out into uncharted waters, making important new decisions and establishing new legal precedents. For example, Dworkin quotes the case of *Spartan Steel & Alloys Ltd* v. *Martin & Co* (1973) in which the court was asked to decide whether economic loss should be allowed following negligent action.

Hart advanced the traditional thesis that normally judges have no duty to take into account any factors other than those established in the rules and principles of statutory law and common law, as accepted by members of the community in question (the rule of recognition). But Dworkin would wish for clearer definitions of the principles of English judicial decisions, if only to overcome a little 'the central problem that . . . sociologists and instrumentalists [have] discussed: do judges always follow rules, even in difficult and controversial cases, or do they sometimes make up new rules and apply them retroactively?' The logical extension of the traditional thesis is that they do on occasion make up new rules – that in controversial or test or hard cases the room for judicial discretion is fairly large. Professor J. A. Griffith would, if from a critical standpoint, not dissent strongly from such an interpretation and has listed a number of cases which illustrate the highly personalised outlook senior judges can bring to important legal actions.

While in the broadest sense Dworkin takes a *liberal* view of legal rules and the constitutional system in both the United Kingdom and the USA, for example, he advocates positive discrimination for black people, he tends to adopt a rather more cautious, almost *conservative* approach to the problem of judicial discretion and power. 'It remains the judge's duty,' he argues, 'even in hard cases, to discover what the rights of the parties are, not to invent new rights retrospectively.'

However, Dworkin disputes that in practice judges either should or, other than very rarely, do make new law, 'either covertly or explicitly'. He doubts whether they do in effect act as 'deputy to the appropriate legislature, enacting the law that they suppose the legislature would enact if seized of the problem.' But where judicial 'discretion' does operate, that discretion must be structured rather than open-ended – in that sense weak rather than strong. It must, in short, be bound by its own set of fundamental principles.

A second edition of *The Concept of Law* was published posthumously in 1994; in the postscript Hart attacks Dworkin's view on positivism, arguing that rules and principles cannot be totally distinguished and that 'law's coercive machinery' is quite separate from its 'moral merits'. But overall Hart thought that the differences between him and Dworkin were not substantial.

Policies and principles

Thus Dworkin distinguishes very clearly between judicial *principle*, which judges may bring to bear with great persuasion and force in the cases before them, and political *policy* which is made elsewhere, and, he adds, this distinction applies no less to controversial, 'hard' cases. Principle will encompass such matters as justice, morality and the rights of the individual. Policy is the Act of Parliament itself, for instance, the introduction of a welfare benefit or the nationalisation of a particular industry. Both policy and principle are different from legal rules.

> I call a 'policy' that kind of standard that sets out a goal to be reached, generally an improvement in some economic, political or social feature of the community (though some goals are negative, in that they stipulate that some present feature is to be protected from adverse change). I call a 'principle' a standard that is to be observed, not because it will advance or secure an economic, political or social situation deemed desirable, but because it is a requirement of justice or fairness or some other dimension of morality. Thus the standard that automobile accidents are to be decreased is a policy, and the standard that no man may profit by his own wrong a principle.

Certainly, as emphasised several times before, no-one can afford to ignore the tremendous importance in the post-war period of parliamentary law over and above common law. Judicial powers of discretion and precedent have been more and more mapped out by statute.

For Dworkin a *rule* is applicable in 'an all-or-nothing fashion'. Rules are precise standards, such as a maximum speed limit on the roads. Principles, on the other hand, 'conflict and interact with one another, so that each principle that is relevant to a particular legal problem provides a reason arguing in favour of, but does not stipulate, a particular solution.' Moreover, a principle, says Dworkin, may be respected by the law, but not necessarily absorbed fully into legal rules. He points out that a man may indeed profit by his own wrong: if a trespasser crosses another's land often enough eventually a private right of way may be recognised – a new legal rule is established. The employee who breaks his contract to take a better job may have to pay damages to his first employer, but it is hardly likely that he will be required to forfeit his new salary. But Dworkin's view of judicial principle begs the vital question – how is it precisely ensured that judges who are effectively appointed for life do not depart from the enforcement of existing individual rights? Dworkin took his arguments a stage further in a subsequent work, *Law's Empire*, expounding his view of law as an integrity, obliging the judge to 'fit' his decision within the framework of superior rules, blending their substance out of convictions about fairness, justice and procedural due process.

One further comment from Professor Dworkin will suffice:

> **Suppose an aircraft manufacturer sues to recover the subsidy that the statute provides. He argues his right to the subsidy; his argument is an argument of principle. He does not argue that the national defense statute was wrong on policy grounds when it was adopted, or that it should have been repealed on policy grounds long ago. His right to a subsidy no longer depends on any argument of policy because the statute made it a matter of principle . . . I propose, nevertheless, the thesis that judicial decisions in civil cases, even in hard cases like *Spartan Steel*, characteristically are and should be generated by principle not policy. . . . The correct view, I believe, is that judges do and should rest their judgments in controversial cases on arguments of political principle, but not on arguments of political policy.**
>
> **. . . America assigns lawyers, as a group, power and influence in a wide variety of matters, notably including government. In Britain you treat your lawyers very well. You dress them up in costumes – though principally middle-aged drag – and when they become judges you give them very wide powers of contempt to protect their dignity. But you give them, or in any case wish to give them, very little power . . . The rule of law, in the conception I support, enriches democracy by adding an independent forum of principle, and that is important not simply because justice may be done there, but because the forum confirms that justice is in the end a matter of individual right, and not independently a matter of the public good.**

Others, it should be said, have developed a 'rights thesis'. For instance, the early twentieth century jurist Wesley Hohfeld talked about four types of rights: claim-rights, where a duty is owed by X. to Y; liberty-rights where there is freedom of any duty to the contrary; powers, which embrace the legal ability to change a legal relation; and immunities, which mean the non-subjection to another's powers, so that in this analysis immunities relate to powers just as liberty-rights stand to claim-rights.

Many academics, however, have not accepted Dworkin's attempts to distinguish between rules, policy and principle, and therefore to narrow down the areas of potential judicial discretion. Professor Sir Rupert Cross has said that Hart's account of judicial behaviour in hard or controversial cases is to be preferred to Dworkin's if only because the latter is too perfectionist, not merely in the sense that few judges are equipped even to begin to fulfil the Herculean task proposed for them, but also because it is unlikely that its performance would produce one uniquely correct answer to many judicial problems. William Twining and David Miers have also expressed their doubts.

> In our view Dworkin's distinction between rules and principles is artificially sharp, for there are relatively few clear examples, in law or elsewhere, of norms that have the 'all-or-nothing' characteristic that he ascribes to rules. No prominent legal positivist who has elucidated law in terms of rules, such as Hart, or of norms, such as Kelsen, has been committed to the view that law is made up solely of categorical precepts. To attribute such a view to 'positivism' is to set up an artificial target for attack. The principles of statutory interpretation, the neighbour principle, and perhaps even the maxims of Equity . . . can, in our view, all be accommodated in a positivist conception of the law.

One Law Lord, Lord Scarman, has had this to say about policy and principle in *McLoughlin* v. *O'Brian* (1982):

> The appeal raises directly a question as to the balance in our law between the functions of judge and legislature. The common law, which in a constitutional context includes judicially developed equity, covers everything which is not covered by statute. It knows no gaps: there can be no *casus omissus*. The function of the court is to decide the case before it, even though the decision may require the extension or adaptation of a principle or in some cases the creation of new law to meet the justice of the case. But, whatever the court decides to do, it starts from a baseline of existing principle and seeks a solution consistent with or analogous to a principle or principles already recognised.
>
> The distinguishing feature of the common law is this judicial development and formation of principle. Policy considerations will have to be weighed: but the objective of the judges is the formulation of principle. And, if principle inexorably requires a decision which entails a degree of policy risk, the court's function is to adjudicate according to principle, leaving policy curtailment to the judgment of Parliament. Here lies the true role of the two law-making institutions in our constitution. By concentrating on principle the judges can keep the common law alive, flexible and consistent, and can keep the legal system clear of policy problems which neither they, nor the forensic process which it is their duty to operate, are equipped to resolve. If principle leads to results which are thought to be socially unacceptable, Parliament can legislate to draw a line or map out a new path.
>
> The real risk to the common law is not its movement to cover new situations and new knowledge but lest it should stand still, halted by a conservative judicial approach. If that should happen, and since the 1966 Practice Direction of the House (*Practice Statement: Judicial Precedent*) it has become less likely, there would be a danger of the law

becoming irrelevant to the consideration, and inept in its treatment, of modern social problems. Justice would be defeated. The common law has, however, avoided this catastrophe by the flexibility given it by generations of judges. Flexibility carries with it, of course, certain risks, notably a degree of uncertainty in the law and the 'floodgates' risk which so impressed the Court of Appeal in the present case.

The importance to be attached to certainty and the size of the 'floodgates' risk vary from one branch of the law to another. What is required of the law in its approach to a commercial transaction will be very different from the approach appropriate to problems of tortious liability for personal injuries. In some branches of the law, notably that now under consideration, the search for certainty can obstruct the law's pursuit of justice, and can become the enemy of the good.

Michael MacGrath, writing in 1985, noted:

Until recently there was no doubt that judges were influenced by, and took cognisance of, extra-legal considerations. Some commentators encouraged this approach, but in recent years the House of Lords has cast considerable doubt on the appropriateness of employing policy considerations in legal reasoning. In *McLoughlin* v. *O'Brian* there was considerable divergence of opinion as to the justiciability of policy considerations, and *dicta* of Lord Roskill in *Junior Books* would appear to indicate that pure policy considerations do not lie within the purview of the judicial domain.

About this old judicial chestnut Lord Salmon had this to say in *Morgans* v. *Launchbury*:

I have always recognised that it is an important function of this House to develop and adapt the common law to meet the changing needs of the time. In an appropriate case we should not shrink from doing so. In the present case, however, the proposed 'development' constitutes such a radical and far-reaching departure from accepted principle that it seems to me to smack of naked legislation . . . In my view this is essentially a matter for the legislature.

Discussion points

1 Is the view of Professor John Mackintosh a reasonable one in relation to modern constitutional developments?

2 Can we differentiate satisfactorily between law and morality?

3 Is it possible for the idea of 'rights' to be conceptually certain?

SOURCES OF LAW, NATURAL JUSTICE AND JUDICIAL REVIEW

'Sources' is perhaps a misleading word, since it implies that law is to be found in some rather special, if not secretive, place. Nonetheless it is convenient to talk generally about the major derivations of the English legal system. Five are examined below (and in Chapter 3) – although it should be pointed out that it is perfectly feasible to increase that number by all manner of sub-divisions. Before, however, those five principal sources are discussed, it is pertinent to note, briefly, the historical nature of justice and the law.

As already noted, the concept of justice lies deep in the conscience of all civilised peoples. What that justice is, however, is a reflection of the customs and laws of that civilisation, and derives from the morality of the people as expounded by their law makers. All civilised societies have had their codes of law, at least from the time of Hammurabi, the founder of the Babylonian Empire in the third millennium BC. As in Mosaic Law, the Hammurabic Code was dictated to him by God, as we know from an ancient Stela now in the Louvre in Paris. It should be remembered that these 'Laws' were not a short set of prohibitions or exhortations, as in the Ten Commandments, but a complete code of conduct for people to observe, as in Leviticus, the third book of the Old Testament.

The majority of Islamic countries today have laws based closely on Koranic Law and throughout Europe, America and Australasia the Christian ethic has been a powerful source of the moral codes upon which the laws were built. Law is the latticework of civilisation and throughout history a few outstanding law makers have illuminated the course of justice, some like Solomon as judges, others such as Justinian as great codifiers.

Across southern Europe the most important factor in moulding legal systems was Roman law, but in England the Saxon tribes had already developed their own legal process whose basic principles were handed down, and survived the Norman Conquest and the influence of the Roman Church to provide the foundations of the common law. Despite some legal 'codes' having been promulgated by Kings such as Offa in Mercia and Alfred in Wessex, among many others, the laws were mostly oral, with much variation of local custom, the main divisions at the time of the Conquest being the Danelaw and the laws of Wessex and Mercia. It is interesting to note that the Scandinavian influence had enhanced the position of women, who could own property and obtain custody of children and a share in the family goods on divorce, often to the dismay of the Church authorities. But after the Conquest the Church was to exercise a greater influence in family disputes, as in other branches of the law.

2.1

The political system and common law

In the first place, as emphasised in Chapter 1, the legal system is an integral part of the political process since the concept of law reinforces political ideas of power and authority. Secondly, in a practical sense it constitutes the means for the orderly settlement of disputes within a particular society and, in the context of international law and European Community (EC) law in particular, between one society and another. The existence of law is thus what distinguishes a developed political state from a situation of anarchy, or at least that is the theory.

Thirdly, as a result of earlier imperial traditions the English legal system, sometimes much altered and modified, remains a pervasive influence across a wide area of the Commonwealth. Perhaps that is a noteworthy tribute to the fundamental flexibility that lies at the very heart of English law. Some Commonwealth countries retain the right of judicial appeal to the United Kingdom.

Fourthly, the English – or in this sense British – legal system is remarkable in that it clearly overlaps with the political system proper. There is no clear separation of powers as enshrined under the American Constitution, no clear-cut divisions of legislature, executive and judiciary that French philosophers such as Montesquieu propounded in the eighteenth century. Instead the executive (that is the government), the Westminster Parliament and the judiciary enjoy a close-knit tripartite relationship. The House of Lords is both a court and part of the legislature. The Lord Chancellor, a political appointee, is a member of the Cabinet and the supreme head of the entire legal system. The Home Secretary is also a member of the Cabinet with wide-ranging legal functions, as well as being a member of the House of Commons. The Attorney-General and Solicitor-General are MPs too, but at the same time they are the government's principal law officers. Judges and judicial institutions are appointed and regulated by political animals and by parliamentary statute, a point only too well illustrated in 1988 in Malaysia, a Commonwealth jurisdiction, when the Prime Minister there secured the dismissal of the Lord President, the country's most senior judge, for purely political reasons, despite the judge's appeal to the Malaysian Crown.

Notwithstanding that overlap between the political and legal systems, is there something of an ambivalent attitude in the popular mind towards political activity on the one hand and legal processes on the other? Perhaps the political system is perceived as concerned with argument and counter-argument, with matters of wheeling and dealing, with shady compromises and with emotional posturing, while the legal system is seen as pure, fair and unbiased. The truth is some way off that mark, but outwardly the crude division remains.

Thus, for example, when the chairman of the Tameside Education Committee in 1976 challenged the Education Secretary's ruling that plans for comprehensive schools were now too far advanced to be altered by a local council whose political control had changed only the previous month, that was the rough and tumble of politics. Yet when the chairman of the Committee was subsequently interviewed on television, he made it clear that a court ruling was a different matter and that the council would respect, albeit reluctantly, the High Court's decision in favour of the Secretary of State (*Secretary of State for Education and Science* v. *Metropolitan Borough of Tameside*). The rule of law would be upheld.

THE 'RULE OF LAW'

The very phrase 'rule of law' owes much to the writings of the constitutionalist A. V. Dicey at the end of the last century. Political stability has for many years been associated with the idea of an ingrained respect for the authority of the law itself. To Dicey the constitution was the result of the 'ordinary law of the land': if there occurred unlawful interference with individual liberty, then the constitution, or political system, should have in-built safeguards to ensure that such abuses were remedied at an early stage. Dicey interpreted the common law in this context – judge-made law acted as a bulwark against tyranny. All individuals and officials were equal before the law, thus avoiding the need for a separate system of administrative courts, and, finally, the 'rule of law' meant the supremacy of 'regular law', as opposed to arbitrary power, presumably including statute law for parliamentary law was 'sovereign' or 'supreme'. In this way the rule of law would prevail.

Dicey viewed the 'Queen in Parliament' as the legal sovereign and thought of the voter, as the political sovereign, although such distinctions today are in practice artificial. It remains true, of course, that Parliament consists of not only the House of Commons and the House of Lords but also the monarch: without the 'safeguard' of the Royal Assent a Bill cannot become an Act. However, it would be extremely unlikely that the Queen or King would refuse to endorse any legislation that had been passed by both Houses. If she or he did, a major constitutional crisis would ensue. As Walter Bagehot, another great constitutional writer of the nineteenth century, once put it, the Queen would have to sign her own death warrant if the two Houses chose to send it to her. That is what is meant by 'limited constitutional monarchy': in political and legislative terms the monarch is more symbolic than real. Dicey owed many of his ideas to those other giants of nineteenth-century constitutional philosophy, John Stuart Mill and John Austin. Austin was particularly concerned with the way in which modern industrial states had developed a sovereign source of law that was widely respected and obeyed.

MAKING LAW

Nowadays, however, both legal and political scientists recognise that there exist other and more subtle cultural and economic forces within all mature legal and political systems. Judges and lawyers can never be totally non-political, however sensitively they may try to deal with politically 'sensitive' matters (as the Industrial

Relations Court showed between 1971 and 1974). In this context the viewpoints of Professors Dworkin and Griffith, for example, have become more pressing in recent years. Politics, it should be emphasised, is as much a series of judgments about the values of society as law is the reflection of the political process itself.

Law can never be seen in isolation from its connected parts. Indeed parliamentary law owes its origin to various influences. In the first place the most obvious is the party factor. Political parties are broad coalitions of similar interests. A party's election manifesto will give some indication of further legislative intentions. If elected to power, the party that then forms the government is expected to implement most of those promises: the electorate has mandated it to do so (the doctrine of the mandate). Most legislation passed by Parliament is introduced by the government; much of it will be politically controversial and will be opposed by the Opposition parties (for example, the Housing Act 1980 which compelled local authorities to give council tenants the opportunity to buy their homes, subsequently the Housing Act 1985 and Housing Associations Act 1985). This is what might be termed 'politicians' law'.

Secondly, a range of pressure groups attempts to persuade government ministers, civil servants and MPs to introduce certain legislation. Pressure groups are basically of two types – interest or sectional groups and promotional or causal groups. The first attempts to defend the interests of a certain section of the community, for example, the CBI, trade unions, the second promotes a particular cause, for example, Liberty (formerly the National Council for Civil Liberties), the League against Cruel Sports. Many groups will fall into both categories for example, the Automobile Association.

Thirdly, the ordinary, backbench Member of Parliament has a limited chance to introduce his own legislation. The best way is to gain one of the 20 or so places in the annual ballot in the Commons for Private Members' Bills, although usually an MP needs government support if he is to have any chance of success. Once an MP has drawn a place he is likely to find himself under considerable pressure from individuals and pressure groups to introduce a particular Bill. Thus the Housing (Homeless Persons) Act 1977 owed something not only to government backing but also to the activities of Shelter (the campaign for the homeless). In a similar way the Abortion Act 1967 was supported by the government, if indirectly, and the Abortion Law Reform Committee.

Fourthly, it is often the Civil Service itself and statutory bodies like the Law Commission which put proposals to the government. This will frequently be non-controversial law in the political sense – in other words it might be called 'lawyers' law'. For example, reforms in such areas as company law, the laws of tort, the law of contract and criminal justice often fall into such a category.

Fifthly, all the above type of legislation is public – that is it relates to the whole community. There are also such things as private Acts that relate only to certain individuals or sections of society. This type of legislation is of limited importance nowadays: it amounts to about 20-30 Bills per session. Most concern a particular locality: in other words a local council will seek to gain statutory powers additional to those it already has under public Acts.

A further illustration of the intertwined nature of British law and British politics can be seen in the establishment in 1965 of the Law Commission (with a separate organisation for Scotland). The Commission, a full-time body reporting to the Lord Chancellor, has exercised a double function. Firstly, it is obliged to prepare suggestions both for the consolidation of parliamentary law wherever overlapping or contradictory Acts exist and for the codification of statute and common law. Secondly, and more importantly, it can make political recommendations: it can suggest to the government specific proposals for law reform. The Law Commission's membership is composed largely of senior lawyers. In addition, since 1959 the Home Secretary has had at his side the Criminal Law Revision Committee. Again this is a lawyer-dominated body, although its record to date has been the more controversial of the two, as well underlined in 1972 when the Committee recommended the abolition of an accused's right of silence under interrogation (without prejudice to a future trial) and the admissibility of 'hearsay' (secondhand) evidence. In respect of civil law reform, the Lord Chancellor has also been assisted since 1952 by the Law Reform Committee. Interestingly in 1980 the chairman of the Law Commission, Sir Michael Kerr, complained that government departments were not sufficiently positive in their approach to the Commission's recommendations. Moreover, he said, codification, the bringing together of all statutes as consolidated and the common law on a particular subject into one code of rules, was an almost impossible task since the very generality that codification involved was alien to traditional legislative practice on specific problems.

By 1994 another chairman, Sir Henry Brooke, was complaining even more strongly, that Parliament was ignoring a large number of Law Commission reports, not least in relation to 'antique and obscure' criminal laws, such as the Offences against the Person Act 1861, as well as trust and landlord and tenant law. Parliament should adopt special procedures to enact Law Commission reforms, he said.

COMMON LAW AND PRECEDENT

English common law dates, so the older authorities remind us, from 'time immemorial'. It is a jumbled collection of popular customs and beliefs developed over the course of many centuries. The gloss to those beliefs has long been given by judges. From the twelfth century onwards the King's own judges toured the country and 'found' or discovered the popular law, that is the common or customary law. That at least is the romantic view. In reality the picture is a little more complicated. Up until the nineteenth century legal scholars did maintain that medieval kings and their judicial representatives simply articulated existing customary practices. In that sense it was possible to view the common law as a collection of general customs nationally applied. In fact it was far more likely that judges arrived at their own conclusions; it was they who made up the law, using their own commonsense. In short, they were – and to some extent still are – policy-makers in their own right. Of course, some customs, especially local ones, did greatly influence judges in particular cases. From early days, however, the courts imposed certain tests in order that a local custom could be recognised by the judges as part of common law. The custom had to date from 'time immemorial', and that meant from before 1189 (the end of the reign of Henry II, who had done so much to develop the system of itinerant, royal justice, and the beginning of that of Richard I). In practice customs that dated from after 1189 were still often accepted by the courts.

Secondly, a custom must have been accepted continuously by the local populace; there should be no record of opposition. Thirdly, people must have felt bound by the custom. Fourthly, the custom should be capable of precise definition and should be 'reasonable'. Lastly, one custom should not conflict with another.

It is also possible to see a local custom as having originally developed from a 'folk-way', which may be defined simply as the traditional behaviour of a certain group of people. If enough people behave in that particular manner for a reasonable period of time, then the folkway has become established and may be alternatively termed a 'custom'. In a broader sense, the term 'folkways' may be used generically – as a label to cover all the manners, customs, morals and mores (habits or values) of a community. It was at the turn of the century that W. G. Sumner wrote his book *Folkways*. Sumner suggested that a folkway or custom although handed down by tradition would nonetheless change to meet new conditions. That change, however, might well occur without any rational reflection or purpose on the part of those making it. For Sumner mores were folkways, in the sense of customs, raised to another plane. 'The Latin word mores seems to be, on the whole, more practically convenient and available than any other . . . as a name for the folkways with the connotations of right and truth in respect to welfare, embodied in them.' Moreover, folkways could also become institutionalised into legal rules and a legal system:

> **When folkways have become institutions or laws they have changed their character and are to be distinguished from the mores . . . Laws and institutions have a rational and practical character, and are more mechanical and utilitarian. The great difference is that institutions and laws have a positive character, while mores are unformulated and undefined.**

As the years went by judges presiding in both civil and criminal disputes inevitably began to look back to earlier times in order to discover what had been judicially decided in situations involving similar circumstances. The outcome of one case would thus establish a yardstick or precedent by which similar cases might be judged in the future.

The decline of common law

From the late nineteenth century, however, given the changing socio-economic conditions of the times, common law has been steadily eroded by parliamentary legislation. Today statutory law is extremely important; it is supreme where a conflict occurs between it and the common law. Hence reference is frequently made to the doctrine of parliamentary supremacy or sovereignty. Nothing in the long run can compete with parliamentary law, but that does not mean to say that judicial precedents have also diminished at the same rate. On the contrary, judicial interpretation of the clauses of a statute remains crucial, particularly when a new Act of Parliament is passed or an existing one amended. The first case – a test case – brought under such an Act will be watched closely by the legal and political professions. The judicial interpretation in that kind of case will, in itself, establish a precedent, but in statutory as opposed to common law. Nonetheless the term 'precedent' is historically associated with the common law. So how do judges make decisions, particularly in common law cases? One way in which they might do so is to use the deductive method. *Deduction* may be regarded as reasoning from the general to the particular. A rule or a theory is developed in the judicial mind, or held by that mind to exist, and as a result that rule leads logically to a particular conclusion given all the circumstances of the case in hand. *Induction* is the opposite: reasoning moves from the particular to the general. The circumstances of the case suggest that a particular rule of law be formulated or found. The inductive approach, however, does not necessarily demand a particular conclusion. It is probably rather more accurate to say that English judges generally proceed by *analogy*, thus avoiding the potential conflicts between deduction and induction.

Analogy is the art of comparison: judges will compare similar problems and similar circumstances. They will see whether two or more apparently like problems might have to be decided differently according to the facts and the circumstances of each case. It is essentially a cautious, pragmatic approach; indeed judges might well be accused of being generally more cautious, or possibly more conservative, than their political masters in Parliament who have been responsible for so much of twentieth-century law. Analogy is reasoning by example: example and comparison have been at the heart of common law over the centuries. In short, analogy is reasoning from the particular to the particular; thus it may be viewed as imperfect or primitive induction.

Ratio decidendi

In every case, therefore, the court arrives at some decision or other. And at the heart of every case there is to be found a fundamental legal rule, the *ratio decidendi*. The phrase *ratio decidendi* is not one of the most helpful in law. In fact it was Austin, one of the leading scholars in jurisprudence in the nineteenth century who brought it into the English legal vocabulary. Literally it might mean 'the reason for a decision', but really the Latin *ratio* means 'principle' or 'rule', in other words the rule of law that is involved in a particular case.

In one sense *ratio decidendi* is at its most obvious in common law civil cases. Statutory law of itself means that Parliament has laid down the legal rules and most criminal legal rules are nowadays parliamentary ones. But in common law it is the judges themselves who are making the rules.

In fact, a judgment very often consists of several legal principles (*rationes*), although inevitably they will be closely related. It would be wrong to suggest that somewhere in the decision of the court lies buried a single magic formula. Nor does it mean to say that the *ratio* is fixed for all time. Changing social circumstances, shifts in public opinion, may well mean that later on the same *ratio* is applied but in a different manner. Or it may mean that an entirely different *ratio* is formulated by the courts. The principle of precedent is simply not that inflexible; if it were, precedent itself would have replaced common law as a source of legal rules. In any case Parliament may intervene and pass an Act which overturns or amends an earlier *ratio decidendi*.

Perhaps, therefore, the process of analogy for the judge is something like this:

1   Does the case or the problem A before me, having heard counsel's arguments, seem similar in outline to any earlier case that has been brought to the attention of the court? Yes, cases B and C seem to be similar.

2   On closer examination cases B and C differ. Case B was based on a somewhat different legal rule from that in case C. The *ratio* of B, if therefore at first sight similar, was at second sight dissimilar.

3   Case C, however, was concerned with the same legal rule as in case A. The *ratio* of case C is relevant to A. In addition the circumstances and the facts between C and A are almost identical: the outcome of case A must therefore be determined by case C (the process of precedent).

An alternative to stage 3, however, might be that the facts and circumstances of A were too divorced from case C. The precedent of case C was not applicable to the situation in case A. Yet even if they were the court might still decline to apply the *ratio* of case C to case A; it was time to change legal direction – precedent would be overthrown. Sir Rupert Cross provided the following definition of *ratio*:

> The *ratio decidendi* of a case is any rule of law expressly or impliedly treated by the judge as a necessary step in reaching his conclusion, having regard to the line of reasoning adopted by him, or a necessary part of his direction to the jury.

Common law is frequently referred to as case-law, since it has evolved almost entirely from disputes brought before the courts. The word 'case-law', however, like 'precedent' and *ratio* must be used with care. Nowadays there are just as many cases concerning the judicial interpretation of Acts of Parliament as there are concerning the application of the common law. And interpretation of an Act may amount in practice to the formulation of new legal rules by the judges themselves, in other words case-law of a different sort.

Sir Rupert Cross's definition of precedent and common or case-law is as follows:

> Case-law consists of the rules and principles stated and acted upon by judges in giving decisions. In a system based on case-law, a judge in a subsequent case *must* have regard to these matters; they are not, as in some other legal systems, merely material which he *may* take into consideration in coming to his decision.

The problems of precedent will be returned to under parliamentary law. The whole question of whether judges 'discover' the law or make it, is obviously not an easy one to answer. In the case of statute law clearly Parliament is the manufacturer, but judges can still fill in the details of the framework, and indeed on occasion give the entire framework a whole new interpretation. In his 1974 Hamlyn Lecture Lord Scarman stressed the importance of the judicial system being prepared to adjust itself to the governmental and parliamentary powers of a modern state:

> **Society . . . asks only that judges transfer their traditional skills, spirit and attitudes from declaring [the common] law, the basis and nature of which no longer suffice to meet society's need, to . . . a modern, statute-based and more activist law.**

In contrast to *ratio*, *obiter dicta* literally means words said on the way, or in passing. That means that in delivering a judgment the court may make comments either with regard to the interpretation or application of a legal rule or as to how Parliament ought to legislate in order to remedy a particular problem. These comments are important but are made in passing – they are not central to the decision in a case, they are not part of the *ratio decidendi*.

Professor Michael Zander has observed:

> **The first thing a lawyer wants to know when inspecting a precedent is whether the proposition of law in which he is interested forms the *ratio decidendi* of the case, or whether it is only something said which is *dictum* or *obiter dictum*. Dicta may be of very great persuasive weight but they cannot under any circumstances be binding on anyone. The most carefully considered and deliberate statement of law by all five Law Lords which is *dictum* cannot bind even the lowliest judge in the land. Technically he is free to go his own way. In practice, of course, weighty *obiter* pronouncements from higher courts are likely to be followed and will certainly be given the greatest attention, but in the strictest theory they are not binding.**

Another view was put by Mr Justice Megarry in *West (Richard) & Partners (Inverness) Ltd* v. *Dick* (1969):

> **Some authorities distinguish between *obiter dicta* and judicial *dicta*. The former are mere passing remarks of the judge, whereas the latter consist of considered enunciations of the judge's opinion of the law on some point which does not arise for decision on the facts of the case before him, and so is not part of the *ratio decidendi*.**

Mr Justice Megarry went on to add a third type of *dictum* – where a judge refers to decisions in unreported cases. 'He is, as it were, a reporter *pro tanto*.' This *dictum*, he said, carried the authority of the judges and of 'an unseen cloud of his judicial brethren'. It was a *dictum* of the highest authority, which other judges should follow.

THE GROWTH OF STATUTE LAW

We have, therefore, in English law two main, and occasionally rival, sources of law – the common law, sometimes known as customary or case-law, and parliamentary or statutory law. But it is the latter which in the end always prevails; there is nothing more supreme than parliamentary law. Would it not make sense, however, to combine these two sources of law? Some progress has been made in this area, especially in the post-war period. Where an Act of Parliament is passed on a particular matter and it incorporates the earlier common law as well as perhaps a series of previous Acts relating to that subject then we can say the law has been codified: the law in respect of that issue may now be found in one place. Codification is traditionally more a feature of continental systems of law, most notably France from the time of Napoleon. There parliamentary or presidential law is the key, not judge-made law. Indeed French judicial decisions do not themselves become a source of law until they are definitely fixed by the repetition of precedents which are in agreement on a single point. *Consolidation* is not to be confused with codification: a consolidating Act brings together earlier Acts on the same subject under one statutory roof, for the sake of simplicity and tidiness. Absorbing common law into statutory law is *codification*, a much more complex task than consolidation.

Where two or more statutes are merged into one, inevitably some of the wording in the original Acts is lost. This may give rise to difficulties of interpretation. In *R. v. Heron* (1982) Lord Scarman observed that when construing a consolidating statute, it is particularly useful to have recourse to the legislative history if a real difficulty arises. 'Consolidation is, or is intended by Parliament to be, the re-enactment "in a more convenient, lucid and economical form" (Lord Simon of Glaisdale) of existing statute law.' Lord Scarman added that there were three types of consolidation: (a) pure consolidation, ie re-enactment; (b) consolidation with corrections and minor improvements; and (c) consolidation with Law Commission amendments.

The essential feature, then, of common law is that although partly based on local and national customs it is fundamentally judge-made law developed over many centuries. In *Parker v. British Airways Board* (1982) Lord Justice Donaldson observed: 'One of the great merits of the common law is that it is usually sufficiently flexible to take account of the changing needs of a continually changing society.' Now it is parliamentary law which is gradually seeing common law off the legal field. But before considering statutory law, it would be appropriate to look at other sources of law first. Perhaps the final word at this stage can be left with Lord Reid, one of the most distinguished judges of the post-war period:

> I suppose that almost every doctrine of the common law was invented by some judge at some period in history, and when he invented it he thought it was plain common-sense – and indeed it generally was originally. But, with the passage of time more technically minded judges have forgotten its origin and developed it in a way that can

> easily cause injustice. In so far as we appellate judges can get the thing
> back on the rails let us do so; if it has gone too far we must pin our
> hopes on Parliament.

'There was a time,' he also observed;

> when it was thought almost indecent to suggest that judges make law
> – they only declare it. Those with a taste for fairy tales seem to have
> thought that in some Aladdin's cave there is hidden the Common Law
> in all its splendour and that on a judge's appointment there descends
> on him knowledge of the magic words Open Sesame. Bad decisions
> are given when the judge has muddled the password and the wrong
> door opens. But we do not believe in fairy tales any more.

2.2

Parliamentary law and delegated legislation

THE RELATIONSHIP BETWEEN THE LORDS AND COMMONS

The concept of the Queen in Parliament apart, the legislative body is divided into two parts – the House of Commons and the House of Lords. The terms 'Lower Chamber (or House)' and 'Upper Chamber' as applied to the Commons and Lords respectively are of only historical significance. The twentieth century has seen a massive decline in the power of the Lords *vis-à-vis* the Commons.

In 1909 the Lords rejected the Liberal Government's budget. The result was two general elections in 1910 on the issue of 'peers versus the people' and a tacit agreement by the King that if necessary he would create enough Liberal peers to swamp the traditional Tory majority. The outcome was the passage of the Parliament Act 1911; it passed through the Lords because under the threat of new Liberal peers being created most of the Conservative peers stayed away. The Act reduced the maximum lifetime of a Parliament to five years from seven, in other words a Prime Minister must call a general election at least once every five years (technically it is the Queen who dissolves Parliament on the advice of the Prime Minister).

As far as the Lords itself was concerned, the 1911 Act did two things. Firstly, any 'money' Bill would become law if the Lords failed to pass it without amendment after one month. On the other hand there have been a number of instances of a money Bill being amended in the Lords and the amendments being accepted by the Commons. The Speaker of the House of Commons decides what constitutes a money Bill – usually it relates to those pieces of legislation dealing with the Budget and public expenditure, such as the annual Finance and Consolidated

Fund Acts, although it should be said the definition is a narrow one – quite often the annual Finance Bill is not so certified. Secondly, as for other legislation, the House of Lords could not indefinitely delay a Bill once the Commons had passed that Bill in three successive parliamentary sessions, where at least two years had elapsed between the second reading of the Bill in the first session and the third reading in the third. The Parliament Act 1949 reduced the period to two sessions and one year respectively. Attlee's Government at that time was afraid that the Lords would hold up various nationalisation measures, particularly one affecting the iron and steel industry. In the case of both money and non-money Bills once the Lords has delayed long enough in accordance with the provisions of the Parliament Acts then the Bill becomes law – it is automatically presented for the Royal Assent. Legislation not covered by these provisions is any Bill designed to lengthen the life of Parliament (this happened at the time of the two World Wars) and private Bills, as well as secondary or delegated legislation which is described below. A simple outright rejection of a Bill is not the same as an amendment, but the 1911 Act provides that a Bill shall be deemed to be rejected by the Lords if not passed without amendment unless such amendments are agreed to by both Houses. It should also be added that under the Salisbury Convention of 1945, the House of Lords will not block legislation which was clearly based on promises in the winning party's election manifesto.

Defeats for the Lords

So far this century the government has had to use the Parliament Act 1911 on only four occasions – to disestablish the Anglican Church in Wales (the Welsh Church Act 1914), to give Ireland a measure of home rule (Government of Ireland Act 1914), to pass the second Parliament Act itself, and the War Crimes Act 1991. (The Irish legislation was not implemented.) During the post-war period there have been several occasions on which the government has come close to utilising the Parliament Act's provisions. This was most notable under the Labour Government of 1974-79. The Trade Union and Labour Relations (Amendment) Act 1976, the Dock Work Regulation Act 1976 (also a trade union measure) and the Aircraft and Shipbuilding Industries Act 1977 (a nationalisation measure) had all run on to the legislative rocks before reaching the statute book. In the end the Lords gave up and the Bills were passed, but only after the government had accepted substantial amendments, especially in the case of the Dock Work and Aircraft Acts. In the former the Lords was helped by the fact that a number of Labour MPs in the Commons, such as Professor J. P. Mackintosh, were opposed to the measure; in the latter the Bill ran into procedural difficulties when the Conservative MP for Tiverton, Mr Robin Maxwell-Hyslop, spotted that the legislation was 'hybrid' – that is partly a private Bill and partly a public Bill.

Defeats for the Commons

In 1969 the Lords effectively wrecked the House of Commons (Redistribution of Seats) Bill. This was part of a constitutionally complicated story that arose out of the reports of the Boundary Commission. There are four Commissions, one each for England, Wales, Scotland and Northern Ireland; they owe their statutory authority to the Parliamentary Constituencies Act 1986 as amended by the Boundary Commissions Act 1992. Their task is to make recommendations every ten to fifteen years to the Home Secretary as to how the numbers and boundaries of parliamentary constituencies should best be adjusted, given today's mobile population. In introducing the Bill, the Labour Home Secretary, Mr James Callaghan, had wished to implement the proposals for London, but postpone the rest of the Commissions' recommendations in order to coincide with local government re-organisation. But the Conservatives and some Labour MPs suspected ulterior motives: the disappearance of a number of inner-city seats with a declining electorate would have been bad news for the Labour Party. Delay followed until the Prime Minister, Mr Harold Wilson, called a surprise general election for June 1970: he lost. The new boundaries did not thus take effect until the general election of February 1974.

Other areas where the House of Lords has made its mark were the Immigration Act 1971 (the position of Commonwealth citizens already resident in the United Kingdom was strengthened), the Education Act 1980 (government proposals to charge for school transport were defeated), the Housing Act 1980 (council homes designated for elderly people were exempted from the 'right to buy' provisions) and the Housing and Building Control Act 1984 (charitable housing and disabled accommodation were also exempted from the 'right to buy' legislation). In 1979 the Lords also strongly criticised the government's Protection of Official Information Bill on the grounds that the Bill was even more draconian than the Official Secrets Act 1911 which it was intended to replace. The Commons was about to voice similar objections, the Bill was introduced into the Lords first, when the Anthony Blunt spy scandal broke. The press was quick to point out that reporting of the scandal would have been more difficult under the proposed legislation than under the existing laws. The government bowed to pressure and withdrew the Bill. Indeed the Commons as well as the Lords may force the government to drop legislation – this happened in 1979 and 1981 in respect of two local government finance Bills – the predecessors of the Local Government, Planning and Land Act 1980 and the Local Government Finance Act 1982. In the case of the earlier Act the Commons' opposition was largely because the Bill had been introduced in the Lords.

What almost sealed the Lords' fate was its rejection in 1968 of the Southern Rhodesia (United Nations Sanctions) Order, a piece of delegated legislation. Economic sanctions against Rhodesia, a colony in rebellion against the Crown from 1965 to 1979, were usually renewed each year by the British Parliament. As a result proposals were drawn up to strip the Lords of its powers still further and to change its composition, but the Commons could not agree on the measure and in 1969 the matter was dropped. In 1997 the new Labour Government renewed its promise to reform the Lords.

Legislative procedure

The procedure for the passage of legislation through both Houses is broadly as follows. The government introduces most legislation into the Commons, but in order to save time some Bills will be introduced into the Lords (the Lord Chancellor, for example, will introduce Bills affecting the legal system, such as the Legal Aid Act 1982 and the Contempt of Court Act 1981). A Bill follows various stages. The First Reading is little more than a formal announcement of the Bill. The Second Reading is a discussion of the major principles of the Bill. Each clause of the Bill will then be examined line by line in a standing committee. Most standing committees are known simply by letters – A, B, C and so on. Membership reflects the political balance in the Commons as a whole. After the Committee Stage comes the Report Stage at which the Commons as a whole considers the standing committee's amendments. A Report Stage will still arise where the Commons itself sits as a committee – the Committee of the Whole House, unless, of course, no amendments in committee have been made: this procedure is usually reserved for important constitutional measures, such as the devolution legislation of 1976-78; the abortive Scotland and Wales Acts 1978 proposed to establish domestic legislative and executive assemblies in Scotland and Wales respectively. The Committee of the Whole House procedure is also used, to save time, on Bills which are not expected to be amended or which are urgent. Final votes are taken at the Third Reading. The procedure is repeated in the House of Lords, although usually the Lords sits as a whole for committee purposes. In the Lords amendments may also be taken at the Third Reading stage.

The Renton Report on the Preparation of Legislation in 1975 made a number of proposals to simplify legislation and to present it in a more user-friendly style, but an innate conservatism within the Parliamentary Counsel's Office has ensured that little has changed in over 20 years. Such issues were returned to by the Rippon Report in 1993, issued by the Hansard Society for Parliamentary Government. Rippon said there were five central principles which guided and governed all the recommendations it made (that included some specific points about procedure in the House of Lords including the role of special standing committees and the appointment of a Delegated Powers Scrutiny Committee), in short:

1 Laws are made for the benefit of the citizens of the state. All citizens directly affected should be involved as fully and openly as possible in the processes by which statute law is prepared.

2 Statute law should be as certain as possible and as intelligible and clear as possible, for the benefit of the citizens to whom it applies.

3 Statute law must be rooted in the authority of Parliament and thoroughly exposed to open democratic scrutiny by the representatives of the people in Parliament.

4 Ignorance of the law is no excuse, therefore the current statute law must be accessible as possible to all who need to know it.

5   The Government needs to be able to secure the passage of its legislation, but to get the law right and intelligible, for the benefit of citizens, is as important as to get it passed quickly.

Retrospective legislation

Normally in the autumn (October or November) the Queen opens the new parliamentary session and in the Speech from the Throne in the Lords she outlines her government's legislative intentions for the year ahead. (Which Bills are included in the legislative programme and how early in the sessional timetable they occur are matters determined by committees of the Cabinet.) Whatever those intentions may be, no Parliament can bind its successors, although the example of EC law since 1973 perhaps provides an exception to that convention. Parliament at a future date can always undo what laws were passed on an earlier occasion; one Act can repeal a previous one. But can an Act have retrospective provisions? In other words can an Act passed in 1998 not just create a new legal rule from 1998 onwards but also have the effect of saying that that legal rule also operated before 1998? It is not a custom for Parliament to pass laws which have retroactive results, but sometimes it deems it to be in the 'national interest' to do so.

The most famous example of a retrospective statute is the War Damage Act 1965. During the Second World War the Army's Commanding Officer in Burma had ordered the destruction of oil installations in and around Rangoon, so as to deny the advancing Japanese the use of industrial resources. The Crown had always possessed the prerogative to enter property in order to take action against an enemy. But it was not clear whether compensation was legally due to persons suffering loss by the Crown's action after hostilities had ceased; moreover, in this case the action had been preventative – it was not part of an actual military encounter. The government warned the owners of the installations – the Burmah Oil Company – that if they persisted in their claims (the company had received limited *ex gratia* compensation) they would have no choice but to ask Parliament to pass a Bill which would effectively put a stop to those claims. Once the House of Lords in its judicial capacity found for the company (*Burmah Oil Company* v. *Lord Advocate*) this was precisely what happened: the War Damage Act 1965 exempted the Crown from claims of the kind that the appellants had brought forward and was made retrospective in effect. Sparing as the use of such legislation may be, 1965 was a good year: the Trade Disputes Act reversed the Lords' decision in *Rookes* v. *Barnard* (a trade union closed shop dispute).

Professor J. A. G. Griffith has suggested that in respect of the Immigration Act 1971 the Law Lords refused to apply the Act's penal sanctions retroactively so as 'to render a person liable to criminal proceedings for acts which were not criminal when he committed them.' Clearly, it must be wrong that a person's liberty can be put at risk by such legislation, but the civil consequences may be as far-reaching – the Burmah Oil Company, one of Britain's oldest established oil 'majors' was virtually bankrupted by the War Damage Act and is no longer involved in oil exploration or production. The Local Government, Planning and Land Act 1980 contained retrospective provisions in respect of the fixing of local government's Rate Support Grant for 1980-81. This was mainly because the government had been forced by backbenchers to drop another Bill with much the same objectives earlier in the same parliamentary session. The Representation of the People Act 1981 was retrospective in respect of the disqualification of prisoners elected to the House of Commons. However, in respect of the Housing and Building Control Bill 1983 the House of Lords deleted from the Bill a clause which could be regarded as retrospective, where the government had proposed to extend its 'right to buy' policy to certain charitable housing associations in receipt of public money under the Housing Act 1974. Further retrospective clauses were contained in the Rate Support Grants Act 1986 and the Local Government Finance Act 1987.

DELEGATED LEGISLATION

Reference has been made earlier to delegated legislation, which is sometimes referred to as subordinate or secondary legislation. Delegated legislation consists mainly of rules and regulations made by government ministers under the authority of an Act of Parliament. It is often convenient if Parliament hands the Minister a partly blank cheque on which can be filled the relevant details. Very often those details are so technical in nature that it would be inappropriate to attempt to incorporate them into a single statute. Sometimes local government enjoys similar statutory authority – it may be allowed to make certain by-laws. On occasion public corporations such as the British Railways Board, may enjoy the powers of delegated legislation.

Delegated legislation may take different legal forms. One such method may be to make an Order in Council; other pieces of delegated legislation may take the form of rules or regulations, for instance. Council here refers to the Privy Council. The Privy Council is largely a historical body that advises the monarch. Its membership is about 400 and is drawn from senior politicians and judges of the United Kingdom and the Commonwealth. A member is known as 'The Right Honourable . . .' All members of the Cabinet are also Privy Councillors. It has few constitutional duties nowadays; when it meets, its proceedings, which are confidential, are usually so brief that no one sits down. It is best known, as seen later, for its role as an appellate court for Commonwealth countries – and, in that capacity, it does sit down!

Virtually all delegated legislation may be generally termed as 'statutory instruments'; statutory instruments, like Acts of Parliament, must be printed and published. Several thousand are produced each year. Statutory instruments do not, however, include rules and by-laws made by public corporations and local authorities. The parent Act, that is the Act that gives authority for the statutory instrument to be made, may require the instrument to be laid before the House. If that is so the instrument will normally be subject to an affirmative or negative vote. A 'negative' instrument will take legal effect if after forty days of being laid before the House no 'prayer' to annul the instrument has been put to the House by an MP and carried. An affirmative vote means that MPs must approve the instrument.

In most cases instruments are laid before both Houses for approval or possible annulment. Whether parliamentary scrutiny of delegated legislation is really adequate remains very much an open question; certainly there have been considerable problems with regard to European Community (EC) law.

INTERPRETATION AND *STARE DECISIS*

Reference has already been made to the very prominent position that statutory law holds in contemporary society. Indeed in *X. v. Morgan-Grampian (Publishers) Ltd* (1990) Lord Donaldson said:

> **Parliament makes the law and it is the duty of the courts to enforce that law, whether or not they agree with it. Every citizen, every corporate body and every authority, whether national or local, is entitled to campaign to change the law, but until the law is changed it is their duty to obey it. That is what parliamentary democracy and the rule of law is all about. Each one of us surrenders a part of his personal freedom of action and choice and in return is protected by the law from the consequences of others seeking to exercise an unfettered freedom of action and choice.**

However, despite the fact that a great deal of the legislation that Parliament passes will reflect the social and economic divide between the two principal political parties, it is also true that an equally significant amount of legislation will be based on ordinary common sense and principles of fairness and reasonableness. In the case of *DPP* v. *Camplin* in 1977 it was held by the Court of Appeal that the trial judge had not properly directed the jury by his interpretation of the relevant section of the Homicide Act 1957. The Act used the phrase 'a reasonable man', but left it to the court to define what it actually meant, in other words to decide what sort of man might reasonably commit murder under severe provocation, thus allowing a charge of murder possibly to be reduced to one of manslaughter.

But the same case – besides illustrating the fact that the term 'reasonable' is enshrined in statutory law as much as it is in common law – highlights only too well the considerable problems that can be involved in judicial *interpretation* of the very clauses of an Act of Parliament. In the *Camplin* case what the Court of Appeal was asked to consider was whether the Crown Court had been right in rejecting the defendant's plea of manslaughter and in reaching the conclusion that a reasonable man, that is one of full age and maturity, would not have acted in the way he, the defendant, a boy of 15, had done, given the same circumstances. The Court of Appeal held that the phrase 'reasonable man' in the Act did not, in this context, mean a 'reasonable adult' but a 'reasonable person of the same age as the accused'. Thus a fundamental point of interpretation was involved – an issue of public policy. It was therefore not surprising that the House of Lords allowed a petition by the Director of Public Prosecutions for leave to appeal to the House on that very point of law. The Lords agreed with the Court of Appeal.

In the controversial jury-vetting case of *R. v. Sheffield Crown Court ex parte Brownlow* (1980) Lord Denning observed:

> **So once again we have here the problem of statutory interpretation. It vexes us daily. Not only us. But also the House of Lords. Even the simplest words give rise to acute differences between us. Half the judges think the interpretation is clear one way. The other half think it is clear the other way . . . Nine times out of ten you will find that judges will agree on what is the sensible result, even though they disagree on the semantic or linguistic result.**

Interpreting laws liberally

The House of Lords (as a judicial body) in the earlier part of the post-war period – from 1945 to about 1957 – was very cautious in appearing to make new law. Rather, it preferred to adhere to the doctrine of substantive formalism – that is to uphold the letter of parliamentary law, if necessary by literal application. In this sense the House of Lords was not concerned with moulding or influencing a body of principles – substantive law – but rather with applying procedures and rules – adjective law.

From time to time, however, the House of Lords and the Court of Appeal (but the latter distinctly more than the former), were prepared to move away from the literal approach. They have been prepared on occasion to make new law in their own right. After five years as a Law Lord, Lord Denning, perhaps the most creative of post-war judges, became, as Master of the Rolls, the head of the Court of Appeal, a post he held from 1962 until retirement in 1982. Literalists may also be called the strict constructionalists – they construe the meaning of a statute, or even of a common law tradition, strictly. In the Lords such a school of thought regained the upper hand from the late 1970s.

Traditionally, there have been three rules or canons regarding the interpretation of statutory law. It should be noted that the Interpretation Act 1978 is concerned only with the definition of technical words and phrases – for example, 'the Crown' and 'sovereign'.

Firstly, the *literal* rule means that the court must give the words of a statute the plainest and most ordinary meaning possible, even if the outcome is slightly perverse. If the law has been badly drafted then that is Parliament's fault. However, Lord Dilhorne in *Black-Clawson International Ltd* v. *Papierwerke Waldhof-Aschaffenburg AG* (1975) noted that in a perfect world the language employed in an Act would not be capable of more than one meaning, but on account of the lack of precision of the English language that was not possible. The literal rule is in one sense a democratic rule: it gained the upper hand in the eighteenth and early nineteenth centuries when politicians felt it was time to cut back on the power that judges had awarded themselves. In *Olgeirsson* v. *Kitching* (1986) a private individual had sold a vehicle to a garage with 38,000 miles recorded, whereas it had done twice the mileage. He was convicted under s.23 of the Trade Descriptions

Act 1968, although s.1, in relation to the principal offender, relates to traders only (applying false descriptions in the course of business). The High Court refused to read s.23 as also applying only to traders (s.23 says another person may be charged even if proceedings are not taken against the trader). 'In the end in this case there are, as I see it, plain words in the statute', held Mr Justice McNeill.

Secondly, as a variation on the first rule, the *golden* rule, means that the court should follow the literal approach as far as possible. But where the result would clearly be absurd then a more sensible meaning must be applied. Adherents of the golden rule are in effect the strict constructionalists.

Thirdly, there is the *mischief* rule. This rule was highlighted by *Heydon's Case* in 1584. By this judges are to ask themselves what was the mischief and defect which the common law did not provide for, what was the state of the common law before the passing of the Act, and how was Parliament intending to remedy that defect. In other words, this rule is more flexible than the first two: the court should look at the whole context of the problem being tackled by the law-makers, especially where doubtful words are present. In *Southern Water Authority* v. *Nature Conservancy Council* (1992) the House of Lords in respect of s.28 of the Wildlife and Countryside Act 1981 had to consider the meaning of 'occupier'. Lord Mustill, applying the mischief rule, considered other provisions of the Act and their effect.

The mischief rule, it might be argued, bears a close relationship to a fourth rule – the modern *purposive* rule. That essentially means that the whole purpose of the Act must be examined and that where difficult sections occur then the spirit of the statute rather than the letter must be emphasised. Where necessary, judges themselves must adapt the Act to its proper and true purpose – the minds of the legislators themselves must be read.

A conflicting approach

In one way all these so-called rules are not so much rules as maxims or overlapping approaches to the interpretation of legislation. The divide – and it is one – comes down to that of either taking words at their everyday face value, with possibly unfortunate results, or interpreting the language widely in order to achieve an apparently more satisfactory outcome as far as society generally is concerned. And both approaches raise the question as to whether words should be examined singly or as a phrase or sentence. Professor H. L. A. Hart has described the problem:

> **Long ago Bentham issued a warning that legal words demanded a special method of elucidation and he enunciated a principle that is the beginning of wisdom in this matter though it is not the end. He said we must never take these words alone, but consider whole sentences in which they play their characteristic role. We must take not the word 'right' but the sentence 'You have a right', not the word 'State' but the sentence 'He is a member or an official of the State'. His warning has largely been disregarded and jurists have continued to hammer away at single words.**

Such problems were well illustrated by the case of *Bromley London Borough Council* v. *Greater London Council* (1982). In 1981 the Labour Party gained control of the Greater London Council (GLC). It was committed to introducing cheap fares on London Transport in order to encourage more people to use buses and the Underground. Rates within the Greater London area went up accordingly. A district council challenged the GLC's action in the courts on the grounds that the rate rise was excessive and that the GLC had broken the fiduciary duty it owed to its ratepayers. The relevant Act was the Transport (London) Act 1969 and the most important section was s.1 under which the GLC was charged with the following task: 'to develop policies and to encourage, organise and, where appropriate, carry out measures, which will promote the provision of integrated, efficient and economic transport facilities and services for Greater London'. The crux of the matter was how far subsidies for London Transport could obtain in the light of the word 'economic'. What exactly did 'economic' mean? Had the legislature intended to abandon earlier legislative principles, that transport operations should as far as possible attempt to break even? Both the Court of Appeal and the House of Lords decided that it had not. Their decision was attacked by the Labour group on the GLC as being, at worst, politically Conservative and, at best, socially behind the times.

Here, for once, the Lords and the Court of Appeal agreed. But there have been many cases where that has not been so (for example, *Express Newspapers Ltd* v. *McShane* and *Duport Steels Ltd* v. *Sirs* – both 1980 trade union cases). In 1979 Professor Michael Zander observed:

> **Ultimately, it may be said that the Law Lords are adopting a more dispassionate, cool, uninvolved attitude which gives prime importance to the statutory words and refuses to become embroiled in the policy behind the words. The Court of Appeal, at least when Lord Denning presides, is more inclined to wear its heart on its sleeve, to take a view on the policy of legislation and to shape its decisions by its sense of the equities. There is no way of saying in the abstract which approach is more often likely to produce a sensible result, but there can be no doubt that whereas the Law Lords have adopted a more restrained approach, Lord Denning's way more obviously requires the judge to judge.**

Since Lord Denning's retirement in 1982, however, the relationship between the two senior courts has been less tempestuous, and in matters of statutory interpretation they have moved towards common ground.

Two further examples of the difficulty of interpreting a single word will suffice. In *R. v. Jones (Keith)* (1987) the captain of a ship loaded with cannabis on a voyage from Lebanon and boarded by customs officers pleaded not guilty to being armed with an offensive weapon contrary to s.86 of the Customs and Excise Management Act 1979 – two pistols were found in the wheelhouse. The Court of Appeal held he was rightly convicted – 'armed' had its ordinary meaning of either physically carrying arms or having them readily available for use. The question for the House of Lords in *Attorney-General's Reference (No 1 of 1988)* (1989) was the meaning of 'obtain' under s.1 of the Company Securities (Insider Dealing) Act 1985; the Court of Appeal and the House of Lords took the wide view that 'obtain' meant receiving or acquiring.

There is also the principle that any ambiguity in a penal statute should be resolved in favour of the defence. That point was explained by Lord Reid in *DPP* v. *Ottewell* (1970) when he said that 'it only applies where after full inquiry and consideration one is left in real doubt'. Ambiguities in statutes should not be construed in a way which does not make good sense, said Lord Templeman in *Waltham Forest London Borough Council* v. *Thomas* (1992), and in *R.* v. *Callender* (1992) the Court of Appeal had reference to the Oxford Dictionary to establish the meaning of 'employment' in the context of s.16 of the Theft Act 1968.

Drafting legislation

When Bills are published, explanatory memoranda are also issued, but strangely these are dropped upon enactment. Then it is a case of the Act, and nothing but the Act. As J. R. Lucas has pointed out, Parliament does not always speak clearly even if it speaks often: 'Legislation which is badly drafted and inadequately scrutinised is often difficult to interpret and often leads to unintended injustices'. Moreover, 'between the publication of a Bill and its application in individual cases, there is relatively little time in Parliament and relatively much in the courts for consideration of expediency, justice and morality to be adduced'. In *Clowser* v. *Chaplin* (1981) a police constable was found to have unlawfully arrested the plaintiff (for failing to provide a breath test under the Road Traffic Act 1972) since the officer had trespassed on private property. The police officer could not enter the premises without a search warrant as provided under the Criminal Law Act 1967 since the offence committed under the breathalyser laws was not an 'arrestable offence' under the Act, that is one carrying a prison sentence of five years or more. Lord Diplock commented:

> **The way in which the 'breathalyser' provisions of the Road Traffic Act 1972 are drafted has enabled motorists to 'cock a snook' at the law . . . The many loop-holes in the law that the ingenuity of defence lawyers has brought to light are, in my view, doing more to bring the criminal law of this country into disrepute than any other legislation. The revision of the 'breathalyser' provisions is under consideration in the Transport Bill now before Parliament. It is for Parliament to make up its mind whether it wants this lamentable state of affairs to continue.**

But *Clowser* v. *Chaplin* was distinguished in *Hart* v. *Chief Constable of Kent* (1983). In the latter case a police officer had already made a lawful arrest under the 1972 Act; it was therefore in order for him to pursue the offender into his house since he had escaped from lawful custody, even though the offender had been standing by his own front door when arrested.

Davis v. Johnson

Perhaps the case which underlined the dilemmas of statutory interpretation most graphically of all was *Davis* v. *Johnson* in 1977–78. The case involved a number of interpretations of the Domestic Violence and Matrimonial Proceedings Act 1976. An unmarried mother, having a joint tenancy of a council flat with a man, the father of her child, left home because of the man's violent behaviour towards her and applied to the County Court for injunctions under the Act to restrain the man from molesting her and to exclude him from the home. A deputy circuit judge granted the applications but within a short time a county court judge rescinded that part of the order which excluded the man from his home. The county court judge took this action following two virtually simultaneous decisions by different judges in the Court of Appeal. In *B* v. *B* (in which the man concerned was the sole tenant of the house) it was held that the Act, on its true construction, simply gave the County Court jurisdiction to grant injunctions of types specified independently of any other relief (in other words the relevant section of the Act was concerned with procedural devices). The Act, the court said, did not alter the substantive law as to the rights of the parties to occupy premises, irrespective of whether those parties were not formally married but were living together as man and wife. Thus an unmarried woman (or man) could not obtain an order excluding her (or his) violent 'partner' from the home unless she (or he) could show that she (or he) had a right by the law of property to exclusive possession of the premises. Within days three different judges of the Court of Appeal followed the decision in *B. v. B.*: in *Cantliff* v. *Jenkins* the judges discharged a county court injunction excluding a man from the home of which he and the woman with whom he had been living were joint tenants. The Court of Appeal considered the decisions of these two cases a month later, at the end of 1977, in *Davis* v. *Johnson*. Quite exceptionally, the Court sat as five judges including the Master of the Rolls, the President of the Family Division of the High Court and the Vice-Chancellor of the Chancery Division. The Court (by a majority of 4-1 but 3-2 on the merits of the case) held that on its true construction the 1976 Act did allow the County Court to grant injunctions to exclude the violent person from the home which the parties, whether married or living together unmarried, shared on a regular basis. It did not matter whether that home was registered in the name of one party only. Thus the court departed from its own decisions in *B. v. B.* and *Cantliff* v. *Jenkins*, even though its decisions were virtually only days old. The Court took the view that *Cantliff* v. *Jenkins* was indistinguishable from *B. v. B.*, although subsequently Lord Diplock in the House of Lords thought that the two cases were distinguishable.

Two points thus arose: was the Court of Appeal bound by its own previous decisions, that is by its own precedents (the rule of *stare decisis*)? This appeared to be so, since the decision in *Young* v. *Bristol Aeroplane Co. Ltd* in 1944 clearly laid down such a rule, subject to three basic exceptions. The exceptions were: where two decisions plainly conflicted with each other; where a decision had been subsequently overtaken by a decision in the House of Lords; and where a previous decision had been given *per incuriam*, in other words negligently. It was this last exception which Lord Denning plainly sought to expand. 'Negligence' is a rather all embracing term; it could certainly mean, for example, that a court had arrived at a wrong decision in an earlier case because insufficient evidence had been brought before it. The Master of the Rolls, Lord Denning, argued that those exceptions had been built upon so much by the Court of Appeal in the post-war period that the rule was hardly any longer a fixed one and that in any case as the House of Lords had in 1966 announced that it was free to depart from its previous decisions, so now should the Court of Appeal. But some of Lord Denning's colleagues argued that the Court of Appeal was bound by its own precedents and that it was up to the House of Lords alone to overrule the Court.

Secondly, was it right for the Court of Appeal, or any other court for that matter, to examine the records of the debates in Parliament (in Hansard) in order to gain a clearer idea of what MPs had in mind when they were debating what turned out to be a poorly framed piece of legislation? Lord Denning clearly thought so, and as far as he was concerned official parliamentary records included reports and debates of Select Committees of Parliament as well as departmental government reports. Technically speaking, until 1980 parliamentary permission was required in order to quote from Hansard.

The House of Lords' reaction and the Practice Statement

The House of Lords upheld the Court of Appeal's decisions in *Davis* v. *Johnson* in respect of their interpretation of s.1 of the 1976 Act but their Lordships took the opportunity to remind the Court that it was indeed bound by its own previous decisions as laid down in the *Young* case and therefore it was up to the Lords to overrule the decisions in *B.* v. *B.* and *Cantliff* v. *Jenkins*. The Lords' own Practice Direction of 1966 was no business of the Court of Appeal. If a precedent is to be binding rather than persuasive, and that is how most precedents are thought of nowadays, then subsequent like cases must follow those previous decisions: the earlier decision must stand – the doctrine of *stare decisis* or binding precedent. In 1966 the House of Lords decided that it, but it alone, was free to depart from its own previous decisions. As the most superior court in the land it did not expect other courts to adopt a similar practice, however. Lower or inferior courts would continue to be bound by their own decisions as well as, of course, by the decisions of superior courts. Earlier decisions of a court in which a trial begins are not binding; that applies to the Magistrates' Court and usually the Crown Court on the criminal side and to the County Court and often the High Court on the civil side. In practice the Civil Division of the Court of Appeal tends to be bound by its previous decisions slightly more than the Criminal Division, but this is partly on account of the historical reorganisation of the criminal appeal process. The decisions of inferior courts can never be binding upon superior courts therefore, although they may be of persuasive importance. Similarly, the decisions of the Judicial Committee of the Privy Council, which deals mainly with appeals from certain Commonwealth countries are strictly speaking only persuasive in respect of British courts, but in practice they may be very important. The Judicial Committee may also depart from its own previous decisions, but it seldom does so.

In *Colchester Estates (Cardiff)* v. *Carlton Industries plc* (1984) it was held that where a judge at first instance was faced with two conflicting decisions of judges of coordinate jurisdiction he should normally treat the legal point at issue as settled by the second judge, unless the third judge was convinced the second judge was wrong in not following the first, for example where some binding or persuasive authority had not been cited in either of the first two cases. In *R. v. Greater Manchester Coroner ex parte Tal* (1984) it was held that in the High Court a divisional court would normally follow the decision of another divisional court but could in rare cases exercise its power to depart from a previous divisional court decision if the court was convinced that the previous decision was wrong, that is where a criminal appeal is made or an application for judicial review is submitted. In *Re Jeffery S Levitt Ltd* (1992) – one High Court judge did not follow the decision of another High Court judge since in the other case certain statutory provisions had not been drawn to the judge's attention and later decisions (including a Court of Appeal case) did not support that judge's views.

The approach in *R. v. Greater Manchester Coroner ex parte Tal* was followed in *R. v. Metropolitan Stipendiary Magistrate ex parte London Waste Regulation Authority* (1993).

The Practice Statement of 1966 reads as follows:

> **Their Lordships regard the use of precedent as an indispensable foundation upon which to decide what is the law and its application to individual cases. It provides at least some degree of certainty upon which individuals can rely in the conduct of their affairs, as well as a basis for orderly development of legal rules.**
>
> **Their Lordships nevertheless recognise that too rigid adherence to precedent may lead to injustice in a particular case and also unduly restrict the proper development of the law. They propose, therefore, to modify their present practice and, while treating former decisions of this House as normally binding, to depart from a previous decision when it appears right to do so.**
>
> **In this connection they will bear in mind the danger of disturbing retrospectively the basis on which contracts, settlements of property and fiscal arrangements have been entered into and also the especial need for certainty as to the criminal law.**
>
> **This announcement is not intended to affect the use of precedent elsewhere than in this House. (*Practice Direction: Judicial Precedent*.)**

The making of such a statement was something of a constitutional novelty: there would have been no doubts about its constitutional status if, however, it had been put into statutory form.

Cassell v. Broome

Some six years before the *Davis* case Lord Denning and the Court of Appeal had been rebuked for trying to ignore a House of Lords decision. In *Cassell* v. *Broome* (1972) Lord Hailsham said:

> I am driven to the conclusion that when the Court of Appeal described the decision in *Rookes* v. *Barnard* as decided *per incuriam* or 'unworkable' they really only meant that they did not agree with it. But, in my view, even if this were not so, it is not open to the Court of Appeal to give gratuitous advice to judges of first instance to ignore decisions of the House of Lords in this way . . . The fact is, and I hope it will never be necessary to say so again, that, in the hierarchical system of courts which exists in this country, it is necessary for each lower tier, including the Court of Appeal, to accept the decisions of the higher tiers.

Of course, it should be added here that it will be more difficult for a court to be bound by the precedent of an earlier case if that case has not been fully reported by one of the law reporting agencies. Many cases, especially when they first come to trial, are not reported at all. Indeed, in 1983 the Court of Appeal made it plain that it would accept submissions only in respect of cases properly reported; it was both costly and time-consuming to examine the transcripts of unreported cases, and such action could be justified only where a very important point of law was raised.

In the *Davis* case Lord Diplock observed:

> Lord Denning [has] conducted what may be described, I hope without offence, as a one man crusade with the object of freeing the Court of Appeal from the shackles which the doctrine of *stare decisis* imposed upon its liberty of decision by the application of the rule laid down in the *Bristol Aeroplane* case to its own previous decisions, or, for that matter, by any decisions of this House itself of which the Court of Appeal disapproved.

In the Court of Appeal, Lord Justice Cumming-Bruce (dissenting from Lord Denning's arguments) remarked:

> If the words of an Act fail to express the intent that Parliament intended, Parliament in its sovereign power can amend the Act. An Act means what the words and phrases selected by the parliamentary draftsmen actually mean, and not what individual members of the two Houses of Parliament may think they mean.

Lord Denning himself remarked in an eloquently phrased speech:

> I would add also that, when the words of the statute are plain, then it is not open to any decision of any court to contradict the statute: because the statute is the final authority on what the law is. No court can depart from the plain words of statute . . . [If] it appears to the Court of Appeal, on further consideration, that a previous decision

was clearly wrong, in my opinion we can depart from it. I would prefer to put it on the ground that this court should take for itself guidelines similar to those taken by the House of Lords; but, if this be not
acceptable, I am of the opinion that we should regard it as an additional exception to those stated in *Young* v. *Bristol Aeroplane Co. Ltd*
(1944), especially as by so doing we can better protect the weak and
do what Parliament intended.

The use of Hansard

The Lords also stated that Hansard and other parliamentary documents should not
be consulted – merely the Act in question and nothing but the Act, the exclusion-
ary rule which dated from 1769. On this point Lord Scarman said:

There are two good reasons why the courts should refuse to have
regard to what is said in Parliament or by Ministers as aids to the
interpretation of a statute. First, such material is an unreliable guide
to the meaning of what is enacted. It promotes confusion, not clarity.
The cut and thrust of debate and the pressures of executive responsibility, essential features of open and responsible government, are not
always conducive to a clear and unbiased explanation of the meaning
of statutory language. And the volume of Parliamentary and ministerial utterances can confuse by its very size. Secondly, counsel are not
permitted to refer to Hansard in argument. So long as this rule is
maintained by Parliament (it is not the creation of the judges), it must
be wrong for the judge to make any judicial use of proceedings in
Parliament for the purposes of interpreting statutes.

Now, however, in *Pepper* v. *Hart* (1993) Lord Griffiths said:

The days have long passed when the courts adopted a strict construc-
tionist view of interpretation which required them to adopt the literal
meaning of the language. The courts now adopt a purposive approach
which seeks to give effect to the true purpose of legislation and are
prepared to look at much extraneous material that bears on the background against which the legislation was enacted.

This case, which involved tax concessions for children of staff educated at Malvern
College, was decided 6-1. with Lord Mackay the Lord Chancellor dissenting; the
Lord Chancellor said the objections to relaxing the Hansard rule were not strong,
but it could lead to an immense increase in the cost of litigation in such cases.

The Lords held that as an aid to construing legislation which was ambiguous or
obscure or the literal meaning of which led to absurdity, then courts could refer to
reports of debates or proceedings in Parliament. But such reference should only be
permitted if it disclosed the mischief aimed at or the legislative intention lying
behind the ambiguous or obscure words. The use of Hansard in such circum-

stances would not impeach or question the freedom of Parliamentary debate and would not be an infringement of article 9 of the Bill of Rights 1688, since it would not amount to a 'questioning' of the freedom of speech or parliamentary debate provided counsel and the judge refrained from impugning or criticising the Minister's statements or his reasoning, since the purpose of the courts in referring to parliamentary material would be to give effect to, rather than thwart through ignorance, the intentions of Parliament and not to question the processes by which such legislation was enacted or to criticise anything said by anyone in Parliament in the course of enacting it. It was thus permissible to refer to the clear statements of legislative intent made in parliamentary proceedings, here for the purpose of construing the ambiguous provisions for taxing benefits of directors and higher-paid employees contained in s.63 of the Finance Act 1976.

Lord Browne-Wilkinson remarked:

> **The courts can now look at White Papers and official reports for the purpose of finding the 'mischief' sought to be corrected, although not at draft clauses or proposals for the remedying of such mischief. A ministerial statement made in Parliament is an equally authoritative source of such information; why should the courts be cut off from this source of information as to the mischief aimed at? In any event, the distinction between looking at reports to identify the mischief aimed at but not to find the intention of Parliament in enacting the legislation is highly artificial . . . There is no logical distinction between the use of ministerial statements introducing subordinate legislation (to which recourse was had in *Pickstone* v. *Freemans plc*, 1989) and such statements made in relation to other statutory provisions which are not in fact subsequently amended. Other common law jurisdictions [in the Commonwealth] have abandoned the rule without adverse consequences.**

Lord Oliver added:

> **Experience shows that [statutory] language – and particularly, language adopted or concurred in under the pressure of a tight parliamentary timetable – is not always a reliable vehicle for the complete or accurate translation of legislative intention; and I have been persuaded . . . that the circumstances of this case demonstrate that there is both the room and the necessity for a limited relaxation of the previously well-settled rule which excludes reference to parliamentary history as an aid to statutory construction.**

Pepper v. *Hart* was immediately applied by the House of Lords in a misleading price case (Dixons at Stratford-upon-Avon, involving an offer of £20 off prices elsewhere) in respect of s.20(1) of Consumer Protection Act 1987 – *R.* v. *Warwickshire County Council ex parte Johnson* (1993). David Miers has commented:

> ***Pepper* v. *Hart* accords primacy to ministerial statements in the event of absurdity, obscurity and ambiguity. To put it mildly, this is a significant break with tradition. . . . In short, *Pepper* v. *Hart* is of the first constitutional importance.**

It should also be added that in *Stubbings* v. *Webb* (1993) the House of Lords ruled that in the light of information to which reference could be made under the new *Pepper* v. *Hart* rule, a court might overrule an earlier decision decided without the benefit of that rule.

2.3   Equity

The term 'equity' has both a technical and a general meaning. First the technical.

Equity dates from the fifteenth century, if not earlier, in the form of the Court of Chancery. Those who were not satisfied with the way in which the common law courts had handled their grievances might petition the king. Such people, of course, were frequently the rich and the powerful. Often it was a case of the common law being defective in its own rules or not being able to deliver the remedy appropriate to the individual's particular needs. But how did this state of affairs first come about? To begin with common law was developed rapidly following the Norman Conquest, too rapidly for some, and in 1258, when Parliament met at Oxford, further development was curtailed by the Provisions of Oxford, arguably a rudimentary form of statute law. As a result common law courts, bound by precedent, were unable to give justice in cases where the strict law was unfair to the plaintiff. To overcome the situation, plaintiffs started to petition the sovereign direct, and such petitions were referred by the King to his Chancellor, whose deputy was the Clerk to the Rolls, the office subsequently called Master of the Rolls, the principal judge in the Chancellor's Court of Chancery.

The petition, 'Let Right be Done', enabled equity to provide a threefold relief from the rigidity of the common law. Chancery exercised exclusive jurisdiction where common law did not recognise the enforcement of rights, concurrent jurisdiction where common law recognised the right, but provided no specific relief, and auxiliary jurisdiction where new procedures were required to augment available remedies.

It is obvious that with two sets of courts, exercising concurrent and in some cases overlapping jurisdiction, there would be conflict, and in fact protests were made in Parliament from the fifteenth century onwards. Nevertheless, the Chancery Court became indispensable, particularly because of its development of the law relating to trusts and wills. Although the distinction between the exclusive, the concurrent and the auxiliary jurisdictions of equity is obsolete since the fusion of equity and the common law under the Supreme Court of Judicature Acts 1873, 1875 and 1925, nevertheless it is necessary to know the historical background, in order to understand the application of the principles of equity.

It sounds as though the court of equity was a knight on a white charger in shining armour, with the common law cast in the role of the Black Knight. In fact, the conflict more resembled the battle between the Red Knight and the White Knight in *Alice through the Looking-Glass*. The first rule that equity established was that 'equity follows the law', that is that where there was a clear rule of law, then the law must be applied. Where there was no clear rule, then equity could intervene to enable a just result and consequently developed a new and parallel set of rules. This development occurred predominantly in matters relating to trusts, wills, land and the wardship of children. So, for instance, at common law a deed could only be varied by another deed; in equity it could be varied by a simple contract and was so applied in *Berry* v. *Berry* (1929). Similarly, where a person is entitled in equity to an interest in land, under an agreement (such as a lease) he is enabled to have his equitable interest turned into a legal estate by an order for specific performance as illustrated in the case of *Walsh* v. *Lonsdale* (1882).

By the eighteenth century the rivalry between the common law and the system of equity had become intense. Moreover, equity no longer provided cheap, efficient solutions. Although there were some reforms in the earlier part of the nineteenth century, these did not work out well in practice, much to the disappointment of the new propertied class of the Industrial Revolution, the self-made men to whom time was money. By the third quarter of the nineteenth century litigants were often trapped between equity on the one hand and the common law on the other.

PARLIAMENTARY INTERVENTION

In 1873 Parliament took a hand in the matter. The two rival systems of courts were merged into one. Where there was a conflict between equity and common law practices in any subsequent case, equity would prevail. But, of course, above both equity and common law would stand any relevant Act of Parliament. Equity was, and in many ways still is, common law's safety-valve. Even now the maxims of equity live on – for instance 'he who comes to equity must come with clean hands', or 'equity looks to the intention and not to the form'. The first rule of thumb means that the complaining party must have a clear conscience in respect of the matter before the court; the second means that equity invariably adopts a less literal or rigid approach than the common law. Other maxims are: 'equity will not suffer a wrong to be without a remedy', 'where there is equal equity the law shall prevail', 'where equities are equal, the first in time shall prevail (*qui prior est tempore, potior est jure*)', 'he who seeks equity must do equity', and 'delay defeats equity (*vigilantibus et non dormientibus lex succurit*)'.

It is said that equity acts *in personam*, not *in rem*; that is the court can act, in appropriate cases, to enforce contracts and trusts relating to property even where the property is not within the jurisdiction. But the court will intervene only if the defendant is within the jurisdiction and the court order can be enforced, and provided always that it is fair, just and reasonable. The principle of relief sought at law is that the plaintiff has suffered loss (for example by breach of contract or tortious act) and is entitled to damages. The principle of relief in equity, however, is that the defendant has improperly made a profit for which it is equitable that he should account to the plaintiff. So at law the damages are measured by the loss suffered by the plaintiff; in equity the extent of the remedy is the improper gain to the defendant, which is frequently measured by directing an account. Since the same court can now order either damages or an account, the plaintiff has the option; he may choose to have an account of profits, or damages, but not both. It was the doctrines of equity, in the Chancery Court, now the Chancery Division, which developed the law of trusts in a flexible manner. Moreover, in law equitable remedies were invoked to supplement procedures, such as discovery and delivery of documents and injunctions, which were not available at common law. While claims in equity did not have to have an origin 'from time immemorial', they had to have a basis in the history of the law; it was not sufficient that 'the justice of the case requires it' *per* Lord Greene in *Ministry of Health* v. *Wintle* (1951).

REMEDIES

Equitable remedies appear to be capable of limitless expansion and adaptation to modern needs, as shown in the matter of Mareva injunctions and Anton Piller orders, mentioned below, which have been developed swiftly in the last few years. Nonetheless, the courts will not extend equitable doctrines, such as relief from forfeiture, too easily, particularly in cases of commercial contracts, as in the case of *Scandinavian Trading Tanker Co. AB* v. *Flota Petrolera Ecuatoriana* (1983), where relief from a time charter clause permitting the ship owners to withdraw the ship for non-payment of hire was claimed; the Court of Appeal, upheld by the House of Lords, declared that certainty in commercial transactions was antipathetic to the equitable doctrine of relief against forfeiture.

Today, therefore, equitable remedies are applied equally in matters of property and trusts and tort and contract, the sort of issues that the Chancery and Queen's Bench Divisions of the High Court handle. Two examples of equitable remedies are promissory estoppel which is a rule of contract law and equitable execution which is a rule that may be applied in bankruptcy hearings. The application of equitable remedies is at the discretion of the court. They will be used if the court thinks it fair, reasonable and just to do so, having regard to all the circumstances of the case. And that is the second and more general meaning of equity. Equity means in a wider sense simply justice, fairness, reasonableness. If something is inequitable, it is unfair and unjust.

One case will illustrate both points. In 1978, in *Cresswell* v. *Potter*, the court was obliged to consider whether the sale of the former matrimonial home by the defendant (the plaintiff's former husband) had, given the circumstances of the case, been executed fairly and judicially. Mr Justice Megarry stated:

> . . . The premises which give rise to the dispute were bought and con-
> veyed to the plaintiff and the defendant as joint tenants in law and
> equity . . . [But] at the end of the day, my conclusion is that this trans-
> action [ie the subsequent sale of the property after the divorce] cannot
> stand. In my judgment the plaintiff has made out her case, and so it is
> for the defendant to prove that the transaction was *fair, just and reason-
> able*. This he has not done' [italics added].

It is also a general principle of equity that the plaintiff should not delay unduly in seeking remedies; indeed it is a matter of equity in the broader sense that inexcusable delay by either party will be injurious to their case, a point underlined in *Antcliffe* v. *Gloucester Health Authority* (1992). In *County and District Properties* v. *Lyell* (1991) the plaintiff was guilty of inexcusable and inordinate delay, but the defendant was estopped from relying on such delay since he had led the plaintiff to believe he would still contest the action despite the delay. Striking out for inordinate delay was also an issue in the Court of Appeal case of *Shtun* v. *Zalejska* (1996). This could even include substantial pre-action delay.

The principles of fairness and reasonableness bring us, conveniently, to natural justice.

2.4

Natural justice and judicial review

Definitions of natural justice are immediately fraught with great difficulties; perhaps the best maxim or rule of thumb would be to say that it is the courts' version of an average person's common sense. Lord Denning said in *R.* v. *Secretary of State for the Home Department ex parte Santillo* (1981) that the rules of natural justice, or of fairness, were not cut and dried. They varied infinitely. What should also be emphasised is that, strictly speaking, natural justice is not so much a source of law as a collection of procedural rules by which legal rules themselves may be considered and applied. In that sense we may refer to 'rules about rules'. In practice, however, an important set of procedures becomes almost a source of law itself, and in this respect it is convenient to consider natural justice at this stage, side by side with the 'true' sources of law.

There are two principal rules of natural justice: *nemo judex in causa sua* (nobody may judge his own case) and *audi alteram partem* (hear the other side: each party to the dispute must be given a fair hearing). In addition, justice must always be seen to be done, as when a case had to be reheard because a magistrate appeared to fall asleep during the original hearing (*R.* v. *Weston-super-Mare Justices ex parte Taylor* (1980)). This cardinal principle of open justice was underlined in the Court of Appeal case of *R.* v. *Avon County Council ex parte Crabtree* (1995). Where a justices' clerk went with the magistrates when they retired for a second time, it could imply that she had participated in the decision, and therefore the convictions were quashed, *R. v. Eccles Justices ex parte Farrelly* (1992). In *Re Crook* (1992) the Court of Appeal said the public should be excluded from a trial only when and to the extent that it is strictly necessary. Similarly, in *H. v. H.* (1982) the Court of Appeal ordered a rehearing in respect of a custody application because the judge had had a private conversation about the case with the welfare officer. As the Court of Appeal observed in *R. v. Chief Registrar of Friendly Societies ex parte New Cross Building Society* (1984) it is only in wholly exceptional circumstances where public knowledge is likely to defeat justice that the courts are justified in proceeding *in camera*. Further, it was a denial of natural justice not to inquire into the defendant's means before imposing a recognisance to keep the peace (here £500) (*R. v. Central Criminal Court ex parte Boulding*, 1984). In a case involving an application for *mandamus*, *R. v. Hendon Justices ex parte DPP* (1992), the High Court said the decision of the justices was so unreasonable that no reasonable bench in like circumstances could have come to the decision. There was a listing error, and the prosecution was dismissed 15 minutes before the prosecutor arrived. The High Court thought the magistrates were deliberately punishing what they saw as the inefficiency of the Crown Prosecution Service. The decision was *Wednesbury* unreasonable (see below).

In *Furnell v. Whangarei High Schools Board* (1973) Lord Morris of Borth-y-Gest said: 'Natural justice is but fairness, writ large and juridically. It has been described as 'fair play in action'. But as was pointed out by Lord Justice Tucker in *Russell v. Duke of Norfolk* (1949) the requirements of natural justice must depend on the circumstances of each particular case and the subject matter under consideration.

In *Crompton v. General Medical Council* (1981) the Judicial Committee of the Privy Council in an appeal from the Disciplinary Committee of the General Medical Council upheld a doctor's claim that he should be allowed to see reports about his 'condition' from two psychiatrists. The Disciplinary Committee had ordered the doctor's name to be erased from the practitioners' register. The Privy Council held that the Committee in refusing the doctor access to the reports had failed to observe the principles of natural justice.

A law examination candidate who was found guilty of attempting to gain an unfair academic advantage, rather than the more serious offence of cheating, could still have the severest penalty imposed on him. But the examination board, when it was deciding the appropriate penalty, should have had before it all the relevant material, including important statements in mitigation. Mr Justice Sedley said that on any view the examination board's decision was surprising and therefore the decision of the Common Professional Examination Board of the defendant university should be quashed – *R. v. Manchester Metropolitan University ex parte Nolan* (1993).

In *Chief Constable of the North Wales Police v. Evans* (1982) the House of Lords held that the dismissal of a police officer by the Chief Constable for North Wales was not in accordance with the rules of natural justice. The Chief Constable had maintained that he had complete discretion to sack a probationary police officer, in this case on account of the facts that E., aged 24, had married a woman 14 years older than himself who had been the former mistress of his uncle, had apparently kept dogs at his police house without permission and had allegedly lived a 'hippy lifestyle'. The Lord Chancellor, Lord Hailsham, said that the Chief Constable had subjected Mr Evans to cavalier treatment; he had not been given a chance to answer the allegations – indeed, he had not been told of the reasons for his dismissal in the first place.

INJUNCTIONS

The courts also have at their disposal a whole range of technical devices that may be used to enforce not only the principles of natural justice but also justice generally. We might almost talk of 'rules about rules about rules'. In private law injunctions are perhaps the best known form of equitable relief developed by the Court of Chancery. An injunction may be a prohibitory one, in other words it orders the defendant to desist from continuing a certain course of action (for example, libel). A variation of this order is the *quia timet* injunction which will restrain the defendant from committing an action which it seems reasonable to believe he might undertake, for instance, wrongful eviction of a tenant by a landlord, as illustrated in *Associated Newspapers plc* v. *Insert Media Ltd* (1990).

A mandatory injunction will compel the defendant to undertake some action or to restore the status quo (for instance, returning a tenancy which was unlawfully taken away). There has also been the twentieth-century development of asking for a simple declaration of the law (or a declaratory judgment) as illustrated in *Gouriet* v. *Union of Post Office Workers* (1977). The House of Lords in *American Cyanamid* v. *Ethicon Ltd* (1975) overruled the Court of Appeal by stating that it was unnecessary for an applicant for an interim injunction to establish a *prima facie* case: it was sufficient to demonstrate that there was a relatively serious issue at stake.

Parallel to injunctions are, in public law, the common law orders (also known as prerogative or Crown orders) of *mandamus* and *prohibition*, whose functions are similar and which nowadays frequently relate to the unlawful actions, or the absence of lawful ones, of public bodies such as a county or district council. The prerogative order of *certiorari* is used to quash a decision of an inferior court or a statutory body where it can be shown that there has occurred a judicial error or a breach of natural justice or an action by a public authority which is *ultra vires* – that is beyond its statutory powers. In *R.* v. *Secretary of State for Transport ex parte Greater London Council* (1985) Mr Justice McNeill, ruling on the financial implications of the transfer of London Regional Transport from the GLC to the Minister, said that the GLC had been denied natural justice in respect of their representations and therefore *certiorari* was appropriate to quash the order, since the Secretary of State, Mr. Nicholas Ridley, had acted unlawfully, irrationally and improperly. In *R.* v. *South Molton Justices ex parte Ankerson* (1989) *certiorari* was granted, since the reasons for the order (here the applicant's binding-over) had not been made clear. The prerogative writ of *habeas corpus* ensures that a person should not be unreasonably detained without being charged with an offence.

Applications for prerogative orders are invariably heard by the Queen's Bench Division of the High Court. All three divisions, Chancery, Family and Queen's Bench, will entertain applications for an injunction or declaration. Injunctions and orders are issued at the discretion of the court, but it is contempt on the part of any party to ignore them once made. The rule of contempt does not apply to a declaration. Frequently the court will be asked to grant an interim (temporary) injunction only, in order to provide some form of interlocutory relief. Applications for such interim or interlocutory injunctions may be made on the strength of the representations of one party only (*ex parte*). Since the Courts and Legal Services Act 1990 (s.3), the County Court judge has power to grant any injunction, but not the Anton Piller or Mareva orders or the prerogative orders. In *Khorasandjian* v. *Bush* (1993) where a boy was pestering and harassing his girl-friend (the defendant) at her parents' house where she was living (the defendant having undergone psychotherapy after suicide attempts) it was submitted that, as the girl had no proprietary interest in the parental home (except that she was a licensee), she could not invoke the tort of private nuisance. The Court of Appeal noted that the power of the County Courts to grant injunctions in cases where the County Court had jurisdiction was the same as the power of the High Court. The statutory authority was now s.37(1) of the Supreme Court Act 1981, which provided that the High Court might by order grant an injunction 'in all cases in which it appears to the court to be just and convenient to do so'. Lord Justice Dillon said that in the light of changing social conditions there was no reason not to grant an injunction.

An interlocutory injunction will often serve its purpose; the parties will not return to court and risk a full trial the result of which might merely be to grant a final injunction, that is to make the interlocutory one permanent. An *ex parte* injunction will be granted in matters of urgency or difficulty, such as where one party has made himself unavailable, perhaps by leaving the country. The practice is to grant an *ex parte* injunction only for a very limited time, say three days or so, and to order a further hearing when the respondent to the application can be present. A court will not grant an injunction if an award of damages appears to be a clearly more appropriate remedy.

MAREVA AND ANTON PILLER ORDERS

Since 1975 the courts have on occasion been prepared to grant what is known as a Mareva injunction. This arose from the case of *Mareva Compania Naviera SA* v. *International Bulkcarriers SA* (1975). The effect of such an injunction is to order third parties such as banks to freeze the assets of one of the two parties to a dispute where there is a chance that those assets will be moved away from the court's jurisdiction, in other words most likely out of the country. If one party has no known assets within the United Kingdom it will be that much more difficult for the other party to enforce damages or costs awarded. The suspension of Exchange Controls in 1979 has increased the danger of such a possibility. 'Assets' include motor vehicles, jewellery, objets d'art and other valuables (*CBS United Kingdom Ltd* v. *Lambert*, 1982). It should also be noted that the Court of Appeal in *Galaxia Maritime SA* v. *Mineralimportexport* (1982) ruled that an injunction could not be granted where the effect would be a substantial interference with the business rights of a third party not directly involved in the dispute.

The injunction has been given statutory recognition by the Supreme Court Act 1981, s.37. In the case of *Z Ltd* v. *A-Z and AA-LL* (1982), where a foreign firm with a London office had been defrauded of £2 million, the Court of Appeal issued guidelines for the granting of a Mareva injunction. In respect of the granting of Mareva injunctions the Court of Appeal has shown it does not approve of the practice of attempting to draw on frozen funds where a defendant company would in any case be supported by a parent company – *Atlas Maritime Co. SA* v. *Avalon Maritime Ltd, The Coral Rose (No3)* (1991).

Following the case of *Anton Piller KG* v. *Manufacturing Processes Ltd* in 1976 the courts have also been prepared to grant, in exceptional circumstances, what has become known as an Anton Piller order. The plaintiff, Piller, was a German computer company which suspected that its trade secrets were being leaked to its commercial rivals by its British agents. An Anton Piller order means that the court instructs the defendant to allow his premises to be searched by the plaintiff's representatives and any relevant material or documents to be seized. Such orders will be granted at private hearings, so that the Press or anyone else cannot let the cat out of the bag by warning the defendant of the impending search. In *ITC Film Distributors Ltd* v. *Video Exchange* (1982) an Anton Piller order was granted in order to seize the illegal copies of feature films. In the *CBS* case the Court of Appeal also laid down guidelines for the ordering of delivery up of goods under Anton Piller where no Mareva injunction had been granted. It is usual for applications for both Mareva and Anton Piller to be made *ex parte* for obvious reasons. Further guidelines about the serving of Anton Piller orders were laid down in *Universal Thermosensors Ltd* v. *Hibben* (1992).

The development of Mareva injunctions and Anton Piller orders shows how interventionist the courts can be, if they are so minded. On the other hand, the courts could be said to be in frequent danger of granting Anton Piller orders too readily, as illustrated by the case of *Columbia Picture Industries* v. *Robinson* (1986), where the solicitors concerned, Hamlins, a well-known firm experienced in such matters, had searched the defendant's premises for suspected pirating of films, and then retained some of the material for three years. The removal and detention of the defendant's business records resulted in his ceasing to trade. Mr Justice Scott found that this was Hamlins' and the plaintiff's intention, 'an improper one [and] an abuse of the Anton Piller procedure'. Whilst the defendant was awarded substantial damages, this was small comfort; the potential for abuse in this area of the law is clearly considerable, and can only ultimately be checked by the courts' constant vigilance to ensure that the party applying for the order discloses all material facts.

Following the 1992 recommendation of the Judge's Council Anton Piller orders were given statutory recognition (s.7 Civil Procedure Act 1997).

JUDICIAL REVIEW

Since 1977 in public law applications for certain orders, for an injunction or for a declaration or damages have been known as applications for judicial review (Order 53 of the Rules of the Supreme Court). Judicial review is the process by which a person aggrieved by a decision of any body or organisation carrying out quasi-judicial functions, or established to perform public acts or duties, may apply to the High Court for relief if the process of the tribunal has been unfair or improper or lacking or exceeding its powers. The process does not extend to acts of 'maladministration' by central or by local government bodies or by the National Health Service, which are, respectively, the province of the Parliamentary Commissioner for Administration, or the Commissioners for Local Administration or the Health Service Commissioner (the Ombudsmen). There are now several thousand applications for judicial review, the average wait for a hearing being over a year.

In 1993 a study by the Public Law Project covering the period 1987-89 and 4,740 cases, showed that 'liberal' judges granted leave in up to 82 per cent of cases, while 'conservative' judges refused up to 79 per cent; the study said that since 1981 applications for judicial review had increased fourfold, but the increase was centred upon homelessness and immigration cases.

Care must be taken to distinguish review from appeal; the former concerns the legality of the process in the original tribunal, whereas appeal concerns the merits of the case and must be made to the appropriate appellate tribunal. The application for review is, initially, to a judge in chambers, made *ex parte*, seeking leave to apply for review and if granted, the Court has the power to make any of the old orders of *mandamus*, *prohibition* or *certiorari*; and in addition the court may now grant declarations and injunctions, including interim injunctions and/or award damages.

In *R. v. Chief Constable of Merseyside Police, ex parte Calveley* (1986), judicial review was allowed where there had been exceptional delay in bringing disciplinary charges against police officers, without requiring them to exercise their right of appeal to the Home Secretary from the Chief Constable's decision. And in *R. v. British Steel and Secretary of State for Trade and Industry ex parte Vardy* (1993) the High Court decided that the plan to close 10 pits without reference to the specific review procedure agreed between the employers and the unions was unlawful.

In *R. v. BBC ex parte Lavelle* (1983) Mr Justice Woolf quoted Order 53, rule 1, produced in 1977, which sets out the cases appropriate for application for judicial review in these terms:

1. An application for (*a*) an order of mandamus, prohibition, or certiorari, or (*b*) an injunction under s.9 of the Administration of Justice (Miscellaneous Provisions) Act 1938 restraining a person from acting in any office in which he is not entitled to act, shall be made by way of an application for judicial review in accordance with the provisions of this Order. 2. An application for a declaration or an injunction, not being an injunction mentioned in paragraph 1(*b*), may be made by way of an

application for judicial review, and on such an application the court may grant the declaration or injunction claimed if it considers that, having regard to (*a*) the nature of the matters in respect of which relief may be granted by way of an order of mandamus, prohibition or certiorari, (*b*) the nature of the persons and bodies against whom relief may be granted by way of such an order, and (*c*) all the circumstances of the case, it would be just and convenient for the declaration or injunction to be granted on an application for judicial review.

Rule 1 has since received statutory confirmation in almost identical terms in s.31 of the Supreme Court Act 1981. There is nothing in rule 1 or s.31 which expressly extends the circumstances in which the prerogative remedies of mandamus, prohibition or certiorari are available. Those remedies were not previously available to enforce private rights but were, what could be described as, public law remedies. They were not appropriate, and in my view remain inappropriate remedies, for enforcing performance of ordinary obligations owed by a master to his servant.

The latter point was illustrated in *R.* v. *Lord Chancellor ex parte Hibbit and Saunders* (1993) where the Lord Chancellor's decision to award, after a national tendering exercise, the contract for court reporting services to a particular firm of shorthand writers was not susceptible to judicial review as it lacked a sufficient public law element

In *R.* v. *Cambridge District Health Authority ex parte B.* (1995) the Court of Appeal said the function of the court on an application for judicial review is to consider the lawfulness of the decision at issue. It is not for the court to decide between conflicting medical opinions or to decide how a health authority's limited budget should be allocated between opposing claims on its resources.

In *An Bord Bainne Co-operative Ltd (Irish Dairy Board)* v. *Milk Marketing Board (No 1)* (1984), concerning the sale of milk at differential prices in the context of the common organisation of the market in milk and milk products under EC regulations, the Court of Appeal held that the procedure of judicial review (Order 53) was wholly inappropriate where a claim for damages was admittedly based on alleged private law rights whether or not it was also based on public law rights. The court held that if they could make good their case on the facts and private law, the court would have no discretion whether or not to grant relief, a point underlined earlier in *Law* v. *National Greyhound Racing Club* (1983), where the defendant company which acted as the judicial body for the conduct of greyhound racing, took action as the result of a doping incident.

Moreover, *R.* v. *Secretary of State for Transport ex parte Factortame (No 1)* (1990) the House of Lords emphasised that s.21(2) of the Crown Proceedings Act 1947 prohibits the granting of injunctions against officers of the Crown in civil proceedings. The Court of Appeal in *R.* v. *Licensing Authority ex parte Smith, Kline & French (No 2)* (1989) had concluded that s.31(2) of the Supreme Court Act 1981, which, for the first time, made declarations and injunctions generally available in judicial review proceedings, was intended to extend the jurisdiction of the court so that interim injunctions in judicial review proceedings could also be granted against the Crown. This point the House of Lords refused to accept, holding that the revised law on judicial review under that Act related to *final* relief. But in *M.* v. *Home Office* (1993) the House of Lords held that Lord Bridge's views in *Factortame (No 1)* (1990) were mistaken and that an injunction, including an interim injunction, could be granted against a minister and officers of the Crown in their departmental capacities, although not, in accordance with tradition, against the 'Crown' directly.

In *O'Reilly* v. *Mackman* (1982) (involving rioting charges and the Board of Visitors' proceedings at Hull Prison) the House of Lords held that as a general rule the Order 53 procedure had to be used if an applicant wished to question whether a public authority had infringed rights to which he was entitled to protection by public law, and that general rule was subject to two exceptions: if the public law issue arose as a collateral issue from a private law claim, or if both parties agreed. Distinguishing, therefore, between private and public law rights is not easy, as illustrated in the case of *Cocks* v. *Thanet District Council* (1982).

Nonetheless in *Ali* v. *Tower Hamlets London Borough Council* (1992) the Court of Appeal held, distinguishing *Cocks* v. *Thanet District Council*, that until the council had completed the process of deciding on suitable accommodation for a homeless person, it was still discharging a public law function, and as such its decisions were only open to challenge via judicial review. Housing allocations are to be challenged by judicial review, the courts seemed to be saying.

Similarly, the case of *R.* v. *Legal Aid Board ex parte Bateman* (1992) showed that decisions of the Legal Aid Board were susceptible to judicial review, providing the interested party had *locus standi*. On the other hand in *R.* v. *Visitors to the Inns of Court ex parte Calder* (1992) the court relied on Lord Diplock's dictum in *Re Racal Communications Ltd* (1981), to the effect that judicial review is not available to remedy mistakes of the High Court itself; High Court judges were sitting as the High Court in their capacity as Visitors to the Inns of Court. But the Court of Appeal took a different line, holding that Visitors' decisions were amenable to judicial review, but only if they had acted outside their jurisdiction or in breach of the rules of natural justice.

In judicial review cases it is important to consider the *locus standi* (or sufficient interest) of the applicant. So in the matter of *R.* v. *Inspectorate of Pollution ex parte Greenpeace (No 1)* and *(No 2)* (1994), which concerned British Nuclear Fuels' testing of reprocessing spent nuclear fuel at the new THORP installation in Cumbria, Greenpeace had *locus standi* since the group enjoyed an international reputation and a significant local membership in Cumbria. This was in contrast to *R* v *Secretary of State for the Environment ex parte Rose Theatre Trust Co* (1990), where a motley group of people had come together to save the Rose Theatre site in London and no individual could show any personal interest in the outcome, a decision of some criticism. Equally, in respect of the Pergau Dam affair in Malaysia (where the British Government gave aid to Malaysia apparently in return for aircraft contracts), the project was economically unsound for British statutory purposes under s.1 of the Overseas Development Act 1980; the applicants were a pressure group of international standing and therefore enjoyed *locus standi* (*R. v. Secretary of State for Foreign and Commonwealth Affairs ex parte World Development Movement Ltd* (1995)).

In *R. v. Cornwall County Council ex parte Huntington* (1992) the County Council had made a public right of way order across the plaintiffs' farm, under the Wildlife and Countryside Act 1981; under Schedule 15 of the Act there was an ouster clause, ie the order could not be challenged after 42 days. The County Council appealed on the grounds that the 1981 Act ousted the common law power of the courts to grant judicial review on general grounds; the High Court, having considered *Anisminic Ltd v. Foreign Compensation Commission* (1969) and *R. v. Secretary of State for the Environment ex parte Ostler* (1976), decided that the grant of leave to apply for judicial review would be set aside. Further interesting points arose in *Lonrho plc v. Tebbit* (1992). The Secretary of State had imposed an undertaking upon the plaintiffs not to acquire more than 30 per cent of the share capital of the target company and this was a matter of public law, since the undertaking had followed a report from the Monopolies and Mergers Commission that the proposed merger of the plaintiff and the target company might be expected to operate against the public interest. But the plaintiff had a private interest in having the undertaking released promptly when it was no longer needed in the public interest, which arguably gave rise to a private law duty on the part of the Secretary of State to exercise reasonable care to release the plaintiff's undertaking promptly when it was no longer needed. The plaintiffs were not required, the Court of Appeal added, to apply for judicial review before bringing a private law right of action in negligence, relying on the House of Lords' decision in *Roy v. Kensington and Chelsea Family Practitioner Committee* (1992).

In *Wandsworth London Borough Council v. Winder* (1984) the defendant objected to a large increase in his weekly rent as being unreasonable; Lord Fraser contrasted *O'Reilly* – there the plaintiffs had not suffered any infringement of their rights in private law (here the tenant complained of the infringement of a contractual right in private law) and, moreover, the plaintiffs had started the proceedings. The difference in the *Cocks* case was that there the plaintiff was prevented from establishing a new private law right. If the public interest required that persons should not be entitled to defend actions brought against them by public authorities where the defence rested on a challenge to a decision by the public authority, then it was for Parliament to change the law, Lord Fraser said.

The general principle of judicial review was stated in *O'Reilly* by Lord Diplock as follows:

Judicial review, now regulated by RSC Order 53, provides the means by which judicial control of administrative action is exercised. The subject matter of every judicial review is a decision made by some person (or body of persons) or else a refusal by him to make a decision.

Lord Diplock said that there were three heads under which could be classified the grounds on which administrative action was subject to control by judicial review – illegality, irrationality and procedural impropriety. The first was substantive *ultra vires*, as in *R. v. Secretary of State for the Environment ex parte Hillingdon Borough Council* (1986), the second objective unreasonableness under the principles in *Associated Provincial Picture Houses* v. *Wednesbury Corporation* (1947), ie *Wednesbury* unreasonableness (a decision so unreasonable that no reasonable authority could come to it), the third being procedural *ultra vires*, which constituted the ground of challenge in the Cheltenham GCHQ case, in other words the rules of natural justice, which in *Ridge* v. *Baldwin* (1964) included the rule against bias (the tribunal has financial interests or special knowledge). Irrelevant financial considerations were seen in the social services case of *R.* v. *Gloucestershire County Council ex parte Barry* (1997).

In *R.* v. *Secretary of State for the Environment ex parte Nottinghamshire County Council* (1986), the House of Lords held that it was constitutionally improper for the courts to review a measure taken by a minister and approved by the House of Commons on the grounds that the measure was unreasonable, unless it could be shown that the Minister had acted in bad faith or for an improper motive. The extent of this restriction was unclear, although in fact it did not mean much in practice. In *R.* v. *Secretary of State for the Environment ex parte Hammersmith and Fulham London Borough Council* (1990), Lord Bridge made it clear that the restriction on judicial review envisaged in the Nottinghamshire case applied only to decisions involving the formulation and implementation of national economic policy which required the approval of the House of Commons. This case involved charge capping under the Local Government Act 1988: where a minister exercised statutory powers in a matter of national economic policy and made administrative decisions which were subject to the approval of the House of Commons, if the decisions were within the statutory powers and requirements, the decisions could not be challenged on the ground of irrationality short of the extremes of bad faith, improper motive or manifest absurdity.

Again, in the *O'Reilly* case Lord Diplock stated that English law had now arrived at a clear division between public and private law – between public rights and private rights:

> **It would as a general rule be contrary to public policy, and as such an abuse of the process of the court, to permit a person seeking to establish that a decision of a public authority infringed rights to which he was entitled to protection under public law to proceed by way of an ordinary action and by this means to evade the provisions of Order 53 for the protection of such authorities.**

In *Cocks*, where the complaint was that the council was in breach of its duty under the Housing (Homeless Persons) Act 1977 to house a homeless person and his family, the House of Lords again held that the plaintiff must use the judicial review procedure. However, in *O'Reilly* Lord Wilberforce gave a warning about the English use of the expression 'public law' and 'private law'. In respect of Order 53 he said, 'Typically, English law fastens not on principles but on remedies. The principle remains intact that public authorities and public servants are, unless clearly exempted, answerable to the ordinary courts for wrongs done to individuals.' And his Lordship repeated his remarks in *Davy* v. *Spelthorne Borough Council* (1984). This case involved a planning dispute between a factory owner and the local authority, and the House of Lords decided unanimously that the decision in *O'Reilly* did not demand that the plaintiff's common law action in negligence (which faced difficulties anyway) be struck out as an abuse of the process of the court, leaving the plaintiff to proceed under Order 53. Lord Keith in respect of judicial review in *R* v *Secretary of State for Trade and Industry ex parte Lonrho* (1989) referred to 'the danger of judges wrongly though unconsciously substituting their own views for the views of the decision-maker who alone is charged and authorised by Parliament to exercise a discretion'.

Judicial review must be made within three months when the grounds for the application first arose, and even that may not be quickly enough (as seen, for example, in *R. v. Stratford-upon-Avon District Council ex parte Jackson*, 1985). John Alder remarked in 1986:

> **Despite the reforms made by the Supreme Court Act 1981, an applicant seeking interim relief in respect of central government action must follow a gruelling obstacle course made up of formalistic technicalities before reaching the substantive merits of the case. First, he must establish that the basis of the particular power or duty that he seeks to challenge is one of public law so as to invoke Order 53. Second he must ensure that the proper respondent is a Crown servant and not the Crown itself. Thirdly he must apparently decide whether certiorari, mandamus or prohibition are available before he can claim an injunction or a declaration.**
>
> **Finally, if the applicant seeks a declaration or injunction, he should preferably establish that his private rights are in issue in order to be sure that the injunction is appropriate. However, this last proposition seems to be a matter within the discretion of the Court. In ordinary litigation injunctions lie only in support of legal or equitable rights but under Order 53 a broader view of standing is taken. Important constitutional issues are thus overlaid by a mass of specific procedural rules. Perhaps the underlying cause of confusion is that English law offers no coherent conceptual basis for a theory of public law. We have no legal concept of the State or of government.**

Writing in 1993, Professor Alder has added this comment in the light of the *Roy* case, about the confusions of the judicial review system.

> **If private rights are always outside the exclusivity principle then, far from being a seminal case, *O'Reilly* v. *Mackman* is reduced to a plati-**

tude. The *O'Reilly* rule now seems to apply to applicants with no private rights at all. The meaning of private right is therefore crucial. The central difficulty is that the notion of right is not cenceptualised as such in English law but is relative, depending upon the cause of action and the particular remedy. In one sense private rights can be contrasted with purely public rights which can be asserted only by the Attorney-General but, in this sense, Order 53 always involves private rights since an applicant must establish sufficient individual standing. . . . The result of *Roy* is that those confined to the public law procedure are amongst the most disadvantaged in society. Pressure groups representing public interest concerns will also be confined to Order 53. It may be appropriate to confine both kinds of litigant to Order 53, but, apart possibly from defences, Order 53 should equally apply to private rights cases if the policies advocated by Lord Diplock are to be taken seriously. The speeches in *Roy* have made the *O'Reilly* v. *Mackman* rule virtually meaningless. Order 53 is exclusive only where no private rights are involved at all, that is in cases where no ordinary action would be possible anyway.

The House of Lords. post-*Roy* and *O'Reilly*, appears to be little further forward in their decision in *Mercury Communications plc* v. *Director-General of Telecommunications* (1996) in establishing the precise limits of public and private law, a point also seen in *R. v. Jockey Club ex parte Aga Khan* (1993). If the relevant activities are more governmental than commercial then it is likely that the decision-making body is a public law body, as seen in *R. v. Legal Aid Board ex parte Donn & Co.* (1996).

It should also be noted in the context of judicial review the importance of the House of Lords' decision in *M. v. Home Office* in 1993, where, following the *Factortame* litigation of 1990, it was decided that injunctive relief did lie against the Crown.

In recent times, it is particularly the Home Office which has fallen foul of judicial review proceedings: in 1996 the court took the view that in respect of the handling of the life sentences for Robert Thompson and Jon Venables (convicted for the Bulger child murder in Bootle) (*R. v. Secretary of State for the Home Department ex parte Venables and Thompson* (1996)) the approach was 'perfunctory' and falling far below the standards a court would adopt. Also in 1996 a judge ordered the Home Secretary, Michael Howard, to reconsider the deportation order on the Saudi dissident Mohammed Al-Masari, and a ban on temporary leave for prisoners to consult their lawyers was reversed. Most notably in 1995 the House of Lords decided the Home Secretary had acted outside his powers when he introduced a tariff-based criminal injuries compensation scheme (*R. v. Secretary of State for the Home Department ex parte Fire Brigades Union* (1995)), and in the same year he was accused of acting unlawfully when he barred the Unification Church leader Sun Myung Moon from entering the United Kingdom, while at the same time almost a High Court judge had found Mr Howard had operated a 'manifestly unjust policy' in delaying consideration of a parole application by five IRA prisoners (*R. v.*

Secretary of State for the Home Department ex parte Norney (1995)). Further, in 1996 the Court of Appeal ruled that social security regulations that removed all entitlement to income-related benefit from asylum-seekers who failed to claim asylum immediately upon arrival in the United Kingdom and from those who were pursuing appeals, were 'uncompromisingly Draconian', and *ultra vires* the Asylum and Immigration Appeals Act 1993 (*R. v. Secretary of State for Social Security ex parte Joint Council for the Welfare of Immigrants and B* (1996)).

DISCUSSION POINTS

1 Examine the Practice Statement (1966) of the House of Lords; do you consider this to be a satisfactory way to conduct judicial affairs?

2 Is there any future for the common law?

3 Why has judicial review in recent years proved so controversial?

h r e e

EUROPEAN LAW

3.1   The work of the European Communities

In 1950 in Paris the French Foreign Minister, Robert Schumann, announced what was then a sensational plan, to place the whole of Franco-German coal and steel output under a common High Authority. This first stage in a rapprochement between France and the defeated Germany marked the nucleus of a much broader European policy of economic co-operation. The European Communities were to be based on three principles – there would be an intergovernmental organisation composed of representatives from member States; the participating States were not to be bound by the organisation's decisions against their will (unanimity would be required in effect); and the implementation of the decisions would be left to the member States themselves. The emphasis upon a new order was highlighted by the fact that Eastern Europe had rapidly fallen under Communist control, through the Soviet Union, perhaps most pointedly in Czechoslovakia in 1948. After the original six members of the European Communities in 1951/1957 (Germany, France, Italy and the Benelux countries), the United Kingdom joined in 1973 along with Ireland and Denmark. The Community was later enlarged to 12 with the accession of Greece in 1981, Spain and Portugal in 1986, and Sweden, Austria and Finland in 1995.

Thus the term 'EC law' denotes in this context the laws and identical institutions of all three European Communities. It should not be confused with the quite separate Council of Europe and the European Convention on Human Rights. In a technical sense all EC law that applies to the United Kingdom is covered by the legislative umbrella of the European Communities Act 1972 (as amended by the European Communities (Finance) Act 1985, the European Communities (Amendment) Act 1986 and the European Communities (Amendment) Act 1993). On the other hand the very accession of the United Kingdom to the Treaty of Rome has posed considerable problems in respect of the contrasting styles of English and European codes of law. When Parliament passed the 1972 Act the United Kingdom acceded to the provisions of the Treaty of Paris (1951) which established the European Coal and Steel Community (ECSC) and the two Treaties of Rome (1957) which founded the EEC (European Economic

Community) and Euratom (European Atomic Energy Community) – including all rules subsequently drawn up by the European Commission and agreed upon by the Council of Ministers (since 1993 the Council of the European Union).

The European Commission – an approximate equivalent of a European Civil Service – has the right to initiate Community legislation within the framework of the treaties. However, the Council of Ministers (consisting of the appropriate national ministerial representatives from each member government) has the right to overrule or change such proposals. The Council has a co-ordinating function, but it plays a key part in the development of economic policy. The ministerial representatives will vary from one meeting to another depending upon which matter is under review, for example finance, transport or agriculture. Each member State holds the presidency of the Council for a six-month term. But the real power rests with the Commission. It should also be added that under Article 2 of the Single European Act 1986 the heads of government of each member State meet twice a year, to review economic and political progress.

The Commission is the body that brings forward EC legislation. There are 20 Commissioners, drawn proportionately from each member State, although they all stress their independence of political parties and governments. The bigger countries (the United Kingdom, France, Germany, Italy and Spain) have two Commissioners each. Commissioners are usually given specific duties, in other words they are rather like departmental ministers, but in essence the Commission is a collective body. The functions of the Commission are therefore colossal – it must not just propose legislation to go before the Council of Ministers after first seeing the opinion of the European Parliament, but also act as the executive body, the European bureaucracy that it is in popular eyes. Moreover it must consult various interests extremely widely, including national governments and their civil services, industry, pressure groups and trade unions. The policy proposals that are then submitted have to be worked up into considerable detail. And from the executive angle it must enforce the laws of the EC, not least in respect of the CAP (the Common Agricultural Policy), the original *raison d'etre* of the Community.

The Commission also prepares the draft budget which the European Parliament has to approve. Between the Council and Commission there is the vital link of COREPER (the Committee of Permanent Representatives), which is a full-time committee of officials from each member State whose task is to screen the proposals coming from the Commission to the Council, so that only the major issues come before the body of ministers.

The European Parliament has the right to be consulted and it also possesses certain budgetary powers – for example, it rejected the draft budget in 1979 and 1984 because it disagreed with the Council's spending priorities; however, it is clear that the Parliament that was directly elected for the first time in 1979 will gradually wish to expand its almost non-existent legislative role, especially since the Single European Act of 1986. Since the Single European Act of 1986 the Parliament has acquired greater delaying powers; it should also be added that it has the power to sack the entire Commission, although this has not been exercised (individual Commissioners cannot be dismissed). The European Parliament now has 626 members with qualified majority voting in the Council of the European Union being 62 out of 87 votes. The use of majority voting in the Council of Ministers has been more common since the passing of the 1986 Act and the Treaty on European Union (the Maastricht Treaty). The total number of votes is 10 each for the United Kingdom, France, Germany and Italy, 8 for Spain and so on. The blocking minority is 26.

The European Court of Justice (the Court of Justice of the European Communities) acts as a kind of referee between individuals, organisations, member States and the Council and Commission in the event of a dispute between any two or more of those bodies in respect of the operation of EC law. There are 15 judges, assisted by nine Advocates-General. There are also 15 judges in the lower court, the Court of First Instance. The Court hears actions by a member State against another member State or by a Community institution against a member State. Actions against a Community institution may be brought by another Community institution or by private parties with *locus standi*.

Equally important under Article 177 of the EEC Treaty (Article 150 of Euratom and Article 141 of ECSC) national courts may refer disputes with a European dimension to the European Court for guidance and advice (the House of Lords is obliged to). Cwmbran Magistrates Court has made a reference under Article 177 over the Shops Act 1950 (Sunday trading) (*Torfaen Borough Council* v. *B & Q plc*, 1990). Guidelines for such references were laid down in *An Bord Bainne Co-operative Ltd (Irish Dairy Board)* v. *Milk Marketing Board (No 2)* (1984). However, the European Court is not directly concerned with the impact of EC law on national, domestic laws. Applying EC law to domestic law is left to the national courts themselves. The first stage is for the United Kingdom court to satisfy itself before referring a question of Community law to the European Court 'that a decision is necessary to enable it to give judgment', to quote the wording of Article 177. The European Court cannot, however, criticise the reasons for the reference made by the national court. The procedures for such references are more complicated than at first they might appear. References are of particular use to the High Court. Article 177(1) in fact reads:

The Court of Justice shall have jurisdiction to give preliminary rulings concerning:
(a) the interpretation of this Treaty;
(b) the validity and interpretation of acts of the institutions of the Community;
(c) the interpretation of the statutes of bodies established by an act of the council, where those statutes so provide.

EC law is both primary and secondary. Primary law is essentially the various parts, that is the articles of the three treaties, with the supplementary annexes and protocols, the 1957 Convention, the 1965 Merger, the 1970 Luxembourg Treaty on Budgetary Matters and the 1972 Treaty of Accession and its annexes, as well as the

1972 Act. Primary law is for the most part self-executing, that is when ratified it becomes directly operative within each member state. In the United Kingdom such matters are covered by the provisions of the European Communities Act. In *Bulmer* v. *Bollinger* (1974) Lord Denning said that the Treaty was like an incoming tide: 'it flows into the estuaries and up the rivers. It cannot be held back'. This point of view was illustrated in *Marleasing, Publico Ministerio v Ratti*, and *Webb* v. *Emo Air Cargo*. In *Marleasing SA* v. *La Comercial Internacional de Alimentation SA* the Court of Justice made it clear that national courts must interpret domestic legislation so as to conform with EC rules, a point raised in *Webb* v. *EMO Air Cargo* (1994) where the House of Lords emphasised that in this process national legislation could not be distorted. However, it was not exactly the case that *Marleasing* was suggesting something revolutionary. In *R.* v. *Secretary of State for Employment ex parte Equal Opportunities Commission* (1995) the House of Lords said part-time workers had to be treated on the same basis as full-time workers for the purposes of EC law.

Secondary law consists of law made by the Council and Commission under the authority of the various treaty articles and therefore again for British purposes is recognised in advance by the 1972 Act. In this way the doctrine or fiction of the supremacy of British statutory law within its own national territory is maintained. Secondary law consists of regulations, directives and decisions, which may be commonly referred to as 'instruments'. Regulations are said to be self-executing since they apply directly to each member state. The European Court of Justice may classify regulations as such by examining their purpose and material content. Directives, on the other hand, are non-self-executing: they are binding as to the result to be achieved, but they leave it to each member government and parliament to decide how best to reach the declared goal. Decisions are directed at specific member States, individuals or undertakings and may be issued after the Court of Justice has considered a particular dispute. The Council and Commission may also issue advisory recommendations and opinions. The House of Commons and the House of Lords each have a Select Committee which scrutinises Community legislation; whether that form of national scrutiny by the Westminster legislature touches more than the tip of the Commission's iceberg is very much open to question. Moreover, the Commission's powers (as those of the European Parliament) were strengthened under the European Communities (Amendment) Act 1986 giving effect to the Single European Act of 1986.

Described like that, EC law in relation to British statutory law seemed likely to provoke a fundamental clash between Europe and a domestic Act of Parliament, due to the traditional doctrine that no government could fetter the absolute power of Parliament's legislative supremacy. When Parliament passed the European Communities Act in 1972, it could not prevent its successors (particularly then a possible future Labour government with an element of anti-European thinking) from legislating in a manner inconsistent with European law. However, as time has passed, the danger of a serious conflict has receded, particularly as political attitudes have changed with a growing realisation of the need for harmonisation of laws in an age of increasing mobility of peoples and, particularly, of communications.

As public awareness of the advantages of integration has increased, and public irritation with bureaucratic delays and the consequent expense of internal frontiers has also increased, so most lawyers and politicians alike became conditioned to the prospect of the single Community envisaged for 1992. The doctrine of parliamentary legislative supremacy remains – but the concept of a unilateral withdrawal by the United Kingdom from the European Community has receded in the past few years (indeed even since the first edition of this book in 1983) to such an extent that it must now be accepted as unlikely in the extreme. The position is now accepted that, as with all international obligations entered into by Parliament, domestic legislation should be enacted, and to some extent interpreted, in a manner that does not conflict with those obligations.

This British, perhaps English, dilemma was recognised by J. P. Warner in *The Law Quarterly Review* in 1977. As he pointed out, the dilemma is not solely an English one, as the famous judgment in 1971 of the Cour de Cassation in *SA Fromagerie Franco-Suisse (Le Ski)* v. *Ministère des Affaires Economiques* showed. The Belgian court held that the EEC Treaty overrode national fiscal legislation, even where that legislation was later in date than the Treaty. Nonetheless Warner made the point in his article that in most member states the dualist theory is accepted. This is certainly reflected in the constitutions of Luxembourg, Ireland, Holland and Denmark, as it is in those of France and Belgium, although in those two countries the national courts at various times have experienced some difficulty in interpreting the Treaty and that has also been true for the Italian Constitutional Court (Consiglio di Stato) and the German courts in respect of the operation of the national Basic Law of Germany. The first reference by the House of Lords of a case to the European Court came in 1979 in *R.* v. *Henn* although the first reference by an English court was in 1974 in respect of the celebrated case of *Van Duyn* v. *Home Office* (concerning the freedom of movement of workers). Every type of English court has now made a reference to the European Court at Luxembourg.

In respect of the first case, it is worth quoting a commentary in the *Financial Times* at length.

> **The smuggling of a large quantity of pornographic films and magazines into this country from Holland . . . has provided the legal world with a unique precedent – the first reference of a case to the European Court of Justice at Luxembourg by the House of Lords . . . When the question of when and how should an English court refer a case first arose in May 1974, Lord Denning laid down some guidelines that have not found universal approval among the judges. In essence, Lord Denning was saying that, unless the point on Community law was really difficult and important, it was much better that English judge should decide the point for himself. This seemingly jingoistic attitude was dictated by the prospect of delays and expense involved in trips by litigants to Luxembourg in the middle of protracted litigation. And with the growing workload of the European Court, there was a proper desire to limit the number of references to those that positively needed**

to be dealt with by the one tribunal specifically allocated that authoritative function . . . A study of the practice of the European Court and the national courts of other member States, before and since our entry, discloses a collaborative forensic process in which a single purpose has been achieved harmoniously between the two courts performing separate roles; the clear division being between interpretation of Community laws by Luxembourg and implementation of those laws by the national courts. By studied judicial courtesy, it has been possible to maintain mutual respect for different judicial responsibilities. Adherence to the separate functions, while collaborating in the performance of complementary roles, is the essence of the partnership envisaged in the interplay of national legal systems and EEC law.

The problem in the *Henn* case centred around the argument that free trade within the EC could only be overriden in 'obscenity' matters if an individual member country had a clear policy of public morality: in English law does such a policy exist? Having received the opinion of the European Court of Justice the House of Lords decided that the United Kingdom did possess just such a policy.

The largest number of references to Luxembourg has come from inferior courts within each member state. This, indeed, is a positive virtue since it allows aspects of European law to be disentangled at an early stage and indeed may actually assist the European Court, overloaded with references as it invariably is, in that such problems can be resolved in their preliminary stages before they have mushroomed into monstrous-sized litigation.

Further, it is not only the courts that are having to follow the guidance of the Community. Parliament, too, is increasingly under pressure to enact statutes in conformity with legislative principles introduced by the EC. A notable recent example of such legislation is the Consumer Protection Act 1987, which is examined in some detail in Chapter 8, and which, as will be seen, was introduced following an EEC Directive. Similar legislation has been introduced in all member countries. Thus the concept of individual State sovereignty is maintained, but more and more in practice, the member States of the EC are incorporating – rather than submitting to – an increasing degree of supranational legislation.

In a searching review of the effect of European law upon the English courts, Peter Oliver has observed in *The Modern Law Review* in 1987:

As the Court of Justice pointed out in *Van Gend en Loos*, Community law depends for its survival as a system of law on effective remedies and procedures for its enforcement before national courts. Without them it would cease to be a body of law and would merely be a code of conduct for the member states and the Community institutions. From the outset the Court has rightly set its face against that. Had it done otherwise, it would have failed to fulfil the task entrusted to it by Article 164 of the Treaty of Rome which provides with majestic simplicity: 'The Court of Justice shall ensure that in the interpretation and application of this Treaty the law is observed'.

At the same time, the impact of Community law on the stock of remedies and procedures available in actions brought against the authorities before the English courts is undoubted. It has provided a most welcome catalyst to gradual developments that have been at work for decades in English constitutional and administrative law, opening up new possibilities for judicial review and limiting the scope of Government immunities.

The Maastricht Treaty added a number of new interests – immigration and freedom of movement of non-EC nationals, the competitiveness of European industry, trans-European networks, education and training, the 'flowering' of national cultures, energy, civil protection and tourism. Economic and social cohesion, research and development, the environment, health, consumer protection and the fisheries policy were given full-blown status as objectives. These were added to familiar items such as competition and the free movement of people, goods, services and capital. The different interests were accorded relative importance by a wide variety of qualifying words, for example, cohesion and industry's competitiveness is to be 'strengthened', R&D (Research and Development) is to be 'promoted', and the establishment and development of networks is to be 'encouraged'.

The European Court will be called upon to give practical meaning to these expressions. Some of them are little more than statements of good intent and others simply empower the Community to act in a particular field.

The celebrated *Factortame* litigation in 1989–90 was a good illustration of the ECJ's influence upon the development of EC law, and is considered further below. But it can be argued that before long the Court will have to grasp the theoretical nettle and insist that EC law is a source of law throughout the Community in the fullest sense of that expression, having the full force of law everywhere, with all necessary national and Community remedies. More generally, the ECJ has not yet gained the momentum to sort out the major confusion at the heart of the theoretical structure of the EC legal system, the problems surrounding the so-called principle of the 'direct effect' of EC law. But the *Factortame* case perhaps means that the courts now regard the question of the sources of law as itself a matter of law to be determined by the courts, not as a matter of fact which has been determined by history.

The Maastricht Treaty was eventually incorporated into British law by the European Communities (Amendment) Act 1993. But the Treaty was surrounded by political controversy, with Lady Thatcher, the former Prime Minister, pursuing a vehemently anti-integrationist line. This coincided with, or was accentuated by, the sterling crisis of September 1992 and the British withdrawal from the ERM (the European Exchange Rate Mechanism). Maastricht epitomised the fact that constitutional changes and membership of a unique international financial club can cut across party lines, a fact underlined by the continuing divisions in the Conservative Party, notably during the general election of 1997.

It might be added here, as a constitutional footnote, that a legal challenge against the ratification of the Maastricht Treaty mounted by the former editor of *The Times*, Lord Rees-Mogg, was emphatically rejected by the High Court, *R.* v. *Secretary of State for Foreign and Commonwealth Affairs ex parte Rees-Mogg* (1994); this was one application for judicial review which fell flat. One of the applicant's arguments was that by ratifying Title V of the Treaty, which establishes a common foreign and security policy among member States, the government would be transferring part of the royal prerogative, to community institutions without statutory authority. Lord Justice Lloyd said that this was the most interesting argument jurisprudentially but also the weakest. Assuming the court has jurisdiction to consider the questions raised and assuming the government could not lawfully transfer any part of the Crown's prerogative powers in relation to foreign affairs without statutory enactment, Title V could not be regarded as transfer of prerogative powers.

3.2   The United Kingdom and the EC

A number of Articles of the EEC Treaty have been held to have direct effect in each member state, including Article 7 (non-discrimination between EC nationals on grounds of nationality), Article 48 (freedom of movement of workers), Article 52 (freedom of EC nationals who are self-employed or members of a profession to establish themselves in another member State, *Reyners* v. *Belgian State*, 1974), Articles 85 & 86 (prohibition on conduct which restricts or distorts competition in the common market), and Article 119 (equal pay between the sexes for equal work, *Defrenne* v. *Sabena Airlines*, 1976). Indeed, it can now be said that most provisions of the Treaties are of direct effect. But the picture is less clear with Directives. Whilst EC Directives may be directly effective, in the case of Regulations direct effect is the norm (under Article 189). In 1970 in *Grad* v. *Finanzamt Traunstein* (1970) the ECJ held that in certain circumstances, and where the rules were clear and without conditions, EC Directives could be invoked directly by individuals before their national courts (in other words they could be directly effective). This European fact of life is increasingly important from 1993 and the completion or harmonisation of the single European market. *Grad* followed on from *Van Gend en Loos* (1963) where Treaty Articles were held to be directly effective. But where Directives allow for implementation within a time limit, then different styles of drafting and interpretation can lead to substantial differences between member states. Academics have made a distinction between direct applicability and direct effect, but this distinction has never been made by the ECJ and is generally of little importance: the key issue is that regulations are intended to take direct effect from stage one.

In the case of *Van Duyn*, mentioned earlier, the plaintiff was a Dutch national who wanted to work for the Church of Scientology in the United Kingdom. The Church had attracted a lot of adverse publicity, and Van Duyn was refused entry. The

European Court held that Article 48 (freedom of movement of workers) and an associated Directive of 1964 were of direct effect, but the Court acknowledged that in the British case there were public policy reasons for excluding Van Duyn. The criteria for Articles to be directly effective are that the wording must be clear and unambiguous, unconditional (that is, not dependent upon the discretion of a member State or the European Commission) and not dependent upon further action. Many Directives cover the field of company and employment law, environment and consumer law, so that public bodies and private individuals are affected equally. However, Article 189, which governs the nature of Directives and Regulations, has led to certain problems. In *Marshall* v. *Southampton and South West Hampshire Area Health Authority* (1986), the European Court held that whilst a Directive might be invoked against the State, even when it acted in a private capacity as an employer (the AHA was found to be an extension of the State), it could not be invoked directly against an 'individual'. One way to avoid the difficulties of Article 189 is to focus on Article 5 of the EC Treaty which obliges member States to take all appropriate measures to ensure fulfilment of the obligations of the Treaty and the actions of the institutions of the Community, as seen in *Harz* v. *Tradax* (1984).

As outlined above, the United Kingdom has a dualist approach to international law, including EC law; in other words international obligations will become binding internally when incorporated or transformed into domestic law by Act of Parliament. It is worth stating the relevant parts of the European Communities Act 1972. Section 2(1) says:

> **All such rights, powers, liabilities, obligations and restrictions from time to time created or arising by or under the Treaties, and all such remedies and procedures from time to time provided for by or under the treaties, as in accordance with the Treaties are without further enactment to be given legal effect or used in the United Kingdom shall be recognised and available in law, and be enforced, allowed and followed accordingly; and the expression 'enforceable Community right' and similar expressions shall be read as referring to one to which this sub-section applies.**

Section 2(2) provides for a general power to implement Community legislation by way of secondary (delegated) legislation. And s.2(4) provides that

> **any enactment passed or to be passed, other than one contained in this part of this Act [in other words where subsections 1 and 2 that give rise to Community obligations] shall be construed and take effect subject to the foregoing provisions of this section.**

Section 2(1) provides for the direct applicability of Commmunity law, and s.2(4) stipulates that national courts must construe domestic law subject to Community obligations arising from s.2(1) and s.2(2). Section 3 goes on to say that national courts must follow all the relevant decisions of the European Court. Not surprisingly, the British courts have on occasion found themselves in something of a tangle over these provisions.

The relationship between EC and domestic law was well illustrated in 1995, in *R. v. Chief Constable of Sussex, ex parte International Traders' Ferry Ltd*, where it was held by the High Court that decisions by a Chief Constable to restrict to a limited number of days police protection for transporting livestock, in the face of disorderly public demonstrations seeking to prevent such exports, were measures having an effect equivalent to quantitative restrictions on exports contrary to Article 34 of the EC Treaty. Whilst under domestic law the Chief Constable had a discretion in the exercise of his duty to keep the peace, under *Wednesbury* principles, and the courts would not normally interfere with a policy decision, his decisions would be quashed as being contrary to Article 34 of the EC Treaty, which, under s.2(1) of the European Communities Act 1972 was also part of United Kingdom domestic law.

The courts have, in short, varied in their attitude. Some have been content to apply EC law directly, without referring to national law and taking their cue from ECJ judgments, as seen in the Court of Appeal's approach in *Macarthys Ltd* v. *Smith* (1979) and *Pickstone* v. *Freemans plc* (1989), both equal pay cases. Other courts have preferred to apply directly effective law by emphasising the correct interpretation of national law, basing such an approach on s.2(4). The House of Lords followed this route in *Garland* v. *British Rail Engineering Ltd* (1983), again in respect of Article 119 and equal pay. However, Lord Diplock did say that domestic law should conform with Community Treaty obligations 'however wide a departure from the *prima facie* meaning of the language might be needed to achieve consistency'. Lord Oliver approved this line in *Pickstone*. The Lords' views in *Garland* and *Pickstone* illustrated how the provisions of the 1972 Act could not be entrenched, notwithstanding what the ECJ said in *Simmenthal SpA* v. *European Commission (No 2)* (1978). So, the courts here have recognised that if Parliament were to attempt to repudiate EC obligations, then the judges would be obliged to give effect to its wishes. But in the meantime the House of Lords has shown that it will 'jettison the words' of a British statute or 'supply the necessary words by implication' to fill a gap in British legislation and to give effect to EC law. Such issues also arose in *Duke* v. *GEC Reliance Ltd* (1988), concerning discriminatory retirement ages, although the Directive concerned was not on the facts directly effective; but here Lord Templeman made it clear that s.2(4) only applied where Community provisions were directly effective, the meaning of a British statute could not be distorted, he said. *Duke* should now be seen as not entirely in line with other House of Lords' decisions. In contrast in *Litster* v. *Forth Dry Dock & Engineering Co Ltd* (1989), concerning the safeguarding of employees' rights in the event of a transfer of undertakings, the House of Lords was prepared to interpret British regulations (to implement EEC Directive 77/187) against their *prima facie* meaning in order to comply with an interpretation of the ECJ.

The key issue is that *Litster* and *Pickstone* have indicated that where national, domestic law has been passed solely to implement EC law (that is an EC Directive), then British courts must interpret that domestic law so as to comply with the Directive, and use the same liberal rules of construction as are applicable to directly effective EC laws; this is in accordance with s.2(4) of the 1972 Act.

The high point of conflict came in the *Factortame* litigation – *R. v. Secretary of State for Transport, ex parte Factortame (No 1)* (1990) and *R. v. Secretary of State for*

Transport, ex parte Factortame Ltd (No 2) (1991). The fisheries policy of the European Community is designed to protect stocks in EC waters by limiting catches, a controversial policy at the best of times. This meant a quota system was to be introduced designed to 'assure each member State relative stability of fishing activities for each of the stocks considered' (Article 4 of EEC Regulation 170/83). The Spanish fishing fleet is the largest in the EC. From 1985 the British Government became concerned that Spanish trawlermen were 'quota-hopping', by registering their boats in the United Kingdom. The Merchant Shipping Act 1988 and the Merchant Shipping (Registration of Fishing Vessels) Regulations 1988 required vessels that had previously registered under the Merchant Shipping Act 1894 to re-register under the new conditions; this meant 95 vessels were unable to re-register. (Part II of the 1988 Act, by s.14, provided that a fishing vessel would only qualify for British registration if it was owned by British citizens resident in the United Kingdom or by companies 75 per cent of whose shareholders and directors were British citizens resident in the United Kingdom.)

The owners of the ships challenged the validity of the legislation as infringing Article 52 of the EEC Treaty and sought judicial review, applying for interim relief through the suspension of the operation of the 1988 Act and the Regulations until the substantive issues had been determined. In 1989 the House of Lords upheld the Court of Appeal and set aside an order of the High Court for interim relief, saying that English courts had no power to make such an interim order against the Crown and that the courts had no power to override an Act of Parliament and grant rights that were not in accordance with the will of Parliament, at least until the question of compatibility with Community law had been determined by the European Court of Justice. However, the House of Lords did ask the ECJ to give a ruling as to whether Community law obliged national courts under Article 5 to grant interim protection of rights claimed under Community law, or gave the national courts the power to do so. In 1989 the ECJ said: 'The full effectiveness of Community law would be . . . impaired if a rule of national law could prevent a court seised of a dispute governed by Community law from granting interim relief in order to ensure the full effectiveness of the judgment to be given on the existence of the rights claimed under Community law.' The ECJ also said: 'Community law must be interpreted as meaning that a national court which, in a case before it concerning Community law, considers that the sole obstacle which precludes it from granting interim relief is a rule of national law must set aside that rule.' The House of Lords gave effect to this ruling.

In separate proceedings, the Commission brought an action against the United Kingdom government on the substantive issues under Article 169. The government made an Order in Council amending s.14 of the 1988 Act.

These issues came down to the nub of the question – in the eyes of the Community the rules of the EC take precedence over rules of domestic, national law, but the general view of the United Kingdom, and its courts, has been that whilst Community law is part of British law, national law is still essentially governed by Westminster. But the House of Lords recognised how Community law could prevail over national law; in the first *Factortame* case Lord Bridge observed:'Under the terms of the Act of 1972 it has always been clear that it was the duty of a United Kingdom court, when delivering final judgment, to override any rule of national law found to be in conflict with any directly enforceable rule of Community law'. This comment underlined his remark in *Factortame (1)* that s.2(1) of the 1972 Act had exactly the same effect as if such a section had been incorporated in the 1988 Act regarding directly enforceable rights.

In the *Factortame (2)* case Lord Bridge further noted:

> **If the supremacy within the European Community of Community law over the national law of the member States was not always inherent in the EEC Treaty it was certainly well established in the jurisprudence of the Court of Justice long before the United Kingdom joined the Community. Thus whatever limitation of its sovereignty Parliament accepted when it enacted the European Communities Act 1972 was entirely voluntary.**

In a celebrated Sunday trading case, *Stoke-on-Trent City Council* v. *B & Q plc* (1991), Mr Justice Hoffmann said:

> **The EEC Treaty is the supreme law of this country, taking precedence over Acts of Parliament. Our entry into the Community meant that (subject to our undoubted but probably theoretical right to withdraw from the Community altogether) Parliament surrendered its sovereign right to legislate contrary to the provisions of the Treaty on matters of social and economic policy which it regulated. The entry into the Community was in itself a high act of social and economic policy, by which the partial surrender of sovereignty was seen as more than compensated by the advantages of membership.**

(The ECJ subsequently ruled that the Shops Act 1950 was not incompatible with Article 30 of the EEC Treaty – *Norwich City Council and Stoke-on-Trent City Council* v. *B & Q plc* (1993); the influence of the *Factortame* cases was also noted in another Sunday trading case – *R.* v. *Lincoln Magistrates Court ex parte Wickes Building Supplies Ltd* (1993). Yet the possibility remains that a United Kingdom Act of Parliament that was expressly designed to override some aspect of Community law would still be given precedence by the British courts.

In 1991 the ECJ ruled that the Merchant Shipping Act 1988 did contravene Community law, since the Act stipulated that those employed on the fishing vessels concerned should reside in the United Kingdom (*R.* v *Secretary of State for Transport ex parte Factortame (No 3)* (1991)). The Court, though, did not criticise the provisions that insisted on management and direction of fishing operations from the United Kingdom. In other words, it was the nationality and residence requirements of the 1988 Act which were not compatible with EC law, not the quota control provisions as such; this was so, even though the 1988 Act came about after the relevant Community obligations. Indeed, the United Kingdom could have used means other than the 1988 Act to guarantee compliance with its international obligations. The British government has recognised that what is required is a change in domestic law, in order to accommodate EC law, and in effect avoid a constitutional difficulty of the first order; thus, at an early stage, after the first *Factortame* case, the contentious nationality parts of the 1988 Act were suspended by a statutory instrument made under s.2(2) of the European Communities Act 1972 (the Merchant Shipping Act 1988 (Amendment) Order, 1989). In 1992 Sir Robin Cooke, the President of the New Zealand Court of Appeal, observed: 'the *Factortame* litigation may be seen as a watershed in the history of English law as significant as the alliance against the claims of the Stuart Kings'. The rules governing registration of merchant ships were also subsequently altered by the Merchant Shipping (Registration etc.) Act 1993.

3.3   The Commission and the Court

As the European Community has developed, so the role of the European Commission in policy and law making has changed. In the early 1960s the Commission had a dynamic role, but the Luxembourg Accords of 1966 diminished its power, whilst the Council of Europe and intergovermentalism generally grew in scope. The Single European Act of 1986 and the internal market of 1992 gave the Commission a new lease of life, in a number of areas – agriculture, social policy, competition, economic union and transport. But more recently the Commission has been weakened by the Maastricht Treaty (which was reviewed at the Intergovernmental Conference in Amsterdam in 1997), with the result that many of its legislative proposals have been diluted or aborted. Much of the Commission's work in the law-making area has been through a complex structure of negotiation and the use of the Article 169 EC procedure. The general criticism of the Commission in recent years is that it has become hidebound by management systems and a technocrat administrative culture, with the result that the Community law has not developed in as a logically coherent way as it might have done.

The European Court's work is in marked contrast: the ECJ has gradually developed a judicial liability system, the recent high water marks of which have been the *Factortame* cases as discussed above and that of *Francovich and Bonifaci* v. *Italy* (1992). In *Francovich* the Court ruled that in the absence of Community provisions, it was up to national legal systems to prescribe measures for legal action to ensure the full protection of Community rights. This has posed problems for the United Kingdom, it appears. In *Kirklees Metropolitan Borough Council* v. *Wickes Building Supplies Limited* (1992) the local council took action under s.47 of the Shops Act 1950 to prevent W. from trading on Sunday. W. argued that Article 30 prohibited such restrictions since this impeded the flow of non-UK goods into the UK market. W. indicated it would cease Sunday trading if the local council gave an undertaking to compensate in damages for the lost trial if the defendants were to win their case, since Community law stated that individual rights must be protected; the Court of Appeal accepted this argument, but the House of Lords reversed that decision, finding in favour of the appellant local authority. The Lords took the view that since *Francovich* a plaintiff could under EC law seek damages from the State for injuries caused by an infringement of Community law, and this obligation rested with, in the United Kingdom, the Crown, not with local authorities. This seems a less than satisfactory interpretation of *Francovich* since Community law enshrines the principle that private individuals have entitlement to 'direct and immediate' protection of their Community rights. What had happened in this case was that certain employees were owed wages when a company had become insolvent. When F. and other applicants failed to obtain the outstanding amounts they commenced an action against the Italian government arguing that it had failed to implement Directive 80/987, which concerned the payment of arrears. The ECJ had ruled that Italy had broken Treaty obligations by not implementing the Directive and the workers sought compensation from the Italian government. The ECJ held that member States should compensate individuals where a Directive had not been put into operation, providing the Directive was conferring rights upon those individuals and the non-implementation or even poor implementation of the Directive had caused such individuals loss.

The European Court of Justice clarified a number of issues relating to State liability in damages in the joint cases of *Brasserie du Pecheur SA* v. *Federal Republic of Germany* and *R.* v. *Secretary of State for Transport ex parte Factortame Ltd (No 4)* (1996). The Court established State liability in damages as a clear principle, including where a national legislature takes positive action to infringe a provision of a Treaty. In short, Community law will confer a right of reparation if three conditions are satisfied: (1) the rule of law infringed must be intended to confer rights on individuals; (2) the breach must be sufficiently serious; and (3) there must be a direct causal link between the breach of the obligations resting on the State and the damage sustained by the injured parties. The quesion of exemplary damages was considered in *R.* v. *Secretary of State for Transport ex parte Factortame Ltd (No 5)* (1997).

Many of the ECJ's judgments have been concerned with member States rather than with individuals, especially where national governments have failed to fulfil Treaty obligations. But the overall aim has been limited, that is to ensure the effectiveness of EC law, and in addition the relationship between the European Court and national courts is pivotal. Underpinning the Court's judicial liability system is Article 5 EC. The weakness of the European Court's work is that it is almost entirely based on individual claims, which is a rather patchwork, *ad hoc* way of developing European law, for the Treaties apart, there is no real framework of legislation.

Francis Snyder noted in 1993:

With regard to ensuring the effectiveness of Community law, the Community system seems to have worked best so far in creating legal

principles and dealing with national administrations. . . . Neither the Commission and the Court of Justice taken together as institutions, nor negotiation and adjudication taken together as processes, despite their merits, are sufficient alone to ensure the effectiveness of Community law in the broader social sense. . . . The legal and political future of the Community is now on the agenda. A debate is emerging as to the Community's institutional and political configuration. This debate is often couched in purely technical terms, especially in legal literature, but nonetheless it inevitably concerns political values and choices.

The work of the ECJ increased sharply during the 1980s and 1990s as EC law has become more complex and the number of disputes grown. Under Article 168a of the EEC Treaty (32d ECSC and 140a Euratom) (all added by Articles 4, 26 and 11 of the Single European Act 1986), the European Council has power, after consulting the European Commission and the European Parliament, to attach to the ECJ a court with jurisdiction to hear and determine at first instance certain classes of action or proceedings brought by legal or natural persons. The Court of First Instance (the CFI) became operational in late 1989. It consists of 15 judges appointed for a six-year term. The CFI is specifically designed to relieve the European Court of its ever-increasing work-load. There is a right of appeal to the European Court on points of law, but actions brought by member States or community institutions or questions referred to the European Court for preliminary rulings (under Article 177) may not be determined or heard by the CFI. The principal heads of jurisdiction of the CFI are: disputes between the Community institutions and their staff; actions against the European Commission by organisations in respect of prices, restrictive agreements and levies; and actions against the European Commission by private parties for the annulment or for failure to act relating to the implementation of competition rules under the EEC Treaty.

3.4   European Human Rights

The Council of Europe was established in 1949. It has acted as a general political forum for the parliamentary nations of Western Europe. It had 23 members by 1990, but with the collapse of communism in central and Eastern Europe, its membership has grown rapidly. One of the major acts of the Council was the drawing up in 1950 of the European Convention for the Protection of Human Rights and Fundamental Freedoms. This was ratified by the British government in 1951, but has never been approved by Parliament. It is therefore not part of English law, although the Labour government elected in 1997 has promised a Bill of Rights. The Convention defined the rights and freedoms of the citizen in a democracy: freedom from torture; freedom from slavery; the right to liberty and security of the person; the right to a fair trial; protection against retrospective legislation; the right to privacy; freedom of thought, religion and conscience; freedom of expression; freedom of assembly and association; the right to marry; the right to an effective legal remedy.

Complaints from individuals or member States may be made to the European Commission of Human Rights (ECHR) which was established in 1954, although not all members of the Council of Europe recognise the competence of the Commission to receive applications from individuals or non-governmental organisations. A substantial number are brought against the United Kingdom. Serious matters may then be passed on to the European Court of Human Rights set up in 1959. To begin with the Court was not very busy and only heard two cases in the next nine years. However, since 1975 the Court has heard a number of cases against the British government, including matters such as prison rules, contempt of court (the *Sunday Times* thalidomide affair), the treatment of IRA prisoners in Northern Ireland (the Maze prison), the rights of mental patients, the Kenyan Asians issue, birching in the Isle of Man, the use of the tawse in Scottish schools, discriminatory laws against homosexuals in Northern Ireland, closed shop practices in British Railways, telephone tapping, immigration rules, sex discrimination, nationalisation without compensation (aircraft and shipbuilding), and censoring prisoners' mail (*Reuben Silver* v. *UK* (1983)). But whatever the judgments of the European Court of Human Rights may be, they are only persuasive; English courts need take virtually no notice of them, for the Convention has no place in common law nor yet in parliamentary law. However, it should be added that the courts are increasingly making reference to the European Convention, as could be seen in the *Spycatcher* litigation in 1989 and the *Anthony Bland* case in 1993. In *R.* v. *Home Secretary ex parte Brind* (1991) Lord Ackner said: 'It is well settled that the Convention may be deployed for the purpose of the resolution of an ambiguity in English primary or subordinate legislation'.

Certain rights under the Convention are absolute, such as Article 3 in respect of the prohibition of torture, inhuman or degrading treatment and punishment. However, some rights are limited in their scope (for instance, Article 4, which deals with the prohibition of slavery, in respect of the definition of forced labour) and others have very clear exceptions (for example, Article 5 (right to liberty) in respect of the preventing of the commission of an offence). Exceptions are made to cover the issues of public morality, the interests of other individuals, including their reputations, national security, public health, public safety, public order, the interests of justice, the economic well-being of the country, territorial integrity, the independence of the judiciary, disorder and crime, confidentiality.

Also, Article 15 allows a country to derogate from its obligations under the Convention in times of war or other occasions of serious emergency. But this provision is not interpreted broadly; for it to operate, there must be a real threat to the organised life of the whole community. Yet not all rights are so caught; for instance Article 7 which prohibits retrospective criminal laws must be maintained, similarly that part of Article 4 which prohibits torture.

The EC is not a signatory of the Convention, but it is fair to say that the Convention has influenced the development of EC laws, as seen in *Nold* v. *Commission of the European Community* (1974) and *Rutili* v. *Minister of the Interior* (1975). It is also of assistance to individuals who challenge the acts of the EC institutions (*National Panasonic (UK) Ltd* v. *Commission of the European Community* (1980)).

The argument of British governments has been that if the Convention were incorporated, this would lead to judicial interference not only at the European level but at the national level too, supposedly a constitutional nightmare. In 1995, the ECHR ruled against the United Kingdom in the Gibraltar case (*McCann, Savage and Farrell* v. *United Kingdom*), although only by a majority of 10-9. This was the first time the European Court of Human Rights decided a case on the most basic human right of all, the right to life under Article 2. The issue concerned the three members of an IRA active service unit who were shot dead in the street by SAS soldiers in Gibraltar who erroneously believed they were on a bombing mission. The Court of Appeal in 1995 expressed reservations about the ban on homosexual members of the armed forces, although it concluded it was not a policy stigmatised by irrationality (*R.* v. *Secretary of State for Defence ex parte Smith*). The decision again raised the issue of the status of the European Convention; Lord Justice Simon Brown told the former soldiers the impact of the Convention on judicial review was relatively limited, and the decision on the future of the armed forces policy must rest with others, notably the Government and Parliament. In *Chahal* v. *United Kingdom* (1996) C. had been held in prison for six years challenging a deportation order. But he was immediately released when the ECHR ruled that Articles 5 and 13 of the Convention had been violated.

Moreover, by Article F(2) of the Treaty on European Union, Community law must respect the fundamental rights guaranteed by the European Convention for the Protection of Human Rights and Fundamental Freedom – all individual member states are party to the European Convention in short (*Re Accession of the Community to the European Human Rights Convention* (1996)). In *P.* v. *S. and Cornwall County Council* (1996) the decision of the European Court of Human Rights in *Rees* (1986) was relied on by the European Court of Justice in deciding that transsexuals fell within the Equal Treatment Directive. In 1997 the ECHR awarded £10,000 to Alison Halford, the former Assistant Chief Constable of Merseyside, in respect of the tapping of her office telephone conversations.

This brings us back, lastly, to Maastricht itself (the Treaty on European Union), as revised by the Treaty of Amsterdam in 1997. The TEU, now that the political obstacles have been cleared, notably in Denmark, France, Germany and the United Kingdom, has had considerable effects upon European law from 1994, although most of the Treaty is a statement of political intent. Indeed the EU (European Union), although relating to the same 15 states, is wider than the EC (European Community), since the TEU covers two matters not in the province of the EC, namely the Common Foreign and Security Policy and also Justice and Home Affairs.

Under Article G of the TEU the term EEC was replaced by EC. The Treaty, originally signed in February 1992, is, of course, part of EC primary law. Under

Articles 102a–109m there are provisions for a process of monetary and economic union. By Article 138e EC a Community Ombudsman was provided for; the Ombudsman may investigate maladministration within Community institutions and is obliged to report annually to the European Parliament. Under Article 189b EC complex procedures were laid down which strengthened the European Parliament's powers in relation to the legislative process in certain areas (for instance, laws on the freedom of movement of workers under Article 49 EC).

DISCUSSION POINTS

1 Is the commentary by the *Financial Times* illustrative of the difficulties of applying European wide concepts to British law?

2 How can the European Communities Act be reconciled with the doctrine of parliamentary supremacy?

3 What reforms to the European Community have been made in the 1990s at Maastricht and Amsterdam?

THE COURTS

4.1   Criminal trials

THE MAGISTRATES' COURT

The Magistrates' Court is the most junior of all courts; in the main it is the lowest rung in the ladder of criminal proceedings. Most of its powers are now governed by the Magistrates' Courts Act 1980. In England and Wales there are approximately 1,000 Magistrates' Courts which are served by 30,000 lay magistrates. There are also about 80 stipendiary justices, in London and the metropolitan cities, who are full-time and paid. The lay magistrates, or justices of the peace, usually have to give up a day of their time every two weeks or so. Although unpaid, they do receive subsistence and travelling allowances, as now provided under the Justices of the Peace Act 1997 (consolidating the Justices of the Peace Act 1979 and provisions of Part IV of the Police and Magistrates' Courts Act 1994).

These courts are extremely important on account of their case-load alone: apart from their limited civil jurisdiction over such family matters as the custody and adoption of children and maintenance orders, magistrates handle about 96 per cent of all criminal cases (including motoring offences). Indictable offences are those triable by a jury at the Crown Court; they therefore tend to be serious offences. Non-indictable offences are dealt with by the Magistrates' Court; they are also called summary offences and they number the best part of three million a year. Over a million of these are motoring offences. Some offences, however, may be triable either way – on indictment or summarily; the procedure is covered by the Criminal Law Act 1977. A good example is that of theft, including petty theft (theft under the value of £20). It should be noted that a significant amount of magistrates' time is taken up with applications under the licensing and betting and gaming laws. The fact that magistrates have jurisdiction over family matters, as the Family Proceedings Court, as well as the County Court and High Court, has led to demands for an integrated separate Family Court.

In 1992 a White Paper, *A New Framework for Local Justice*, was published. Its proposed reorganisation included the creation of a magistrates' courts inspectorate with lay members to raise standards of service, and a new layer of senior managers, paid according to performance. The courts continue to be a local service but are being overhauled to improve performance. Lay people who are not magistrates are involved in running the courts through committees. The Lord Chancellor has power to intervene if any court seriously or consistently underperforms and the committee responsible fails to act. The White Paper sought to preserve magistrates' judicial independence, the erosion of which had been at the core of magistrates' concerns over earlier proposals. Lord Mackay, the then Lord Chancellor, said that the reforms were the 'most important' in the organisation of the courts for more than 40 years. The new service would 'demand and reward excellence' and would bring about a 'less parochial service'.

(From 1995 every court, apart from the Magistrates' Courts and coroners' courts, came under the control of a new body, the Court Service Agency. The judges traditionally are not involved in court administration, but in this instance consultative committees have been created between the judges at three levels and the agency itself).

The result was the Police and Magistrates' Courts Act 1994 – a controversial piece of legislation and much amended in Parliament. It made changes to the constitution of police authorities and also attempted to bring a greater degree of efficiency and scrutiny to the operation of magistrates' courts. Specifically, under Part IV of the Act, by s.69, two or more courts' committees may be merged. The Magistrates may ask the Lord Chancellor for permission to merge. The Lord Chancellor will grant permission if the order is likely to contribute to an overall increase in efficiency of the court area. By s.70 lay people (a maximum of two) may be co-opted on to magistrates' courts committees, and by ss.73–74 the Lord Chancellor may direct magistrates' committees to undertake specified steps, and may ask for reports and plans.

A justices' chief executive for each committee has to be appointed and approved by the Lord Chancellor (s.75), and s.86 established Her Majesty's Magistrates' Courts Service Inspectorate together with a Chief Inspector. The reorganised magistrates' committees undertake training under the supervision of the Judicial Studies Board, and their accounts are subject to review by the Audit Commission.

Under the Criminal Justice and Public Order Act 1994, it was proposed to abolish committal proceedings as recommended by the Runciman Commission in 1993 (see below), and replace them with transfer proceedings, but this was reversed by the Criminal Procedure and Investigations Act 1996, an acute example of a sloppy legislative process.

After a great deal of public criticism a programme of training was introduced for magistrates in 1966 and there are now also a number of compulsory refresher courses. Notwithstanding the 1994 reforms, above, most Lord Chancellors continue to express confidence in the system of lay magistrates; it is they who are responsible for appointing magistrates in the first place. The Lord Chancellor, who as a member of the government is the political head of the legal system, receives recommendations through area committees made up of existing magistrates. In

1988 the Lord Chancellor, Lord Mackay, decided that the 878 people on the 95 local advisory committees who interview candidates for the magistracy and recommend them for appointment should be made public. The committees were given until 1992 to disclose names.

In 1977 *The Guardian* commented:

> **Magistrates are criticised for being conservative, middle-aged or elderly, with a host of barely concealed prejudices against blacks, drug offenders and homosexuals. Research ten years ago showed that the average age of a magistrate was 56, and that 77 per cent were drawn from the professional and managerial classes. 'The compulsory training of magistrates has had a profound effect in bringing magistrates from being pure amateurs to a quite considerable degree of professionalism', says Louis Blom-Cooper, the chairman of the Howard League for Penal Reform. But still left in the magisterial system is too high a degree of amateurism. They are nice, ordinary people on the whole who have no kind of idea what it is to administer criminal justice. This means that one gets a spatchcock system in which some courts, particularly those in London, are really quite good but when one gets away from London the standards are very variable indeed.**

In any case lay magistrates themselves are very much guided by the clerk to the court, who is normally a legally qualified, full-time official. However, in this context the chairman of the bench may exercise an important role.

One difficulty has been to maintain consistency in sentencing practices. A *Which?* survey in 1989, for example, found that Tiverton magistrates fined twice the amount for speeding than Exeter JPs 15 miles away. And in 1992 Liberty found wide variations in magistrates' sentencing practices. Its survey, *Unequal before the Law*, showed that offenders in Devon and Cornwall were far more likely to go jail (7.27 per cent) than in Dyfed-Powys (2.9 per cent). Of the percentage of males aged 21 and over who were sent straight to prison, Exeter and Plymouth were amongst the top ten, at 13.22 per cent and 11.66 per cent, but Yeovil was only 0.81 per cent and Shepton Mallet actually 0 per cent.

A 1990 study by Professor Shari Diamond showed that the 63 stipendiary JPs (46 in London) were tougher in their sentencing than lay JPs, perhaps showing that the community wants sentencing based on 'just deserts', and stipendiaries were more in touch with what the public wants.

A more worrying survey came from the Lord Chancellor's Department/Duchy of Lancaster itself in 1992. This found that magistrates were largely Conservative; the lack of women JPs supporting Labour was most acute. In Bristol, as much Labour as Conservative, 142 JPs said they were Tory and 85 Labour. LCD officials said that Labour supporters were more likely to be employees who had difficulty getting time off work and could ill-afford to lose wages, even for one day a fortnight. Critics say the selection committees are still dominated by magistrates, who tend to favour like-minded applicants. Further figures published by the Lord Chancellor's Department in 1995 showed little change: of 30,952 magistrates in England and Wales, 45 per cent were Conservatives, 22 per cent Labour, 16 per cent Liberal and 17 per cent no party.

Be that as it may, the crucial decision that Magistrates' Courts have to make once a defendant is brought to court by summons, warrant or from police detention is whether they have the power to try the accused at all. They may well have the right to try the 'offender' without reference to another court. There are a number of offences which may be tried either by magistrates alone or by a jury in the Crown Court. Following the James Report of 1975 the range was reduced by the Criminal Law Act 1977 and further reduced by the Criminal Justice Act 1988. If the accused decides to elect for jury trial, then the magistrates must accept that. If, however, he does not express a preference for a Crown Court trial, the magistrates may still decide that it would be appropriate for the person to be tried by jury. Even where the defendant is tried summarily, he may still be sent to the Crown Court for sentencing if the Magistrates' Court wishes to impose a punishment more severe than its statutory powers allow. Nonetheless wherever the case is sent to the Crown Court for trial, magistrates must first undertake committal proceedings – they must determine whether a prosecution has presented enough evidence to establish a *prima facie* case, whether in fact there is any case to answer in the Crown Court. In serious or complex fraud cases committal proceedings may be dispensed with and a preliminary hearing may instead take place in the Crown Court before the judge alone (Criminal Justice Act 1987). This can also occur in cases involving child abuse.

It can be argued that committal proceedings are a wasteful legal procedure. In 1981 the Royal Commission on Criminal Procedure (the Philips Report) and in 1993 the Royal Commission on Criminal Justice (the Runciman Report) recommended their abolition, but, as indicated above, a legislative mess ensued from 1994 to 1996. Under the Criminal Justice Act 1967 reforms were instituted to speed up the process. These reforms were consolidated under the Magistrates' Courts Act 1980. Very seldomly the prosecution may seek leave from the High Court to prefer a 'voluntary bill of indictment'. This means that the case goes straight to the Crown Court for trial. This will occur where the accused threatens to disrupt committal proceedings as illustrated in *R. v. Raymond* (1981), where it is convenient that the accused stands trial with others who have already been committed to the Crown Court, or where the magistrates' refusal to commit a person for trial appears to be clearly questionable. This last example arose in the so-called Prosser Case in 1981 when a bill of indictment was successfully obtained after a Birmingham stipendiary magistrate had refused to commit several prison officers for trial for the alleged murder of a prisoner, one Prosser (*R. v. Jackson*). The bill of indictment procedure is a statutory one (the Administration of Justice (Miscellaneous Provisions) Act 1933).

Section 49 of the Criminal Procedure and Investigations Act 1996 amends the mode of trial procedure so that for triable either way offences in practice a greater number will be heard by magistrates' courts. The transfer for trial proceedings, designed to replace committal proceedings, under the Criminal Justice and Public Order Act 1994, were abolished under s.44 (Part V) of the 1996 legislation. The committal stage is now modified and old-style oral hearings are abolished. This does put defendants at a disadvantage in so far as weak prosecution witnesses cannot be tested until the jury stage. Also of note is that the principle of *autrefois acquit* was amended in a limited way (for instance where the accused was guilty of intimidating a juror) under s.54 of the 1996 Act, so that following an acquittal fresh proceedings may be brought.

Part III (ss.29–33) of the Act provides that the Crown Court may order a preparatory hearing in a case which is complex or lengthy; this appears to be additional to the recent Plea and Directions Hearing (PDH) rules. The *Practice Direction (Crown Court: Plea and Directions Hearings)* (1995) made it clear it applied to all cases except serious fraud. The magistrates' court had to commit the defendant to appear in the Crown Court on a specific date for an initial PDH, the purpose being to ensure all necessary steps had been taken and that the court had sufficient information to fix a trial date. The PDH should normally be held in open court, with all the defendants present.

There have been a number of arguments about whether jury trial is more advantageous to the accused than trial by magistrates. The former can be considerably more expensive for the defendant where he has a choice of courts; on the other hand, most lawyers would probably agree that the chances of acquittal are higher before a jury than before the bench. Lord Mackay in 1992 said too many cases found their way to the Crown Court, Magistrates' Courts should hear more triable either way cases, and that was a matter that was being re-considered by the Conservative Government in early 1997 and probably will also be examined by the new Labour Government.

The House of Lords in *R. v. Brentwood Justices ex parte Nicholls* (1991) held that where a number of defendants appearing before the magistrates are jointly charged with an offence that is triable either summarily or on indictment, and one defendant elects trial on indictment, but one or more others consent to summary trial, the justices are not bound to commit all the defendants together for trial on indictment.

Appeals may be made from the Magistrates' Court to the Crown Court in respect of conviction and sentence. On appeal sentences may be reduced or, more rarely, increased. However, if only a point of law is involved, or an alleged procedural error, then appeal may be made directly to the High Court (the Divisional Court of the Queen's Bench Division), possibly with an opportunity to appeal to the House of Lords where the point of law is serious enough to warrant their Lordships' attention. This latter form of procedure is known as a case stated appeal.

THE CROWN COURT

The Crown Court deals with a wide range of serious criminal cases and it came into existence under the Courts Act 1971. This Act provided for a major re-organisation of the court structure at senior level, abolishing the higher criminal

Courts of Assize and Quarter Sessions in the process. The Crown Court is part of a federation of courts known as the Supreme Court (formerly the Supreme Court of Judicature). The Supreme Court's overall organisation is detailed by the Supreme Court Act 1981. The other courts belonging to the Supreme Court are the Court of Appeal and the High Court of Justice, including the Divisional Courts of the High Court. Three different classes of judges sit in the Crown Court. Firstly, there are High Court judges who are normally judges of the Queen's Bench Division. However, most Crown Court judges are circuit judges. The judges of the County Courts, which deal with civil matters, are also circuit judges. There are approximately 500 circuit judges in total, and still a shortage (England and Wales are divided into a number of circuits or regions each of which is presided over by a Queen's Bench judge). Lastly, there are part-time judges, known as Recorders, who normally try criminal cases. A Recorder is expected to serve a minimum of 20 days a year. Under the Administration of Justice Act 1977 either a barrister or solicitor may be appointed as a Recorder; they must be of at least 10 years' standing. A circuit judge must also be a barrister of at least ten years' standing, or a Recorder who has held office for three years.

There are four classes of criminal offences tried by Crown Courts sitting in principal towns throughout England, Wales and Northern Ireland. Class 1 cases must be tried by a High Court judge – for example, the offences of murder and spying. Class 2 offences will normally be tried by a High Court judge but he may assign the case to a circuit judge or Recorder – for instance, manslaughter, rape, incestuous acts, infanticide and acts which cause very serious bodily harm. Class 3 cases may be tried by any one of the three types of judges listed above; the offences here will include robbery and serious burglary. Finally, Class 4 offences, such as theft, assault causing bodily harm, reckless driving and incitement to racial hatred, will usually be tried by a circuit judge or a Recorder. Class 4 offences are by and large those triable either way. Some Crown Courts are more 'senior' than others, depending upon which class of offences they are able to try.

Despite the subsequent delays in Crown Court procedure, the rationalisation of the criminal court structure in 1971 was an important step forward, not least because the Assize system itself dated from the time of Henry II. Now the overlapping jurisdiction between Assizes and Quarter Sessions has been removed and the Crown Court, particularly in terms of first- and second-tier centres, is located in towns geographically accessible. The very buildings, too, have been made more user-friendly and there is an extensive court building programme. The Beeching Report of 1969 which led to the passage of the 1971 Act had drawn sharp attention to the deplorable conditions under which the system operated:

Accused persons, litigants, witnesses, jurors, police officers, and even solicitors and counsel conferring with clients, all jostle together in embarrassing proximity in halls and corridors which, far from providing any elements of comfort, may well be stacked with the paraphernalia associated with other uses of the building, such as dismantled staging parts of a boxing ring, or the music stands for a brass band contest.

APPEALS

A defendant who has been convicted at the Crown Court may appeal to the Court of Appeal (Criminal Division) under s.9 of the Criminal Appeal Act 1968 in respect of sentence. All the original grounds for appeal were contained in the 1968 Act, but following the recommendations of the Runciman Report in 1993, the law was amended by the Criminal Appeal Act 1995.

Under s.1 of the Criminal Appeal Act 1995 an appeal against conviction may be made only with leave of the Court of Appeal, or if the trial judge grants a certificate that the case is fit for appeal

Section 2 of the Criminal Appeal Act 1995 introduced a single ground against conviction – an appeal should be allowed if the conviction is 'unsafe'. 'Unsafe' is not defined.

With regard to fresh evidence, under s.23(2) of the 1968 Act, the Court of Appeal is under a duty to receive fresh evidence, if evidence is likely to be credible, and would have been admissible at trial, and there is a 'reasonable explanation' for failure to adduce the evidence at trial.

Under s.23(1) the Court of Appeal has a discretion to receive fresh evidence if it thinks it necessary or expedient in the interests of justice. This section is not much used, since in theory s.23(1) permits the court to re-hear the entire case; the Court of Appeal will usually receive fresh evidence only if the conditions in s.23(2) are satisfied.

Section 4 of Criminal Appeal Act 1995 Act substituted the phrase 'capable of belief' for 'likely to be credible' in s.23(2) of the 1968 Act.

Under s.7 of the 1968 Act the court may order a re-trial following appeal against conviction if a re-trial is considered in the interests of justice. The power to order a re-trial is generally available, whether the appeal is on the basis of fresh evidence, or because of some irregularity, or misdirection in the trial.

In addition, the Court of Appeal has inherent powers, independent of the 1968 Act, to issue a writ of *venire de novo*, that is the original trial was a nullity – see *R. v. Rose (Newton)* (1982). Irregularity has to be very fundamental in this instance.

With regard to lenient sentences the Attorney-General may refer a case to the Court of Appeal where he considers the sentence 'unduly lenient' (ss.35–36 of the Criminal Justice Act 1988).

Under Part II of the 1995 Act, there has been established the Criminal Cases Review Commission (the CCRC), which began work in 1997. The Commission took over the Home Secretary's powers to refer troublesome cases back to the Court of Appeal in the wake of the Birmingham Six, Guildford Four, Maguire Seven (and latterly the Bridgewater Three) and other miscarriages of justice.

Also s.5 (under Part I) of the 1995 Act inserted s.23A into the 1968 Act, enabling the Court of Appeal to direct the CCRC to investigate and report to the court on any relevant matters that should be resolved.

Section 8 and Schedule 1 of the Act established the CCRC and made provision as to its membership and procedure, and ss.13–14 set out the conditions and other factors to be considered for the making of references by the Commission under ss.9–12; s15 deals with investigations by the Commission following a direction of the Court of Appeal.

In *R. v. Graham (H K)* (1996) the Court of Appeal considered the changes introduced by the Criminal Appeal Act 1995, including s.2, regarding unsafe verdicts.

BALDWIN AND MCCONVILLE'S CRITIQUE

In 1981 two academics from Birmingham University, John Baldwin and Michael McConville, published a study of Crown Court prosecutions in London and Birmingham, *Courts, Prosecution and Conviction*. They found that in 8 per cent of the Birmingham cases and in 6 per cent of the London cases the standard of evidence was found wanting. Sometimes, however, this was a result of the police being pressurised to prosecute, especially by large stores for shop-lifting offences. In such cases the police hoped that the defendant would either plead guilty or put up a poor show before a jury or be dealt with by way of a summary hearing before the magistrates. Out of 807 cases studied the judge had directed an acquittal in 181. The police accepted this as the right course in the majority of those acquittals. The police were reluctant to drop a case once a charge had been preferred, for if they did so they admitted that the evidence was fundamentally weak and thereby ran a risk of being sued in tort for malicious prosecution or false imprisonment. Indeed, on a general basis, the Crown Court judges throw out nearly half the cases, without a trial, which says much still about committal proceedings. In nearly half the cases studied the main evidence against the accused was identification by a witness or the victim. Forensic evidence played a significant part in only about 5 per cent of cases.

The researchers also expressed doubts about the adversarial nature of the English legal process. An adversarial system means that the two sides to a dispute come to court on equal terms and they, or their respective legal representatives, do most of the arguing. The judge and, where appropriate, the jury do most of the listening before making up their minds. The French system can be described as an inquisitorial one: there the judge plays a much more active part in rooting out the truth. The equivalent of barristers and solicitors play a more muted role. Baldwin and McConville suggested that as a result of police and court practices, committal and Crown Court proceedings were, in effect, becoming more inquisitorial than adversarial. Baldwin and McConville also voiced concern about the unsatisfactory way in which verbal confessions to the police were used as evidence. Even written confessions were sometimes 'guided' by the police and defendants subsequently regretted the form of their confessions. This point had been underlined by the Maxwell Confait murder case. Three London youths of limited intelligence had been persuaded to make written confessions to the effect that they had murdered Confait, a transvestite prostitute. The Court of Appeal eventually quashed their conviction and the case led to an official inquiry (the Fisher Report). The 1993 Runciman Report also expressed concern about confession evidence and lack of corroboration as well as a certain amount of intimidatory techniques used in police interviews, highlighted in the Cardiff Three case. The report was critical of the fact that 59 per cent of all Crown Court acquittals were judge ordered (before trial) or judge acquitted (during the trial) on account of poor prosecution evidence, which did not reflect highly on committal proceedings or the work of the police and the Crown Prosecution Service (the CPS).

Under s.76 of the Police and Criminal Evidence Act 1984 any confession obtained by oppression is inadmissible, that is by torture, inhuman or degrading treatment and the use or threat of violence, 'degrading treatment' being a concept taken from the European Convention on Human Rights. Broadly speaking, beyond that the court must decide what may be inadmissible evidence, in the context of unreliable confessions. Under the same Act, by s.78, the court has a general power to exclude evidence which would have an adverse effect on the fairness of the case, the court's discretion here is thus very broad. In *R. v. Fuller* (1987) the Court of Appeal, in interpreting s.76, adopted the Oxford English Dictionary definition of oppression.

4.2   Civil trials

THE COUNTY COURT

County courts were established by the County Courts Act 1846 and exist in most towns of a reasonable size. However, their lineage is long. At common law a local County Court used to exercise a considerable jurisdiction in respect of land and small debts, but the County Courts fell into disuse from the time of Henry II with the establishment of Assize courts. From the reign of James I onwards local small debt courts were progressively established and these were made the basis of the statutory system of 1846.

The general jurisdiction is now derived from the County Courts Act 1984, together with special jurisdiction from a wide variety of statutes, some of which confer exclusive jurisdiction on the County Courts. Certain County Courts have jurisdiction in admiralty, bankruptcy and race relations matters. Also, nearly 200 courts in the larger towns have had jurisdiction in divorces since the Matrimonial Causes Act 1967. When a divorce became defended it was formerly transferred to the High Court, and where undefended divorces were complex they were also transferred, but since 1986 under the Matrimonial and Family Proceedings Act 1984 as amended by the Matrimonial Proceedings (Transfers) Act 1988 all County Courts designated for divorce hearings automatically hear defended divorce suits, which generally are no longer tried in the High Court. Magistrates' Courts have concurrent jurisdiction in a number of family matters, such as adoption, guardianship, matrimonial and domestic violence, but generally they have very limited civil jurisdiction.

Some cases start in the County Court in their own right, others in the High Court, but both courts have overlapping jurisdiction. The High Court deals with about half a million civil cases a year. However, it should be noted that just 1 per cent of High Court and 10 per cent of County Court cases actually reach trial stage; in other words, they are 'settled out of court'. Under the Administration of Justice Act 1982 a judgment or order of the High Court may be enforced in the County Court, and vice versa. Under s.40 of the County Courts Act 1984 the High Court can transfer certain business to the County Court, but a Practice Direction during 1988 made it clear that complicated cases of fact or of expert evidence, fatal accident cases, jury trials, claims against the police or cases involving a novel point of law would not be transferred. Where a case has been transferred from the High Court to the County Court, the latter court has a discretion to award costs on the High Court scale, as appropriate – *Forey* v. *London Buses Ltd* (1991).

LIMITATION

In all civil cases proceedings must be brought within a limited period on account of the fact that evidence will wane as time passes. Furthermore it is not considered fair to the potential defendant to keep him in indefinite legal suspense. The rules are governed by the Limitation Act 1980. The limitation rules are quite complex, but as a general guide it can be said that actions for personal injury must be brought within three years. Contractual disputes are limited to six (from the time the breach complained of occurs), as are tortious actions other than those for personal injury and latent damage in buildings. Six years also apply to actions for loss of mortgage or rent and breaches of trust, although for certain breaches of trust, such as fraudulent breach, there is no limitation. For recovery of land the limit is 12 years.

In contrast there is generally no time bar to criminal proceedings, but there are certain exceptions – for example under the Food Act 1984 there is a three-year limitation period. Certain motoring offences are subject to a time bar. *Halford* v. *Brookes* (1991) was an unusual case in so far as it concerned civil proceedings for murder, and s.33 of the Limitation Act 1980 the Court of Appeal ruled gave the court discretion to allow proceedings to commence outside the limitation period.

SMALL CLAIMS

An important part in the County Court's jurisdiction is played by the district judge (formerly the registrar). For the trial itself the normal practice – as in the High Court – is for a single judge to hear the case. In any event the district judge will deal with all the interlocutory matters, that is he or she will conduct a pre-trial review, clearing the legal decks for the trial proper and fixing a date for the case to be heard. It is at this stage that the litigants often settle out of court. In addition the district judge has had the power since the Administration of Justice Act 1973 to hear disputes that involve small claims. The aim was to help those disputants who might not have sought legal redress on account of the fact that the costs of a trial could often outweigh any damages sought.

Whether, however, County Courts really have sufficient time and resources at their disposal to give much more than a cursory examination to the complaint, is probably still very much open to question. However, it is possible to argue that 'palm tree justice is better than no justice at all'. The upper limit to small claims arbitration is now £3,000. The small claims procedure has certainly become popular, with the greater part of a half a million cases being disposed of. In 1986 the Lord Chancellor published a consultation paper, as part of his Civil Justice Review. It found that in over two-thirds of small cases both parties were either private individuals or small businesses and that the facility was well understood by the public. However, there was too great an inconsistency between courts in the time taken to dispense with cases and in the way they were handled; registrars should hold a single hearing, act more 'inquisitorially' and undergo systematic training, and there should be a publicly available manual, the report said.

The Lay Representatives (Rights of Audience) Order 1992, made under s.11 of the Courts and Legal Services Act 1990 gives lay representatives rights of audience in small claims cases dealt with by arbitration in County Courts, although they cannot be heard if the person represented does not attend the hearing.

APPEALS

A County Court judge may hear appeals against the orders of a district judge; similarly a judge sitting in chambers in the High Court may hear appeals against the orders of the High Court's equivalent of a registrar, the Master. An appeal against a County Court judge's decision will lie, as in the case of the High Court, to the Civil Division of the Court of Appeal. Leave to appeal is usually as of right under s.7 of the Courts and Legal Services Act 1990. If there has been a serious irregularity at the original trial or if fresh evidence comes to light, either party in the County Court can apply for a new hearing. However, there is no right of appeal from a County Court decision in a small claims case or in matters concerning land disputes where the land in question is of low taxable value. An appeal on a point of law is a different matter.

The County Court may not face the same pressures as the Crown Court, but its judges do belong to the same group – circuit judges. In his speech to the annual conference of the Law Society in 1984, the Master of the Rolls suggested the establishment of civil lay justices, whose job would be to take over some of the work of the County Court, which then in turn could relieve pressures on the High Court. Surprisingly, this idea has not yet been pursued.

Civil Courts

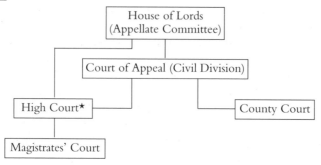

Criminal Courts

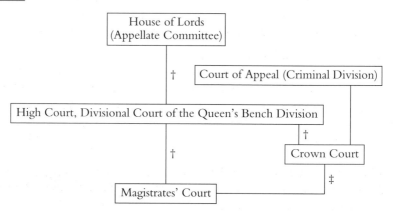

*   Direct (leap-frog) appeal from High Court to
House of Lords is under the Administration of
Justice Act 1969
†   Appeal by case stated
‡   Appeal or committal for trial or sentencing

FIGURE 2 *The court structure*

THE HIGH COURT

The High Court of Justice is a division of the Supreme Court which includes the
Crown Court and both divisions – civil and criminal – of the Court of Appeal.
Both the Court of Appeal and the High Court are housed at the Royal Courts of
Justice or 'Law Courts' in the Strand in London. As a result of the Administration
of Justice Act 1970 the High Court is organised in three divisions – Queen's
Bench, Chancery and Family. As already stated above, when appeals to those divisions are involved, invariably on points of law and to the Queen's Bench Division
most of all, those divisions are known, somewhat clumsily, as Divisional Courts –
hence the Divisional Court of the Queen's Bench Division, and so on.

Before 1971 there existed a Probate, Divorce and Admiralty Division dealing with what was popularly called 'wills, wives and wrecks'. However, under the 1970 Act's reorganisation Probate and Divorce were transformed into 'Family' and Admiralty was given its own court within the Queen's Bench Division which now also contains the Commercial Court. The Chancery Division, whose nominal head is the Lord Chancellor, traces its lineage to the Court of Chancery and the system of equity. Among the most important functions of the Chancery Division are matters covering partnerships, mortgages, trusts, deeds, minors and the partition of land. In 1981 the Chancery Division of the High Court came in for considerable official criticism, to the effect that it was administratively badly organised. Changes were subsequently made, but the criticism is illustrative of the fact that in a technological age courts are notoriously slow to adapt to new procedures. In 1988 a report, by a committee of judges and officials under the President of the Family Division, called for greater flexibility in allocating cases between High Court judges by abolishing its divisions and creating a unified structure.

The Family Division deals with problems which are self-evident by its very name – all matrimonial matters and disputes and issues relating to the care and adoption of children. The Queen's Bench Division deals with a wide range of issues under contract law and the law of torts. To some extent all three divisions exercise overlapping or concurrent jurisdiction. Barristers usually specialise within one of the three divisions. What Peter Archer said a number of years ago still holds true:

The chief distinction lies between those who practise in the Chancery Division and those who concentrate on the common law side. The former are usually to be found in Lincoln's Inn, and there, as a general rule, may be seen men whose talent is to express themselves with precision on paper and who by long concentration can produce a careful analysis of an intricate problem. In the Temple, which is the home of the common lawyers, are the less retiring counsel, the advocates, who make their reputations by cross-examination or by argument in court. The wits of the Chancery bar express the difference by declaring that they and their fellows 'think without speaking', leaving the role of the men from across Fleet Street to be inferred.

While barristers may stay within one division for the whole of their professional lives judges may enjoy greater mobility. Apart from the Lord Chancellor, the nominal head of the Chancery Division, the Lord Chief Justice, who presides over the Queen's Bench Division, the Vice-Chancellor of the Chancery Division and the President of the Family Division, there are approximately 90 remaining High Court judges (puisne judges). Most judges are assigned to the Queen's Bench Division. From 1992 their work-load was monitored. The High Court may also sit outside London; when it does it resides in the most important (first-tier) Crown Court towns. Thus it is mainly Queen's Bench judges who tour on circuit and, as we have seen, they have the right to try the more serious of Crown Court cases. Appeals from the High Court will normally lie to the Court of Appeal (Civil Division). However, the Administration of Justice Act 1969 made provision for an appeal to lie to the House of Lords. The qualifications to this 'leap-frog-ging' procedure are that the High Court decision has been made by a single judge, that the judge has certified that a point of law of fundamental public importance is involved and that the House of Lords itself agrees. Lastly, under the Administration of Justice Act 1982, Recorders may sit as judges in the High Court from time to time, in order to assist in the transaction of business.

CIVIL JUSTICE REVIEW

In 1988 the Civil Justice Review committee, set up by Lord Hailsham when Lord Chancellor, and under the chairmanship of Sir Maurice Hodgson, a businessman, issued wide-ranging recommendations. Although the committee left untouched much of the civil justice system, it did make some notable suggestions, some of which required implementation by primary legislation. As Lord Hailsham himself has said, rises in personal injury and commercial cases have put a strain on civil lit-igation: existing delays in each field cannot be justified and the case for a thorough overhaul of jurisdiction, procedure and evidence was urgent and overwhelming. This Civil Justice Review led directly to the Courts and Legal Services Act 1990, a note of which is given at the end of the following chapter. The Civil Justice Review also added:

1 Litigants in small claims, housing or debt cases in the County Court should have a statutory right to be assisted by a lay representative of their choice. Court forms and leaflets should be simplified, advice agencies should be encouraged to have duty representatives and an experimental scheme of early evening arbitration should be conducted at a small number of trial centres.

2 In personal injury cases the Lord Chancellor should consider a system of no-fault compensation for less serious road accidents to be financed by personal insurance.

3 Simplified procedures should be introduced in respect of housing cases, and in particular both judges and registrars should receive more training in housing work; rent assessment panels should be integrated into the national structure of courts and tribunals administered by the Lord Chancellor.

4 One of the law reform agencies should study the problem of representative or class actions, to enable better procedures to be introduced for cases where large numbers of litigants have a common basis to their claims.

In 1993 a joint committee of the Bar and the Law Society published a review (the Heilbron Report) which was highly critical of the complexity of civil justice, and amongst other things recommended a reorganisation of the High Court, including the merging of the Chancery and Queen's Bench Divisions.

The Civil Justice Review culminated in the Woolf Report, *Access to Justice*, in 1996.

The Report by Lord Woolf argued that there should be a fundamental transfer in the responsibility for the management of civil litigation from litigants and their advisers to the courts. Litigation would be divided into fast-track cases £3,000 to £10,000 (that is above the revised small claims limit except in the case of personal injuries), and multi-track for those over £10,000. Fast-track cases would be subject to a streamlined procedure including an abbreviated trial, normally restricted to three hours (but at the most a day), within 20 to 30 weeks.

A case should not be included in the fast track if it raises issues of public importance, or is a test case, or oral evidence from experts is necessary, or it requires substantial documentary evidence. Moreover, in fast track cases where possible a single expert should be instructed, and the appointment if necessary will be made by the court. Maximum legal costs on the fast-track procedure should be £2,500 excluding VAT and disbursements.

In multi-track cases the court can (a) fix a case management conference; (b) issue directions in writing for the preparation of the case; (c) fix a date for the trial; (d) specify a period within which it is intended that the trial shall take place; (e) fix a pre-trial review. Also the possibility of Alternative Dispute Resolution (ADR) must be considered; the judge will be able to take into account the litigant's unreasonable refusal to attempt ADR, which will have a bearing upon costs to be awarded. Lord Woolf stressed the role of ADR as well as a re-examination of the relationship of the Ombudsman to the courts (judicial review). New rules will, *inter alia*, provide that only the Lord Chancellor and the Head of Civil Justice will be able to issue Practice Directions to ensure that case management systems are uniform and consistent. Sanctions will be imposed by judges where lawyers fail to meet strict deadlines. Lawyers must explain to their clients how their charges for litigation are calculated. In addition courts, in making orders for costs, should pay greater regard than they do at present to the manner in which the successful party has conducted the proceedings and the outcome of individual issues.

A Civil Justice Council should be established to contribute to the development of the proposed reforms. Judges should be nominated for appropriate areas of specialisation; judges who specialise in areas such as medical negligence and housing should be given appropriate training. The possibility of providing joint training with the legal profession, under the general aegis of the Judicial Studies Board, should be explored. Consideration should be given to (1) the way in which members of the professions who are experienced in litigation and who retire at an early age can be involved as 'civil magistrates' or otherwise, in support of the civil justice system; (2) referral of decisions to the House of Lords or Court of Appeal to ensure proper development of the law.

Under s.6 of the Civil Procedure Act 1997, a Civil Justice Council has been established to keep the civil justice system under review, to consider how to make the system more accessible, fair and efficient, and to advise the Lord Chancellor and the judiciary on future developments.

4.3

The Appeal Process

THE COURT OF APPEAL

Since the Criminal Appeal Act 1966 (as consolidated by the Criminal Appeal Act 1968) there has existed a single Court of Appeal with Civil and Criminal Divisions. (A separate Court of Criminal Appeal had existed prior to the 1966 Act from 1907.) Under the Supreme Court Act 1981 the Civil Division is presided over by the Master of the Rolls and the Criminal Division by the Lord Chief Justice. Besides the Master of the Rolls and the Lord Chief Justice there are approximately 30 Lords Justices of Appeal, as well as a number of *ex officio* members. The latter include the Lord Chancellor and ex-Lord Chancellors, Lords of Appeal in Ordinary (the Law Lords), the Vice-Chancellor of Chancery and the President of the Family Division. (There are about 90 High Court judges.) The Court of Appeal normally sits as a bench of three although in controversial cases, such as *Davis* v. *Johnson*, a bench of five may be convened, perhaps including one or two *ex officio* Law Lords. However, since 1982 more frequent use has been made of two judges only, in order to speed up business; this was at the direction of the new Master of the Rolls, Sir John Donaldson. Only about 25 per cent of appeals succeed.

Recently, the increasing number of appeals in the Court of Appeal has resulted in further delays in hearings; the same is true of the High Court, especially in the Queen's Bench Division. Appeals lie from the Crown Court on the criminal side and from the County Court and High Court on the civil side. On occasion High Court judges may be required to hear criminal appeals on account of the case-load, but they will be required to hear civil appeals comparatively infrequently. Appeals are permitted from the Court of Appeal to the House of Lords: either the Court of Appeal itself or the Appeal Committee of the Lords must give its consent.

The usual procedure in the Court of Appeal is for each judge to give his own opinion and the majority view prevails. In a comparatively straightforward appeal, on which there is unanimity, one or more of the statements may simply read 'I concur'. The hearing is more informal than in the trial courts, especially in relation to civil cases. Usually the appeals are heard on the basis of the transcripts of the original trial and arguments from counsel. The Court is reluctant to admit fresh evidence unless it is of a material nature. However, even if the Court is persuaded of the merits of certain technical submissions, it may in the interests of justice still refuse to overturn the lower court's decision, especially in criminal cases. Nonetheless, if fresh evidence submitted is of a particularly material kind, then a re-trial may be ordered. If the Court of Appeal decides that there was some very grave defect in the original trial (the judge was drunk, for example), then it may order a new trial (*venire de novo*). Technically it is not a re-trial because the original 'trial' had been a nullity from the very beginning. This power is used only extremely rarely. In *R.* v. *McKenna* (1960) the judge told the jury he had to catch a train urgently and unless they returned a verdict within a few minutes they would have to be detained until the following day. The jury quickly returned a guilty verdict. The Court of Criminal Appeal quashed the conviction on the grounds that there had been a material irregularity, but not on the grounds that the whole trial was a nullity. In *R. v. Rose (Newton)* (1982) the Court of Appeal took the same line and quashed a conviction for murder. In that case the trial judge had sent a message to the jury to tell them if they did not hurry up he would discharge them.

A similar point arose in 1984 when a Crown Court judge was criticised by the Court of Appeal for 'his extraordinary and irregular' behaviour during the trial of two black teenager brothers accused of assaulting the police. The appeal judges quashed the conviction. According to prosecution and defence counsel, the Assistant Recorder told them he found the trial 'distasteful' and said nothing was to be gained by the Crown seeking a conviction. He asked if the case could be shortened and went on to refer to his friendship with the Metropolitan Police Commissioner.

Under s.43 of the Criminal Justice Act 1988 the Court of Appeal was given wider powers to order a retrial where it is satisfied that it is in the interests of justice to do so. As noted earlier, under ss.35 and 36 a case may be referred to the Court of Appeal (with its leave) by the Attorney-General where he considers that the sentence passed by the Crown Court is unduly lenient. The Court of Appeal may quash the sentence and substitute for it any sentence which it thinks appropriate and which the Crown Court had power to pass. A reference on a point of law may be made to the House of Lords. In 1985 £121,000 was paid to Geoffrey Davis who had spent 16 years in prison for the murder of an 84 year-old woman after being convicted mainly on evidence from a discredited Home Office forensic scientist; the Criminal Justice Act 1988 made provisions for a scheme of statutory compensation, although the statutory scheme was not properly established until the Criminal Injuries Compensation Scheme Act 1995 was passed.

In *R. v. Callaghan* (1988) the Court of Appeal, on a reference from the Home Secretary, in considering an appeal against conviction by the six appellants who had been convicted of murder in the IRA 1974 Birmingham pub bombings case, declined to overturn the conviction and noted that in any case it would have been highly unsatisfactory to order a re-trial 13 years after the original trial. The major problem with the Court of Appeal, John Spencer has argued, is that four panels of senior judges in London can barely handle nearly 2,000 appeals against Crown Court convictions, and therefore the tendency is for them to favour appeals on technical points, as opposed to genuine miscarriages of justice, a point also underlined by Ludovic Kennedy in his campaigns against wrongful convictions. The difficulties since 1989 involving the Court of Appeal, especially in relation to the cases of the Birmingham Six (*R. v. Callaghan* (1988) and *R. v. McIlkenny* (1991)), the Guildford Four (*R. v. Armstrong* (1989)), the Maguire Seven (*R. v. Maguire* (1992)), Judith Ward (the M62 bombing – *R. v. Ward* (1992)), the Tottenham Three (*R. v. Silcott* (1991)), as well as the Cardiff Three (*R. v. Miller*), Stefan Kiszko and the Swansea Two (*R. v. Darvell*) in 1992 and the Taylor sisters in 1993, led to the establishment of the Runciman Commission which reported in 1993.

As indicated above, s.7 of the Criminal Appeal Act 1968 was amended by s.43 of the Criminal Justice Act 1988, which means the Court of Appeal can order a retrial for any reason. The record of the Court of Appeal since 1950 has been rather dismal, as outlined by Bob Woffinden in his 1989 study, *Miscarriages of Justice*. In the Luton Post Office case (Cooper and McMahon), after five separate unsuccessful appeal hearings, the Home Secretary was obliged to exercise the prerogative to release the men. Both the Scott Henderson Inquiry and Brabin Inquiry found Timothy Evans to have been guilty. The Jolly Inquiry found Walter Rowland guilty of murder and he was subsequently executed. The Hawser Report into the Hanratty case failed to command public confidence. The Fisher inquiry into the Maxwell Confait murder found that the appellants were probably guilty; some years later this conclusion had to be repudiated by the then Home Secretary in the House of Commons. (Timothy Evans was probably the most famous victim of a miscarriage of justice – he was hanged in 1950 for the alleged murder of his baby daughter. In 1966, thanks largely to the efforts of Sir Ludovic Kennedy, Evans was granted a posthumous free pardon.) In 1993 Derek Bentley was given a limited posthumous pardon over his death sentence in 1953 for the murder of a policeman; the new Home Secretary, Michael Howard took this decision after the High Court had criticised his predecessor, Kenneth Clarke, for failing to recognise that the prerogative of mercy was capable of being exercised in many different circumstances (*R. v. Secretary of State for the Home Department ex parte Bentley*).

The Maguire Seven were entitled to compensation of £500,000 in 1990, the previous highest compensation being £121,000 to Geoffrey Davis in 1985, as noted above. Awards are by virtue of the Criminal Justice Act 1988 which put compensation for wrongful convictions on a statutory footing. Before the Act compensation was by *ex gratia* payment at the discretion of the Home Secretary. The Home Secretary still acts as a filter and there is no right of appeal if he decides compensation is not warranted. If he decides there is a case, he refers it to an independent assessor to evaluate the claim. To qualify a claimant must have been pardoned or had his conviction quashed on appeal or on a reference to the Court of Appeal. The pardon or quashing of the conviction must have been based on a newly-discovered fact showing beyond reasonable doubt that there was a miscarriage of justice. In addition, the claimant must not be to blame for the late emergence of the fact showing he was innocent.

In 1992 it was announced that Lord Justice Farquharson was to chair the newly established Criminal Justice Consultative Council, whilst the Lord Chief Justice, Lord Taylor, said that judges should treat jurors, witnesses, litigants and their relatives much more considerately and sensitively. On miscarriages of justice, Lord Taylor said that trial judges needed, however strong the evidence appeared and from whatever source, 'to be seen to leave issues of fact fairly to the jury'. He added: 'I hope that one benefit from these traumatic recent cases will be a greater vigilance by trial judges and the Court of Appeal, recognising that appearances may sometimes belie the truth'. The Criminal Appeal Act 1995 was the outcome of the Runciman Report (see below).

THE HOUSE OF LORDS

The House of Commons and the House of Lords together form the High Court of Parliament, which acts primarily as a deliberative and legislative body. However, both Houses have jurisdiction over persons committing any breach of the privileges of the House or its members. In addition the House of Lords exercises original jurisdiction in regard to peerage claims.

The House of Lords is also the supreme court of appeal for civil cases in Great Britain and Northern Ireland, and in criminal matters for England, Wales and Northern Ireland. An appeal to the House of Lords requires the permission of the Court of Appeal or in certain cases from the High Court or Divisional Court for a so-called leap-frog appeal under the provisions of the Administration of Justice Act 1969, Part I. The House of Lords can itself give leave for an appeal where the lower court has refused permission, the procedure being by way of a petition to the Appeal Committee, which is not to be confused with the Appellate Committee, which is the 'court' of the House. As observed earlier, appeals to the House are generally only permitted where it is certified that there is some point of law of general public importance and that the case merits the consideration of the House of Lords. Lord Roskill in *Wilson* v. *Colchester Justices* (1985) made the following observation:

There are a multitude of reasons why, in a particular case, leave to appeal may be refused by an Appeal Committee. I shall not attempt to embark on an exhaustive list for it would be impossible to do so.

One reason may be that the particular case raises no question of general principle but turns on its own facts. Another may be that the facts of the particular case are not suitable as a foundation for determining some question of general principle. Your Lordships' House is only able, in any given year, to hear and determine a limited number of cases and it is important for the evolution of the law as a whole that those cases should be carefully chosen. Conversely, the fact that leave to appeal is given is not of itself an indication that the judgments below are thought to be wrong. It may well be that leave is given in order that the relevant law may be authoritatively restated in clearer terms. It is not difficult to find in the books examples of cases where, after leave to appeal has been refused in one case, another case will later arise in which leave to appeal has been given as a result of which the decision against which to appeal was originally refused is shown to have been wrong. But that of itself does not mean that the initial refusal of leave was wrong.

The House of Lords hears about 70 cases a year. A third of all civil appeals are revenue (taxation) cases. Lord Devlin, perhaps the finest legal brain this century, simply retired at the youthful age of 58: 'For the most part the work was dreary beyond belief. All those revenue cases'. Until 1948 appeals to the House of Lords were heard in the chamber of the House. Since that time they have been heard by one of the two Appellate Committees, which normally consist of five Lords of Appeal in Ordinary, generally known as the Law Lords. (The appeal committees comprise only three Law Lords, which report their recommendations to the Appellate Committee.) By convention no lay peer exercises his or her right to sit on the Appellate Committee: that privilege is now reserved for members of the House who have held high judicial office, principally ex-Lord Chancellors, plus, of course, the ten special peers, the Lords of Appeal in Ordinary, two of whom are from Scotland. In 1987, unusually, a Scottish Law Lord, Lord Mackay of Clashfern, was appointed Lord Chancellor in succession to Lord Havers. The minimum qualification for a Lord of Appeal in Ordinary is to have been a barrister for 15 years or to have been a judge in the Supreme Court for two. The Lord Chancellor, or at least his Department, determines which Law Lord hears which appeal, and this, of course, is an important power.

The procedure in the Lords is quite informal; strange as it may seem in the final court of appeal there are, at least for the judges, no wigs, gowns or robes. At the conclusion of the hearing before the Appellate Committee, the Law Lords reserve their judgment, and will then provide written opinions. These opinions are read by the other members of the court who may then amend their own opinions. Judgment is then given in the appeal in the chamber of the House of Lords, with the Lord Chancellor or the senior Law Lord in the case seated on the Woolsack. The Law Lords attend, and in order of seniority give verbally the conclusion of their individual written opinions in the form of brief speeches. As in parliamentary debate the question is then put as to whether the order appealed from, be reversed or affirmed.

As in the Court of Appeal (or indeed a Magistrates' Court or tribunal with several members) the House of Lords operates by majority judgment. Thus an appellant may win or lose by merely three votes to two (sometimes after obtaining a unanimous decision in the Court of Appeal) and a number of controversial cases have underlined this very point (for example *Donoghue* v. *Stevenson*, *R.* v. *Lemon*, and *Home Office* v. *Harman*). This immediately begs the question as to whether it is fair or right that an individual's whole future may hang by the thread of just one vote. The answer – unsatisfactory as it may seem – is that the buck must eventually stop somewhere; there is a danger of overloading the system with too great a chain of appellate courts. Moreover, when a case goes to the House of Lords the decision will often turn upon a very intricate point of law. It is unlikely for a case to reach that stage in the first place if that were not so.

In very controversial cases, in those which involve a point of law of exceptional public importance, it has been known for seven judges to sit, but this occurs extremely rarely nowadays. *Broome* v. *Cassell & Co. Ltd* (1972) (the PQ17 convoy libel action) was one such case and *Pepper.* v. *Hart* (1993) another.

It has been questioned whether there is a necessity for a higher appellate jurisdiction above the Court of Appeal. Cases that eventually find their way to the House of Lords clearly take up a great deal of time and money, and it is right the value of such an additional tier should be questioned. The reason for this additional level of jurisdiction lies in the distinction between review and supervision. In normal cases it is appropriate for any aggrieved litigant to have a right to a review of his particular case by an appellate court. In a few cases it is for the public benefit that a supervisory court should be in a position to lay down a body of precedent to guide lower courts and develop case-law in accordance with contemporary needs. The first-tier appeal courts, with relatively large case-loads, emphasise review at the expense of supervision, though they do, in fact, exercise an important law-making role. But the House of Lords deals with a very small number of appeals selected by a rigorous sieving process which, as stated above, means in practice it only hears cases involving 'points of law of general public importance'. It also has the benefit of the judgments of the courts below, which serve to highlight the central issues. The Law Lords are thus in a position to 'make law' on the grand scale, though on the whole they exercise this function with studied self-restraint .

It should also be remembered that it is frequent government practice to appoint a Law Lord to chair a Royal Commission or a tribunal inquiry. This at least ensures that the close relationship between the Government, the judiciary and Parliament is maintained. It keeps the Law Lords in touch with certain aspects of public affairs.

THE JUDICIAL COMMITTEE OF THE PRIVY COUNCIL

The Judicial Committee of the Privy Council dates from 1833 and the extent of its legal jurisdiction has waxed and waned. Today it can hear appeals from Ecclesiastical Courts and certain tribunals of a professional nature such as the Disciplinary Committee of the General Medical Council. It also hears appeals from the Isle of Man and the Channel Islands. However, it is chiefly known for its role as an imperial left-over – the hearing of appeals from Commonwealth countries. The number of countries in the Commonwealth that have retained this 'last-ditch' link has steadily diminished during the post-war period. The principal areas of the independent Commonwealth that have retained the right of final appeal to the Privy Council are Jamaica and New Zealand, and, until 1986, Australia and Malaysia. The Privy Council deals with a few dozen such appeals a year.

The members of the Committee are the Lord Chancellor, Lords of Appeal in Ordinary, all Privy Councillors who have held high judicial office and a number of senior Commonwealth judges. Since 1966 Committee members have been allowed to give dissenting opinions. The Committee's judgments are technically recommendations to the whole Privy Council; what it says is given practical effect by the mechanism of an Order in Council.

In 1963, Peter Archer, subsequently Solicitor-General in the 1974–79 Labour government, remarked:

There is a strong body of opinion which advocates the setting up of a Commonwealth court of appeal, on the pattern of the Judicial

Committee, but including the best judicial talent from every part of the Commonwealth. Yet this is, in itself, a compliment to the work of the Committee, whose personnel consisted largely of the men who, in the House of Lords, were deciding the disputes of individual citizens and whose minds had been trained in the British courts.

Whether, however, the Commonwealth role of the Judicial Committee will survive in the longer term is a matter still very much open to doubt.

The Judicial Committee is noticeably more chary about overturning Commonwealth decisions in respect of criminal matters than it is in respect of civil cases. In recent years it has upheld the use of the death penalty in such countries as Singapore, Jamaica and Trinidad and Tobago.

Courts Charter

Lastly, as a general point note should be made of the Courts Charter 1992. It recommended:

1 improved friendliness and co-operation in courts, and prompt reply to letters;

2 proceedings in Magistrates' Courts should take no more than five weeks to first appearance, three weeks in a youth court; for a defendant in custody there should be no more than eight weeks between a first hearing at a Magistrates' Court and committal for trial to the Crown Court;

3 in the Crown Court if a defendant is in custody the trial should start within eight weeks of the case being committed for trial to the Crown Court;

4 for a defendant on bail the trial should start within 16 weeks of committal for trial to the Crown Court.

In short, the Courts Charter of 1992 set deadlines within which court staff must respond to or carry out steps in major areas of court business like divorce, probate and debt collection. Court staff had to become more accessible to the public and a complaints procedure was published. It also requires courts to publish the time within which they can provide a hearing in a civil case once the parties are ready for trial. As far as criminal cases are concerned, the Charter sets out guidelines for the timetable in bringing cases forward for trial and also deals with arrangements and levels of service which aim to help and ease the strains which inevitably fall on jurors, witnesses and victims. For example, witnesses who are worried about appearing in court will be shown a courtroom before the case starts and, wherever accommodation allows for it, the defence and prosecution sides will be provided with separate waiting areas.

4.4

The Runciman Report
1993

Following the release of the Birmingham Six, the Royal Commission on Criminal Justice was set up. Its report made 352 proposals, but not all of these were unanimous; Professor Michael Zander issued his own note of dissent on some issues. The Report's findings were not universally welcomed, Lord Scarman, for instance, being particularly opposed to the proposal to give magistrates the right to determine whether an accused can go to trial, whilst Professor Simon Lee called its attitude to research 'disastrous'. 'It mostly avoids doctrinal as well as theoretical analysis, referring tricky questions instead to the Law Commission.' Chris Mullin, the MP who campaigned vigorously on behalf of the Birmingham Six, as well as the Guildford Four and Maguire Seven, commented:

> **The Commission's report is a disappointment. The single greatest omission is the failure to outlaw convictions based on uncorroborated confessions. The commission is content to make do with video recordings and warnings by the judge. This overlooks the clear lessons of recent history. The key to obtaining a false confession is to reduce the suspect to such a degree of terror that he or she will say whatever is required once the formal recorded interview commences.**
>
> **In the Guildford case, Paul Hill says he confessed because the police offered to release his pregnant girl-friend. Gerry Conlon says he confessed because of threats to his sister and mother. Both these confessions, which were the sole basis of conviction, would still have been forthcoming if the interview had been recorded. The report says: 'A small number of police officers have been proved to be dishonest in fabricating confessions'. This is nonsense. The scale of the fraud and perjury uncovered in the Birmingham and Guildford cases is massive.**
>
> **In the Guildford case the Crown counsel, Lord Havers, said that, if the defendants were telling the truth, then the police must have engaged in 'a really gigantic conspiracy'. In the Birmingham case the trial judge, Lord Bridge, said that for the defendants to be telling the truth, the police would have to have been involved in a conspiracy 'unprecedented in the annals of criminal history'. The commission has utterly underestimated the scale of the problem. Many police operations, particularly those involving elite detective squads, regard perjury as a way of life. 'There is nothing wrong with perjury, committed by an honest police officer in the aid of good cause', a senior official of the Police Federation said recently – to me of all people.**
>
> **...There is much that is good in this report, but were anyone to ask if it would prevent another Birmingham Six or Guildford Four tragedy, I regret that I would have to say no.**

THE REPORT'S MAJOR RECOMMENDATIONS

1 There should a new tribunal to consider alleged miscarriages of justice, and this body would take over the role of the Home Secretary in deciding whether to refer cases to the Court of Appeal and would be able to set its own rules for selecting cases for consideration. The Criminal Cases Review Authority would hear about 700–800 cases a year, and it would be given the power to supervise further police investigation of cases. The chairman would be appointed by the Queen on the advice of the Prime Minister, but would not be a judge. Its membership of both lawyers and laypersons would be appointed by the Lord Chancellor. It would report annually to Parliament and the only power the Home Secretary would be left with is the exercise of the royal prerogative of mercy.

The Commission said the tribunal should be able to interview prisoners who believe they have been the victims of miscarriages of justice. The Commission recommended that the tribunal should be able to order that an investigation is carried out by a police force different from the one that investigated the orginal offence. This is similar to the procedures operated by the Police Complaints Authority.

At the same time the present grounds for referral to the Court of Appeal should be replaced by 'a single broad ground which would give the court flexibility to consider all categories of appeal [and] to decide whether the conviction is or may be unsafe'. In future the Court of Appeal would be allowed to consider 'errors by trial lawyers' if it believes these have rendered the conviction unsafe. At present this is confined to cases of 'flagrantly incompetent advocacy'. The Commission said: 'What matters is whether the particular decision, whether reasonable or unreasonable, caused a miscarriage of justice.' A majority of commission members rejected a minority proposal for an automatic retrial where errors by trial lawyers were sufficient to affect the trial but not to render the conviction unsafe. The test for receiving fresh evidence should in future be 'whether it is capable of belief'. It is also proposed that senior circuit judges nominated by the Lord Chief Justice would be able to sit as members of the Court of Appeal. The requirement that, before an appeal can go to the House of Lords, the Court of Appeal must say that the case involves a matter of general public importance should be dropped.

2 Defendants will be expected to disclose the substance of their case before a Crown Court trial or risk an adverse comment from the judge to the jury. But there should be no restrictions on the right to silence at the police station. The decision to insist that the defence disclose the substance of its case before the trial is to reduce what the police term 'defence ambushes' which leave the prosecution little chance to challenge defence contentions. 'We hope that this would keep to the minimum those cases where the defendant withholds his defence until the last possible moment in the hope of confusing the jury or evading the investigation of fabricated defence.' The Commission recommended that if the defence introduces a late change or departs from the strategy it has disclosed it should face adverse comment. The disclosure issue split the Commission, with Professor Michael Zander issuing a note of dissent that the principle that the burden of proof lies with the prosecution should be maintained, saying it is not the 'job of the defendant to be helpful either to the prosecution or to the system'.

The prosecution will also be required to disclose its evidence to the defence as long as the material is relevant to the likely line of defence. To protect informants the prosecution may be able to apply for a ruling on non-disclosure of sensitive material. The Criminal Justice and Public Order Act 1994 (ss33–34) actually went further than Runciman in the 'abolition' of the right to silence. Advance disclosure of evidence was dealt with by the Criminal Procedure and Investigations Act 1996.

3 The right of defendants to insist upon a jury trial (in triable either way offences) should be removed to the magistrates themselves. Cases would continue to go to the Crown Court where both the prosecution and defence agree they should be tried on indictment. Where the defence do not agree with the Crown Prosecution's proposal on which court should try the case the magistrates will decide. The magistrates would decide on the basis of such factors as the gravity of the offence, the defendant's past record, the complexity of the case and the likely effect on the defendant including sentence. The Commission says that the bulk of affected cases would involve theft or handling stolen goods worth less than £100, going equipped to steal or similar non-indictable offences. But offences which are 'triable either way' also include assault causing bodily harm, criminal damage, sexual assaults and arson. Research showed that judges were three times more likely to impose custodial sentences than magistrates. The Commission also supported a suggestion from the Commission for Racial Equality that up to three jurors should be from the same ethnic minority as the defendant or the victim.

There would be pre-trial hearings to determine and clarify issues in advance of a trial as is now the procedure in civil courts. Committal proceedings would be abolished.

Professor Zander, in his dissenting note, argued these proposals would increase delays and costs.

4 A majority of the Commission said that confession evidence, unsupported by any other evidence, was allowable to secure a conviction, as long as it was credible and passed all the tests laid down by the Police and Criminal Evidence Act 1984. The judge should, however, give a warning to the jury where uncorroborated confession evidence is involved. The police would be allowed to continue questioning suspects after they had been charged, as long as the usual caution had been repeated and the accused had been afforded the chance of having a solicitor present, but the Commission was particularly horrified by a tape of a police interview it heard in the Cardiff Three case, where a long and highly repetitive series of questions was put to a suspect in a loud and aggressive way until a damaging admission was obtained.

5   A new national DNA bank containing the 'genetic fingerprints' of all those convicted of serious criminal offences was proposed, and the police should be allowed to take saliva samples from suspects without their consent in order to identify offenders through the DNA data bank. The Report also recommended that public forensic laboratories should be equally available to defence and prosecution, and that the defence should be given an enforceable right of access to material held by the prosecution. Both considerations were at the heart of the Birmingham Six case. The Commission says an independent body should be established to keep a national data base of DNA samples, separate from police records of convicted persons, so that the 'uniqueness' of a particular genetic fingerprint can be checked. There should be set up a Forensic Science Advisory Council to oversee the standards and provision of forensic services.

6   There should be a more open system of plea bargaining. The Commission noted that sentence discounts of between 25 and 30 per cent were common practice in Crown Courts. But the system would not go as far as the American system where the prosecution can suggest the appropriate sentence: 'we agree that to face defendants with a choice between what they might get on an immediate plea of guilty and what they might get if found guilty by the jury does amount to unacceptable pressure'. In chambers the judge would answer the question: 'What would be the maximum sentence if my client were to plead guilty at this stage?', but not any other. If the defendant then pleaded guilty, the case would move to open court.

7   Jury trials were to be retained for serious fraud cases. The Serious Fraud Office (SFO), which came under severe criticism in 1993 for its handling of the Asil Nadir (Polly Peck) case, should possibly be merged with the Fraud Investigation Group (FIG) of the Crown Prosecution Service. The FIG cannot use s.2 of the Criminal Justice Act 1987 which allows the SFO to compel defendants to give interviews and produce documents even after they have been charged, on pain of imprisonment. The Commission accepted the SFO's suggestion that the courts should be allowed to bring City regulators into the plea-bargaining process. In return for guilty pleas, defendants would agree to accept 'severe regulatory penalties' instead of jail sentences. These could include fines and disqualification from office. The Commission said it was seriously concerned that the powers and resources for investigating serious and complex fraud were 'not available to all those charged with the task', particularly when the number of offences and amounts involved were increasing.

8   The Commission asked for an increase in funds to train judges, including training in the awareness of race and gender. Refresher course should be held every three years and there should be a formal system of appraisal of the judiciary. '[We] find it surprising that full-time judges seldom if ever observe trials conducted by their colleagues.' Judges would be able to impose cost penalties and reduce fees as well as urge formal disciplinary measures for incompetence in court. The Crown Prosecution Service 'could do more to prepare cases better', and to ensure weak cases do not get to court. Solicitors' services at police stations were often inadequate. New barristers might be restricted as to what cases they could undertake –

during the second six months of pupillage they should not appear in a jury case or in the Court of Appeal unless led by a senior barrister.

9 Section 8 of the Contempt of Court Act 1981 should be amended to enable research into juries' reasons. There should be further research to establish how far members of ethnic minority communities suffer discrimination within the criminal justice system. Police performance should not be assessed unduly on the basis of arrest or conviction rates; performance measures should be based on quality of work. Code C of the Police and Criminal Evidence Act 1984 should be amended to encourage police to inform the solicitor of the general nature of the case and *prima facie* evidence. Acquittal in a criminal court should no longer be a bar to police disciplinary proceedings on the same facts. The Commission also made a number of detailed recommendations affecting juries, including the fact that clergymen should now be eligible for jury service; the jury should be given greater assistance by the judge, including more documentary and technological aid. In respect of fraud trials s.10(3) of the Criminal Justice Act 1987 should be amended to permit judges to put the issues before the jury at the outset of a long fraud case.

OTHER RECOMMENDATIONS

These included a help-line for police to report malpractice among colleagues; on the spot fines for minor offences, as in Scotland; a 30-minute time limit on barristers' closing speeches, and judges to act firmly to control 'bullying and intimidatory tactics' by counsel; new rules of conduct to ensure barristers read papers promptly; a review of fees for lawyers doing criminal legal aid work; a greater admission of hearsay evidence, subject to further investigation by the Law Commission; and the defendant's previous convictions to be made known to the jury where the facts in the case are admitted, otherwise the Law Commission should look at the rule governing the admissibility of evidence relating to the defendant's previous convictions.

DISCUSSION POINTS

1 Did the Runciman Report tackle the real issues affecting miscarriages of justice?

2 Does the appeal process work satisfactorily?

3 Should lay participation in the judicial system be extended?

5 Five

AGENTS OF THE LAW AND ACCESS TO THE LAW

5.1   Judges

For many centuries judges have been appointed by the Crown. Nowadays minimum qualifications are laid down by statute; under the Act of Settlement of 1700, judges held office *quamdiu se bene gesserint* – as long as they were of good behaviour and that rule has been continued by more recent Acts. Judges cannot be removed from office on account of political considerations – the independence of the judiciary is, at least theoretically, guaranteed. A senior judge (a judge of the High Court or above) may only be removed by the Queen or after an address has been successfully presented to both Houses of Parliament. However, since the Administration of Justice Act 1973 the Lord Chancellor has had power to enforce the retirement of senior judges on account of incapacity. The Judicial Pensions Act 1959 provided that all future senior judges had to retire at 75. A circuit judge normally retired at 72; circuit judges and Recorders may also be removed by the Lord Chancellor for either misbehaviour or incapacity (the Courts Act 1971) as happened with Judge Bruce Campbell, who was convicted of smuggling in 1983. 'Misbehaviour' means any behaviour which is inconsistent with judicial behaviour. All judges from 1994 retire at 70, but 75 for exceptional cases in certain instances, under s.26 of the Judicial Pensions and Retirement Act 1993. No judges have been removed from office by an address of both Houses of Parliament since 1830 when Sir Jonah Barrington was removed after his conviction for appropriating for his own use funds paid into court.

Nonetheless it is fair to say that, in contrast to their political masters, judges in the United Kingdom appear to be held in fairly high public esteem, as a number of polls conducted on such matters have indicated, for example as long ago as the Granada Television *State of the Nation* survey in 1973. In other countries, though, the position of the judiciary may be much more closely allied to the ideology of the dominant political party irrespective of whether that party considers itself to be revolutionary or established. But 'independence' from political interference does not mean that judges hold no political convictions. On the contrary, as barristers, in their younger days, a number have stood as parliamentary candidates, chiefly in the Conservative interest.

Religious convictions may also have a bearing upon judicial outlook. Such principles are usually Christian, but sometimes not (for instance, in the 1970s Judge Christmas Humphreys was a leading British Buddhist). Lord Denning once observed that, although religion, law and morals could be separated, they were nevertheless still very dependent on each other. Without religion there could be no morality, and without morality there could be no law. In *Shaw* v. *DPP* (1962) Lord Hodson noted that even if Christianity were not part of the law of England, the common law certainly had its roots in Christianity, as well illustrated by the very institution of marriage and all its obligations.

GRIFFITH'S CRITICISMS

Professor J. A. G. Griffith has taken the argument a stage further. He has argued in *The Politics of the Judiciary* that by their very background and training judges are not only socially but also politically conservative and this is particularly reflected in controversial or hard cases. About Griffith's line of argument Professor Ronald Dworkin has commented:

> There are those who think that British judges do make political decisions. But that is not to say that they should. Professor Griffith thinks it inevitable, as I understand him, that the judiciary will play a political role in a capitalist or semi-capitalist state. But he does not count this as a virtue of capitalism; on the contrary he treats the political role of judges as deplorable. It may be that a few judges and academics – including perhaps Lord Denning – do think that judges ought to be more political than the conventional view recommends. But that remains very much an eccentric – some would say dangerous – minority view.

Griffith himself has made the following observation:

> Judges, like the rest of us, have views of where the public interest lies. And those views differ little from one judge to another. This is not surprising. Three out of four senior judges were educated at independent schools and at Oxford or Cambridge. Four out of five are from upper or upper middle class families. But more importantly, all judges are appointed from among the ranks of successful and rich barristers after twenty-five or more years' practice.

In 1987 a survey of 465 judges revealed that of the 11 Law Lords, nine went to public school and eight to Oxford or Cambridge; of the 23 Court of Appeal judges, 20 attended public school and Oxbridge, while for 79 High Court judges the figures were 42 and 53 respectively. Griffith went on to say:

> Sometimes the judges are immodest in their claims. A few years ago Viscount Simonds, delivering judgment in a case where the charge

was a conspiracy to corrupt public morals, said: 'I entertain no doubt that there remains in the courts of law a residual power to enforce the supreme and fundamental purpose of the law, to conserve not only the safety and order but also the moral welfare of the State.

Griffith also pointed out that in 1968 in a secrets case Lord Reid stated that it would not be appropriate to disclose information to those who had inadequate knowledge or some axe to grind. In a 1974 case Lord Diplock noted in passing (*obiter dicta*) that the Race Relations Act, desirable in principle as it was, did restrict the liberty of the individual who under common law, he suggested, had been able to lead his life as he chose.

Judges are seen as an integral part of the government of the State. Rules are made by the government or, through the common law, by the judiciary. These rules are 'the law' and that phrase gives them a supra-political respectability . . . Liberal thinking among the judiciary has . . . shown itself only occasionally and then only in minority judgments or dissents. The protection of the public interest in the preservation of a stable society is how the judges see their role.

However, in an interview with *The Observer* in 1993 Sir Thomas Bingham, the new Master of the Rolls, denied that judges were of a conservative disposition, in the political sense too or that they were remote, patrician figures; indeed, given the long period of one party rule, and Mrs Thatcher's tendency to test the limit of her authority, judges, Sir Thomas claimed, had become much more constitutionally aware, even anti-Government.

One leading lawyer, Lord Gifford QC, has also written about judges in these words: 'Their ignorance of whole areas of British life is shattering. They receive no training whatever which might help them to recognise and overcome their prejudices.' Judges should be selected from a wide social range, including the young, solicitors and academic lawyers, who should all undergo substantial training, Gifford argued. In 1988 a Judges' Council was created as a policy-making body for High Court and Court of Appeal judges. It is a non-statutory body whose task is to co-ordinate all aspects of the responsibility of the judiciary for the administration of justice.

A few judges have been prepared to talk about their constitutional views and about their approach to statutory interpretation. Lord Scarman, in his advocacy of a Bill of Rights, and Lord Devlin, in his discourse about the jury and appeals system, have been notable examples. Lord Denning has frequently spoken to the media about the need, on occasion, to interpret Acts of Parliament flexibly if justice is to be properly done. But the more senior judges become the more difficult it may be to practise such openness. 'When Lord Widgery became Lord Chief Justice in 1971 he told *The Times* he thought it no bad thing if judges were occasionally to speak to the press. He no longer thinks so,' noted another newspaper in 1977. On the other hand if judges are constantly talking to the press they could quickly tarnish their generally high reputation for courtroom impartiality, it is claimed, and that was certainly the view Lord Chancellor Hailsham took in 1985–86 when one northern circuit judge, Judge James Pickles, delivered a series of stinging rebukes about the London-dominated legal establishment, and in so doing became an almost instant celebrity. However, in 1987 the new Lord Chancellor, Lord Mackay, indicated that he was prepared to see a relaxation of the 'Kilmuir Rules', so called after an earlier Lord Chancellor, which prevented judges speaking out openly on political matters. Lord Mackay's short-lived predecessor, Lord Havers, had opined that 99 per cent of the judges were happy with the Kilmuir Rules. Shortly after Lord Mackay's announcement, Sir Nicolas Browne-Wilkinson, the Vice-Chancellor, warned against the executive's drive for 'efficiency': 'Justice is not capable of being measured out by an accountant's computer'. Lord Mackay said that he would not lay down hard and fast rules about what judges could say in public: 'Judges should be free to speak to the press, or television, subject to being able to do so without in any way prejudicing their performing of their judicial work.'

Lord Mackay was given a taste of his own medicine in early 1989, when his three Green Papers on the reform of the legal profession, attracted a storm of unprecedented judicial criticism, notably led by Lord Chief Justice Lane who found the proposals constitutionally sinister, a rather extravagant phrase in the circumstances.

Whether judges are in tune with the kind of daily life the majority of people live is debatable; whether they need to be is questionable. Perhaps a greater proportion of women among the senior members of the judiciary would lead to rather different attitudes. Yet as *The Guardian* pointed out at the end of 1977, there were just two female High Court judges out of 83, and both of those sat in the Family Division. Twenty years later there were just seven High Court female judges and one in the Court of Appeal. The same article commented: 'the late Mr Justice Harman used to dress up in old clothes and a cap in order to go to the pubs and listen to what "the common man" was talking about'. It might also be noted that the first circuit judge who had been a solicitor was appointed to the High Court in 1993.

In 1992 Lord Williams, the chairman of the Bar, attacked the way in which judges were appointed. Secret files were kept by the Lord Chancellor's Department: 'the cruellest error may be in it. You cannot put it right. It is carefully kept under lock and key by a graduate of the Franz Kafka school of management'. Lord Williams said two lists were kept: an A list of those likely to become High Court judges and a B list of those 'who pick their noses' and were thought unsuitable. The last time he looked at the B list he was able to agree that one barrister named was quite unsuitable – he had been dead four years. In the summer of 1993 Lord Mackay, the Lord Chancellor, announced that vacancies for judges would be publicly advertised.

In a similar vein, Malcolm Dean, of *The Guardian*, in late 1992 noted:

Drawn so exclusively from the ranks of the Bar, the main emphasis is still on advocacy, one of the least appropriate attributes for a presid-

ing judge whose role is to listen astutely, defuse emotion, counterbalance bias, prevent excessive domination from one side, and weigh up the motives of the participants.

The booklet, *Judicial Appointments*, The Lord Chancellor's Policies and Procedures, in 1986, said:

A guiding principle of the Lord Chancellor's approach is that, as far as possible, no one person's view about a candidate, whether positive or negative, should be regarded as decisive in itself, however authoritative or eminent the person giving it. By contrast, the independent view of a spread of observers and colleagues in a position to assess the candidate's work and personality over a sufficiently long time is treated as having great weight, especially if it reveals a consensus or a clear predominance of view. This approach is applied extensively in relation to the appointments of High Court and Circuit Judges and their associated part-time appointments, and to the appointment of Queen's Counsel. It is being progressively applied, as circumstances allow, to other appointments in the courts and tribunals.

From 1995 a new procedure was adopted for appointing judges, although it should be said the changes were not major. This includes advertising the judicial posts in newspapers. The Select Committee on Home Affairs considered the question of judicial appointments, including magistrates, in considerable detail in 1996.

It only needs a few judicial errors to make unfortunate headlines. So, for example, in 1993 in *R. v. Chapman and Bond* Judge Binns at Norwich Crown Court imposed a five year sentence upon the appellants who for twenty minutes had held a man against whom they had a grievance; the Court of Appeal said that the judge's sentence was grossly disproportionate and that six months may have been more commensurate. Earlier Judge Prosser had attracted attention when he let a 15 year-old rapist go free after ordering him to pay for a holiday for his schoolgirl victim, and Judge Starforth Hill said that a 9 year-old victim of a sexual attack was 'not entirely an angel'. In respect of the latter case, *Attorney-General's Reference (No 13 of 1993) (1993)*, the Lord Chief Justice, Lord Taylor deplored the way the judge's comment had been extracted out of context and seized upon by the media, but nonetheless the judge's remarks were unacceptable. In 1988, Judge Sir Harold Cassel refused to jail a former policeman for the indecent assault of his 12 year-old step-daughter – he was publicly rebuked by the Lord Chancellor and retired early on medical grounds. In 1996 Judge Alistair McCallum attracted criticism when he halted the trial of a policeman accused of grabbing at the breasts of two of his colleagues, saying he should have had a 'sound ticking-off' instead. In 1998 Lord Justice Harman was retired after taking 20 months to deliver a judgment, having lost some of his notes.

Lord Williams, the former chairman of the Bar, has said that training for judges is 'inappropriately scanty'. The Royal Commission of 1993 (the Runciman Report) has made detailed recommendations for the improved training of judges.

5.2

The Crown Prosecution Service and the Attorney-General

Following the 1981 Philips Report, the Prosecution of Offences Act 1985 established a system of Crown Prosecutors to parallel that of the Procurators-Fiscal in Scotland. Crown Prosecutors may be either barristers or solicitors. The new system got off to a shaky start because of a shortage of staff, especially in London, and young, inexperienced lawyers were overloaded with cases.

But the police are still responsible for initiating prosecutions, so despite the powers of the Crown Prosecution Service, where a person was told by the police that he would not be prosecuted, it was held to be an abuse of process that he was prosecuted (*R.* v. *Croydon Justices ex parte Dean* (1993)).

The Director of Public Prosecutions (DPP) is responsible for the Crown Prosecution Service (CPS), and the aim has been to ensure greater consistency and efficiency in prosecution practice. Only the most complex cases as well as those of public interest will be referred to the DPP's office (the headquarters of the CPS) or to the Attorney-General, such as terrorist crimes, official secrets cases, company fraud, attempted murder, major drugs offences. (The Serious Fraud Office, set up under the Criminal Justice Act 1987, is also answerable to the DPP.) The 1985 Act (s.10) imposed a duty on the DPP to issue a Code for Crown Prosecutors giving guidance on the general principles to be applied in arriving at their decision whether to proceed with criminal cases begun by the police and on the choice of charges. As already noted, the police still have an initial role in prosecuting, and this distinguishes the new English system from the Scotish system. The DPP must report annually to Parliament.

The Code for Crown Prosecutors was revised in 1994, is shorter, less detailed and less technical. The new Code emphasises that 'realistic prospect of conviction' is an objective test. A prosecution may be in the public interest if there is a likelihood of a substantial sentence, but other factors include the position of the victim and the defendant and whether the offence is a common one in the area in which it has been committed. Equally the offence may not be in the public interest if the defendant is elderly or suffering from mental illness, or has put right the harm or loss caused. A long delay between the offence taking place and the date of the trial is also a factor against prosecution, unless the offence is serious. A serious charge should never be brought simply in the hope that the defendant will plead guilty to a less serious one.

The lingering criticism of the new system is that it is centrally controlled, under the Attorney-General, is short of staff and excessively bureaucratic and leaves the police still with too great a power in pressing charges, although the Crown Prosecutor under s.23 can stop proceedings which the police have already commenced; the biggest danger, therefore, is that young, inexperienced Crown

Prosecutors are seen as a 'rubber stamp' for police decisions and that a lot of important paperwork is handled inefficiently by legally unqualified clerks.

The CPS was heavily criticised by the House of Commons Public Accounts Committee in 1990; it noted that there were wide local variations in the way cases were dropped (the average being 7.5 per cent). The CPS's role in serious fraud prosecutions, alongside that of the Serious Fraud Office, has run into public controversy, as seen in the difficulties in the prosecutions from 1989 to 1993 in the cases of Barlow Clowes, County NatWest/Blue Arrow, Guinness, BCCI, Maxwell, and Brent Walker. The Blue Arrow case cost £35 million and the Guinness cases over £25 million; both were preceded by expensive DTI (Department of Trade and Industry) enquiries. In the Guinness, Barlow Clowes and Blue Arrow cases 26 people and three companies were charged, but only six convictions obtained. The Serious Fraud Office has very considerable powers of investigation, including the seizure of documents under s.2 of the Criminal Justice Act 1987.

Generally Crown Prosecutors do not have rights of audience in the Crown Court, this is still virtually a place for barristers in private practice; but the Act does not preclude the possibility. Counsel are instructed by the Crown Prosecutors, whose main role is therefore preparing and conducting all cases heard before the magistrates, once charges are preferred. In deciding whether to prosecute the DPP and the CPS followed a rule of thumb, namely that a case should proceed where there was a 51 per cent chance of winning; but in evidence in 1990 to the Commons Home Affairs Committee the DPP said that all the circumstances of the case would be looked at, and the 51 per cent rule no longer applied. But how 'independent' from the police is the CPS and is the new system so very different from the old network of private prosecuting solicitors or experienced police officers prosecuting on their own?

THE ATTORNEY-GENERAL AND THE DIRECTOR OF PUBLIC PROSECUTIONS

Although as a member of the government the Attorney-General may sit on the Legislation and Home Affairs Committees of the Cabinet and may be involved in extensive consultations with senior government ministers, as was the case in the Crossman Diaries affair, and perhaps later, in 1987, over the Wright memoirs, he is not actually a member of the Cabinet itself. The Attorney-General is the government's chief Law Officer and his deputy is the Solicitor-General. He advises the government on legislative proposals and on criminal proceedings which have a political or public element. He may take advice from his colleagues in the government but he cannot be instructed by them.

The Attorney-General's consent is required where an individual wishes to stop a possible breach of the law – a relator action. It should also be mentioned that on occasion local authorities may seek to enjoin the Attorney-General to a relator action, although since the Local Government Act 1972 local government has enjoyed greater powers to bring proceedings in its own name to enforce public rights. The problems associated with this particular aspect of the law were well illustrated in the case of *Solihull Metropolitan Council* v. *Maxfern Ltd* (1977) in which the local council sought to prevent certain premises within its area being used as a Sunday market. The issue was raised again in the case of *Kent County Council* v. *Batchelor* the following year, 1978, in which the County Council sought to bring an end to continual breaches of a tree preservation order. Indeed in a 1984 case involving breaches of the Shops Act 1950 (Sunday trading) in respect of local authorities' powers of enforcement under the Local Government Act 1972 by way of civil remedy, the House of Lords established the power of local councils to enforce the criminal law via the civil courts. They rejected the constitutional theory that only the Attorney-General had the right to institute civil proceedings in aid of the public law (*Stoke-on-Trent City Council* v. *B & Q (Retail) Ltd*, 1984). In *Norwich City Council and Stoke-on-Trent City Council* v. *B & Q plc* (1993) the European Court of Justice on a preliminary ruling under Article 177 by the House of Lords said that Article 30 of the Treaty did not restrict national legislation prohibiting retailers from opening their premises on Sundays.

NOLLE PROSEQUI

The Attorney-General has the power to stop proceedings for any indictable offence by entering a *nolle prosequi* ('do not prosecute'). This is what happened in 1982 when Mrs Whitehouse prosecuted Mr Michael Bogdanov, the director of the play *Romans in Britain*, under the Sexual Offences Act 1956. The play included a simulated act of homosexual rape.

The Director of Public Prosecutions is generally responsible to the Attorney-General for the conduct of affairs in his department and he will invariably consult with the Attorney in serious cases with which he is directly concerned. The theory is that the DPP is involved where the offence is grave or where it appears desirable to have some uniformity in prosecuting policy. The DPP's office was established under the Prosecution of Offences Act 1879 (now 1985). The DPP is appointed by the Attorney-General. He undertakes a considerable number of prosecutions himself and is constantly required to give advice to the police, his own Crown Prosecutors, as well as to central government departments and magistrates' clerks.

Offences which must be referred to the DPP include certain violations of the fair trading laws, and the ill-treatment of mental patients. Offences which must be referred to the Attorney-General include corruption, possessing explosive substances, hijacking, and breaches of the Official Secrets and Theatre Acts. In most cases the DPP or the Attorney-General is required by the relevant statute to give his consent to the prosecution but in a few the DPP or the Attorney-General, or exceptionally a government Minister, must prosecute themselves. There are over 100 such referrable offences.

The DPP or Crown Prosecutor has the authority to take over any prosecution. In the case of a summary trial the Attorney-General has the power to instruct the

DPP to do just that; then if no evidence is offered against the accused the case is dropped (an equivalent to a *nolle prosequi*). The Attorney-General also has the power to instruct the DPP to take over any prosecution commenced by a private individual. The offering of no evidence can be a controversial matter, but as stressed in *Raymond* v. *Attorney-General* (1982) the Prosecution of Offences Act provides a safeguard in that the Attorney-General as the DPP's superior is answerable to Parliament for any abuse of power by the DPP. 'Private prosecutions' amount to about 25 per cent of the total, including 6 per cent by retail stores, 1 per cent by individuals and the remaining 18 per cent by the Post Office, DSS and other government bodies and local authorities.

There are, of course, certain advantages to be gained from having prosecutions split several ways between those eligible to initiate them – the Crown Prosecution Service, the Serious Fraud Office, the individual, the Attorney-General, the Director of Public Prosecutions, a government department, local authorities or other bodies named by statute. At least, it can be argued, it means that legal and political power is not concentrated in the hands of one agency, but in practice the Crown Prosecutors fulfil the most important role.

5.3   The Lord Chancellor

The Lord Chancellor, a political appointee and member of the Cabinet, is the supreme head of the entire legal system, although as has already been seen other members of the government – like the Attorney-General and the Home Secretary – also exercise considerable judicial power. The Lord Chancellor recommends to the Prime Minister the appointment of the most senior judges, including those in the Court of Appeal, the House of Lords and the Lord Chief Justice. Other senior appointments the Lord Chancellor makes directly himself. No appointments are made nowadays on grounds of political consideration. In the case of those other senior appointments the Lord Chancellor will normally consult with the Lord Chief Justice, the Master of the Rolls, the President of the Family Division and the Vice-Chancellor of the Chancery Division. In 1992, Lord Mackay acknowledged the shortage of judges and delays, after criticisms from the Lord Chief Justice, Lord Taylor, in his BBC Dimbleby Lecture.

In evidence to the Select Committee on Home Affairs in 1992, the Lord Chancellor, Lord Mackay said:

> **I have responsibilities as head of the judiciary, as Speaker of the House of Lords, and as a member of the Cabinet. I think it is extremely important for the working of our democratic institutions that there should be in the Cabinet a person who represents in a particular way the system of justice. I think it is also very helpful that there should be, at**

the head of the judiciary, someone who can be accountable to Parliament and can hold office in such a way that if Parliament is dissatisfied with the way in which its responsibilities are being discharged he could be relieved of his office without the necessity which protects all holders of permanent judicial office. I think it is also convenient that should be linked with the speakership of the House of Lords because of the very special nature of that House and the fact that I may act as Speaker and still participate in debates. I also act as Chairman of the Appeal Committee, if I sit on the Appeal Committee or the Appellate Committee, as well as acting as Chairman of the Judicial Committee of the Privy Council. I think this link is important and I believe it is one which has served the constitutional arrangements well in the past. It imposes a heavy responsibility on the holder of the office.

The Lord Chancellor is also a judge – a Law Lord. However, most Lord Chancellors do not take an active part in the judicial proceedings of the Upper House and it is – or was – a convention that ex-Lord Chancellors take little part, even though they too are Law Lords. Lord Hailsham, Lord Chancellor in Mr Heath's government of 1970-74 and in Mrs Thatcher's government from 1979 to 1987, proved a notable exception to such 'rules'. As seen from Lord Mackay's evidence to the Select Committee the Lord Chancellor performs yet another role: he acts as Speaker in the House of Lords. He thus combines executive, legislative and judicial powers perfectly. As Lord Elwyn-Jones (the Labour Lord Chancellor from 1974–79) has said, 'The benefit of the office is that you can be a universal joint in the machinery. My vote infringes the separation of powers . . . but it allows the maintenance of the separation of powers to flourish.'

The Lord Chancellor is also responsible for the work of the Council on Tribunals and the Law Commission. Another duty has been to oversee the entire legal aid scheme (this is examined later). Finally, he has the power to appoint the Official Solicitor of the Supreme Court. The Official Solicitor's main work is to ensure that minors, the mentally ill and those charged with contempt of court are properly represented. The office attracted the greatest publicity in 1972 when the leaders of an unofficial dock strike (the 'Pentonville Five') were, following the Official Solicitor's intervention, released from prison where they had been sent for contempt of the National Industrial Relations Court (*Churchman* v. *Joint Shop Stewards' Committee*).

5.4   Juries

The modern English jury now owes its statutory existence to the Juries Act 1974, although it is important to realise that certain important reforms were instituted during the previous decade. In 1965 the Morris Committee reported on the constitution of juries, and some of its recommendations were put into legislative effect. Under the Criminal Justice Act 1967 majority verdicts were introduced; thus in the normal jury of 12, verdicts of 11-1 or 10-2 are allowed after a minimum of two hours' consideration of the evidence. Only 6-7 per cent of jury decisions are by a majority verdict. Juries cannot fall below nine in number in a criminal trial; majority verdicts are also possible on the basis of 10-1 or 9-1. The Courts Act 1971 extended majority verdicts to juries in civil cases; in such cases juries are nowadays normally of the same size (12). However, the size of a Coroner's jury still varies.

The function of the jury is to decide on the guilt or innocence of the accused on the facts; jurors must take the law from the judge, but it was held in *Berry* v. *R.* (1992) that the jury is entitled at any stage to the judge's help on the facts as well as the law; the jury is used infrequently in civil cases nowadays, most notably in libel cases. The problem – for the jury at least – of overly long trials was seen in *R.* v. *Wright* (1995), here one that lasted 17 months.

Under the Criminal Justice Act 1972, the property qualification for jurors was abolished. Now anyone on the electoral register between the ages of 18 and 65 is eligible for jury service. Under s.119 of the Criminal Justice Act 1988 the upper age limit was raised to 70, although those over 65 may be excused jury service as of right. Under the Juries (Disqualification) Act 1984 anyone sentenced to life imprisonment or to a fixed term of five years or more is disqualified from jury service for life. Anyone sentenced to a lesser custodial sentence, a supended sentence or a Community Service Order is disqualified from jury service for 10 years from the end of their sentence. For those given a probation order the period is five years. Certain people in vital occupations, such as doctors can be excused service as of right, while others may be given a discretionary excusal if they have a good enough reason, for example illness, business appointments or even sitting examinations, but otherwise jury service is compulsory. Lord Devlin once remarked that the English jury was 'male, middle-aged, middle-minded and middle-class', but that is hardly applicable nowadays.

The use of the jury in English law stretches far into history. However, it was only by the beginning of the nineteenth century that it was settled that jurors should not have personal knowledge of the accused; until the eighteenth century the juror's function was invariably to assist the judge with an intimate assessment of the defendant's character, good or bad. In *R.* v. *Gough* (1993) the question for the Court of Appeal and the House of Lords was whether there was a real risk of bias where a juror was the next door neighbour of the defendant's brother. The test for bias in *Gough* was well illustrated by the first coroner's inquest into the Marchioness riverboat disaster in 1989 (*R.* v. *Inner West London Coroner ex parte Dallaglio* (1994)). The use of the jury has, however, declined to some extent. As indicated above, on the civil side juries are best known in the more serious defamation cases. Juries most frequently appear in criminal cases in the Crown Courts. In 1986 the Roskill Report recommended the abolition of a right to jury trial in complex fraud cases, but the government did not adopt the proposal. However, since the Serious Fraud Office has run into controversy this issue has come back into the political limelight. In 1993 and 1998 the Lord Chancellor and the Home Office issued Consultation Papers on long (fraud) trials.

Lord Denning, however, has argued that some jurors are not up to the task, and commenting on the 1988 incident when some jurors were intimidated at a trial in Leeds Crown Court, he remarked: 'You may get girls or lads of 18 serving on a jury who may be an easy prey to bribery or intimidation'.

During the empanelling of selected jurors, counsel for the defence or the defendant was able to make a number of peremptory challenges: he had the right to object to jurors without giving reasons. The maximum number of peremptory challenges used to be seven but this was reduced to three under the Criminal Law Act 1977 on account of alleged abuse of the procedure at the Central Criminal Court in London (the Old Bailey); however, the right to peremptory challenge was abolished by the Criminal Justice Act 1988 (s.118). The prosecution does not have a right of peremptory challenge, although like the defence it can challenge the whole body (array) of assembled jurors or, more usually, it may examine individual jurors for partiality. In practice, though, the prosecution does not have to prove cause when it asks jurors to whom it objects to 'stand by for the Crown': this simply means those particular jurors fall to the back of the queue. Normally the power of the prosecution to ask jurors to stand by for the Crown is only used in jury vetting cases. The 1973 Judges' Practice Direction stated that it was contrary to established practice for jurors to be excused on general grounds such as race, religion, political opinions or occupation. Louis Blom-Cooper has argued that juries' acquittals ought to be appealed against (for instance, over the acquittal in 1991 of Patrick Pottle and Michael Randle for having organised the escape of the spy, George Blake, from jail 25 years previously).

JURY-VETTING

During the 'ABC' official secrets trial in 1978 (*Attorney-General* v. *Aubrey, Berry and Campbell*) it was suggested in the media that the Crown had been screening jurors for their political beliefs. This matter came to a head after a participant in a late-night television chat-show revealed that the foreman of the jury had at one time been a member of a special military division (the SAS). As a result the jury was dismissed and the trial restarted in view of the 'prejudicial' information that had been broadcast. A few weeks later the Attorney-General (Sam Silkin) issued a lengthy statement regarding police checks on potential jurors. He remarked:

> **No investigation of a panel should be made save with the personal authority of the Director of Public Prosecutions or his deputy, who should notify the Attorney-General when such authority is given. Since August 1975 the Attorney-General has been notified of only 25 cases in which a jury check has been authorised by the Director of Public Prosecutions.**

Writing in *The Observer* Mr Silkin later said that guidelines on jury-vetting had been issued in 1975 to the police, DPP and Home Secretary only because he and the Home Secretary had become aware of the practice in 1974. They had both agreed that to forbid it altogether might open the door to corruption or intimidation. Under the guidelines, published in 1978, only the DPP or his deputy could authorise a check on jurors in three types of cases – official secrets, terrorism and gang warfare (organised crime). The trial or pre-trial judge had to be asked if he agreed. The Criminal Record Office would make checks of criminal records, the defence being entitled to receive relevant details. If checks of either Special Branch or local CID files cast doubt on a potential juror's fairness, then the Crown could exercise its right to stand the juror by; alternatively it could warn the defence in order that the juror might be challenged. In his *Observer* article Mr Silkin argued that it was a myth to say that limited jury checks were unfair; they dated from at least 1948. Where checks were permitted, the Attorney-General had to be notified.

There the whole matter might have rested had not three events immediately pushed jury-vetting back to the front page. In the first place it was revealed that the Chief Constable of Northamptonshire had condoned widespread use of un-authorised jury-vetting (*R. v. Mason* (1980)). Secondly, a row blew up in Sheffield Crown Court. There Judge Pickles granted two policemen charged with assault the right to vet the jury panel. He ordered the Chief Constable of South Yorkshire to supply to the defendants' solicitors details of any previous convictions of members of the jury panel. The Chief Constable unsuccessfully applied for an order of *certiorari* to quash the judge's order. Lord Denning in the Court of Appeal (*R. v. Sheffield Crown Court ex parte Brownlow* (1980)) felt that the order of the judge had been a bad one and that on balance the Court of Appeal had the power to quash the judge's order, the Divisional Court having declined to do so. But Lords Justices Shaw and Brandon thought otherwise. Lord Denning said: 'To my mind it is unconstitutional for the police authorities to engage in "jury vetting" . . . If this sort of thing is to be allowed, what comes of a man's right of privacy?' Lord Denning noted, with evident distaste, that in the United States jurors before being sworn could be cross-examined about their occupations, previous convictions or general beliefs. Lord Justice Brandon had serious doubts as to whether there should be jury-vetting at all – by either the prosecution or the defence. Following the Sheffield case, one Chief Constable, Mr Barry Pain of Kent, called for a wider use of jury-vetting.

The third matter concerned the so-called 'Anarchists' Trial' of 1979 (*R. v. Bennett*). *The Guardian* supplied extensive details in September of that year on how vetting had been carried out on 93 potential jurors without their knowledge; one example was: 'Isobel K had something to do with 39 boxes of stolen razor blades nine years ago'. The newspaper's revelations caused a sensation and Judge King-Hamilton referred the matter to the DPP. The pre-trial judge, Mr Justice Gibbens, had already caused a stir by stating that he was powerless to prevent jury-vetting. 'Anyone may do anything the law does not forbid', he said. He also admitted the incaution of an earlier remark when he had promised legal aid for the defence's use of private detectives in the vetting process.

An editorial in *The Guardian* said: 'What must be condemned – and has been by the Lindop Committee which looked into the subject recently – is the use of information collected for one purpose to serve a different purpose altogether . . .

Who is so free of peccadillos that his life history must be examined every time he fills in a form?' The result was that Judge King-Hamilton decided to discharge the entire jury panel of 93. *The Guardian*, he said, had wasted the court's time and much public money. The DPP and the Attorney-General agreed that vetting of the replacement panel should nonetheless take place.

At the end of 1979 the Attorney-General announced that future investigations on jurors could only take place with his personal approval. In 1980 revised guidelines were issued. The new guidelines confirmed that the DPP would have to obtain the Attorney-General's express permission for checks upon any potential juror, and in respect of two types of cases only, those where national security was involved and part of the evidence was likely to be heard in camera (in secret) and those of a terrorist nature. The defence should be told, at least in general terms, why a juror might be inimical to their interests if the Crown decided not to stand that particular juror by. Judges should not order security checks on a juror, even if alerted by other members of the jury, and certainly not without letting defence counsel know (*R. v. Obellim* (1997)).

THE 'EFFICIENCY' OF JURIES

Do, however, juries perform a useful legal and social function? How do they really work? Professor W. R. Cornish suggested in 1971 that juries had been generally kept away from the probings of disinterested researchers:

> **The rational way, for instance, of assessing whether the broader selection of jurors would produce too many disagreements and unacceptable verdicts would be to attempt some actual comparisons. But that is impossible to organise outside the laboratory of the social psychologist, [although] one branch of the great Chicago Jury Project studies the functioning of juries by playing tape recordings of trials to experimental jury groups.**

Professor Michael Zander supported the Conservative Home Secretary's proposals in 1997 to restrict the right of trial by jury in triable either way offences, on grounds of efficiency, not least because in many cases the result was 'cracked trials', that is a change to a guilty plea at the last moment.

It has also been suggested that one basic difficulty with the jury system is that jurors hear only the admissible evidence relevant to a particular defendant and not all the facts relevant to the crime, with the result that verdicts may sometimes be based on an incomplete or even an inaccurate picture of events. However, Zander has expressed his academic confidence in the operation of the jury system. Zander once commented:

> **It is not surprising that the judge took a stern view of the case of the juror who walked out after several days of evidence because he could**

not bring himself to make up his mind. If that sort of thing began to catch on, the administration of criminal justice could collapse for lack of jurors. Yet the dilemma of knowing how to decide a case must be a common one for a conscientious juror. Most laymen are unfamiliar with the surroundings, the language, the technicalities, even the geography of the court and the identities of the participants in the drama of a trial. They receive little or no guidance as to the nature of their duties. In a study of nearly 200 acquittals at the Old Bailey and the Inner London Crown Court, I found, for instance, that prosecution lawyers agreed in most cases with the defence that acquittal was justified in the light of the evidence (or lack of it) presented to the court. In a study by the Oxford Penal Research Unit it was found that mock juries monitored after they had listened to a real trial performed soberly and rationally and normally agreed with the real jury. In spite of their difficulties, therefore, jurors seem to do their job extremely well and generally to the satisfaction of most observers of the system.

But in 1979 research published by John Baldwin and Michael McConville (of Birmingham University) suggested that 36 per cent of acquittals and 5 per cent of convictions by juries were 'questionable'. Zander, on the other hand, interpreted their research as running almost parallel to the studies of Kalven and Zeisel involving some 3,576 American criminal trials (the 1966 Chicago University Project). Kalven and Zeisel, Zander argued, showed that judge and jury agreed on 75 per cent of the verdicts, whereas Baldwin and McConville showed that in Birmingham Crown Court judge and jury agreed on 85 per cent of the verdicts. Zander went on to say that, on 1977 figures for the Crown Courts, 66 per cent of defendants plead guilty, 19 per cent are found guilty by the jury, 6 per cent are acquitted on directions from the judge and 9 per cent are acquitted by the jury. In respect of the last category Zander commented: 'In the overwhelming majority of cases neither the judge nor the lawyers nor even the police raised any doubts about the jury's verdict . . . [but] in a small minority of cases, most of which end in acquittal, the jury's verdict is not readily explicable'. Research undertaken by the Vera Institute of Justice in New York has pointed towards similar conclusions.

Lord Scarman has observed:

The weakness of the English system arises from overemphasis on the trial itself as the critical period for determining guilt or innocence, and from consequent lack of judicial involvement in the pre-trial preparation, which may be still more critical. An eminent Scots judge once commented to me that 'You in England do not pay enough attention to the merits of a case before trial'. He may have had in mind the Scottish 'judicial examination', but certainly he was correct about the absence of any continuous judicial control of pre-trial preparation. Save for committal proceedings in the magistrates court, which are frequently bypassed or a mere formality, there is in most cases none.

In research carried out for the Runciman Report of 1993, it was found in a survey of some 3,000 Crown Court cases that jurors and most defendants thought judges and barristers did a good job, while lawyers and judges thought that juries had a good understanding of even complex scientific evidence. There were convictions in eight per cent of cases that defence lawyers thought weak, six per cent that prosecution barristers thought weak and four per cent that judges thought weak. Also, the survey, by Professor Zander and Paul Henderson, found that 31 defendants said they had pleaded guilty to offences they had not committed; their reasons were varied: to avoid a trial, to gain a less severe sentence, because they had been advised to, and in one case because of 'hellish' police questioning. In about one-third of the cases the client was being dealt with by clerks rather than solicitors and a significant number met their counsel for the first time on the morning of the trial.

The reasonless verdict means that the appellate body is understandably reluctant to say that the jurors were wrong and much of the current problem of miscarriages of justice is directly traceable to the Court of Appeal's inability to scrutinise the trial court's verdict. However, there are critics of moving towards a more inquisitorial pre-trial hearing; for example, Torquil Dick-Erikson in 1990 wrote: 'a false confession obtained inquisitorially is practically unassailable: the investigating judge passes it on to a colleague, who, in the secrecy of his office and with no public debate, decides whether to commit the case to trial'.

The Contempt of Court Act 1981 prohibits the secrets of the juryroom from being published in any form. The juror may be prosecuted, as may the person soliciting the information. In *Attorney-General* v. *Associated Newspapers* (1994) it was made clear that the prohibition under s.8 of the Contempt of Court Act 1981, on the disclosure of the statements, opinions and arguments of jurors during their deliberations in legal proceedings, applied not just to jurors themselves, but to anyone who sought to publish or reveal such material. The publishers of *The Mail on Sunday*, its editor, and a journalist, were fined £30,000, £20,000 and £10,000 respectively. The offending article revealed the statements, opinions and arguments, during their deliberations, of some of the jurors in the year-long Blue Arrow fraud trial (*R. v. NatWest Investment Bank* (1992)).

In *R. v Young (Stephen)* (1994) four jurors at Hove Crown Court met in a hotel room and conducted a session with a Ouija board, purporting to ask questions of and to receive answers from one of the deceased. Although under s.8 of the Contempt of Court Act 1981 inquiries could not be made as to what went on inside the jury-room at court, here it was a matter of overnight accommodation and therefore a re-trial was ordered by the Court of Appeal.

Under ss.40-43 of the Criminal Justice and Public Order Act 1994 amendments were made to the jury rules, and under s.51 a new offence of tampering with the jury was created.

5.5   Barristers and solicitors

The traditional picture of the English lawyer is that the solicitor is the general practitioner, confined mainly to the office, the front-line individual, and the barrister is the specialist adviser much of whose time is taken up with courtroom appearances. Zander has noted:

> **This picture, however, is increasingly misleading. Many solicitors, perhaps most, are specialists at least in conveyancing, probate and commercial work. Some solicitors do a great deal of advocacy; some barristers do mostly paper work and rarely appear in court. Barristers are now permitted to do solicitors' work in free legal advice centres and for overseas clients. The lines of demarcation are increasingly blurred.**

Zander went on to remark that while the two professions remained divided, while there was no fusion between the two sectors, lack of coordination would continue – barristers would still complain about the poor quality of instructions received from solicitors' firms, and solicitors would complain about last-minute changes of counsel. Solicitors have rights of audience in the magistrates' court and the County Court, but only very limited rights in the Crown Court, High Court and Court of Appeal.

Support for fusion has come from a variety of quarters, including, for example, the TUC. In its evidence to the Royal Commission on Legal Services (the Benson Report of 1979) the Trades Union Congress argued that fusion would enable firms to provide efficient and cheaper services; it was of the opinion that specialisms would best be maintained and enhanced within a united legal profession. Certainly, with the recent trends towards mergers amongst solicitors' firms, so individual solicitors will increasingly concentrate on specialist areas, and with new Law Society and Legal Aid Board rules in relation to minimum standards in certain areas of work, including franchising, the smaller firm is under greater pressure. And the question has also been raised as to how far solicitors should be able to form partnerships with other professions such as accountants. Since 1988 the Law Society has permitted solicitors to form arrangements with building societies, estate agents and housing developers for the introduction of new work, but the code prohibits solicitors participating in 'all-in' conveyancing packages fixed by institutions in the house buyers' market. A direct relationship between the client and the solicitor has to continue. Section 66 of the Courts and Legal Services Act 1990 allows for the creation of multi-disciplinary partnerships, in respect of both solicitors and barristers.

The Mummery Report in 1990 argued that the public interest in maintaining a ban on such partnerships far outweighed any competing private or public interest in lifting it. The Mummery Report created three categories of barristers:

1 independent practising barristers who receive instructions only from solicitors and other professionals;

2 employed barristers who receive instructions from their employers but not from their employers' clients;

3 non-practising barristers in employment are able to provide legal services to their employers' clients but only if they do not hold themselves out as practising barristers.

Direct referral to barristers may be made by Citizens Advice Bureaux and from 1997 by other advice agencies.

As far as persons wishing to train as a solicitor are concerned they will normally have a degree, although school-leavers with good A levels and mature candidates with work experience (not necessarily in law) may also qualify. Each trainee must serve under 'articles of clerkship', that is he has to work in a solicitor's office, and must also pass the examinations of the Law Society, the solicitors' professional body. A person with a law degree may take the shortest route to the examinations, a person with a non-law degree slightly longer. A non-graduate will have to be trained (or, as it was known, serve under articles) for four years, as opposed to the graduate's two years. Most solicitors now work in partnerships. The larger the partnership the more an individual solicitor can specialise, as indicated above.

The Lord Chancellor's Advisory Committee in Legal Education and Conduct in the light of the Benson Report of 1979 and the Marre Report of 1988 issued a consultation paper on continuing professional development in 1996.

By the mid-1980s the Law Society lost much credibility following the Glanville Davies affair, which concerned overcharging on a vast scale, in fact by £130,000. It reorganised its complaints machinery, with the introduction of the Solicitors Complaints Bureau (the SCB). It should be added though that in respect of purely negligent work, the proper course of action is to sue for professional negligence through the courts, not an easy task. Section 21 of the Courts and Legal Services Act 1990 gave the Lord Chancellor powers to appoint a Legal Services Ombudsman, and this was done with effect from January 1991. The Ombudsman can investigate any allegation which is properly made to him and which relates to the way in which a complaint made to a professional body in respect of a person authorised to deliver legal services under the Act has been dealt with by that professional body. Crucially, under s.22 of the Act there is, in effect, power for the Ombudsman, notwithstanding the general principle outlined above, to exercise his discretion to investigate negligence cases, at least small negligence cases. Under s.23 the LSO has considerable powers in recommending compensation but the complainant cannot necessarily enforce that compensation.

From 1991 the SCB could award £1,000 for work not of a professional standard. The Legal Services Ombudsman (LSO) in his first report (in 1992) said delays, lack of information, failure to reply to letters and disregard for instructions were at the heart of most complaints. Solicitors needed to be 'completely frank with clients when they take instructions'. More than 90 per cent of the cases involved criticisms of the SCB which was set up in 1986. Many people still felt that where there was a dispute about facts, the Bureau was more inclined to accept the solicitor's version of events than their own. In 1991 the LSO received 870 complaints – 815 about solicitors, 50 about barristers and five about licensed conveyancers. In one-third of the cases the LSO favoured the complainants. Most were concerned with lack of information and costs. In 14 per cent of cases the LSO was dissatisfied with the way the complaint was handled by the SCB. In the same year the SCB received 16,983 complaints. The number of complaints has remained stubbornly high since then, for instance in 1996 OSS (the Office for the Supervision of Solicitors, successor to the SCB) received approximately 19,000 complaints. A new practice rule has required solicitors to have their own in-house complaints procedures. The main causes for complaint, the SCB found, were shoddy professional work and poor communications. Litigation and divorce and matrimonial work accounted for 44 per cent of complaints about poor service.

By 1992 complaints to the LSO about 'delay and excessive administration costs' in the administration of wills moved up from fourth to second place, behind divorce and family proceedings, in the league table of work prompting complaints. Despite the new so-called 'written professional standard' urging solicitors to advise clients on costs, this was still not always happening. Most of the sums of compensation given were between £250 and £500. Although the Bar had no formal complaints machinery apart from its disciplinary procedure, the Ombudsman took the view that he could investigate complaints about the way the Bar Council handled complaints, including those about a barrister's conduct, so long as these did not undermine 'the finality of any judicial decision' in a case.

In 1996 the Legal Services Ombudsman accused solcitors of adopting a 'legalistic and defensive stance' when faced with complaints instead of settling them quickly if they were at all justified. Barristers were not a great deal better; they lived a 'blinkered existence', unaware of the distress caused to clients by brusque treatment. In 1996 the SCB was revamped as the OSS (Office for the Supervision of Solicitors). Compensation may be awarded against barristers for inadequate service, up to £2000, from 1997 under a Bar Council scheme. The Bar has frequently been accused of high fees, long-winded and inept advocacy in court, shoddy case preparation and a lack of any complaints system.

By 1993 a number of solicitors' firms were adopting practice management standards (in accordance with BS5750) and staff appraisal techniques. Practice management standards are voluntary, but not for those seeking a legal aid franchise; the Legal Aid Board has incorporated the standards into its franchising requirements, which in turn affected Law Society rules.

It can be argued that if the solicitors' profession is to respond to the future needs of society then it will have to embrace the idea of multi-disciplinary partnerships, if only to recapture some of the business ground lost to accountants. But some solicitors would argue this would destroy their professional independence.

Practising barristers, though, are self-employed. The intending barrister must join one of the four Inns of Court (Lincoln's Inn, Inner Temple, Middle Temple and Gray's Inn). It is from the Inns that barristers rent the chambers they work in, sharing expenses and the services of a clerk and other support staff. Once the intending barrister has passed the Bar examinations (again the route is easier for law graduates than for non-law graduates and very difficult for non-graduates), he is 'called to the Bar'. He must then serve a year's pupillage or apprenticeship with a practising barrister. Obtaining that first vital step of pupillage is often very difficult for the young barrister; the early years may be financially hard.

By the mid-1970s pressure was building up to introduce more competition into lawyers' practices by allowing them to advertise openly in the media. Eventually, in 1984, the Law Society relaxed its rules, and solicitors were now allowed to advertise their charges and services, including on radio, but excluding television. From 1987 solicitors were allowed to advertise in any medium, and in the same year barristers decided that they too could advertise their services. Another 'competitive' approach might be to encourage in appropriately simple cases the use of lay advocates; 'unprofessional' as that suggestion might seem, it could, however, bring a further competitive edge to the established lawyers' practices. The Court of Appeal established in the case of *McKenzie* v. *McKenzie* in 1970 that every party had a right to have beside him or her for assistance and advice – a friend who might well be legally unqualified. The Court of Appeal in *R.* v. *Leicester City Justices ex parte Barrow* (1991) emphasised that McKenzie friends had to be allowed: justice must be administered fairly and unless the interests of justice otherwise required, it must be administered openly and its administration must not only be fair but be seen to be fair. The McKenzie friend could take notes and give quiet advice about the conduct of the case – such assistance was a basic part of procedural justice and not within the discretion of the court, but the adviser must not use the position for ulterior motives or disrupt the proceedings of the court, for example, causing the party to waste time, advising the introduction of irrelevant issues or the asking of irrelevant or repetitious questions. However, an application for the assistance of a friend can be refused for good reason: *R.* v. *Wolverhampton Stipendiary Magistrates ex parte Mould* (1992).

A committee under the chairmanship of Lady Marre was set up by the two branches of the legal profession in 1986 to examine the future of both solicitors and barristers. Amongst its recommendations in 1988 were:

1 Standard fees for legal aid work should be supported wherever practicable.

2 A joint Legal Education Council should be established by both branches of the legal profession to consider the future of legal education, especially vocational training and specialisation.

3 Mandatory grants should be provided for the vocational stage of training, and continuing education should be introduced for all qualified lawyers, including older members of both branches.

4   Solicitors should have full rights of audience in the Crown Court (the barristers on the Committee produced a note of dissent about this), but rights of audience should not for the time being extend to lawyers employed by the Crown Prosecution Service. (Historically, in the more remote areas (eg Barnstaple and Truro), some solicitors have already had rights of audience in the Crown Court.)

5   Professions other than solicitors should be allowed to brief barristers directly and employed barristers should have direct access on behalf of their employer to a practising barrister.

In its 1992-93 Annual Report the Lord Chancellor's Advisory Committee on Legal Education outlined the widest-ranging investigation into legal education (including law degrees at universities) since the Ormrod Committee reported in 1971. The future of legal education from undergraduate level upwards is still under review.

Early in 1989 the Lord Chancellor published three Green Papers on the future of the legal profession, which led to the Courts and Legal Services Act 1990, noted at the end of this chapter.

The strength of the independent Bar is that it still maintains a dominance over advocacy, not by any means weakened by the Courts and Legal Services Act 1990; it has representation in Parliament, and close contacts with the Government, particularly through the offices of the Attorney-General and Solicitor-General. On the other hand, whilst the Inns of Court are financially well-endowed, the organisation of the Bar is complicated, and it recruits over-whelmingly from a privileged social class, through the pupillage system. The real dilemma is whether an independent Bar should or could meet a challenge from the Law Society and other quarters that may result in near-fusion, by way of equal rights of audience, common legal education, partnerships and direct lay access; there is also the question as to whether employed barristers in industry, the CPS or the universities should have rights of audience. The 1995 equality code for the Bar aimed to stamp out racial and sexual discrimination and to rid the profession of the 'old boy network'.

5.6   Arbitrators

In the commercial world, where the financial stakes are often high, it may be in the interests of the contracting parties to agree that an arbitrator should be appointed to settle a dispute, should one arise.

There are four chief advantages to arbitration: firstly, parties to arbitration can make their own rules of conduct and therefore the hearing may be as formal or informal as they like, thus saving time and money on the disputants' part.

Secondly, as the parties can choose a specialist arbitrator, they do not have to spend time educating the judge about technical issues. Thirdly, the hearing is in private and commercial organisations may prefer not to wash their dirty linen in public, and lastly, except in exceptional circumstances, the arbitration award is final and binding.

An appeal against the award itself can ordinarily be made only with the consent of the other party or by leave of the court; but judicial interpretation of the 1979 Act has in practice varied widely from one court to another. As was clearly shown in *The Nema* case (1981) (*Pioneer Shipping Ltd* v. *BTP Tioxide Ltd*), the first to come before the Court of Appeal under the Arbitration Act 1979, the appellate judges, both in the Court of Appeal and the House of Lords, have interpreted their discretion narrowly: they prefer to accept the decision of the arbitrator as final wherever possible. This has been in marked contrast to the practice of the Commercial Court (part of the Queen's Bench Division of the High Court). The *Financial Times* commented in 1981:

> **The [1979] Act allowed parties to international contracts to exclude the possibility of an appeal when making the arbitration agreement – though not in respect of marine, insurance and commodity disputes. But even in these areas of London arbitration, appeals were made more difficult by introducing a screening procedure: judges can refuse to deal with appeals against awards unless it is apparent on first reading that the arbitrator has gone wrong on a question of law in a way affecting substantially the interests of the complaining party.**

The criticism of London arbitration is that the parties and lawyers involved frequently treat it as a rehearsal for litigation. Although London arbitration does have a world-wide reputation for impartiality, in contrast the Paris-based ICC (International Chamber of Commerce) selects its 'umpires' from third countries. In *Warde* v. *Feedex International Incorporated* (1983) the High Court ruled that if one party requested a reasoned award, the arbitrator should give reasons, save in very exceptional circumstances.

Where a question of EC law arises in an arbitration, then leave to appeal from the award may be given if the point is new, is capable of serious argument, and is of potentially great importance and far-reaching effect. This was the Court of Appeal's decision in *Bulk Oil (Zug) AG* v. *Sun International Ltd* (1984) where the contract provided 'destination . . . always in line with exporting country's government policy'. At a North Sea oil terminal Sun refused to load a cargo of crude oil because the destination was Israel, and it appeared the export of such oil to Israel was contrary to the policy of the UK government. An arbitrator could not refer any question to the European Court, there would first have to be an appeal from the award.

In the field of international arbitration the leading bodies of arbitrators are the LCIA (the London Court of International Arbitration, notably in relation to civil engineering disputes and the like), the LMAA (London Maritime Arbitrators'

Association – many arbitrations are maritime in nature) and GAFTA (the Grain and Feed Trade Association). Over 10,000 arbitrations take place in London each year. Of course, this particular form of arbitration is not the only form known to the law; we have already seen the popular small claims procedures in the County Court, as established in 1973, whilst trading standards officers can refer serious complaints to the Office of Fair Trading. In 1986 the London Bar Arbitration Scheme was established, to enable litigants to avoid the expense of lengthy court hearings, and to settle under a special code of procedure. And there are various forms of industrial arbitration – for example, under the government's Advisory, Conciliation and Arbitration Service (ACAS). For instance, a conciliation officer from ACAS is obliged to attempt to settle an individual employment grievance before it reaches an industrial tribunal. Moreover, especially in the business world, increasing use is being made of other alternative routes to litigation, under the generic title of Alternative Dispute Resolution (ADR).

ADR is a way of avoiding lengthy and costly litigation, especially in the commercial sector. In 1991 the CBI gave its backing to the Centre for Dispute Resolution, which has dealt with a wide variety of claims including patents and shipping. ICI, Reed International, Sony and Ciba-Geigy are among its members. ADR is being considered by many as an alternative to expensive and time-consuming litigation (especially in commercial and construction litigation involving parties doing long-term business with each other). The four Cs of ADR are: consensus (ie both sides have to agree to non-binding ADR), continuity of business relations (ie not to refuse to deal with each other in the future), control (ie look for a commercial result, rather than a legal result), and confidentiality (ie no publicity). One approach will be through a mini-trial. This involves a panel (with a third-party neutral adviser, and one executive from each party – with each executive having power to settle the case). There will be presentations made by each side's lawyers, but the presentations will be short and to the point. The executives will then try and negotiate a solution (helped by the neutral adviser); they try to find an outcome that satisfies them both from a commercial point of view – and not necessarily from a legal point of view. Thus, there may be agreements on future business, and on the terms of other contracts (ie provisions that a court could never include). An alternative to a mini-trial is mediation; once again, the key-note is that each side assigns an executive who has power to settle the case (and who preferably should not have been previously involved). ADR is ideally suited to straightforward construction disputes in which the parties want to resolve the issues, and get on with life (preferably without incurring large trial costs, and without prejudicing their future working relationship).

Alternative Dispute Resolution was considered in some detail by a report from the General Council of the Bar in 1991, the Beldam Committee, and was returned to in some detail in the 1996 Woolf Report, *Access to Justice*.

More fundamentally, international arbitration is premised on a distrust of developing countries and their courts. It is characterised by a more informal approach to so-called legal technicalities. International arbitration converts disputes with significant legal, regulatory and policy dimensions into purely private contractual dis-

LEGAL ADVICE AND AID **149**

agreements. Courts, whose duty it is to administer justice pursuant to law and policy, are replaced with private arbitration panels that often see their mission as merely to settle disagreements in accordance with 'general' legal principles and prevailing business practices that favour transnational corporations.

> **Finality, confidentiality and speed are often said to be the main advantages of arbitration over litigation. [But] Professor Goode comments: 'If I were asked by foreign parties whether they could rely on an English arbitration award being final if all the rules of natural justice, procedure and jurisdiction had been followed, my answer would have to be God only knows'**

the *Financial Times* noted in 1991.

It should also be observed that the Arbitration Act 1996 has now reformed earlier arbitration law; in particular, as Lord Bingham has said, the Act is a new departure, a hopeful attempt at laying down a clear, flexible, fair, accessible and modern set of rules to govern the conduct of arbitration. The Act also gives abitral tribunals a new power to make provisional orders.

5.7   Legal advice and aid

The cost of going to law is often sufficient to deter people from commencing litigation in the first place. As the well-worn remark usually attributed to Mr Justice Darling puts it, 'the law, like the Ritz Hotel, is open to all'. The costs may include legal advice from a solicitor, the solicitor's and a barrister's pre-trial work, representation in court, court fees and the costs of the other party if you lose. By the time a case reaches the Court of Appeal or the House of Lords a five figure bill would not be unknown.

In civil cases the costs of the successful party are usually paid by the losing party, who, of course, must also foot his own bill. The costs are therefore met between the parties themselves (*inter partes*). However, a winning party in a civil action does not necessarily have all his fees paid. It is likely that he will still be out of pocket to some extent; the court has different methods of assessing costs and they can be complicated. But in 1986 Order 62 of the Supreme Court said the entitlement to costs, by the successful party, on the 'standard basis', was not what was 'necessary and proper' as before, but now 'reasonably incurred', meaning that there should be little difference between the solicitor's bill and what the successful litigant recovers from his opponent.

COSTS OF A TRIAL

In criminal cases costs are governed by the Costs in Criminal Cases Act 1973. The costs will be met either *inter partes*, as in civil cases, or out of 'central funds', that is the Government pays. For summary offences the costs may only be met *inter partes*; in indictable cases it may be *inter partes* or central funds or possibly a mixture of both. This means that if a defendant is convicted for a summary offence he must pay the prosecution's costs as well as his own. If the defendant is convicted for an indictable offence he may still have to pay the prosecution's costs, but they might be met out of central funds (or it might be a mixture of both). If the defendant is acquitted, costs for a summary offence must be met by the prosecution. In the case of an indictable offence the costs may be met either by the prosecution or more likely out of central funds. Of course, whenever costs fall upon the prosecution they still in effect come out of the public purse. The court may, however, decide that an acquitted defendant should still make a financial contribution towards costs, 'having regard to the applicant's resources and commitments'.

The power to order an acquitted defendant to contribute towards the costs of the trial are covered by the Indictments Act 1915 and the Prosecution of Offences Act 1985. In 1981 the Lord Chief Justice issued a Practice Direction which stated that the court should normally make an order for the defendant's costs to be met out of central funds (where it had the power to do so) unless the defendant's conduct had brought suspicion on himself or where the defendant had misled the prosecution into thinking that the case against him was stronger than it was. Similarly, an exception might be made where there was ample evidence to support a conviction but the defendant had been acquitted on a technicality which had no merit. In addition the prosecution might have to pay the costs of the trial where it had acted spitefully or had continued proceedings without reasonable cause.

The individual may, however, receive State help, either as a defendant in a criminal trial or as a plaintiff or defendant in a civil case. The legal aid and advice scheme costs many hundreds of million pounds a year, a constant headache for the Lord Chancellor who is in overall charge of the funding.

The State system of legal aid and advice was developed slowly through four Acts of Parliament – the Legal Aid and Advice Act 1949, which controlled civil proceedings, the Legal Aid Act 1964, which was concerned with aiding a successful litigant in civil cases who was not in receipt of legal aid, the Criminal Justice Act 1967, which governed legal aid in criminal cases, and the Legal Advice and Assistance Act 1972, which provided free advice, short of actual legal representation in court, for those on low incomes. All these statutory provisions were consolidated in the Legal Aid Act 1974.

The 1972 Act also provided for the establishment of local law centres wherever there was a clear need for unmet services. In 1979 the Benson Report recommended a nationwide network of state-funded law centres, but this was never implemented; there are about 50 centres in England and Wales, often funded by local councils and dealing with housing, immigration, welfare and employment matters, issues which not all solicitors' firms have been keen to pursue.

Under the Legal Aid Act 1979 (as amended by the Administration of Justice Act 1985) Parliament delegated to the Lord Chancellor powers to vary the advice and civil aid limits so as to ensure the whole system was flexible enough to keep up with the ravages of inflation and changes in general economic circumstances. The Legal Aid Act 1988 has attempted to deal further with this problem and it replaced all previous such legislation.

Criminal cases

Legal aid for appearances in criminal cases is established by determining what constitutes 'the interests of justice'. This applies only to persons charged, not to people bringing private prosecutions who must pay their own way. Thus a person who brings a private prosecution is liable not only for his own costs but also, should he lose, for the defendant's. If a charge of murder is involved, or if there is a prosecution appeal to the House of Lords, then the defendant must automatically be granted legal aid. And should there be doubt about making a legal aid order at any stage in criminal proceedings then the decision must be resolved in the applicant's favour.

In the Crown Courts, up until 1982, nearly all defendants as a matter of course were granted full legal aid. Where the legally aided defendant was acquitted the Legal Aid Fund was reimbursed by the prosecution or central funds; in most cases, therefore, it became a matter of one public fund paying another.

The real variations in the granting of legal aid arise in the Magistrates' Court. A defendant is far more likely to appear unrepresented before a magistrate than before a judge. The Legal Aid Act 1982 attempted to overcome this problem by providing for a scheme of duty solicitors in Magistrates' Courts, with the establishment of committees whose members include both a magistrate and a clerk to the court. Twenty-four hour duty solicitors were a safeguard to the police's revised powers of detention under the Police and Criminal Evidence Act 1984, but the separate funding has posed problems. Up to a point the duty solicitor scheme also counters criticism about lack of the law centres envisaged under the 1972 and 1974 Acts. But of course, law centres have many responsibilities other than to provide representation for a defendant in the Magistrates' Court. In 1989 a critical research study by Andrew Sanders and Lee Bridges of Birmingham University revealed a low quality of service to suspects by duty solicitors, a criticism that was very much echoed by the Runciman Report in 1993. Only 25 per cent of suspects in police custody took up their right under PACE to receive advice from a solicitor.

In addition, the Legal Aid Act 1982 introduced new procedures for requiring defendants in criminal cases to contribute towards the costs of a trial, where the applicant was not in receipt of income support. If the defendant is acquitted, then the contributions will usually be refunded, unless the accused has brought the prosecution on himself or been acquitted on a mere technicality.

In a spot check on Magistrates' Courts in 1996, out of 20 courts, only one (Plymouth) had it seems investigated all defendants' financial circumstances properly, according to the National Audit Office. The auditors also found that no one would take responsibility for running the criminal legal aid system. The Lord Chancellor had already introduced regulations in 1995 requiring justices' clerks to keep records of all applications for criminal legal aid.

Civil cases

As far as civil legal aid is concerned then it is more a question of an individual's financial circumstances. Someone in receipt of income support or who has a low income and little capital will qualify for a full legal aid order covering both pre-trial work and the costs of the court hearing. Someone who is better off may receive limited aid but as a rough guide anyone in a professional occupation is unlikely to qualify in total or in part. To qualify at all the individual's financial circumstances must fall below the upper limits for disposable income and capital. 'Disposable income' means the income after allowances for tax, dependants and other outgoings are made. 'Disposable capital' means the capital a person has after deducting the value of his or her principal place of residence and household furnishings. A legal aid order will not be made if the 'merits of the case' are inadequate, that is if a *prima facie* case is not established.

The 1972 Act introduced the Law Society's much-debated 'Green Form' scheme; this meant that people with little capital and a low income could receive free up to £25 worth of a solicitor's time in advice on virtually any kind of legal problem. Originally some people qualified in part: they would have to pay something towards the cost. The Legal Aid Board's Annual Report for 1991-92 noted:

> **Despite the introduction and/or growth of other schemes over the last ten years, the 'Green Form' scheme of legal advice and assistance and its 'ABWOR' offshoot, assistance by way of representation, remain the most widely used of the legal aid schemes, accounting for almost 50% of all acts of advice, assistance or representation paid for out of the Fund each year.'**

ABWOR covers the costs of a solicitor preparing a case and representing the client in most civil cases in magistrates' courts; it is also available for hearings before the Mental Health Review Tribunals, as well as to prisoners facing disciplinary charges and to discretionary lifers who cases are referred to the Parole Board. All proceedings under the Children Act 1989 are covered by legal aid.

Civil legal aid is available for all courts dealing with civil cases but only a handful of tribunals – the Employment Appeal Tribunal, the Lands Tribunal, Mental Health Review Tribunals, the Commons Commissioners and, in certain instances, the Restrictive Practices Court. Legal aid is not available for defamation actions, nor for small claims (under £3,000).

THE LEGAL AID ACT 1988

This statute established the Legal Aid Board which from 1989 took over the functions performed by the Law Society's legal aid administration, and criminal legal aid will be transferred to it as and when the Lord Chancellor considers it appropriate. (Five groups administer legal aid within the LAB – M4, Midlands, North West, North East, London & Brighton.) Part I gives some rather vague definitions, that is 'advice' means oral/written advice in relation to any particular circumstances, 'assistance' means the taking of any steps a person might take in this context, including steps with respect to proceedings and 'representation' is representation for the purpose of proceedings including such assistance given in preliminary steps to any proceedings. Part II of the Act established the Legal Aid Board, which has up to 17 members appointed by the Lord Chancellor. The Board has the power to hive off areas of advice (Green Form) work by competitive tender, but some organisations, like the Citizens Advice Bureaux, have been less than happy about this prospect. A legal aid fund similar to the previous fund administered by the Law Society was established under Part II.

Part III provided that entitlement to advice and assistance shall be dependent upon financial eligibility and enables regulations to be made; it also maintains the previous arrangements whereby solicitors must obtain approval from the legal aid authorities before any advice and assistance can be given beyond the initial cost limit. Applicants were liable to pay a contribution towards the cost of the advice and assistance, but since 1993 the Green Form is limited to those below income support level who will receive free advice.

Part IV of the Act sets out the provisions for legally aided representation before the civil courts; applicants must satisfy the 'merits' test and may be obliged to make a contribution towards the costs of the case. (Successful unassisted defendants may have their costs met out of the Legal Aid Fund.) Under s.15 of the Legal Aid Act 1988 the merits of the case include the question would only a trivial advantage be gained (ie a moral victory alone)? Would a solicitor not normally be employed (eg is it a small claims arbitration)? Is finance available from some other source (eg trade unions)? Is there an arguable case? Section 18 provides for an unassisted successful defendant to be aided by the Legal Aid Fund, but Lord Denning said in *Hanning* v. *Maitland (No 2)* (1970) that this should exclude insurance companies and 'commercial companies who are in a considerable way of business; and wealthy folk who can meet the costs without feeling it'. (See also *Kelly* v. *London Transport Executive* (1982).)

Part V of the Act maintains the 'interests of justice' test for legally aided representation in criminal cases and the system of contributions introduced under the 1982 Act. The 'interests of justice' criteria are the so-called 'Widgery Criteria', and under s.22 of the Act include the potential loss of livelihood and damage to reputation, whether a substantial question of law is involved, whether the accused is unable to understand the proceedings and the nature of the defence. Responsibility for criminal legal aid may be transferred to the Legal Aid Board from the courts if the Lord Chancellor agrees.

The 1988 Act, which swept away previous legislation, that is the 1974, 1979 and 1982 Legal Aid Acts, gives the Lord Chancellor wide powers to determine the scales for legal aid and advice and to set the amount of remuneration for solicitors and barristers undertaking legal aid work. The Act did not extend legal aid to tribunal representation, nor did it extend the system of law centres, nor did it tackle the problem of 'class' actions as highlighted by the Opren arthritis drug case. However, legally-aided multi-party actions have been allowed from 1992.

From 1993 the fixed fee interview of £5, which some solicitors' firms ran, was abolished. Instead there are local referral schemes in conjunction with law centres and the NACAB (National Association of Citizens Advice Bureaux). The length of interviews are up to half an hour, with maximum fees not to exceed £25. However, a number of solicitors continue to give initial free interviews and from 1993 the Law Society launched its *Lawyers for Business* scheme, under which free preliminary consultation is given by some solicitors for the self-employed, those working already in a business or freelance.

PROBLEMS OF COST

The British system of legal aid, at least until the substantial restrictions introduced by Lord Mackay in 1993, is the most generous in Europe, if not the world. The only European country that approaches a British comparison is the Netherlands, although when the nature of State/private insurance schemes is taken into account the Danish and Swedish systems also bear examination.

The real difficulty of the British scheme has been its escalating costs. Legal aid cost £100 million in 1981 but £900 million by 1991, and £2 billion by 1996. So the disposable income limit for full civil legal aid was reduced in April 1993 from £3,060 to £2,294. Meanwhile, for criminal legal aid solicitors were faced with the introduction of standard fees. Moreover, as the Criminal Justice Act 1991 put more emphasis upon community rather upon custodial sentences, so magistrates were refusing, under national guidelines, to grant legal aid in summary cases. (In 1992 research from Birmingham University showed how the granting of legal aid varied amongst Magistrates' Courts.) The changes in civil and criminal legal aid were challenged by the Law Society under judicial review, but in both instances the High Court and the Court of Appeal threw out the applications, clearly saying that under s.34 of the Legal Aid Act 1988 the Lord Chancellor was within his powers to make such changes, even if the Law Society had not been fully consulted by him at an earlier stage, *R. v. Lord Chancellor ex parte the Law Society (No 1)* (1993) and *R. v. Lord Chancellor ex parte the Law Society (No 2)* (1993). For what it is worth, in 1993 the House of Commons Public Accounts Committee was severely critical of the cuts in legal aid.

Then there has been the question of block-funding (franchising) (ie blocks of contracts for legal aid work). Proposals were outlined in 1992. Franchising will probably help the bigger firms. Lord Mackay also indicated that he wanted to reduce legal aid on divorce matters. Couples would be encouraged to use mediation, possibly with incentives to reach agreement. An experimental franchise system has been running in the Birmingham area since 1990. In some circumstances franchised solicitors would be able to decide whether to grant legal aid. The Law

Society has indicated its reservations about certain legal work being transferred to para-legal advice agencies:

> **For example, there are several firms of solicitors in Bude, but no advice centre; the nearest is at Launceston, 16 miles away, but it is not open five days a week; at Okehampton, the CAB is open five days a week, but it is 30 miles away. Clients in rural areas in particular [would] be put to enormous inconvenience. The lack of public transport, and where it is available, its cost, [could] cause hardship to many clients and deter many people from obtaining advice.'**

During 1991 the Legal Aid Board visited six towns, such as Barnstaple in Devon, and its 1991–1992 Annual Report noted:

> **We learned that solicitors in private practice and advice sector workers have widely differing perceptions of the levels and areas of need in their locality. We also realised that the advice sector could have a valuable role to play in providing information about need for legal help. We believe it is likely that the advice sector is the first and perhaps only port of call for many of those needing help outside the mainstream areas of work for solicitors. As a result, advice workers may have a much better appreciation of the legal needs of the community in these areas than solicitors in private practice. It is important that this knowledge is used to demonstrate the existence of areas of need to those able to provide help. Unless solicitors are aware of the levels and areas of need, market forces cannot operate to meet demand. This is the sort of exercise we think a legal services committee could promote.**

The original proposal was that franchises would be awarded only to firms doing more than £40,000 worth of legal aid work a year. That proposal has been abolished; instead, franchising contracts are to be offered to firms that meet certain legal and business management criteria. This will include legal resources (eg the scope of the library, and office management procedures), and also 'consumer friendliness' (eg policy on home visits, opening hours, waiting areas). The idea is that each firm appoints a supervisor who oversees up to two areas of work (no more). It seems that a minimum of five years qualification will be needed before one can become a 'supervisor' (although there will be special rules for non-solicitor advisers, such as CABx). What is worrying for many firms is that there appears to have been no decision on whether they will have to undertake a wide variety of legal aid work, or whether they can simply specialise in one or two categories. Also, the five-year qualification rule is seen as unreasonably strict, as is the limitation on two areas of practice per supervisor; both rules may well work against small and new firms.

In a 1992 report, the Legal Action Group said: 'The current position – in which the distribution of solicitors' offices and advice agencies is dictated by market forces and the vagaries of local authority generosity and solvency – is self-evidently unsatisfactory'. The LAG recommended the extension of regional legal services throughout the country. The duty solicitor scheme in courts and police stations set up in 1986 was the last creative development in the legal aid scheme, the Report said. In fact, the duty solicitor scheme covers about a quarter of a million defendants each year.

THE 1994–96 'REFORMS'

In 1996 the Lord Chancellor published a White Paper, following an earlier Green Paper in 1995 and a consultation document in 1994 on legal aid for the apparently wealthy which was a consequence of certain high profile criminal trials such as Brent Walker and Barlow Clowes and civil cases such as Arab Monetary Fund (Jawad Hashim) where the legal aid bill had reached very high proportions. As a result a number of rule changes were already made in 1996, for example the capital value of the principal place of residence above £100,000 would be taken into account, in any part of the country.

The White Paper made it clear that the extended principles of legal aid would embrace providing any help, not just from lawyers, that could either prevent court proceedings or questions that would demand a legal solution from arising, or promote their settlement or other disposal, in accordance with the law and in a way that would produce an enforceable result. Earlier proposals to extend legal aid to tribunals were now dropped. The Lord Chancellor would allocate separate, pre-determined budgets for criminal, family and non-family civil legal aid to the Legal Aid Board. The Lord Chancellor would give directions about priorities to the Legal Aid Board and in that regard the budgets would be allocated on a regional basis.

Most legal aid services would now be provided under contracts between the Legal Aid Board and providers in the private or voluntary sectors, and all contracts would include quality standards, building upon the Legal Aid Board's franchising initiative. In civil and family matters contracts would include mediation in family matters and franchised advice agencies would be able to obtain contracts to provide advice and assistance in their areas of expertise.

In respect of granting civil legal aid, the Lord Chancellor would be able to make regulations setting out the criteria. Where legal aid is refused or withdrawn, the applicant will be able to ask the Legal Aid Board to review the decision, and there will be a right of appeal. All financially eligible applicants would pay a fixed contribution, except those on income support. Those people covered by legal expenses insurance would not be eligible for legal aid, and the possibility of reaching a conditional fee agreement might also be taken into account.

Subject to the successful completion of the trial period, the government proposed to extend the scope of conditional fees to cover most types of civil case involving a financial claim. In criminal cases new arrangements for contracting criminal cases would be considered and tested, and contracts for more substantial Crown Court work would probably be based on an agreed price per case, with one-off contracts for very expensive cases. In the longer term the Legal Aid Board, rather than the courts, will determine applications for criminal legal aid.

5.8   The Courts and Legal Services Act 1990

This Act, already alluded to, appeared, at least at the time it was passed, to be one of the most significant pieces of legal reform in the post-war period. Its main provisions are as follows.

Part I deals with procedure in the civil courts. Principally, this Part deals with provisions implementing the Civil Justice Review and amendments to certain family proceedings as a result of the Children Act 1989. Under s.2 there has occurred a major transfer of business from the High Court to the County Court, notably personal injuries cases. The upper limit of County Court jurisdiction was raised from £5,000 generally to £25,000, but County Courts can deal with *all* contract, tort and recovery of land actions regardless of value. Rules of evidence were also changed, not least to deal with small claims cases (now £3,000 upper limit) in a more open way, being heard by registrars, now called district judges under s.74 (Part III) of the Act. Also, in respect of representation, under s.11, the Act has provided that in housing, debt and small claims, there can be unrestricted rights of audience, although the court would retain power to exclude an unsuitable representative.

Part II deals with legal services. Under ss.19 and 20 there has been established the Lord Chancellor's Advisory Committee on Legal Education and Conduct. This is a committee of 17, largely lay persons, but chaired by a senior judge, whose task is to prescribe the rules for the education and training of all sectors of the legal profession, as they affect court work. But within that committee four senior judges (the Lord Chief Justice, the Master of the Rolls, the President of the Family Division and the Vice-Chancellor, the 'designated judges') have to agree as to which members of the legal profession may exercise rights of audience and rights to conduct litigation (ss.27–29). These are the controversial powers which have seen a number of solicitors being allowed practising certificates (to conduct cases in the Crown Court and the senior courts); in the same way the Crown Prosecution Service is arguing for parallel extended rights of audience, but hitherto with a conspicuous lack of success, the Lord Chancellor's advisory committee taking the view that Crown Prosecutors, and other solicitors in the public service such as local government, would be insufficently neutral for senior prosecutions; this has not been a problem, however, in Scotland.

Under s.34 the Authorised Conveyancing Practitioners Board was established in respect of property work (licensed conveyancers). Under ss.21 and 22 the office of the Legal Services Ombudsman was established, and specifically under s.43 a Conveyancing Ombudsman is provided for, who must deal with complaints in the first instance against authorised practitioners in connection with the provision by them of conveyancing services.

Section 66 allows for multi-disciplinary and multi-national partnerships, whilst under s.58 conditional fees arrangements are allowed (that is agreements on fees to be paid only in the event that the litigation is successful, but full-scale contingent fees, as presaged by one of the 1989 Green Papers, were not included in the Act). In respect of s.58, the Lord Chancellor agreed in 1993 that there could be a limited operation of conditional fees, on a basis of 'no win, no fee', primarily in the area of personal injury work, together with insolvency and European Court of Human Rights cases, but possibly later to cover breach of privacy and defamation actions; the successful lawyers in such cases would be entitled to a 100% bonus of their normal fees, but this is not the same as American-style contingency fees whereby the winning lawyer is entitled to part of the damages awarded. In practice, of course, people will still be liable for the other party's costs if they lose their case. Where damages are often only £2,000 to £3,000 (in contrast to the much larger awards in American courts), nothing may be left after taking out costs, which does not make it worthwhile embarking on litigation in the first place. From 1995 the Law Society introduced the Accident Line Protect scheme, which is based on a low, single premium since it is available to clients of solicitors on the Law Society's panel of expert litigators; it is for personal injury actions, but not medical negligence cases. If a conditional fee case is won, then lawyers can impose a 100 per cent uplift of fees, but the Law Society recommends a 25 per cent maximum of the client's compensation. Only very strong accident cases will be taken on, however, outside of those paid for by legal aid or privately. Conditional fees have come in for a great of criticism, not least in respect of the uplift in fees. Professor Zander has said: 'The idea that a winning litigant would have to pay most or even all the damages to his lawyer seems preposterous . . . For most clients conditional fees will just be a con.'

Part III of the Act deals with largely technical matters regarding judicial offices and judicial pensions.

Part IV amends the Solicitors Act 1974; notably under s.93 (and Schedule 15) the Solicitors Complaints Bureau (now OSS) was given power to award up to £1,000 to clients who have been victims of a solicitor's 'shoddy work'. Part V covers arbitration; under s.102 an arbitrator or umpire is given the power to dismiss a claim for lack of prosecution. Part VI is about miscellaneous matters, the most important of which is that under s.110 the Parliamentary Commissioner for Administration now has the right to investigate maladministration in courts and tribunals.

DISCUSSION POINTS

1 Discuss whether the proposals to reform legal aid are realistic.

2 Is there any future for a divided legal profession?

3 Can ADR really develop over the next few years?

6six CRIMINAL LAW

6.1 Crime and society

Social deviance in general may be viewed as the failure to change society in a number of ways, and criminal behaviour in particular is an acute form of deviance. Deviance can be defined as conduct which does not follow the normal aggregate patterns of behaviour. Indeed it tries to untie the bundle of social rules or norms that invariably holds society together. Thus crime can be judged only in relation to the behavioural codes, written and unwritten, that most people understand and accept. Criminal behaviour is seen as sufficiently serious or deviant or immoral for the majority of society to want to ban it. Of course, what may be outlawed one year may not have been the year before. Public opinion is not set for all time and parliamentary legislation reflects changing habits or norms. Moreover, new forms of potentially criminal activity arise, with the result that Parliament and the courts in time respond to those too; a good example here is the Protection of Children Act 1978 which prohibited the taking of indecent photographs of children.

Professor J. B. Mays has emphasised that public opinion is influenced by writers, thinkers, politicians, the mass media and by pressure groups such as the Howard League for Penal Reform.

> **Definitions of what is to be regarded as criminal, moreover, can change quite radically over the years. Crime is hence a relative concept . . . Since legal codes can be seen to change with cultures, time and place, our assessment of the seriousness of any offence (perhaps other than homicide) will inevitably be relative and flexible.**

However, a number of qualifications must be made when talking about criminal deviance in general. Firstly, similar actions may not all be classed as 'criminal'. For example, prostitution itself is not unlawful, although a prostitute may be regarded as a social deviant. But organised prostitution is; it is a criminal offence to solicit or to live off the immoral earnings of another.

Secondly, the detection of criminal deviance can never be consistent. Crime may well be class based. In an age when much of society is supposed to be 'on the fiddle' or 'on the make', the gap between middle-class, white-collar crime and working-class, blue-collar crime is a wide one. The middle-classes, with their higher educational standards, are faced with a number of opportunities to practise subtle deviance – for example, tax avoidance, embezzlement or fraud. But, so the argument runs, the working-classes have few such chances: the petty thief epitomises the less educated member of society. At a meeting of Commonwealth Law Ministers in 1980 twenty-five different types of 'white-collar' or commercial crimes were listed, including corporate fraud, exchange control violations, fraudulent insurance claims, social security fraud, credit card fraud, tax evasion and copyright violations (pirating). In 1995 the Employment Policy Institute claimed that Britain's departure from full employment and the emergence of mass unemployment from the mid-1970s had coincided with a strong trend in recorded crime.

Thirdly, the more the activity concerned is a 'victimless' one, the greater the chance that society will regard the action as socially rather than legally deviant. Large department stores could 'afford' to bear the losses incurred by 'shoplifting', but snatching an old lady's purse might evoke greater sympathy. But, as indicated above, attitudes do change; now a large number of stores display signs which warn the public that shoplifting is theft.

Fourthly, there is the police's own detection rate; this has hovered around the 30 per cent mark for the last 10 years. In 1996 it reached the low of 26 per cent, but with great variation, for instance the clear-up rate was 57 per cent in Dyfed-Powys. The national clear-up rate for 'serious' crime, including homicide, rape and aggravated burglary, was 50 per cent. Some types of sexual and drug offences are extremely unlikely to be reported to the police, and the incidence of acts committed in private is clearly greater than the number of such crimes the police actually get to hear about. But it is also a matter of the patterning of police activity and surveillance. It could be argued that as long as county-wide constabularies remain in existence there will always be considerable variation between the forces in the application of resources to less serious crime. Thus after dealing with theft, injury and road traffic offences one local authority's policy may be to concentrate its remaining energies upon investigating drug offences, but another authority will concentrate on underage drinking and other infringements of the licensing laws. Local variations in crime patterns as reported and investigated may therefore say more about the nature of a police force than about the sort of criminals and deviants who live in a particular area. The police are increasing the use of formal cautions for minor offences, rather than prosecuting offenders – a practice backed by the Crown Prosecution Service.

VIEWING CRIME POSITIVELY

Emile Durkheim, the so-called father of sociology, would have taken a rather optimistic view of criminal behaviour. He believed that deviance was a 'natural' feature of organised society; it was a safety-valve that released the in-built tensions of human nature. Durkheim argued that we should not view crime negatively, as a force solely causing disruption in society, but, rather, positively. Popular sentiments could be expressed against criminal actions and the perpetrators of them. The majority could thus rally round the flag of normative solidarity; the behavioural rules of the majority would be restated and, if necessary, redefined. Durkheim believed that it was no occasion for self-congratulation when the crime rate dropped noticeably below the average level, for we would be certain that that apparent progress was associated with some social disorder. Durkheim also believed, rather simplistically it would now seem, that as societies advanced, so laws would become more compensatory in nature and less penal, the latter being reserved for more 'primitive' communities.

But even if Durkheim was right, the way in which popular sentiment, or even outrage, is expressed against crime may lack consistency. After all there is a world of difference between being privately fined by the Inland Revenue Commissioners for tax evasion and becoming stigmatised by a court appearance. In any case there is an inherent danger in viewing crime positively: such an approach could soon lead to accusations of 'softness' towards the deviant. For instance, Sir Richard Jackson, one-time Assistant Commissioner of the Metropolitan Police, has remarked:

> **For glossy magazines to print glamorised pictures of criminals; for journalists and sociologists to write articles making heroes out of petty crooks and brutal thugs; for radio and television producers to put out programmes which deride and attack the police while deliberately working up sympathy for thieves and murderers – such behaviour seems to me either irresponsible or malicious.**

Sir Richard's comments illustrate the point made by Paul Rock in his inquiry into deviant behaviour, namely that since all deviance is supposedly a discredited activity, those who are prepared to justify it, however noble or laudable their intentions, may also find themselves under attack. This was certainly the case in 1968 when amid some controversy the Wootton Committee recommended a relaxation in the penalties for the use of cannabis, partly, it could be argued, on the basis of evidence taken from drug-users themselves. As Rock has said, by publicly casting a particular role as deviant, an authoritative law-maker can translate the role player into a morally degraded outsider.

Whatever may be the truth or otherwise in the substance of Sir Richard's remarks, there is little doubt that the mass media are powerful opinion-shapers. Some deviance is deemed 'newsworthy' for no apparent logic; other forms of deviancy may be safely passed over in the interests of impartiality and political balance. How deviancy and deviant events are assessed and described rests very much in the hands of news editors.

ANOMIE

For many years sociologists and criminologists have tried to explain the real cause of crime and deviance and why the incidence of criminal actions appears to vary from one social group to another. R. K. Merton's theory of anomie is clearly one that is now well-established. Merton paid particular attention to the role of social competition and stress as factors causing individuals to take the first step down the deviant path. In a modern society the overall emphasis is upon 'momentary success', on 'getting ahead' by fair means or foul – that was the basis of Merton's comments in the 1950s about the great American Dream, the 'Dream' being the collective belief that individuals, no matter how humble or deprived their backgrounds, should strive to succeed, that by 'hard work' everyone should eventually reach a position to realise his long-term aspirations. In the American Dream there is 'no final stopping point'. In reality, Merton emphasised, it is easier for the son of a corporation president than for a Harlem slum boy to reach his declared goals. Hence, he said, we have a convenient explanation of the higher rate of detected crime amongst the lower social strata. Once some people realise their dreams will not be fulfilled, they reject the rules of the game, they give up competing, they opt out. Established conventions and social rules (or norms) are disregarded; a state of normlessness or 'anomie' sets in.

Yet Merton's theory has come in for much criticism, both in America and in the United Kingdom. Many sociologists and criminologists have suggested that anomie is no more prevalent amongst the working-class than amongst the middle-class. 'Getting ahead' – and using deviant means to do so – may be a common aim of both groups. In the former it is usually limited to material success, in the latter there are the additional factors of social recognition and the enhancement of personal status.

THE GENERAL AIMS OF PUNISHMENT

The object of Gilbert and Sullivan's Mikado – his sublime object – was 'to let the punishment fit the crime', but it was never clear how it exactly fitted. No sentencing policy, no form of punishment, can ever be totally rational – there will inevitably be a large element of subjective judgement. While most sentencing powers are now contained in the Powers of Criminal Courts Act 1973, there is often a vital difference between what the courts can do and what they will do. Indeed the current trend is towards shorter sentences of imprisonment.

The underlying aims of punishing the individual are hard to define let alone analyse. However, as Sir Rupert Cross has pointed out in his standard work on the English sentencing system, punishment by the State can only be justified if there are in its objective two key elements, namely the reduction of crime and the promotion of respect for the criminal code. The first element, Cross says, is commonly associated with utilitarian theories and the second with retributive theories, 'but they are in reality mutually dependent. If punishment is to deter it may only do so by giving offenders their deserts; but the only reason for giving offenders their deserts is that it deters.' While, as Cross says, sentencing philosophy may owe a great deal to the writings of Hegel and Kant, contemporary legislators make considerable attempts to base modern forms of punishment on the notions of fairness, proportionality, prevention, individual and general deterrence, and education and reform.

Fairness is a difficult quality to define accurately, since there is something of a double-edged quality to it. We all want to be fair in the sense that we must encourage the law-abiding to remain so – we must be fair, in other words, to those who do *not* break the law. Equally, we may also wish to be equitably disposed towards a person who must be punished in order to uphold a principle and yet whose wrong was hardly more than venial. Furthermore, what do we do about someone who breaks a law on the grounds that he views it as a rule which is morally repugnant? Then there arises a yawning gap between legal justice and moral (or 'true') justice. This question of fairness and justice arose in *R. v. Secretary of State for Home Department ex parte Walsh* (1991) where it was held that in order to achieve fairness and equality of treatment among life-prisoners, the Home Secretary is under a obligation to disclose the length of the tariff period to satisfy the requirements of retribution and deterrence to the prisoner.

As far as *proportionality* is concerned, we are back again to *The Mikado*. There has never been much quarrel about the need to grade crime according to the severity of the consequences it brings to society. But there is no exact science: the grading of crime – and even more the grading of punishment – owes much to historical accident.

Prevention and *deterrence* are very much interrelated. A sentence may be aimed at preventing the offender from committing further acts, hence the use of life sentences. Alternatively, a sentence may be aimed at deterring an offender from committing further crimes, but because the guilty person is not actually shut away for a long period the sentencers' hopes may sometimes prove to be wishful thinking. Sentencing in order to deter potential criminals as much as the offender, is a well-established, utilitarian aim. Suffice it to say, however, that from the point of view of general deterrence there is still much controversy surrounding the efficacy of punishment, both in terms of fines and imprisonment. It could be argued that the rate of crime depends far more on the risk involved, on the detection rate, than on paper penalties. Further reforms have been instituted under the Crime (Sentences) Act 1997, and also the Proceeds of Crime Act 1995.

GRADING PUNISHMENT

On what basis, though, can we grade offences themselves and therefore the punishment of those offences? The first, according to Sir Rupert Cross, is that of social danger. Crime – as opposed to an action in contract or tort – is a menace to society generally, and in that context the handler of stolen goods is more of a menace than the actual thief, since without receivers there would be fewer thieves. Furthermore, social attitudes about the nature of menace change; the blackmailer is probably regarded as a more wicked person today than before. In a similar way alarm is another element in the grading of crime – for example, burglary is treated more seriously than theft; before the Theft Act 1968 burglary could only be committed in houses at night as if to indicate in the eyes of the law the alarming nature of darkness. Cross distinguishes a third factor: it is not so much menace as social disapproval; *social disapproval* frequently is directed towards such actions as sexual offences.

The distinction, however, between crimes that register mere disapproval and those that cause menace is not as wide as may first appear; it is arguable whether the distinction is helpful at all. Further, the questions of harm done and the inherent wickedness of the crime are two other important factors that need to be taken into consideration. Hence murder is more serious than manslaughter – the harm may be the same in effect, but the degree of wickedness may be different, if, that is, wickedness depends upon actual intent. Thus although the *actus reus* (the guilty action) may be identical in several instances, the intentional wrongdoer is invariably regarded as the greater menace, as a more significant danger to society than one who is extremely reckless. The nature of the crime, and therefore the nature of the punishment, will turn upon the extent of mens rea (intent or guilty knowledge). Lastly, it must be remembered that sentencing will also depend upon such personal variables as the record of the offender, social position (*ie* will a man or woman well-known in society endure greater shame and disgrace than an ordinary person, the man on the Clapham omnibus), the offender's contrition, cooperation with the police and social circumstances, for example, a broken home or drug addiction. In the final resort there is always some room to temper 'justice' with 'mercy'.

PLEA-BARGAINING

One other factor that has come to notice in recent years is 'plea-bargaining'. In 1977 a study by John Baldwin and Michael McConville based on trials at Birmingham Crown Court showed that out of a sample of 121 defendants (all of whom had intended to plead not guilty but had changed their minds) 71 per cent had changed their plea on account of pressure of some kind, while in 35 cases (29 per cent) there had been no pressure at all. In 22 (18 per cent) the change of plea was the result of a bargain, involving either the prosecution counsel or judge or both – that is acceptance of an offer regarding length of sentence. In a further 16 cases (13 per cent) the defendants stated that their counsel had made an implicit deal with the judge. And in 48 cases (40 per cent) there had been no deal or bargain regarding the sentence but barristers had nonetheless exerted some kind of influence regarding the changing of a plea. The authors wrote:

> **Case 75, for example: the barrister said, 'I'll do a deal for you; you won't get more than two years in prison. The judge knows what's going on but we can't tell you. We have our ways of doing deals and if you plead guilty now the judge will be lenient – otherwise you will get four years. In these 'nod and a wink' bargains the defendant assumes**

> naturally that the barrister is merely echoing the thoughts of the judge
> . . . It is not correct to say that plea-bargaining does not exist in
> England to any significant degree. And our study suggests there are in
> Birmingham a very small number of judges (all of circuit judge status
> or lower) who are not unwilling to involve themselves in such bargains.
>
> That is point one. Point two concerns the influence of defence coun-
> sel on the decision to plead guilty . . . Forty-eight defendants gave as
> their reason for changing plea advice from counsel. Our investigations
> of these cases disclose evidence of questionable conduct on the part of
> a small number of barristers.

Later in the same year the Court of Appeal (with two Law Lords sitting) in the case of *R.* v. *Atkinson* ruled that plea-bargaining had no place in English law. (The trial judge had felt unable to reduce the sentence because at an earlier stage the defendant had refused to change his plea.) However, as Zander has pointed out, in the case of *R.* v. *de Haan* in 1967 the Court of Appeal had held that a confession of guilt should be reflected in the sentence awarded. The Court took a similar view about plea-bargaining in *R.* v. *Turner* in 1970 and in *R.* v. *Cain* in 1976. But it could be argued that there is some difference between actual plea-bargaining and merely tailoring a sentence to fit an act of genuine contrition. It is doubtful whether the problem of striking bargains about pleas will disappear that readily. Without some form of plea-bargaining the courts could well grind to a halt. A year after the Birmingham research the Court of Appeal felt obliged once more – in *R.* v. *Winterflood* – to draw attention to the undesirability of discussions taking place between counsel and judge in private during the course of the trial. Earlier in 1978, in *R.* v. *Llewellyn* a similar point had been stressed. Plea-bargaining was again stressed by the Court of Appeal to be unacceptable in *R.* v. *Thompson* (1995). Nearly 90 per cent of barristers and two-thirds of judges favour a formal system of plea-bargaining, a survey of Crown Court trials by Professor Michael Zander for the Royal Commission on Criminal Justice (the Runciman Report of 1993) has indicated. The study, based upon questionnaires sent to participants in every Crown Court trial in England and Wales during a two week period, also found almost universal approval for the jury system. Little evidence was found of jurors being unable to understand evidence, although judges, barristers and defence solicitors said they had been surprised by the jury's verdict in about 15 per cent of cases. The police and the Crown Prosecution Service said they were surprised by the verdict in about 25 per cent of cases. The police found half of all acquittals surprising but thought that only 8 per cent of jury decisions were inexplicable in the light of the evidence.

In 53 cases heard during the two weeks the defence barrister voiced concern that an innocent defendant had pleaded guilty either in the hope of getting a discount on sentence or a reduction in the indictment. Grossed up, this would mean that there were more than 1,000 such inconsistent pleaders in Crown Courts each year. Seventy per cent of defendants who pleaded guilty said they had committed the offence charged and a further 17 per cent said they had committed a similar offence. But 13 per cent claimed not to have committed the offence for which they had pleaded guilty. Prosecution barristers thought in 67 guilty-plea cases that the defendant would have stood a fair chance of being acquitted if he had pleaded not guilty. Grossed up, that would mean 1,700 such cases a year. In 89 cases, equivalent to well over 2,000 cases a year, the prosecution barrister thought the case was too weak and should not have been brought. Judges felt there were 116 (more than 3,000 a year) cases which were too weak.

The case of *R. v. Warth* (1991) emphasised the importance of a judge saying nothing that could appear to induce a plea of guilty. The judge should examine the defendant in open court to confirm the plea is voluntary, and the defendant should be able to withdraw his plea or appeal against conviction. The English criminal justice system accepts plea negotiation between prosecution and defence, it was held, provided it does not extend beyond seeking to know the type of sentence the judge has in mind.

IMPRISONMENT

The severest penalty is, of course, imprisonment. The deprivation of liberty involves hardship for the criminal and probably for friends, family and relations too. Adults cannot be sent to prison, however, for a first offence if they are not legally represented in court, unless they have not availed themselves of the opportunity to apply for legal aid, or if they have been refused because they could afford to pay themselves. About 21 per cent of those sentenced to prison have committed offences involving violence.

As a general rule magistrates may not commit a person to imprisonment for a period exceeding six months, even though they have been compelled since the Criminal Law Act 1977 to deal with a heavier workload. Problems do arise, however, when Magistrates' Courts are faced with an aggregate of consecutive terms for related offences. Under the Magistrates' Courts Act 1980 the total of the individual terms imposed should not exceed one year, although calculating the aggregate of terms is not always as straightforward as it may seem, not least where further terms are imposed in default of the payment of fines (as illustrated in the case of *R. v. Metropolitan Stipendiary Magistrate for South Westminster ex parte Green* (1977)). Imprisonment is, of course, refined by the system of parole which has itself been the subject of much review and change over the last 30 years or so, starting with the Criminal Justice Act 1967 which introduced parole.

PROBATION

A different form of supervision is the *probation* order. No sentence is involved in this case, but the offender is obliged to report regularly to a probation officer to account for the way he is rehabilitating himself within the community (the Probation Service is a division of the Home Office). A probation order will be for a period of between six months and three years. A number of conditions may be attached to a probation order. In 1990 the Commons Public Accounts Committee said the courts continued to send too many people to prison because of a lack of confidence in the Probation Service.

DISCHARGE

Alternatively, the court may give the offender an absolute discharge. The offender has been guilty of a wrongdoing, but because of the very minor nature of the case or possibly the special circumstances involved, the offender's copy-book is in effect not blotted at all. Or the offender may be discharged conditionally; in other words he must behave himself, for if he does not he will be brought back to court and fined or punished in some other way. (Similarly, a person who breaks a probation order may be fined or compelled to undertake community service.) The offender might be bound over to keep the peace and such binding-over may well involve his entering into his own recognisance or that of a surety. An ancient common law power, binding-over has long been recognised by various statutes. Binding-over is not restricted to an accused person; anyone appearing before the court, whether as a witness or in some other capacity, may be made the subject of such an order. The bind-over has become rather controversial of late.

Two cases illustrate the point. In *R. v. Saunders* (1980) a young woman was convicted at Bristol Crown Court of stealing a National Savings bank-book. She was a British citizen who had a boyfriend in Ulster. She indicated to the court her willingness to live in Northern Ireland and to be bound over on that condition. The court ordered her bound over in her own recognisance of £50 and to come up for judgment unless she proceeded to Ulster and stayed outside England and Wales for a period of three years. Six months later she returned to Wales. On her arrest the court then had the power to sentence her for theft or to order forfeiture of her £50 or both. In 1982, Croydon Crown Court decided to bind over a black youth convicted of theft on the condition that he went to Jamaica for five years; *R. v. Williams (Carl)*. But the Court of Appeal quashed the order. It made it clear that the power to send a person to another country should be used only seldomly, that the accused had to consent freely, and that he had to be sent to a country of which he was a citizen or where he lived most of the time or whose government was willing to admit the accused for the sake of his well-being.

The court may defer passing sentence if the offence in question carries a potential maximum imprisonment of not more than six months; in other words the sentence may be postponed, a variation on suspended sentences except that in those cases sentence is actually passed although not put into operation.

In *R. v. George* (1984) the Court of Appeal laid down the following guidelines as to when a deferred sentence should be passed:

1 the purpose of deferment is to enable the court to take into account the defendant's conduct after conviction or any change in his circumstances;

2 in many cases a short probation order may be preferable to a deferred sentence. A deferment is, however, more appropriate where the conduct required of the defendant is not sufficiently specific to be made the subject of a condition imposed as part of a probation order;

3 the court should make clear to the defendant (ideally in writing) the purpose of deferring sentence and the conduct expected of him during deferment. The court should keep a careful note of these matters;

4 at the expiration of the period of deferment the sentencing court should determine if the defendant has substantially conformed with the expectations of the deferring court. If he has, the defendant may legitimately expect that an immediate custodial sentence will not be imposed. If he has not, the court should state with precision in what respects he has failed.

A further variation within non-custodial sentencing is that of the Community Service Order (CSO). The court may order any offender over the age of 16 to undertake specific, unpaid work that will be of benefit to the community over a period of 12 months, and for a minimum of 40 hours and a maximum of 240. The Criminal Justice Act 1982 amended the Powers of Criminal Courts Act 1973 by reducing the minimum age from 17 to 16. The supervision of such orders is undertaken by the Probation Service and any breach of the order by the offender will make him liable to fines or other punishments. CSOs are comparatively cheap to administer and also genuinely rehabilitative.

FINES

Of course, the most common form of non-custodial punishment is that of monetary deprivation – the fine. The maximum that a court may impose is frequently laid down by statute and a number of limits were substantially revised by the Criminal Law Act 1977. Too many different maxima may lead to anomalies and injustice. It is not surprising, therefore, that the Criminal Justice Act 1982 rationalised the system of fines. A 'standard scale' was introduced: the scale consists of five levels.

The courts may attach a number of conditions to fines – for example, the offender may be required to have a regular sum deducted from his weekly or monthly earnings; he may be required to be supervised in this connection by a probation officer. The offender may also be made the subject of a compensation order (for injury or damage suffered by another person as a result of the wrongdoing) or a restoration order (returning stolen goods or goods bought out of the proceeds of stolen property) or a criminal bankruptcy where others can be shown to have suffered substantial losses. Since the Criminal Justice Act 1982 compensation orders may be made in their own right, rather than in addition to some other form of punishment. The

Criminal Justice Act 1988 took this a stage further, by strengthening the powers to make compensation orders under the Powers of Criminal Courts Act 1973 (s.35), as amended by s.67 of the Criminal Justice Act 1982. The 1988 Act (s.104) requires the court, when sentencing, to give reasons for not making an award in cases which involve personal injury, loss or damage; it also enables a compensation order to be made in favour of the relative of a deceased person to the extent of funeral expenses and the standard bereavement award. Note should also be made here of the fact that since 1964 the Criminal Injuries Compensation Board has given discretionary awards to victims of criminal violence. The government of the day established the body and it is financed with money voted by Parliament. It is now statute based, since the passing of the Criminal Justice Act 1988 and the Criminal Injuries Compensation Scheme Act 1995.

YOUNG OFFENDERS

A 'young offender' strictly means any person under the age of 21, although for many purposes here it is the age of 18 that applies. A 'child' is a person under 14 and a 'young person' between 14 and 18. A 'juvenile' is anyone under the age of 18 (until 1992 it was 17). The Criminal Justice Act 1982 introduced new procedures for dealing with young offenders. The normal rule is that no such individual may be sent to prison, as the Act says, 'for any reason'. But there are exceptions. The court must give reasons in open court as to why it was inappropriate to impose a non-custodial sentence. In addition, any court must first normally obtain a social enquiry report in respect of a young offender – the 1982 Act defined such a report as one made 'by a probation officer or by a social worker of a local authority social services department' about the person in question and his circumstances.

The Criminal Justice Act 1991 (and subsequent legislation) introduced further significant reforms in sentencing, in respect of both young and adult offenders. Amongst other things the Juvenile Court was replaced by the Youth Court. Part I of the Criminal Justice and Public Order Act 1994 introduced new procedures for dealing with young offenders.

6.2   The nature of criminal law

A crime is an offence against the whole of society; it is a wrongful act or omission, serious enough for the wrongdoer to be punished by the rest of the community. It has already been observed that the civil law is concerned with wrongful acts or omissions too. However, there the object is not to punish, but rather to compensate the aggrieved person for the loss he has suffered. Of course, a tortious or contractual wrong in civil law is of interest to society at large; society lays down a framework of legal codes and within that framework the individuals must settle their disputes. Thus it is customary to talk of a 'civil wrong' rather than a 'civil offence'. The word 'offence' invariably means a crime, although sometimes just to make it absolutely clear the phrase 'criminal offence' is used instead. A crime is also a 'wrong' in the broadest sense, but it is simpler and easier to think of an 'offence' as a criminal act or omission and a 'wrong' as a civil one. Therein lies another problem, however: certain legal problems may be both criminal and civil in nature. Indeed the same act may be not only criminal but also doubly civil, that is a tort and a breach of contract. Common examples of wrongs which are both civil and criminal are assault or battery (both offences against the person) or motoring accidents which will usually constitute a criminal offence and may well give rise to a civil action in negligence. The two leading branches of the civil law – tort and contract – are considered in Chapters 8 and 9.

The dividing line between criminal offences and civil wrongs is not always easy to draw. Nowadays, however, it is Parliament which decides what constitutes a crime; most criminal law is now derived from one or more statutes. Obviously an offence such as murder must be a crime, but it is not always clear whether other matters, such as euthanasia, drug abuse and sexual 'deviation', should be; the controversies in recent years surrounding cannabis and homosexuality underline the point. Similarly, is it right to classify a parking 'offence' as a crime? It is a long way removed from murder; most members of the public would hardly regard such an activity as a 'true' crime. Nonetheless there would be real practical difficulties in treating misuse of drugs and parking on yellow lines as merely civil wrongs. For example, parking on a yellow line might not affect an individual alone, in the civil sense, unless an obstruction was clearly caused, like the blocking of a person's driveway. Rather it is for the benefit of the public generally to have streets uncongested by traffic. The point at issue is not whether certain activities should be regarded as civil rather than criminal offences but whether they should be regarded as unlawful in any sense.

Again, smoking cannabis, especially in private, could hardly be deemed as directly harming a second individual, unless that individual was persuaded to do the same or suffered from the effects of being close to the fumes. Yet society has decided that not only is smoking cannabis a bad example to set others, but also it is necessary to protect the individual from self-inflicted misfortune. In other words much of the criminal code will be based upon a sense of paternalism: others know what is best for the individual; the individual must be looked after and protected from his or her own potential foolishness. But the greater the degree of paternalism, the more may that society be described as moving away from liberalism and towards autocracy. In any case another point for not decriminalising certain activities is that civil actions for the individual may be extremely expensive. Thus some 'grey' areas, such as the breach of planning laws or health and safety legislation, are kept within the province of crime. Criminal law, therefore, in the widest sense covers a multitude of activities and sins – from murder, rape, arson, theft and damage to property to the less overtly criminal matters of careless motoring, pollution, selling unfit food or serving alcohol to a teenager. Not all of these criminal rules can be covered here, but the major part of substantive crime is – the most recognisable criminal acts are examined in detail in the following sections.

CRIME AND CIVIL WRONGS

If, however, there are practical difficulties in regarding some activities as civil wrongs rather than criminal offences, equally there are real problems in making certain apparently reprehensible actions criminal in the first place. For instance, a doctor who performs an operation carelessly – as illustrated in the *Lim Poh Choo* case at the very beginning – is not guilty of a crime but merely of civil negligence. However horrible the results of a negligent action may be, the important consideration is that the doctor or other wrongdoer did not *intend* to commit harm. Moreover, the very concept of negligence is so broad – it encompasses very minor wrongs as well as those that bring about injury on a grand scale, such as the thalidomide tragedy – that it makes any criminal definition difficult. In addition, some actions may be morally repulsive but not unlawful in either the civil or the criminal sense. For example, telling lies is not unlawful in itself. The effect of telling lies is not precisely measurable and it is too commonplace to be made a wrong. If it were a crime the whole world would be behind bars; if it were a civil wrong we should all be continually compensating each other. All that society can do is to strive to improve general standards of conduct and to outlaw specific instances of lying – such as criminal fraud and civil deceit.

As for the classification of crime the Criminal Law Act 1967, as seen earlier, introduced the concept of 'arrestable' and 'non-arrestable' offences, thus abolishing the old distinction between felonies (serious crime) and misdemeanours (minor offences). An arrestable offence is one for which no specific arrest warrant is required: a police officer can arrest without a magistrate's warrant for a suspected crime carrying a maximum of five years' imprisonment or more or where the penalty is fixed by law, as in the case of murder (Murder (Abolition of Death Penalty) Act 1965), treason (Treason Act 1814) and piracy with violence (Piracy Act 1837). In fact the law of treason was unaffected by the Criminal Law Act and it therefore remains a separate category in its own right.

Another way of classification, as again we have seen earlier, is by the manner of trial. Offences may be indictable, summary or triable either way. Indictable offences are those tried by a jury in the Crown Court; summary offences are dealt with by the Magistrates' Court. Indictable offences therefore may be generally regarded as serious and summary cases as less serious or minor.

Classification may also be made according to source, in other words common law or statutory crime.

ACTUS REUS AND MENS REA

Two essential concepts in the operation of the criminal law are those of *actus reus* and *mens rea*. A conviction cannot be secured unless it is shown that both factors were present. *Actus reus* means the 'guilty action': in other words the accused must be shown to have committed an act or omission which is criminal in nature; it is not sufficient to show that he has merely committed an act which appears to be wrongful. Secondly, it must also be shown that he intended to commit an offence – the *mens rea* or 'guilty mind'. Intent or intention do, however, carry certain problems of definition: it may not always be a matter of deliberate intention – inattention, recklessness or some other state of mind will suffice to constitute the *mens rea*. Thus if a person is charged with murder but the jury is not convinced beyond reasonable doubt that the death was not caused accidentally, then the accused must be acquitted: the intention to kill was not present. A charge of manslaughter, though, might be a different matter. Normally there can be no crime where either the *actus reus* or *mens rea* is absent; this rule is applied without exception in respect of the *actus reus*, but it can be qualified in the case of *mens rea*. The *actus reus* is, approximately, the physical element of the crime, the *mens rea* the mental element, as seen in R. v. *White* (1910), where the accused put potassium cyanide into his mother's drink; but his mother died from a heart attack, not from the poison, although the glass was partly empty. There was no completed *actus reus* in respect of murder, although *mens rea* could be held to have existed: the *actus reus* may have been partial but was certainly not total. Moreover, there can be no crime committed if the act is not done voluntarily; such a defence is known as automatism. In other words there is a breakdown in the apparent connection between the act committed and the intention to commit it. Insanity – as a 'disease of the mind' – would be one such example; others are sudden illness – for example, a man has a heart attack while driving a car and as a result crashes into another vehicle, as underlined in *Hill* v. *Baxter* (1958). The *mens rea* is absent, although the *actus reus* appears to have taken place. It can, however, be argued that voluntariness is technically part of the *actus reus* rather than the *mens rea*.

The question of sufficient *mens rea*, as seen in *Kingston* (1994), was also of note in *Yip Chiu-Cheung* v. R. (1994). In the former case the House of Lords emphasised that involuntary intoxication is a defence if, and only if, the defendant is so drunk or drugged that he does not know what he is doing; here the Lords overturned an unreported decision of the Court of Appeal. In *Yip* the Privy Council said that conspiracy can be committed even where one of the parties is an undercover agent.

Usually a crime will be a positive act, but an *actus reus* may on occasion simply be an omission, or a failure to perform a duty. For example, in R. v. *Pittwood* (1902) a railway-crossing keeper forgot to shut the gate and went to lunch. A train struck a cart and the gate-keeper was convicted of manslaughter. In R. v. *Gibbins and Proctor* (1918) a child was denied food and the child's father and the woman with whom he was living were found guilty of murder; the failure to look after a child adequately is an offence under the Children and Young Persons Act 1933.

Intention

Of the two terms, *actus reus* and *mens rea*, the latter is the more difficult concept. Usually the most common definition of *mens rea* is 'guilty intention', but it may mean other things, according to the particular circumstances of the *actus*. Intention may be said to be primary, direct or dominant on the one hand or secondary, oblique or tangential on the other. For example, in *Hyam* v. *DPP* (1975) the intention of the accused was to frighten another woman into leaving the neighbourhood in Coventry. In fact by setting fire to the building she had killed the woman's children. It was decided that the accused knew that it was very probable that deaths or injury would result from the fire and therefore it was right to convict of murder, even if the intention to do so had not been the dominant one in respect of the wrongful act. The difficulty, however, for the judge in directing the jury is to decide whether an oblique intention is always sufficient to constitute *mens rea* as underlined in *R.* v. *Mohan* (1976) and *R.* v. *Belfon* (1976) – the cases involved wanton driving and wounding with intent respectively.

How oblique can 'oblique' be? In *Hyam* v. *DPP* (and it should be emphasised that *Hyam*, a controversial case, was decided by a bare majority) Lord Hailsham leaned towards adopting the relatively narrow test of 'moral certainty'.

Hyam is now regarded as 'bad' law, and the courts seem as far as ever from providing watertight definitions of the key concepts of 'intention' and 'recklessness'. This leaves an important part of the criminal law in an unsatisfactory state, although the Law Commission is waiting in the wings with a solution.

In his speech, however, Lord Dilhorne appeared to take a more circumspect but wider view, that foresight of probability was by itself sufficient to constitute an oblique intention in this context. He observed:

> **A man may do an act with a number of intentions. If he does it deliberately and intentionally, knowing that when he does it it is highly probable that grievous bodily harm will result, I think most people would say and be justified in saying that whatever other intentions he may have had as well, he at least intended grievous bodily harm.**

Later on, Lord Diplock, who was one of the dissenting judges in *Hyam*, commented in *Whitehouse* v. *Lemon*:

> **When Stephen (*History of the Criminal Law of England*) was writing in 1883, he did not then regard it as settled law that, where intention to produce a particular result was a necessary element of an offence, no distinction was to be drawn in law between the state of mind of one who did an act because he desired it to produce that particular result and the state of mind of one who, when he did the act, was aware that it was likely to produce that result but was prepared to take the risk that it might do so, in order to achieve some other purpose which provided his motive for doing what he did. It is by now well-settled law that both states of mind constitute 'intention' in the sense in which that expression is used in the definition of a crime whether at common law or in a statute. Any doubts on this matter were finally laid to rest by the decision of this House in *R.* v. *Hyam*.**

Any such hopes quickly proved false, for along came *Moloney* and *Hancock*, which are discussed further under the section on murder. If there is intention then the *actus reus* has been committed, as illustrated in *R. v. Kingston* (1995), where a man with paedophiliac tendencies was under the influence of secretly administered drugs.

Recklessness

Another form of *mens rea* is that of recklessness. The offender may not intend what happens, or rather the result of what he does, but he is extremely careless – he is irresponsible to the point of recklessness, even if he does not foresee that some harmful result of his action is probable or likely. Thus the wider the concept of oblique intention is drawn, the closer it will approximate to recklessness, as perhaps suggested by their Lordships' remarks above. Recklessness may be described as subjective or objective. Subjective recklessness means that the offender has consciously undertaken an unjustified risk: he knows harm may result although it is not necessarily probable or likely; if it were it might constitute oblique intention in the broadest sense.

Objective recklessness means the taking of an unjustified risk the consequences of which he is unaware or does not foresee but ought to have. Objective recklessness may be negligence in this context. It is important to stress that the risk must be unjustified – knowledge of the risk alone does not necessarily amount to recklessness. For instance, if a man waves a gun at a person with the object of frightening him and the gun goes off injuring or killing that person, he may be judged as obliquely intending to cause physical harm if he knew it was loaded; if he did not know it was loaded but did not bother to check, then he would probably be judged as having been criminally reckless. In both cases the waving of a gun without being sure that it is unloaded is an unjustified risk; on the other hand the risk may be known but justifiably taken in order to assist the other person, a third person or the risk-taker himself. For example, if A. waved a gun, which turned out to be loaded, in order to deter C. from attacking B. but in the excitement he pulled the trigger and shot B., it might well be that there was insufficient recklessness to constitute *mens rea*.

In *R. v. Lawrence* Lord Diplock commented:

> I turn now to the *mens rea*. My task is greatly simplified by what has already been said about the concept of recklessness in criminal law in *R. v. Caldwell*. Warning was there given against adopting the simplistic approach of treating all problems of criminal liability as soluble by classifying the test of liability as being either 'subjective' or 'objective'. Recklessness on the part of the doer of an act does presuppose that there is something in the circumstances that would have drawn the attention of an ordinary prudent individual to the possibility that his act was capable of causing the kind of serious harmful consequences that the section which creates the offence was intended to prevent, and that the risk of those harmful consequences occurring was not so slight that an ordinary prudent indivdual would feel justified in treating them

as negligible. It is only when this is so that the doer of the act is acting 'recklessly' if, before doing the act, he either fails to give any thought to the possibility of there being any such risk or, having recognized that there was such risk, he nevertheless goes on to do it.

Lawrence and *Caldwell*

In *Cunningham* (1957) a man inadvertently – in the process of robbing a gas meter – poisoned his girlfriend. He did not foresee the consequences of his action. In *Caldwell* (1982) the accused started a fire in a hotel whose proprietor he disliked. He was charged with arson under the Criminal Damage Act 1971, which under s.1(1) provides that 'a person who without lawful excuse destroys or damages any property belonging to another intending to destroy or damage any such property or being reckless as to whether any such property would be destroyed or damaged shall be guilty of an offence'. Lord Diplock, in the House of Lords, said that a person was guilty under the Act if:

(1) he does an act which in fact creates an obvious risk that property will be destroyed or damaged and

(2) when he does the act he either *has not given any thought to the possibility of there being any such risk* or has recognised that there was some risk involved and has nonetheless gone on to do it.

The first part of the second limb, italics added here, appeared to move the concept of recklessness towards an objective test, in other words negligence, although it can be argued that negligence, unlike pure Caldwell-type recklessness, includes averting to the *possibility* of risk, but unreasonably concluding the risk does not exist.

Caldwell was followed in Lawrence (1982), a reckless driving case – *Cunningham*-type recklessness thus receded into the legal distance. The decisions in Caldwell and Lawrence were controversial to say the least, and further consideration will be given to these cases below.

In *R.* v. *R.* (1984), an arson case, the Court of Appeal held that it was not obliged to decide that the ordinary prudent man in cases of recklessness was one who shared the age, sex and other such characteristics which would affect his recognition of risk, but it had to take the same line as the Divisional Court in *Elliott* v. *C.* (1983) in view of the definition of recklessness in *Lawrence* and the fact that the Lords had refused leave to appeal in *Elliott* (which was followed in *Cole* in 1994), where a girl of 14 of limited intelligence, who had been out all night, ignited white spirit on a carpet, burning down a garden shed, and was convicted of arson.

Negligence

If negligence is to constitute *mens rea* then it must be shown that the consequence of an action must have been reasonably foreseen – the test is what in those circumstances would the reasonable man have done or what avoiding action, if any, might he have taken? Negligence in *mens rea* usually relates to manslaughter, although as will be seen it is an important and broad concept in the civil law of tort. Nonetheless, negligence as *mens rea* has been the subject of some controversy for both the legal profession and academic writers; some object to negligence being regarded as part of *mens rea* at all, although offences under the Road Traffic Act 1988 turn upon objective standards of care, and therefore, conversely, negligence. Other Acts where negligence is a relevant consideration are the Trade Descriptions Act 1968 and the Misuse of Drugs Act 1971.

Basic intent, mistake and other terminology

Other terminology is employed in *mens rea*, and sometimes confusingly so. For example, judges often refer to 'basic intent'. This is a broad phrase; in *DPP.* v. *Morgan* Lord Simon said: 'By 'crimes of basic intent'. I mean those crimes whose definition expresses (or, more often implies) a *mens rea* which does not go beyond the *actus reus*.' In other words 'basic intent' means recklessness or intention: it is 'basic *mens rea*'. The phrase 'further (or ulterior) intention' is employed to describe a consequence which does not relate directly to the *actus reus* concerned. Thus it is a wrong, invariably a civil one, to trespass, but if a person trespasses with the intention of stealing then he is guilty of the crime of burglary; it is unlikely that it is a crime to trespass in itself, except in very specific instances, for trespass by itself is normally a civil wrong only. Usually ulterior intention means intention; recklessness, at least in the *Cunningham* sense, here will not suffice. In *DPP.* v. *Luft* (1976) the accused had committed unauthorised expenditure in order to prevent a candidate for the National Front from being elected; logically therefore the ulterior intention was to improve the chances of any of the other candidates even if the wrongdoer was indifferent as to which would be successful.

However, it should also be noted that it is not always necessary to prove *mens rea* as well as *actus reus*. In this case the crime is one of strict liability which is discussed below. And indeed, the court may on occasion find proof of *mens rea* for a less serious offence sufficient for that with which the accused is charged. This is most notable in the cases of murder and grievous bodily harm.

Furthermore, if the accused makes a mistake, if what he does is unintentional with regard to that particular victim, there is usually still sufficient *mens rea* to warrant a conviction. In *The Queen* v. *Latimer* (1886) L., a soldier, was involved in a pub quarrel. He intended to hit E. with his belt, but in the reflex from hitting E. the belt hit and severely wounded the face of R. who was standing near to E. L. was convicted of maliciously wounding R. This aspect of *mens rea* is sometimes known as the doctrine of 'unforeseen victim or mode' or 'transferred malice'. The doctrine of transferred malice was reemphasised in *Attorney-General's Reference (No 3 of 1994)* (1996). But the doctrine is limited: it cannot operate where the *actus reus* and *mens rea* do not coincide, that is both *actus* and *mens* must relate to the same crime. It is not usual for a conviction to be obtained if a person who commits an action which results in harm, the *actus reus*, can be shown to have a *mens rea* in respect of a different crime, except where the *mens rea* is broad, that is recklessness rather than deliberate intention is proved. In *R. v. Pembliton* (1874) P. was fighting in the street outside a pub. A crowd of 40-50 people gathered. He broke a pane of glass, but he was not convicted of malicious damage, since his real intention had been to injure the others in the fight: the stone he had thrown was aimed at them, not at the window. If, however, the jury had found him guilty of recklessness, then the charge would have been proved. Lord Coleridge said:

> **If the jury had found that the prisoner had been guilty of throwing the stone recklessly, knowing that there was a window near which it might probably hit, I should have been disposed to interfere with the conviction, yet, as they have found that he threw the stone at the people he had been fighting with intending to strike them and not intending to break the window, I think that the conviction must be quashed.**

In *Latimer* the court distinguished *Pembliton* on the grounds that in the latter case there was no intention to damage any property at all. Mistake here is in the accidental sense, that is an error of judgement.

The case of *R. v. Mitchell* (1983) illustrated the problem of the 'unforeseen victim'. Here the appellant forced himself into a Post Office queue. He then hit a man who fell against an 89 year-old woman who broke her femur. She underwent an operation but died. The Court of Appeal said that in respect of a charge of manslaughter an unlawful and dangerous act did not have to be aimed at the deceased.

Mistake

At common law it has long been a rule that a reasonable and honest belief in circumstances which, if true, would have made the act with which the accused is charged an innocent one, does constitute a good defence. It is summed up by the Latin maxim, *actus non facit reum, nisi mens sit rea* (a person does not commit an unlawful act unless his state of mind is guilty). The rule, a controversial one, is sometimes referred to as the rule in *R. v. Tolson* (1889); more recently it has been given approval by the House of Lords in *Sweet* v. *Parsley* (1970). This type of mistake is concerned with law or fact.

In *R. v. Taaffe* (1984) the House of Lords held that where the defendant had believed he was not smuggling cannabis but currency, the defendant's mistake of law could not convert the importation of currency into a criminal offence when such currency was not the subject of any prohibition. (The defendant drove a car into the green lane of the Sheerness ferry terminal and said there was nothing to declare. The car was searched, and in the spare tyre were found five packages containing cannabis resin. The defendant was then searched, and a further three packages were found strapped to his back and under his clothing.) The House of Lords said that the principle that a man must be judged on the facts as he believed them to be was an accepted principle of the criminal law when the state of man's mind and his knowledge were ingredients of the offence with which he was charged.

Can, however, a distinction be made between a mistake of law and a mistake of fact? Mistake or ignorance of the law is generally no defence (*ignorantia juris non excusat*). A reasonable person, a person of discretion should be familiar with the legal code; that was how William Blackstone saw it in the eighteenth century. For John Austin, another leading legal philosopher, in the nineteenth century, the problem could be approached from the opposite direction, negatively – it was simply hard to disprove ignorance. Foreign visitors are no more exempt from the rule than British citizens. But in other countries, such as Norway, ignorance of the law is a defence. J. C. Smith and Brian Hogan have said: 'Such rules seem to have much to commend them, compared with the rigid and uncompromising attitude of English law. They seek to relate guilt to moral responsibility in a way which our rule does not.' One important exception is provided by the Statutory Instruments Act 1946: it is a defence to argue that the relevant piece of delegated legislation was not published at the time the 'offence' was committed, unless the government had taken reasonable steps to bring it to the notice of the public or to that of persons likely to be affected by it.

A mistake of fact

A mistake of fact is, though, a defence; it may point to an absence of the requisite *mens rea*. Mistake of fact and mistake of law may, however, not always be easily distinguished. In *DPP* v. *Morgan* (1976) the House of Lords held that it was a defence in rape to argue that it was honestly if mistakenly believed that consent to sexual intercourse had been given, the *mens rea* for rape demanding proof of either direct intention or recklessness but not mere negligence. Indeed in those crimes where negligence is sufficient to constitute *mens rea* then the mistake must be shown to be a reasonable one if liability is to be avoided, whereas the test of reasonableness is not a relevant consideration in respect of recklessness and intention, including, it would appear, *Caldwell*-type or objective recklessness. The problems of mistake and reasonableness were also illustrated in *Albert* v. *Lavin* (1982), a case referred to earlier.

In *R.* v. *Smith (David)* (1974) a genuine but mistaken belief as to the ownership of damaged property (the accused believed it to be his) was held to be a defence. In contrast, in bigamy it is a defence to show honest *and* reasonable belief that there are no restrictions on the availability to marry: if X. thinks R., his wife, was lost at sea, for example, and he marries P., then he may not be guilty of bigamy if R., it later transpires, was rescued after all. The cases of *R.* v. *Tolson* and *R.* v. *Gould (No 2)* (1968) have illustrated this dilemma. Similar defences are available in theft and fraud; for instance, if the accused genuinely believed he had the right to take property from another person, then that may act as a defence. Mistake as to the civil law may help to establish a defence in criminal law, a point underlined in the *Smith* case. Bad professional advice, however, as to a particular criminal rule will not serve as a defence, except in so far as the sentence imposed may be a light one; the accused, of course, would still have the right to sue his adviser, such as a solicitor, for civil negligence.

Malice

The word 'maliciously' raises certain difficulties in relation to *mens rea* and *actus reus*. So, too, do other words, like 'knowingly', 'motive' and 'wilfully'. Motive is not the same as intention, a matter that has also been stressed in the law of tort. A man intends to steal and does so, but the motive for his theft is hunger or starvation. Motive is thus an irrelevant consideration in crime: the fact that the person who steals from a millionaire is poor is not to be taken into account; if it were the whole basis of the criminal code would change overnight. In the civil law of tort malice in the sense of improper motive is generally irrelevant as will be discussed in Chapter 8; it is not the motive that matters, but the harm caused. Malice might be described as *secondary* intention.

The word 'maliciously', like 'knowingly' and to a lesser extent 'wilfully', is to be found in various statutes. It no longer means 'wickedly' but is probably best interpreted as denoting recklessness or intention, while 'wilfully' points to intention alone − 'wilfully' most frequently occurs in respect of the wilful obstruction of the police in the exercise of their duties. Professor J. A. Andrews has said this about the word 'wilful'.

> It should be observed that in civil cases the word most frequently appears adjectively, qualifying liability for neglect, default or misconduct. In the criminal law the adverb 'wilfully' is used much more frequently than the adjectival form 'wilful'. One of the most important sections in which it is used is section 1 of the Children and Young Persons Act 1933 which makes it an offence where someone having the care of a child or young person under the age of sixteen 'wilfully assaults, ill-treats, neglects, abandons or exposes him . . . in a manner likely to cause him unnecessary suffering or injury to health'. It is only recently that the House of Lords has had the opportunity to review the expression 'wilfully neglects' in the criminal law and to bring its meaning into line with that which has prevailed in the civil law. [In *R. v. Sheppard* Lord Diplock] defined the phrase 'wilful neglect' as importing the need to establish recklessness − itself an unfortunately ambiguous word in the criminal law and one to which Lord Diplock chose to give a different meaning again within a few months in *R. v. Caldwell* − and not simply the need to show negligence as defined in the civil law. Although *R. v. Sheppard* can be taken to have resolved the meaning of 'wilful' and 'wilfully' in the context of omission, the case is not necessarily authority on the interpretation of the word when associated with positive conduct. Indeed this point was made by Lord Diplock.

'Knowingly' is frequently used in Acts of Parliament. It has been suggested by Lord Devlin in *Roper* v. *Taylor's Central Garages (Exeter) Ltd* (1951) as merely expressing what is normally implied. It may also be interpreted, he said, in three senses. The most obvious way is actual knowlege: the accused intended something to happen (the deliberate intention of *mens rea*). Second degree knowledge is where the wrongdoer has shut his eyes to the problem, where he deliberately fails to make further enquiries, where he appears not to care in the slightest about the consequences of the act. This state of mind is sometimes called 'wilful blindness', or connivance: it is in effect recklessness. Third degree knowledge, sometimes known as constructive knowledge, is simple ignorance, carelessness in the sense of not knowing (but he ought to have known) rather than pretending that he is unaware of the risk; it is innocent rather than deliberate failure to make enquiries. Constructive knowledge is essentially negligence and therefore rarely part of the criminal law.

Statutory terms

Acts of Parliament also use other words; three fairly common ones are 'permitting', 'suffering' and 'allowing', which are self-explanatory and may be taken to mean one and the same thing. The accused may permit (or suffer or allow) his premises to be used for smoking cannabis (*R*. v. *Souter* (1971)) or his vehicle to be used despite faulty brakes (*Fransman* v. *Sexton* (1965)). In the *Souter* case the accused put up a notice saying that the police would be called if any illegal drugs were found in his house, although drug addicts were allowed to use his living-room. The Court of Appeal held that 'permit' meant actual knowledge that the premises were being used for smoking cannabis or shutting his eyes to the obvious or not caring whether such smoking was taking place. In the *Sexton* case the High Court held that knowledge was an essential part of 'permitting'; mere negligence would not suffice. Recklessly sending out a faulty car or not caring what would happen would impute knowledge.

'Fraudulently' and 'corruptly' are also important words used in Acts; they have specific meanings. Corruption will be noted later, under obscenity. The concept also occurs in relation to election malpractices and the bribery and corruption of public officials and elected representatives (for example, the Public Bodies Corrupt Practices Act 1889 and the Prevention of Corruption Acts 1906 and 1916). Whether 'possession' is sufficient to establish *mens rea* is debatable – the word is frequently used in relation to having a measure of physical control over prohibited drugs (Misuse of Drugs Act 1971). The word 'causing' or 'causes' is another statutory favourite; here there is requirement of proof of a positive act ('permission' does not require such proof). It usually relates to the responsibility of actions by third parties (vicarious liability is discussed in more detail below). In *F. J. H. Wrothwell Ltd* v. *Yorkshire Water Authority* (1983) it was held the word 'cause' was a simple English word and did not become anything different when used in a statute. Here the defendant company had breached the Rivers (Prevention of Pollution) Act 1975. The word 'cause' was to be given its ordinary, common sense meaning and any attempt to introduce refinements was to be deprecated, the Court of Appeal said; if other factors, such as the laws of nature or Acts of God were to be taken into account, that was part of the exercise of common sense and it was unwise to build them into propositions of law, for each case depended on its own facts. The Law Commission in 1978 and 1985 recommended statutory definition of such terms as knowledge, intention and recklessness, and it is submitted that were this to occur the scope for the confusing and imprecise use of these words would be greatly reduced. But it is unlikely that Parliament will act in the foreseeable future.

Coincidence

Time is an important factor in *mens rea* and *actus reus*: there should be coincidence or contemporaneity between the two. A long gap between *mens rea* and *actus reus* may not lead to a conviction. This is not always easy for the court to decide, as illustrated in *R. v. Church* (1966) where in a fight C., having knocked N. unconscious and believing her to be dead, threw her into the river. In fact N. was not dead but nonetheless drowned. It appeared that a fight had taken place as a result of N.'s taunting of C on account of his sexual failure with her in his van.

In *R. v. Le Brun* (1991) D. had an argument with his wife in the street and hit her; he then attempted to move her but dropped her; she died. *R. v. Church* was applied. In *R. v. Cheshire* (1991) it was held that in respect of subsequent medical negligence, the negligent treatment had to be independent of D.'s acts for the chain of causation to collapse.

Before passing on to 'Burden of proof', further consideration is given to the special problems raised by *Caldwell/Lawrence*.

Criticisms of *Lawrence/Caldwell*

The decisions of the House of Lords in *Lawrence* and *Caldwell* have hardly been greeted with universal approval by academic commentators since 1981. The term 'recklessness' is not one of fine legal art. For example, in *R. v. Sheppard* Lord Diplock defined 'wilful neglect', of a child, as one denoting the need to establish recklessness, whereas in *Caldwell* his Lordship, according to Professor Andrews, used 'recklessness' in a different way.

The principal criticism of the *Caldwell/Lawrence* judgments, and of Lord Diplock in particular, is that the result has been to widen the meaning of recklessness, and despite what Lord Diplock said, to endow it with an objective interpretation, thus taking the term close to 'negligence'. The consequence is a harsh one, for if recklessness is to mean negligence in the criminal law, undoubtedly more defendants will be convicted. Indeed, the less *mens rea* or a guilty state of mind is to be imported into an offence, the more is the defendant strictly, or absolutely, liable for his 'misdeeds'. Of course, both terms, negligence and recklessness, and especially the former, may be interpreted differently in civil and criminal law. In general terms it may be fairly said that recklessness in criminal law means that the defendant deliberately pursues a course of action which probably (rather than possibly) will create serious and harmful consequences; the defendant may or may not be aware of the consequences of his action, or possibly omission, the point being that he has pressed on regardless – he could not care less, he is recklessly careless. Negligence means, however, that he was careless in an accidental sense, yet the consequences are still sufficiently grave, if not as serious or harmful as the consequences of recklessness, to impose liability. Given all the circumstances, the defendant in negligence does little more than his incompetent best, but the chances are he would have stopped what he was doing if he fully appreciated the consequences of his action or omission. Omission, here, will more likely constitute negligence rather than recklessness. In civil law we might refer to 'mere negligence', implying that the root of the defendant's action is more providential than criminal negligence, that the defendant, while still careless, and perhaps seriously so, to the point of being reckless, has nonetheless not canvassed, or been wilfully blind to, the *probability* of harm, but only the *possibility* of damage, or if he was not aware of the possibility of damage, he should have been according to the lights of the 'reasonable man', providing that the degree of possible damage is not too far removed from the original stage of foreseeability (the test of remoteness of damage in tort). Moreover, the concepts of recklessness and negligence are, of course, testing different 'wrongs' or 'offences' in the civil and criminal branches of law.

In criminal law the critics have not minced their words regarding *Caldwell/Lawrence* recklessness. In *Lawrence (Stephen)* the defendant while driving a motor cycle along an urban street after nightfall collided with and killed a pedestrian. In *Caldwell* the defendant set fire by night to a residential hotel where he had been employed and against the proprietor of which he bore a grudge. In the latter case the certified question of law was whether evidence of self-induced intoxication was a relevant defence under s.1(2) of the Criminal Damage Act 1971. Professor J. C. Smith said: 'The House of Lords has a dismal record in criminal cases. All too often their Lordships' decisions have to be reversed by legislation . . . The present decision [*Caldwell*] could well be another. Can we really afford the House of Lords as an appellate criminal court?'

What then is the nature of the 'new recklessness', and is it limited merely to cases with which *Caldwell* and *Lawrence* were concerned, that is statutory recklessness in respect of the Criminal Damage Act 1971 and the Road Traffic Act 1972? Does it, for instance, extend to rape and the defence of mistake (as in *Morgan*)? It should be noted that the Road Traffic Act 1991 has re-introduced, by s.1, the offence of dangerous driving and under s.3 creates the offence of causing death by careless driving when under the influence of drink or drugs. 'Reckless driving' was abolished under the 1991 Act.

L. H. Leigh and J. Temkin have argued that the House of Lords has attempted to install a regime of *mens rea* based upon concepts of moral wickedness, subjective in some respects, objective in others, difficult to apply consistently and for that reason alone more objectionable than the definition which it has partially replaced.

> **In reaching his formulation of the mental state, Lord Diplock had first to discard what had become, in both reported cases and academic writings, the accepted test of recklessness, namely, whether the accused foresaw the risk and took it unjustifiably. In doing so, his Lordship rejected the argument that the formulation of recklessness in *Cunningham* was intended to be exhaustive. Lord Diplock does not deny that malice, the word used in the Malicious Damage Act 1861,**

> imports recklessness, Rather, he treats recklessness as having an ambit
> which goes from cases of actual foresight to cases of particularly
> wrongful inadvertence, and treats malice as referring only to that
> aspect of recklessness which requires advertence.

The writers argue that Lord Diplock is guilty of the modern fetish of invoking popular conceptions of words as the universal answer to problems of interpretation; thus he selects the wide dictionary definition of recklessness, as denoting 'careless, regardless, heedless of the possible consequences of one's acts'. 'So viewed, recklessness would hardly differ from negligence.' In this way it is argued that *Sheppard* was a true precursor of *Caldwell/Lawrence*. Of course, it is important to remember that under s.8 of the Criminal Justice Act 1967 a jury may infer intention or foreseeability, having regard to all the evidence, in respect of the defendant.

Leigh and Temkin conclude that they agree with Professor Glanville Williams that the test of recklessness has a subjective meaning, but think that it is whether the accused had the capacity to have appreciated the risk had he thought of it when calm and sober.

> It follows that we accept neither Professor J. C. Smith's assertion that
> liability is purely objective, nor that of Mr Syrota that an accused who
> can show that he was not capable of appreciating the risk by reason of
> such factors as excitement, rage, or exhaustion is entitled to be acquit-
> ted, or Professor Griew who, more cautiously, stresses shock, stress or
> fatigue on the basis that these do not warrant censure. Some of these
> factors, for example driving while enraged or fatigued, should proba-
> bly be considered as aggravating circumstances. Mental illness stands
> on a special footing as may the taking of a medically prescribed drug.

The writers also pertinently and rightly add:

> Nor . . . is it inconceivable that courts may pick and choose between
> definitions for the purpose of interpreting different statutory provi-
> sions; precisely that was done in *Belfon* concerning intent.

To what extent has the *Caldwell* definition of recklessness affected other areas of the criminal law? In the first place it could well be argued that the word 'recklessly' in s.14 of the Trade Descriptions Act 1968 should be construed on *Caldwell/Lawrence* lines, something almost presaged in the earlier case of *MFI Warehouses Ltd* v. *Nattrass* (1973). Another important area is that of rape and criminal assault.

In respect of the former, Temkin has argued that the effect of *Caldwell/Lawrence* is to widen the grounds on which a man accused of rape may be judged as having acted recklessly. The defendant was already reckless if he realised that the woman was not perhaps consenting but hoped that she was or that he realised that the woman was not perhaps consenting but was determined to have intercourse regardless or where he deliberately closed his mind to the risk or where indeed his mind was a total blank on the subject. Now, it is argued, that post-*Caldwell* the defendant is also reckless where he believes the woman is consenting but it does not occur to him that she might not be. Recent cases have illustrated the considerable difficulties the courts have found themselves in regarding rape – in *Pigg* it appears an objective line was taken, while in *Mohammed Bashir* there appears a subjective gloss. The issue again came to the fore in *R. v. Satnam and Kewal* (1984). In *R. v. Satnam and Kewal* the victim was a 13 year-old girl who worked part-time in a shop where S. worked. S. and K. committed rape while taking her for a drive in a car one evening, it was alleged. However, Temkin's comments must be treated with some caution, since the courts in *Satnam* and in other subsequent cases have distanced themselves from the decision in *Pigg*. The facts in *Pigg* were that the defendant was charged with attempted rape of two girls aged 15 and 17 whilst pretending to be an official at the local holiday camp in Filey; Lord Lane noted: 'it is apparent that the girls were subjected to a catalogue of almost every sexual indignity of which one can think'.

Temkin also stated that the law of mistake in England had not been transformed in the manner anticipated after *Morgan*. (Mistake is examined immediately below.) *Morgan* established that an honest, albeit unreasonable, mistake was a good defence to rape.

> **On the contrary, in a series of cases the courts have insisted that the defendant's mistake must be a reasonable one. Most recently in *Phekoo* it was suggested that *Morgan* stands alone and that whilst an honest but unreasonable mistake may suffice to excuse a defendant for rape, the same principle does not apply with respect to other offences. The view taken here is that there is no reason why rape should be singled out in this manner and good reason for requiring that a mistaken belief in consent to sexual intercourse should be a reasonable one.**

Since that was written, however, the cases of *Kimber* and *Williams* have been decided.

In *R. v. Kimber* (1983) the appellant was observed to have approached a female patient in a mental hospital. He spoke to her and showed her money. A few minutes later, having followed him down a lane, she was seen in a distressed state, naked from the waist down. The defendant admitted interfering with her, but he claimed she had consented. He was charged with indecent assault under s.14 of the Sexual Offences Act 1956. The Court of Appeal held that it was the appellant's belief, not the grounds on which it was based, or whether or not it was reasonable, that went to negative the intent (as in *Morgan*). Thus Professor Smith commented:

> **The importance of the principles in *Morgan* had been somewhat diminished by the decision in *Caldwell*, though even that decision recognises that the existence of an actual belief in facts inconsistent with the *actus reus* is an answer to the charge of an offence requiring intention or recklessness. Moreover, *Caldwell* applies only to statutory**

offences defined expressly to require recklessness. It does not apply to all those offences against the person where the *mens rea* word is 'maliciously'. It is not certain whether it will be applied to common law offences but it is submitted that it should not. Its application to offences of assault, for example, would mean that we should have two different tests of recklessness in the law of offences against the person which would add appreciably to the existing chaos.

The point Professor Smith was making was underlined in the case of *W (A Minor)* v. *Dolbey* (1983). Here the defendant, aged 15, spent some time shooting bottles with his brother's air rifle. He then met R. in a doorway of a barn, whom he told there were no pellets in the gun. D. fired the gun and a pellet hit R. between the eyes, wounding him. D. was charged with unlawfully and maliciously wounding R., contrary to s.20 of the Offences against the Person Act 1861. The Queen's Bench Divisional Court held that in order to establish that a defendant had acted maliciously it had to be shown that he actually foresaw that a particular kind of harm might be done to his victim. In *Caldwell* Lord Diplock, after referring to the definition of malice given by Professor C. S. Kenny in his *Outlines of Criminal Law*, was careful to distinguish recklessness from malice. It was clear that no guidance could be derived from the meaning of recklessness in order to define malice, and that in respect of the latter the definition in *Cunningham* still stood. Thus if the defendant honestly believed the gun was not loaded then although he may have been reckless in not checking first, he did not foresee the harm done and was therefore not malicious. Recklessness under the 1861 Act is subjective, for in this context it appears irrelevant that the risk was extremely obvious to the reasonably minded person. It may well be, however, that to some degree *Caldwell* and *Morgan* are in conflict in respect of the defence of mistake.

In *R. v. Williams (Gladstone)* (1984) M. saw a youth seizing a woman's handbag. He caught the youth and was seen by the appellant to be knocking him to the ground. M. passed himself off as a policeman but failed to produce a warrant card. A struggle ensued and the appellant punched M. on the face. The appellant, charged with assault occasioning actual bodily harm, argued that he honestly believed that M. was unlawfully assaulting the youth. The Court of Appeal held that a mistake as to the facts honestly held did not have to be reasonable by objective standards. In the case of mistake arising from voluntary intoxication, it can be argued that this rule, in *Williams*, applies only to an offence of 'specific intent' and not to one of 'basic intent' or gross negligence (manslaughter), where the mistake would have to be a reasonable one in an objective sense, although George Syrota has argued that it seems fair to assume that the principle established in *Morgan* (an honest but unreasonable mistake negatives indifference to risk) may be applied in cases of manslaughter as well as in rape. The rules in *Gladstone Williams* were reiterated in *R. v. Owino* (1995).

Finally, not everyone has greeted the decisions in *Caldwell/Lawrence* with stinging criticism. For example, Jenny McEwan and St John Robilliard have made the following observations:

Professor Smith suggests that the meaning of 'recklessness' in offences such as assault may be different from the _Caldwell_ interpretation which may apply only to statutory crimes. Such a distinction would in our view be unjustifiable in principle and would result in hideous and unnecessary confusion. There seems to us nothing in the decision in _Caldwell_ or in _Lawrence_ to suggest that recklessness means different things according to whether the offence is of common law or statutory origin or as between different statutes. . . . The House of Lords cannot be accused of flouting the settled intention of Parliament or of disregarding established authorities. The Court of Appeal is much more susceptible to attack, in our view, in that . . . it tried to find excuses to ignore relevant and important statements by the House of Lords on _mens rea_. Further attempts by any judges or academics to escape by raising arbitrary distinctions should be deplored and resisted. We suggest that the House of Lords has simply ensured that the public is protected by preventing the accused from being placed in too favourable a position as a result of the [Criminal Justice Act 1967].

The 'lacuna' problem in the _Caldwell/Lawrence_ definition of recklessness, that is where A. has considered whether there is a risk, concluded there was none and proceeded to his cost, has not been fully tested in the courts. In _Chief Constable of Avon and Somerset Constabulary_ v. _Shimmen_ (1986) S., on the way from a pub in Bristol, tried to impress his friends by narrowly missing a shop window with a kick. He smashed the window and caused £500 worth of damage. S., an expert in Korean self-defence, realised there was some outside risk, so he was convicted. In _R._ v. _Reid_ (1992) Lord Browne-Wilkinson thought that there might be some revision of Caldwell at a later date. Lord Goff said : 'I accept that, if the defendant is addressing his mind to the possibility of risk and suffers from a _bona fide_ mistake as to specific facts which if true would have excluded the risk, he cannot be described as reckless'. This seems to recognise the lacuna problem in the _Caldwell_ test for recklessness. The Court of Appeal held, not entirely convincingly, in _R._ v. _Merrick_ (1996) that in respect of the lacuna argument only steps taken that were aimed at stopping the risk arising would, for these purposes of recklessness, suffice. This case concerned the removal of television cabling; as this was an aggravated offence, under s.1(2) of the Criminal Damage Act 1971, the 'lawful excuse' provisions of s.5(2) did not apply. (The issues of aggravated criminal damage also arose on appeal in _R._ v. _Webster and Warwick_ (1995).)

While the exact wording of the model direction in _Lawrence_ is not binding and may need modification in particular circumstances, the case remains essentially good law, as Professor Smith has pointed out. So, in respect of the subjective test, the risk need not be an obvious one, because the defendant has actively perceived the risk.

As reckless driving has been replaced by dangerous driving, the _Lawrence_ test has no future, in any event. However, the instant case [_Reid_] also throws light on the sister-case of _Caldwell_ and may be a har-

binger of a reconsideration of that case. It should not be assumed that, as *Lawrence* was substantially upheld, the same fate would necessarily await *Caldwell*: the saga of *Caldwell* recklessness continues with obstinacy on both sides of the argument. . . . The solution would be to remove the word [recklessness] altogether from the judicial vocabulary.

BURDEN OF PROOF

It is for the prosecution to prove *mens rea* and *actus reus* beyond reasonable doubt; the burden of proof lies upon the Crown. That includes charges of murder, as established in *Woolmington* v. *DPP* in 1935. The burden of proof shifts to the defence in three instances. Firstly, where he wishes to plead insanity the accused must prove it (the *M'Naghten* case); of course, it may be difficult for an insane person to prove he was insane at the time of the *actus reus* – it would take sanity to do so thereby destroying any semblance of insanity, the original 'Catch 22'. (The *M'Naghten Rules* are discussed below.) Secondly, Parliament may deliberately shift the burden of proof; under the Prevention of Crime Act 1953, for instance, it is for the defendant to show why he was carrying an offensive weapon in a public place. Thirdly, Parliament may exempt certain groups or classes of persons from criminal liability, but the burden of proof is upon the accused to show that he enjoys such exemption, as seen in *R.* v. *Edwards* (1975). This case involved the unauthorised sale of liquor in a Brixton basement fitted up as a bar.

Moreover, the prosecution may be assisted in its case by presumptions of either law or fact. A criminal intention may be inferred if certain facts have already been proved, unless the accused offers a reasonable explanation: such a presumption of fact may be known as a provisional presumption. If the jury is obliged to presume a fact, then that presumption is one of law and it may be rebuttable or irrebuttable. Thus in law it is provided that no child under 10 is capable of committing a crime, and that presumption is irrebuttable. But in other cases a presumption in law may be rebutted if sufficient evidence is adduced; for instance, although a child born to a married couple is presumed legitimate this may be rebutted by evidence. It is also important to note that nowadays the court, or rather the jury, is not necessarily required to infer intention on the basis that a reasonable man would have foreseen the outcome of his action. The Criminal Justice Act 1967 (s.8) provides:

A court or jury in determining whether a person has committed an offence a) shall not be bound in law to infer that he intended or foresaw a result of his actions by reason only of its being a natural and probable consequence of those actions, but b) shall decide whether he did intend or foresee that result by reference to all the evidence, drawing such inferences from the evidence as appear proper in the circumstances.

STRICT LIABILITY

In some crimes it is sufficient to prove the illegal action alone, the *actus reus* being enough to incur liability; the proof of intention, recklessness or negligence (*mens rea*) is unnecessary: the accused is strictly liable for his wrongful action and for any harm caused. Direct physical harm to another may not even be the issue, the public harm may be that the act alone was unlawful. It is, though, a little misleading to suggest that *mens rea* is an entirely superfluous matter in such crimes; in the first place there may be other circumstances or elements of the *actus* for which proof of *mens rea* still needs to be adduced, although they may be secondary to the dominant issue in respect of the charges preferred. In the second place intention must usually be shown: X. intended to carry out an action; he did not intend that action to cause harm, nor was his state of mind reckless. Nonetheless he intended to act and he did act: he is strictly liable, but liability is not absolute; if liability were absolute then a defence such as compulsion could not be raised (that is X. claims Y. forced him at gunpoint to undertake a wrongful action or, perhaps, first made him drunk). This point was highlighted in *R.* v. *Larsonneur* (1933) where an alien deported from Ireland unlawfully entered the United Kingdom. The accused, a French subject, was in fact brought to Holyhead by the Irish Free State police. But, surprisingly, she was found guilty: the Court of Criminal Appeal held that the circumstances of her return were immaterial.

Strict liability usually relates to statutory offences. The chief offences at common law have been public nuisance, criminal libel (defamation) and conceivably blasphemous libel, and criminal contempt of court. The latter has now been overtaken by the Contempt of Court Act 1981. Public nuisance is in many ways overshadowed by its civil relation, private nuisance, as is criminal libel in respect of defamation. Public nuisance and criminal libel are discussed under tort, and blasphemous libel later in this chapter. With regard to libel suffice it to say at this point that criminal libel consists of defamatory remarks or statements that appear permanently to injure an individual's reputation. Blasphemous libel concerns any comment or statement that abuses the doctrines of Christianity and the Church of England, or Christ or God, and in so doing outrages and insults Christians; but there is no need to prove intention to outrage (*R.* v. *Lemon*). Strictly speaking blasphemous, seditious and obscene libel are all branches of criminal libel.

Many statutory strict liability cases arise under regulations dealing with the sale of food and drink. In *Hobbs* v. *Winchester Corporation* (1910) the plaintiff was in effect judged to be guilty of selling unfit meat under the Public Health Act 1875. (In this civil action the plaintiff was suing the defendants for compensation for the destruction of the meat.) Lord Justice Kennedy said:

> **The natural inference from the statute and its object is that the peril to the butcher from innocently selling unsound meat is deemed by the legislature to be much less than the peril to the public which would follow from the necessity of proving in each case a *mens rea* . . . If a**

man chooses for profit to engage in a business which involves the offering for sale of that which may be deadly or injurious to health he must take that risk.

The judge's remarks underline the point that strict liability often results where a statute omits mention of such a word as 'knowingly', but not always because, as noted above, *mens rea* may be implied by the court, and that will remain so until Parliament itself decides to define *mens rea*. Other Acts, like the Contempt of Court Act 1981, define strict liability in context. In *Cundy* v. *Le Cocq* (1884) it was immaterial that the wrongdoer did not realize that the person to whom he had served a drink was already drunk; he had still breached the provisions of the Licensing Act 1872.

Thus under the Salmon and Freshwater Fisheries Act 1975 the placing of a 'fixed engine' in certain waters is one of strict liability (*Champion* v. *Maughan* (1984)) and so too is selling gold, described as such, without a hallmark, where the offence was 'regulatory and quasi-criminal', under the Hallmarking Act 1973 (*Chilvers* v. *Rayner*, (1984)). In *Sweet* v. *Parsley* (1970), where the defendant was prosecuted for allowing cannabis to be smoked in a farmhouse, without her knowledge, the conviction was overturned by the House of Lords, Lord Reid saying that if a statute was silent as to *mens rea*, there is a presumption that *mens rea* is required, unless the statute specifically says not, that strict liability is sufficient. But in *Pharmaceutical Society* v. *Storkwain Ltd* (1985), the House of Lords held that a pharmacist who supplied controlled medicines against a forged prescription was guilty of an indictable offence under the Medicines Act 1968 since the requirement of a 'guilty mind' was absent from one section of the Act whilst present in other sections.

Implying strict liability

Mr Justice Wright in *Sherras* v. *De Rutzen* (1895) (another liquor case) thought that strict liability could be inferred where the statute was silent in those acts which, in the language of Mr Justice Lush, in *Davies* v. *Harvey* (1874), were not criminal in any real sense, but were acts which in the public interest were prohibited under a penalty. He went on to say that such statutes would normally be those concerned with revenue (taxation) and the sale of food. In other words, Acts whose object was to eradicate or control some general social ill would be interpreted by the courts as not requiring proof of *mens rea*. So, it is an offence of strict liability (*Kirkland* v. *Robinson* (1987)) under s.1(2) of the Wildlife and Countryside Act 1981 to possess live wild birds. Pollution is another good example. In *Alphacell Ltd* v. *Woodward* (1972) a company was found guilty of causing pollution under the Rivers (Prevention of Pollution) Act 1951 even though it was not negligent in the care of its settling tanks. The company was unaware that vegetation had stopped the pumps from working normally. *Alphacell* was effectively followed in *National Rivers Authority* v. *Alfred McAlpine Homes East Ltd* (1994), which concerned pollution of the River Medway by wet cement. Prior to the Misuse of Drugs Act 1971 a number of cases concerning drugs showed that the strict liability rule operated in respect of the Dangerous Drugs (Prevention of Misuse) Act 1964.

The 1971 Act allows the accused to argue that he did not know that the substance he possessed was a prohibited (controlled) drug. The Act says that he shall be acquitted 'if he proves that he neither believed nor suspected nor had reason to suspect that the substance or product in question was a controlled drug'. The same Act provides for the offence of knowingly to permit or suffer the smoking of cannabis on the premises the accused occupies or manages, which, again, hardly amounts to strict liability.

Another aspect of strict liability is that sometimes the question will be asked as to whether the imposition of the rule would aid the enforcement of law, a point underlined in *Lim Chin Aik* v. *The Queen* (1963), a Privy Council case concerning Singaporean immigration rules.

> **It is not enough in their Lordships' opinion merely to label the statute as one dealing with a grave social evil and from that to infer that strict liability was intended. It is pertinent also to inquire whether putting the defendant under strict liability will assist in the enforcement of the regulations. That means that there must be something he can do, directly or indirectly, by supervision or inspection, by improvement of his business methods or by exhorting those whom he may be expected to influence or control, which will promote the observance of the regulations. Unless this is so there is no reason in penalising him, and it cannot be inferred that the legislature imposed strict liability merely in order to find a luckless victim.**

Lord Evershed continued: 'Their Lordships prefer [this principle] to the alternative view that strict liability follows simply from the nature of the subject-matter and that persons whose conduct is beyond any sort of criticism can be dealt with by the imposition of a nominal penalty'. The court also added that the maxim 'ignorance of the law is no excuse' could not apply since there was no provision to enable the appellant to discover whether an order had been made against him.

Quasi-crimes

It should be stressed that the concept of strict liability in criminal law is a controversial one, the main arguments in its favour being the special protection of the public from various evils and the conviction of wrongdoers who might otherwise escape punishment. Arguments against are that it is a harsh, unjust rule and that too many people whose conduct was basically innocent are convicted. Some suggestions have been made for a compromise, for a modification of the rule, as Lord Diplock did in *Sweet* v. *Parsley* (1970) by drawing upon Australian practice. The Law Commission report on the mental element in crime, referred to above, also put forward suggestions.

In the Privy Council case of *Gammon (Hong Kong) Ltd* v. *Attorney-General of Hong Kong* (1984), which concerned building regulations, Lord Scarman said that the law, in this case, could be stated in five propositions:

1 in criminal law there was always a presumption that *mens rea* was required before a person could be found guilty;

2 the presumption was especially strong where the offence was 'truly criminal';

3 the presumption applied to statutory offences, and could only be displaced expressly or impliedly by the effect of the statute concerned;

4 the presumption could be displaced where the statute was concerned with an issue of social concern, and public safety was such an issue; and

5 even where a statute was concerned with such an issue, the presumption of *mens rea* stood unless it could also be shown that the creation of strict liability would be effective to promote the object of the statute by encouraging greater vigilance to prevent the commission of the prohibited act.

In *Denham* v. *Scott* (1983) the defendant was convicted under s.23 of the Theft Act 1968 of publishing a public advertisement offering a reward for the return of stolen goods using words to the effect that no questions would be asked. The Queen's Bench Divisional Court said that the offence fell into the class of quasi-criminal offences and a conviction did not result in any stigma; the offence was one of strict liability.

Defences

A few statutes do provide a defence to strict liability, in so far as the accused can argue that he took all reasonable care, that there was no sense in which there had been negligence. This 'no negligence' defence that is occasionally allowed is akin to the Australian 'halfway house' approach. As seen above, under the Misuse of Drugs Act 1971 the accused may show that he was totally unaware that the substance in his possession was a controlled drug. Under the Trade Descriptions Act 1968 the accused may show that he acted mistakenly or accidentally, provided he had still attempted to avoid the consequences of his action. The dilemmas of strict liability were well illustrated in the 1981 cases of *R.* v. *Phekoo* and *R.* v. *Sheppard*. The former concerned the Protection from Eviction Act 1977; the defendant mistakenly believed two residential occupiers of a house he owned had no right to be there and he put pressure on them to leave. The second case concerned the Children and Young Persons Act 1933 and the wilful neglect of a child. In that case Lord Diplock said:

The climate of both parliamentary and judicial opinion has been growing less favourable to the recognition of absolute offences over the last few decades, a trend to which section 1 of the Homicide Act 1957 and section 8 of the Criminal Justice Act 1967 bear witness in the case of Parliament, and, in the case of the judiciary, is illustrated by the speeches in this House in *Sweet* v. *Parsley*.

PARTICIPATION: ACCOMPLICE

The person who commits the crime is the perpetrator, the principal, and two or more persons may be perpetrators, for example, 'gang rape' or conspiracy, or even a driving offence where one steered and the other changed gear (*Tyler* v. *Whatmore* (1976)). In other instances the second party is precisely that: he plays a secondary role, assists the principal or perpetrator, in short he is the accomplice. To prosecute an accomplice does not mean that the perpetrator must have been tried or convicted, but it must be shown that the main or principal offence had been committed and that the accused intended to encourage or aid the commission (or omission) of the act. An acquittal of the principal offender does not necessarily debar a conviction of an accomplice, especially where there are separate trials in different courts. But if there is no *actus reus*, no principal offence, then there can be no accomplice, as shown in *Thornton* v. *Mitchell* (1940). A bus driver reversed his vehicle and knocked down two pedestrians. The driver had relied on signals given by his conductor. He was not proven to be negligent and therefore the conductor was not guilty of aiding or abetting him. The accomplice must be shown to have full *mens rea*, even where the principal offence is one of strict liability. Negligence will not constitute *mens rea*. The relevant statute is the Accessories and Abettors Act 1861, as amended by the Criminal Law Acts 1967 and 1977. A party to a joint enterprise is different from a mere aider or abettor (*R.* v. *Stewart and Schofield* (1995)). The Court of Appeal in *R.* v. *Bamborough* (1996), following *Stewart*, emphasised that liability concerning joint enterprise for murder would be interpreted widely, that is even if fatal injuries inflicted are different from what was contemplated by the secondary party.

Aid or encouragement embraces other terms such as 'counselling', 'abetting' or 'procuring'. If a person procures the commission of an offence, it normally means that he ensures that it is effected, perhaps even unbeknown to the perpetrator, as well as giving all due assistance before the actual commission. However, the person who at first sight may appear to be an accomplice sometimes turns out to be the principal and thus the person who appears to be the principal is merely an innocent agent. If L. drops poison into a drink which he knows M. will give to N., it is L. who is guilty of murder, not M. But in some offences the concept of 'innocent agent' would appear to be impossible to apply, for example bigamy and rape, although not where the perpetrator acts under duress. That does not, however, mean to say that an accomplice cannot exist in bigamy or rape; for example, in the latter case holding down a woman while another commits rape is the act of an accomplice (*R.* v. *Clarkson*, 1971).

In *R.* v. *Bourne* (1952) the accused compelled his wife to commit bestiality with a dog; B. was tried on his own for abetting her and was convicted. Similarly, in *R.* v. *Cogan and Leak* (1976) the accused compelled his wife to have sex with C. C.'s conviction for rape was quashed, but the husband was convicted as aider and abettor. Inadvertent *Caldwell/Lawrence* recklessness is not enough for being an accomplice: D2, wanting D1 to stay the night, laced his drink, but he drove off; her conviction for procuring D1's driving with excess alcohol was quashed in *Blakely and Sutton* v. *DPP* (1991).

Causal links

If the accused is charged with *procuring* an offence, then a causal connection between his secondary action and the principal offence (primary action) must be established. A direct causal link does not have to be established where the question is one of *abetting* (counselling) but rather consensus: here the accomplice encourages the principal offender, either before or at the time of commission of the offence, to undertake the wrongful action, and the principal offender is in agreement, as seen in *R. v. Calhaem* (1985), where a private investigator was hired by the accused to kill the mistress of a man with whom the accused was infatuated. If the accomplice *aids* the principal he gives direct assistance rather than active encouragement; there is not necessarily any consensus between them. Sometimes, however, 'aiding' and 'abetting' are regarded as meaning much the same thing. *Counselling* usually means encouragement prior to the act rather than encouragement at the time of the act. If the encouragement or counselling is proved to have been ineffective then a charge of incitement may be more appropriate.

Moreover, a person can hardly be an accomplice after an offence has been committed; he cannot assist in a murder which has already taken place. Since the Criminal Law Act 1967 it is not an offence to be an accessory to a crime after it has taken place (an accessory after the fact).

It should be said that the *Attorney-General's Reference (No 1 of 1975)* (1975) made it clear that *aid* and *abet* and so on have different meanings. Lord Widgery said that Parliament would not have wasted time using four words where three would do. In respect of 'procuring' this means that there does not have to be a consensus between the secondary participant and the perpetrator.

There is no general and legally enforceable duty on the private citizen to report crimes, except in the case of treason. Merely being in the vicinity while an offence is in the course of being committed will not suffice; to be an accomplice demands an active not a passive role. On the other hand a deliberate if voluntary presence at, say, an unlawful event, for example cock-fighting, would probably amount to aiding or abetting. Similarly, simple inactivity may lead to a conviction, but the party who fails to act must have some interest in the matter concerned, as shown in the Australian case of *R. v. Russell* (1933) where a husband watched his wife drown herself and their children in a swimming-pool; the accused was found guilty of manslaughter. In that context the intent to encourage or aid may be indirect; the accomplice, as outlined in *DPP for Northern Ireland v. Lynch* (1975), may not particularly care as to the exact outcome of his secondary action but his presence alone may be sufficient to encourage the commission of the principal offence. In *R. v. Sharp* (1987) the appellant was convicted of manslaughter, being a member of a gang who robbed a number of post offices, at the last of which the postmaster was killed. The appellant argued that he had wanted to pull out of the last robbery when he saw guns loaded into the car, and claimed duress. But the Court of Appeal dismissed the appeal, for he had voluntarily joined a criminal gang. The courts do not 'discover' any longer new common law crimes, but defences to crime in common law are a different matter.

Knowledge of the crime

If the accused knows that a criminal offence will be committed as the result of his action but is not sure precisely what offence, then he will be guilty of being an accomplice if the offence is not too remote from that action – for example, murder, manslaughter and possibly serious wounding are related but an offence such as fraud would probably be too far removed from the accused's knowledge that his action was designed to cause someone physical harm. He need not know the details of the principal offence but there must be a relationship between that offence and the secondary action, as illustrated in *R. v. Bainbridge* (1960), where cutting equipment was sold which was later used to rob a bank. In *Davies* v. *DPP* (1954) the accused was involved in a gang fight in London, but he did not know another member of his gang was carrying a knife which fatally wounded a third person. Although guilty of an assault, he was found not guilty of being an accomplice to murder. On the other hand the relationship between the primary action and the secondary action was shown to be sufficiently close in *Maxwell* v. *DPP for Northern Ireland* (1979). The appellant was a member of the Ulster Volunteer Force (UVF), an illegal Protestant para-military organisation. He was told to drive his car to a remote rural area, in fact to the Crosskeys Inn at Toomebridge in County Antrim. The inn was run by Roman Catholics. Other members of the UVF followed in another car; one of these men placed a bomb in the hallway of the pub, although the attack was a failure since the landlord's son threw the bomb into the road. The House of Lords held that although the appellant need not have known precisely what the other members of the UVF were going to do, as a UVF man himself he must have known that he was taking part in some kind of terrorist attack. He was, therefore, an accomplice. In a case where a risk of a killing or the infliction of serious bodily harm crosses the mind of the accused it is for the jury to decide whether the risk as recognised by the accused is sufficient to make him a party to the crime committed by the principal. The jury needs to bear in mind that the accused might genuinely have considered and dismissed a risk as negligible (*Chan Wing-Siu* v. *The Queen* (1984)). Overall *Chan Wing-Siu* (which involved three assailants armed with knives bursting into a prostitute's flat, intent on robbery, with one of them murdering the prostitute's husband) was followed in *R. v. Ward* (1986) and *R. v. Hyde* (1990) and approved by the Privy Council in *Hui Chi-ming* (1992). In *Hui* H. was one of a group persuaded by P. to seek out a man who had been intimidating P.'s girlfriend; P. struck the man with a metal pipe and was convicted of manslaughter and two years later H. was indicted for murder. In *Hyde* it was said that if a secondary party continues to participate in the use of force, without necessarily agreeing to such conduct being used, then he too is guilty of murder (here three people kicking and punching a man outside a public house). Lord Lane observed:

> There are two main types of joint enterprise cases where death results to the victim. The first is where the primary object is to do some kind of physical injury to the victim. The second is where the primary object is not to cause physical injury to any victim, but, for example, to commit burglary. The victim is assaulted and killed as a (possibly

> unwelcome) incident of the burglary. The latter type of case may pose more complications than the former, but the principle is, in each case the same. . . . If B. realises (without agreeing to such conduct being used) that A. may kill or intentionally inflict serious injury, but nevertheless continues to participate with A. in the venture, that will amount to a sufficient mental element for B. to be guilty of murder if A., with the requisite intent, kills in the course of the venture.

Any withdrawal by the accomplice from the crime must be clear, although he could still remain liable for incitement or conspiracy. This was illustrated in *R. v. Becarra* (1976) (followed in *Baker* (1994)) where one burglar gave a knife to his companion to use if necessary: his companion killed the nightwatchman and the accused had not withdrawn as aider/abettor by merely saying 'Come on, let's go', with accompanying movement. In *R. v. Slack* (1989) D. and E. broke into the home of a frail old lady, in order to rob her. E. supplied a knife to D. who murdered V. In respect of E. it sufficed if he contemplated the possibility that such death or grievous bodily harm might be deliberately inflicted by D. and that either (1) E. tacitly agreed that, if necessary, this violence should be done as part of the joint enterprise or (2) E. lent himself to the infliction of such harm. This point was applied in *R. v. Hyde*. In *R. v. Rook* (1993) the accomplice remained liable where he failed to turn up for a contract killing but did nothing to indicate a change of mind.

It is occasionally possible for the accused to argue that he was an 'accomplice' in order to entrap the true criminals; but a private citizen must be even more careful than a police officer if this defence is to be used successfully. In *R. v. Bickley* (1909) a police spy acted as the 'victim' – the accused unlawfully supplied a noxious substance to her with the intent to procure her miscarriage. Equally, the accused may attempt to show that he took active steps to withdraw from or renounce participation, but that does not rule out a charge of conspiracy or incitement. The 'true criminal' may not use entrapment as a defence, except to mitigate the sentence, a point reaffirmed by the House of Lords in *R. v. Sang* in 1979; the case concerned forged banknotes. A similar point arose in *R. v. Smurthwaite and Gill* (1993), concerning soliciting to murder spouses, where the Court of Appeal held the entrapment defence rule was unaffected by s.78 of the Police and Criminal Evidence Act 1984.

The Court of Appeal in *R. v. Jefferson and Skerritt* (1993) made it clear the offence of aiding and abetting was applicable to all Acts unless specifically excluded by statute.

CAPACITY AND DEFENCES

1 Children (minors)

A minor for most legal purposes is a person under the age of 18. No child under the age of 10 , in the eyes of the law, is capable of committing a crime (Children and Young Persons Act 1963) (*doli incapax*). However, the child may be placed in care under the Children and Young Persons Act 1969 and the Children Act 1989.

For those aged between 10 and 14 the position is more complicated. Such a minor (or infant) may be convicted only if it can be shown that not only was there an *actus reus* with some form of *mens rea*, but also present was a 'mischievous discretion'; in other words the child fully realised that what he was doing was morally wrong even if he did not know it was legally wrong. Sometimes 'mischievous discretion' is referred to as 'malice' in this context. In *R. v. Gorrie* (1919) the jury was told by the judge that they must be satisfied that the accused, a boy of 13 knew that what he was doing was 'gravely wrong, seriously wrong' and not merely wrong, as would suffice for someone over 14. The boy in question had stabbed another with a penknife; the victim died later from pneumonia and septic poisoning and a charge of manslaughter was preferred. The defendant had been cutting a piece of wood with the knife and ran after the boy in horseplay, which occasioned a small wound in the victim's buttock. The victim did not mention the incident at home until it was too late. The accused was acquitted.

In *C. (A minor) v. DPP* (1995) the House of Lords said that the *doli incapax* rule was still part of English law.

2 Corporations

A company or corporation – and sometimes an unincorporated body like a trade union or employers' association – may be criminally liable in the same way as an ordinary individual is. But clearly there are limitations: it is difficult to conceive of a situation where a non-physical entity can be prosecuted, for example, for rape or bigamy. It is only over the last hundred years or so that the courts have recognised that the concepts of *mens rea* and punishment can sometimes apply as much to an artificial body as to a real one.

However, the perception of corporations not being capable of criminal acts has begun to shift lately, especially in the light of the 193 deaths in the Zeebrugge ferry disaster in 1987. There followed the King's Cross Underground tragedy, and it appears that there were gross management failures in both cases. In 1988 the Llandeilo inquest into the British Rail accident on a flooded line in West Wales the year before returned, like the Zeebrugge inquest, a verdict of unlawful death. As Celia Wells has said, 'Modern accidents are often caused by failure to heed simple warnings of impending risk. Since modern technology makes the consequences of such failure horrific, there is no reason why the imposition of criminal liability should not reflect that'. The DPP, in 1989, dismissed the possibility of prosecutions against London Underground, but not against Townsend Thoresen in the Zeebrugge case, although the Zeebrugge case subsequently collapsed. Professor Michael Zander commented in 1990:

> **As a result of the Zeebrugge case (193 dead), then, corporate manslaughter is legally admissible as a charge in an English court. But it looks harder than ever to prove it. And there is little prospect of any change in the law. No matter how great their desire for what they see as justice, the victims of future disasters will probably have to be content with remedies in the civil courts.**

In late 1994 OLL Ltd (formerly Active Leisure and Learning Ltd) became the first company in English legal history to be convicted of homicide, and was fined £60,000. This concerned the deaths in 1993 of four teenagers in a canoe trip off Lyme Regis. The weather forecast had not been checked, there were no distress flares provided and the only safety equipment for the instructors was a whistle.

In 1995 a second inquest jury decided that the 51 people who died as a result of a collision between the Marchioness river boat and another vessel (the Bow Belle) on the River Thames in 1989 were unlawfully killed.

The most common way in which a corporation is held criminally liable is for breach of a specific statutory duty. Equally, a corporation may be made strictly liable in criminal law; it may be judged vicariously liable, and it may be charged with acting as an accomplice (*DPP* v. *Kent and Sussex Contractors Ltd* (1994)). Lord Denning observed in *H L Bolton (Engineering) Co. Ltd* v. *P J Graham & Sons Ltd* (1957):

> **A company may in many ways be likened to a human body. It has a brain and a nerve centre which controls what it does. It also has hands which hold the tools and act in accordance with directions from the centre. Some of the people in the company are mere servants and agents who are nothing more than hands to do the work and cannot be said to represent the mind or will. Others are directors and managers who represent the directing mind and will of the company and control what it does. The state of mind of these managers is the state of mind of the company and is treated by the law as such.**

In *Tesco Supermarkets Ltd* v. *Nattrass* (1972) Lord Reid suggested that a company may only be directly liable, as opposed to vicariously so, for the actions of the board of directors, the managing director and perhaps other superior officers who carried out management functions and spoke and acted as the company. Lord Dilhorne said in the same case that direct company liability occurred where a person was in actual control of the operations of a company or of part of them.

As *The Modern Law Review*, in May 1984, noted:

> **Both civil and criminal law have encountered difficulties in using this 'identification' approach. Which managers other than directors, for example, are part of the 'nerve centre'? In regard both to negligence and to criminal offences the functional tendency has grown to include whatever layers of management are appropriate to the issue. The 'fault' of top management below the board may be personal to the company but that of superior employees is not; and the knowledge of a servant is not that of the company for the purpose of aiding and abetting. Shareholders, even when voting in general meetings, are not identifiable with 'the company' itself; and the company will be directly procured to act in breach of contract only when the inducement reaches it in the form of a person 'who has authority on the company's behalf to make contracts', not any other managerial agent.**

In a situation where the defendants were charged with stealing property from a company, of which they were the only directors and shareholders, the trial judge directed their acquittal, since they could not in effect steal from themselves. But the Court of Appeal thought otherwise – the victim company was a separate person, *Attorney-General's Reference (No 2 of 1982)* (1984).

A company cannot be prosecuted where the punishment does not afford any possibility of a fine but only of imprisonment; murder is therefore excluded, although manslaughter may not be, as seen with Zeebrugge. In *Deutsche Genossenschaftsbank v. Burnhope* (1995) the House of Lords held the company had committed theft because its directing mind and will (in short the chairman) had committed theft, albeit through an innocent agent.

The criminal liability of corporations has developed piecemeal over the years, and its rationale in terms of social policy is possibly open to question. Is it right, for instance, to make taxpayers, consumers or shareholders carry the burden of the fines imposed, when the harm done was in practice the result of actions committed by one or more individuals? On the other hand imposing a penalty upon an organisation as a whole, particularly a large one, does expose that corporation to the glare of unwelcome publicity. Many statutes now provide for the criminal liability of a corporation through specified officers within that organisation – for instance, director, manager, secretary and so on. A statute may also allow as a defence proof of care and diligence undertaken by the company's officer.

3 Insanity

Reference has already been made to the *M'Naghten Rules*. The accused is always presumed to be sane. He must show that he suffers from a 'disease of the mind' a difficult enough mental and legal concept to determine. This kind of disease will have rendered him incapable of rational thought: the accused did not realise that what he was doing was wrong. Disease of the mind may include brain disease. A judge can only rarely raise the issue of insanity of his own accord (*R. v. Dickie* (1984)). That the effects of drugs or alcohol do not constitute such a disease, was illustrated in *R. v. Tandy* (1989). Here D., an alcoholic, drank a bottle of vodka and then strangled her daughter. The Court of Appeal said that alcoholism could be treated as a disease for the purpose of diminished responsibility if D.'s intellectual or emotional impairment was caused by the damage of alcoholism itself or by drinking rendered involuntary by the alcoholism. Drinking on a particular day would be involuntary only if D. could not resist taking the first drink of the day. In this case, for obvious reasons, the accused was reluctant to assert that she was insane within the *M'Naghten Rules*.

However, under the Mental Health Act 1983 the Home Secretary has the power to commit a person to a mental hospital, providing two or more doctors certify that the accused is suffering from mental illness or severe mental impairment before the trial commences. Or the accused may be found unfit to plead at the commencement of the trial under ss.4 and 4A of the Criminal Procedure (Insanity) Act 1964 as substituted by the Criminal Procedure (Insanity and

Unfitness to Plead) Act 1991, in which case he may be committed to hospital (Mental Health Act 1983), if, following the provisions of the 1991 Act, he is found to have done the act; if he is found not to have done the act, he goes free. The 1991 Act allows not just for a hospital or guardianship order under the Mental Health Act 1983, but also for a supervision and treatment order (Schedule 2) or an order for an absolute discharge under s.55 of the 1964 Act as amended.

Section I of the Criminal Procedure (Insanity and Unfitness to Plead) Act 1991 has not changed the criteria for being found not guilty by reason of insanity. However, s.1 requires that a jury shall not return a special verdict except on the written or oral evidence of two medical practitioners, one of whom must be approved as having experience in the diagnosis and treatment of mental disorder. The aim, in effect, is to ensure a closer fit between the criteria by which a person will be found not guilty by reason of insanity and the concepts of mental disorder which are necessary for detention under the Mental Health Act 1983.

Under s.5 (2)(b) of the Criminal Procedure (Insanity and Unfitness to Plead) Act 1991 the court has a discretion parallel to the powers of disposal for a person found unfit to plead, as indicated above, that is to deal with the accused person found 'not guilty by reason of insanity' when the special verdict relates to an offence where the sentence is not fixed by law − if the case is suitable the court may make a guardianship order within the meaning of the Mental Health Act 1983 or a supervision and treatment order, or make an order for the accused's absolute discharge. But there remain problems where the sentence is fixed by law, ie murder, and in respect of the inherent nature of the *M'Naghten Rules*, plus the fact that the term insanity is still used where the defence of non–insane automatism collapses. The Act does not apply to Magistrates' Courts, who have powers under s.37 of the Mental Health Act 1983 to make a hospital or a guardianship order without convicting an accused person.

So, the *M'Naghten Rules* only come into operation once the trial has commenced and they relate not so much to the question of the accused's insanity at the time of the trial (the accused may now be sane) as to the state of his mind at the time the wrong was committed. The Rules date from the case of that name in 1843: one Daniel M'Naghten killed the private secretary to Sir Robert Peel instead of the Prime Minister himself; he was acquitted on the grounds of insanity. If the accused can show at the time that he lacked rationality, that he did not understand the nature and quality of his action or indeed not realise it was wrong to any degree, then, the Rules say, he should normally be acquitted as he was devoid of the requisite *mens rea*; 'wrong' here means legally wrong, not purely morally wrong (*Attorney-General for State of South Australia* v. *Brown* (1960)). Even if the accused is found not guilty on grounds of insanity he will still be sent to a secure mental hospital by the Home Secretary and kept there indefinitely under the 1964, 1983 and 1991 Acts. Few plead insanity, partly on account of this bleak future. The *N'Naghten Rules* have come in for considerable criticism over the years, as indicated in 1975 by the Butler Report.

A mere 'irresistible impulse' does not fall within the Rules. In *R.* v. *Kopsch* (1925) Lord Chief Justice Hewart observed that if the fantastic theory of uncontrollable impulse were to become part of the criminal law, it would be merely subversive. In this case the accused had strangled a woman, with whom he was on intimate terms, at her own request with his tie. He was convicted of murder.

Summary trials in the Magistrates' Court follow a different procedure from the Crown Court, but in practice the provisions of the Mental Health Act 1983 ensure that the accused may still be detained in an appropriate institution.

Of the two tests of insanity, it should be stressed that it is the second which has caused the courts the most difficulty, that is whether at the time of the act the accused knew that what he was doing was legally, or possibly morally, wrong. The first test, as stated above, is whether the accused was aware of what he was doing at all; in other words did he realise the nature and quality of the action? In *R.* v. *Codère* (1916) the appellant was a lieutenant in the Canadian army. He was convicted of the brutal murder of another soldier, one Ozanne. O's head was smashed and nearly severed and it had 45 cuts on the face. C. appealed on grounds of insanity. Lord Chief Justice Reading observed:

> **In approaching the facts it is right to say that undoubtedly on the evidence the appellant is possessed of a mind of very inferior quality. He was always known as being abnormal mentally; he was called in Quebec and in the regiment 'Le fou Codère' . . . It is said that 'quality' is to be regarded as characterising the moral, as contrasted with the physical, aspect of the deed. The Court cannot agree with that view of the meaning of the words 'nature and quality.' The Court is of opinion that in using the language 'nature and quality' the judges were only dealing with the physical character of the act, and were not intending to distinguish between the physical and moral aspects of the act. That is the law as it has been laid down by judges in many directions to juries, and as the Court understands it to be at the present time.**

Such difficulties of definition were again clear in *R.* v. *Windle* (1952). Lord Chief Justice Goddard delivered the following judgement:

> **The appellant was convicted before Devlin J. at Birmingham Assizes of the murder of his wife. He is a man of little resolution and weak character who was married to a woman 18 years older than himself. His married life was very unhappy. His wife, in the opinion of the doctors, though they never saw her, must have been certifiable, and was always talking about committing suicide. The appellant became obsessed with this and discussed it with his workmates until they were tired of hearing him, and on one occasion, just before this crime was committed, one of them said, 'Give her a dozen aspirins.' On the day of the crime the appellant seems to have given the woman a hundred**

aspirin tablets, which was a fatal dose. Later, he told the police that he supposed he would be hanged for it.

In the opinion of the court, there is no doubt that the word 'wrong' in the *M'Naghten Rules* means contrary to law and does not have some vague meaning which may vary according to the opinion of different persons whether a particular act might not be justified. There seems to have been no doubt in this case that it could not be challenged that the appellant knew that what he was doing was contrary to law.

But not all Commonwealth countries have followed *Windle*. Most notably the High Court of Australia in *Stapleton* v. *The Queen* (1952) felt that 'wrong' meant morally wrong by the ordinary standards of the reasonable man, and not legally wrong. This case concerned the murder of a policeman in the Northern Territory by a man whose Tasmanian family had a history of mental deficiency and abnormality. In its lengthy, if complex, historical survey the court said:

[The relevant words in *M'Naghten*] are not to be construed as a legislative declaration and their meaning, if any difficulty exists about it, is best ascertained by looking at the authorities upon which the statement of the judges was founded. How the law had been understood for a century past appears from the reports of a number of trials not excluding the report of the trial of M'Naghten himself (*R.* v. *M'Naghten*).

What appears is that an incapacity to know the difference between good and evil was, if it was the outcome of mental disease, a test of irresponsibility. It is true that among the different expressions used there sometimes appears a reference to knowledge that the act committed was against the 'laws of God and man'. But the context leaves no doubt that this expression is referring to the canons of right and wrong and not to the criminal law.

In *R.* v. *Sullivan* (1984) the defendant while suffering from an epileptic fit kicked an elderly friend inflicting severe injuries. The Court of Appeal and the House of Lords held that it was proper to return the special verdict of 'not guilty by reason of insanity', since the assailant was suffering from a 'disease of the mind' within the M'Naghten Rules, in other words automatism by reason of insanity as opposed to non-insane automatism (automatism simpliciter).

In *R.* v. *Burgess* (1991) it was held that sleep-walking violence could amount to insanity, a point not totally dissimilar to the facts in *Hennessey* (1989). Here, in *Burgess*, B. fell in love with the victim, who lived in a flat above his. One night, after watching a violent video together, they both fell asleep. The victim woke to find that Burgess had broken a bottle over her head. He then dropped the video recorder onto her and started to strangle her. She stopped this only by shouting out that she loved him. Burgess was charged with wounding with intent, contrary to the Offences against the Person Act 1861, s.18. His defence was that he had caused the injuries whilst sleep-walking.

The Court of Appeal decided that a defence of somnambulism constituted insane automatism. It was a disease of the mind because it came from within. It was irrelevant that it was only temporary and that there was no recorded case of recurrence with serious violence. The mandatory hospital order was justified because sleep-walking was a mental disorder which had manifested itself in violence and suitable treatment could be provided within a hospital.

Burgess is an important case which reverses a number of earlier decisions where somnambulism had been regarded as amounting to *non-insane* automatism. This was the *obiter* view of the House of Lords in *Bratty* v. *Attorney-General for Northern Ireland* (1963). Nevertheless the approach in *Burgess*, it can be argued, is consistent with more recent developments in the law of insanity. In *Sullivan* (1984) the House of Lords had decided that it was irrelevant whether the disease of the mind was organic or functional, permanent or transient or intermittent. Also, in *Quick* (1973) the crucial distinction between insane and non-insane automatism was held to depend on whether the cause of the disease was internal or external. Generally sleep-walking is regarded as coming from within.

Celia Wells has commented:

> **The Rules and the special verdict which follows seem blunt instruments with which to achieve [a] purpose. Do epileptics present a danger, and is it greater than that presented by diabetics? Lord Diplock is, however, able both to attribute to the Rules a purpose not necessarily borne out by history and to admit that 'it is natural to feel reluctant to attach the label of insanity to a sufferer from psychomotor epilepsy of the kind to which Mr Sullivan was subject'.**

One final point about insanity, an evidential one. Unusually for criminal law, the burden of proof here is generally the civil one of the balance of probabilities, rather than beyond reasonable doubt. The prosecution cannot raise the issue of insanity except in the case of pre-trial proceedings (fitness to plead). But if the defence pleads diminished responsibility, the prosecution may raise the question of insanity, or where the defence pleads insanity on a murder charge, then the prosecution may raise the issue of diminished responsibility (Criminal Procedure (Insanity) Act 1964, s.6).

4 Diminished responsibility

In respect of 'murder' the Homicide Act 1957 provides that a person may instead be convicted of the less serious offence of manslaughter on grounds of 'diminished responsibility'. The proof does not have to be beyond reasonable doubt but on the balance of probabilities; the effect is that the court is left with a wide discretion as to the nature of the punishment. There are several elements to diminished responsibility. The accused must show that he was suffering from some abnormality of the mind (as opposed to disease) at the time of the killing. Abnormality of the mind means what the ordinary, reasonable person would understand to be abnormal. Section 2 the 1957 Act reads:

Where a person kills or is a party to the killing of another, he shall not be convicted of murder if he was suffering from such abnormality of mind (whether arising from a condition of arrested or retarded development of mind or any inherent causes or inducted by disease or injury) as substantially impaired his mental responsibility for his acts and omissions in doing or being a party to the killing.

In *R. v. Byrne* (1960) Lord Parker noted:

Abnormality of the mind . . . means a state of mind so different from that of ordinary human beings that the reasonable man would term it abnormal. It appears to us to be wide enough to cover the mind's activities in all its aspects, not only the perception of physical acts and matters, and the ability to form a rational judgement whether an act is right or wrong, but also the ability to exercise willpower to control physical acts in accordance with that rational judgement.

In *R. v. Ahluwalia* (1992) the appellant had been the subject of an arranged marriage; her husband had beaten and taunted her over a number of years. Eventually she poured petrol over him and set him alight. The trial judge had rightly directed the jury that provocation involved the *sudden* loss of self-control, but a re-trial would be ordered since she may have had an arguable case on grounds of diminished responsibility. The case is in contrast to *R. v. Thornton* (1992) (see below).

In *R. v. Egan* (1992) the appellant was virtually subnormal, and having drunk a large amount of alcohol entered the house of an elderly woman (possibly with intent to rob) and killed her. His defence to the murder charge rested on diminished responsibility which failed: the jury had to ignore D.'s intoxicated state and instead consider whether the accused whilst carrying out the killing would still have been suffering from diminished responsibility.

'Irresistible impulse' would fall within the concept of diminished responsibility. In *R. v. Byrne* the accused strangled a young woman and mutilated her body on account of an abnormal sexual impulse. Care is usually taken to distinguish very carefully between insanity under the *M'Naghten Rules* and diminished responsibility: in the latter case the accused may be perfectly capable of appreciating the quality or nature of the act and the wrong he is committing, but he is still under an overwhelming urge to commit the offence (hence diminished responsibility may be argued in defence even in a premeditated killing). The defence of diminished responsibility has been employed successfully in such instances of manslaughter as mercy killing and 'crimes of passion', thus largely replacing insanity as a defence.

In *R. v. Gittens* (1984) the defendant, suffering from a depressive illness on account of hereditary factors and psychological injury, took drink and drugs. Because of the consequent abnormality of the mind, he killed his wife and daughter-in-law. The Court of Appeal substituted convictions of manslaughter for murder, on account of diminished responsibility. As in *Egan* later it emphasised that intoxication should be disregarded in deciding whether the defendant's mind is abnormal for the purposes of diminished responsibility, but the case well illustrated the thin dividing lines between the various 'mental defences'.

5 Mistake and automatism

Both these defences have been outlined under *actus reus* and *mens rea* above; however, a few more words may be added about the latter. (Mistake is also considered below in the context of duress and provocation.) Automatism must mean that the accused undertook his act in a totally involuntary state. Thus in *Hill* v. *Baxter* (1958) it was suggested that a motorist who was attacked by a swarm of bees might well lose complete control over the vehicle; a driver suddenly suffering from a stroke or heart attack or an epileptic fit might also raise the defence of automatism. But if there was any chance of the accused taking avoiding action, then, of course, the defence of automatism will fail (*Kay* v. *Butterworth* (1945) and *R.* v. *Quick* (1973)). In *Bratty* v. *Attorney-General for Northern Ireland* (1963) Lord Denning suggested that automatism should be interpreted relatively narrowly, that it should be limited to unconscious acts, spasms and convulsions.

G. J. Bennett and Professor Brian Hogan have observed:

> **In *R.* v. *Sullivan* Lord Diplock said that it was natural to feel reluctance to attach the label of insanity to a sufferer from psychomotor epilepsy but he was clear that only Parliament, and not the courts, could do anything about it. So Lord Denning's restriction of automatism to such things as spasms, reflex actions and convulsions needs to be qualified to the extent that if the cause of the spasm or convulsion is a disease of the mind it is only the qualified form of acquittal on the grounds of insanity that is available, and on all but the most serious of charges the defendant will want to sidestep that by pleading guilty. The instances where automatism would lead to an unqualified acquittal might thus be reduced almost to vanishing point. . . . The common-sense answer has suggested itself to the courts, and in particular to Lord Diplock in *Sullivan*, that if the loss of conscious control is attributable to an external factor (other than the consumption of intoxicants) then automatism may be available; if it is attributable to internal factors then an acquittal is available only on the ground of insanity.**

In *R.* v. *Bailey* (1983) the Court of Appeal held that self-induced automatism other than that due to intoxication from alcohol or drugs might provide a defence to crimes of basic intent, and it would be up to the prosecution to show that the required element of recklessness existed. (Recklessness here looks like a subjective test pre-*Caldwell*.) Lord Justice Griffiths observed that automatism resulting from intoxication by alcohol or drugs did not negative the *mens rea* necessary for crimes of basic intent since the accused's conduct was reckless and recklessness was enough to constitute the necessary *mens rea* in assault cases where no specific intent formed part of the charge. ('Specific intent' is discussed below under 'intoxication'.)

There might be material distinctions, Lord Justice Griffiths continued, between someone who consumed alcohol or took drugs and one who failed to take sufficient food after insulin to avert hypoglycaemia. It was common knowledge that those who took excessive alcohol or certain drugs might become aggressive or do dangerous, unpredictable things – they must be able to foresee the risks of causing harm to others. The same could not be said of a man who failed to take food after an insulin injection. If he did appreciate the risk that such a failure might lead to aggressive, unpredictable and uncontrollable conduct and he nevertheless deliberately ran the risk or otherwise disregarded it, that amounted to recklessness. It was not common knowledge even among diabetics that such was a consequence of a failure to take food, the judge concluded.

There might be the possibility of non-insane automatism in cases where a temporary impairment which was not self-induced by drink or drugs arose from some external physical factor such as a blow on the head or the administration of an anaesthetic for therapeutic purposes. In *R. v. Hennessy* (1989) Lord Chief Justice Lane said that stress, anxiety and depression could be the result of the operation of external factors but they were not in themselves, separately or together, external factors of the kind capable in law of causing or contributing to a state of automatism. The Court of Appeal dismissed an appeal by H. against conviction of taking a conveyance, contrary to s.12 of the Theft Act 1968, and driving whilst disqualified; H. was an insulin-dependent diabetic and was suffering from hypoglycaemia, so that he sought to rely on the defence of non-insane automatism. The appellant had told the police that, if he managed to drive on the open road, he would have given them a real run for their money. Lord Lane said that the trial judge had rightly concluded that it was a case of legal 'insanity' within the *M'Naghten Rules*.

The cases of *Sullivan* and *Hennessy* show that the law's view of insanity does not parallel that of the psychiatrist. Only where the cause arose from an external factor, such as a blow on the head or possibly failure to take the correct medicine, could there be non-insane automatism which would lead to a complete acquittal.

6 Intoxication

Drunkenness, or a similar state of irresponsibility brought on by drugs, is not a defence in its own right, but in certain instances it is an important argument, particularly where it can be shown that a mistake has been made. The accused must show that the degree of intoxication had meant that he lacked the necessary *mens rea* to form the act and it is for the prosecution to rebut that argument. In *DPP* v. *Beard* (1920) the accused, who pleaded drunkenness, was convicted of murder when he raped a 13 year-old girl and in doing so placed his hand over her mouth to stop her screaming. As a result she suffocated and died. The Court of Appeal reduced the conviction to manslaughter but the House of Lords restored it to murder. The argument of intoxication may be used where the prosecution must show that the accused had a 'specific intent' to commit the offence in question or where it has apparently led to a disease of the mind (as defined under the *M'Naghten Rules*). The argument may also be employed if it can be shown that the drink or drug was taken involuntarily, for example, gin is added to unadulterated tonic water or where the accused has been forced to take a drink or drug. Voluntary intoxication falling outside the *M'Naghten Rules* is no defence in those crimes which do not require proof of specific intent, unless, it might be suggested, voluntary intoxication indicates the accused made a mistake of fact. In *Jaggard* v. *Dickinson* (1981) the defendant relied on s.5 of the Criminal Damage Act 1971 to be acquitted of criminal damage; when drunk she broke into what she thought was a friend's house. But the contrary was held in *R.* v. *O'Grady* (1987), where Lord Chief Justice Lane said that if the jury was satisfied that the defendant was mistaken in his belief that any force was necessary to defend himself and the mistake was caused by voluntarily induced intoxication then the defence must fail – it did not matter whether the offence was of 'basic' or 'specific' intent. But, *obiter*, the Court of Appeal added that a sober man mistakenly believing he was in immediate danger of death from an attacker could be acquitted of both murder and manslaughter if his 'reaction was a reasonable one'. The victim was a friend of the appellant; both had consumed large quantities of alcohol, leading to a fatal fight between them.

O'Grady was considered in *R.* v. *O'Connor* (1991) where D., because of self-induced intoxication, formed a mistaken belief that he was using force to defend himself, and his plea of self-defence had failed. However, the judge should have directed the jury that self-induced drunkenness could have the effect of preventing the appellant from forming a specific intent. The conviction for murder was therefore unsafe. Professor Smith said:

> **the illogicality of the dictum in *O'Grady* could hardly be better illustrated than by the present case. The jury is not entitled to take into account the fact that the defendant was drunk in deciding whether he intended to act in self-defence but they must take it into account in deciding whether he intended to cause serious serious bodily harm. As well as being completely illogical, it must be extremely difficult for the jury to understand and apply.**

In *R.* v. *Woods* (1982) the Court of Appeal said: 'The law as a matter of social policy has declared that self-induced intoxication is not a legally relevant matter to be taken into account in deciding as to whether or not a woman consents to intercourse'. But in *R.* v. *Hardie (Paul Deverall)* (1985) – an arson case – the Court of Appeal took the line that a commonplace drug like valium (here the defendant had taken about five tablets) was wholly different in kind from drugs which were liable to cause unpredictability or aggressiveness, although in certain cases the taking of a sedative or sorporific drug could not be an answer, for example in a case of reckless (now dangerous) driving. This hardly seems to accord with the strict interpretation of *Caldwell*.

So, the qualification of 'specific intent', is an important one. Thus in a crime not requiring proof of 'specific intent', it is no argument to say that drunkenness caused an 'irresistible impulse' or led to a state of automatism. Defining 'specific intent', however, has caused the courts some problems. To date Parliament has not defined specific intent: the matter has been left to the courts to decide. Crimes which require proof of specific intent are murder, wounding or causing grievous bodily harm with intent, theft, robbery, burglary with intent to steal, handling stolen goods, criminal damage to property with the aim of endangering life, forgery of cheques, the aiding and abetting of or attempt to commit any offence. Certain attempts at clarifying the term 'specific intent' have been made, but they have not always been helpful. For example, in *DPP* v. *Majewski*, which reaffirmed and extended the *dicta* in *Beard*, it was suggested that the *mens rea* in a crime of specific intent required proof of some purposive element (Lord Simon) or that crimes not requiring proof of specific intent were those committed recklessly (Lord Elwyn-Jones). Offences not requiring proof of specific intent include manslaughter; assault occasioning actual bodily harm; assault on a police officer in the execution of his or her duty; indecent assault; common assault; rape; criminal damage to property; taking a conveyance without the owner's consent; and maliciously wounding or inflicting grievous bodily harm.

In respect of intoxication (*Majewski*) the fault element appears to be less than that for inadvertent recklessness under the *Caldwell* test or gross negligence under *Adomako*. This is not helpful to have two different tests, even if the difference is perhaps marginal; it was even less helpful to have only one substantive judgment in *Adomako* (1994), from Lord Mackay, the Lord Chancellor, which gave no real guidelines for the jury in respect of recklessness.

Like insanity the defence of intoxication is one that can often cause considerable problems for the courts. This was illustrated in *R.* v. *Sheehan and Moore* (1975). Here the appellants, who had both had a great deal to drink, were charged with the murder of N. They poured petrol over N.'s derelict house and set fire to it, but N. escaped. They then pursued N. and S. poured petrol over N. himself and set light to him. The trial judge, Mr Justice Caulfield, in his summing-up at Lincoln Crown Court said: 'Drunkenness is only a defence to an act which would otherwise be criminal if a person has drunk so much that he is incapable of forming that intention to do the particular act.' He then went on to say to the jury: 'All these matters you will consider and it may be that you will conclude that these men were perfectly capable of forming the intention either to kill or cause grievous bodily harm or to attack [N.].' The Court of Appeal held, however, that the jury should have regard to all the evidence and as a result should feel sure that S. and M. had had the intent either to kill N. or to inflict upon him grievous bodily harm, whereas, the judge's direction was misleading in that it suggested to the jury that the onus was upon S. and M. to show that they were incapable of forming the necessary intention. Thus a conviction for manslaughter was substituted.

The *O'Grady* case is less than helpful; the judgment of the Court of Appeal on such a complicated issue as intoxication was breathtakingly brief. J. C. Smith has commented:

> **The decision proceeds on the assumption that self-defence is a complete defence on a charge of homicide or not a defence at all. It is submitted**

that this assumption is unfounded. Take first the case of a sober person who mistakenly believes that he is the victim of a deadly attack and, using no more force than would be reasonable if the facts were as he believes them to be, kills his assailant or supposed assailant. Since *Gladstone Williams* it is clear that he has a defence to a charge of murder. It does not necessarily follow that he has a defence to a charge of manslaughter. If he was grossly negligent in making the mistake, assuming the offence of manslaughter by gross negligence still exists, he would appear guilty of manslaughter.

The same conclusion would appear to follow in the case of a defendant who makes the mistake because he is drunk – the drunken mistake can hardly be regarded as other than a grossly negligent one. But even if it be the case that manslaughter by gross negligence is no longer part of our law, the drunken defendant may still be liable simply on the ground that he is reckless within the doctrine of *Caldwell*: a reasonable person who gave thought to the matter would have been aware that he was *not* the victim of a deadly attack. Manslaughter may certainly be committed by *Caldwell* recklessness. Perhaps, however, the defendant could say he was not *Caldwell* reckless, because he *had* given thought to the matter and concluded he was under deadly attack . . . The answer then is that he may still be liable under the principle of *Majewski*. Since manslaughter is a crime of so-called 'basic intent' a plea based on the absence of recklessness through intoxication must fail.

7 Necessity, self-defence and duress

The accused may argue necessity as a defence: he acted in order to protect himself (self-defence) or property or to prevent some violent act being committed against a third party. It is a defence which has caused considerable difficulties for English law. Under the Road Traffic Regulation Act 1967 fire engines, ambulances and police cars may be driven above the normal speed limit. But apart from certain statutory provisions such as the 1967 Act, it is unclear as to how far the defence exists, if at all, at common law. In *R. v. Vantandillo* (1815) it was suggested that it might be a defence to argue necessity where a mother carried her seriously ill child through the streets in order to seek medical assistance, although at the same time she exposed members of the public to a contagious disease. The defence of necessity was also considered in *DPP v. Harris* (1995). In *R. v. Dudley and Stephens* (1884) three shipwrecked sailors and a cabin-boy were adrift on the open seas for nearly three weeks without food. S., supported by D. but not by the third man, killed the cabin-boy. All three fed themselves from the boy's body. Four days later they were rescued. Later D. and S. were charged with murder; it was accepted by the court that the men would probably have died within the four days had they not eaten and that the boy would have died first being the weakest. Nonetheless, they were convicted of murder but the sentence was later reduced to six months' imprisonment. In *R. v. Martin* (1989) the Court of Appeal allowed the defence of necessity in respect of a conviction for driving whilst disqualified on account of the fact that the defendant's wife had suicidal tendencies. The defendant's stepson was late for work and in danger of losing his job; this apparently made Martin's wife distraught enough to threaten to commit suicide if Martin did not drive the son to work.

In *R. v. Cousins* (1982) the appellant threatened to kill another but argued that he had a lawful excuse within the terms of the Offences against the Person Act 1861 by reason of self-defence, for he believed an attack was planned on himself which he wished to forestall. He also argued that he was generally seeking to prevent crime under the Criminal Law Act 1967. The facts were as follows:

> On 23 April 1981 William Reed, a notoriously violent man, was attacked and beaten up when leaving a public house where the appellant had been. There was no evidence that the appellant had anything to do with this assault as a result of which William Reed was detained in hospital for a few days. On the afternoon of 29 April 1981, the appellant, carrying a double-barrelled shotgun, came to the Reeds' home where he inquired as to the whereabouts of Kelly Reed, the son of Mr and Mrs Reed. Mr Reed asked the appellant what he was going to do with the gun and, according to him, the reply was, 'I am coming after Kelly with a gun. When I see him I'm going to kill him. I'm going to blow his brains out, when I see him.' Mrs Reed confirmed this evidence. She said that the appellant had pointed the gun at her husband's head and said: 'I am after your Kelly. I want to see Kelly because he is after me and I'm going to blow his head off.' Both Mr and Mrs Reed said that they believed the appellant intended to carry out the threat he had made and the appellant in cross-examination conceded that he meant them to do so. He said: 'I went to the Reeds to make a threat . . . I intended Reed should believe the threat and that was to kill their son Kelly if he came anywhere near any of my family or me'.

Under further examination the appellant stated that he believed that Kelly Reed and a cousin had put out a contract because they had heard that the appellant was the man who had beaten up William Reed. The Court of Appeal, allowing the appeal, held that in the light of the Criminal Law Act 1967 (s.3) and the common law recognition of the lawfulness of the use of reasonable means for self-defence, a lawful excuse could exist under the Offences against the Person Act 1861, but the threat must be reasonable in all the circumstances and it was a matter for the jury to decide. Here, therefore, there is no Australian 'half-way house': self-defence can acquit for murder, but not reduce the charge to manslaughter.

In *R. v. Barrett (Alan)* (1981) the Court of Appeal made it clear that the amount of reasonable force used in self-defence was based on an objective and not subjective standard. It is even conceivable that making petrol bombs can be a matter of self-defence, such as where riots are taking place, *Attorney-General's Reference (No 2 of*

1983),(1984). In *Beckford* v. *R.* (1988), where the unarmed victim begged the policeman not to shoot him, but the policeman believed the victim was firing upon him, the Privy Council, considering the appeal from Jamaica, said that the test for self-defence was that a person might use such force as was reasonable in the circumstances as he honestly believed them to be. So, in *Beckford*, in respect of an honest *mistake*, a subjective test prevails. The reasoning of the Privy Council in *Beckford* is *ad hoc*, A. P. Simester argued in a 1992 review. 'The Privy Council rested their advice upon a peculiar view of *Morgan*', for *Morgan* affirmed that mistakes going to supervening defences, including self-defence, had to be reasonable.

But the amount of force used must always be reasonable, that is not excessive in an objective sense, as seen in *Barrett* and as underlined in *R.* v. *Whyte* (1987) where a stabbing was an over-reaction for a punch in the face, particularly as the knife had already been opened before the alleged attack on the defendant. In the cases of *Gladstone Williams* and *Beckford* the issue was the genuine if mistaken and seemingly unreasonable belief in the need for self-defence in the first place, rather than the amount of force as such then applied in self-defence.

In *Williams* (1987) the defendant was charged with occasioning actual bodily harm but he argued that he genuinely believed that the victim was unlawfully attacking another man; in fact the victim was attempting to make a citizen's arrest of the other man for robbery. The Court of Appeal held that to be guilty the defendant had to apply unlawful force, so that a genuine, albeit mistaken, belief in circumstances which would have rendered the force lawful would thus be a defence, and it was for the Crown to disprove the belief beyond reasonable doubt.

These points were returned to in *R.* v. *Scarlett* (1993); here the appellant was the licensee of a pub in Halifax which the deceased had entered 10 minutes after closing time, the worse for drink. S. used force to eject him, the deceased falling down some steps into the street, striking his head fatally as he did so. The judge had directed the jury that if they concluded that the accused had used more force than was necessary in the circumstances then the appellant was guilty of manslaughter. But Lord Justice Beldam, in the Court of Appeal, said that there seemed no logical basis for distinguishing between a person who objectively was not justified in using force at all but mistakenly believed that he was and another who was in fact justified in using force but mistakenly believed that the circumstances called for a degree of force objectively regarded as unnecessary. The directions to the jury were therefore inadequate and the conviction would be quashed. *Owino* (1996) made it clear that *Scarlett* had not changed the rule in *Gladstone Williams*.

No exceptions in respect of the degree of force allowed for self-defence could be allowed for serving soldiers or police officers, the House of Lords held in *R.* v. *Clegg* (1995). Here a soldier opened fire on a car that had been driven through a check-point in Northern Ireland, the fourth shot killing one of the occupants. So, was a soldier on duty, who kills a person with the requisite intention for murder, but who is, except for the use of excessive force, entitled to rely on self-defence, guilty of murder or manslaughter? The House of Lords held the charge could not be reduced from murder to manslaughter where the force used was excessive and unreasonable. This was a matter for the legislature. However, the House of Lords had not hesitated to change the law in respect of marital rape (*R. v. R.*, 1991). Private Clegg was released after two years, and in 1997 fresh evidence led to a reference to the Court of Appeal; a retrial was ordered in 1998.

Duress

Very closely related to necessity is the defence of duress. The term 'compulsion' is also used instead of 'duress', as is 'coercion', although the latter, as explained below, can have a special meaning. It simply means that a person is forced or threatened with force to undertake a criminal action. It now appears that such a defence may be raised in respect of any crime except murder. It is not a defence to certain instances of treason. Some people, of course, might be better equipped than others in resisting duress; what has to be taken into account by the courts is what is a reasonable reaction to force or threats in all the circumstances. Where a person has a means of escape, then the argument of duress will falter, if not fail altogether (*R. v. Gill* (1963)); but again some people might be better escaping than others – the man with a wooden leg will have more difficulty in climbing through a high window than an Olympic athlete. The *Gill* case involved the theft of a lorry which the accused was 'forced' to drive. The case of *R. v. Hudson* (1971) concerned two girls charged with perjury on account of giving false evidence in court; they had seen a man in the public gallery who, they believed, might injure them. The Court of Appeal observed that it was always open to the prosecution to show that the accused failed to take an opportunity – depending on his age and circumstances – which might render the threat ineffective. Duress remains, however, a difficult defence. In *Subramaniam v. Public Prosecutor* (1956) the appellant, charged with unlawful possession of ammunition, pleaded that he had been compelled by terrorists in Malaya to accept ammunition, for he feared for his own safety if he refused their demand.

In *R. v. Graham (Paul)* (1982) the Court of Appeal explained what the test should be in respect of duress. The defendant, a homosexual who had been drinking and taking drugs, was involved with his homosexual partner in killing his wife by strangling her with electric flex attached to a coffee percolator. The prosecution, at trial, conceded that it was open to the defendant to raise the defence of duress, that is fear of King, his partner, although the charge was one of murder.

> **In other words, they were not prepared to take the point that the defence of duress is not available to a principal in the first degree to murder. Consequently, the interesting question raised by the decisions in Director of Public Prosecutions for Northern Ireland v. Lynch (1975) and Abbott v. The Queen (1977) was not argued before us. We do not have to decide it. We pause only to observe that the jury would no doubt have been puzzled to learn that whether the appellant was to be convicted of murder or acquitted altogether might depend on whether the plug came off the end of the percolator flex when he began to pull it. (Lord Chief Justice Lane).**

The Court of Appeal held that the test (the question of murder apart) was a double one, firstly a subjective part, then an objective one, as follows.

> **(1) Was the defendant, or may he have been, impelled to act as he did because, as a result of what he reasonably believed King had said or done, he had good cause to fear that if he did not so act King would kill him or (if this is to be added) cause him serious physical injury? (2) If so, have the prosecution made the jury sure that a sober person of reasonable firmness, sharing the characteristics of the defendant, would not have responded to whatever he reasonably believed King said or did by taking part in the killing? The fact that a defendant's will to resist has been eroded by the voluntary consumption of drink or drugs or both is not relevant to this test.**
>
> **As a matter of public policy, it seems to us essential to limit the defence of duress by means of an objective criterion formulated in terms of reasonableness. Consistency of approach in defences to criminal liability is obviously desirable. Provocation and duress are analogous. In provocation the words or actions of one person break the self-control of another. In duress the words or actions of one person break the will of another. The law requires a defendant to have the self-control reasonably to be expected of the ordinary citizen in his situation. It should likewise require him to have the steadfastness reasonably to be expected of the ordinary citizen in his situation. So too with self-defence, in which the law permits the use of no more force than is reasonable in the circumstances. And, in general, if a mistake is to excuse what would otherwise be criminal, the mistake must be a reasonable one.**

The House of Lords, however, later went further. In *R. v. Howe* (1987), departing from its previous decision in *Lynch*, it held that the defence of duress was not available to a person charged with murder, whether as a principal in the first degree (the actual killer) or as principal in the second degree (an aider and abettor). The Lord Chancellor, Lord Hailsham, did not accept that it was either good morals, good policy or good law to suggest, as did the majority in *Lynch*, that the ordinary man of reasonable fortitude was not to be supposed to be capable of heroism if he was asked to take an innocent life rather than sacrifice his own. In murder cases the available mechanisms, his Lordship added, were today both more flexible and more sophisticated, a lot of comfort, it might be added, to the ordinary 'hero'; Lord Hailsham's reasoning seems to be flawed in several respects.

> **The House really had to go forward or back, as Lord Bridge said. The decisions in both *Lynch* and *Abbott* could not rationally be left standing together so that, on a charge of murder, duress could be a defence to one who aided, abetted, counselled or procured the killing, but not to the actual killer. Sadly, but predictably, the House has gone the wrong way – backward. The decision is supported by some unconvincing arguments. (*The Criminal Law Review*).**

The facts in *Howe* were that Howe and Bannister with two other men (Bailey and Murray) had attacked Elgar, a youth of 17. H. and B. had virtually kicked E. to death, but it was Bailey who strangled him. The four men's second victim, Pollitt, was also killed by strangulation and H. and B. had pulled the cord. A third victim escaped. In the conjoined appeal of *Burke*, B. had shot the victim at point blank range at C's request. B. alleged that Clarkson had threatened his life if he did not carry out the killing.

In *R. v. Conway* (1986) the Court of Appeal made it clear that a driver, who was charged with reckless driving and admitted driving fast and over the speed limit, could raise the defence of duress of circumstances where the facts established that he was constrained by circumstances to drive as he did to avoid death or serious bodily harm to himself or some other person. In such a case the jury must be left to decide if, from an objective standpoint, the driver had acted in order to avoid a threat of death or serious injury. This essentially is a defence of necessity, as illustrated in the parallel case of *R. v. Martin* (1989). Indeed, in *Conway* Lord Justice Woolf stated that whether the term 'duress of circumstances' was called duress or necessity did not matter; the circumstances had to be such that the accused objectively acted as he did to avoid death or serious bodily harm to himself or some other person.

In *Martin* the Court of Appeal held that the defence of necessity is available only if the defendant can objectively be said to be acting reasonably and proportionately to avoid the threat of death or serious injury; moreover, it is for the jury to determine whether because of what the defendant reasonably believed he had good cause to fear death or serious injury; and if so whether a person of reasonable firmness, sharing the characteristics of the accused, would have responded as the defendant did.

In *R. v. Pommell* (1995) and *R. v. Ali* (1995) the Court of Appeal stressed that the doctrine of duress of circumstances did not just relate to road traffic offences, and was subject to the same principles as duress by threats. In *Bowen* (1996) it was made clear that low intelligence was of no relevance for purposes of duress and coercion.

The House of Lords, by a majority of three to two, has upheld the finding of the Court of Appeal that duress is no defence to *attempted* murder. Lord Jauncey commented that in the present climate of violence and terrorism it would probably be a good idea if Parliament reviewed the availability of duress in all serious crimes: *R. v. Gotts* (1992). The main difficulty now centres around s.18 of the Offences against the Person Act 1861. Gotts was also charged under s.18 with wounding with intent. Had the jury found that he had not intended to kill, but only to cause grievous bodily harm, they would have had to acquit him of attempted murder. The next step would have been to consider whether duress was available to a charge under s.18. It would appear that as the law stands the defence would be allowed. But if the victim then died within a year and a day from the initial attack (as the law then stood), Gotts would be retried for murder and duress excluded. This would appear to be nonsensical, for a defence to be relevant at one stage and not so at the next. Professor Smith has suggested that it would be possible to allow duress as a defence to murder where the accused intended to cause grievous bodily harm, but not where he intended to kill. It is unlikely this distinction would find favour with the courts or indeed with Parliament.

'Coercion' is sometimes used to mean marital duress – a wife is forced by her husband to commit a crime (Criminal Justice Act 1925). The wife must prove such coercion whereas in duress proper the burden or onus is effectively upon the prosecution to disprove it. It appears that the legislators' thoughts behind the relevant section of the 1925 Act was that coercion, in the marital context, could embrace mental or spiritual compulsion, whereas duress denoted purely physical compulsion.

Professor Smith has commented:

> **When Stephen wrote his *History of the Criminal Law of England* in 1883 he remarked on how little authority there was on the subject of duress (or 'compulsion' as he called it) and that, in nearly 30 years' experience of criminal law at the bar and on the bench, he never heard of the defence being made, except in the special case of married women. It is perhaps a sad commentary on our times that the defence now appears so prominently in the law reports.**

8 Impossibility

In rare instances it may be a defence to argue that it was impossible to perform a certain duty, invariably a statutory one.

6.3

Inchoate offences (incitement, conspiracy and attempt)

1 INCITEMENT

Incitement is the suggestion to or the persuasion of another to commit a crime. The persuasion, which does not necessarily have to succeed, may be accompanied by threats or other forms of improper pressure. Nonetheless, incitement is mere encouragement rather than positive assistance; it falls short of aiding and abetting (the act of an accomplice). Incitement really applies to where a crime is not committed as such, as in conspiracy and attempt. In a sense incitement is passive whereas aiding and abetting is active: while incitement involves some element of persuasion or pressure, aiding and abetting need not, for to be an accomplice a more weighty test is applied – was the accused in effect as guilty of the crime as the principal offender, did he, for example, hand another a gun in the full knowledge or agreement that a third person would be killed as a result?

Under the Criminal Law Act 1977 an incitement to commit an offence will be tried summarily or on indictment according to whether the offence itself is triable summarily or on indictment (or either way). It is not a crime to incite others to conspire, although it is an offence to incite others to commit incitement (*R. v. Sirat* (1986)), and conspiracy to incite is also an offence. It also appears under the 1977 Act that there is no offence of inciting others to aid and abet. Equally there can be no conspiracy to aid and abet (*R. v. Hollinshead* (1985)). And it is hardly possible to incite others to attempt to commit a crime, since in that context 'commit' and 'attempt' are indistinguishable.

Incitement, like conspiracy and attempt, may be termed an inchoate offence since the main or substantive crime to which it relates does not necessarily have to be committed.

2 CONSPIRACY

For many years – until the passage of the Criminal Law Act in 1977 – conspiracy was a common law crime. It was usually interpreted as an agreement between two or more people to commit an unlawful act or a lawful one by unlawful means. The term 'unlawful' embraced the civil law as much as it did the criminal. The 1977 Act is something of a half-way house towards total statutory reform of conspiracy. Under the 1977 Act common law conspiracy has been abolished, subject to certain exceptions. Statutory conspiracy is simply an agreement to commit any criminal offence; the means may be lawful or unlawful. It is triable only on indictment. The most important exception is conspiracy to defraud at common law; the Act specifically preserves this conspiracy, and 'to defraud' could cover a multitude of sins, including theft and forgery. As indicated later, it also appears that the Act preserves the common law conspiracies of corruption of public morals and outraging public decency. The Act, however, is not the most clearly drafted. The three common law conspiracies are dealt with below, although a note here is called for on recent developments in the first (to defraud).

In *R. v. Ayres* (1984), which concerned conspiracy to defraud an insurance company by claiming a lorry had been stolen, the House of Lords noted that criminal conspiracies were of four kinds only:

1 a conspiracy to commit one or more substantive criminal offences contrary to s.1 of the 1977 Act;

2 a conspiracy made an offence as such by some other enactment;

3 a common law conspiracy to defraud (s.5);

4 a common law conspiracy to corrupt public morals or outrage public decency (s.5).

Only in exceptional circumstances need a fraudulent agreement be charged as a common law conspiracy to defraud.

The muddled decision in *Ayres* led to many prosecutors feeling that fraudsters would escape conviction more easily. Indeed, in *R. v. Cooke* (1986), where British Railways staff were charged with conspiracy to defraud, by making sales of food and drink not the property of BR to passengers on a Penzance to Paddington train, the House of Lords held that a conspiracy to defraud at common law might still be charged where the evidence pointed that way, even if the evidence also disclosed a distinct statutory conspiracy to commit a substantive offence. Lord Bridge tried to clarify the language he had used in *Ayres* and pointed out that conspiracy to defraud at common law covers those situations where a fraud undertaken by A. alone would not be a crime, but only with B. perpetrated on C. would it be a crime, or indeed where A. and B. could only be charged with statutory conspiracy to commit minor statutory offences. The Criminal Justice Act 1987 (s.12) therefore enacted that where two or more people agreed to commit an offence, that would not preclude a charge of conspiracy to defraud, the penalty being up to 10 years' imprisonment, or a fine or both.

Certain other difficulties arise with the offence of conspiracy. For example, the parties concerned may not be able to foresee all the consequences of the act if their agreement is put into operation. It is conceivable, too, that while the requisite *mens rea* might be established for the commission of the principal crime, there is insufficient *mens rea* for its conspiracy. The 1977 Act makes a person liable for conspiracy only on the basis of actual knowledge of the circumstances relevant to the commission of the substantive offence and the intention to commit that particular crime. In respect of the common law conspiracies preserved under the 1977 Act it may be that recklessness is sufficient to constitute the requisite *mens rea*, but clear intent is certainly preferable. Thus while recklessness might well be sufficient to prove *mens rea* for the substantive offence, conspiracy to commit that offence will be held to exist only on proof of actual intention.

A person who ostensibly agreed with others who intended to pursue a course of conduct which necessarily involved the commission of an offence, while reserving to himself a private intention only to go part of the way in assisting in the commission of the offence, had the necessary guilty mind to support a conviction for conspiracy under s.1 of the Criminal Law Act 1977 (as amended by s.5 of the Criminal Attempts Act 1981), the Court of Appeal upheld by the House of Lords ruled in *R. v. Anderson (William Ronald)* (1985) (effecting a prisoner's escape).

A continuing crime

Conspiracy is a continuing crime; so an agreement to suspend terrorist activities during the Irish ceasefire from 1994 did not negate criminal conspiracy (*R. v. O'Hadmaill* (1996)). The various parties do not have to join a conspiracy at the same time; it is enough that at some point two or more are in agreement to commit an offence. A husband and wife count as one person for the purposes of criminal conspiracy, but not civil conspiracy in tort. Where three or more are involved it is not necessary to show that they all met and agreed; as long as two are in touch with each other, that is sufficient – the conspiracy may be a series or chain of inter-related agreements. A person under the age of criminal responsibility or the intended victim cannot be guilty of statutory conspiracy. The Criminal Attempts Act 1981 makes it clear that impossibility is no defence to statutory conspiracy; it may not be a defence in common law conspiracy. For example, if X. and Y. conspire to lock Z. inside a room without food or water, their intention is clear: they have agreed to kill Z. by the process of starvation. They also have the appropriate knowledge: the door is locked, the windows shuttered and barred. But Z., knows of a secret passage and escapes. X. and Y. were completely unaware of the passage's existence. They could therefore be held guilty of conspiracy to murder. Similarly, it would amount to conspiracy to have sex with a girl believed to be under 16 when in fact she is 17.

Where the substantive offence is successfully committed, it is unlikely that charges of conspiracy will be added. To do so would complicate matters unnecessarily; usually a charge of conspiracy is brought where the substantive offence has not been committed either at all or successfully.

Common law conspiracy

The three common law conspiracies may now be briefly considered. In conspiracy to defraud, the problems of which have already been noted above, it has been held that actual deceit is not a vital factor, for deceit (deception) is but one aspect of fraud itself. In *Scott* v. *Metropolitan Police Commissioner* (1975) the accused was found guilty of conspiracy to defraud, since he had agreed with employees of cinema owners that they should abstract films without the consent of either the cinema owners or the owners of the copyright.

Further, it is enough to show that the 'victim' did not suffer actual economic loss, but that his economic interests were simply put at risk, as seen in *Wai Yu-tsang* v. *R.* (1991). Similarly, it is conspiracy to defraud where it is intended to deceive a person in the performance of his public duties, even though it is not that person who suffers economically but the public at large, as illustrated in *DPP* v. *Withers* (1975) and *Welham* v. *DPP* (1961). In this instance some form of deception is involved, unlike theft, and the public official may be deceived into undertaking some action which barely involves economic considerations – for example, the release of confidential information, although even here the information concerned might be used eventually for financial gain. In *R.* v. *Landy* (1981) it was held that dishonesty was an essential ingredient in conspiracy to defraud. In this case, which involved a number of bank directors, it is notable that the Court of Appeal observed that counsel's closing speeches should not be prolix and a judge's summing-up should be clear, concise and intelligible. If it was overloaded with detail, whether of fact or law, and followed no obvious plan, it would not have the attributes it ought to have.

Conspiracy to corrupt public morals was best outlined in *Shaw* v. *DPP* (1962) (the 'Ladies' Directory' case). 'Lawyers have not yet come to terms with the principle that an agreement should not be indictable as a conspiracy unless it is an agreement to do something that would be an offence if done by an individual', said

Professor J. C. Smith, commenting on the *Attorney-General's Reference* (*No 1 of 1985* (1986)). Conspiracy to outrage public decency was similarly examined in *Knuller* v. *DPP* (1973). The former appears to mean any act designed to deprave or corrupt reasonable members of the public, to undermine, as Lord Simonds put it in *Shaw*, the 'moral welfare of the State'. To outrage public decency appears to mean offending standards of decency in public places – that includes the sale of books, newspapers and other literature. In *R.* v. *Lunderbach* (1991) the appellant was convicted of outraging public decency, by masturbating in a children's park.

After some doubts recent cases confirm that there is a substantive offence of outraging public decency, for instance *R.* v. *May* (1989); in *R.* v. *Rowley* (1991) where the accused, having left a series of notes in public places designed to lure boys for immoral purposes, was convicted of committing an act of outraging public decency, it was accepted the common law offence of outraging public decency existed. The cases of *R.* v. *Gibson* and *R.* v. *Sylveire* (1990) concerned convictions for the offences of outraging public decency at common law, as falling outside the 1959 Act, here an exhibition of earrings made from a freeze-dried human foetus.

Logically, it appears unjust for one person involved in a conspiracy to be convicted and for the other to be acquitted; either there is a conspiracy or there is not. On the other hand the evidence brought against X. may simply be stronger than that brought against Y.; X. may confess, Y. may deny the charge (*DPP* v. *Shannon* (1975)). The 1977 Act has made it clear that the acquittal of one is not a bar to the conviction of another, 'unless under all the circumstances of the case his conviction is inconsistent with the acquittal of the other person or persons in question'. What is agreed to be done, not what is actually done is the crucial factor, as Lord Justice Woolf pointed out in *R.* v. *Bolton* (1991).

In *R.* v. *Edwards* (1991) E. had agreed to supply amphetamine but it was possible he intended to supply ephedrine; he could not be convicted of conspiracy to supply amphetamine if there was doubt about his intention.

A common law conspiracy may be punishable at the discretion of the judges. A statutory conspiracy can only receive the maximum sentence of the substantive offence, but in the case of murder or any other offence for which the sentence is fixed by law or an indictable offence which is punishable with imprisonment but without a maximum term then the maximum sentence is life imprisonment.

Under the 1977 Act where the substantive offence has been committed and is subject to a limitation period within which any prosecution must be brought, then any prosecution for statutory conspiracy in relation to that offence is also subject to the same time-bar.

		A Crime?
1	Aiding/Abetting an Attempt	Yes
2	Attempting aiding/abetting	No
3	Attempting conspiracy	No
4	Incitement to conspire	No
5	Incitement to incite	Yes
6	Incitement to aid/abet	Unlikely
7	Conspiracy to aid/abet	No
8	Incitement to attempt	Theoretically
9	Attempting incitement	Yes
10	Conspiracy to incite	Yes
11	Aiding/Abetting incitement	Yes
12	Aiding/Abetting conspiracy	Yes
13	Conspiracy to attempt	Yes

3 ATTEMPT

It is an offence for an individual to attempt to commit a crime. Thus the *mens rea* is intention, not recklessness. But it may be argued that a man should be guilty of attempted rape, if he is reckless as to whether the woman is in fact consenting, and the same principle (recklessness being sufficient *mens rea* for attempt) might extend to the offence under s.1(2) of the Criminal Damage Act 1971, a point indirectly raised in *R.* v. *O'Toole* (1987). The attempt must be direct (perpetration) and not incidental or preliminary (preparation) – as seen in *DPP* v. *Stonehouse* (1977) where a well-known politician in financial difficulties faked his death in order that his innocent wife should benefit from certain life assurance policies. The common law has now been replaced by the Criminal Attempts Act 1981. This Act attempts to bring some sense of rationality to an area of criminal law that has frequently seemed to suffer from judicial confusion. In *R.* v. *Button* (1900) the accused impersonated an athlete of average ability; he was given long starts and being a good runner won the races. He was convicted of attempting to obtain money (the prizes) by false pretences. But in *R.* v. *Robinson* (1915) the accused, who had faked a robbery in his shop in order to claim insurance money, was found not guilty of attempting to obtain money by false pretences; Robinson was judged as merely preparing the necessary evidence to attempt to make a false claim on the insurance company, since the fraud was discovered and he was arrested before he had a chance to make the claim.

The 1981 Act makes it a criminal attempt for a person with an intent to commit an indictable offence to undertake an act which is more than 'merely preparatory to the commission of the offence'. *R. v. Jones* (1990) was a case of attempted murder, where the judge was correct in leaving it to the jury to conclude whether D. had 'done an act which is more than merely preparatory to the commission of murder'. The case followed *R. v. Gullefer* (1990); here G. bet money on a greyhound which he subsequently observed to be losing the race. In order to ensure that the race was declared void, so that the bookmaker would return his £18 stake, G. jumped onto the racetrack to distract the greyhounds as they rounded the final bend. In the event, the race was declared valid so G. was unable to seek a refund of his stake. The Court of Appeal held that G. was so far from completing the offence that no reasonable properly directed jury could have found him to have passed the preparatory stage. *Jones* decided that the tests used before the Act were no longer to be applied.

In *Jones* (1990) the appellant had climbed into the victim's car and pointed a loaded sawn-off shotgun at him; his conviction for attempted murder was upheld, although it was argued that his conduct was insufficiently proximate in that at least three more actions were required to be carried out before the full offence could have occurred, eg removing the gun's safety catch. But in *R. v. Campbell* (1991) the accused was found not guilty of attempted robbery, since his presence outside a post office was insufficiently proximate. A rather awkward case is *R. v. Griffin* (1993); G. was charged with attempting to take her two children out of local authority care, under s.1 of the Child Abduction Act 1984. She had bought single ferry tickets to the Irish Republic, which action was judged as more than merely preparatory.

The proximity test for attempts was illustrated in *R. v. Geddes* (1996), where the accused had entered school grounds and was found in a boys' toilet by a member of staff. He ran off; it was held by the Court of Appeal that only limited preparations had been made, that is his actions were only merely preparatory.

A person may be guilty of attempting to commit an offence even though the facts are such that the commission of the offence is impossible, thus solving the problem of the 'empty pocket' attempt; if a thief put his hand in an empty pocket he formerly could not be accused of attempted theft since there was nothing to steal. It is not an offence under the Act to attempt to aid, abet, counsel or procure or to attempt offences under the Criminal Law Act 1967 (assisting offenders and concealing arrestable offences) or to attempt conspiracy. But the Act did not remove from criminal responsibility the act of aiding and abetting to attempt a crime (*R. v. Dunnington* 1984)). Also, attempting incitement is an offence under the Act, although, conversely, in *R. v. Fitzmaurice* (1983) the Court of Appeal appears to have ruled that incitement to commit an impossible crime is an offence at common law, at least where the crime appears possible rather than impossible. The Act's poor drafting soon led to a battle in the courts. As Lord Hailsham said, the Act 'had formed a tilting yard for a joust of almost unexampled ferocity between two of the most distinguished professors of English criminal law'. In *R. v. Shivpuri* (1986) a man believed he was importing from India a controlled drug (heroin or diamorphine) contrary to the Customs and Excise Management Act 1979. In fact the substances were not drugs but some vegetable material akin to snuff. The Court of Appeal held that he was rightly convicted of attempt, that is attempting the impossible, under the 1981 Act. The House of Lords agreed, and in so doing overruled its decision in *Anderton* v. *Ryan* (1985), a case of handling a stolen video recorder. The overruling, following harsh academic criticism, was in accordance with the terms of the 1966 Practice Statement.

So it is no longer vital to distinguish between someone who tries to do something which in fact is no offence (for example, trying to kill a man already dead) and someone who tries to do something which is an offence but fails (for instance, trying to shoot someone alive with a blank bullet). Lord Bridge observed: 'The language in which Professor Glanville Williams criticised the decision in *Anderton* v. *Ryan* was not conspicuous for its moderation but it would be foolish on that account not to recognise its force and churlish not to acknowledge the assistance we have gained from it'. Lord Bridge also regretted not paying greater regard to the Law Commission report that had led to the 1981 Act.

A criminal attempt is an indictable offence, although under the 1981 Act an offence of interference with a vehicle is triable summarily.

6.4   Homicide

1 MURDER

Murder is one aspect of homicide; others include manslaughter, infanticide and genocide. Murder, like manslaughter and infanticide, is the unlawful killing of another. Coke defined murder in his *Institute of the Laws of England* as follows: 'Murder is when a man of sound memory, and of the age of discretion, unlawfully killeth within any county of the realm any reasonable creature *in rerum natura* under the king's peace, with malice aforethought, either expressed by the party or implied by the law . . . ' Formerly, death did not need to be immediate but it had to occur within a year and a day after the wrongful action if a charge of murder, manslaughter or infanticide was to be successfully preferred. This rule has sometimes led to difficulties. For instance, in *R.* v. *Dyson* (1908) the accused injured a child in November 1906; then he injured it again in December 1907. The child died in March 1908. The conviction of the accused was quashed because the jury had been wrongly directed by the judge: it should have been asked whether the injuries of 1907 hastened the child's death, rather than being told that it could convict on the basis of the 1906 injuries alone. Today one of the greyest areas of the law is how far the denial of medical aid, such as the switching off of a life-support machine, might amount to murder or manslaughter, and how far certain drugs might give relief of pain yet at the same time shorten a person's life. The *Anthony Bland* case was discussed in the first chapter. The year and a day rule was abolished by the Law Reform (Year and a Day Rule) Act 1996; but the Attorney-General must give his consent to prosecutions where death results beyond three years.

The 'person' killed must be a human being; a freak may not constitute a human being, nor will an unborn child, although here an offence may be committed under the Abortion Act 1967 or the Infant Life (Preservation) Act 1929. For a child to be 'born', it must have totally left the mother's womb, but it does not have to be immediately breathing.

A British citizen can be tried in a British court for a murder or manslaughter committed anywhere in the world.

Unless any contributory negligence of the victim or a third party is so gross or extreme as to prevent the accused's action from being the substantial cause of death, then the accused may still be convicted of murder, and the same rule applies to other branches of homicide. For example, in *R. v. Benge* (1865) the accused was a foreman platelayer who having misread a timetable took up a section of railway track at the very time a train was due. The accident resulted in several deaths and B was convicted of manslaughter, despite the fact that others had been negligent – the flagman who stood at the wrong place and the train-driver himself. On the other hand it would be a defence to argue that some intervening act so destroyed the chain of causation that X. could not be guilty of murder, although attempted murder would be a different matter. The same principle, *novus actus interveniens*, applies in tort. Suppose X. removes a stair-rod; he calls Y., his elderly mother, to come downstairs. Y., however, is fond of neat gin and in descending the stairs she sways, trips over before reaching the loose carpet, knocks her head on the bannisters and dies. X. can hardly be held responsible for her death, even though he may have welcomed it, for normally she descended the stairs safely, albeit in an alcoholic haze. In contrast, in *R. v. Blaue* (1975) the accused was held guilty of manslaughter; he had stabbed the victim, but she might well have lived had she not been a Jehovah's Witness and refused a blood transfusion. The wrong-doer must therefore take the victim as he finds them; again a similar rule, the 'egg-shell skull' rule, operates in tort. In *Dear* (1996) D. may have worsened the situation by interfering with his wounds, but they were still the cause of his death.

In a much older case, *R. v. Wall* (1800), a colonial governor was held guilty for the death of a man unlawfully flogged although there was evidence to suggest that the victim had guaranteed his demise by consuming a large amount of spirit. In *R. v. Michael* (1840) the act of an innocent London child was not held to break the chain of causation. Here the accused, M., delivered a bottle of medicine to S., who was paid to look after her child, G. M. wished to kill G., and in fact the 'medicine' was laudanum. S. put the 'medicine' on one side; in her brief absence K., aged five and one of S.'s own children, gave the poison to G. who promptly died. M. was convicted of murder. In *Thabo Meli* v. *R.* (1954), a Lesotho case, the accused clearly intended to murder the victim and having done so would push him over a cliff to fake an accident. This they did, but in fact they had not killed the victim at the top of the cliff – they had simply made him unconscious. In fact the victim died later from exposure. The Privy Council, however, regarded the actions as inextricably linked and it upheld a conviction for murder. In *R. v. Le Brun* (1991), *Thabo Meli* was distinguished on the basis that in *Le Brun* there was no preconceived plan to kill his wife and to dispose of the body; the case was more similar to *R. v. Church* (1966). The principles of causation were restated in *R. v. Mellor* (1996), where the appellant unsuccessfully argued that the death of an elderly man was really due not to his actions but to the failure of the medical attendants at the hospital to administer sufficient oxygen.

In *R. v. Fisher* (1987) the Court of Appeal quashed a conviction for manslaughter, thus confirming the principle of *R. v. Williams* (*Gladstone*) (1984) that a defendant who relies on self-defence is to be judged on the facts as he believed them to be. The judge should have allowed the issue of lawful justification to go to the jury. In *Fisher* the appellant was a doorman at a gay night-club. He intervened in a fight and was bitten by the deceased. He pushed and carried the victim down staircases and left him in the street where he was later found to be dead. The appellant thought the deceased's bite presented a threat of AIDS and he had punched him as a result (this might have caused the death). The case was different, therefore, from *Thabo Meli* or *Church* where one act was done with *mens rea* and the death was partly caused by a second act. Here the appellant's conduct was one process.

The chain of causation

Can medical treatment act as an intervening event, so breaking the chain of causation? In *R. v. Jordan* (1956) the victim, who had been stabbed eight days before his death, was given 'palpably wrong' treatment in hospital. It was held that that was the true cause of death, not the stab wound which, by that stage, had virtually healed. But if a drug is not administered negligently, yet nonetheless brings about the victim's death, then the accused may still be guilty of murder (if there was malice aforethought) or manslaughter (if there was not). The drug was given to save the victim's life, but no-one could foresee that the drug would have the opposite effect; the victim would have died anyway. In *R. v. Malcherek* (1981) the switching off of a life-support machine when the victim was to all intent and purposes 'dead', was held not to have broken the chain of causation; a similar issue arose in the Hillsborough tragedy case of *Airedale NHS Trust v. Bland* (1993) (*Bland* was applied in *Frenchay NHS Healthcare Trust v. S.* (1994).) 'Dead' here means brain death; the heart may, though, go on beating. In this case the accused, after a quarrel at a flat in Poole, had stabbed his wife nine times with a kitchen knife. The essential point is was the reaction within the range of responses that would not break the chain (*Corbett* (1996)?

In *R. v. Cheshire* (1991) the accused shot the victim who suffered from serious injuries, but the victim should have made a full recovery. However the surgeons did not notice that his windpipe was becoming blocked. Did their negligence break the chain of causation? This seemed like *Jordan*. But the Court of Appeal said that the acts of the accused need not be the sole or even the main cause of the victim's death as long as they contributed significantly to that result. The complication in *Cheshire* was a rare one, although the mistake by the hospital staff did bring about the death; the appellant's acts remained the significant cause of death. The doctors were negligent but not grossly negligent, in other words reckless; doctors could not be held reckless by juries in this context. At what stage is there liability – is it somewhere between negligence and recklessness? But overall this seems an unsatisfactory decision and in conflict with *Jordan*. Professor Smith noted: 'there is one thing for which we should be very grateful to the Court of Appeal. The idea that the test of causation should incorporate the concept of recklessness in its present horrific state is too dreadful to contemplate. At least the idea seems to have been strangled at birth.'

In *R. v. Williams* (1992) the appellants were the driver and passengers in a car which picked up P., a hitchhiker. The facts were disputed and there was a lack of direct evidence. However, it seemed that, following various threats to P., he jumped out of the car at 30mph and died. When the victim was killed while escaping from threatening demands for money, a jury can convict of manslaughter only if the threats were a cause of the death. Thus the jury must consider whether the victim's actions were so unreasonable and disproportionate to the threats that they constituted an unforseeable intervening cause which broke the chain of causation. In this instance the manslaughter convictions were quashed and so, for other reasons, were those for robbery.

In *R. v. Pitts* (1842) it was held that a person was guilty of murder if a victim had taken evasive action, such as throwing himself into a river, and thus drowning, on account of justified fear of immediate violence being done to him by the accused; the chain of causation held.

Intention

As indicated above the *mens rea* for murder is known as 'malice aforethought'. This is a broad and misleading phrase, since malice does not have to be present in the sense of ill-will, nor premeditation in the sense of planning the murder. 'Malice aforethought' means an intention to kill or to cause grievous bodily harm. Thus it is sufficient in murder to show that the accused had intent to cause very serious bodily harm, there is no need to prove an intention to kill or to endanger life as such (*R. v. Cunningham* (1981) and *R. v. Vickers* (1975)). The accused might well have failed to foresee what the reasonable man would have foreseen (*DPP v. Smith* (1963) and *Hyam v. DPP* (1975)). In the *Vickers* case a burglar of a shop was caught by its elderly owner; he struck her several times, although the force used was not particularly excessive. Nonetheless she died as a result and the accused was convicted of murder in accordance with the provisions of the Homicide Act 1957.

In *Hyam* (1975) the accused, who was the lover of J., set fire to the house of B., J.'s new friend. In so doing two of B.'s children were killed and H. was convicted of murder. The House of Lords was divided in *Hyam* but in *Cunningham* it was made clear that *Hyam*, *Vickers* (1975) and *Smith* (1961) had been rightly decided:

proof of an intention to cause grievous bodily harm was sufficient for a conviction of murder. In *Cunningham* (1981) the accused attacked the victim in a Margate public house, repeatedly hitting him with a chair. The deceased died later from his injuries. The accused wrongly suspected the victim, an Iranian, of sexually associating with his girlfriend. (Lord Hailsham, the Lord Chancellor, in approving the decisions in *Hyam*, *Vickers* and *Smith*, took care to emphasise that the doctrine of *stare decisis* (judicial precedent) was indispensable to the workings of the Lords, the 1966 Practice Statement notwithstanding. 'Especially must this be so in criminal law, where certainty is indeed a condition of it commanding and retaining respect.') In *Smith* the accused deliberately drove his car away with a policeman clinging to it; the officer later fell off and was killed by another vehicle in the oncoming traffic. The House of Lords overruled the Court of Appeal and reinstated a conviction of murder in place of manslaughter.

All this might suggest the law was settled on this point. But as indicated earlier in this chapter *Hyam* was regarded as a controversial case and it was effectively overruled in the South Wales miners' case of *Hancock* (1986). The *Hancock* case concerned striking South Wales miners who threw a lump of concrete at a taxi carrying a working miner; the concrete smashed the windscreen and killed the driver. On appeal, verdicts of manslaughter were substituted for murder. In *Hancock* the Law Lords clarified the rulings in *R. v. Moloney* (1985) on intention, disapproving the dictum of Lord Bridge in the latter. So, the terms 'probability', 'foresight' and 'intention' that bedevilled *Smith*, *Hyam* and to some extent *Cunningham* came back to haunt their Lordships. In the *Moloney* case the defendant had been drinking heavily along with his stepfather and in a 'lark' after a party fired a twelve-bore shotgun at his stepfather, to whom he was deeply attached and who died instantly.

> **Lord Bridge's speech in *Moloney* must go down as one of the finest examples of judicial legerdemain since records were kept. The real villain of the piece, Lord Bridge disclosed, was the learned editor of *Archbold* who not only sought to state the ratio of *Hyam* in the text . . . but compounded his folly by fabricating quotation marks around it**

was the comment of the *All England Law Reports Annual Review* in 1985. Their Lordships in *Hancock* were evidently unhappy at Lord Bridge's explanation of *Hyam*. The House decided a reference to 'probability' was necessary – that where it was necessary for the judge to direct the jury on the issue of intent, the trial judge should refer to probability and explain to the jury that the greater the probability of consequence the more likely it was that the consequence was foreseen, and that if it was foreseen the more likely it was that it was intended. In *R. v. Nedrick* (1986) the Court of Appeal returned to the problem.

In the *Nedrick* case, the appellant who had a grudge against a woman, without warning, poured paraffin through the letter-box and on to the front door of her house and set it alight. As a result the house was burnt down and one of her children died. Lord Chief Justice Lane, in giving guidance for juries, said that the jury must decide the defendant's intention on consideration of all the evidence: how probable was the consequence resulting from the defendant's voluntary act, and did he foresee the consequence? If he did not appreciate death or really serious harm was likely, then there was an absence of intention. But if the defendant realised death or serious injury was a virtual certainty, then the jury might infer that he intended to kill or seriously harm, even though he might not have desired that result. In *R. v. Walker and Hayles* (1990) the Court of Appeal accepted a direction to the jury using the phrase 'very high degree of probability' instead of 'virtual certainty', although the latter was to be preferred. But are the two phrases synonymous or is the test of a very high degree of probability a lower standard? *Nedrick* was followed in *R. v. Scalley* (1995). In *Mahmood* (1994) the Court of Appeal quashed the conviction of B. since he could not have foreseen A.'s further action in leaving the stolen car with its engine running with the result it moved away and killed a baby.

In *Hui Chi-ming* v. *R.* (1991), the Privy Council ruled that the contemplation of two parties to a crime does not have to be the same, although in most cases this will be so. In this case of murder it was enough that the secondary party, H., could foresee that P. might use a pipe to cause serious bodily harm.

The punishment for murder has been modified over the years. The Homicide Act 1957 drew a distinction between capital and non-capital murders. Then the Murder (Abolition of Death Penalty) Act 1965 abolished the death penalty and now the only sentence for all types of murder is life imprisonment. The judge may recommend to the Home Secretary a minimum period of imprisonment before the latter exercises his discretion whether to release the offender on licence (Prison Act 1952).

2 MANSLAUGHTER

Manslaughter is the other principal type of unlawful killing. It is punishable with any sentence, ranging from life imprisonment to an absolute discharge. Manslaughter is either voluntary or involuntary. It should be added that at common law juries have always been able to return verdicts of manslaughter on indictments alleging murder, and this was not changed by the Criminal Law Act 1967, s.6(2) (*R. v. Saunders* (1987)).

Voluntary manslaughter means that the killing took place with 'malice aforethought', but in such circumstances as to reduce the crime from one of murder. The three situations covered by the Homicide Act 1957 are that the accused was acting under diminished responsibility as discussed earlier; that the killing was in pursuance of the 'suicide pact'; and that the accused acted under provocation. Provocation and diminished responsibility can be raised as parallel defences. While the Suicide Act 1961 abolished self-murder as a crime, it is still an offence to aid and abet a suicide, the maximum sentence being 14 years' imprisonment. A 'suicide pact' means that two or more people agree to die together, although that does not necessarily mean that each has to take his own life.

Provocation

Provocation is a common law rule which has been amended by the 1957 Act. Its principal meaning is the sudden loss of self-control by the accused, who has been unduly provoked by another, usually the victim but sometimes a third party, having regard to what the behaviour of the reasonable man might be in all the circumstances. A confession of adultery is probably insufficient provocation (*Holmes* v. *DPP* (1946)). Catching a husband, wife, fiancé, fiancée or lover in the act (*in flagrante delicto*) may amount to provocation, particularly in the case of a spouse. In *Bedder* v. *DPP* (1954) a young man of 18 attempted but failed to have sexual intercourse with a prostitute. On account of his impotence the prostitute severely taunted him; B. stabbed the prostitute to death. Taunting is not unlawful but presumably is immoral. The Lords held that the reasonable man would not have acted in that way, since most men were not sexually impotent. The logical extension of the argument is that most 'reasonable' men are not disfigured, midgets, perpetually drunk or over-excitable.

The *Bedder* case appeared to suggest that the 'reasonable' man was the 'average' man, the person who had the physical and mental characteristics of the majority of the population, rather than being a man of reasonable behaviour whatever his particular, individual disabilities might be. In *DPP* v. *Camplin* (1978) the Lords adopted the latter test: what, in other words, would be the reaction of the reasonable man in those particular circumstances given the fact that he is sexually impotent? In *Camplin* a 15 year-old boy was buggered against his will by K., some 40 years his senior. The older man then laughed at him; the boy seized a chapatti pan and fatally cracked K.'s skull. The Lords said that the test to be applied was not that of the reasonable man, but that of what a reasonable 15 year-old boy would have done in all the circumstances, having taken into account any unusual characteristics of the accused. Unusual characteristics would include physical or mental matters, such as height, disfigurement, colour, impotence but not general considerations such as over-excitability or intoxication. The key point was that *Bedder* was decided before the Homicide Act was passed in 1957. 'The question', the Act says, 'whether the provocation was enough to make a reasonable man do as he did shall be left to be determined by the jury.' A state of intoxication may, however, be relevant to provocation, if that provocation owes something to a mistake of fact arising from a drunken condition, as illustrated by *R*. v. *Letenock* (1917), where one soldier stabbed another.

Provocation might even allow a degree of planning or co-ordination, as seen in *R*. v. *Pearson (William)* (1992) where abused sons killed their father with a sledgehammer, which was distinguished in *R*. v. *McKechnie, Gibbons and Dixon* (1992). In *Pearson* what was relevant to one brother's defence (provocation) was the ill-treatment handed out to his brother, whom he came home to protect, although he had been absent for eight years. *Thornton* (1992), following *Camplin*, showed that provocation over a long period is acceptable, if it leads to a sudden loss of self-control; here a woman had been brutally treated by her husband over a period of months.

In *Roberts* (1990) a 23 year-old man who was very deaf killed another as a result of taunts; so the *Camplin* test was again applied, ie how would the hypothetical reasonable 23 year-old deaf man have reacted, but evidence that certain deaf people are violently irrational was not relevant.

However, cooling-off periods seem to be less important, as seen in *Baillie* (1995), where D. fetched a gun from his attic and then drove to the victim's house to shoot him. The question of provocation is always one for the jury (*Cambridge* (1994) and *Rossiter* (1994)), although the judge must decide whether there is sufficient evidence for the jury to consider (*Cox* (1995) and *Burgess and McLean* (1995)).

Provocation should arise from clear actions or words (*Acott* (1997)), but can we allow for eccentric behaviour? In *R. v. Dryden* (1995) the appellant had built a bungalow without planning permission; a dispute arose with the result that the accused shot dead the council's chief planning officer. The *Camplin* test also arose in the House of Lords' case of *R. v. Morhall* (1995) where the matter of glue-sniffing being a characteristic of the reasonable man was considered; self-induced intoxication, for reasons of public policy, could not be relied upon where the defence of provocation was raised. In *R. v. Thornton (No 2)* (1996) the Court of Appeal ordered a retrial, in respect of the importance being attached to the battered woman syndrome. The Privy Council held in *Luc Thiet Thuan* v. *R.* (1996) that a defendant's mental infirmity which impaired or reduced the power of self-control below that of an ordinary man was not a factor to be attributed to the reasonable man. In short, the court was following the *Camplin* test, but following the cases of *Ahluwalia* and *Thornton (No 2)* what constitutes background issues to provocation is less than clear as far as the judges are concerned.

Involuntary manslaughter

Involuntary manslaughter, as stated earlier, embraces those areas of homicide where the killing has not taken place with malice aforethought. It basically falls into two categories: constructive manslaughter and criminal negligence. Constructive manslaughter means that the accused intended to undertake an act which was both unlawful and dangerous with the result that it was likely to cause physical injury although not necessarily of a serious kind. It is very unlikely that the act is unlawful where the victim has consented to the risk of harm, for example, a rugby player may expect to incur injury. Similarly, a parent or schoolteacher (*in loco parentis*) may use a reasonable amount of force in order to discipline a child. But in *R. v. Sharmpal Singh* (1962), a Kenyan case, a woman's consent to sexual intercourse was no defence to the excessive amount of force used which resulted in her death. Squeezing his wife's neck and throat could not be regarded as sexual embrace by the accused; the degree of force was an unlawful act. The matter of an accident being the consequence of lawful activity, and not amounting to constructive manslaughter (here death from septicaemia after sexual activity) was considered in *R. v. Slingsby* (1995).

In the controversial case of *DPP* v. *Newbury* (1976) two boys threw a paving stone from a bridge into the path of an oncoming train. The stone smashed a window and killed the guard. The Lords decided that a conviction for constructive manslaughter was in order, even if the boys, who were not under the influence of drink or drugs, could not foresee the consequences of their action. 'Unlawful' does not, however, apply to mere negligence, that would be a civil matter, nor to gross negligence which falls under the second type of involuntary manslaughter and is considered below.

An 'unlawful act' means a criminal offence and probably one that is clearly identifiable. In *R.* v. *Larkin* (1943) the accused aimed to frighten his mistress's boyfriend with a razor. His mistress was drunk and fell against the razor, fatally cutting her throat. A failure to act where there is a duty to do so will probably amount to constructive manslaughter, although in *R.* v. *Lowe* (1973) the Court of Appeal held that an omission was not sufficient, in the sense that manslaughter by negligence required proof of a high degree of negligence, amounting to recklessness. In contrast in *R.* v. *Dalby* (1982) the Court of Appeal held that the accused had not caused the victim direct injury, since although he had supplied his friend, also a drug addict, with a dangerous drug, the deceased had taken it completely of his own accord; it therefore quashed the conviction of manslaughter. The Court said that where a charge of manslaughter was based on an unlawful and dangerous act, it must be an act directed at the victim and likely to cause immediate injury, however slight. *Dalby* (a subjective test) is difficult to reconcile with *Newbury* (an objective one). However, *Mitchell* (1983) and *Pagett* (1983) confirmed the doctrine of transferred malice applies to manslaughter. (In *Pagett* the accused held a girl in front of him as a shield and shot at the police who returned fire and killed the girl.) In *R.* v. *Goodfellow* (1986) the defendant, wishing to be rehoused, set fire to his council house and caused the death of his wife, child and friend. The act was not 'directed at' the deceased; the conviction stood, on the grounds of an unlawful act and reckless manslaughter.

The second type of involuntary manslaughter is that of criminal negligence. The death may be caused either by the accused's gross negligence or by his recklessness. Ordinary or mere negligence constitutes only civil liability, and therefore is a defence to manslaughter. Whether, however, negligence should be criminal in any sense is a matter for some debate. In *R.* v. *Finney* (1874) the accused was an attendant at a lunatic asylum. The victim was told to get out of the bath he had been washing in; the victim understood but made no attempt to do so. The attendant turned on the hot water tap in mistake for the cold one; the victim was scalded to death. Gross negligence means total inadvertence to the consequences of his otherwise lawful action, a culpable disregard of what the reasonable man would foresee. The courts have frequently confused the terms 'negligence' and 'recklessness'. However, it is probably best to think of gross negligence as objective recklessness, that is in the *Caldwell/Lawrence* sense, as underlined in *Kong Cheuk Kwan* v. *R.* (1986) where two hydrofoils collided in clear open sea between Hong Kong and Macao, leading to two deaths. Subjective recklessness may, though, still amount to manslaughter by criminal negligence.

Subjective recklessness means that the accused could foresee the possibility, if not certainty, or risk, of the likelihood of death, whereas objective recklessness means he did not see or perhaps did not want to see. In subjective recklessness the accused has pressed ahead: he has taken the risk although he is aware of the possible consequences. In *R. v. Pike* (1961) the accused, a gas meter collector, had given carbon tetrachloride to a number of women for the purposes of sexual performance. He soaked a rag in the substance which the women would inhale before intercourse. But on this occasion the victim died; the others had merely temporarily lost consciousness. In *R. v. Stone and Dobinson* (1977) the accused was a man in his late sixties who was virtually incapable of looking after himself. He lived with his mistress, D., 24 years his junior; she was also socially inadequate. His sister came to live with them. She became bed-ridden. Despite the fact that S. and D. were urged by neighbours to summon help from the health or social services authorities, they did nothing and allowed her to die unnecessarily.

In *R. v. Prentice, Adomako and Holloway* (1993) two of the cases involved doctors administering treatment which resulted in the death of patients, the third an electrician wiring up a wrongly earthed central heating system which delivered a lethal shock. Lord Taylor, the Lord Chief Justice, in the Court of Appeal, said that the wide definition of recklessness in *Caldwell/Lawrence* had caused problems in regard to involuntary manslaughter involving breach of duty. In their Lordships' judgment the proper test was the gross negligence test established in *Andrews* v. *DPP* (1937) and *Stone and Dobinson* (1977). Accordingly, except in motor manslaughter, which remained governed by *Lawrence*, the ingredients of involuntary manslaughter by breach of duty which had to be proved were:

1 the existence of the duty;

2 a breach of that duty, causing death; and

3 gross negligence which the jury considered justified a criminal conviction.

It was not possible, said Lord Taylor, to prescribe a standard jury direction, but a finding of gross negligence could include the following factors:

1 indifference to an obvious risk of injury to health;

2 actual foresight of the risk plus a determination to run it;

3 an appreciation of the risk with an intention to avoid it, but coupled with such a high degree of negligence in the attempted avoidance as the jury considered justified conviction;

4 inattention or failure to advert to a serious risk which went beyond 'mere inadvertence' in respect of an obvious and important matter which was the defendant's duty to address.

Motor manslaughter

The question of 'motor manslaughter', a comparatively rare charge, arose in *R. v. Seymour* (1983). Here S. drove a lorry so as to push his car a certain distance. He had loaned this car to a woman who, getting out of the vehicle, was crushed to death. He was prosecuted for both reckless driving and manslaughter. His conviction for manslaughter was upheld in the House of Lords. The requirement of a 'very high risk' in *Seymour* is *obiter* (*per* Lord Roskill) and appears to be inconsistent with Lawrence. The House of Lords in *Adomako* made it clear that the *Lawrence* direction no longer applied to manslaughter, whether motor manslaughter or any other.

Defences

There are certain defences which are common to both murder and manslaughter. In the first place the carrying out of the sentence of the court is lawful – the executioner is simply doing his job. Secondly, under the Criminal Law Act 1967 it is lawful to use reasonable force to prevent a crime or to assist or effect a lawful arrest. However, the occasions on which it is reasonable to kill or cause grievous bodily harm ought to be few and far between. Thirdly, at common law there is a right of self-defence, although this right might be exercised in relation to the prevention of a crime under the 1967 Act. Again the degree of force exercised should be reasonable in the light of all the circumstances. Self-defence will be a bad argument, of course, where it is the accused who had provoked the killing. A similar defence is available to the person who seeks to protect property. The major difficulty here is what is meant by not only 'reasonable' but also 'in all the circumstances', for the circumstances of the accused may have been very different from those of the victim; a perceived threat is very much an individual matter. 'Reasonable' applies in two ways: firstly, was it reasonable in all the circumstances to use force at all, and secondly, if so was the degree of force used not excessive in all the circumstances?

There are seven other offences related to homicide now considered below.

3 SOLICITATION

Under the Offences against the Person Act 1861 (s.4), as amended by the Criminal Law Act 1977, it is an offence to solicit, encourage or persuade another to murder a third person. This statutory provision is virtually identical to the common law on incitement, although it does extend to murders committed abroad including those committed by aliens temporarily resident in the United Kingdom.

4 THREATS

It is an offence under the 1861 Act (s.16)(as again amended in 1977) to threaten to kill another; the threat must cause the person to whom the threat is communicated to fear for his life or that of a third person. The maximum term is 10 years' imprisonment.

5 SUICIDE PACTS AND COMPLICITY

As stated earlier it is no longer a crime to commit suicide (Suicide Act 1961). However, under the Act if anyone aids, abets, counsels or procures the suicide or attempted suicide of another, then he is liable to be imprisoned for up to 14 years; such an offence is known as 'complicity in suicide'. As also mentioned above the Homicide Act 1957 provides for a charge of manslaughter rather than murder where X. kills Y., or is a party to Y.'s death by Z., in pursuance of a suicide pact.

6 CONCEALMENT OF BIRTH

Under the Offences against the Person Act 1861 (s.60) it is an offence punishable by up to two years' imprisonment to conceal the birth of a child by secretly disposing of its body, where that child died before, at or after its birth. Under the common law it is an offence to dispose of a dead body in order to avoid an inquest. To make false statements about a death or birth is an offence under the Perjury Act 1911 and the failure to give information required by law about a death or birth is an offence under the Births and Deaths Registration Act 1953.

7 INFANTICIDE

Under the Infanticide Act 1938 a mother may be guilty of infanticide, effectively manslaughter, rather than murder. This rule applies where she causes the death of her child before it is one year old and while the balance of her mind is disturbed as a result of the effects of childbirth.

8 CHILD DESTRUCTION AND ABORTION

Although it is not murder to kill a child before it is born, it is an offence under the Offences against the Person Act 1861 (s.58) (as amended by the Abortion Act 1967) to abort a potential birth; that offence is known as 'procuring a miscarriage'. To kill a child in the process of being born is known as 'child destruction' and it is an offence under the Infant Life (Preservation) Act 1929. Both offences carry a maximum sentence of life imprisonment.

Under the 1861 Act (s.58) it is an offence for a pregnant woman to use an instrument or other means or to take poison or a noxious substance in order to procure the miscarriage; but she cannot be guilty if she mistakenly believes herself to be pregnant. It is equally an offence for another to cause the woman's miscarriage or merely to intend to procure a miscarriage even if the woman is mistakenly believed to be pregnant. Under the 1967 Act as amended in 1990 it is lawful deliberately to cause a miscarriage (an abortion) if the continuation of the pregnancy would involve a substantial risk of injury to her physical or mental health or possibly to that of her other children. The abortion must be carried out in an NHS hospital or in an approved private establishment, and two registered doctors must agree on the desirability for the abortion.

The Abortion Act 1967 provided no defence to the offence of child destruction under the 1929 Act. Under the latter Act it is an offence not just to destroy a child in the process of being born but also to kill a 'viable' child, that is one capable of being born. The 1929 Act states: 'Evidence that a woman had at any material time been pregnant for a period of twenty-eight weeks or more shall be prima facie proof that she was at that time pregnant of a child capable of being born alive.' The amended Abortion Act 1967 (under s.37(1) of the Human Fertilisation and Embryology Act 1990) now distinguishes between pregnancies of less than 24 weeks duration, and those that have lasted longer; and it provides that in three cases, one of which is that two registered medical practitioners have certified that they believe 'that there is a substantial risk that if the child were born it would suffer from such physical or mental abnormalities as to be seriously handicapped', those destroying the child shall have, it would seem, a defence to a charge under the 1929 Act as well as to one of procuring an abortion under s.58 of the Offences against the Person Act 1861. The other two cases are, in effect, where there is a likelihood of grave permanent injury to the physical or mental health of the pregnant woman (or risk to her life if the pregnancy continued) or, similarly, injury to any existing children of her family. The legal protection hitherto given to the lives of children capable of being born alive has now been drastically curtailed. The statutory criteria are noticeably vague in some areas. When is a risk substantial and when are handicaps serious?

By s.37(4) of the Human Fertilisation and Embryology Act 1990 it is provided that no offence is committed under the 1929 Act if the abortion is carried out by a doctor in accordance with the Abortion Act. In practice, therefore, the 1929 Act will only be relevant where the foetus is destroyed other than in the course of a lawful abortion.

9 GENOCIDE

The Genocide Act 1969 makes it an offence, punishable by up to 14 years' imprisonment, to commit any act designed to destroy partially or totally a national, ethnic, racial or religious group. Where any member of such a group is killed then the sentence may be one of life imprisonment.

6.5

Non-fatal offences against the person

1 ASSAULT AND BATTERY ('COMMON ASSAULT')

'Assault' is a term that is sometimes used generally, to mean both assault and battery. Both assault and battery are covered by the Offences against the Person Act 1861, as amended by the Criminal Justice Act 1988. Under s.39 of the 1988 Act 'common assault' is a summary offence only, which carries a maximum six months imprisonment or a level 5 fine or both. In the strict sense an assault is the reckless or intentional causing of a person to fear that he will be subjected to unlawful violence. A battery is the application of force to another. Both assault and battery are also tortious wrongs in civil law (trespass to the person). However, in *DPP* v. *Little* (1991) the High Court held that assault at common law did not survive the 1861 Act (as amended by s.39 of the Criminal Justice Act 1988). *Lynsey* (1995) said common assault means assault or battery.

For an assault to be effective, it is essential that the 'victim' must be within range. Shaking a fist at someone in a moving train from a position on the station platform will hardly constitute a wrong. In battery the force used must be positive, not negative; it will not be a battery to refuse to step aside from the path of a jogger, for instance, providing the jogger has clear vision ahead of him.

Silent malicious telephone calls can constitute an assault under s.47 of the 1861 Act (see below under aggravated assault), the House of Lords held in 1997 (*R.* v. *Ireland*), although assault traditionally has required proof that the victim has apprehended immediate physical violence; obscene calls can amount to an assault it was held in *R.* v. *Gelder* (1994).

Deliberate intention or recklessness will constitute the requisite *mens rea*; but mere negligence will not – that will be sufficient to bring a civil action. Recklessness is in the subjective sense, it is not an objective test of what the reasonable man would have foreseen in like circumstances; the accused knew the risk he was taking. Of course, even if *mens rea* is established the police may not prosecute – if, for example, the injury or fear caused was slight.

Consent is a valid defence in both assault and battery. In *R.* v. *Clarence* (1888) the accused had sexual intercourse with his wife. She did not know he was infected with venereal disease, but nonetheless she had consented to intercourse. A mistaken but honest belief that a person has consented to the use or threat of force is still a defence; the belief does not necessarily have to be a reasonable one. Duress, however, will probably cancel out the effect of consent. Equally, there is a limit to the amount of force to which a person may consent; it is not a defence to argue that a person consented to be murdered and it is therefore not a defence to argue that a person consented to excessive force. Thus participation in sports becomes a difficult legal problem: the rugby player expects to be injured from time to time, but he does not consent to have a boot deliberately struck at his head. In *R. v. Donovan* (1934) the accused in indecent circumstances beat a 17 year-old girl with a cane for pleasure, but consent could not be deemed as having been given since it was likely that the blows would occasion actual bodily harm, indeed the accused may have intended them to do so. (The accused was acquitted on account of a procedural error.)

R. v. Brown (1993) was a particularly controversial case: consensual sado-masochistic acts in private between homosexuals involving the infliction of actual bodily harm nonetheless constituted offences under ss.20 and 47 of the Offences against the Person Act 1861, the House of Lords held by 3–2. Lord Templeman said there was a difference between violence which was incidental and violence which was inflicted for the indulgence of cruelty. Society was entitled and bound to protect itself against a cult of violence. Pleasure derived from the infliction of pain was an evil thing, cruelty was uncivilised. Lord Jauncey said that a line had to be drawn somewhere between those injuries which a person could consent to have inflicted upon himself and those which were so serious that consent was immaterial. In his Lordship's opinion that line properly fell to be drawn between assault at common law and the offence of assault occasioning actual bodily harm created by s.47 of the 1861 Act. Lord Jauncey added that if in the light of the Wolfenden Report of 1957 Parliament had decided to make certain practices lawful they had not been included in the Sexual Offences Act 1967. Lord Lowry said that sado-masochistic homosexual activities were not conducive to the welfare of society, but Lord Mustill (dissenting) thought the sole question was whether in the light of the Offences against the Person Act 1861 consensual private acts were offences against the existing law of violence, to which there must be a negative response. Lord Slynn (dissenting) said it was a matter of policy for the legislature to decide. It was not for the courts in the interests of 'paternalism' to introduce into existing statutory crimes relating to offences against the person, concepts which did not properly fit there. The difficulty with the Law Lords' speeches is that, apart from the issues of moral paternalism involved, the decisions were based on rather wide-ranging and ill co-ordinated points of law.

In a very questionable decision, *R. v. Wilson* (1996), the Court of Appeal did not follow *Brown*, on the grounds that although the accused had used a hot knife to brand his initials on her buttocks (subsequently noticed by a doctor during a medical examination) his wife had instigated the activity, and there was no 'aggressive intent' (whatever that might mean in the context of *mens rea*).

Secondly, parents and teachers *(in loco parentis)* have a right physically to punish children. The force used must be reasonable in degree according to the circumstances, nor must it be given for purely spiteful reasons.

Thirdly, self-defence is a valid argument; so too is reasonable force used to prevent a crime or to effect an arrest under the Criminal Law Act 1967.

Aggravated assaults

Some offences are regarded as aggravated assaults; 'assault' here includes battery. Under the Police Act 1964 assaulting a police officer in the execution of his duty, or a person assisting him, attracts a heavier punishment – a fine or six months' imprisonment or both. The normal maximum punishment for assault or battery is a fine or two months' imprisonment. Resisting or wilfully (intentionally) obstructing the officer, or a person assisting him, may also amount to aggravated assault. It is possible for common (ordinary) assault or battery to be tried on indictment with a maximum of one year's imprisonment under the Offences against the Person Act 1861. Similarly, under the Offences against the Person Act 1861 it is an offence punishable with up to two years' imprisonment to assault another person with the intention to resist or hinder arrest. Deciding whether a police officer's action amounts to an execution of his official duty is not always an easy task. For instance, in *R. v. Prebble* (1858) a constable responded to the request of the landlord and assisted in ejecting certain people from a barn attached to the pub; one of those turned out assaulted the officer. But the court held that he was not acting in the execution of his duty: there appeared little likelihood of a breach of the peace and there was no nuisance. Thus the assault in question was a common one, not an aggravated one. The police have no general power to detain for questioning; it is lawful therefore to use reasonable force to escape from such detention. Similarly, to refuse to answer a police officer's questions is not obstruction (*Rice* v. *Connolly* (1966)) but to give a false story is.

In considering whether a defendant was guilty of 'wilful' obstruction of a constable in the execution of his duty, a court has to be satisfied that the defendant's conduct made it more difficult for the police officer to carry out his duty and that the defendant intended this to be so. Here the defendant's friend was arrested in Bristol for being drunk and disorderly. The defendant opened the van door at the rear to ask where his friend was being taken, and thus prevented the police from driving away (*Lewis* v. *Cox* (1984)). The High Court directed his conviction, the magistrates having acquitted the defendant.

Under the 1861 Act (s.47) an aggravated assault is also one which causes actual bodily harm, an offence punishable by up to five years' imprisonment. The harm involved need not be serious; a bruise or a scratch is sufficient. Actual bodily harm also includes a nervous or hysterical condition as illustrated in *R. v. Miller* (1954) and *R* v. *Chan-Fook* (1993). The harm caused must be foreseen by the reasonable man, but not necessarily by the accused as underlined in *R. v. Roberts* (1971), where the accused interfered with a girl's clothes while she was in a moving car; she jumped out and was injured. Under the Theft Act 1968 an assault with intent to rob is punishable with life imprisonment; under the Sexual Offences Act 1956 an assault with intent to commit buggery is punishable by up to 10 years' imprisonment. Indecent assault is also an aggravated assault.

2 WOUNDING AND GRIEVOUS BODILY HARM

The offences of wounding and inflicting grievous bodily harm are covered by the Offences against the Person Act 1861 (s.20) as amended by the Criminal Law Act 1967. Wounding means that the complete skin – outer and inner – must be broken (*Moriarty* v. *Brookes* (1834)); the rupture of internal blood vessels is not sufficient to constitute a wound under the 1861 Act (*C(A Minor)* v. *Eisenhower* (1983)), where the defendant, aged 15, was involved in an incident in which C. was hit in the eye by an air gun pellet. A wounding is always the result of an assault or battery. 'Grievous bodily harm' means serious harm, in other words its natural meaning is used by the courts (*DPP* v. *Smith* (1961)). Again an assault or battery is normally the precondition for grievous bodily harm. However, in *R.* v. *Martin* (1881) no direct assault took place: the accused had put out the gas lights in a theatre not long before the performance had finished, and he had also blocked the exit by pulling an iron bar across the door. The audience panicked and rushed down the stairs; those at the front sustained injuries by being crushed against the iron bar. The accused had intended to cause terror and thus was found guilty of inflicting grievous bodily harm. In *R.* v. *Lewis* (1970) a husband shouted at his wife through the locked front door; he threatened to kill her and hearing the sound of breaking glass she jumped out of the window. As the flat was on the third floor she broke both legs. The accused was likewise convicted, although the wife was not in danger of immediate violence – in the strict sense of assault. The maximum penalty is five years' imprisonment.

In *R.* v. *Halliday* (1889) Lord Chief Justice Coleridge said: 'If a man creates in another's mind an immediate sense of danger which causes such person to try to escape, and in so doing he injures himself, the person who creates such a state of mind is responsible for the injuries which result'. In *R.* v. *Wilson (Clarence)* (1983) the House of Lords, overruling the Court of Appeal, made it clear that it was open to the jury on a charge of inflicting grievous bodily harm (s.20) to return a verdict of not guilty, but guilty of assault occasioning actual bodily harm (s.47).

The 1861 Act (as amended) also makes it an offence (s.18) to wound or cause grievous bodily harm with intent to cause grievous bodily harm or on account of the intention to resist or prevent a lawful arrest. The maximum penalty is life imprisonment. Here the word 'cause' is used rather than 'inflict'. The difference is normally taken to mean that bodily harm is not inflicted unless it is the result of an assault or battery, whereas bodily harm caused with intent may not necessarily be the direct result of an assault or battery, despite the cases of *Martin* and *Lewis* described above, which since *Wilson*, would not probably be decided in the same way.

Thus there are essentially four offences: wounding, wounding with intent to cause grievous bodily harm, inflicting grievous bodily harm and causing grievous bodily harm with intent. All four must be shown to have been committed unlawfully and maliciously. The word 'maliciously' is not particularly helpful; in this case it does not mean with ill-will, spite or on account of some improper motive. In respect of wounding and inflicting grievous bodily harm it underlines the fact that the accused acted intentionally or recklessly in the subjective sense but that he did not necessarily foresee the full results of his action, only that they appeared minor. But, wounding with intent or causing grievous bodily harm with intent means deliberate, direct intention; recklessness will not suffice. In this instance it appears the word 'maliciously' becomes redundant, as the Court of Appeal suggested in *R. v. Mowatt* (1968). However, the word 'maliciously' is an important qualification to causing grievous bodily harm as a result of resisting arrest, for if 'malice' in this context – in the sense of foreseeing the consequences of his action – is not shown to be present then the accused cannot be convicted under the more serious charge (carrying the maximum term of life imprisonment) but perhaps instead under the less serious one (carrying the maximum term of five years).

Further issues arose in the cases of *Spratt*, *Savage* and *Parmenter*. In *DPP v. Parmenter* (1991) Lord Ackner said the House of Lords in its conclusion on the meaning of 'recklessly' in the Criminal Damage Act 1971, accepted that *R. v. Cunningham* (1957) (subject to the *Mowatt* (1968) gloss), correctly stated the law in relation to the 1861 Act. Therefore, in order to establish an offence under s.20 the prosecution must prove either the defendant intended or that he actually foresaw that his act would cause harm.

In the Court of Appeal Lord Justice Mustill had said that if the *Cunningham* subjective test combined with the low level of intent prescribed by *Mowatt* was applied to s.47 in the same way as to s.20, the moral overtones of the two offences became indistinguishable and the differences between the two depended upon variations between the levels of physical injury suffered in the individual case, which often was the result of chance. Second, it was impossible to contemplate the instant appeal without dismay. At a time when 'middle-rank' criminal violence was a dismal feature of modern urban life, and when convictions and pleas of guilty on charges under s.47 occupied so much of the Crown Court lists, it seemed scarcely credible that 129 years after the enactment of the Offences against the Person Act three appeals should come before the Court of Appeal which revealed the law to be so impenetrable.

What had happened in *Parmenter* was that the Court of Appeal had to require the House of Lords to clear up the problems created by the conflicting decisions in *Spratt* (1991) and *Savage* (1991). Although the maximum sentences under ss.20 and 47 were the same, the Court of Appeal recognised that the two offences were seen in quite different terms by defendants and their advisers contemplating guilty pleas, and by sentencers.

The result was that in the combined appeals of *Savage* and *Parmenter* (1991) the House of Lords took the view that for s.20 offences, 'maliciously' denoted *Cunningham*-type recklessness. The House of Lords did not see fit to depart from Lord Justice Diplock's test of foreseeability of some harm being caused, even if of a minor nature, where he used both a subjective and an objective approach to the question, although taken as a whole, Lord Ackner said, Lord Diplock's judgment enshrined a subjective approach.

Lord Ackner said that for a s.47 offence there was no need to prove foresight of actual bodily harm, and similarly in murder the *actus reus* requires a killing, but the *mens rea* is satisfied by intention to cause grievous bodily harm. So to make a change in respect of a s.20 offence would make the offence one of very limited scope.

The House of Lords re-emphasised in *R. v. Mandair* (1994) that a charge under s.18 of the Offences against the Person Act 1861 included one under s.20. The difficult distinction, however, is that between s.20, s.39 and s.47. But since 1994 there are guidelines for the police and the CPS on this matter. 'Cause' and 'inflict' appear to mean one and the same thing (*Burstow* (1997) and *Ireland* (1997)).

In respect of ss.20 and 47 in *DDP v. K. (a minor)* (1990), where a schoolboy panicked and hid acid in a hot air dryer which another boy subsequently used and was burned when the acid squirted into his face, Lord Justice Parker wrongly gave the word 'recklessly' the *Caldwell* meaning. In *Spratt* (1991) the Court of Appeal held that the law had been correctly stated in *Venna*: the prosecution must prove that the accused actually foresaw that what he was doing could result in the application of unlawful force on another. It would appear that in *Savage* and *Parmenter* the House of Lords agreed with the Court of Appeal's approach in *Spratt*, but the Lords overruled *Spratt* on another point. In *Spratt*, D. had fired an air pistol from his flat and two pellets had struck a girl playing outside; he had pleaded guilty to a s.47 charge on the grounds that he was reckless in so far as he had given no thought to the possibility of a girl playing outside.

Moreover, is the *mens rea* for assault occasioning actual bodily harm (s47) any more than that required for common assault? In *Savage* the accused threw the contents of a glass of beer over the victim but also the glass itself, with the result that the glass cut the victim on the wrist. Whilst there was no proof that the defendant was aware that her action might cause actual bodily harm, it was sufficient that there was a causal connection between the assault and the bodily harm, no further *mens rea* was required, as seen in *R. v. Roberts* (1971). In *Spratt* the issue was less clear, but in *Parmenter* the House of Lords favoured *Savage* and *Roberts*. In *Parmenter* D. had originally been convicted under s.20 for the rough treatment he had given to his three month-old son.

So, out of the maze the position can be restated:

1 common assault (under s.39 of the Criminal Justice Act 1988) requires proof of an intention to apply unlawful force, or to cause the victim to fear the immediate application of unlawful force, or subjective *Cunningham*-type recklessness as to whether such force may be so applied;

2 assault occasioning actual bodily harm (s.47), which carries five years imprisonment has the same *mens rea*, but some bodily harm must have been caused by the assault;

3 s.20 offences require proof that the accused intended to cause some harm even if slight, or was *Cunningham* reckless as to whether such harm might be caused, and in practice s.20 is seen as a more serious offence than s.47;

4   s18 requires foresight of some bodily harm but also proof that the defendant intended to commit some grievous bodily harm, or to resist arrest, the latter being also via *Cunningham* recklessness.

Section 47 carries a sentence potentially four-and-a-half times greater than that for common assault, the *mens rea* being the same, although s.47 requires proof of some harm, even if slight. The House of Lords could have overruled *Mowatt* and stipulated that there should be foresight of a wound or grievous bodily harm under s.20, and equally it could have been laid down that the accused should foresee some harm for a conviction under s.47. However, this really is a matter for legislation.

Of course, the offences under s.18 are clearly meant to be the more serious, as they carry a penalty of life imprisonment, whereas under ss.47 and 20 it is five years' maximum. But the overlapping sections of the Act do not lend themselves to clarity, as seen above.

3   OTHER NON-FATAL OFFENCES

1   Under the Offences against the Person Act 1861 (s.23) it is a crime to administer a poison or noxious substance to another person, thereby endangering life or inflicting grievous bodily harm. The administration must be intentional or reckless in the *Cunningham* sense. The maximum sentence is 10 years. Under s.24 it is merely an offence to administer the poison or noxious thing, with the ulterior intent to injure, aggrieve or annoy; s.24 carries a maximum of five years' imprisonment.

2   False imprisonment is a crime as well as a tort; but it is more usually the latter and is examined in detail in the next chapter. It is not entirely clear whether the tort can be committed through an innocent third party, but it is virtually certain that the crime may be. Kidnapping is often regarded as an aggravated form of false imprisonment.

In *R. v. D.* (1984) the House of Lords, overruling the Court of Appeal, held that a parent who snatched his own unmarried minor child in contravention of a court order was liable to be convicted of kidnapping. In this case the defendant, a New Zealander, took his young daughter, a ward of court, to New Zealand and Ireland. This was the first case, apparently, where a father had been convicted at trial of kidnapping his own child. Lord Brandon said that the common law, while generally immutable in its principles, unless different principles were laid down by statute, was not immutable in the way in which it adapted, developed and applied those principles in a radically changing world, and against the background of radically changed social conventions and conditions.

Two recent Acts of Parliament, as subsequently amended by the Family Law Act 1986, have taken this matter further. First, the Child Abduction Act 1984 as amended also by the Children Act 1989 imposes criminal liability in 'intentional child snatching' cases by making it an offence for anyone who is a parent or guardian to take or send a child under 16 out of the United Kingdom without obtaining the 'appropriate consent', that is of other parents or the court. The Act also makes it an offence to abduct a child from those with lawful control of it. The maximum term of imprisonment is seven years and the DPP's consent is required to any prosecution, as it is under the Act to the common law offence of kidnapping. Under the 1984 Act the principle of *Prince* appears to apply, regarding strict liability as to age: the defendant must 'show' that he believed the child was 16, otherwise the rule of strict liability will operate. Subjective recklessness will apply, where no thought was given to the child's age as seen in *R.* v. *Mousir* (1987). *R.* v. *Hutchins* (1988) established that kidnapping and false imprisonment could be committed by recklessness alone. The Child Abduction and Custody Act 1985 gave statutory effect to The Hague Convention on the Civil Aspects of International Child Abduction.

3 The Firearms Act 1968 (as subsequently amended by Firearms (Amendment) Acts 1988, 1994 and 1997) has as its aim the limitation of crime. It contains detailed provisions as to who may purchase what, if any, type of weapon. For example, anyone sentenced to a term of imprisonment for three years or more may not be sold or possess a firearm; a drunk or insane person may not be sold a firearm. The Firearms Act 1982 extended such regulations to imitation and readily convertible firearms. Certain weapons, of course, are prohibited for any civilian use. To use a firearm, whether real or imitation, to resist or prevent arrest is an offence punishable with life imprisonment; so too is the possession of a real firearm or ammunition with intent to endanger life or cause serious injury to property. Possession of a firearm (real or imitation) at the time of committing a specified offence or being arrested for it is punishable by a maximum of 14 years' imprisonment. The Act lists the specified offences under such other Acts as the Theft Act 1968 and the Sexual Offences Act 1956. These are, therefore, offences of strict liability.

Under the Firearms Act it is also an offence to trespass in any building without reasonable excuse while carrying a firearm (five years' imprisonment) or to trespass on land without a reasonable excuse whilst carrying a firearm (three months' imprisonment). Under the same Act it is also punishable with five years' imprisonment for a person without lawful authority or reasonable excuse to have with him in a public place a loaded shot gun or air weapon, or any other firearm loaded or unloaded together with suitable ammunition.

Offensive weapons

Under the Prevention of Crime Act 1953 it is an offence merely to carry an offensive weapon in a public place, without lawful authority or reasonable excuse. An offensive weapon is defined as one which is made or adapted for causing injury or is intended to be used to cause injury. A flick-knife, for example, has been held to constitute an offensive weapon (*Gibson* v. *Wales* (1983)). The phrase 'lawful authority' has posed a problem of interpretation for the courts, but it would clearly include the soldier or police officer with a weapon. Similarly 'reasonable excuse' is not the clearest of phrases. It does not appear to mean what the reasonable man would regard as excusable, but rather whether the weapon was carried because the accused felt under an immediate, as opposed to a general, danger of attack. A 'public place' means any place to which the public may be admitted, with or without payment, and the highway and open spaces. An outside landing in a block of estate flats was held to be a public place in *Knox v. Anderton* (1983). The Offensive Weapons Act 1996 (s.2) has increased the penalties for carrying an offensive weapon without lawful authority or reasonable excuse.

Smuggling an offensive weapon is covered by s.86 of the Customs and Excise Management Act 1979 (three years' imprisonment). Bomb hoaxes are now directly covered by the Criminal Law Act 1977 with a maximum term of five years' imprisonment.

Under s.139 of the Criminal Justice Act 1988 a new offence was created: that of having an article with a blade or sharp point, except a small folding penknife, in a public place; s.140 amended the Police and Criminal Evidence Act 1984 to extend police powers of stop and search to include articles in relation to the commission of an offence under s.139. The punishment is a level 3 fine. It is a defence to show that the blades were for use at work, or for religious purposes, or were part of national costume. An article with a cutting edge that exceeded three inches was caught under s.139 in *Godwin v. DPP* (1993).

Threats

Under the Malicious Communications Act 1988 it is an offence for any person to send to another a letter or other article which conveys a message which is indecent or grossly offensive, a threat, or information which is false and known to be false by the sender, or any other article which is indecent or grossly offensive. The sender's purpose must be to cause distress or anxiety to the recipient, although a person is not guilty if he can show that the threat was used to reinforce a demand which he believed he had reasonable grounds for making and that he believed that the use of the threat was a proper means of reinforcing the demand. A person guilty of an offence shall be liable to a level 4 fine.

Torture

Under ss.134 and 135 of the Criminal Justice Act 1988 an offence of torture, attracting life imprisonment, is created. Prosecution requires the consent of the Attorney-General, and the enactment enabled the United Kingdom to ratify the United Nations *Convention against Torture and other Criminal, Inhuman and Degrading Treatment or Punishment*, signed in 1985. Torture is defined as the intentional inflicting of severe pain or suffering on another in the performance or purported performance of the accused's official duties.

6.6   Theft and similar offences

1 THEFT

The law of theft and related offences was codified by the Theft Act 1968 and amended by the Theft Act 1978. Theft consists of the dishonest appropriation of another's property (the *actus reus*) with the intention (*mens rea*) of permanently depriving that other person or persons of its use (s.1). Forgery does, not, however, fall within the scope of the Acts. Theft, triable either way, is punishable with a maximum of seven years' imprisonment on indictment (s.26 of the Criminal Justice Act 1991). There is clearly a close relationship between appropriation and the tortious wrong of conversion, but the key difference is that conversion is usually thought of as 'borrowing', while permanent deprivation is the basic feature of theft. It is possible for one 'spouse' to steal from another, but the DPP's consent must be given for such prosecutions. Further, a partner can steal from fellow partners for partners are co-owners of their property (*R. v. Bonner* (1970)).

The goods or property stolen do not necessarily have to belong to the person from whom they are taken. The victim may enjoy lawful possession rather than outright ownership – for example, the driver of a car. Neither ownership nor possession need entail physical control: the owner (X.) of a boat may be away from the vessel for much of the year or may have allowed a friend (Y.) to use it for a particular period of time. X. or Y. would have a right of repossession against the thief, but neither need have been physically present on the vessel, although 'possession' usually denotes some form of control. Physical control, however, in a gratuitous sense, would not amount to lawful possession: sitting in a deck chair on the deck of a boat does not amount to lawful possession of the chair although there is an element of physical control. Suppose the chair had a sunshade and a thief stole the shade while the person was asleep in the chair and the owner of the boat was below deck. It would be the owner, not the dozing guest, who would have the right to repossession. Theft, therefore, is concerned as much with the assumption of proprietary rights and interests as with the assumption of physical control.

Proprietary interests

Proprietary interests (s.5) include 'legal interests' (the trustee) and 'equitable interests' (the beneficiary) where property is under a trust, in other words wherever there is some kind of fiduciary relationship; thus B. may own certain property for the benefit or interest of A. Proprietary interests may conflict with those of the true owner and lead to a charge of theft. For example, in *R. v. Turner (No 2)* (1971) the owner of a car returned to a garage where he had left his car for repairs and removed it without paying as he had previously promised. He was convicted of stealing the car since he intended dishonest appropriation. Similarly, if X. minds goods for Y. (bailment) and then uses them without permission, he will have appropriated the goods and be guilty of theft. Moreover, if Y. takes his goods from X., his bailee, he may still steal them, if say, the agreed period of bailment has not come to an end, since X. is in lawful possession – he has a sufficient proprietorial interest (as shown in *Turner*).

An owner or lawful possessor need not, though, be aware of what is actually in his possession, but such items can still be stolen; so, too, can apparently 'unwanted' items, as seen in *R. v. Woodman* (1974) which involved scrap metal left on disused premises. Something that is apparently 'valueless' or 'unwanted' is not the same as something clearly 'abandoned'. Anyone who regards property as abandoned must do so with great caution.

Destruction of goods

The taking of goods amounts to theft; so may their complete destruction. But damage or partial destruction will more likely fall under the Criminal Damage Act 1971. Selling another's goods without permission is also, of course, misappropriation; receiving (handling stolen goods) is theft, providing *mens rea* is present. The mere receipt or acquisition of goods does not constitute theft, however, unless the person concerned subsequently intends to deprive another of lawful ownership or possession. In *R. v. Skipp* (1975) the accused collected three loads of goods by misrepresenting himself as a haulage contractor; the accused did not steal the goods when he collected them, but when he took the goods to different place, the Court of Appeal held. However, in *Gomez* (1993) the House of Lords overruled *Skipp* and *Fritschy* (1985) (the latter concerned the collection of krugerrands from London to Switzerland) as being inconsistent with *Lawrence* (below).

As shown in *Edwards v. Ddin* (1976) the motorist who is served with petrol does not appropriate the petrol and cannot be guilty of theft, although he may be guilty of making off without payment. A *bona fide* purchaser who has innocently purchased stolen goods is not guilty of theft (s.3) when he subsequently assumes proprietary or possessory 'rights', although X. can sue P. for their return. It may also be an appropriation, and therefore theft, if a person wrongly claims to have a lawful title to goods which are not in his physical possession, providing, of course, he intends permanently to deprive the owner or possessor of his property, as illustrated in *R. v. Pitham* (1976).

Property

'Property' includes intangible as well as tangible matters (s.4), including, for example, gas stored in pipes. Electricity cannot as such be stolen, but it is an offence under the 1968 Act (s.13) dishonestly to use, waste or divert electricity; the offence carries a maximum punishment of five years' imprisonment. In *R. v. McCreadle and Tume* (1992) abstracting electricity was proven when there was no actual notification to the electricity company by the squatter on the premises and the squatters were moving out just when the police arrived.

Cheques and money are also property and may too be misappropriated; but financial transactions may give rise to difficult considerations. In *R. v. Hall* (1973) a travel agent received money from his clients as deposits for flights to America. None of the customers received their tickets and the monies in question were never refunded. The Court of Appeal overturned his conviction for theft since it accepted the argument that although he had acted dishonestly the sums of money had been paid into the firm's general account and that the clients were not concerned as such with what happened to the money they had paid over but rather with the non-delivery of tickets. It would have been a different matter if the monies had been paid into a special account, to be used only for their air tickets. In contrast, in *R. v. Meech* (1974) the accused was convicted of stealing money from McC. McC. had obtained a cheque by fraud and asked the accused, M., to cash it for him. M. paid the cheque into his account but upon discovering the fraud withdrew the money. Instead of handing over the money to McC., with the help of P. and J., M. staged a robbery and pretended the money was stolen from him. M., P. and J. were convicted of theft and the judgment was upheld by the Court of Appeal. McC.'s fraud was irrelevant to the fact that theft had taken place. The 1968 Act provides that where a person 'receives property from or on account of another, and is under an obligation to the other to retain and deal with that property or its proceeds in a particular way, the property or proceeds shall be regarded (as against him) as belonging to the other', s.5(3).

A further illustration of s.5(3) of the Theft Act 1968 was seen in *Wain* (1995); here the defendant was convicted in respect of raising money for charity from Yorkshire Television involving dishonoured cheques. Under s.5(3) 'obligation' is a legal one, not merely moral, as seen in *Dubar* (1995), the *dicta* in *Hall* being disapproved.

Appropriation

The 1968 Act specifically provides that where property is obtained on account of another's mistake and the person who receives that property is then under a legal obligation to restore it in kind or in value, and omits to do so, he will be regarded as intending permanently to deprive the other of the property, that is he is guilty of theft, s.5(4). This particular provision of the Act is concerned with ownership mistakenly transferred, not mere possession. But the mistake is not concerned with the value of the goods — an old picture turns out to be a Constable, for instance — nor with one of identity, but rather with some other material fact. Mistake in the sense of a genuine belief by C. that D. would have consented to the appropriation does mean that C. did not act dishonestly. But consent is not a valid defence if it has been given on account of the other's fraud, although that is subject to qualification. In *R. v. Lawrence (Alan)* (1972) a taxi-driver who knowingly took more than the legal fare from a foreign visitor was convicted of theft. The visitor was an Italian student who was charged £7 instead of 53p for a journey from Victoria railway station in London. Consent given to appropriation through intimidation is not a valid consent, and it is most likely that the accused may be convicted of theft, although such a situation can overlap with blackmail and deception both of which are discussed below. In *R. v. Gomez* (1993) Lord Lowry strongly dissented and said that in his view the Eighth Report of the Criminal Law Revision Committee revealed a desire to maintain a distinction between theft and obtaining property by deception, and that this distinction would be lost if *Lawrence* were to be reaffirmed.

In *Anderton* v. *Burnside* and R. v. *Morris (David)* (1983) the House of Lords held that the combined acts of switching price labels – in this instance on goods in a supermarket – and removing goods from a shelf and placing them in a receptacle provided by the store did constitute a dishonest appropriation for the purposes of the Theft Act 1968 (s.l). Lord Roskill commented that it was wrong to introduce into this branch of the criminal law questions whether particular contracts were void or voidable on the ground of mistake or fraud or whether any mistake was sufficiently fundamental to vitiate a contract. They were not relevant questions under the 1968 Act. It could be argued, however, that the House of Lords, was construing the meaning, in this instance, of s.1 widely. Normally placing goods in a wire basket or trolley provided by the store is not an appropriation no matter how dishonest a person's intention may be. It does not usurp the owner's rights since the store expects the shopper to do that act (*Eddy* v. *Niman* (1981)). However, removing goods and placing them in an unauthorised receptacle, for example, one's coat pocket, could be an appropriation (*R.* v. *Mcpherson* (1973)). Both these decisions were approved of by the House of Lords in *Anderton* v. *Burnside*. In *Dobson* v. *General Accident Fire and Life Assurance Corporation plc* (1990), P. handed over a watch and a ring to R. (a rogue) in exchange for a building society cheque, which he subsequently discovered to have been stolen and thus to be worthless. Whilst admittedly R. had obtained the goods by deception (a peril against which P. was not insured), could he also be said to have stolen the goods (so that P. could recover against the defendant which was his insurance company)? The Court of Appeal held yes, and said that the decision in *Lawrence* (1972) should be applied even if there was difficulty in reconciling it with the later case of *Morris* (1984). But a differently constituted Court of Appeal preferred *Lawrence* to *Morris* in R. v. *Shuck* (1992).

In R. v. *Gomez* (1993) electrical goods were supplied on two stolen building society cheques, to the value of some £17,000; an act done with the authority or consent of the owner could amount to an appropriation of goods for the purpose of the Theft Act 1968 where such authority or consent had been obtained by deception, it was held. In the civil case (Lord Keith said, for the majority, Lord Lowry dissenting) of *Dobson* v. *General Accident Fire and Life Assurance Corporation plc* (1990), the Court of Appeal had considered the apparent conflict between *Lawrence* and *Morris* and applied *Lawrence*. There was no material distinction between the facts of *Dobson*, which had been correctly decided, and those of the instant case. *Lawrence*, which also made it clear that it was irrelevant that what had happened might also have constituted the offence of obtaining property by deception under s.15(1) of the 1968 Act, had been a clear decision of the House of Lords on the construction of 'appropriate' in s.1(1) that had stood for 12 years when doubt had been thrown on it by *obiter dicta* in *Morris*. *Lawrence* had to be regarded as authoritative and correct, and there was no question of it now being right to depart from it.

The effect of the *Gomez* decision is to make consent irrelevant in considering appropriation. Lord Browne-Wilkinson said: 'For myself, I regard the word 'appropriation' in isolation as being an objective description of the act done irrespective of the mental state of either the owner or the accused'. Thus merely placing an item in a basket provided by a supermarket may be an appropriation. Lord Keith said:

> In my opinion Lord Roskill in *Morris* was undoubtedly right when he said . . . that the assumption by the defendant of any rights of an owner could amount to an appropriation within the meaning of s.3(1), and that the removal of an article from the shelf and the changing of the price label on it constituted the assumption of one of the rights of the owner and hence an appropriation within the meaning of the subsection. But there are observations in the passage which, with the greatest possible respect to Lord Roskill, I must regard unnecessary for the decision of the case and as being incorrect. . . . [The *Lawrence* case] is a clear decision to the contrary, since it laid down unequivocally that an act may be an appropriation notwithstanding that it is done with the consent of the owner; it does not appear to me that any sensible distinction can be made in this context between consent and authorisation.

Lord Lowry, dissenting, stressed: 'Some cases can be prosecuted under s.15, but it is fallacious, having regard to what I perceive as the true meaning of appropriation, to say that cases of obtaining by deception can be prosecuted under s.1'.

One comment, in *The Cambridge Law Journal* in 1993, has tartly said:

> A person is, needless to say, entitled to deal with another's property, even to the extent of depriving him permanently of it, if he has his consent to doing so, *volenti non fit injuria*, unless that consent is obtained by duress or by deceit, that is, tortiously. It was because, and only because, Lord Roskill failed to add this last and important qualification that his well-known statement in *Morris* that an act expressly or implicitly authorised by the owner could never amount to an appropriation was, as Lord Keith says, erroneous. But it is just as misleading for Lord Keith now to say that consent to or authorisation by the owner of the taking by the accused is irrelevant, and for Lord Browne-Wilkinson to say (quite preposterously) that the word 'appropriation' is simply an objective description of the act done irrespective of the mental state of either the owner or the accused. It would indeed be difficult to find a clearer case of two pots calling the kettle black. But it is high time to call a halt to all the wearisome carping at judicial decisions interpreting the Acts and to be, instead, constructive. For the Acts were, as the experience of the last 25 years has amply demonstrated, execrably drafted. The judges and justices' clerks who have had to wrestle with them deserve better: not only in the matter of 'appropriation', but also in, for instance, those of 'dishonesty' (s.2

having, from the start, been seen to be inadequate); 'property' (s.4 resembling a Chinese puzzle); 'belonging to another' (s.5 omitting what it should include, and including what it should omit); 'intent permanently to deprive' (s.6 is a regular dog's breakfast); and robbery (s.8 is pointlessly complicated).

In *R. v. Gallasso* (1993) D. was a nurse who was responsible for the care of mentally handicapped patients and received cheques of behalf of one of them, V.; D. opened a third trust account in V.'s name with the same society and paid in a cheque for V., the prosecution alleging that this was done to make easier unauthorised withdrawals. D. was held not guilty of theft, but Professor J. C. Smith has argued this decision is inconsistent with *Gomez*, since if D. appropriated the cheque with unlawful intent, then she stole it.

In *Attorney-General's Reference (No 1 of 1983)* (1985), where D.'s employer, P., mistakenly instructed his bank to credit to D.'s account a sum of £74 in excess of her proper entitlement, the Court of Appeal held that if and when D. discovered the error, D. had to restore the value of the property (the sum being a chose in action). An intention not to restore would amount to one permanently to deprive another.

Appropriation of land

Under the Theft Act 1968, s.4(2), a person cannot be guilty of the appropriation of land, for example, by moving a boundary fence, for it is thought that the civil law provides adequate remedies. But a person may be guilty of theft in three instances: where a person is in a fiduciary position of trust, such as a personal representative or trustee; where a person is not in lawful possession of the land; where a tenant appropriates fixtures (for example, a shed or sockets). Nor is a person guilty of theft for picking wild flowers or the like, unless intending to sell what he picks or use them for some other commercial purpose, s.4(3). (He may, though, be guilty of an offence under the Wildlife and Countryside Act 1981, as amended by the Wildlife and Countryside (Amendment) Act 1991.) Wild animals not tamed nor ordinarily kept in captivity cannot be regarded as being in anyone's possession, s.4(4). The 1968 Act and the Poaching Prevention Act 1862 do not, however, preclude the offence of poaching wild animals found on another's land.

Mens rea of theft

Finally, the *mens rea* of theft consists of an intention dishonestly to deprive permanently another of property. 'Dishonesty', however, may mean different things to different people. The 1968 Act, s.2(1), says that a person's appropriation of another's property is not to be regarded as dishonest:

(*a*) if he appropriates the property in the belief that he has in law the right to deprive the other of it, on behalf of himself or of a third person; or

(*b*) if he appropriates the property in the belief that he would have the other's consent if the other knew of the appropriation and the circumstances of it; or

(c) (except where the property came to him as the trustee or personal representative) if he appropriates the property in the belief that the person to whom the property belongs cannot be discovered by taking reasonable steps.

Omissions are as much a part of theft as dishonest positive acts; so in *R. v. Firth* (1990) a doctor was held to have deceived a hospital contrary to the Theft Act 1978 s.2(1) by failing to inform the hospital that certain patients were private patients.

Section 2(2) says: 'A person's appropriation of property belonging to another may be dishonest notwithstanding that he is willing to pay for the property.' Thus in (a) if someone genuinely but mistakenly believes property to be his, he is not guilty of theft. The mistake may be one of fact or law. In (b) a person is not guilty of theft if, for example, he believes his friend or acquaintance had impliedly given him permission to take the property. And in (c) the honest finder of goods is protected from a conviction for theft, providing he remains honest in respect of his actions or inactions. Is the test of dishonesty, however, that of the reasonable man? The answer appears that there is no objective standard of reasonableness, but equally the subjective test is limited. This can be seen in *R. v. Ghosh* (1982) which concerned a locum surgeon claiming fees by deception, a decision which has attracted some adverse comments on the grounds that it faces in two directions. Lord Lane, Lord Chief Justice, commented as follows:

> **In determining whether the prosecution has proved that the defendant was acting dishonestly, a jury must first of all decide whether according to the ordinary standards of reasonable and honest people what was done was dishonest. If it was not dishonest by those standards, that is the end of the matter and the prosecution fails.**
>
> **If it was dishonest by those standards, then the jury must consider whether the defendant himself must have realised that what he was doing was by those standards dishonest. In most cases, where the actions are obviously dishonest by ordinary standards, there will be no doubt about it. It will be obvious that the defendant himself knew that he was acting dishonestly. It is dishonest for a defendant to act in a way which he knows ordinary people consider to be dishonest, even if he asserts or genuinely believes that he is morally justified in acting as he did. For example, Robin Hood or those ardent anti-vivisectionists who remove animals from vivisection laboratories are acting dishonestly, even though they may consider themselves to be morally justified in doing what they do, because they know that ordinary people would consider these actions to be dishonest.**
>
> **Cases which might be described as borderline, such as *Boggeln v. Williams* (1978), will depend upon the view taken by the jury as to whether the defendant may have believed what he was doing was in accordance with the ordinary man's idea of honesty. A jury might have come to the conclusion that the defendant in that case was disobedient or impudent, but not dishonest in what he did.**

Permanency of deprivation

In addition, 'permanent deprivation' may be difficult to prove in its strictest sense – as in the case of goods being abandoned by the taker at a later stage, but in circumstances which make recovery virtually impossible. To meet this problem the Theft Act 1968 (under s.6) further provides:

> **1. A person appropriating property belonging to another without meaning the other permanently to lose the thing itself is nevertheless to be regarded as having the intention of permanently depriving the other of it if his intention is to treat the thing as his own to dispose of regardless of the other's rights, and a borrowing or lending of it may amount to so treating it if, but only if, the borrowing or lending is for a period and in circumstances making it equivalent to an outright taking or disposal. 2. Without prejudice to the generality of subsection 1 above, where a person, having possession or control (lawfully or not) of property belonging to another, parts with the property under a condition as to its return which he may not be able to perform, this (if done for the purposes of his own and without the other's authority) amounts to treating the property as his own to dispose of regardless of the other's rights.**

In *R. v. Easom* (1971) the accused took a handbag from a seat in front of him in a cinema. It had been placed there as a trap by a policewoman. He sorted through the contents, found nothing of value and put it back on the floor. The Court of Appeal quashed his conviction for theft, since although he appropriated the handbag and its contents it was for a brief period – there was no intention of permanently depriving the owner of those particular pieces of property. Nor, as can be seen, could s.6 apply for what amounted to a matter of minutes. There is a difficulty in deciding what is a short period of time and what is not. 'Borrowing' goods for a year might well amount to permanent deprival; for five years almost certainly. However, concentration upon the time element can well become both irrelevant and misleading: in fact the central question more properly turns upon an intention to return, at whatever stage in the future, or an intention to appropriate permanently. It should also be added that *Easom* was decided before the passage of the Criminal Attempts Act 1981 which as already seen was designed to cover the 'empty pocket' situations. Of course, borrowing may mean that all the goodness of the item has disappeared, *R. v. Lloyd* (1985).

2 ROBBERY

Robbery is aggravated theft – it is stealing by means of force or the threat of force. (However, the taking of conveyances ('joy-riding' as it is inaptly named) is also aggravated theft and covered by s.12A of the 1968 Act, as inserted by the Aggravated Vehicle-Taking Act 1992, but fault on the part of D. does not have to be proved, *Dawes* v. *DPP* (1995).) Robbery is defined by the Theft Act 1968 (s.8):

1. A person is guilty of robbery if he steals, and immediately before or at the time of doing so, and in order to do so, he uses force on any person or puts or seeks to put any person in fear of being then and there subjected to force. 2. A person guilty of robbery, or of an assault with intent to rob, shall on conviction on indictment be liable to imprisonment for life.

The force or threat used need not amount to an assault: the victim does not have necessarily to apprehend violence; it is force as a fact which matters. The force used may be on a third party in order to effect the appropriation of another's property – for example, holding a person hostage or in detention or at gun-point so that the other delivers up the goods. The phrase 'immediately before or at the time of doing so' under the Act can give rise to a number of interpretations, depending on the circumstances of the case. The requisite time element can be said to be present as long as the theft is in progress, but not after it has been completed. It is for the jury to adopt a commonsense view of the problem and decide when the theft is actually completed (*R*. v. *Hale* (1979)). The jury must also decide whether force in a factual sense has been used or threatened. The amount of force may be very small. *Hale* was confirmed in *R*. v. *Lockley* (1995).

3 BURGLARY AND AGGRAVATED BURGLARY

Under the Theft Act 1968 (s.9) there are two offences of burglary. Firstly, a person is guilty of burglary if he enters a building as a trespasser with intent to steal or to inflict grievous bodily harm on any person or commit rape in that building or do unlawful damage to the building or its contents. A 'building' includes a vehicle or vessel normally inhabited (for example, a caravan or house-boat). Secondly, a person is guilty if having entered a building as a trespasser he steals or attempts to steal or inflicts or attempts to inflict grievous bodily harm on any person inside. (Murder, as an offence greater than grievous bodily harm, must logically fall within s.9.) Both offences are punishable by up to 14 years. The accused must know that he enters a building as a trespasser or at the very least is reckless as to whether he has implied permission to enter or not, as seen in *R*. v. *Collins* (1973) where a naked woman thought that a naked man at her window was her friend – she beckoned him in and sexual intercourse took place before the error was discovered by her. If he honestly but mistakenly believes that consent has been given to enter then there is no burglary. Consent to enter as a result of fraud is not, of course, a valid consent. Moreover, a consent given for one purpose may not be used for another – if it is burglary is committed (as in *R*. v. *Jones and Smith* (1976) where the 'trespasser' entered his father's house in order to steal a television set – he went beyond the bounds of the permission that had been given).

Under the Act 'building' also includes a part of the building. For example, a department store is open to the public, but the offices on the fifth floor, part of the same building, are not. A cash-till, whether full or empty, is not within the public area (*R*. v. *Walkington* (1979)). The same principle applies to hotels: a guest has a right to occupy a room and common areas such as the restaurant or foyer, but not the manager's private office or other guests' bedrooms. In *R. v. Laing* (1995) the appellant was found in the stock room of a department store after the store had closed; he was convicted of burglary. In *Ryan* (1996) it was sufficient that D. had his head and one arm inside a window for the purposes of burglary.

Aggravated burglary under the 1968 Act (s.10) is burglary committed with any firearm or imitation firearm, any weapon of offence, or any explosive. A firearm includes an airgun or air pistol, a weapon of offence any instrument made or adapted to cause injury to or incapacitate a person. Aggravated burglary is punishable by life imprisonment.

4 DECEPTION

The Theft Act (ss.15 and 16) provides: 'A person who by any deception dishonestly obtains property belonging to another, with the intention of permanently depriving the other of it, shall on conviction on indictment be liable to imprisonment for a term not exceeding ten years'. Property here will include land. 'A person who by any deception dishonestly obtains for himself or another any pecuniary advantage shall on conviction on indictment be liable to imprisonment for a term not exceeding five years'. 'For the purposes of this section 'deception' means any deception (whether deliberate or reckless) by words or conduct as to the present intentions of the person using the deception or any other person'. Deception may occur at any stage during the borrowing of goods for the purpose of s.15 of the Theft Act – *R. v. Coady* (1996).

So in *R. v. Callender* (1992) preparing accounts for small businessmen when not professionally qualified to do so fell within s.16 of the Theft Act 1968. In *R. v. Miller* (1992) the Court of Appeal said that the appellant was rightly convicted under s.15 of the Theft Act 1968, since he had operated as an unlicensed taxi-driver at London airports, posing as an authorised driver and charging ten times the normal fares.

As can be seen, the deception may be either deliberate or reckless in the subjective (*Cunningham*) sense. But the negligence of a reasonable man does not constitute deception. A deception is practised where it is clear that a person has obtained dishonestly the ownership, possession or control of the other's property. The misrepresentor does not have to be the beneficiary of the deception – a third party will suffice. It has been established that a person who obtains goods from a retailer by dishonestly using a credit card or cheque card is guilty of deception (*R. v. Lambie* (1981), and *Commissioner of Police for the Metropolis* v. *Charles* (1977)). In the first case the defendant had a credit card limit of £200, but exceeded this by over £800. In the latter case the accused used his cheque card to back 25 cheques in a gambling club. In *First Sport* v. *Barclays Bank plc* (1993) the Court of Appeal held that a bank must honour a forged cheque when backed by a cheque guarantee card. Similarly, in *R. v. Beck* (1985) the Court of Appeal held that the offence of procuring the execution of a valuable security by deception, contrary to s.20 of the Theft Act 1968, could be committed even if the deception alleged was not practised upon the persons who executed the valuable security as they knew of its falsity, but upon someone with whom their legal or commercial obligations were such that the jury could nevertheless decide it caused them to execute. This case involved the cashing-in of a large number of stolen Visa travellers' cheques and the unlawful use of a Diners Club card. A post-dated cheque can indicate deception in respect of the obtaining of property or a pecuniary advantage, as one ordinarily dated, since in both instances the person making out the cheque may know it will not be honoured by the bank (*R.* v. *Gilmartin* (1983)). In *Rozeik* (1996) the managers were the company so they could not be deceived (cf *Lambie*).

However, *R.* v. *Manjdadria* (1993) showed that obtaining a loan by way of jointly owned property as security (of £12,000) need not be caught by s.20 of the Theft Act 1968 (execution of a valuable security) since there was no identifiable document that was a valuable security.

In another cheque card case, that of *R.* v. *Navvabi* (1968) the defendant was accused of stealing sums of £50 and £100 from two banks by drawing cheques in false names on accounts with inadequate funds and handing them to the casino with a cheque card to guarantee payment. According to the prosecution the movement of theft was when a cheque was handed to the casino and N. was convicted. But the Court of Appeal quashed the convictions, ruling that a person cannot steal property until he appropriates it (s.1 of the 1968 Act) and that Mr Navvabi had not appropriated the bank's funds nor was the delivery of the cheque to the casino an appropriation, nor the use of a cheque card. A charge under s.16 of the Theft Act 1968 (obtaining a pecuniary advantage by deception) would have been more appropriate, but this was hardly of comfort to the bank manager.

The difficulties of proving obtaining property by deception when electronic transfer is involved (here the case was concerned with 40 mortgage applications at a time of a rising house market) were illustrated in the House of Lords' decision (overruling the Court of Appeal) in *R.* v. *Preddy and Slade* (1996). As a result of this decision s.15 of the 1968 Act was amended by the Theft (Amendment) Act 1996, which adds s.15A creating a new offence of obtaining a money transfer by deception. The 1996 Act creates a new offence too (s.24A) of dishonestly retaining a wrongful credit.

Misrepresentation

As it is in the civil law of contract and tort silence, that is a misrepresentation by concealment or omission, does not generally amount to deceit (deception). But the failure to correct a true statement which subsequently becomes false does amount to deception (*DPP* v. *Ray* (1974)). That is not to say, however, that an implied pretence cannot amount to a deception as much as an express one. The deception will usually be a misrepresentation of fact, but on occasion it may also be a misrepresentation of law. The word 'fraud' is sometimes applied to deception, but in effect it has a broader meaning: it embraces blackmail, cheating, false acounting, forgery, the suppression of documents and aspects of theft.

It should be added here that while certain debts may be 'legally unenforceable' under contract law, because, for example, the debtor is under 18 or the contract concerns gambling, it does not follow that the debtor is not criminally liable for deception. The Act states that obtaining a pecuniary advantage occurs where a person is given the opportunity to earn remuneration or greater remuneration by employment or by holding an office or to win money by betting. In the case of property the *mens rea* must, as seen from the relevant sections of the Act above, include obtaining it dishonestly and intending the other persons to be permanently deprived. In the case of pecuniary advantage it must be obtained dishonestly and for the benefit of the accused or another.

Making off without payment

The Theft Act 1978 amended the 1968 Act and made it an offence to obtain services by deception (s.1), to evade liablity by deception (s.2), and to make off without payment (s.3). The first two offences are punishable with a maximum of five years' imprisonment, the third by two. The services in question must be such that they confer a benefit upon the accused or a third party on the basis that they are paid for, or will be paid for. Evading a financial liability means that the accused obtains the remission of the whole or part of a legally enforceable debt whether in fact his own or another's, or that he clearly induces the creditor to wait for or forgo payment with the intention of permanent default in whole or in part by himself or another, or that the accused obtains an exemption (the whole debt) or abatement (part of the debt) of a (future) liability to pay. The accused may obtain an exemption or abatement for himself or another or create the cirumstances whereby another obtains exemption or abatement. An exemption or abatement does not have to relate to an existing debt: it may refer to a liability to pay which might arise in the future. The *mens rea* for both offences is essentially the same as that of obtaining a pecuniary advantage. In *R. v. Firth* (1989) the House of Lords held that the offence of dishonestly obtaining exemption or abatement of liability to make a payment, contrary to s.2(1)(c) of the Theft Act 1968, could be committed irrespective of whether the act was one of commission or omission and could be committed before any liability to pay had come into existence. Making off without payment means deliberately avoiding payment on the spot, as in the case of collecting goods or leaving a hotel without paying the bill. There is a certain amount of overlap between the various sections of the 1978 Act and between it and the 1968 Act – they are not mutually exclusive in respect of the charges that may be preferred. In *R. v. Aziz* (1993) D. and B. took a taxi to a nightclub; they thought the ride was worth £4 and refused to pay the fare of £15 charged; it was said that in this context payment 'on the spot' meant 'there and then'. In *R. v. Allen (Christopher)* (1985) the defendant booked a room in a London hotel for 10 nights. He stayed on for nearly a month, and the bill came to £1,300. He explained to the hotel that he was in financial difficulties, that he would return to move his belongings and would leave his Australian passport as security for the debt. When he arrived he was arrested, but he claimed he genuinely hoped to pay the bill and denied acting dishonestly. The Lords, looking at all the evidence and the thirteenth report of the Criminal Law Revision Committee which had led to the 1978 Act, ruled that the accused was not guilty.

5 FALSIFICATION

The Theft Act 1968 (under s.17) provides:

> **1. Where a person dishonestly, with a view to gain for himself or another or with intent to cause loss to another, (*a*) destroys, defaces, conceals or falsifies any account or any record or document made or required for any accounting purpose; or (*b*) in furnishing information for any purpose produces or makes use of any account, or any such record or document as aforesaid, which to his knowledge is or may be misleading, false or deceptive in a material particular; he shall on conviction on indictment, be liable to imprisonment for a term not exceeding seven years. 2. For purposes of this section a person who makes or concurs in making in an account or other document an entry which is or may be misleading, false or deceptive in a material particular, or who omits or concurs in omitting a material particular from an account or other document, is to be treated as falsifying the account or document.**

As can be seen, s.17 is specifically concerned with financial accounts. A document need only be partly required for accounting purposes as seen in *R. v. Shama* (1990), where an international telephone operator dishonestly failed to complete all the charge tickets required. Section 19 makes it an offence punishable by seven years for an officer of a body corporate (in effect company directors) or an officer of an unincorporated association deliberately to make a false financial statement. Section 20 provides for a similar term of punishment for a person who dishonestly destroys, conceals or defaces valuable securities, wills or other documents, with a view to gain for himself or another. In *R. v. King* (1991), the Court of Appeal upheld convictions under s.20 for inducing a bank to make mortgage advances on false valuations of a property, and *King* was approved by Lord Ackner in the House of Lords in *Kassim* (1992). In *Kassim* K. had opened a bank account and was also given an Access card. He incurred an overdraft of £8,338 and credit of £943 on Access. The bank honoured the debts. However, the House of Lords did not think a wide interpretation of s.20(2) as given in *Beck* was appropriate; it accepted the defendant's view that the word 'execution' meant the victim should actually do something to the face of the document.

6 TEMPORARY DEPRIVATION

Under the Theft Act 1968 (s.11) it is an offence punishable by up to five years' imprisonment to remove without lawful authority articles from a place open to the public – in other words temporarily to remove any part of a collection of paintings or the like on display to the public. 'A place' means a building or the grounds within a building; a park is not a place in this context. 'An article' means an object kept specifically for purposes of display, and that includes any such item kept in store. The section relates only to non-commercial exhibitions such as museums and art galleries.

Section 12 provides a punishment of up to three years' imprisonment for the taking of a conveyance without lawful authority or the consent of the owner. A conveyance is not just a car: any 'vehicle' designed to convey people is a conveyance – an aeroplane, a boat, a bus are all conveyances. Bicycles and other pedal cycles are also conveyances, but here the punishment is a summary one (a fine). The taking must be for his own use or that of another person. The accused may drive it or be driven by someone else. It is not an offence, though, for someone to be carried on a pedal cycle unlawfully taken by another. The 'unlawful taking' is limited by a subjective test: it is a defence for the accused to argue that he honestly believed that he had lawful authority to take the conveyance or that the owner's consent was impliedly given. It is irrelevant that the belief was an unreasonable one. Recklessness, however, would tend to point to a lack of honest belief. Similarly, it must be shown that a person being carried in a conveyance driven by another was fully aware that the conveyance had been unlawfully taken. Where the accused has lawfully borrowed the vehicle he is guilty if he breaks the conditions of the bailment or employment – such as an agreed route, time-limit or purpose (*R.* v. *Peart*, (1970), *R.* v. *McGill* (1970) and *McKnight* v. *Davies* (1974)).

7 BLACKMAIL

Section 21 of the Theft Act 1968 provides that the offence of blackmail is punishable by a maximum of 14 years' imprisonment. The offence is defined as one where a person, 'with a view to gain for himself or another or with intent to cause loss to another, makes any unwarranted demand with menaces unless the person making it does so in the belief that he has reasonable grounds for making the demand, and that the use of menaces is a proper means of reinforcing the demand'. The two qualifications clearly constitute a totally subjective and perhaps therefore unfair test: the accused is to be judged, if this point arises, by his standards. The Act also states that the nature of the act or omission is immaterial and that it is irrelevant whether the menaces relate or not to the action to be taken by the person making the demand. Usually a demand will be for money or property. The demand may be made in a variety of fashions; indeed, it may be implied or expressed. It has been established that a demand is made once a letter is posted, not when it is received (*Treacy* v. *DPP* (1971)). The 'menace' appears to mean the threat of any 'action detrimental to or unpleasant to the person addressed' (*per* Lord Wright in *Thorne* v. *Motor Trade Association* (1937)). But the important point is that the accused must intend that the victim will respond to the threat; if he does not, then there is no offence. The test is whether the mind of an ordinary person of normal stability would be affected by the threat as far as the accused is concerned (*R. v. Clear* (1968)). If that is the intent it does not matter that the person concerned does not in fact respond to the threat. If the victim is of a timid disposition, it is irrelevant that a person of greater firmness may not have given in to the threats, as illustrated in *R. v. Garwood* (1978) where the defendant seized hold of S., a youth of 18, by the shirt and demanded money (£30) and jewellery. In other words this is similar to the 'egg-shell skull' rule in tort.

Under the Administration of Justice Act 1970 it is a summary offence unlawfully to harass debtors. What constitutes unlawful harassment will be determined by an objective test, that of the reasonable man.

8 POSSESSION (GOING EQUIPPED)

The Theft Act under s.25 makes it an offence punishable by three years imprisonment for a person to have with him (other than at his home) any article for the purpose of burglary, theft, deception or the taking and driving away of a conveyance. An 'article' could cover a large number of different items or instruments; many articles, apparently innocent in appearance, could be used for criminal purposes, a difficult point to prove. The accused must know he has the article and intends to use it, although the crime need not be a specific one – going equipped with the general object of burglary or theft or so on is sufficient. In *R. v. Doukas* (1978) the defendant, a wine waiter at the Cunard Hotel in London, was found guilty under s.25 since he took his own wine to work in order to sell to guests as the hotel's own alcohol and to pocket the profit. Going equipped was illustrated in *Re McAngus* (1994). And in *R. v. Goodwin* (1996) the appellant was convicted of going equipped where he used Kenyan coins that were identical to British 50p coins but worth much less so as to play on the gaming machines.

9 HANDLING STOLEN GOODS

The 1968 Act by s.22 provides:

> **1. A person handles stolen goods if (otherwise than in the course of stealing) knowing or believing them to be stolen goods he dishonestly receives the goods, or dishonestly undertakes or assists in their retention, removal, disposal or realisation by or for the benefit of another person, or if he arranges to do so. 2. A person guilty of handling stolen goods shall on conviction on indictment be liable to imprisonment for a term not exceeding fourteen years.**

The draughtsman appears to have muddled this section of the Act. The meaning of 'knowing' and 'believing' was considered in *R. v. Hall (Edward)* (1985), where the appellant who was an antique dealer, was found in his mother's flat in London with two other men and some articles worth about £26,000, which had been stolen the previous night from a mansion in Gloucestershire. The word 'believing' is superfluous, since the courts will not convict merely on strong suspicion alone that the goods are stolen.

In *R. v. Bloxham* (1982) the accused in early 1977 agreed to buy a car for £1300. He paid £500 on account, the balance to be paid when the registration documents were delivered; these he never received. In fact the car was stolen and fitted with false number plates. The defendant admitted to the police that by mid-1977 he had suspected the car was stolen. At the end of the year he sold the car for £200 to a stranger. He was charged with handling stolen goods contrary to s.22 in that he had dishonestly undertaken or assisted in the disposal or realisation of the stolen vehicle by or for the benefit of the unknown purchaser. The House of Lords allowed his appeal against conviction. It ruled that the single offence created by the second half of s.22(1) contemplated its committal in relation to the four activities specified – retention, removal, disposal, realisation – in one or other of two ways. Firstly, the offender himself might undertake the activity for the benefit of another person. Secondly, the activity might be undertaken by another person and the offender might assist him. Accordingly, a purchaser, as such, of stolen goods could not be 'another person' within the subsection since his act of purchase could not sensibly be described as a disposal or realisation of the goods by him. Equally, although the sale to him could be described as a disposal or realisation for his benefit, the transaction was not within the ambit of the subsection.

'Goods' means money, property, but not land where the area in question is not severed. 'Stolen goods' include those obtained by theft, blackmail, deception or by similar criminal acts in another country. It does follow, however, that a person accused of handling stolen goods must be acquitted automatically if the original 'thief' has been acquitted. Section 24 provides:

> **But no goods shall be regarded as having continued to be stolen goods after they have been restored to the person from whom they were stolen or to other lawful possession or custody, or after that person and any other person claiming through him have otherwise ceased as regards those goods to have any right to restitution in respect of the theft.**

Once goods, originally stolen, are placed in the possession of the lawful owner or possessor, such as the police, then the goods are no longer stolen and receiving or handling such 'stolen' goods becomes impossible. Where a person ceases to have any right to restitution, it effectively means a person avoids his right to lawful ownership (voidable title). This matter is directly related to the tort of wrongful interference with goods; under the Torts (Interference with Goods) Act 1977 the court may make a specific order for the redelivery of goods (restitution). If the aggrieved party waives his right to such an order, then the goods are no longer stolen. Section 24 also provides that handling stolen goods may apply to those goods which although not originally stolen have been exchanged for such goods and therefore for these purposes become stolen, unless the 'receiver' is neither the thief nor a handler, that is he does not know that the goods have been exchanged for stolen ones.

'Handling' is often thought of as 'receiving'. But as the Act makes clear it also embraces undertaking or assisting in the retention, removal, disposal or realisation of the goods by or for the benefit of another, or arranging to receive, undertake or assist. If no such benefit is intended, then receipt of goods alone is sufficient for the offence of handling (or arranging to receive). Receipt will usually involve some form of physical possession or control. An example of assistance occurred in *R. v. Kanwar* (1982): here the accused was convicted of dishonestly assisting in the retention of stolen goods for the benefit of her husband. The husband had brought stolen goods into their house at a time when she was in hospital. Later on when the police arrived with a search warrant, she told them that certain articles were lawfully hers. But merely using goods in the possession of another does not constitute assistance; there must be an intentional and dishonest act. However, in the *Kanwar* case the accused had told lies; if she had remained silent, for there is no general obligation to assist the police with information, a conviction would have been virtually impossible.

It is not usually the case that thieves are handlers as well. But it is possible to charge a thief with handling, too, where he keeps or moves the goods for the benefit of another. Similarly, X. might pass goods to Z. for safe-keeping; after a week Z. returns them to X., who is now a receiver as well as a thief. Thus the offences of theft and handling are not mutually exclusive. However, the general rule was set out in the guidence issued by the Court of Appeal in *R. v. Shelton* (1986), where the appellant had obtained money on cheques from a cheque book stolen earlier the same day. The court said:

> **1 the practice of charging theft and handling as alternatives should continue whenever there was a real possibility that the evidence might support one rather than the other; 2 there was a danger that juries might be confused by reference to second or later appropriations since the issue in every case was whether the defendant had in fact appropriated property belonging to another. If he had done so, it was irrelevant how he came to make the appropriation provided it was in the course of theft; 3 the jury should be told that a handler can be a thief, but he cannot be convicted of being both a thief and a handler; 4 handling was the more serious offence; 5 in the unlikely event of the jury not agreeing whether theft or handling had been proved, they should be discharged.**

Finally, it must also be underlined that for a charge of handling to be preferred successfully, the prosecution must show that the accused knew the goods were stolen or believed they were; it is not enough simply to assert that the defendant ought to have known or even suspected that they were stolen or simply ignored the situation. The test for *mens rea* is thus a subjective one. So, suspicion that the goods were stolen, even coupled with the fact that the defendant shut his eyes to the circumstances, is not sufficient although these matters may be taken into account by a jury when deciding whether or not the necessary belief existed. This was underlined in a case involving a mare valued at £700 stolen from livery stables; the appellant sold her the next day for £480 in cash (R. v. *Moys*, 1984).

The handling must be done 'dishonestly'. Such a word adds little to the *mens rea*, but it is important where the accused knew or believed the goods to be stolen but intended to return them to the owner or pass them to the police. Because of the difficulty in proving the requisite *mens rea* for handling offences, the Theft Act 1968 (s.27) allows the prosecution to introduce evidence which shows that the accused has been guilty of theft or handling during the previous five years, a point illustrated in an antiques and objets d'art case – R. v. *Fowler* (1987). *Fowler* underlined how controversial s.27 is and how sparingly it should be used.

Section 28 of the 1968 Act empowers the court, if it thinks fit, to order the return of the stolen goods to the lawful owner or possessor and any innocent purchaser to be appropriately compensated (restitution). Such a procedure avoids the necessity of a civil action as well in tort. Parallel powers also exist under the Police (Property) Act 1897 and the Powers of Criminal Courts Act 1973. There is a strong case for extending the 1973 Act's provisions to provide compensation for the victim's family.

6.7   Criminal damage

The Criminal Damage Act 1971 provides that a person who 'without lawful excuse destroys or damages any property belonging to another intending to destroy or damage any such property or being reckless as to whether any such property would be destroyed or damaged shall be guilty of an offence; s.1(1). The maximum term of imprisonment is 10 years, but under the Criminal Justice Act 1988 damage under £5000 is a summary offence only. 'Damage' need not always mean actual physical impairment. Property may be damaged if, for example, some part of it is removed, such as a battery from a car. Property may only be tangible articles and includes wild creatures kept in captivity. It does not, though, include mushrooms growing wild or the flowers, fruit or foliage of wild plants. Property 'belonging to another' means property over which another has custody or control or in which he has any proprietary right or interest (that includes the property of a corporation). Property also 'belongs' to a person if that person has a charge on it. A person cannot commit criminal damage on his own property, unless, of course, he is only a co-owner. The *mens rea* for the offence is intention or recklessness. Recklessness here is, since *Caldwell*, objective. The doctrine of transferred malice is applicable to criminal damage.

As the Act makes plain a person may destroy or damage another's property with lawful excuse, which was considered in *Johnson* v. *DPP* (1994). A 'lawful excuse', s.5(2), would include consent from the other person, implied or express, as well as a form of necessity, that is the accused takes action in order to protect his own or another's property, or rights or interest in such property. The excuse is lawful providing the accused believes in what he is doing; it is immaterial that the belief is unjustified. The accused must also honestly believe that the means of protection adopted are 'reasonable having regard to all the circumstances'; the latter phrase still constitutes, however, a subjective rather than an objective test. The 'danger' to the property must be immediate, not distant. In *R. v. Denton* (1981) the appellant set fire to the business premises of T., at T.'s request since the firm was in financial difficulties and T., the appellant's employers, apparently intended to make a false insurance claim. The Court of Appeal held that no offence was committed under the 1971 Act where a person arranged to set fire to his own premises, even though such an action involved an inchoate attempt to commit fraud. The appellant thus had a 'lawful excuse', but s.5(2) does not apply to ss.1(2), 2(b) or 3(b). The question of lawful excuse, in relation to s.5(5), arose in *Lloyd* v. *DPP* (1992), where L. found his car wheel clamped and, after a heated dispute with the security firm, sawed through the chains securing the clamps; it was held, under s.1(1), that L. should not have damaged the clamps.

The 1971 Act also makes it an offence, s.1(2), for a person without lawful excuse to destroy or damage any property, whether belonging to that person or another, where he intends 'to destroy or damage any property or [is] reckless as to whether any property would be destroyed or damaged; and [intends] by the destruction or damage to endanger the life of another or [is] reckless as to whether the life of another would be thereby endangered'. This offence clearly overlaps with that of attempted murder, although the *mens rea* is wider in the sense that recklessness is sufficient. The maximum sentence is life imprisonment. The problems of s.1(2) were illustrated in *Merrick* (1996).

In *R. v. Steer* (1987), the defendant disagreed on a number of occasions with his business partner; as a result he visited his partner's home, rang the doorbell and fired at the bedroom window where his partner and wife appeared. Not surprisingly the window was broken and the defendant pleaded guilty to criminal damage, but he was also charged under s.1(2) and convicted. The Court of Appeal, upheld by the House of Lords, quashed the conviction, since the endangerment of life should be caused by the damaging of the property, and a smashed window would hardly suffice in these circumstances. But if the defendant had intended to kill he would have been guilty of murder or attempted murder, or guilty of manslaughter if he had killed recklessly. Yet as the shot missed, the offence would be no more than common assault. In *Attorney-General's Reference (No 3 of 1992)* (1994) the Court of Appeal held it was sufficient that the accused was reckless as to whether life was endangered under s.1(2) of the Criminal Damage Act 1971 for the purposes of attempted arson, providing there were steps more than merely preparatory to causing criminal damage with intent.

ARSON

Arson, s.1(3), is any destruction or damage of property by fire and is thus covered by either of the two first sub-sections of the 1971 Act quoted above, so the maximum sentence for arson is life imprisonment. Any threat made to another (*a*) to destroy or damage property or that of a third party or (*b*) to destroy or damage the accused's own property in a manner that is likely to endanger the life of the other person or a third party is also an offence (s.2) under the 1971 Act, punishable by 10 years' imprisonment. The threat must be made without lawful excuse and must be intended to cause the other to fear that it would be carried out.

In *R. v. Miller (James)* (1983) the House of Lords held that in cases where an accused was initially unaware that he had done something which was the original cause of a risk of damage to the property of another, then he would be guilty under the Criminal Damage Act 1971 if, once aware that what was happening had resulted from his own act, he did not take steps to prevent or reduce the risk of damage. In this case the appellant fell asleep on a mattress with a lighted cigarette. He woke up to find the mattress on fire. He then simply went into another room and fell asleep again. When he woke up he found that the police and fire brigade had arrived. 'I hadn't got anything to put the fire out with, so I just left it', the accused said. And in *R. v. Sangha* (1988) where the defendant set fire to furniture in an empty flat, the defendant's conviction under the 1971 Act (that is he was reckless whether life would be endangered, in the *Caldwell* sense) was upheld by the Court of Appeal even though there was only a very small chance of the fire spreading outside the flat.

The punishment of 10 years' imprisonment also applies to a person who has anything in his custody or under his control intending (s.3) without lawful excuse to use it or cause or permit another to use it in order '(*a*) to destroy or damage any property belonging to some other person; or (*b*) to destroy or damage his own or the user's property in a way which he knows is likely to endanger the life of some other person'. A conditional intent, in the sense of use of the article to cause damage if it proves necessary at some future date, will also suffice.

The Criminal Damage Act 1971 has not affected the offences under the Explosive Substances Act 1883 and certain sections of the Malicious Damage Act 1861 are still extant. The 1861 Act covers obstruction of a railway line and endangering of shipping, the 1883 Act damage caused by explosions. A person may make an explosive substance if he can show its making had a lawful object, inside or outside of the United Kingdom (*R. v. Berry* (1984)). Under the Powers of Criminal Courts Act 1973 the court may make a compensation order in respect of loss of damage to property.

6.8   Public morality

1 BLASPHEMY

It is a blasphemous libel under the common law to publish certain matters; the words concerned may be oral or written. Any matter which outrages or insults Christian feelings, although not the feelings of people belonging to different religions, is blasphemy. In R. v. *Chief Metropolitan Stipendiary Magistrate ex parte Choudhury* (1991) it was held the blasphemy laws do not cover Islam (the Salman Rushdie affair). The accused must have intended to publish the material in question, but he need not have intended to cause outrage or insult. Arguably, to that limited extent the offence is one of strict liability. These points were underlined in R. v. *Lemon* (*Whitehouse* v. *Gay News*) (1978), the first case of blasphemy for over half a century, which concerned the publication of a poem in *Gay News* suggesting *inter alia* that Christ had indulged in promiscuous homosexual practices. The prosection was brought privately by Mrs Mary Whitehouse. However, the Lords did not think that the offence was one of strict liability. It also noted that a tendency to cause a breach of the peace was not a necessary element in the offence of publishing a blasphemous libel.

2 FREEDOM FROM OBSCENITY

The law on obscenity is little short of a mess, as the Williams Report found in 1979. The Report felt existing laws were out of date. It argued for a new all-embracing statute; and it was particularly mindful of the effects of 'obscenity' upon young people. Pornography, obscenity, indecency, immorality – both the public and the legal system are fond of using a variety of different terms to cover much the same problem. The real difficulty with drawing up any law to cover obscenity is that public attitudes do shift, perceptibly if not dramatically. What might be regarded as depraved or corrupt one day, could become if not totally normal at least acceptable the next.

The 1959 Act

For a long time common law recognised the offence of obscene libel, but in 1959 Parliament intervened. The Obscene Publications Act provided that it was an offence to publish material that was obscene or to handle such material for gain, an article being deemed obscene if 'its effect [was], if taken as a whole, such as to tend to deprave and corrupt persons who [were] likely having regard to all relevant circumstances to read it'. The Act was put to the test the following year in the case of *Lady Chatterley's Lover*, a racy novel by D. H. Lawrence (*R. v. Penguin Books Ltd*, 1961). Perhaps a change in the public mood was already under way, for the jury acquitted the defendants, having heard counsel for the prosecution in his opening address ask them whether it was the kind of book they would wish either their wives or their servants to read. Where a defendant has had obscene articles for gain contrary to s.2(1) of the 1959 Act, then the jury must be satisfied that the effect of any of those contemplated publications would be to deprave and corrupt a more than negligible proportion of those likely to see the relevant matter. Part VII of the Criminal Justice and Public Order Act 1994 has amended the 1959 legislation and the Protection of Children Act 1978.

The 1959 Act says (s.4) that one test of obscenity shall be that the book must be taken as a whole: salacious extracts must be considered in context. Moreover, if it can be shown that the published work is in the interests of science, art or literature or other objects of learning, then the defence can use such grounds to justify publication. And if it can be shown that a person suffers aversion or revulsion, then it can be argued that the work has not tended to corrupt or deprave. The 1959 Act also provided that the accused might legitimately argue that he was unaware that the matter was obscene, that he had not examined the matter but had merely handled it. However, following a flood of pornographic literature from overseas in the early 1960s, Parliament passed the Obscene Publications Act in 1964. The control or possession of obscene material *for gain* is clearly an offence under the 1964 Act.

The 1959 Act also provides that obscene material may be confiscated if magistrates issue a search warrant. The articles must, though, be kept for the purpose of gain; this process is known as 'forfeiture proceedings'. Despite parliamentary protests about the seizure of the eighteenth century work, *Fanny Hill*, the 1964 legislation did nothing to amend forfeiture. Indeed one Member of Parliament, Sir Cyril Black, used the same procedure in 1966 in respect of *Last Exit to Brooklyn*, a book which contained explicit descriptions about homosexual behaviour. The publishers of the book were then unsuccessfully prosecuted, the Court of Appeal overturning the jury's verdict (*R. v. Calder and Boyars Ltd* (1969)). The Court of Appeal was able to do this on a point of law – the trial judge had misdirected the jury. Under the Criminal Justice Act 1967 a private individual can longer commence proceedings for forfeiture; the DPP, or the police acting on his behalf, must lay the relevant information before the magistrates. The main criticism of forfeiture is that it undercuts the right to a trial by jury.

A number of other points that have arisen from judicial interpretation of the 1959 and 1964 Acts should be noted. Firstly, it is no defence to say that persons already addicted to pornography are incapable of being corrupted or depraved further (*DPP v. Whyte* (1972)) or that obscene material has therapeutic value (*R. v. Jordan* 1977)). Secondly, a publication describing the 'merits' of drug-taking can also be judged obscene, as shown by the decision in the case of *John Calder (Publications) Ltd v. Powell* in 1965; in the same way published material which could induce violent behaviour is illegal (*DPP v. A & BC Chewing Gum Ltd* (1968)). The last case was concerned with the effect of depravity upon children. The standards may well be different: what might corrupt children might not corrupt adults. The point was underlined by the prosecution of the editors of the 'underground' magazine *Oz* regarding the *Oz No.28 School Kids Issue*, to which school children themselves had been invited to contribute (*R.* v. *Anderson* (1972)); similar matters arose in the case of *Handyside* v. *United Kingdom* (1976). It is clear from the *Oz* prosecution that, unlike books, magazines or periodicals do not have to be considered *in toto*: it is sufficient that one article is judged obscene for the whole publication to become obscene.

Other legislation

While indeed under the 1959 Act 'obscene' does not for the purpose of conviction necessarily mean shocking, repulsive or lewd, it does carry that wider definition in respect of matter sent through the post as covered by the Post Office Act 1953 and the Unsolicited Goods and Services Act 1971. It should be noted, however, that horror comics and the like are covered by the Children and Young Persons (Harmful Publications) Act 1955. The consent of the DPP for prosecutions under this Act is absolute, whereas anyone can bring a prosecution under the 1959 Act, although the Attorney-General's permission is required in respect of theatrical productions and the DPP's in respect of films. Under the Customs Consolidation Act 1876 and related statutes customs officers may seize obscene material, as the case of *R.* v. *Henn* (1980) mentioned earlier has well illustrated. Under the Protection of Children Act 1978 it is an offence to take an indecent photograph or film of a person under 16, or to distribute such material.

In 1984 *The Guardian* wrote:

> **Eight years ago Customs and Excise seized an edition of the work of the artist Thomas Rowlandson, apparently unaware of the fact that the originals were hanging in the George V collection at Windsor Castle. And more than a decade earlier, in 1964, Sir Dingle Foot QC, who was to become a law officer in the first Wilson administration, bought a copy of *The Perfumed Garden* at Heathrow Airport, prior to departure abroad. He returned with the book, which was promptly confiscated. He was told that he was seeking to bring an indecent article into the United Kingdom. Since then the Customs Department has altered its procedures and single copies of obscene or indecent books or other articles imported in baggage tend not to be seized. The Home Office was responsible for framing the Obscene Publication Acts of 1959 and 1964, but it is, strangely, the Treasury, which has responsibilty for the manner in which Customs officers interpret 'obscenity' and 'indecency'.**

The Criminal Law Act 1977 extended the obscenity laws to include film-shows – 'cinematograph exhibitions'. This includes film, videos and sound track. (The 1959 Act in this context had very restricted provisions; photographs were not, of course, excluded – indeed books and magazines themselves might include photographs; and negatives of photographic material were covered by the 1964 Act.) This provision in the Act had partly been presaged by the case of *DPP* v. *Jacey Ltd* in 1957, even though the film in question – *More About the Language of Love* – had been awarded an X certificate by the Greater London Council. However, it should be remembered that the types of certificates awarded by the British Board of Film Classification are advisory, the Board originally being the poodle of the film industry itself. (The British Board of Film Censors became the British Board of Film Classification in 1984.) Under the Cinematograph Act 1909 county councils were given the power to inspect the quality of the celluloid for fire-risk hazards. But the councils soon became more interested in what they saw on the film and the Act was therefore interpreted rather broadly. The Cinematograph Act 1952 recognised this situation and gave local councils the power to inspect and license non-inflammable films. Since the Local Government Act 1972 it is district rather than county councils which perform this heady task; the same Act abolished the right of delegation to local magistrates. The aim of the 1977 Act was to regulate the growth of unlicensed premises and commercial clubs showing obscene films. The DPP's consent to prosecute or to commence forfeiture proceedings is necessary where the film is 16mm or over. The Cinematograph (Amendment) Act 1982 excluded exhibitions of moving pictures promoted for private gain from certain exemptions under the 1909 and 1952 Acts; it also reformed the procedures for granting licences (including appeals) and it gave the police and officials of the licensing and fire authorities clear powers of entry to the relevant premises. The legislation relating to cinemas in this context was consolidated under the Cinemas Act 1985.

Under the Theatres Act 1968 the Lord Chamberlain's powers to censor all varieties of stage productions were swept away. The Act states that plays must not include obscene performances. Nonetheless it makes some wide exceptions in respect of the artistic merits and aims of the play, and the West End of London has borne eloquent testimony to that provision; hence the attempt by some MPs to include theatres in the Criminal Law Act 1977.

Cases of blasphemous libel are extremely rare at common law; the *Gay News* trial of 1977–78 has been referred to earlier. In 1985 the Law Commission recommended the abolition of the crime of blasphemy, along with criminal libel as a whole.

In respect of the broadcasting authorities, a single unified Broadcasting Standards Commission was established under the Broadcasting Act 1996.

Common Law provisions

Despite the regulation of obscenity by statute law, unsatisfactory in many respects as that regulation may be, it appears that there remain two common law rules – that of conspiring to corrupt public morals and conspiring to outrage public decency. The former was underlined by the decision in *Shaw* v. *DPP* in 1962 (the Ladies' Directory case) which involved the publication of a list of prostitutes for discriminating clients. The latter was emphasised 10 years later in the test case of *Knuller Ltd* v. *DPP* which involved advertisements for those desiring homosexual relationships. It is not entirely clear as to what extent those common law provisions have now been absorbed into the Criminal Law Act 1977.

The Indecent Displays (Control) Act 1981 makes it an offence to show in public indecent advertisements or displays: the Act is directed at hoardings and the like outside cinemas. This would include displays on private property visible from public places. Under the Local Government (Miscellaneous Provisions) Act 1982 local authorities have the power to grant or refuse licences for sex establishments. Under the 1982 Act it was necessary for the prosecutor to prove that the accused knew not only that the premises were being used as a sex establishment but also that no licence had been granted, held the House of Lords in *Westminster City Council* v. *Croyalgrange Ltd* (1986), although as Mr Justice Devlin had said in *Roper* v. *Taylor's Central Garages (Exeter) Ltd* (1951), such knowlege could often be proved by showing that a defendant had deliberately shut his eyes to the facts and had failed to make reasonable inquiries.

The Video Recordings Act 1984 lays down a system of classification for video works, including those not suitable for under 18 year-olds. It is a criminal offence to supply or possess an unclassified video, that is a 'video nasty', and the court may order the forfeiture of such videos; the Video Recordings Act 1993 provides for a three month time-limit for prosecutions under the 1984 Act.

6.9   Public order and the national interest

It has long been a cherished right in the United Kingdom that people should be able to associate politically and industrially without let or hindrance. Trade unions were given this power over a century ago under the Trade Union Act 1871, although the right to picket peacefully has been the subject of much legislative change over the years. Under the Public Order Act 1936 it is an offence to organise or participate in organisations whose functions would appear to be quasi-military. The Prevention of Terrorism (Temporary Provisions) Act 1989 makes it an offence to belong to the IRA, INLA, IPLO, UDA, UVF, UFF and the Red Hand Commandos. Moreover, the holding of meetings is sometimes regulated by local by-laws made under the authority of an Act of Parliament.

Processions and public meetings in the open may in practice be limited by the police on the grounds that they may cause an obstruction of the highway, 'obstruction' being a notoriously loose word to define. The Highways Act 1980 makes it an offence wilfully to obstruct a highway without lawful authority or excuse; the Police Act 1964 makes it illegal to obstruct the police, while the Criminal Law Act 1977 makes it illegal to join a conspiracy – for example, to obstruct police officers.

The main area of the law is now covered by the Public Order Act 1986.

1 PUBLIC ORDER ACT 1986

The 1986 Act now comprehensively covers the area of public order and was the first major review of such legislation for half a century – when the 1936 Act had been passed to deal with the fascist 'threat' of Sir Oswald Mosley and his black-shirts.

The reasons for the statutory reform are to be seen in the experience of police forces throughout the country over the last decade or so, in coping with industrial disputes, inner city riots and the growth of football hooliganism. For example, in the 1984-85 miners' dispute there were 137 charges of riot, but no-one was convicted, under the old law; there were also 509 charges of unlawful assembly.

One major aim of the new Act was to bring some sense of rationality and coherence to this area of the law. So the old common law offences of riot, rout, affray and unlawful assembly have all been abolished and replaced with new offences of riot, violent disorder, affray, causing fear of violence, and offensive conduct.

The Act does not abolish the common law matters of public nuisance and breach of the peace; it is not, therefore, a codifying measure.

a) Violent disorder

This was a wholly new offence, upon which, at the time the Bill was being passed, the Government placed considerable emphasis. Under s.2, where

> **three or more persons who are present together use or threaten violence and the conduct of them (taken together) is such as would cause a person of reasonable firmness present at the scene to fear for his personal safety, each of the persons using or threatening unlawful violence is guilty of violent disorder.**

As with riot, no person of reasonable firmness need actually be present, and the offence may be committed in private as well as in public, so, perhaps paradoxically, a bystander may never be likely to be in a particular private place, yet the offence of violent disorder is still committed. Violence is not strictly defined under the Act, but s.8 gives it an extended meaning, so that 'other violent conduct' is included, which, for example, the Act states, includes missile throwing. Under s.6 the defendant must be shown to have *mens rea* in respect of his own conduct; it does not have to be shown that he has *mens rea* in respect of its consequences. He must intend to use violence or be (subjectively) aware that his conduct could be violent. The three people present do not, curiously, have to be threatened with violence simultaneously. Also, under s.6 the accused shall be taken to be aware of that of which he would have been aware if not intoxicated; so self-induced intoxication amongst, say, football fans is not a legal escape route, and this applies to offences under (**b**) to (**e**) too. The maximum penalty is five years' imprisonment.

b) Riot

Riot is committed where 12 or more people present together use or threaten violence (s.1). Violence has the extended meaning, under s.8, as in violent disorder above, so that would embrace violence towards property and violent conduct causing fear of injury whether or not intended to injure, including 'other violent conduct' such as missile throwing.

There must be a 'common purpose' and, as with violent disorder, their conduct must be such as would cause a person of reasonable firmness at the scene to fear for his safety. Only each person actually using violence is guilty, for up to 10 years' imprisonment, but once a riot quickly develops someone 'involved' would have to dissociate himself rapidly to avoid conviction. This offence would appear to cover gang fights and pitched battles, although a riot cannot be committed if some of the 12 people concerned were acting in self-defence, but this is difficult to distinguish in a mêlée, a point that is of some relevance, too, to the offence of violent disorder. Riot and affray can take place in private places – so, in a club or a college, a serious disturbance will constitute a riot. A prosecution for riot may only be by or with the consent of the DPP; surprisingly, this requirement does not occur in relation to violent disorder, although in practice the police would be expected to consult closely with the DPP's office (ie the Crown Prosecution Service).

Under the Riot (Damages) Act 1886 compensation may be awarded from the police fund for damage caused by a riot to houses, shops or other buildings, or property inside such premises. The riot, however, must also have been a tumult; in other words the scale of the riot was such that the attention of the police was, or should have been, attracted to the commotion caused.

c) Affray

Here, under s.3, the offence hardly differs from the previous two offences; it is essentially aimed at those who fight in public in a way that alarms bystanders, but as with riot and violent disorder the bystander, the 'person of reasonable firmness', need not actually be present. In respect of affray the meaning of a person of reasonable firmness was illustrated in *R.* v. *Sanchez* (1996).

Only violence, s.8 lays down, towards the person, although that would include missile throwing, will suffice, whereas violence towards property will be sufficient in riot and violent disorder. Like riot, affray would cover pitched street battles, as well as such instances as revenge attacks on individuals and attacks in pubs and seaside resorts. On the other hand, the offence may be committed by a person alone; also, the threat cannot be made simply by the use of words, as opposed to a combination of words and gestures (for instance, shaking a fist). The maximum term of imprisonment is three years.

d) Causing fear of violence

Section 4 of the Act replaced the old breach of the peace provisions of the 1936 legislation, and creates a new offence of causing fear of, or provoking the immediate use of, unlawful violence by threatening, abusive or insulting words or behaviour to another, or the distribution or display of writings or signs to another which are threatening, abusive or insulting. The maximum term of imprisonment is six months, or a fine, or both.

A number of problems are thrown up by s.4. In the first place it is not entirely clear how this provision differs from the common law breach of the peace, which the Act does no more to abolish than the Police and Criminal Evidence Act 1984 as seen earlier. Secondly, no offence is committed, as stated above, inside a 'domestic dwelling'. The point of this provision is to exclude domestic disputes. On the other hand, if insulting words are shouted at a person in a garden from a house, then an offence is committed. In *Atkin* v. *DPP* (1989) the defendant told customs officers that the bailiff outside in the car was 'a dead 'un', but the threat was not direct, nor was it in *Chappell* v. *DPP* (1989) in respect of writing contained in an envelope; the belief involved must be that of the person threatened, *Loade* v. *DPP* (1990).

Thirdly, the *mens rea* is not entirely clear, but it would appear the accused must intend to use the words or behave insultingly and so on or be aware that the words or behaviour may be insulting, threatening or abusive, a subjective test. The proviso regarding self-induced intoxication outlined under s.2 (violent disorder) also applies here, as stated earlier, and below (s.5). 'Violence' has the full meaning, under s.8, as in riot and violent disorder. The fear of violence under s.4 is probably wider than the fear, at least as far as property damage is concerned, under breach of the peace.

As the Act is relatively new much of the case law will be irrelevant. However, some of the principles of breach of the peace cases will be applicable.

A police officer may arrest without a warrant anyone whom he reasonably suspects is committing an offence under s.4. If the officer has reasonable grounds for suspecting that the offence under s.4 has been committed by an individual, then he may arrest him, but only if the officer believes that service of a summons is either impracticable or inappropriate because one of the general arrest conditions under s.25 of the Police and Criminal Evidence Act 1984 is satisfied.

In contrast riot and violent disorder are arrestable offences, under s.24 of the Police and Criminal Evidence Act 1984. But as the maximum penalty for affray is three years, this is too low to satisfy s.24. Instead, s.3 of the Public Order Act 1986 provides a limited statutory power of arrest: a constable may arrest without warrant anyone he reasonably suspects is committing an affray. But it is also likely that riot, violent disorder or affray impinges upon breach of the peace, so that the common law power of arrest is activated, as outlined below. By virtue of s.154 of the Criminal Justice and Public Order Act 1994, s.4A of the 1986 Act has created the further offence of intentional harassment, alarm and distress.

e) Harassment, alarm or distress

Section 5 created a new offence of causing harassment, alarm or distress. The offence is committed by using words or behaviour which are threatening, abusive or insulting, or using 'disorderly' behaviour, or displaying writings or signs which are threatening, abusive or insulting, within the hearing or sight of a person likely to be caused harassment, alarm or distress. In *Chambers and Edwards* v. *DPP* (1995) it was noted that under s.5 'disorderly behaviour' was not defined in the Act and therefore had to be given its ordinary and everyday meaning.

This offence therefore covers minor acts of hooliganism or anti-social behaviour, for example kicking over dustbins, banging on windows, shouting abuse at bus queues, or late night rowdy behaviour. A major problem with this section is that it tries to protect the weak and vulnerable but they are unlikely persons to be willing to appear in court. The offence may take place in a private or public place, with the same exception as for (**d**).

The *mens rea* is not totally clear, but one major difference with s.4 is that the conduct need not be directed 'towards another', which could appear to make the question of whether or not the actors were aware of the existence of others a matter of strict liability. But the better view would be that the person who honestly believes there is no risk of his conduct being threatening is not guilty (a subjective, *Ghosh* test).

There are three defences:

1 the accused may prove he had no reason to believe that there was any person within hearing or sight who was likely to be caused harassment (and so on);

2 he may prove he was inside a dwelling and had no reason to believe the words or behaviour would be heard or seen by a person outside; and

3 he may prove his conduct was reasonable.

The last defence is pretty vague, and for all defences the standard of proof is the civil one – on the balance of probabilities, as opposed to beyond reasonable doubt, with the burden of proof being on the defendant.

The maximum penalty is a fine (up to level 3 on the scale of fines). The police are given a special power of arrest where a person persists in offensive conduct after a warning has been given. This has been criticised as resurrecting the old 'sus' law.

The offence under s.5 might pose a threat to individual freedoms if the police and the courts interpret it strictly. Merely tiresome behaviour in public could become caught by the Act. Whilst codification of the law is to be welcomed, not least in criminal law, the danger of very vague drafting of statutes, especially in the area of civil liberties, is to be deprecated. 'The very process of reducing the common law to statutory language is fraught with the possibilities that it will afford counsel the chance to make clever semantic points of little moral merit,' A. T. H. Smith has commented.

Even policemen can be alarmed or distressed under s.5 of the Public Order Act 1986 it was held in *DPP* v. *Orum* (1989). The Protection from Harassment Act 1997 has created further and serious offences of harassment, with provision also for a civil remedy.

2 BREACH OF THE PEACE

As stated above, the common law 'offence' of breach of the peace is not abolished, by either the 1984 or 1986 legislation. At common law a police officer, or anyone else, may arrest without a warrant a person who commits a breach of the peace in his presence, or a person who has been guilty of such a breach, providing there is a reasonable belief that a renewal of it is threatened, or a person whom he reasonably believes will commit a breach of the peace in the immediate future as seen in *Lewis* v. *Chief Constable of Greater Manchester* (1991). The Court of Appeal in *R.* v. *Howell* (1981) said: 'We cannot accept that there can be a breach of the peace unless there has been an act done or threatened which actually harms a person, or in his presence his property, or is likely to cause such harm, or which puts someone in fear of such harm being done.' A mere disturbance will not constitute a breach of the peace; on the other hand, an action might constitute a breach of the peace which would not amount to 'threatening, abusive or insulting' behaviour in the offences described above. The dividing line is unsatisfactorily thin. In *Brutus* v. *Cozens* (1973) the accused disrupted a tennis match at Wimbledon by running on to No. 2 Court and distributing leaflets. This angered some of the spectators who tried to hit him as he was taken away. But the House of Lords upheld the finding by the magistrates that although his behaviour was irritating it was not abusive or insulting. Under the old law, s.5 of the 1936 Act used virtually the same language as s.4 of the 1986 Act, except the s.4 offence covers private as well as public places and uses the phrase 'unlawful violence' instead of 'breach of the peace'. So as the 'tennis fan' did not use threatening, abusive or insulting behaviour in *Brutus*, so he was not guilty of breach of the peace under s.5 of the 1936 Act. But now that s.4 of the 1986 Act has replaced s.5, and common law breach of the peace is still at large, might such behaviour now amount to breach of the peace? The failure to deal with common law breach of the peace under the 1986 Act may well prove to be its undoing, and illustrates, yet again in the criminal law, the spatchcock approach to statutory reform. In *R.* v. *Morpeth Justices ex parte Ward* (1992) a breach of the peace was caused by anti-blood sports campaigners; there was an entitlement to protest but not in a manner likely to cause violence. In *McConnell* v. *Chief Constable of the Greater Manchester Police* (1990) the Court of Appeal emphasised that a breach of the peace can take place on private premises.

In *Parkin* v. *Norman* (1982) the defendant was found masturbating in a public lavatory, apparently to attract the attention of the other person present, who happened to be a plain-clothes police officer. It was held by the High Court that on the facts neither the police officer nor the accused were likely to breach the peace, and therefore the conviction was quashed. 'Likely', the Court said, was not the same as 'liable'. In *R.* v. *Chief Constable of Devon and Cornwall ex parte Central Electricity Generating Board* (1982), Lord Denning observed:

> **There is a breach of the peace whenever a person who is lawfully carrying out his work is unlawfully and physically prevented by another from doing it. He is entitled by law peacefully to go on with his work**

> **on his lawful occasions. If anyone unlawfully and physically obstructs the worker – by laying down or chaining himself to a rig or the like – he is guilty of a breach of the peace.**

In this instance the CEGB wished to survey land for a nuclear power station in Cornwall, but the Board's representatives found their way blocked by protestors and the Chief Constable of Devon and Cornwall was not inclined to take action. In *Masterton* v. *Holden* (1986) two men late at night, in fact at 1.55 am in Oxford Street in London, were at a bus stop and seen to be cuddling and kissing. Two couples came by and one of the men shouted: 'You filthy sods. How dare you in front of our girls?' The men at the bus stop were arrested and charged with insulting behaviour occasioning a breach of the peace under s.54 of the Metropolitan Police Act 1839. The High Court, although it thought the behaviour might be better classified as offensive or disgusting, not therefore an offence, found that the magistrates were entitled to conclude that the behaviour was insulting to other people in the street.

In *Cheeseman* v. *DPP* (1991) C. masturbated himself in a public toilet and was watched by two members of the vice squad. He was charged under s.28 of the Town Police Clauses Act 1847 in that he wilfully and indecently exposed his person in a street to the annoyance of passengers; the charges were not successful.

Section 6 of the Theatres Act 1968 provides that if a public performance of a play involves the use of threatening, abusive or insulting words or behaviour, any person who presented that performance is guilty of a summary offence if he did so with intent to provoke a breach of the peace, or if indeed the performance was likely to occasion a breach. The presenter of the play must take his audience as he finds them. The maximum penalty is six months' imprisonment or a fine (up to scale 5) or both. The Attorney-General must give his consent to any prosecution.

Despite opposition to the clause in the House of Lords, s.43 of the Education (No. 2) Act 1986 provides that the responsible authorities in universities and colleges 'shall take such steps as are reasonably practicable to ensure that freedom of speech within the law is secured for members, students and employees of the establishment and for visiting speakers'. The clause resulted from a number of rowdy occasions over the previous 20 years when visiting speakers of a political persuasion often unacceptable to the student caucus were given rough treatment. In *R.* v. *University of Liverpool ex parte Caesar-Gordon* (1990) the university was not entitled to take into account threats of public disorder outside the confines of the university by persons who were not within its control.

Part IV of the Public Order Act 1986, ss.30–37, deals with exclusion orders. (Part I of the Act has been covered in section 1 above; Part II deals with processions and assemblies – see section 4 below; and Part III deals with racial hatred – see section 3 below.) An exclusion order may be made in addition to any other sentence or order (including probation and discharge) in any case where the offence satisfies one of three conditions:

1 that the offence was committed while the offender was at a football ground or was entering or leaving within the prescribed period (two hours before the start of the match or one hour after). The nature of the offence is immaterial – it is not necessary that violence should be involved;

2 that the offence involved the use or threat of violence to a person or property, or involved the use of offensive, threatening or abusive behaviour likely to cause alarm, or involved the stirring up of racial hatred, and was committed while the accused or victim was on the way to a football match;

3 that the offence was an offence against the Sporting Events (Control of Alcohol etc) Act 1985, as amended by the Sporting Events (Control of Alcohol etc)(Amendment) Act 1992.

The exclusion order prohibits the offender from entering any premises for the purpose of attending any football match as prescribed by the Secretary of State. The order will last for a minimum of three months, but there is no maximum. While the order is in effect, it is a summary offence for the person to whom it applies to enter premises and he may be arrested without a warrant if he attempts to do so.

The offences under the 1985 and 1986 legislation just described are, of course, not part of common law breach of the peace, but it is convenient to include them at this stage, and they do have certain breach of the peace features.

3 RACIAL HATRED

Part III of the Public Order Act 1986 provides six offences in this area. Two of them are entirely new. Section 17 provides that racial hatred means hatred against a group of persons defined by reference to colour, race, nationality (including citizenship) or ethnic or national origins. Racial groups here may constitute religious groups, but for the purposes of the Act religious groups do not constitute racial ones.

An important point under this part of the Act is that none of the six offences require an intent to provoke a breach of the peace, nor proof that racial hatred was actually stirred up. It is sufficient that the accused intended to stir up racial hatred, or that such hatred was likely to be stirred up, having regard to all the circumstances, and whether or not the accused realised this would be likely, in other words an objective test. If the accused was addressing an audience all of whom, to a man, were avowedly racists, then the prosecution would have no case.

It should also be mentioned here that Part III of the Act, rather oddly, extends only to Great Britain, not to the United Kingdom, in other words Northern Ireland is excluded.

All the offences under Part III require that the material, words or behaviour in question are 'threatening, abusive or insulting', a perhaps overly restricted condition. The six offences are as follows:

1   Section 18 makes it an offence where a person uses words or behaviour, or dis-
    plays written material, which in each case is threatening, abusive or insulting, if
    he intends to stir up racial hatred, or if racial hatred is likely to be stirred up
    thereby; the offence may be committed in a public or private place, in the sense
    of offences under s.4 or s.5 as seen earlier. It also is an arrestable offence with-
    out a warrant (originally there was no such power of arrest in respect of the
    other five offences under Part III), where a police officer reasonably suspects
    someone is committing an offence under s.18. The accused has a defence if he
    was not aware that his action was threatening (and so on).

2   Section 19 provides that a parallel offence is committed where a person publishes
    or distributes such written material to the public or a section of the public, the lat-
    ter terms, as well as publication and distribution, unfortunately not being defined
    by the Act, although presumably a family group or members of a comparable unit
    are exempt, but not members of a private club; it is a defence under s.19 for the
    accused to prove that he was not aware of the content of the material nor had any
    reason to suspect its contents – this defence is designed to aid the 'innocent pub-
    lisher', such as a newsagent. In respect of s.19, s.155 of The Criminal Justice and
    Public Order Act 1994 has now made this an arrestable offence.

3   Under s.20 it is an offence to present or direct a public performance of a play
    which involves the use of threatening, abusive or insulting words or behaviour,
    with an intent to stir up racial hatred, or where, having regard to all the circum-
    stances, in particular taking the performance as a whole, racial hatred is likely to
    be stirred up. An actor's unscripted addition to the play is also caught by the sec-
    tion, and the actor would be guilty of a s.20 offence. Plays include operas and
    ballet. The accused has a defence if he did not know and had no reason to know
    that the performance would so offend, or that words or behaviour were threat-
    ening, abusive or insulting, or that it was likely that racial hatred would be
    stirred up – the first defence essentially covering unauthorised departures from
    the script; the second offending, in rare cases, a particular section of the audience
    which could not be anticipated; the third, in a similar way, the totally unexpect-
    ed stirring up racial hatred via what appeared a completely 'innocent' play.

4   Section 21 relates to recordings. This new offence is committed where a person
    distributes, shows, or plays a recording of visual images or sounds which are
    threatening, abusive or insulting, subject to the same 'intent' and 'likelihood'
    conditions as the previous offences. The distribution must be to the public or a
    section of the public. Broadcasting and cable services are excluded from the
    ambit of s.21 and dealt with under s.22; in a defence parallel to that under s.19,
    the accused may show that he was not aware of the content of the recording
    and had no reason to suspect that it was threatening, abusive or insulting.

5   Section 22 deals with broadcasting: incitement to racial hatred through broad-
    casting, on radio or television, of a programme by the BBC or ITC (the
    Independent Television Commission) or the Radio Authority was not in itself
    an offence. But such visual images or sounds occurring through DBS (Direct
    Broadcasting by Satellite) or, for example, by cable programmes were an

offence, subject to the 'intent' and 'likelihood' conditions again. The BBC and the former IBA (Independent Broadcasting Authority) were excluded because the Government felt they had their own systems of control and were answerable to Parliament, not entirely plausible reasons, as underlined by the recognition of the Broadcasting Complaints Commission and the establishment of the Broadcasting Standards Council under the Broadcasting Act 1990. Indeed, the 1990 Act removed the original exemption for the BBC and IBA(ITC). It is a defence under the section for the accused to prove that he did not know and had no reasonable cause to suspect that the programme would involve the use of the offending material and that it was not reasonably practicable for him to remove it, and there are other defences in this section. It is submitted that the defences to all these sections are poorly drafted, and suffer from cumbersome phraseology, not sitting easily with the 'likelihood' part of the offences.

6   Under s.23 there is the offence of possession of racially inflammatory material. This is committed where a person has in his possession written material, or a recording, which is threatening (and so on) with a view to its display, distribution, broadcasting (and so on), again subject to the 'intent' and 'likelihood' conditions. Again, the BBC and IBA were originally exempted, until the amendments made under the Broadcasting Act 1990. 'Possession' is, unfortunately, not defined. There is a similar defence, as under s.19 in particular – the accused may argue that he was not aware of the content nor had reason to be suspicious, a defence of use to warehouses. On the other hand, it would appear that librarians and education authorities may well be caught by the section, since such people would be expected to have examined the material more closely in the course of their professional duties.

Under s.24 magistrates may issue a search warrant in respect of a suspected s.23 offence, and under s.25 a court may order the forfeiture of materials or recordings where a person is convicted of an offence under s.18 relating to the display of written materials, or an offence under s.19, s.21 or s.23. Section 28 provides for the criminal liability of a corporation (company), but not for unincorporated associations (including political parties). Under s.26 provisions in Part III do not apply to fair and accurate reports of proceedings in Parliament, or fair, accurate and contemporaneous reports of judicial proceedings, the latter provision being designed to stop racists from distributing at a later stage verbatim reports of trials for Part III offences.

A prosecution for any Part III offence can only be brought by or with the consent of the Attorney-General, which does raise the question of political bias in politically sensitive cases; the DPP would, surely, have been a better figure in this instance. The requirement of the Attorney-General's fiat could deter the police from pursuing charges. A private individual might try to bring a *relator* action, but this is fraught with difficulty, as seen earlier in the *Gouriet* case.

The offences under Part III are triable either way, that is up to two years' imprisonment on indictment (six months on summary conviction) or a fine or both.

4 PROCESSIONS AND ASSEMBLIES

The right to assemble freely, to demonstrate peacefully and to organise marches is one of the most important hallmarks of a free society, and cherished not least in the United Kingdom for the last 100 years or more. But there is no clearly stated right so to do. The United Kingdom may be a party to the European Convention, but it is not, yet, part of statutory law. The number of processions and demonstrations has grown markedly since the 1960s, as seen at the time of the Vietnam War protests and the Civil Rights movement in Ulster. A minority has led to violence, but a greater concern, almost, has been the amount of police resources required with the accompanying cost to the taxpayer.

Part II of the Public Order Act 1986 now deals with this area, under ss.11–16.

Under s.16 a public procession is defined as a procession in a public place, that is any highway or place to which the public, or a section of it, has a right of access, expressly or impliedly, for payment or without. So, footpaths, roads, bridges, parks are all included. But, alas, the Act ducks the question of what a procession is. Under s.11 written notice must be given of public processions intended to demonstrate support of, or opposition to, any person or body of persons, or to publicise a cause or campaign, or to mark or commemorate any event, unless it is not reasonably practicable to give advance notice. Notice should be given to the police not less than six clear days before the date of the procession, or as soon as is practicable. This is an important provision since it would appear that the marches resulting in the most serious disorder were often the ones the police had no prior knowledge of and learned about by accident.

There are some exemptions to the giving of notice requirement, particularly where a procession is 'commonly or customarily held', a vague phrase. This would seem to cover annual processions on set days, such as local carnivals and May Fairs like the Hobby Horse procession through Padstow in Cornwall, as well as Remembrance Sunday marches and educational processions such as graduation in Oxford.

The other exemption of notice, where it is not reasonably practicable to give advance notice, is also not clear, but presumably would relate to those situations where a reaction at short notice is in order in respect of some political event or crisis.

If the notice is not given, then the organisers are guilty of a summary offence (a fine up to level 3).

The accused may argue that he did not know or had no reason to suspect the failure to satisfy the requirements, or a difference in date, time or route. The test is an objective one, and is not generous to the defendant.

Section 12 gives the most senior police officer on the spot (conceivably this could be someone of quite junior rank) the power to impose conditions, once the procession has started or is assembling. The officer must reasonably believe that serious public disorder, or serious damage to property or serious disruption to the life of the community will result, or that the purpose of the organisers is intimidation.

The terms 'disruption' and 'intimidation' in particular remain to be tested in the courts. Failing to comply with such a condition is a summary offence, leading to three months' imprisonment, or a fine (level 4) or both, for the organiser, but merely a level 3 fine for a participant. Section 12 does not detract from existing statutory powers, some of which are local, for instance under the Metropolitan Police Act 1839 or the Town Police Clauses Act 1847, or from common law powers (that is for breach of the peace).

Section 13 follows the old procedures under the 1936 Act, that is a Chief Constable may apply to the district council for an order prohibiting all, or certain, processions within a local area for up to three months. If the council grants the order it must also be approved by the Home Secretary. In London the Metropolitan Commissioner makes the order himself, subject to the consent of the Home Secretary. Under s.13 certain processions are covered by the phrase 'class of public procession', which is an uncertain phrase in a sensitive area. The chief officer concerned does not have to give his grounds for requesting a ban, but he must reasonably believe that the powers under s.12 will be insufficient to prevent serious public disorder resulting. A blanket or class ban does mean that the innocent march may also be caught. The punishments are the same as for those outlined under s.12.

Under s.14 there is a new power for a senior police officer to impose conditions in relation to public assemblies.

It should be emphasised the new powers under s.14 do not replace the common law power to disperse an assembly (breach of the peace) but are superimposed upon the common law, a very untidy approach.

It is not easy either to distinguish between a public assembly and a public procession. A gathering in Trafalgar Square is an assembly, but it is likely a procession will have preceded it. Certainly there are more public assemblies than processions, particularly with changing social behaviour, as reflected in mass industrial picketing (such as the Grunwick dispute in London in 1976–77 and the miners' strike in 1984–85), pop festivals, political demonstrations outside embassies, and, with the growth of pressure groups, mass lobbying of Parliament. Such changes in the social climate have put extra demands upon the police, as notably illustrated in the 1979 General Election when an anti-National Front demonstration in Southall in London had nearly as many policemen present as the 3,000 demonstrators (one of whom was killed).

Under s.14 a public assembly means a gathering of 20 or more people in a public place wholly or partly open to the air (s.16). The senior police officer may impose conditions on the same grounds as those outlined for a procession (as above), and, again, 'senior police officer' means the most senior in rank present at the scene, or the Chief Constable if the assembly is still intended. Section 14 may yet prove to be something of a blunderbuss in dealing with small demonstrations, and it may be the police prefer to rely on obstruction and breach of the peace powers.

A constable in uniform may arrest without warrant anyone whom he reasonably suspects is committing an offence under ss.12, 13 or 14. These powers appear rather unnecessary in the light of the powers to arrest for breach of the peace and under the Police and Criminal Evidence Act 1984 (s.25).

Under s.15 a chief constable (or equivalent) may delegate his powers to a deputy or assistant chief constable in respect of ss.12, 13 or 14.

In respect of decisions made under ss.12-14 (conditions or ban), these may be challenged by way of judicial review (Order 53). As seen earlier, under Chapter 2, applications for judicial review are not always straightforward, although in this context there should be less of a problem since the issue concerns a public authority acting in respect of public 'rights'. However, *ultra vires* or unreasonableness will have to be proved, and the latter in accordance with the strict *Wednesbury* principles (*Associated Provincial Picture Houses Ltd* v. *Wednesbury Corporation* (1948)), that is that no reasonable body of persons could possibly have made such a decision. Of course, it must be said that an application for judicial review may be heard too late for the applicant, the relevant day may have come and gone. Whilst the courts do sometimes grant injunctions or orders with remarkable alacrity, there is no guarantee. This might be especially so where local inhabitants seek *mandamus* to compel a chief constable to ban a procession.

It should also be added that ss.70-71 of the Criminal Justice and Public Order Act 1994 introduced further restrictions on what are termed trespassory assemblies, by the way of amending s.14 of the 1986 Act. This could be seen in *DPP* v. *Jones (Margaret)* (1997), where a demonstration occurred near Stonehenge within an area covered by a s.14A order, it being held that there was no right in law for members of the public to hold a peaceful, non-obstructive assembly on the public highway.

5 PUBLIC NUISANCE

The offence is triable either way. This common law matter is discussed under tort since in practice the main effect of the crime is to give an aggrieved person the right to bring a civil action for damages. The *mens rea* for public nuisance is certainly intention or recklessness; it may also include criminal negligence. Negligence alone suffices where a civil action results. It is also an offence intentionally and unreasonably to obstruct a public highway, crossing or thoroughfare under the Highways Act 1980 and the Town Police Clauses Act 1847. Under the Public Meeting Act 1908 it is an offence to behave in a disorderly way at any lawful public meeting with the intent of stopping the business of the meeting; the Act was designed to deal with the suffragette problem, but nowadays is little used. The Representation of the People Act 1983 provides for a similar offence at election meetings. The Rights of Way Act 1990 has amended Part IX of the Highways Act 1980; by s.131A a person who, without lawful authority or excuse, so disturbs the surface of (a) footpath, (b) a bridleway or (c) any other highway which consists of or comprises a carriageway other than a made-up carriageway, as to render it inconvenient for the exercise of the public right of way is guilty of an offence and liable to a fine not exceeding level 3 on the standard scale. The offence of public nuisance has been further extended by the provisions of the Noise Act 1996.

6 ENTERING AND REMAINING ON PROPERTY

Under the Criminal Law Act 1977 (s.6) it is an offence triable summarily for any person without lawful authority to use or threaten violence for the purpose of securing entry into any premises for himself or for any other person, 'provided that (a) there is someone present on those premises at the time who is opposed to the entry which the violence is intended to secure; and (b) the person using or threatening the violence knows that that is the case.'

'Violence' is not the same as 'force' for the purposes of entry to property. Smashing a door down is violent; forcing a Yale-type lock with a piece of wire or plastic is not, it would appear. But the distinction, it is submitted, has little merit. It is lawful, however, to use reasonable force to eject a trespasser or to defend property from unlawful entry. The degree of force allowed depends on the circumstances of the case. Thus violence could be met with violence.

'Premises' covers any building or part thereof, and any land 'ancillary to a building.' A 'building' means any immovable structure or one that is mobile but designed or adapted for residential purposes, such as a caravan or house-boat. The person present does not have to be the owner or occupier; a guest or even another trespasser is sufficient. The *mens rea* of the offence is that violence is used or threatened either intentionally or recklessly in order to secure entry subject to the fact that the accused is aware of the other person's opposition; that opposition is usually overt, but it may on occasion be implied – for example, a person who has bolted his door and then falls asleep would presumably be opposed to another's entry. Those who may enter lawfully but violently include court officials, bailiffs and police officers. A private individual may only re-enter his own premises peacefully; failing that he must use the civil courts to gain an order for re-possession. But where the premises concerned are the person's residential accommodation – as opposed to business premises, or perhaps a second home, depending on the distance from the principal place of residence – then reasonable force may be used to secure re-entry; it is the right of the 'displaced residential occupier' to do so. If such force is used then it should be employed as soon as possible after the occupier has discovered he was displaced. An unreasonable delay could be interpreted to mean that the occupier has impliedly recognised the trespasser's possession.

Adverse occupation of premises

The 1977 Act (s.7) as amended by ss.72–73 of the Criminal Justice and Public Order Act 1994, also provides for the adverse occupation of premises, as seen in *R. v. Forest Justices ex parte Madeline Michelle Hartman* (1991). This means that a trespasser is guilty of an offence if he fails to leave any premises once requested to do so by a displaced residential occupier of the premises or by an individual who is a 'protected intending occupier' of the premises. The latter person must hold a written statement signed by himself and witnessed by a magistrate or a commissioner for oaths. The purpose of the statement is that the police can verify his interest in the property before effecting a forcible entry. The statement must also say that the aggrieved person requires the premises himself for residential occupation. The interest in the property must be the purchase of the freehold or a leasehold of 21 years or over. An intending occupier may also be a person with authorisation from a local council, a housing association or similar body. In this case an appropriate certificate must be provided rather than a sworn statement. The defendant may submit that he did not believe the person to be a displaced residential occupier or a protected intending occupier; this line of argument is unlikely to impress the courts except in rare cases. He may also argue that the person concerned failed to produce the relevant certificate or statement. Thirdly, it may be argued that the accused was not occupying any residential part of the premises that are in the main non-residential.

Under the same Act it is a summary offence to trespass with a weapon without lawful authority or reasonable excuse. Similarly, it is a summary offence under the Act for a person to trespass upon any diplomatic mission (a foreign embassy or the like). A person who lawfully enters such a building will be guilty of the offence where he fails to leave once requested to do so. But a prosecution may only be brought with the Attorney-General's consent. A police constable may not enter diplomatic premises without a search warrant.

It is a summary offence, too, under the Act for a person to resist or intentionally to obstruct a court official in the course of enforcing an order for the repossession of premises. It is a defence for the accused to argue that he did not honestly believe the official to be an officer of the court (a subjective test, of an honest mistake). The Protection from Eviction Act 1977 makes it an offence punishable on indictment by up to two years' imprisonment to evict or harass a person lawfully occupying premises for residential purposes. The offence is also triable summarily.

7 AGGRAVATED TRESPASS

Notwithstanding the provisions under the 1977 Act, above, s.39 of the Public Order Act 1986 has taken the matter a stage further. This section of the Act largely came about because of the invasion of a farm in Somerset by a hippy convoy, which in the words of the Home Secretary resembled 'nothing more than a band of medieval brigands who have no respect for the law or the rights of others'. Section 39 has now been replaced in broadly similar terms by ss.61-62 of the Criminal Justice and Public Order Act 1994. It should also be added that ss.63-66 of the 1994 Act give the police powers over the holding of 'raves', whilst ss.68-69 give them even wider powers in respect of specifically aggravated trespass, these latter sections being aimed at certain groups such as hunt saboteurs or motorway protesters – the senior police officer at the scene can direct people not to re-enter the land within a period of three months.

With regard to the more general provisions of the former s.39, now ss.61-62 of the 1994 Act, the senior police officer present at the scene has the power to direct trespassers to leave if four conditions are satisfied: that he must reasonably believe that two or more persons, having entered the land as trespassers, are present with the common purpose of residing there (the first two conditions). With respect to the first condition the trespassers are such in civil law, initially, and it must be said that the police are normally not concerned with civil trespass. Thus where lawful visitors stay beyond the permitted period and become trespassers, they are not included in s.61, for it must be a case of trespassers *ab initio*. Land may include common land and agricultural buildings, but not any other type of buildings and certainly not residential premises. 'Residing' is not defined under the Act, but it would not include walkers and bird-watchers and the like.

Thirdly, the police officer must reasonably believe that reasonable steps have been taken on behalf of the occupier to ask the trespasser to leave. Fourthly, he must also believe that any of the trespassers have caused damage to property on the land or used threatening, abusive or insulting words or behaviour to the occupier or a member of his family or his employee or agent, or that the trespassers have brought between them six (formerly 12) or more vehicles on to the land.

Obviously, the trespass will have already taken place, although a police officer might prevent entry in the first place under breach of peace powers. If a trespasser fails to leave, after being directed to do so, as soon as reasonably practicable, or having left he enters the land again as a trespasser within a three month period, then he commits an offence under ss.61–62. The accused must know the direction applies to him, or be wilfully blind that such a direction has been given. He may argue that he was not a trespasser or had a reasonable excuse. A uniformed constable who reasonably suspects that a person is committing the offence may arrest without a warrant. The maximum punishment is three months' imprisonment or a fine (level 4) or both.

It might be argued that the law, by ss.61–69, has been made more cumbersome, and that this was a matter best left to civil remedies. But the argument that civil remedies themselves are often slow and expensive is compelling, and to give the police some role here does not seem entirely unreasonable.

8 LIBEL

Criminal libel at common law is punishable by up to one year's imprisonment on indictment. Under the Libel Act 1843, however, to publish a libel which the accused knows to be untrue is punishable by two years. For an action to be brought for criminal libel rather than civil libel it is necessary to show that the words complained of are very serious and that it is in the public interest to bring such an action. A breach of the peace need not have occurred as the result of the libel, or be likely to occur; but evidence that this is so might assist the prosecutor's case. Libel is a controversial branch of criminal law and it is also examined under the tort of defamation. The defendant must show the statement was true and made in the public interest; to argue 'truth' alone or 'fair comment' is not sufficient.

OFFENCES AFFECTING THE NATIONAL INTEREST

There are a number of offences which affect the security of the State or at the very least are international in character.

1 Piracy and hijacking

The Tokyo Convention Act 1967 enacted the Convention of that name. This international agreement defined piracy as follows:

> **Article 15: Piracy consists of any of the following acts: 1. Any illegal acts of violence, detention or any act of depredation, committed for private ends by the crew or the passengers of a private ship or a private aircraft, and directed:** *a*) **on the high seas, against another ship or aircraft, or against persons or property on board such ship or aircraft;** *b*) **against a ship, aircraft persons or property in a place outside the jurisdiction of any state; 2. Any act of voluntary participation in the operation of a ship or of an aircraft with knowledge of facts making it a pirate ship or aircraft; 3) Any act of inciting or intentionally facilitating an act described in sub-paragraph 1. or sub-paragraph 2. of this article. Article 16: The acts of piracy as defined in Article 15, committed by a warship, government ship or government aircraft whose crew had mutinied and taken control of the ship or aircraft is considered a pirate ship or aircraft if it is intended by the persons in dominant control to be used for the purpose of committing one of the acts referred to in Article 15. The same applies if the ship or aircraft has been used to commit any such act so long as it remains under the control of the persons guilty of that act.**

The Act stipulates that the above provisions, as set out in a schedule to the Act, 'shall be treated as constituting part of the Law of nations'. Presumably if other statutory domestic, national law conflicted with that part of the convention, the existing national law would prevail, since the 1967 Act is not prescriptive, but rather it provides a detailed definition of piracy. There are a number of older statutes, such as the Piracy Acts of 1698 and 1721. The former, for instance, covers revolts on a ship and the latter Act trading with or assisting pirates. There are varying punishments for piracy under the Offences at Sea Act 1799 and the Piracy Act 1837. The variation will partly depend on whether the act is committed on the high seas (in extra-territorial waters) or not. Normally the same punishment is meted out as if the offence were committed on land. Life imprisonment is possible for the more serious offences and the death penalty where there is an intent to murder or endanger life.

Under the Tokyo Convention Act 1967 any offence committed on board a British controlled aircraft in flight is deemed to have taken place in the United Kingdom. The Aviation Security Act 1982 (as amended by the Aviation and Maritime Security Act 1990) makes it an offence punishable by life imprisonment to take unlawful control of an aircraft in flight irrespective of whether the aircraft is British or not, or unlawfully and intentionally to destroy, damage or endanger an aircraft in flight. Prosecutions require the consent of the Attorney-General. The 1982 Act states:

> **A person on board an aircraft in flight who unlawfully, by the use of force or by threats of any kind, seizes the aircraft or exercises control of it commits the offence of hijacking, whatever his nationality, whatever the State in which the aircraft is registered and whether the aircraft is in the United Kingdom or elsewhere.**

Similarly, hostage-taking is punishable with life imprisonment, and again a prosecution requires the consent of the Attorney-General; the Taking of Hostages Act 1982 enacted the New York Convention on this matter of 1979:

> **A person, whatever his nationality, who, in the United Kingdom or elsewhere (_a_) detains any other person ('the hostage'), and (_b_) in order to compel a State, international governmental organisation or person to do or abstain from doing any act, threatens to kill, injure or continue to detain the hostage, commits an offence.**

2 Treason

Treason is punishable by death. It is covered by the Treason Act 1351. It is treason to compass the death of the King, the Queen or the male heir to the throne. To compass means to demonstrate in some way an intention to kill. That would include the written or spoken word. It is also treason 'to violate the King's companion [wife] or the King's eldest daughter unmarried or the wife [of] the King's eldest son and heir,' as well as to 'levy war against the King in his realm' and to 'be adherent to the King's enemies in his realm giving to them aid and comfort in the realm, or elsewhere'. A small-scale limited revolt, confined to a particular locality would probably constitute a riot rather than treason. In respect of the fourth type of treason it is not necessary that war has been formally declared; a state of hostilities will suffice. The Treason Felony Act 1848 effectively made life imprisonment an alternative punishment for the third and fourth types of treason. A British citizen may commit treason anywhere in the world, but the possibilities are more restricted for Commonwealth citizens and aliens. Prosecutions for treason are very rare indeed.

3 Sedition

Strictly speaking there is no offence of sedition but at common law there are the offences of seditious libel and seditious words. The former consists of a written publication made with a seditious intention, the latter an oral publication with the same intention. A seditious intention was defined by Sir James Stephen and quoted approvingly by the judge in _R. v. Burns_ (1886):

> a seditious intention is an intention to bring into hatred or contempt or to excite disaffection against the person of Her Majesty, her heirs or successors, or the government and constitution of the United Kingdom as by law established, or either House of Parliament, or the administration of justice, or to excite Her Majesty's subjects to attempt, otherwise than by lawful means, the alteration of any matter in Church or State by law established, or to raise discontent or disaffection among Her Majesty's subjects, or to promote feelings of ill-will and hostility between different classes of her subject.

The words published must have the effect of causing, or having a tendency to cause, public disorder. The test is the effect upon the ordinary, reasonable man; the particular audience to whom the words are addressed need not react positively for the publication to be seditious. Conversely, if a particular audience is incited, as opposed to ordinary, reasonable men, that is sufficient. The *mens rea* must be intention in respect of such consequences. It appears recklessness will not suffice any more than negligence. Moreover, the accused must intend to bring about disorder or disaffection through violence. Sedition is an indictable offence, punishable by a fine and imprisonment at the court's discretion.

4 Official secrets

Section 1 of the Official Secrets Act 1911 (as amended) provides that espionage or a related offence is punishable by 14 years' imprisonment.

> 1. If any person for any purpose prejudicial to the safety or interests of the State – (*a*) approaches, inspects, passes over, or is in the neighbourhood of, or enters any prohibited place within the meaning of this Act, or (*b*) makes any sketch, plan, model, or note which is calculated to be or might be or is intended to be directly or indirectly useful to an enemy; or (*c*) obtains, collects, records or publishes or communicates to any other person any secret official code word or pass word, or any sketch, plan, model, article, or note, or other document or information which is calculated to be or might be or is intended to be directly or indirectly useful to an enemy; he shall be guilty of an offence. 2. On a prosecution under this section it shall not be necessary to show that the accused person was guilty of any particular act tending to show a purpose prejudicial to the safety or interests of the State, and, notwithstanding that no such act is proved against him, he may be convicted if, from the circumstances of the case, or his conduct, or his known character as proved, it appears that his purpose was a purpose prejudicial to the safety or interests of the State; and if any sketch, plan, model, article, note, document, or information relating to or used in any prohibited place within the meaning of this Act or anything in such a place, or any secret official code word or pass word, is made, obtained, collected, recorded, published or communicated by any person other than a person acting

> **under lawful authority, it shall be deemed to have been made, obtained, collected, recorded, published, or communicated for a purpose prejudicial to the safety or interests of the State unless the contrary is proved.**

A 'prohibited place' means a dockyard, air base, army camp, signal station and the like. The test for *mens rea* in respect of the phrase 'prejudicial to the interests of the State' is an objective one, although the word 'purpose' has subjective connotations.

The Official Secrets Act 1989, which replaced s.2 of the 1911 Act, had attracted criticism for its 'catch-all' quality (see the Franks Report 1972).

5 Terrorism

The Lloyd Report (of the inquiry into legislation against terrorism) was published in 1996. The current position is that as a result of the difficulties in Northern Ireland Parliament has passed the Prevention of Terrorism (Temporary Provisions) Act 1989, as amended by the Prevention of Terrorism (Additional Powers) Act 1996. The Act (s.2) makes it unlawful for any person to belong or profess to belong to a proscribed organisation; solicit or invite support for a proscribed organisation, other than support with money or other property; or arrange or assist in the arrangement or management of, or address, any meeting of three or more persons (whether or not it is a meeting to which the public are admitted) knowing that the meeting is to support or to further the activities of a proscribed organisation, or is to be addressed by a person belonging or professing to belong to a proscribed organisation. Terrorism is defined as the use of violence for political ends and includes any use of violence for the purpose of putting the public and any section of the public in fear (s.20 of the 1989 Act and s.66 of the Northern Ireland (Emergency Provisions) Act 1991).

The offence, triable either way, is punishable on indictment by a maximum of 10 years' imprisonment or a fine or both. The UVF (Ulster Volunteer Force), UFF (Ulster Freedom Fighters), the Red Hand Commando and the UDA (Ulster Defence Association) on the 'loyalist' side, and the IRA (Irish Republican Army), INLA (Irish National Liberation Army) and the defunct IPLO (Irish People's Liberation Organisation) on the Republican side, are proscribed organisations under the 1991 Act in respect of Northern Ireland, but in general only the IRA and INLA for the rest of the United Kingdom under the 1989 Act. The 1989 Act also made it an offence to loan or donate money or property for the purposes of acts of terrorism connected with the affairs of Northern Ireland or unreasonably to fail to disclose information that would be of material assistance to the authorities.

Part IV of the Criminal Justice Act 1993 under ss.36–48 substantially amended the Northern Ireland (Emergency Provisions) Act 1991 in respect of the financing of terrorist activities, particularly in relation to confiscation orders, compensation and offences relating to the proceeds of terrorist-related activities. The law here has now been consolidated under the Northern Ireland (Emergency Provisions) Act 1996.

Section 49 of the 1993 Act has amended s.9 of the Prevention of Terrorism (Temporary Provisions) Act 1989, in respect of contributions towards acts of terrorism. Financial assistance for terrorism is unlawful, where a person 'uses or has possession of, whether for consideration or not, any money or other property', and a person 'who uses or has possession of money or other property shall be taken to be concerned in a transaction or arrangement'. Section 50 deals with amendments to s.17 of the 1989 Act, in respect of the investigation of terrorist activities. For s.17(2) there was substituted the following clause:

(2) A person is guilty of an offence if, knowing or having reasonable cause to suspect that a constable is acting, or is proposing to act, in connection with a terrorist investigation which is being, or is about to be, conducted, he (*a*) discloses to any other person information or any other matter which is likely to prejudice the investigation or proposed investigation, or (*b*) falsifies, conceals or destroys or otherwise disposes of, or causes or permits the falsification, concealment, destruction or disposal of, material which is likely to be relevant to the investigation, or proposed investigation.

Section 51 by way of textual amendment (s.18A) supplemented s.18 of the 1989 Act in relation to the failure to disclose knowledge or suspicion of financial assistance to terrorism; essentially a person is guilty of an offence if he knows, or suspects, that another is providing financial assistance for terrorism. Under s.18 of the 1989 Act it is an offence to fail to disclose information that would be of material assistance to the authorities. The Northern Ireland (Emergency Provisions) Act 1991 added, under s.27, the following offence, punishable by life imprisonment: 'any person who directs at any level the activities of an organisation which is concerned in the commission of acts of terrorism is guilty of an offence'. As indicated in the previous section, overall the 1989 Act is primarily geared towards offences in Great Britain, whilst the 1996 Act, which in many ways parallels the 1989 Act, largely relates to Northern Ireland.

It is an offence to wear in public any item of dress or wear or carry any article that causes reasonable persons to fear that the accused is a member of a proscribed organisation, under both the 1996 and the 1989 Acts. The Public Order Act 1936 has a parallel but rather narrower provision in respect of the wearing of uniforms (s.1).

The police have special powers to detain suspected terrorists under the 1989 Act under Part IV and under Part II the Home Secretary or Northern Ireland Secretary may make an order excluding such a person from Northern Ireland or from the rest or whole of the United Kingdom. This occurred in 1982, for example, and a major political row developed as a result, when Mr William Whitelaw, the Home Secretary, banned members of the Northern Irish Sinn Fein (the political wing of the IRA) from visiting the mainland. They had been invited to County Hall in London by certain members of the GLC (the Greater London Council). The exclusion order lasts for a maximum of three years and can be renewed only on fresh intelligence.

The Suppression of Terrorism Act 1978 enacted the European Convention the Suppression of Terrorism. The Act is primarily concerned with extradition proceedings in respect of offences that are non-political in character, as defined under the Act.

DISCUSSION POINTS

1 Will the courts ever be able to deal satisfactorily with the concept of recklessness?

2 Are the public order offences too Draconian?

3 Discuss how the law of theft might be improved.

7 *Seven*

CIVIL LAW: TORT

7.1   The nature of tort

TORT, CONTRACT AND CRIME

Tort is closely related to criminal law: if tort is, in shorthand, a civil wrong, it may also have criminal connections. Tortious liability arises from a breach of a duty of care owed by members of society to each other – to their neighbours. Such duties are fixed by law and any breach is compensated by the award of damages in the courts.

The breach of that duty is of interest to society generally as well as to the individual member of it who has suffered damage – damage may include personal injury. Crime and tort may therefore overlap in such matters as assault and battery, theft and the wrongful interference with goods, damage to property and trespass to land, and aspects of negligence, nuisance and libel. However, other matters like slander and occupiers' liability are branches of the civil law in their own right.

Whether an action by an individual constitutes a criminal or civil wrong may quite simply be determined by the work-load of the police. A slap on the face, therefore, will most likely give rise to an action in tort pure and simple, while a severe blow to the head would more probably result in a prosecution in the criminal courts and perhaps civil proceedings too. The Criminal Injuries Compensation Board may award victims of violent crime financial redress; that, however, does not deprive the victim of his right to sue the assailant in tort for damages, although frequently the defendant is unable to pay the sum the court may wish to award: Lord Mustill noted the 'peculiarly British conception of the separation of powers' in R. v. *Secretary of State for the Home Department ex parte Fire Brigades Union* (1995).

In practice concurrent civil and criminal proceedings can cause difficulty. For example, in the case of *Jefferson Ltd* v. *Bhetcha* (1979), involving the misappropriation of cheques, it was held that a plaintiff could not be debarred from pursuing a civil action even if that meant the defendant would be bound to disclose his line of defence in contemporaneous criminal proceedings, although it is true that

under the Supreme Court Act 1981 an order may be made to 'grant a stay of proceedings', that is postpone the civil action.

Moreover, it should also be noted that Parliament may decide to legislate against
concurrent civil and criminal remedies in certain instances; for example, under the
Offences against the Person Act 1861, summary criminal proceedings for an assault,
whether resulting in a conviction or not, bar any subsequent civil proceedings.

Since crime consists of offences against the whole of society, the wrongdoer must
be punished by the State. Tort, however, is more concerned with individual
harm. Whereas the fines imposed upon guilty defendants in criminal cases are
punitive damages that the State sees fit to exact in the interests of everyone, in tort
the successful plaintiff will normally be awarded compensatory damages up to the
full value of his total loss. Yet nothing in English law is that straightforward, for
sometimes a court in a civil case will impose exemplary damages, as a warning, an
example for those who might be contemplating further tortious actions of a similar
nature; the possibility of awarding exemplary damages was emphasised in the case
of *Rookes* v. *Barnard* (1964). Exemplary damages are punitive: the plaintiff receives
more than he actually lost.

Tort overlaps, too, with the law of contract, as the celebrated case of *Donoghue* v.
Stevenson (1932) illustrated. However, a plaintiff may need to consider very carefully whether he brings an action under contract or under tort, especially in
respect of the rules governing remoteness of damage caused (was the damage done
really foreseeable by the defendant?) and the time limits within which cases must
be commenced. Actions under bailment, the minding of a person's goods by
another, constitute an interesting example of tortious and contractual overlap
where such goods are lost or stolen. In a similar way there is an overlap between
contract and crime, as, for example, where goods have been sold through fraudulent misrepresentation. Furthermore, cases can occur which have criminal, tortious
and contractual elements; employers' negligent actions in respect of safety at work,
actions which result in injury to their employees, are a good example. It is up to
the plaintiff to decide whether to proceed under contract or under tort (*Henderson*
v. *Merrett Syndicates Ltd* (1994)).

The difference between tort and the law of contract can be roughly summed up as
follows: under tort an individual is liable under clear rules of law imposed upon
him for a whole range of actions, and is liable to virtually all neighbours, to everyone, yet to no-one in particular. Under a contract two or more individuals have
voluntarily entered into some kind of agreement, they have created their own
legal relations, and disputes between the parties concerned will therefore be settled
within broad, if distinctive, legal parameters.

Contract law, it could be argued, is a much more cohesive body of law than tort.
Indeed, it might be more accurate to speak about the law of 'torts' rather than
'tort'. Is there, in other words, a common form of liability in all torts, a common
theme, or is it more accurate to talk in terms of a 'bundle of torts' that are not particularly interrelated. Of the two leading historical figures in the study of tort (or
torts) Winfield took the former view. But Salmond took the latter standpoint: 'for

Salmond there was no English law of tort; there was merely an English law of torts, that is, a list of acts and omissions'.

To say that contract law forms a more cohesive body of law almost implies that tort is more open-ended, more loosely framed. To a certain extent that it is true, old torts can easily die, new ones may be rapidly born as social attitudes change. One area of tortious liability which in effect has been greatly reduced is that of negligence. A whole field of social security legislation now covers industrial injury, sickness and other matters. And it is not just a question of state-run insurance; private insurance – for road accidents or injuries at work for example – has also greatly developed through the century in the absence of a comprehensive scheme of no-fault insurance. Insurance companies have also promoted cases to recover damages paid to their injured insured parties. W. V. Rogers has commented:

> **However, it is almost certain that the majority of writers, but not necessarily the majority of those affected, favour radical reform and the total or partial abolition of the law of tort so far as it relates to compensation for personal injuries. Many commentators, it is true, have concentrated their attention on one or two classes of accident only, especially road accidents and industrial accidents, on the ground that these are numerically the most important. Others, however, would extend their proposals so that all accidental injuries, and even disease as well, should receive similar treatment for the law governing social security to the exclusion of the law of tort.**

It was precisely this sort of debate that the Pearson Report attempted to answer in 1978. Should all the recommendations of the Commission ever be given legislative life then the law of tort – primarily in the field of negligence – would once again become the subject of much change. The Administration of Justice Act 1982 gave a small part of the Pearson Report statutory effect; so, too, has the Consumer Protection Act 1987. But whether the system of tort in relation to negligence can really cope with modern problems is questionable. As David McIntosh has said,

> **Society as a whole needs to rethink its position on how it copes with life's accidents, whether they are disasters, such as the Abbeystead waterworks explosion in 1984, the Bradford City Football Club fire and the Manchester Airport disaster in 1985, the Zeebrugge ferry disaster and the King's Cross Underground fire in 1987, the side effects of medicines, or the consequences of everyday accidents at work or on the roads.**

(There were also the West Wales (Llandeilo) rail tragedy in 1987, the Piper Alpha oil rig explosion in 1988, the Pan-Am air crash at Lockerbie in 1988, the Clapham Junction rail crash in 1989, the British Midland (M1) air crash in 1989, the Thames river barge tragedy (the Marchioness) in 1989, the Chinook (North Sea) helicopter crash in 1986 and the Super Puma (North Sea) helicopter crash in 1992, the Purley railway accident in 1989, the Hillsborough (Sheffield) football disaster in 1989.) However, the cost of funding a comprehensive no-fault compulsory universal insurance scheme would be a heavy financial burden and necessitate an increase of taxation on social security contributions that would prove politically difficult for any government to introduce.

Finally, in relation to the Pearson Report, it should be remembered that while the bulk of the law of tort, like the law of contract, is still based upon common law principles, in other words upon judicial interpretation of the cases that come before the courts, parliamentary law has inevitably become ever more important, as evidenced, for example, by the Defamation Act 1952, the Occupiers' Liability Act 1957 and the Torts (Interference with Goods) Act 1977.

The discussion in the following sections covers the major areas of tortious liability – from defamation to negligence, from nuisance to trespass of various kinds. First, though, a brief note on remedies and defences.

'DAMAGE' AND REMEDIES IN TORT

Some torts may be described as 'actionable *per se*'. The phrase 'actionable *per se*' has given rise to some misunderstanding, but fundamentally it applies to the historical division of torts into trespass and case. Trespass actions constituted those where injury caused – whether intentionally or by carelessness – was direct. 'Actions on the case' related far more to consequential injury. Thus nowadays in trespass actions, including libel and in certain circumstances slander as well as trespass to the person, land and, for the most part, goods, it is sufficient to prove that a wrong took place. The plaintiff need not prove actual damage. (Actual – or particular – damage is sometimes referred to as special damage; this is an unhelpful phrase since it can be confused with 'special damages' as noted below.) Thus if X. walks across Y.'s land as a trespasser, it is sufficient to show that X. did precisely that, that he interfered with Y.'s private enjoyment of his own property. No physical damage might have resulted but X.'s walking was enough for Y. to have good grounds for action. Trespass is therefore actionable in its own right: it can be a question of *injuria sine damno* (a wrong without damage).

The usual remedy in tort is the award of damages, although a plaintiff may be awarded an injunction restraining the defendant from further commissions of the tort, or the wrong may be put right by an order for specific restitution – restoring that which is withheld from the plaintiff. Combinations of these remedies are, of course, possible, but awarding damages is the most commonplace.

If no actual damage has resulted to the plaintiff, the action will not succeed. But in those instances where the tort is actionable *per se*, damages will still be awarded even if no actual or particular damage has been suffered. Damages in this context will, however, be nominal. Of course, nominal damages may also be awarded in actions on the case, in other words in torts *not* actionable *per se*, if the loss or damage which the plaintiff has incurred is very slight, but nonetheless in those cases the damage done must still be proved, it is not presumed.

If damages awarded by the court are not nominal they can be said to be substantial and generally such damages can be classified as general and special. Special damages are meant to cover the plaintiff's actual financial loss up to the date of the trial, including loss of earnings and medical expenses. Special damages relate to the particular circumstances of the case and must therefore be strictly pleaded. General damages, on the other hand, will constitute those awarded for normal losses, in other words they cover the harm the court would expect a plaintiff to suffer generally once actual damage had been proved. Thus general damages do not have to be specially pleaded, they are to that extent presumed by the court; general damages will cover such things as loss of reputation, physical injury, including pain and other suffering, as well as the loss of future earnings. The distinction between special and general damages, especially in relation to pecuniary losses, has come in for some criticism. Prospective damages is the term applied to damages which cover future loss. Damages may be recovered for loss resulting from a foreseeable fall in the market the Court of Appeal said in *Banque Bruxelles Lambert SA* v. *Eagle Star Insurance Co. Ltd* (1996), but the House of Lords held that such market losses were not recoverable on the grounds that it was not a matter in relation to which a valuer owed a lender a duty of care (*South Australia Asset Management* v. *York Montague Ltd* (1996)). Moreover, once damages have been settled and a claim finally decided, under the principle of *res judicata* parallel claims between the same parties will not be entertained by the courts.

Special and general damages will normally be compensatory, that is they will cover the true and total value of the loss (*restitutio in integrum*), but as indicated above exemplary damages may also be awarded by way of a public warning – exemplary damages are therefore punitive and criminal in nature. The relatively narrow interpretation of exemplary damages as laid down in *Rookes* v. *Barnard* and reasserted in *Cassell & Co. Ltd* v. *Broome* (1972) has been criticised in a number of Commonwealth courts.

Damages may also be aggravated: these are damages awarded when it is clear that the injury committed has been made worse by the manner in which it was done. The malicious motive of the defendant would also apply here, although as we will see the motive of the defendant is usually irrelevant in tort. The case of *White* v. *Metropolitan Police Commissioner* (1982), discussed later on, is a good illustration of aggravated damages. Such damages will increase the total amount normally awarded by the court. A variation of aggravated damages is the parasitic element in an award. Parasitic damages are awarded for losses that are in turn dependent upon the success of another and more central cause or action. The distinction between parasitic damages and aggravated damages is thus largely an academic one; while the former term is widely recognised in the USA, it is one expressly discouraged in English courts.

An interesting example of exemplary damages occurred in 1975 in the case of *Drane* v. *Evangelou* (1978) in which the trial judge commented that the landlord had arranged the eviction of his tenant, who brought an action effectively for trespass to property, and that 'monstrous behaviour called for exemplary damages of £1,000'. The Court of Appeal upheld the judgment in 1977 and its *obiter dicta* were notable in respect of both aggravated and exemplary damages. Nonetheless as Lord Denning said in an earlier case, *Taylor* v. *Bristol Omnibus Co. Ltd* (1975), judges 'should look at the total figure [of damages awarded] in the round, so as to be able to cure any overlapping or other source of error'. *AB (or Gibbons)* v. *South West Water Services* (1993) which involved a contaminated water supply at Camelford in Cornwall, made it clear that exemplary damages were not available in public nuisance, in contrast to private nuisance – *Guppys (Bridport) Ltd* v. *Brookling* (1983). But in the case of Kenneth Hsu in 1997, the Court of Appeal reduced the exemplary damages awarded by a High Court jury from £250,000 to £50,000, signalling this was the ceiling for damages for oppressive, arbitrary or unconstitutional behaviour by public servants.

The question of assessing damages in today's inflationary society is a difficult one, not least in actions based upon negligence as the case of *Lim Poh Choo* v. *Camden and Islington Area Health Authority* well illustrated in 1979 and in the same year that of *Walker* v. *John McLean & Sons Ltd.* 'The courts are not infrequently having to face the prospect of assessing damages to a person who has been converted by an accident (usually on the roads) from a healthy, intelligent bread-winner into an unemployable handicap upon his family or institutions for the infirm', Rogers has commentated. The Damages Act 1996 allows for the award of provisional damages and structured settlements.

The 'damage' committed in the first place may be defined by statute – as stressed earlier not all tort is based upon common law. But Parliament too may experience difficulty in defining such a term closely, as *Fothergill* v. *Monarch Airlines Ltd*, which involved a torn suitcase, illustrated in respect of the Carriage by Air and Road Act 1979. Lastly, any damage committed in tort must generally have been caused directly by the defendant; it must not be too remote, it must be reasonably foreseeable. This problem is one which is examined in detail under the tort of negligence, since as will be seen, the concept of reasonable foreseeability and remoteness of damage is central to that particular tort.

GENERAL DEFENCES IN TORT

1 *Volenti non fit injuria*

It has long been established in English law that the defendant may argue that the plaintiff deliberately undertook a risk, and in so doing waived his rights against the defendant. This defence usually relates to physical harm caused, as in negligence. The defendant must show that in agreeing to run the physical gauntlet the plaintiff intended the assumption of risk to be legally binding.

Games and sporting events frequently fall into this category (as seen in *Condon* v. *Basi* (1985), involving a tackle in an amateur football game): the participant in a boxing match can hardly sue for trespass to the person. A greyer area is where a doctor has to perform an emergency operation and the patient is not in a fit or conscious condition to give permission. Similarly, spectators at a race or a game are in something of an uncertain position (*Wooldridge* v. *Sumner* (1963), and *Wilks* v. *Cheltenham Home Guard Motor Cycle and Light Car Club* (1971)).

The age of the participant in a sport might be crucial. So, in *Affutu-Nartoy* v. *Clarke* (1984) it was held to be a breach of a duty of care for a school teacher to contact physically a 15 year-old boy in a game of rugby, where a high tackle, although permissible under the rules of the game, was dangerous and therefore unlawful. However, in *Van Oppen* v. *Clerk to the Trustees of the Bedford Charity (Harper Trust)* (1990), a 16 year-old boy suffered spinal injuries when tackling another in a rugby game, but the court held adequate instruction had been given and there was no duty to insure the boy against the risk of injury. It is the duty of the organiser of such events not unnecessarily to add to the hazards inherent in the sport, as noted in *Latchford* v. *Spedeworth International Ltd* (1983) where the plaintiff's car in a race hit a concrete flower-bed which had not been sufficiently screened off.

On the other hand certain assumptions of risk have been excluded by Parliament – for example, the Road Traffic Act 1988 imposes liabilities in respect of passengers carried in cars (third parties); similar legislation covers buses and trains. Even here, however, things are not straightforward, for accepting lifts from an obviously drunken driver (*Dann* v. *Hamilton* (1939)) or from a driver who displayed a warning notice in his car (*Buckpitt* v. *Oates* (1968)) used to be sufficient in raising the defence of *volenti non fit injuria*, but *volenti* is excluded as a defence in motoring cases under s.149 of the Road Traffic Act 1988. And this points towards an important qualification to the doctrine: mere knowledge of the risk does not imply consent. In *Smith* v. *Baker* (1891) the plaintiff knew of the risk of a crane swinging large stones over his head, but he did not assume the risk in the sense that no warning was given to him when the crane was about to move.

In *Morris* v. *Murray* (1990) it was held that if a passenger agrees to travel in an aircraft when he knows, and it is obvious, that the pilot is very drunk, he cannot afterwards claim damages for personal injuries caused by the pilot's negligence. That applies even if the passenger himself is drunk when he agrees but is capable of knowing what he is doing and of appreciating the risks involved.

On *volenti* Richard Kidner in 1991 noted:

> **This doctrine has met with disfavour for some time although it is occasionally applied where the risk is glaringly obvious. There has been a long debate, beginning with *Dann* v. *Hamilton*, as to whether it should be applied where the plaintiff is aware of the defendant's disability. Most cases of this kind involve drunken drivers, but that debate is rather sterile as it is now clear that the Road Traffic Act prevents the application of the *volenti* doctrine in road accident cases [s.149(3) of the 1988 Act]. It is often said that the doctrine applies but for the statutory exclusion, and indeed it has been applied in similar circumstances where the statutory bar does not apply [*Morris* v. *Murray* (1990)].**

In *Pitts* v. *Hunt* (1991) in respect of s.149 of the Road Traffic Act 1988, it was clear that there was no such thing as 100 per cent contributory negligence. In *Morris* v. *Murray* (1990) the pilot had consumed the equivalent of 17 whiskies, his blood alcohol level being over three times the legal car limit, and the aircraft was only airborne for a few minutes.

It should also be noted that under the Unfair Contract Terms Act 1977, s.2(1), liability cannot be excluded in respect of death or injury resulting from negligence in the course of 'business'. And s.2(3) of the Act states: 'Where a contract term or notice purports to exclude or restrict liability from negligence, a person's agreement to or awareness of it is not of itself to be taken as indicating his voluntary acceptance of any risk'. Some occupations (fireman, North Sea oil diver) are naturally hazardous (*Bowater* v. *Rowley Regis Corporation* (1944)), but health and safety at work regulations may limit the use of *volenti* as a defence. In *Thompson* v. *T Lohan (Plant Hire) Ltd* (1987) the second defendants hired an excavator with a driver from the first defendants. The driver negligently killed the plaintiff's husband who was also an employee of the first defendants, against whom the plaintiff obtained damages. The Court of Appeal held that, in accordance with their agreement, the first defendants were entitled to be indemnified by the second defendants, and this was not contrary to the provisions of the 1977 Act.

Consent must be freely given; consent obtained by force or fraud will not stand the test. Conversely, the plaintiff's consent to an illegal act may amount to a valid *volens* or defence. In tort as in contract the legal maxim *ex turpi causa non oritur actio* is important, although it is of more significance to contract; similarly, the defence itself should not be based on illegality, for that is contrary to public policy. Further, consent may be difficult to prove in employment situations where 'the act to which the servant is said to be *volens* arises out of his ordinary duty' (*per* Lord Goddard of Bowater).

In *Sherrard* v. *British Gates (and Timber) Ltd* (1984) it was held that there was no provision in English law to compensate a person who sustained injury when he lent a helping hand unless it could be shown that there was a fault on the part of the other party. This case was about an accident whilst helping to load and move logs with a tractor – the plaintiff was an expert tractor driver, although the plaintiff was actually and legally a neighbour and some duty of care was therefore owed to him by the defendant company unless in the circumstances that duty was abrogated. The duty was to ensure there was a safe system of working and that the plaintiff was not exposed to risk of injury; there was no breach of duty by the company because there was no reasonably foreseeable risk of injury. The tractor driver was an expert driver.

Assumption of risk will normally not apply as a defence to those situations in which the bystander is under a moral duty to go to the aid of a stranger in distress (as shown in *Haynes* v. *Harwood* (1935) – a policeman tried to stop two unattended horses in the street; the horses had bolted, having had a stone thrown at them). And if the first rescuer fails, liability may still be owed to a second (*Horsley* v. *MacLaren* (1971)), where the argument was about whether the first rescuer owed a duty of care to the second rescuer). In rescue cases the person in difficulty has caused a broad duty of care to be owed to others. Knowledge of the risk alone, however, might establish that the plaintiff was partly to blame (contributory negligence – see below) or that the damage done was too remote a consequence to foresee from the negligent action committeed – some other intervening event had occurred (*novus actus interveniens* – see below).

2 Novus actus interveniens

In some cases there may be an act which occurs between the defendant's original wrongful act and the damage suffered by the plaintiff. Such an act committed by the plaintiff or a third party is called a *novus actus* (or *nova causa*) *interveniens* and in some circumstances it may so change the course of events that the defendant cannot be held liable for the damage. An example of such an intervening act occurred in *Singleton Abbey* v. *Paludina* (1927) where the *Paludina*, while moored in port, was driven by a high wind against the *Singleton Abbey* setting it adrift. The *Singleton Abbey,* some minutes later, when manoeuvring back to its mooring, collided with another ship and was damaged. The court held that the manoeuvring was a *novus actus interveniens* which broke the chain of causation between the original negligence of the *Paludina* and the damage to the *Singleton Abbey*. This case contrasts with another maritime one: *SS Temple Bar* v. *MV Guildford* (1956). These two ships collided due to the negligence of the *Temple Bar*. The *Guildford* refused the offer of a tow by the *Temple Bar* and waited several hours for a tug to take it into harbour, but sank before it could be towed into the harbour. It was held that the decision to wait for a tug was reasonable in the circumstances and it was not a *novus actus interveniens*, so the *Temple Bar* remained liable for its negligence.

The defendant may still be liable

In *Emeh* v. *Kensington and Chelsea and Westminster Area Health Authority* (1985) where a sterilisation operation had been negligently performed so that the woman became pregnant, her conscious decision thereafter not to have an abortion did not prevent her from claiming damages against the surgeons for the pregnancy and its consequences, the Court of Appeal held. But the trial judge had held the plaintiff's conduct in refusing to consider an abortion was so unreasonable as to eclipse the defendant's breach of duty, and that that conduct was a *novus actus interveniens* in the chain of causation of her pregnancy. In *Salih* v. *Enfield Health Authority* (1991), which involved the parents of a child born severely damaged suffering from congenital rubella syndrome, through admitted medical negligence, the Court of Appeal stressed the need to assess damages according to the basic principles of tort, in contrast to the substantial award under *Emeh* (1984).

In another sterilisation case (*Udale* v. *Bloomsbury Area Health Authority* (1983)) the plaintiff was entitled to damages for pain and suffering and loss of earnings during the unexpected pregnancy, but not for the cost of the child's upbringing to the age of 16, since the birth was of a normal, healthy boy which the family had welcomed.

Udale was not followed in *Thake* v. *Maurice* (1986) where the plaintiffs already had five children and were living in straitened circumstances. An award was made for the birth and upkeep of the child, but on a moderate basis, for breach of a contractual (collateral) warranty. The case differed from ordinary 'medical negligence' since the plaintiffs 'put their case boldly in contract', said the trial judge, Mr Justice Peter Pain. But the Court of Appeal reversed his decision in part; it said it was not a case of breach of contract but was one of negligence and accordingly increased the damages by £1,500. *Thake* v. *Maurice* was applied in *Allen* v. *Bloomsbury Health Authority* (1993).

The fact that there is an intervening act does not always absolve the defendant. If the act could have been reasonably foreseen by the defendant, he will remain liable. An example of this is the old case of *Scott* v. *Shepherd* (1773), where the defendant threw a lighted squib on to a stall in Milborne Port. The fact that two other people in turn picked it up and threw it in alarm for their own safety, did not break the chain of causation when, after the second person threw the squib, it exploded in a man's face and injured him. The defendant was held liable since the onward throwing was reasonably foreseeable.

As we have seen in *Haynes* v. *Harwood* (1935), a policeman tried to stop runaway horses and as a result was injured. The defendant was held liable because he had left the horses unattended and the action by the policeman was reasonably foreseeable; the damage caused to the policeman was not too remote from the original negligent act of leaving the horses on their own. It was therefore not a *novus actus interveniens*. Similarly, in *Chadwick* v. *British Railways Board* (1967), the defendants were held liable for the mental disorder of the plaintiff's husband that was a result of his playing an important role at the site of a railway accident near his home: his action was to be expected, it was neither *novus* nor *volens* in this context; on the contrary it was reasonably foreseeable.

A case illustrating the *novus* principle more precisely was that of *Knightley* v. *Johns* (1982). Here a car was driven carelessly and crashed in a tunnel. A police inspector forgot to close off the tunnel and two constables, one of whom was the plaintiff, rode their motor-bikes against the flow of the traffic in order to do so. Another car struck the plaintiff. It was held that the driver of the first car was not liable for the plaintiff's injuries, the chain of causation had been broken; the police inspector, however, was liable. Where the intervention is by someone who lacks full tortious responsibility, for example, a child, the courts have held that the defendant remains liable (*Bebee* v. *Sales* (1916)). The defendant will also remain liable if he himself committed the intervening act, or authorised or instigated another person to commit the act. In *Topp* v. *London Country Bus (South West) Ltd* (1993) the defendant company was not liable for the theft of an unattended mini-bus, although keys had been left in the ignition at a bus stop; it was the act of a third party which led to the plaintiff's wife being knocked down and killed.

3 Contributory negligence

Under the Law Reform (Contributory Negligence) Act 1945 the defendant may argue that the plaintiff was partially responsible for the harm suffered. In hearing this argument the court must have regard to what a reasonable man would have done in all the circumstances: whether, for example, avoiding action could have been taken, whether it was sensible to try to escape in a particular way, whether some or all of the blame can be imputed to the plaintiff's servant, agent or spouse (*Lampert* v. *Eastern National Omnibus Co. Ltd* (1954)), or whether a child was owed protection by an accompanying adult (*Oliver* v. *Birmingham and Midland Omnibus Co. Ltd*, (1933)).

In *Sayers* v. *Harlow UDC* (1958) it was reasonable for a woman trapped in a public lavatory to make attempts to escape, but it was not sensible to stand on the toilet-roll holder in so doing.

Contributory negligence may be a defence in trespass to the person; it is not a defence in deceit. Blame will not be apportioned where it appears that one of the parties is less than 10 per cent to blame. *Volenti non fit injuria* is not a defence to breach of statutory duty, but contributory negligence may reduce the damages.

In *Barrett* v. *Ministry of Defence* (1995) the Court of Appeal held the defendant one-third liable for the death of a naval airman who became very drunk at his birthday party, since medical assistance was not summoned and the supervision provided was inadequate.

4 Public interest

There is no fully developed tort of confidence as such, although in *Seager* v. *Copydex Ltd* (1967) it was affirmed that disclosure of private confidential information was tortious. Nonetheless it may be a defence to an action for breach of confidence to argue that it was in the public interest to release certain information. This was the theme in the case of *British Steel Corporation* v. *Granada Television Ltd* (1980). Here, as we have seen earlier, the television company used BSC classified documents in one of their programmes and refused to name their source. It was conceded that there might be cases in which the public had an interest in the free flow of information, even if that meant protecting the source responsible for the breach of confidence. A similar line was taken in *Schering Chemicals Ltd* v. *Falkman Ltd* (1981). Lord Denning dissented on the grounds that public interests can outweigh private interests. In this case Thames Television made a film about a controversial pregnancy drug on the basis of confidential information. As seen earlier, breach of confidence has been highlighted by the *Spycatcher* affair.

Conversely, the government can 'hinder' the plaintiff's action by resisting disclosure of certain documents on the grounds that it would not be in the public interest to reveal secrets (the doctrine of Crown privilege or public interest immunity). This may make it difficult for the plaintiff to prove negligence, for example. In *Ellis* v. *Home Office* (1953) the Government refused to release medical reports about an inmate of Winchester Prison. In *Duncan* v. *Cammell Laird and Co.* (1942) the Government refused to release the design plans of a submarine which sank during sea trials. Confidential documents may, however, still be used in judicial proceedings, but restricted to those proceedings only.

5 Mistake

Mistake is generally not a defence in tort (contract is a different matter). Mistake, of course, about the law (*ignorantia juris non excusat*), will not amount to a good defence, but mistake about facts may on occasion be allowed; it will most likely apply in malicious prosecution, false imprisonment, defamation, vicarious liability and deceit (misrepresentation).

6 Act of God

This is not so much a general defence as a specific one: it embraces extraordinary events − like a flash flood. It is relevant to the rule in *Rylands* v. *Fletcher* (strict liability), as seen in section 8.9.

7 Inevitable accident

This defence − an uncertain one − is concerned with the argument that the consequences of a tortious action, usually a negligent action, were not at all foreseeable at the time the action took place, nor were they intended. It usually applies to trespass, whether to land, goods or the person.

8 Self-protection

The courts are always prepared to take into account that it was reasonable, having regard to all the circumstances, to use force to protect the person or property. But the amount of force used must not be excessive. This particularly applies to trespass and occupiers' liability.

9 Necessity

The defendant may not have been under threat (as in self-protection) but nonetheless undertook tortious action in order to protect himself or others from unfortunate consequences that he could see arising. Here we are back to medical assistance given to unconscious patients. Also, action designed to stop fire from spreading or to save a ship by throwing things overboard will fall into this category. In *Cope* v. *Sharpe* (1912) fire broke out on the plaintiff's land, but the defendant had reasonably committed trespass in order to protect game in respect of which his master had shooting rights. Following the controversial case of *Burmah Oil Co. (Burmah Trading) Ltd* v. *Lord Advocate* (1965) (concerning the destruction of oil installations by the British Army in South-East Asia in order to hinder the Japanese occupation of Burma in the Second World War), the War Damage Act 1965 was passed which states that the government is immune from claims in respect of the damage to or the destruction of property caused by its own war-time actions. In *Rigby* v. *Chief Constable of Northamptonshire* (1985), a gunsmith's shop owned by the plaintiff was badly damaged by fire caused by a canister of CS gas fired by the police to flush out a dangerous psychopath, but unfortunately this was during 1977 when the fire service was on strike and no fire appliance was in immediate attendance. The defence of necessity was successfully employed in relation to claims in trespass and *Rylands* (it being conceded by the plaintiff that a claim of nuisance added nothing to trespass). But the plaintiff succeeded in negligence.

10 Statutory authority

Acts of Parliament will sometimes lay down penalties in criminal and/or civil law for their breach. But not every Act does so and it is then up to the courts to decide whether the Act does imply a right of tortious action. Where a clear duty is laid down the courts will presume that there is that right (*Square* v. *Model Farm Dairies (Bournemouth) Ltd* (1939)). Where there is doubt the courts will have to look at the Act as a whole and all of the relevant existing common law (*Anns* v. *Merton London Borough* (1977)). In *Atkinson* v. *Newcastle Waterworks Co.* (1877) the defendants had not kept a certain water supply at the right pressure. The relevant statute provided a £10 penalty. As a result water could not be brought to the plaintiff's house which was on fire. The court took the view that the company was not liable, since Parliament had not intended the water company to be liable for fire at large. If there appears to be a breach of statutory duty, then it must be shown that there was a duty of care owed to the plaintiff and that the injury must be the kind the Act contemplated (*Chipchase* v. *British Titan Products Co* (1956), *Hartley* v. *Mayoh and Co* (1954) and *Ginty* v. *Belmont Building Supplies* (1959)). Breach of a statutory duty is sometimes referred to as 'statutory negligence', *per* Lord Wright, as seen in *Lochgelly Iron and Coal Co.* v. *M'Mullan* (1934). However, ordinary negligence as we shall see turns upon the notion of reasonable foresight (could the consequences of careless action have been anticipated?), whereas statutory duties and their breach vary according to the responsibilities laid down by the individual Acts, as in the case of factory legislation.

In *Stovin* v. *Wise (Norfolk County Council, Third Party)* (1996) where the council had become aware of a road junction danger and had decided to allocate resources to deal with the matter, then there was a common law duty to resolve the matter as quickly as possible, the Court of Appeal held. But the House of Lords, by a bare majority, although disapproving of the narrow lines drawn between positive acts and omissions, and reviewing *Anns*, thought that a statutory 'may' could not be turned into a common law 'ought'. Thus it appears more difficult to argue for a common law liability regarding a failure to exercise a statutory power rather than to perform a statutory duty. A breach of statutory duty, Lord Hoffmann said for the majority, did not automatically give rise to an action or to an action for common law negligence. The *Stovin* case followed that of *X* v. *Bedfordshire County Council* (1995), which had illustrated the decisions in *Anns* and *Dorset Yacht Co.* were being heavily restricted in favour of not imposing civil liability upon public authorities (see *Hill* v. *Chief Constable of West Yorkshire* and *Murphy* v. *Brentwood District Council* below). The issues in *Stovin* raised the old and ever unanswered question (despite the best efforts of Professor Dworkin, as seen in Chapter 1) of the difference between policy and principle.

It is indeed a defence, providing the statute is clear in its intention, express or implied, to argue that statutory authority overrides what otherwise might constitute a tortious action. In *Department of Transport* v. *North West Water Authority* (1983) the House of Lords held where water had escaped from a main under a main road, thereby causing the highway damage, the defendant authority had used all reasonable diligence to prevent the main becoming a nuisance, having regard to the fact that the Public Utilities Street Works Act 1950 (s.18) did not impose a form of strict liability.

11 Waiver and limitation

It is a defence in tort to argue that the plaintiff had already waived his right to bring an action, or that there has been accord and satisfaction. Waiver may not apply to all torts; it does apply to deceit and trespass to goods and land. Accord and satisfaction mean that the plaintiff has already been compensated in some way – by apology, by compensation or by some other means, which had been accepted.

Under the Limitation Act 1980 it is a defence to show that the action is 'out of time'. Normally the period is six years from the date of the cause of the action, but three years in the case of personal injuries, and formerly three years since the Administration of Justice Act 1985 for defamation, now reduced to one year by s.5 of the Defamation Act 1996. The court can rarely dismiss an application for delay if proceedings are brought within the time limit. In torts actionable *per se* the time limit commences from the moment the wrong was committed. In other torts it runs from when damage occurred, although, of course, some torts may be concerned with continuing harm, for example, nuisance and false imprisonment, in which case time runs from when the wrong stops, the tort of conversion (of goods) excepted. A thief cannot use the defence of limitation in conversion, but a *bona fide* purchaser for value will acquire title to the stolen property six years from purchase; but the original owner will always be able to claim against the thief, without limitation, although deprived of the actual goods.

The limitation period for certain other torts is specially restricted. For recovery of land it is 12 years. For damage caused by collision at sea or in the air it is two (Maritime Conventions Act 1911, Merchant Shipping Act 1979 and Carriage by Air Act 1961). Injury caused by radiation has a 30 year limitation (Nuclear Installations (Licensing and Insurance) Act 1959 as consolidated by the 1965 Act). Claims for contribution between joint tort-feasors has a cut-off point of two years from when the right to contribution first accrued – for example, B. can try to claim from A. within two years from when judgment is given against B.; it is one year for sea collisions.

All these limitation periods may be lengthened if there is a recognisable disability, such as being detained in enemy territory. Infancy is also treated as such (the 'disability' ends, obviously, at 18) and mental disorder (within the terms of the Mental Health Act 1983). Time runs from the moment the plaintiff's disability ends or from his prior death.

But harm may be committed without the plaintiff having had a reasonable opportunity of discovering it; yet the limitation period may have already commenced, as illustrated in *Sparham-Souter* v. *Town and Country Developments (Essex) Ltd* (1976) which involved cracks appearing slowly in a house. Where the tortious action has been concealed by fraud, then the limitation period runs from the time that the fraud was discovered. In the case of personal injuries, including mental conditions, or death caused by negligence, nuisance or a similar wrong, then the period of three years may run from the time the injury was actually *discovered* by the plaintiff. This is an important consideration for those situations where the injury is of a cumulative nature – for example, lung disease caused by asbestos or coal-mine dust (pneumoconiosis or silicosis). Thus the seeds of the damage may have been planted in year X; the damage may have started to occur in earnest in X + 2, but it could not reasonably have been discovered until X + 4, normally outside the limitation period. The Pneumoconiosis etc (Workers' Compensation) Act 1979 provided for lump sum payments to persons disabled by pneumoconiosis, byssinosis or diffuse mesothelioma. By the Social Security Act 1985 the Secretary of State was given powers to add other diseases to the 1979 list.

Conversely, a dormant disease may subsequently affect the courts' attitude towards deciding damages. In *Jobling* v. *Associated Dairies Ltd* (1981) the plaintiff was employed by the defendants as the manager of a butcher's shop. He slipped in the course of his work and injured his back. But by the time the action had come to trial the plaintiff was found to be suffering from myelopathy, a condition unconnected with the accident, but which would have in any event proved totally disabling. The House of Lords upholding the Court of Appeal, reduced the damages awarded accordingly.

In *Brooks* v. *J & P Coates (UK) Ltd* (1984) the plaintiff waited 15 years before bringing an action for breach of a statutory duty under the Factories Act 1961 (inhalation of dust). The High Court held that the action was not statute barred under the Limitation Act 1980, since the plaintiff was blameless in delaying and the balance of prejudice lay in his favour.

In personal injury cases the court has a clear general power to override the limitation periods if it thinks it equitable to do so. This might include cases of a procedural error by legal advisers, notwithstanding the plaintiff's right to sue such advisers in negligence (misrepresentation). This unfettered discretion was strongly underlined by *Firman* v. *Ellis* (1978) (a road accident case which involved a procedural slip by a solicitor) and *Thompson* v. *Brown* (1981). The second case involved the collapse of scaffolding on to a bricklayer; the solicitor mislaid the file. In *Thompson* the court recognised the right the plaintiff had to sue his own solicitor in negligence, but it felt the consequential requirement that the plaintiff would have to find new solicitors to instruct was undesirable, bearing in mind the accompanying costs and anxiety. However, such limitation discretion was not allowed by the House of Lords in the case of *Donovan* v. *Gwentoys Ltd* (1990), and in *Stubbings* v. *Webb* (1993) the House of Lords said that an action for rape and indecent assault was trespass to the person and was therefore time-barred by the six-year period; the three year test did not apply. The six-year period had run from the age of majority; the plaintiff was now aged 36. Discretion to override the limitation rules, under s.33 of the 1980 Act, also arose in the mass product liability claims in the Opren drug litigation (*Nash* v. *Eli Lilly* (1993)).

7.2   Defamation

A defamatory statement or action or gesture is one which injures the reputation of another person or persons. In *Sim* v. *Stretch* (1936) Lord Atkin noted that a defamatory statement was one which tended to lower a person in the estimation of right-thinking members of society, or to cause those right-thinking persons to shun and avoid him. On the other hand public opinion is never static; what is defamatory one day may not be the day after. In *Telnikoff* v. *Matusevitch* (1991), the plaintiff wrote an article for a newspaper criticising the BBC's Russian Service for recruiting too many employees from ethnic minorities of the Soviet Union and not enough from people who associate themselves 'ethnically, spiritually or religiously with the Russian people'. In respect of a defence of fair comment the House of Lords held that an objective test was the right one, and that it was for the plaintiff to prove that the evidence was more consistent with the existence of malice than its absence. The decision might be interpreted as an important support of fair comment as part of free speech.

Much of the law of defamation is now covered by statute – the Libel Acts 1843 and 1845, the Defamation Acts 1952 and 1996 and the Theatres Act 1968. However, despite suggestions made in 1975 for abolition of the distinction, it continues to be divided into two parts – libel and slander. Legal aid is not available for defamation actions. The judge will always decide whether there is a case to answer; if the matter proceeds to a full trial, a jury may be involved, in which case the final decision is theirs. In any case trial by jury is not available in cases worth under £10,000 since the Defamation Act 1996 (ss.8–9), for which there is a rapid procedure.

In *Beta Construction* v. *Channel 4 Television Co. Ltd* (1990), the Court of Appeal set out a number of factors in deciding whether under s.69 of the Supreme Court Act 1981 trial by judge alone ought to be ordered in a libel action – the court has to direct its attention to the issue of the efficient administration of justice, including significant expense.

Libel consists of a defamatory statement which is permanent in some form or other; thus such things as writing, printing, statues, pictures and records can fall into the libellous category. In the case of *Youssoupoff* v. *Metro-Goldwyn-Mayer* (1934) it was established that films also fell into that division of defamation; the same has also been established for radio and television broacasts under the Defamation Act 1952 and for plays under the Theatres Act 1968.

The scale of damages, and who can sue, has proved something of a maze in recent years. In *Rantzen* v. *Mirror Group Newspapers* (1993) the Court of Appeal cut excessive libel damages from £250,000 to £110,000 under s.8 of the Courts and Legal Services Act 1990, whilst in *Derbyshire County Council* v. *Times Newspapers Ltd* (1993) Lord Keith, in the House of Lords, said the conclusion must be that under the common law a local authority did not have the right to maintain *any* action for damages for defamation. There was no difference in principle between English law on the subject and Article 10 of the European Convention on Human Rights; it followed that *Bognor Regis UDC* v. *Campion* (1972) was wrongly decided and should be overruled. In 1987 £500,000 was awarded by the jury in the Jeffrey Archer case, where *The Star* had alleged that the deputy chairman of the Conservative Party had paid a prostitute for sex and then lied about the matter publicly. In *Aldington* v. *Tolstoy* (1989) record libel damages of £1.5 million were awarded, but following the *Roache* v. *News Group Newspapers Ltd* case (1992) and the recommendation of an advisory committee (in *Roache* the actor who played Ken Barlow in the television soap *Coronation Street* was described as 'boring' and was awarded £50,000 damages) the Lord Chancellor announced reforms in the law of defamation, principally that there should be a new procedure for an 'offer of amends' where damages would be fixed by a judge and not a jury, plus a new summary procedure where the plaintiffs could claim damages up to a fixed ceiling, and the abolition of the rule under which the defendants could adduce evidence of discreditable acts by the plaintiff so as to mitigate the damages payable.

The ECHR in *Tolstoy Miloslavsky* v. UK (1995) (see *Tolstoy* v. *Aldington* (1996)) said that the award of £1.5 million amounted to a violation of Article 10 of the Convention. The issue again came to the fore in *John* v. *Mirror Group Newspapers Ltd* (1995) where out of £350,000 total damages awarded £275,000 were exemplary damages.

The Lord Chancellor also accepted other proposals from the committee, the Supreme Court Procedure Committee under the chairmanship of Lord Justice Neill; for instance, judges would be empowered to rule as to whether words complained of are capable of bearing a particular meaning; the limitation period would generally be reduced to one year; protection to media reports afforded by s.7 of the Defamation Act 1952 would be extended to similar reports from abroad. The outcome was the Defamation Act 1996.

CRIMINAL LIBEL

Two other aspects of libel may be noted briefly at this stage. Libel can also take a criminal form. Criminal libel actions are fairly rare beasts; such actions may involve elements of disorder, but by no means necessarily as the case of *Private Eye* illustrated in 1976 (*Goldsmith* v. *Pressdram Ltd*). In the case of *Gleaves* v. *Deakin* (1979) the House of Lords recommended, *obiter*, that the law of criminal libel should be amended so that prosecutions could only be brought with the consent of the Attorney-General or the Director of Public Prosecutions. Unlike civil libel an alleged criminal libel does not have to be read or heard by a third party. Under criminal libel it may even be an offence to libel the dead. A criminal libel action can be launched by anyone and once the prosecution has established that the alleged libel is, *prima facie*, serious and was published by the accused, then the defendant must prove that what he had published or broadcast was both true and in the public interest. Mr Gleaves's action concerned the book *Johnny Go Home*, the subject of a controversial film by Yorkshire Television. Mr Gleaves, the self-styled 'Bishop of Medway', had run a hostel for young homeless people in London. While Mr Gleaves did not require the Attorney-General's or DPP's permission to launch his action of criminal libel, the leave of a judge is required under the Law of Libel Amendment Act 1888 (s.8) in respect of any publication in a newspaper. In 1980 the Attorney-General intervened: under *nolle prosequi* he forbade Mr Gleaves to launch any further criminal libel actions in respect of *Johnny Go Home*.

Secondly, there occur even more rarely cases of blasphemous libel (a criminal matter) as the celebrated prosecution of *Gay News* in 1978 evidenced (*R v. Lemon*). Thirdly, there is obscene libel (under the Obscene Publications Act 1959) which is also a criminal matter. Both matters have been examined earlier.

SLANDER

Slander consists of an attack made in a transient form; thus gestures and the spoken word would fall into the slanderous category. Yet to say that slander is addressed to the ear and libel to the eye is a crude over-simplification; the distinction between the two branches of defamation is by no means a straightforward one.

In defamation the general rule is that libel is actionable *per se*, slander is not. But there are exceptions in slander. Slander is actionable *per se* if the defendant has imputed that the plaintiff has committed an indictable criminal offence, but actual damage must be proved where a crime punishable by fine only is imputed. Secondly, slander imputing a person has a contagious disease, including venereal disease, leprosy and the plague, is actionable *per se*. So too is that which imputes unchastity in a woman, including adultery and lesbianism (Slander of Women Act 1891). Lastly, slander is also actionable *per se* under the Defamation Act 1952 (s.2) in respect of words spoken or written that are calculated to disparage a person in the exercise of his professional, commercial or official duties.

Defamation will involve holding a person up to hatred, contempt or ridicule. Such categories will include remarks that relate to alleged misconduct or dishonesty, as was well established in the case of *Cassidy* v. *Daily Mirror Newspapers Ltd* (1929). This case involved a newspaper photograph and caption capable of the interpretation that the plaintiff was her husband's mistress.

INNUENDOS

On the other hand many words in all languages are capable of several interpretations, ambiguity may abound: the context in which the words complained of are used is all important. Words may be *prima facie* defamatory, but if an ambiguity exists, the plaintiff must explain in the plea the defamatory innuendo which he views as attached to the words used by the defendant – this is sometimes called the popular or false innuendo. If, however, the words complained of are totally ordinary and innocent at face value, then the plaintiff must set out in the pleadings the nature of the evidence he will produce to prove that an apparently normal usage of words was in fact defamatory. The second type of innuendo is referred to as the true innuendo.

In *Charleston* v. *News Group Newspapers* (1995) the plaintiffs were actors in a long-running Australian serial shown on British televsion. Photographs of the plaintiffs' faces superimposed on the near-naked bodies of models in pornographic poses were not defamatory the House of Lords held.

The cases of *Allsop* v. *Church of England Newspaper Ltd* (1972) – in which the argument centred around the word 'bent' as applied to a broadcaster – and *Tolley* v. *J. S. Fry & Sons Ltd* (1931), which involved a famous golfer, without his permission, advertising a bar of chocolate, underline the difficulties of linguistic interpretation – the innuendo. In *Skuse* v. *Granada Television* (1993) the natural and ordinary meaning of the words and images in a *World in Action* programme about the soundness of the convictions of the Birmingham Six, bore the defamatory meaning that Dr Skuse (the Home Office scientist involved) failed to show the knowledge and care to be expected of him.

But it is equally important to note that defamation actions will not succeed where the words in dispute prove to be ones that constitute mere vulgar abuse in everyday language, as illustrated in the case of *Lane* v. *Holloway* (1968), where the words 'shut up you monkey-faced tart' shouted late at night in a Dorchester street would probably not have amounted to defamation. This case actually concerned assault and contributory negligence, but the endearing vocabulary is illustrative for these purposes. The difference between mere insults and defamation were considered in *Berkoff* v. *Burchill* (1996).

An alleged defamatory statement must refer to the plaintiff and if it is clear to the court that the relevant words cannot conceivably refer to the plaintiff, then the case will not proceed further. For example, references made to a large group of people without naming any one of its individual members do not constitute actions in defamation, as noted in the case of *Knupffer* v. *London Express Newspaper Ltd* (1944). Thus to say that all lawyers are crooks is too much of a generality to be actionable at law.

Journalists and authors, however, must be careful to ensure that names used in their writings do not refer to others of the same name, accidental as those references may well be. The point has been highlighted in a number of cases, such as *Newstead* v. *London Express Newspaper Ltd* (1939) which involved a printed reference to the trial of Harold Newstead, 'a Camberwell man', for bigamy. Unfortunately for the newspaper concerned, there was another Harold Newstead living in Camberwell, not a bigamist but a hairdresser. It is true, however, that only nominal damages were awarded in this instance.

It should also be noted that disclosure of a defamatory statement by the person making that statement to his or her spouse does not constitute publication, in other words the spouse cannot count as the essential third person; but if the statement is communicated by the originator of the defamatory statement to the wife or husband of the person about whom the statement is made, then publication is held to exist. Without publication an action for defamation will not lie. Publication may include the dictation of a letter to a secretary.

Defences

There are a number of other defences in the law of defamation, although it is possible to discern elements of strict liability in defamation. If a tort is one of strict liability, then subject to certain defences it is just bad luck for the defendant that the harm he has 'caused' was done innocently and was not the result of any carelessness (negligence) on his part. In other words, the plaintiff does not have to prove that the defendant was at fault; it is enough that harm has occurred. Thus strict liability applies to the escape of dangerous things (fire, water and animals) and formerly also to defamation. Liability in defamation was strict since the underlying philosophy in law was that the interest of the defendant in publishing is secondary to the plaintiff's interest in protecting his reputation.

In other torts the *fault* of the defendant must be established; liability is 'ordinary'. But in such torts even if the carelessness of the defendant is established, he may still escape liability, or a great part of it, if it can be shown that the damage that resulted from his action was not reasonably foreseeable or if the chain of causation was broken in some way (*novus actus interveniens*). Of course, no defendant can be liable for damage *ad infinitum*; the chain of causation must not be too elaborate. The damage complained of must not be too remote from the original action, it must be proximate and direct. Subject to that proviso, however, in torts of strict liability the defendant will be liable for all direct consequences of his action, innocuous as that action originally may have been.

Strictness of liability is not the same as a tort being actionable *per se*, since in torts actionable *per se* the proof of actual damage is not necessary, although it is essential nowadays to prove the fault of the defendant. Libel is therefore the rare tort for which liability is strict, at least in part, and which is actionable *per se*.

However, it should also be added that over the years the rules of strict liability in tort have been much amended, for example, by the Defamation Acts 1952 and 1996 itself. The modern trend in the courts has been towards the dictum 'no liability without fault'.

Innocent dissemination

In the first place the defence of *innocent dissemination* may be raised: the handlers of defamatory material, such as librarians, news vendors and booksellers, may plead that they were totally unaware that they were circulating defamatory matter. This defence has not, understandably, been available to publishers and printers, for they are just as strictly liable as the author. However, s.1 of the Defamation Act 1996 has introduced a statutory defence of innocent defamation – D. may show that he took reasonable care in relation to its publication, and did not know that what he did caused or contributed to the publication of the defamatory statement.

Justification

The plaintiff's action will also fail if the defendant can successfully plead *justification*, in other words what he said or wrote was true. Thus it may be an unfortunate fact of life that a person with malicious motives in mind will expose, truthfully, an early misdeed of another who has since led a perfectly blameless life. It is not, though, a defence which should be used lightly – if it is used unsuccessfully the court may well decide to award aggravated damages. Nonetheless it is sufficient to show that the remark in question was substantially true, a point established in the case of *Alexander* v. *North Eastern Rly Co.* as long ago as 1865 (the case involved certain inaccuracies in the reporting of the prison sentence of the plaintiff). Moreover, under the Defamation Act 1952 (s.5) it is clear that the press, private individuals and others may still use the defence of justification even if the truth of one of several charges is not proved, with the proviso that the plaintiff's reputation is not materially injured. A newspaper may therefore be allowed a few factual errors if what it says remains essentially true, as illustrated in *Redgrave* v. *The Observer Ltd* (1978). (Miss Redgrave, her brother and four other members of the Workers' Revolutionary Party brought a libel action against *The Observer* in respect of events occurring at the party's political school in Derbyshire. The newspaper article was part true, part untrue, but the part that was not true did not materially injure the plaintiff's reputation.) The same provision applies under the Act in respect of the defence of fair comment, where the words complained of consist partly of allegations of fact and partly of opinion – again not all the facts stated have to be true, as noted in the cases of *Broadway Approvals Ltd* v. *Odhams Press Ltd* (1965). The one principal exception to the defence of justification is that under the Rehabilitation of Offenders Act 1974 damages may be recovered by an ex-prisoner for the malicious publication of his previous conviction.

Justification – that is establishing the truth of what was said – does not apply to statements of fact alone; the defence can also be used in respect of statements of opinion, but in this respect it is a defence which must be used with particular caution. Justifying an opinion is not very different from the defence of *fair comment*. In *Polly Peck (Holdings) plc* v. *Threlford* (1986) it was held that a defendant may justify all the allegations in a publication if a jury find they have a 'common sting'. Where a defence of justification is relied upon, then the defendant must clearly state the meaning he seeks to justify (*Lucas-Box* v. *News Group Ltd* (1986)). Pleading in libel cases had become an 'artificial minuet' – in every case the pleadings should define the issues, said Lord Justice Parker in *Singh* v. *Gillard* (1988).

Fair comment

To employ the defence of fair comment, however, the defendant must establish the honesty of his claims, whereas in justification the emphasis is placed upon truth. On the other hand the presence of malice (spite, ill-will, improper motive) in the making of that 'fair' comment will usually destroy that defence. It should be noted that 'malice' in the sense of improper motive – the term is sometimes used simply to mean intention – is generally irrelevant in tortious actions. However, it is legitimate for a plaintiff to attempt to show that the defendant acted for malicious reasons in respect of the torts of malicious prosecution, injurious (malicious) falsehood, and to a lesser extent in defamation and nuisance.

The defence of fair comment will also collapse if it is shown that the defendant has imputed that the plaintiff is dishonest, corrupt, immoral or untruthful, the leading case being that of *Campbell* v. *Spottiswoode* (1863). Such imputation has to be justified or reasonably inferred from the facts. This particular defence can only succeed if the plaintiff in addition can establish that 'fair comment' was made in the public interest. Thus the private affairs of relatively unknown people are unlikely to fall within this category, but comments upon political, literary or judicial figures or upon other men or women of public affairs do. It is for the judge to decide whether the comment in question is in fact in the public interest.

Absolute privilege

Another major defence is *privilege*. Privilege is of two types – absolute and qualified.

There are a number of circumstances which attract absolute protection, even if the statements concerned are false and defamatory and even where they are made maliciously. Thus on certain occasions the public interest is put above any safeguarding of the reputation that an individual might normally expect to enjoy. Any statement made in the course of the proceedings of either House of Parliament – including committees – is covered by absolute privilege. Moreover, absolute privilege extends to any reports and papers authorised by either House as well as to the reproduction of such reports in full – for instance by the mass media. Therein lies a problem, especially in an age of instant news: an editor's omission of just a few non-essential words from the reproduction of parliamentary reports, papers or proceedings will be enough to turn the privilege into a qualified one. Such was the difficulty the media found themselves in in respect of the ABC trial (*R* v. *Aubrey, Berry and Campbell* (1978)), even though the relevant information was to be found in Hansard. Reports and communications by the Ombudsman (the Parliamentary Commissioner for Administration) are also, under the Parliamentary Commissioner Act 1967, the subject of absolute privilege, as are the local equivalent (the Local Commissioners for Administration) under the Local Government Act 1974. The publication of parliamentary reports and proceedings is covered by the Parliamentary Papers Act 1840.

Absolute privilege also extends to all judicial proceedings. That rule probably includes the relationship between solicitor and client, although whether that situation is qualified rather than absolute has not been totally settled by the House of Lords and Court of Appeal. The Lords in *Minter* v. *Priest* (1930) left the question open. Fair and accurate reports published contemporaneously in a newspaper or on television or radio in respect of judicial proceedings within the United Kingdom attract absolute privilege too, in accordance with the provisions of the Law of Libel Amendment Act 1888 as amended by the Defamation Act 1952 (s.8). This has been restated by the Defamation Act 1996, ss.14–15, and crucially s.15 has extended statutory qualified privilege to all forms of the media. Judicial proceedings embrace tribunals as well as courts, as underlined by the case of *Trapp* v. *Mackie* (1979). Dr Trapp was a headmaster who had been dismissed from his post; a local inquiry was held to investigate the reasons for his dismissal. Dr Trapp brought an action against Mr Mackie for the allegedly 'maliciously false evidence' he gave at the inquiry; Mr Mackie was Chairman of the Aberdeenshire Education Committee.

Other situations that fall into the category of absolute privilege include communications between husband and wife, as well as between one officer of State and another. What an 'officer of State' exactly constitutes is not totally clear. However, the relationship would embrace that of a Minister of the Crown to a senior civil servant (but how senior?) and the relationships between senior military personnel would also be included, as well as reports from High Commissioners of Commonwealth states to the relevant Prime Minister. It is likely, however, that statements by officials of foreign governments resident in the United Kingdom would attract only qualified privilege, unless made within the same embassy.

Qualified privilege

Qualified privilege is a more difficult concept to define and some legal authorities have argued that it differs little from the defence of fair comment. In *Adam* v. *Ward* (1917) Lord Atkinson commented that qualified privilege was occasioned where a person had some kind of social or moral duty to communicate with another who had an interest or duty to receive that statement – in other words there was an element of reciprocity. *Kingshott* v. *Associated Kent Newspapers* (1990) concerned a planning inquiry into the ferry terminal for Sally Lines at Ramsgate and a newspaper report. In the light of *Adam* v. *Ward*, what did principle require? When, as in the present case, the question was whether a defendant newspaper could show that it did not lose its privilege because the matter published was not of public concern, and the publication was not for the public benefit, no issue of law was raised and the answer depended on a judgment of the significance of the matter reported and the public consequences of publication; those, the court said, would seem to be factual judgments which a jury was well fitted to make and in accordance with long established principle should make. It was for the jury to decide whether the report was accurate and fair (ie qualified privilege) under s.7 of the 1952 Act.

As in fair comment the defence of qualified privilege can be destroyed by the plaintiff establishing malicious motives on the part of the defendant, although the procedure varies slightly. The existence of malice is a matter for the jury, the existence of a privileged occasion is one for the judge. Evidence of malice has to be overwhelming (*Herbage* v. *Pressdram Ltd* (1984)).

Qualified privilege will relate to statements made in the performance of an official duty – for instance, the occasion of the employer giving a confidential reference about an employee. Statements made about a matter of common concern to two or more people may also attract qualified privilege, although what constitutes a 'common interest' can pose problems. Business or commercial letters might well fall into this category. However, although it was stated above that the sender of a letter 'publishes' it once that letter had been dictated to his secretary, or given to the care of other members of the staff, the occasion will probably attract qualified privilege.

In *Blackshaw* v. *Lord* (1983) the jury awarded £45,000 damages where *The Daily Telegraph* alleged that a senior civil servant had resigned on account of incompetence. The story arose from a public session of a Commons committee – hence the defendants argued the occasion was one of qualified privilege. But the jury concluded that it was not a fair and accurate report that had been given. The Court of Appeal noted that where, as in this case, damaging allegations or charges had been made and were still under investigation, or where the defamatory statement was based upon inference or conjecture, there was no duty to publish.

In addition, qualified privilege extends to fair and accurate reporting of parliamentary proceedings; such reporting includes impressionistic sketches. Extracts from parliamentary papers and any other documents of a public nature also fall into this category. It has already been seen above that fair and accurate reporting of judicial proceedings by newspapers and the broadcasting authorities attracts an absolute privilege under statutory law.

Moreover, under s.13 of the Defamation Act 1996, parliamentary privilege may be waived in order that MPs and peers may pursue a defamation action, a point illustrated by the disastrous episode of Neil Hamilton against *The Guardian* in 1996–97. (Hamilton subsequently lost his seat in the General Election of 1997 to Martin Bell, a distinguished BBC correspondent who stood as an Independent on an anti-corruption ticket.) Absolute privilege still attaches to things spoken in Parliament.

Under the Defamation Act 1952 (s.7) certain other reports – of a fair and accurate nature – either in newspapers or on television or radio are afforded qualified privilege, as seen in the *Sally Lines* case above. But the statements concerned are, under the Act, divided into two categories: those which are privileged without explanation or contradiction and those which are privileged subject to explanation or contradiction. The first category embraces fair and accurate reporting of parliamentary and judicial proceedings in British colonies (the Act says 'Dominions') and of proceedings in international organisations, both political and judicial, of which the United Kingdom is a member. The second category covers fair and accurate reports of proceedings in trade, professional, industrial and sporting associations, as well as of lawful public meetings, local authorities and public inquiries and at general meetings of public companies. The qualification attached to the second category means that the defence of qualified privilege will fail if the plaintiff can show that he requested the defendant to publish a statement by way of explanation or contradiction and that the defendant refused or neglected so to do. Under s.10 of the Act statements made at election meetings are not privileged.

Apology

Under the Libel Act 1843 the defendant may prove that he offered to make or actually made an *apology* to the plaintiff for a defamatory remark and may therefore use that apology as evidence in mitigation of damages. Furthermore, although liability in defamation is primarily strict, the Defamation Act 1952 (s.4) provided for cases of *unintentional defamation* – in other words a statement published which was not intended to be understood to refer to the plaintiff or which was not *prima facie* defamatory and therefore the publisher would not know of circumstances under which the statement could be understood to be defamatory to the plaintiff. In such a situation the publisher may make an offer of *amends*, that is correction of the words complained of together with a suitable apology. The publisher should also notify distributors of the correction made. In practice the publisher often went further and offered to withdraw the text in part or totally and make an *ex gratia* payment to the plaintiff. If an offer of amends is rejected the defendant may use such rejection by the plaintiff as a defence in court. Section 4 has now been repealed by ss.2-4 of the Defamation Act 1996, which makes clear that an offer must mean an offer to make and publish a suitable correction and apology and to pay compensation

It has been a rule that special (actual) damage in slander not actionable *per se* is too remote if it is a result not of the original slander but merely of other people's repetition. This principle appeared to be established in 1830 in *Ward* v. *Weeks*. Thus a plaintiff might have no grounds for action if, for example, he attempts to show that business profits have declined as a result of repetition of an ordinary slander, unless there is authorised repetition. But nowadays a republisher may have to show his republication is fair and accurate – *Brent Walker Group plc* v. *Time Out Ltd* (1991), whilst a professional critic is never in the same position as the man on the Clapham omnibus – *McQuire* v. *Western Morning News* (1903). Moreover, in *Slipper* v. *BBC* (1991) it was held that *Ward* v. *Weeks* was not authority for the proposition that there was a rule of law to the effect that there was no liability on the part of the original publisher of a libel in respect of its republication unless the republication was authorised by that original publisher. The law relating to republication in defamation cases was but an example of the rules of *novus actus interveniens* in all cases of tort or, where applicable, breaches of contract where that issue arose.

In *Slipper* v. *BBC*, the plaintiff was a senior police officer who had been unsuccessful in trying to extradite one of the Great Train Robbers from Brazil. A film of his attempts was shown on national television and reviews appeared in the press. The plaintiff claimed the reviews of the film repeated libels in the film itself, namely it portrayed him as an incompetent police officer and buffoon. Was the repetition a *novus actus*, was the damage too remote? The Court of Appeal refused to strike out the plaintiff's claim.

Lastly, note should also be made of the proposals put forward in 1975 to reform the law of defamation. The Committee on Defamation suggested, *inter alia*, that the laws of libel and slander should be merged, that the defence of justification should be changed to that of *truth* and fair comment to simply *comment*. But as indicated earlier, it is the more recent 1992 Neill reforms which took precedence in 1996.

7.3   Misrepresentation

'Misrepresentation' is a convenient generic term to apply to a bundle of related torts. Some of these torts are economic in nature, but the full range of economic torts is not covered in this particular work. The torts in question are deceit, negligent misstatement or misrepresentation, malicious or injurious falsehood and passing off; the last mentioned is occasionally seen as a branch of malicious falsehood.

Deceit (or civil fraud) is the deliberate or reckless misrepresentation of *fact* by word or action to another. The defendant does not care whether that statement is true or false; in all probability he knows it to be false. The plaintiff has relied upon that misrepresentation which has *not* necessarily been communicated to a third party. Actual damage must result in some form. Contributory negligence is not a defence in deceit.

Negligent misstatement may appear to be structurally similar to deceit but here the misrepresentation is carelessly but innocently made, as opposed to recklessly or fraudulently. As in deceit the plaintiff must have relied upon the representation and damage must have resulted.

In contrast defamation is more concerned with a person's reputation and is tied up with *opinion* as much as fact. Defamation might cause economic harm, but not necessarily so, for libel and certain forms of slander are actionable *per se*. In all cases the words complained of must have been communicated to a third party.

In malicious falsehood for an action to succeed there must again be a misstatement of fact; the misstatement, unlike deceit, must be made not just deliberately or recklessly but maliciously. The statement must cause, or be calculated to cause, actual damage. Here the statement is communicated to a third party, but usually with the intention of harming the plaintiff's commercial or economic standing (it is essentially an economic tort), rather than his personal reputation as in defamation proper.

DECEIT

If a plaintiff sues for deceit he must show that he relied on a misrepresentation of fact that was made by the defendant deliberately or recklessly. Such a misrepresentation may be transmitted to the plaintiff through a third party; indeed the plaintiff may simply be one of a whole group of people, possibly the entire public, to whom the false representation has been conveyed. On the other hand it is a defence to show that it was not intended that the statement should either come to the plaintiff's attention or be acted upon, as illustrated by *Peek* v. *Gurney* (1873) which involved the purchase of shares from an existing shareholder in a company part of whose prospectus had been false. Conversely, the plaintiff must show that he has acted upon that statement to his detriment and that the defendant knew, or ought to have known, he would do so. Thus, if it is known that the plaintiff is likely to act upon the representation, the defendant will be presumed to have intended the plaintiff should so act. In *Langridge* v. *Levy* (1837) the father of the plaintiff purchased a gun deceitfully claimed by the defendant to be sound. The plaintiff was subsequently injured when the barrel burst and the court held the defendant liable for deceit. The misrepresentation, however, must be a false statement – mere broken promises will not suffice. And honestly held opinion is not deceit. Injury may encompass nervous shock as well as pecuniary loss (*Wilkinson* v. *Downton* (1897)).

Normally, silence or inaction cannot amount to deceit. In other words if the plaintiff has been labouring under a misconception and no-one enlightens him, that may be just plain bad luck. But not always so, for partial non-disclosure may indeed give rise to an action: a statement that leaves certain things unsaid might lead the plaintiff, and therefore the defendant, into dangerous waters. *Suppressio veri* may amount to *suggestio falsi*, as established in *Arkwright* v. *Newbold* (1881). There is also a duty to correct false statements that were initially true. A false statement which subsequently becomes true is not, of course, actionable, providing the plaintiff has relied on the statement after it has become true. Such a responsibility – to tell the whole story – frequently arises out of contract. Further, if there exists a fiduciary relationship (this is examined below, under negligent misstatement) the person in a position of trust would probably be under a duty to advise the 'dependant' accordingly, and not to allow silence to lead the other into a course of action detrimental to him. In any case, equity has come to the rescue here, or at least partially so. This was recognised in the case of *Nocton* v. *Lord Ashburton* (1914) (a solicitor gave misleading advice). The case established that where a fiduciary relationship existed, or by implication other special circumstances, then the defendant could be liable for 'constructive fraud', a non-tortious civil wrong in equity, in which case the plaintiff would receive an indemnity (rather than damages) for losses hitherto incurred. In addition, the 'dependant' does not have to be a firm client, he may be a potential customer and no more; yet a fiduciary relationship can still exist, as illustrated by *Woods* v. *Martins Bank Ltd* (1959).

It should also be mentioned here that it is not a sufficient defence to argue that the plaintiff acted so carelessly that he allowed himself to be deceived. This point was underlined by the case of *Central Railway of Venezuela* v. *Kisch* (1867); here the plaintiff could have discovered the fraud in a company's prospectus had he gone to their head office to inspect other documents to which the prospectus referred. But he was under no duty to do so, and it would not be reasonable to expect most people to undertake that amount of checking-up.

How the tort developed

The tort of deceit owes its origins to the case of *Pasley* v. *Freeman* in 1789, but it was firmly established by that of *Derry* v. *Peek* a century later. Here the directors of a tramway company wrongly issued a prospectus which indicated that they had parliamentary approval to run steam-driven trams in Plymouth (they were anticipating approval). The key point was that Parliament had made its consent subject to the sanction of the Board of Trade. The directors believed this to be a mere formality; the Board of Trade did not issue its consent and as a result the plaintiff lost money. Nonetheless the Lords (reversing the Court of Appeal) did not allow the action to succeed, for the defendants had only been careless – they had not wilfully or recklessly made a false statement. The case established that deceit, by and large, means the conscious making of a false statement, in contrast to a simply careless or negligent statement.

But there are certain exceptions to that rule; mere carelessness may amount to deceit. Firstly, there may exist a fiduciary relationship as already outlined above. Secondly, there may be a contractual obligation between the parties concerned, sometimes express as in insurance proposals, but frequently only implied, which covers the duties of making careful statements. This contractual obligation, however, will only affect the contracting parties, not third persons. Thirdly, an action will still lie when a structure, possibly a building, is represented to be safe but in fact it results in physical harm. Strictly, however, liability here will fall under the head of liability for chattels (goods) or occupier's liability. Fourthly, Parliament may impose a duty that in certain situations accurate information must be given. The result of *Derry* v. *Peek* was that the Directors' Liability Act 1890 was passed which covered negligent statements in company prospectuses (this is now part of the Companies Act 1985).

Fifthly, there is the problem of a principal's liability for the misrepresentation of the agent. The general rule appears to be that the principal, although innocent, may be vicariously liable for the wilfully false representations of the agent. One leading case here is that of *London County Freehold and Leasehold Properties Ltd* v. *Berkeley Property and Investment Co. Ltd* (1936). Clearly, the principal will be liable if he wilfully uses an innocent agent, *Ludgater* v. *Love* (1881), but there has been some difficulty in respect of the situation where an agent innocently makes a false representation and the principal is in a position to correct that statement but has no reason to believe that the agent will act in that way. The logic appears to point for no liability on the part of either principal or agent but the apparently conflicting arguments in the cases of *Gordon Hill Trust Ltd* v. *Segall* (1941) and *Armstrong* v. *Strain* (1952) muddied the waters. Of course, principal and agent may be jointly liable for a falsity – each knew what the other was doing.

Sixthly, under equity the principle of estoppel may operate. This means that liability would still be imposed where A. has acted to his detriment on the false but innocently made statement of B. who had given that representation on the strength of the forgery or fraud of C. But it must be stressed that this argument must be treated with circumspection.

Seventhly, under the Misrepresentation Act 1967 it is possible to sue for damages if a misrepresentation, albeit innocently made, induces the plaintiff to enter a contract and suffer loss as a result – as if, in other words, that misrepresentation had been made fraudulently. This Act is discussed in more detail under negligent misstatement below and in the next chapter.

Finally, two other points should be noted. First, under the Statute of Frauds Amendment Act 1828 (Lord Tenterden's Act) there can be no action in respect of a wilfully false statement that is made by A. to B. in respect of the creditworthiness of C., unless that statement is made in writing by the defendant. In *UBAF Ltd* v. *European American Banking Corporation* (1984) the Court of Appeal ruled that where an agent is authorised to sign on behalf of a company in the conduct of its business, his signature in the normal course of his duties is the company's signature for the purpose of an action against it for fraudulent misrepresentation as to the creditworthiness of another. In this instance credit was secured in respect of two Panamanian companies who later defaulted. Credit may include ability, trade and character; the objective must be to obtain for C. credit, money, goods or the like. The Act only applies to fraudulent representations, not to negligent misstatement. Secondly, there is the problem of ambiguity, for if the defendant meant a statement to be understood differently from the interpretation of the plaintiff, and that second meaning is a reasonable meaning, then the action will probably fail.

NEGLIGENT MISSTATEMENT

Subject to the exceptions listed above, *Derry* v. *Peek* appeared to establish that at common law innocent misrepresentations were not actionable; the position could be changed only by parliamentary intervention. Thus the tort of negligent misstatement is a comparatively new one. It was established by the case of *Hedley Byrne and Co. Ltd* v. *Heller and Partners Ltd* (1964) in the early 1960s. In this case HB were advertising agents who wanted to make sure that a client (Easipower Ltd) was creditworthy. E.'s bankers, H.P., gave a satisfactory reference to H.B.'s bankers, the National Provincial Bank, although the statement was accompanied by a disclaimer of responsibility. As a result of relying upon the statement H.B. suffered loss of approximately £17,000. H.B. could not sue under the general principles of negligence since they did not cover purely economic (pecuniary) loss resulting from careless *statements*, although just before *Hedley Byrne*, in *Clayton* v. *Woodman & Son (Builders) Ltd* (1962), it was firmly established that physical damage arising from a negligent misstatement was actionable. Indeed, in negligence proper economic loss arising from physical harm caused by careless *actions* has also been questioned in the courts: in 1966 in *Weller and Co.* v. *Foot and Mouth Disease Research Institute* cattle auctioneers lost business because of an escaped virus, but their claim was refused because it would have opened the floodgates to many other claims. But in *SCM (United Kingdom) Ltd* v. *W. J. Whittall and Son Ltd* (1971) and *Spartan Steel and Alloys Ltd* v. *Martin and Co. (Contractors) Ltd* (1973) – both cases were concerned with the careless cutting of an electric power cable – economic loss, including the appropriate loss of profit, was clearly allowed. This matter is considered more fully below, under the tort of negligence.

Nor could Hedley Byrne sue under deceit, since, as we have already seen, that usually demands the presence of fraudulent intentions. Now, however, in the most important extension of the laws of negligence since *Donoghue* v. *Stevenson* (where the manufacturer rather than the retailer of a faulty bottle of ginger pop was held liable) it was held that where a 'special relationship' exists between the parties concerned, where professional skills and advice are involved, then a liability does occur for statements made carelessly, albeit innocently. *Hedley Byrne* revived the much older case of *Cann* v. *Willson* (1888) which had been subsequently over-ruled. There a property on which a loan was to be raised had been carelessly over-valued. *Hedley Byrne* also reaffirmed that where a fiduciary relationship exists liability may well arise from careless statements, as we have already seen under deceit. Thus *Hedley Byrne*, it could be argued, was essentially an extension of the fiduciary relationship principle. But what exactly constitutes a 'special relationship' and how does it differ from a 'fiduciary relationship'? The answers to both these questions are by no means clear. A fiduciary relationship means that one person is in a position of dependence upon another, he trusts that person, he has to rely upon him and such a relationship usually involves the person in a superior position having control or an influence over the other's money, property or proprietorial interests. A 'special relationship' widens the scope of responsibility, for it appears to cover all professional situations, so-called. In practice, however, there may be little difference between 'special' and 'fiduciary'. A person who possesses a particular skill will clearly have his advice heeded by those who do not have that skill, this was the basis of the *Hedley Byrne* judgment. So a doctor advising a patient, an accountant or valuer advising a client, a teacher advising a student, an engineer advising a customer would all appear to be covered by the *Hedley Byrne* principle: the professional list is almost endless. In *Gold* v. *Haringey Health Authority* (1987) a claim for negligent misrepresentation by a consultant obstetrician failed since the statement that the sterilisation operation was 'irreversible' could not reasonably be construed as a guarantee of success.

In *Al Saudi Banque* v. *Clark Pixley* (1990) the court held that the auditors of a company owed no duty of care to banks who relied on the company's published accounts. But in *Punjab National Bank* v. *de Boinville* (1992) the Court of Appeal held that under *Caparo*, which is noted below, insurance brokers did owe a duty of care not just to their client but to the plaintiff bank who, to the brokers's knowledge, intended to become an assignee of the insurance policy which the brokers had been instructed to place; there was clear proximity – a close financial interest. *McNaughton James Papers Group Ltd* v. *Hicks Anderson & Co.* (1991) concerned a firm of accountants which prepared, at short notice, draft accounts of their client company for the company's chairman; it owed no duty of care to a bidder who took the company over after having inspected those accounts. Where, therefore, the accounts were found to contain errors the accountants were not liable in negligence to the bidder. In *Morgan Crucible plc* v. *Hill Samuel Bank Ltd* (1991) it was held that if the directors and financial advisers of the target company made express representations to a known bidder, then they owed a duty of care not to be negligent.

In *Sidaway* v. *The Board of Governors of the Bethlem Royal Hospital and the Maudsley Hospital* (1985) it was held that a fiduciary relationship did not exist where a neuro-surgeon had advised his patient to the best of his ability in respect of the risk of spinal injury in an operation for back pain. Lord Justice Browne-Wilkinson said:

> **There is no ground for extending the limited doctrine of informed consent outside the field of property rights in which it is established. The doctrine is in each case based on the principle that the person said to be in a fiduciary position may have abused his position of trust to make a personal profit for himself. That principle has no application to the present type of case where there is no suggestion that the doctor is abusing this position for the purpose of making a personal profit.**

The House of Lords upheld the Court of Appeal's verdict. Lord Templeman said: 'I do not subscribe to the theory that the patient is entitled to know everything nor to the theory that the doctor is entitled to decide everything'. Notwithstanding responsible medical opinion, a patient's right to decide whether to consent to the treatment was so obvious that no prudent medical man could fail to warn of the risk save in emergency or some other sound clinical reason for non-disclosure. Lord Scarman was rather more sympathetic towards the American practice of 'informed consent', but the speeches of their Lordships overall leave the medical profession in something of an uncertain position. In effect a doctor who fails to warn his patient of a 10 per cent (or more) risk of serious personal injury will be in trouble.

Moreover, the law does not always distinguish between different competencies within the same profession. In *Wilsher* v. *Essex Area Health Authority* (1988) the law required, said the Court of Appeal, of the junior hospital the same standard of care as was expected of his more senior colleagues – inexperience could not be a defence to an action for medical negligence. Here a premature baby was born nearly blind. So, what is said or done by a junior must be taken as to represent the words or actions of a superior. But a contrasting position may be offered in *Luxmoore-May* v. *Messenger May Baverstock (A Firm)* (1990). Here, two small paintings were handed over for examination at Christie's and returned to the defendants' representative after a few minutes, nothing favourable being said about them. At the defendants' auction they were sold for £840; they subsequently sold at Sotheby's for £88,000. The trial judge found for the plaintiffs on the grounds that no competent auctioneers, exercising proper skill and care, would have valued the paintings as the defendants did. But the Court of Appeal disagreed; the defendants and their fine arts consultant were not negligent in failing to spot the paintings' 'Stubbs' potential. The trial judge demanded too high a standard of skill on the part of the defendants and on the part of their fine arts consultant since the professional position of a provincial auctioneer is analogous to that of a general medical practitioner rather than to that of a specialist.

The role of the professional person

Does the professional person have to be, however, in the business of giving advice or information? In a Privy Council case, *Mutual Life and Citizens' Assurance* v.

Evatt (1971) the majority took that view, which appeared to narrow the effect of *Hedley Byrne*. But a few years later *Esso Petroleum Co. Ltd* v. *Mardon* (1976) appeared to give *Hedley Byrne* as broad an interpretation as possible. At the present time anyone holding himself out to possess specialist skill or information may be liable for a negligent misstatement made to another who it is realised will rely on the information given (that might include known third parties). Moreover, where the defendant himself has some financial interest, direct or indirect, in the matter concerned, then liability will be even more difficult to avoid. On the other hand, an express disclaimer by the defendant will weaken the plaintiff's case, which is why *Hedley Byrne* still failed in their action; nor will the courts look favourably on claims concerning advice casually solicited – for example, on a train journey or at a social gathering, unless the defendant was quite willing to have his advice relied upon. In a contractual situation a disclaimer may well be prohibited under the provisions of ss.2(1), 3, 11 and 13 of the Unfair Contract Terms Act 1977. Similarly, under ss.2(2), 11 and 13 of the Act, where non-contractual notices are concerned, then the test under the Act applies when liability arose or but for notice would have arisen, meaning that the business representor will always be liable for death or personal injury, and for other losses if the reasonableness test is satisfied. So, the salient features of successful, if at times confusing, cases after *Hedley Byrne* were that the defendant giving the advice or information was fully aware of the nature of the transaction which the plaintiff contemplated, knew that the advice would be communicated to the plaintiff, and knew that he would rely on it when deciding whether to go ahead with the transaction.

Reliance on the accuracy of the statement is the key factor it was stated in *Caparo Industries plc* v. *Dickman* (1990). The House of Lords ruled that shareholders who, relying on negligently prepared accounts, purchased shares and suffered, had no claim in negligence against the auditors. This applied to both existing shareholders and potential investors. Caparo had begun to purchase shares in Fidelity plc, manufacturers of electrical equipment; the appellants were the accountants, Touche Ross and Co. Fidelity's audited accounts had suggested the company had made a profit of £1.3 million, whereas in fact it had made a loss of £400,000. The Law Lords preferred a narrow interpretation to the broader principles of *Anns* (1977) and found unhelpful concepts such as 'relationships equivalent to contract' and even 'proximity'. Lord Bridge said that the law approached a duty of care to avoid injury to the person or property differently from a duty of care to avoid causing purely economic loss. The situation was entirely different where a statement was put into more or less general circulation and might foreseeably be relied on by strangers to the maker of the statement for a variety of purposes which the maker had no reason to anticipate, hence the essential ingredient of 'proximity'. The creation of an unlimited duty would be for Parliament, not the courts, to take.

Lord Oliver was of the opinion that there was no reason in policy or principle why any special relationship should be held to arise simply because the company was susceptible to predators in the market. 'I think it has to be recognised that to search for any single formula which will serve as a general test of liability is to pursue a 'will-o-the-wisp'.' Lord Bridge added:

> While recognising ... the importance of the underlying general princi-
> ples common to the whole field of negligence, I think the law has now
> moved in the direction of attaching greater significance to the more
> traditional categorisation of distinct and recognisable situations as
> guides to the existence, the scope and the limits of the varied duties of
> care which the law imposes. What can be deduced from the *Hedley
> Byrne* case, therefore, is that the necessary relationship between the
> maker of the statement or giver of advice (the adviser) and the recipi-
> ent who acts in reliance upon it (the advisee) may typically be held to
> exist where (1) the advice is required for a purpose, whether particu-
> larly specified or generally described, which is made known, either
> actually or inferentially, to the adviser at the time when the advice is
> given; (2) the adviser knows, either actually or inferentially, that his
> advice will be communicated to the advisee, either specifically or as a
> member of an ascertainable class, in order that it should be used by
> the advisee for that purpose; (3) it is known either actually or inferen-
> tially, that the advice so communicated is likely to be acted upon by
> the advisee for that purpose without independent inquiry, and (4) it is
> so acted upon by the advisee to his detriment. That is not, of course,
> to suggest that these conditions are either conclusive or exclusive, but
> merely that the actual decision in the case does not warrant any
> broader propositions.

Caparo Industries v. *Dickman* was applied in *Galoo Ltd* v. *Bright Grahame Murray* (1995).

And what of the personnel of the law itself? Judges in the exercise of their judicial office are given complete immunity, so too are arbitrators, members of tribunals and the like (*Sutcliffe* v. *Thackrah* 1974 and *Arenson* v. *Casson, Beckman, Rutley and Co.* (1977)). Witnesses, jurors and advocates also enjoy immunity in respect of things said during judicial proceedings. A barrister cannot be sued for breach of contract, for his fees have long been regarded as an honorarium, nor can he be sued in negligence in respect of conduct during a trial (*Rondel* v. *Worsley*) but he may be sued for pre-trial work which is not intimately bound up with the case itself (*Saif Ali* v. *Sydney Mitchell* (1980)). It was thought until recently that a solici-tor could be sued only in contract, not in tort. But in *Ross* v. *Caunters* (1980) (the action concerned the negligent preparation of a will) the judge said:

> There is no longer any rule that a solicitor who is negligent in profes-
> sional work can be liable only to a client in contract; he may be liable
> both to his client and to others for the tort of negligence. The basis of
> the solicitor's liability to others is either an extension of the *Hedley
> Byrne* principle or, more probably, a direct application of the principle
> of *Donoghue* v. *Stevenson*.

The possibility of liability to third parties where a solicitor owes such a duty of care was underlined in *Al-Kandari* v. *J Brown & Co.* (1988), where the plaintiff's husband removed their two children to Kuwait. The defendant firm of solicitors, on the plaintiff's husband's request, had instructed agents in London to take his passport to the Kuwaiti Embassy to have his children's names removed. The agents were told that the passport was not to leave their possession; it did and the husband forcibly removed the children from the jurisdiction. The Court of Appeal agreed with the trial judge in that he had decided that a duty of care was owed by the defendants to the plaintiff and that it had been breached, but it overruled him on the question of remoteness of damage: the Court of Appeal held that the damage caused was a natural and probable consequence of the breach. In *White* v. *Jones* (1995) the Court of Appeal said that a solicitor who through inexcusable delay failed to draw up a will before the testator's death was liable in negligence to the disappointed prospective beneficiaries. Here the testator's two daughters were disinherited and claimed the financial loss from the solicitor. The Vice-Chancellor pointed out that the thrust of the speeches in both *Caparo* and *Murphy* was against any hard and fast boundary and held that there was a special relationship between a solicitor and an intended beneficiary which should attract a liability if the solicitor was negligent. The House of Lords, by a bare majority, upheld the decisions, although the speeches are not entirely easy to follow. Lord Browne-Wilkinson was prepared to extend the category of special relationship (*Hedley Byrne*) and fiduciary duties (*Nocton* v. *Lord Ashburton*), in the latter it not being necessary to prove foreseeable reliance by the plaintiff before a claim in negligence might be allowed.

Where a solicitor acts as an advocate in court then it appears from *Rondel* that he enjoys the same immunity from liability in contract and negligence as a barrister. But in view of the fact that it is the solicitor who is the 'front line' person, and that it is he who engages the barrister, his immunity in respect of pre-trial work is probably less than that of the barrister (*Somasundram* v. *M Julius Melchior & Co* (1989)). In any case s.62(1) of the Courts and Legal Services Act 1990 provides that advocates other than barristers enjoy the same immunity from liability in negligence as barristers, whilst s.62(2) says that such acts or omissions accorded immunity in negligence shall not give rise to an action for breach of contract.

The Court of Appeal in *First National Commercial Bank* v. *Loxleys* (1996) considered further the effect of disclaimers in the context of *Hedley Byrne* following the House of Lords' decision in *Henderson* v. *Merrett Syndicates* (1994). In *Goodwill* v. *British Pregnancy Advisory Service* (1996) where M. underwent a vasectomy operation arranged by the defendants and later made the plaintiff pregnant, the defendants owed no Hedley Byrne type duty of care to the plaintiff, and moreover her own doctor had warned her of the very slight chance of pregnancy notwithstanding M.'s operation.

In *Possfund Custodian Trustee Ltd* v. *Diamond* (1996) subsequent purchasers as well as original purchasers could be covered by the terms of a prospectus. And where a local council gave the wrong information to the owner of premises, that alterations had to be carried out under the Food Safety Act 1990, then the council was liable under Hedley Byrne for the wasted expenditure (*Welton* v. *North Cornwall District Council* (1996)). In *Allied Maples Group Ltd* v. *Simmons and Simmons* (1995), which concerned property development, the plaintiffs brought an action against the defendant solicitors; the plaintiff could recover if it can be shown under the causation/'but for' test that he had a substantial as opposed to speculative chance of acquiring a benefit. *Hedley Byrne* was again considered, by the House of Lords in *South Australia Asset Management Corporation* v. *York Montague Ltd* (1996), where it was held that there was no liability for a fall in the property market in respect of negligent valuation.

Misrepresentation Act 1967

A further couple of points must be noted. Firstly, a few years after *Hedley Byrne* came the Misrepresentation Act 1967. This has an important bearing both upon this tort and upon the law of contract. If a person enters into a contract as a result of a misrepresentation and suffers harm as a result, then under the Act he will be entitled to damages as if the representation had been made deceitfully (fraudulently). The burden of proof shifts to the defendant: it is up to him to show that the representation was reasonable and that he honestly believed in it. The plaintiff may also be allowed to rescind (avoid) the contract. If, however, the misstatement was both innocent and non-negligent then the aggrieved person may be entitled to rescission with equitable indemnification (indemnity) – that is he can bring contractual obligations to an end and obtain out-of-pocket expenses, but cannot be awarded damages for the general harm caused in relying upon the representation or for the monies he would have expected to receive under the terms of the contract. (Rescission is an established remedy in the law of contract.) The 1967 Act, though, does allow the court to award damages as an alternative to rescission, in other words the contract continues, as far as possible.

If the misstatement is transmitted to a third party, from A. to C. through B., can that third person sue the original representor? For instance, can an insurance company sue a doctor in respect of a negligent misstatement made to a patient who subsequently seeks life assurance on the basis of that representation? The answer is not totally clear; since *Hedley Byrne* there has been no case clearly deciding this point alone. In *Yianni* v. *Edwin Evans & Sons* (1981) the court held that a duty was owed to third parties. In this case the plaintiffs bought a £15,000 house with an advance from the Halifax Building Society. The survey carried out by the defendants on behalf of the society suggested the property was sound. Nine months later subsidence occurred which cost £18,000 to repair. A similar issue arose in *Smith* concerning a property at the 'lower end' of the market, which turned out to have dangerous chimneys; a disclaimer by the surveyor did not, said the Court of Appeal, satisfy the test of reasonableness under s.11(3) of the Unfair Contract Terms Act 1977. But the Court of Appeal took a contrary view in the similar case of *Harris* which concerned a purchase of a house that was found to be settling.

In the conjoined appeals to the House of Lords, *Smith* v. *Eric Bush (a firm)* and *Harris* v. *Wyre Forest District Council* (1989), Lord Griffiths said: 'the existence of the common law duty to take reasonable care . . . is to be judged by considering whether it would exist 'but for' the notice excluding liability'. Lord Griffiths acknowledged that the same approach was being taken as in *Phillips Products* v. *Hyland*. *Smith* and *Harris* were referred to in respect of s.13 of the Unfair Contract Terms Act 1977 in *Johnstone* v. *Bloomsbury Health Authority* (1991); with regard to statements made 'without responsibility', s.13 provides that s.2 of the 1977 Act also prevents 'excluding or restricting liability by reference to terms and notices which exclude or restrict the relevant obligation or duty', although, of course, such a disclaimer may be reasonable in all the circumstances and therefore still effective. Here a junior hospital doctor had contracted to work 40 hours a week but also to be available for up to a further 48 hours a week on average, the validity of which he sought to challenge.

In *Smith/Harris*, in respect of the matter of reasonableness it would appear the defendants did not satisfy their Lordships, bearing in mind the great expense of the alternative (a full structural survey) and the fairly elementary inspection which is all that can reasonably be expected on a basic building society valuation, which might nonetheless reveal disturbing features of the property. Lord Griffiths referred to the availability of insurance to distribute the risk but both he and Lord Templeman indicated that they were dissatisfied with the much higher fees charged for the middle-range 'valuation with responsibility', considering the degree of risk of liability. But the emphasis in these cases was on 'typical house purchases', dwellings 'of modest value' or ones 'at the lower end of the market', and that different considerations applied to commercial or industrial property or even 'very expensive houses', for in those cases Lord Griffiths' view was that it might be reasonable to restrict liability to the level of insurance cover or even to exclude it altogether and Lord Jauncey doubted whether there would be sufficient indication of reliance upon the mortgagee's surveyor by the purchaser.

Essentially, in *Smith/Harris* the House of Lords asked whether the parties were of equal bargaining power, whether it was practicable to obtain advice from an alternative source, how difficult was the task for which liability was being excluded (ie visual inspections), what were the practical consequences of a decision on the question of reasonableness, ie was it easier for the valuers than the purchasers to bear the burden? It did not matter whether the valuer was employed by a building society, a local authority or an independent firm, or acted on his own account. But the liability was only owed to the purchaser of the house and not to subsequent purchasers.

In *Roberts* v. *J Hampson & Co.* (1989) the plaintiffs were awarded £5,000 damages (£3,500 for the difference in valuation and £1,500 for disturbance) against a building society surveyor who had found a certain amount of dampness and rot but had failed to notice the full extent, notwithstanding that the plaintiffs had chosen the most limited survey, that is what was essentially a valuation for the building society.

Where physical harm results a duty is owed to the third party, but the position is not so certain in respect of purely economic loss. If, though, it is clear that known third parties will rely on the statement then liability will be incurred under *Hedley Byrne*, but most third parties do not enjoy close relationships with the party making the statement (the representor); in the *Hedley Byrne* case, as has been seen, the misstatement was actually made to Hedley Byrne's bankers, the National Provincial, who then passed it on to their clients. All that can be said is that liability will probably occur if the misstatement is the true source of the economic loss caused and if there is reasonable proximity in the relationship between A. and C.

In *Chaudhry* v. *Prabhakar* the Court of Appeal applied the *Hedley Byrne* principles. In this 1988 case the plaintiff was awarded £5,526 damages plus interest in respect of a worthless car she had bought (the car had been involved in a serious accident) on the first defendant's advice from the second defendant, Mr Singh Jandoo, trading as Jandoo Autocrafts. The plaintiff was a 26 year-old accountant who knew nothing about the mechanical side of cars.

Ewan McKendrick has noted:

> **It is no easy task to discern the limits of *Hedley Byrne*. Is it the case that there is one rule for those who give advice (consulting engineers and architects) but another rule for those who build, with the liability of the former being more extensive than the liability of the latter? If *Pirelli* is now a *Hedley Byrne* case then it would appear that this is indeed the case. *Murphy* tells us that the second purchaser has no cause of action against the local authority building inspector and *D & F Estates* informs us that he has no cause of action in tort against the builder. But, according to the House of Lords in *Smith* v. *Eric S Bush*, the second purchaser may have a cause of action against the surveyor, at least where the house is a 'modest' one. But why is it that the purchaser only has a claim at common law against the surveyor employed by the building society? The House of Lords in both *Anns* v. *Merton London Borough Council* and *Murphy* was at pains to emphasise that the liability of the local authority could not be greater than the liability of the builder, whose primary fault it was. If this is so, why is the liability of the surveyor at common law greater than the liability of the builder (even to the extent that the surveyor is prevented by the operation of s.2(2) of the Unfair Contract Terms Act 1977 from excluding liability towards the mortgagor)?**
>
> **Further, why is a building society surveyor liable when a local authority inspector is not? What is the difference between the two? The answer of the House of Lords would appear to be that there is no relationship of proximity between a local authority inspector and a house owner, while there is such a relationship between a surveyor and a mortgagor. Is the relationship between the house owner and the building inspector . . . not as proximate as the relationship between the plaintiff and the surveyor in *Smith* v. *Eric Bush*? If so, should the local authority inspector not be liable to the house owner on ordinary *Hedley Byrne* principles?**
>
> **At least thus far, their Lordships have not shown any inclination to reconsider *Hedley Byrne*, although their approach to it may be said to**

be inconsistent. On the one hand, *Caparo Industries plc* v. *Dickman* evidences a desire to cut back on the scope of *Hedley Byrne*, whereas the inclusion of *Pirelli* and *Junior Books Ltd* v. *Veitchi Co. Ltd* within its province increases its scope. So, at least for now, *Hedley Byrne* survives. The question which must be posed is: why does it continue to survive?

(*Pirelli* and *Junior Books* are considered under section 8.7.)

SLANDER OF TITLE (MALICIOUS FALSEHOOD)

Injurious falsehood (or malicious falsehood as the Defamation Act 1952 prefers) consists of a misrepresentation made about the plaintiff to others which causes, or is calculated to cause, economic loss. The statement has to be made with malice, that is with some dishonest or improper motive. Common law has always required that it is necessary to prove actual damage, but the 1952 Act provides if the words are calculated to cause pecuniary loss and are published in writing or some other permanent form then actual damage does not have to be proved; even writing is not a requirement if the statement relates to the plaintiff's profession, office or trade.

Slander of title and slander of goods are the most common forms of malicious falsehood; the former consists of a statement which wrongly challenges the plaintiff's title to immovable property. Slander of goods is a statement which questions the plaintiff's right to personal, moveable property or certain intangibles like trade marks and copyright. 'Mere puffs' – claims made during the course of normal commercial rivalry (such as advertising) – are not usually actionable. In *Greers Ltd* v. *Pearman and Corder Ltd* (1922) the defendants were shown to have acted maliciously since they had alleged that the plaintiffs had used their trade mark for chocolates and yet had given up exclusive use of the words some time before. The dispute may also be about a trade name, as in the leading case of *Royal Baking Powder Co.* v. *Wright, Crossley & Co.* (1900).

It is not precisely clear, however, as to how far malice stretches beyond deliberate recklessness or falsity – the key factors in deceit or fraud. Obviously it is not the same as simple carelessness or innocent negligence. Recklessness – not caring whether the statement is true or false – may be borderline; knowledge of the falsity of a statement may suffice, but certainly a dishonest or improper motive – often spite – will constitute malice. Of course, as said earlier, one essential difference between deceit and malicious falsehood is that in the former the misstatement is usually communicated directly to the plaintiff; in the latter he has learned of it through others.

Damages may not always be an appropriate remedy; rather the court will prefer to grant an injunction, or simply a declaratory judgment as to who does have the rightful title.

The following two cases illustrate malicious falsehood in the broadest context. In *Ratcliffe* v. *Evans* (1892) the defendant was held liable for falsely and maliciously publishing a newspaper statement to the effect that the plaintiff had ceased trading (with the inevitable results). In *Grappelli* v. *Derek Block (Holdings) Ltd* (1981) the Court of Appeal distinguished between defamation and injurious falsehood. The defendants made up a spurious excuse that the plaintiff, an international musician, was 'seriously ill' and would probably never tour again, in order to avoid the responsibilities of cancelling concerts they had arranged without authority. To allege illness is not defamatory, but that did not eliminate the claim of injurious falsehood if loss could be proved. In *Joyce* v. *Sengupta* (1993) concerning a report in the *Today* newspaper about a maid to the Royal Family, the Court of Appeal said the fact that the statement was defamatory did not exclude a cause of action for malicious falsehood, although the law would ensure that a plaintiff did not recover damages twice over for the same loss.

PASSING OFF

Passing off is an economic or commercial tort. It is sometimes viewed as a form of injurious falsehood. Quite simply it means a wrong that is committed in order to mislead or confuse members of the public in respect of commodities or businesses. The imitation of trade names and trade marks is the most common occurrence. It is a well established tort and there have been a considerable number of cases before the courts this century. It should be noted here that under the Trade Marks Act 1938 (as amended by the Trade Marks (Amendment) Act 1984 and the Patents, Designs and Marks Act 1986) (together with the Trade Marks Act 1994) an action for passing off may still be brought even if the trade mark is not registered; patents are covered by the Patents Act 1977. The deliberate copying of another's work (as opposed to name imitation) was covered by the Copyright Act 1956 and the Design Copyright Act 1968. The problems caused by the copying of film on video gave rise to the Copyright Act 1956 (Amendment) Act 1982 and computer programs and their storage to the Copyright (Computer Software) Amendment Act 1985. The 1956, 1968, 1982 and 1985 Acts were consolidated under the Copyright, Designs and Patents Act 1988. Essentially infringing copyright is a variation of conversion. While an action for passing off may be successful, it does not follow that one brought under the 1988 Act will also be, given the same circumstances.

The tort is designed not only to protect the consumer but also to prevent unfair competition. In the celebrated case of *Bollinger* v. *Costa Brava Wine Co. Ltd* (1960) it was established that producers of champagne could not use that name if the wine came from outside the Champagne district in France. This case illustrated how internationally based the tort of passing off can be. In *Maxim's Ltd* v. *Dye* (1977) the famous restaurant in Paris successfully prevented one operating under the same name in Norfolk. In *White Hudson and Co. Ltd* v. *Asian Organisation Ltd* (1964) the Privy Council decided that similarly wrapped cough sweets in Singapore did amount to passing off since most people in Singapore were unable to distinguish between different English words on the front of the wrappers. In

My Kinda Bones Ltd (trading as Chicago Rib Shack) v. *Dr Pepper's Stove Co. Ltd (trading as Dr Pepper's Manhattan Rib Shack)* (1984) the plaintiffs argued that on account of advance publicity they had acquired goodwill with potential customers to entitle them to be granted an injunction restraining the defendants from also opening a restaurant in London with the phrase 'rib shack' in its title. A similar point, in respect of one or two identical words within different phrases, arose in the 'Egg Flip' case. The Lords took the view that the British-produced 'Keeling's Old English Advocaat' could be confused with the well-established Dutch drink Warnink's 'Advocaat' which has a different constitution – it was a matter of unfair trading (*Erven Warnink Besloten Vennootschap* v. *J Townend & Sons (Hull) Ltd* (1979)). Lord Diplock said that the essential elements in passing off were:

1 a misrepresentation,

2 made by a trader in the course of trade,

3 to prospective customers or ultimate consumers,

4 calculated to injure (as a reasonably foreseeable consequence) the business or goodwill of another trader, and

5 causing actual or probable damage.

If, though, the two parties are not in the same trade, then similar or identical names may not amount to passing off. For example, in *Granada Group Ltd* v. *Ford Motor Co. Ltd* (1972) the court took the view that the public was able to distinguish between an entertainment organisation and the brand name of a car. In *Cadbury-Schweppes Pty Ltd* v. *Pub Squash Co. Pty Ltd* (1981) it was held that Australian consumers were able to distinguish two lemon drinks 'Pub Squash' and 'Solo', although the 'get-up' and advertising campaigns were very similar. But in the leading case of *Parker-Knoll Ltd* v. *Knoll International Ltd* (1962) it was a different matter, for both companies were manufacturers of furniture.

Equally, in *Reckitt and Coleman Ltd* v. *Borden Inc* (1990) the sellers of Jif lemon juice were not entitled, the House of Lords held, to a monopoly in lemon-shaped plastic containers, but the rules of passing off did prevent a competitor from selling lemon juice in a similar container if the public bought his product in the belief that it was the 'Jif Lemon'. The competitor must take adequate steps to differentiate packaging so that the customer was not misled; the House of Lords in effect agreed with the Court of Appeal which had upheld injunctions against the second and third defendants in two *quia timet* actions for passing off.

Passing off is usually concerned with words, as illustrated by the cases so far mentioned. One word will suffice, but as the *White Hudson* and *Jif Lemon* cases demonstrated appearance and colour can also be equally important. This was again emphasised in cases involving medical tablets that were ordinary in colour (yellow and white) on the one hand (it was fair to copy such tablets) and distinctively coloured ones on the other *Roche Products Ltd* v. *Berk Pharmaceuticals* (1973) and *F L Hoffmann-La Roche and Co. AG* v. *DDSA Pharmaceuticals Ltd* (1972).

Passing off is in theory actionable *per se* – but potential damage ought to be proved. The remedy will usually therefore be that of an injunction in equity and nominal damages under common law. That assumes, however, the passing off was innocent, but if fraud (deceit) is manifestly present then rather more than nominal damages may be the outcome, and the onus of proving passing off becomes a much lighter one for the plaintiff. Rarely, actual (special) damage may be a direct consideration where it appears that more than more negligible confusion has occurred. Innocent confusion will more likely apply to everyday and straightforward language, fraudulent confusion to distinctive titles.

In the *Advocaat* case Lord Diplock and Lord Fraser had made it clear that if an action were to be based on mere fear of damage it was not enough that the fear should exist, it had to be based on substantial grounds. This point came to the fore in *Stringfellow* v. *McCain Foods (GB) Ltd* (1984) where the plaintiff ran a high-class London nightclub and the defendant had commenced marketing potato chips under the same name. Surprisingly, the Court of Appeal in *Harrods Ltd* v. *Harrodian School* (1996) felt the Harrodian School (on the site of Harrods former sports club) would not be confused with Harrods and therefore an action for passing off would not lie.

The use of a person's own name, even if it does lead to confusion will, however, not make for a good action in passing off. That may include stage or assumed names, as underlined by *Jay's Ltd* v. *Jacobi* (1933) where the defendant had long been known locally as 'Mrs Jay' and she was therefore not prevented from setting up in business as 'Jays'. (Jay's and Jays raise an interesting point – the small alteration of a name, say by the position of an apostrophe, designed to mislead, will be actionable and is known as 'garnishing'.)

Finally, there will always be instances of similar names which can amount only to sheer inconvenience: in *Day* v. *Brownrigg* (1878) the plaintiff was not successful against his next door neighbour who changed the name of his house also to read as 'Ashford Lodge'.

7.4   Abuse of legal procedures

FALSE IMPRISONMENT (WRONGFUL ARREST)

False imprisonment is the unlawful physical restraint of a person. False merely signifies 'wrong', that is without lawful excuse. Imprisonment is the prevention of free movement, but that does not necessarily mean the literal putting in prison. Examples of false imprisonment can be locking a class in its classroom after the time for dismissal; preventing someone from leaving his own house; or even putting up barricades in the street if this prevents a person from leaving the enclosed area. Wrongful arrest, strictly speaking therefore, is only one aspect of false imprisonment. Although as we saw earlier arrest itself does not have to involve physical contact or force, a person must be told he is under arrest. However, in general terms false imprisonment is frequently referred to as wrongful arrest.

The definition in the old *Termes de la Ley* is

> the restraint of a man's liberty whether it be in the open field, or in the stocks or cage in the street, or in a man's own house, as well as in the common gaol. And in all these places the party so restrained is said to be a prisoner, so long as he hath not his liberty freely to go at all times to all places whither he will, without bail or mainprize.

This definition was accepted by the Court of Appeal in *Meering* v. *Grahame – White Aviation Co. Ltd* (1920).

When a person has been so 'imprisoned' it does not matter that he was unaware of it at the time, the tort has still been committed. In *Meering*'s case Lord Justice Atkin said,

> It appears to me that a person could be imprisoned without his knowing it. I think a person can be imprisoned while he is asleep, while he is in a state of drunkenness, while he is unconscious and while he is a lunatic . . . Of course the damage might be diminished and would be affected by the question whether he was conscious of it or not.

The court's attitude probably arises from the fact that interference with personal liberty is considered a serious matter.

The length of imprisonment may be very short, but a tortious action will still have taken place; damages, however, may reflect the period of imprisonment. Where embarrassment or humiliation has been caused to the plaintiff, the court may award exemplary or aggravated damages, as will be seen in an example below. False imprisonment, derived as it is from trespass, is actionable *per se*.

Imprisonment is 'total'

An action will also only succeed if the imprisonment is total. If the plaintiff is afforded a means of escape he is under a duty to take it, but the escape route must be a reasonable one. For example, on the assumption that the plaintiff is not elderly and is physically fit a large open window at ground floor level would probably amount to a reasonable means of escape, but hardly one on the fifth floor. In *Bird* v. *Jones* (1845) the defendants enclosed part of the public footpath on Hammersmith Bridge for seating to watch a regatta on the river. The plaintiff insisted on using this part of the footpath and climbed into the enclosure. The defendants refused to let him through but told him he could go back into the carriageway and cross on the other side of the bridge if he wished. He declined to do so and remained in the enclosure for half an hour. The defendants were held not to have committed the tort of false imprisonment since the plaintiff had means of leaving.

Where a person enters premises under a contract in which there is a reasonable condition imposed upon his manner of leaving, it is not false imprisonment if the defendant refuses to allow him to leave unless he complies with the condition. In *Robinson* v. *Balmain Ferry Co. Ltd* (1910) the plaintiff paid for entry to the defendant's wharf in order to cross the river by one of their ferry boats. Since there was no ferry boat for the next 20 minutes, he decided to leave the wharf and was directed to the exit turnstile. There he refused to pay the exit charge and the defendant declined to let him leave the wharf unless he did pay. This was held not to be false imprisonment: 'There is no law requiring the defendants to make the exit from their premises gratuitous to people who come there upon a definite contract which involves their leaving the wharf by another way . . . ' The court regarded the charge for exit reasonable, but it is very doubtful this decision would stand up to legal scrutiny nowadays.

Nor will an action lie where the plaintiff has brought imprisonment upon himself, by trespassing, for instance, and falling into a quarry or pit. Similarly, in *Herd* v. *Weardale Steel Coal and Coke Co. Ltd* (1915) there was no false imprisonment; although a miner had decided to stop work the coal company refused to bring the pit cage up earlier than normal (*volenti non fit injuria*). Imprisonment, of course, does not have to take place in a building; in a variety of cases the courts have held that ships, cars and ski-lifts, for instance, can fulfil the purpose just as well. Indeed the geographical area may be large, as in the case of airport buildings (*Kuchenmeister* v. *Home Office* (1958)), although the scale of damages may reflect how restricted the area of confinement is.

Defences

The main defence is that the plaintiff has been lawfully arrested, and here it is important to emphasise (notwithstanding complex outcomes) that the rules for arrests are basically laid down by s.24 of the Police and Criminal Evidence Act 1984, formerly s.2 of the Criminal Law Act 1967, which distinguishes between arrestable and non-arrestable offences. Where an arrestable offence has been committed private citizens and police officers can arrest anyone they reasonably suspect of committing the offence. A Privy Council case made it clear that the arrestor must have reasonable suspicion at the time of the arrest, otherwise it would constitute false imprisonment (*Shaaban Bin Hussein* v. *Chong Fook Kam* (1970)). Police officers are protected from proceedings for false imprisonment even if they make an arrest when no actual arrestable offence has been committed, provided they can show they had *reasonable* grounds for suspecting that an offence had been committed.

In *Wershof* v. *Commissioner of Police for the Metropolis* (1978) the plaintiff was a young solicitor who was asked by his brother to go to the family jewellers' shop one Saturday afternoon. At the shop a police officer believed he had found a stolen ring which he wished to remove to the police station. The plaintiff told the police officer that he was a solicitor; he asked for a receipt for the ring but the police officer refused to give one. The solicitor in turn refused to part with the ring. As a result the officer, having arrested the solicitor for obstructing him in the course of his duties under the Police Act 1964, marched the plaintiff to a car and drove him to the police station. The plaintiff was locked in a room at the station, but after about an hour had passed a police sergeant charged him with obstruction and released him on bail.

At the subsequent hearing at the Magistrates' Court the plaintiff was acquitted of obstruction. The plaintiff brought an action against the police for (1) assault, (2) false imprisonment and (3) malicious prosecution. The Police Commissioner conceded that the arrest could not have been made under the terms of the Criminal Law Act 1967 since there was no question of an arrestable offence having been committed. However, at common law an arrest without a warrant is possible if it appears that a breach of the peace might ensue. The court found against the police and for the plaintiff on two counts. On the first count the police officer was guilty of an assault and on the second of false imprisonment. The court took the view that it had been unreasonable not to give a receipt for the ring as requested, that the arrest was wrong since there was no likelihood of a breach of the peace ensuing and therefore in the circumstances the force applied to effect the arrest had also been unnecessary, although not excessive.

However, on the third count, that of malicious prosecution, the court did not find for the plaintiff. It took the view that although the police did not have reasonable and probable cause for bringing the charge of obstruction, the officer concerned had not acted maliciously. He had believed that he was right to seize the ring just as the sergeant believed he was right to charge the plaintiff. Wershof was awarded a total of £1,000 damages.

In *White* v. *Metropolitan Police Commissioner* (1982) the two plaintiffs were each awarded £20,000 exemplary damages, £6,500 and £4,500 aggravated damages and £197 special damages each, for assault, false imprisonment and malicious prosecution. The facts were that at 12:45 am the police entered the plaintiffs' house. A search warrant had been issued to search the house for stolen goods, but the police made a mistake as to which house was being kept under observation. They therefore sought to justify their powers of entry under the Criminal Law Act 1967 (reasonable suspicion that a burglary or theft was taking place at the plaintiffs' house). Both plaintiffs were beaten over the head with truncheons and forcibly taken to the police station in their nightclothes (one was unconscious upon arrival). They were then falsely charged with assaulting police officers in the execution of their duty. Mr Justice Mars-Jones commented:

> The plaintiffs were prosecuted for offences which the relevant police witnesses knew they had not committed, knowing that their entry was illegal and that the violence to which they subjected the plaintiffs was either entirely uncalled for or grossly excessive. And the prosecutions were brought in order to escape the consequences of their own wrongful acts. That was a monstrously wicked thing to do.

Such malicious prosecution, the judge continued, also called for aggravated damages. For the distress, anxiety and damage to reputation which the prosecution caused, the plaintiffs would be awarded £2,500 each. In *Rookes* v. *Barnard* (1964) one of the categories for which exemplary damages could be awarded was cases of oppressive, arbitrary or unconstitutional acts by government servants. Police officers were servants of the government for this purpose and the case fell into the category where exemplary damages could and should be awarded, Mr Justice Mars-Jones added. Such shameful things called for punishment. Conduct of the kind in the present case could do gross damage to race relations, the judge concluded.

In *Hayward* v. *Commissioner of Police of the Metropolis* (1984) the plaintiff was awarded £1,750 for four and a half hours detention. The plaintiff, an antique dealer from Devon, was on a day trip to London, where he was unlawfully arrested. The judge said that the plaintiff was a typical, ordinary respectable Englishman. He was well dressed, articulate and not over assertive. There was nothing that would suggest that he was dishonest. But in *Mohammed-Holgate* v. *Duke* (1983), where the plaintiff was suspected of the burglary of jewellery, £1,000 was awarded by the Portsmouth County Court for six hours detention. However, the House of Lords held that a police constable in exercising his discretion under s.2 of the Criminal Law Act 1967 whether or not to arrest a person whom he reasonably suspected of having committed an arrestable offence, was entitled to take into consideration as a relevant matter the fact that the suspect was more likely to tell the truth if she were detained for questioning at a police station than if she were questioned at her own home. The lawfulness of the way in which the decision to arrest (or not) was exercised could not be questioned in court except under the principles of 'reasonableness' laid down by Lord Greene MR in *Associated Provincial Picture Houses Ltd* v. *Wednesbury Corporation* (1948), in respect either of proceedings for judicial review or of founding a cause of action at common law for damages for false imprisonment.

In *Davidson* v. *Chief Constable of North Wales* (1994) a store detective reasonably thought the plaintiff and her friend had left a branch of Woolworths without paying for a cassette; the police arrested the plaintiff for shop-lifting although this was not the case. The plaintiff's claim for wrongful arrest against the police failed since there had been reasonable action under s.24 of the Police and Criminal Evidence Act 1984. The basis of reasonable suspicion for a police officer arresting for an arrestable offence was seen in *O'Hara* v. *Chief Constable of the Royal Ulster Constabulary* (1996).

MALICIOUS PROSECUTION

When a plaintiff sues for malicious prosecution, he must show that he has been unsuccessfully prosecuted by the defendant, that the defendant had no reasonable cause to prosecute and that the defendant did so on account of malicious motives. The plaintiff must also prove special (actual) damage. This latter point is by no means easy to prove, and not surprisingly actions for malicious prosecution are few and far between, and successful actions are even rarer. 'Actual damage' might encompass the slight or social stigma that a person suffers as a result of being maliciously prosecuted. Moreover, deciding in this context who is the actual 'prosecutor' – when in most criminal matters the police act on the basis of assertions made and evidence received – is not necessarily a straightforward matter. No action for malicious prosecution will lie if, of course, a person is convicted, even if there is no right of appeal and even where that prosecution was originally brought about through fraud.

The plaintiff must show that the prosecutor did not have a reasonable or just cause; in other words, the plaintiff has to establish a negative. The judge is concerned with the objective part of the problem – was there a reasonable cause of action in fact? The jury – malicious prosecution like defamation, but unlike virtually any other branch of tort, may require a jury – must provide the answer to the subjective part – that is whether the prosecutor believed he was acting reasonably.

The shorthand expression for malice is, as we have seen before, 'an improper motive'. As Winfield and Jolowicz have said

> **Judicial attempts to define malice have not been completely successful. 'Some other motive than a desire to bring to justice a person whom he [the accuser] honestly believes to be guilty' seems to overlook the fact that motives are often mixed. Moreover, anger is not malice; indeed, it is one of the motives on which the law relies in order to secure the prosecution of criminals**

If the prosecutor has no desire to vindicate justice, then it may be held that malice exists. Malice, then, is clearly not the same as the want or lack of a reasonable cause; indeed those two potential factors must always be separated out by the court, for a prosecutor can still honestly believe in a person's guilt, in other words he did not act maliciously, even if no probable cause can be demonstrated. Malicious motives may embrace such things as the wish to deter a person from bringing a civil action against the prosecutor, or a desire to stop a witness from speaking his mind. And the other side of the same coin is that a prosecutor or accuser may act maliciously (he might thoroughly hate the person accused), yet reasonable cause may still be shown, in which case no action for malicious prosecution will lie (*Brown* v. *Hawkes* (1891)).

In *Martin* v. *Watson* (1995) the House of Lords held that the person responsible for supplying false and malicious information is equally liable under malicious prosecution (see also *Davidson* v. *Chief Constable of North Wales* (1994)). The defendant was responsible for the prosecution rather than the prosecutor himself; the matter concerned a complaint of indecent exposure.

To sum up, a prosecutor may have a reasonable and probable cause in fact and a conviction, of course, will be self-evident. If this is so, any improper motives on the prosecutor's part will be quite irrelevant. If, though, it can be seen that the prosecutor did not have a reasonable cause *and* if it can also be shown, and this is the more difficult part, that he did not reasonably believe in that cause, that in other words he initiated an unreasonable prosecution not out of genuine if misguided belief but on account of an improper motive, then an action for malicious prosecution will lie.

The term 'malicious prosecution' will normally relate to actual legal proceedings, but it might also embrace an arrest or search warrant. By its very wording the term relates to malicious criminal proceedings, but logically there is no reason why actions should not also embrace malicious civil proceedings; so far the law has avoided such a general proposition, although it is clear that it is a tort to institute winding up or bankruptcy proceedings without reasonable cause and maliciously.

Finally, the court will naturally not entertain what it considers to be vexatious or frivolous proceedings. Special (actual) damage must, as stated above, be proved by the plaintiff – that may include the damage done to his reputation (scandal), but that is much less easy to determine than may appear at first sight, since in one sense all criminal proceedings reflect upon a person's standing in society. Damage may also embrace endangering a person's life or liberty or encroaching upon property, in other words the plaintiff has suffered some form of financial loss.

7.5   Trespass to the Person

Trespass to the person is a common law tort. The word 'trespass' originally meant no more than 'wrong' and any trespass to the person was actionable *per se*. This meant, as we have previously noted, that in order for a right of action to lie the simple fact of the trespass was enough; it was not necessary to show that the plaintiff had suffered any damage.

In modern times there have been two important developments in the tort of trespass to the person. Firstly, it appears that it has become necessary to establish either an intentional act or some form of negligence on the part of the defendant. An unintentional act without negligence is probably not a trespass. This proposition emerged from the case of *Stanley* v. *Powell* (1891). In that case the defendant, who was one of a shooting party, fired at a pheasant, but accidentally struck and wounded the plaintiff when a pellet glanced off a tree. The jury found that the defendant was not guilty of negligence in firing as he did, and the judge on that finding held that the defendant was not liable even if the action were brought under the tort of trespass. In short, the incident amounted to an inevitable accident. This case was at first instance and has been criticised but nevertheless it was followed by the Court of Appeal in the case of the *National Coal Board* v. *Evans* (1951). More recently, but again at first instance, Mr Justice Diplock in *Fowler* v. *Lanning* (1959) held that an action for trespass to the person did not lie if the injury to the plaintiff was caused unintentionally and without negligence on the defendant's part. It is important to note, however, that this point has not yet been taken to the House of Lords so that it cannot be stated with finality.

The second change is that while trespass to the person can be committed negligently, the trend has been for such cases to be brought under the tort of negligence. This has occurred to such an extent that the law of negligence has largely superseded trespass to the person as the cause of action where negligence is alleged. Lord Denning in *Letang* v. *Cooper* (1965) put the position as being beyond even this when he said, 'When the injury is not inflicted intentionally but negligently, I would say that the only cause of action is negligence and not trespass'. This statement was, however, only *obiter* and probably a plaintiff in such a case could choose to frame his claim under either tort.

There are three main forms of trespass to the person: assault, battery and false imprisonment which has already been examined in the previous section. In addition there is an extension made by *Wilkinson* v. *Downton* (1897) which, although not strictly speaking a trespass, is conveniently dealt with in this section. It is important to note that assault and battery are two separate rights of action with distinct and different legal meanings.

ASSAULT

This in its legal sense has a strict meaning which differs from its everyday connotation. At law an assault is an act which causes any reasonable person to fear that force will be used against him. It does not involve physical contact, and this point distinguishes it from battery.

There are many examples of acts which have been held to constitute an assault. These include waving a fist at someone; throwing a stone at a person; raising a stick or other implement as though to strike someone; and throwing water at a person. Where no actual contact is made, the act is an assault, but once contact is made, that is, when the blow lands or the stone or water touch their target, the act becomes battery. Thus an interception of a blow by a third person (*Stephens* v. *Myers* (1830)) would constitute an assault rather than a battery. Another clear example of an assault is pointing a loaded gun at another person who is within shooting range. Where the gun is unloaded, however, there is a doubt as to whether it amounts to an assault. In the old civil case of *Blake* v. *Barnard* (1840) it was held that pointing an unloaded gun was not an assault, but in criminal cases it has been clearly held that such an action could amount to a common law assault. The outcome of a modern civil case on such a point cannot be forecast, although common sense demands that there should be a distinction drawn between cases where the victim knows the gun is unloaded, and those where he does not, since in the latter case any reasonable person would have cause to fear that force would be used against him.

Normally words alone cannot constitute an assault, there must be some movement or physical act. On the other hand, words can negative apparently threatening actions which would otherwise amount to an assault. An example of this is in the old case of *Turbervell* v. *Savadge* (1669) where the defendant laid his hand on his sword and said, 'If it were not assize time, I would not take such language from you'. As it was assize time it was held that there was no assault. Moreover, it is possible to commit assault by one or more silent telephone calls (*R* v. *Ireland* (1997)).

BATTERY

This is the unlawful use of force against another person. Force in this sense means physical contact. Examples include punching or slapping another person; striking someone with a stick or other implement; spitting in their face; hitting them with a missile; and pulling off their clothing. Provided there is an element of 'force' in the strict technical sense, it is not necessary to prove a physical hurt or injury to the plaintiff. However, trivial matters – such as back-slapping, a handshake, the accidental brushing of shoulders – will be treated as having implied consent. Members of the medical profession may not be immune either, if a patient feels that unnecessary force has been used in an operation or similar circumstances (*Chatterton* v. *Gerson* (1980)), although usually, as noted earlier, the defence of *volenti non fit injuria* would apply.

In *Wilson* v. *Pringle* (1986) the plaintiff and the defendant were both schoolboys aged 13; the former suffered serious injury as a result of the other having intentionally jumped upon him, but the defendant claimed that he had merely pulled the plaintiff's schoolbag off his shoulder in the course of horseplay. The Court of Appeal held that battery was an intentional and hostile touching, or contact with, one person by another and that an intention alone by the assailant to injure the other was not an essential element of the tort; whether touching or contact was hostile was a question of fact for the court. In reaching its decision the Court of Appeal paid particular attention to the decision in *Collins* v. *Wilcock* (1984), where Lord Justice Goff said that the test must be whether the physical contact has 'gone beyond generally accepted standards of conduct; and the answer to that question will depend on the facts of the particular case'. In *Collins* a woman police officer suspected that a woman was soliciting contrary to the Street Offences Act 1959; the officer tried to question her and took hold of her arm, which the woman proceeded to scratch. The woman's appeal against being convicted of assaulting a police officer in the execution of her duty was allowed – the police officer had gone beyond the scope of her duty and had therefore committed a battery.

DEFENCES

There are various defences to the torts of assault and battery, the main one of which is self-defence. A person can use reasonable force when it is necessary for his own defence, or for the defence of property owned or occupied. What is reasonable depends on the circumstances of each case. It is also a defence that a parent, guardian or teacher uses only reasonable force when chastising a child. Consent is another defence; if the victim consents to the act, no tort has been committed (*volenti non fit injuria*). It may also be a defence to argue that under the

Offences against the Person Act 1861 summary criminal proceedings act as a bar to any subsequent civil proceedings. Statutory authority may also constitute a defence, such as the taking of breath tests under the Road Traffic Act 1988. Further, as we have seen in *Stanley* v. *Powell* (1891), 'inevitable accident' may prove a sufficient defence.

Wilkinson v. *Downton*

The idea of trespass to the person was extended at the end of the last century in the case of *Wilkinson* v. *Downton* (1897), where as a practical joke the defendant told the plaintiff her husband had been seriously injured. As a result the plaintiff suffered nervous shock and had a serious illness. Mr Justice Wright, giving judgment for the plaintiff felt that the case was without precedent and said the verdict could be supported on that basis.

> **The defendant has . . . wilfully done an act calculated to cause physical harm to the plaintiff, that is to say, to infringe her legal right to personal safety, and has in fact thereby caused physical harm to her. That proposition without more appears to me to state a good cause of action, there being no justification alleged for the act.**

This judgment was approved by the Court of Appeal in *Janvier* v. *Sweeney* (1919). However, in the case of *D* v. *NSPCC* (1978), Lord Denning felt that the principle in *Wilkinson* v. *Downton* could not be extended to include statements made honestly and in good faith. The facts of *D* v. *NSPCC* (1978) were that an inspector, acting on information, called at a house and told the mother of a 14 month-old child that they had had an allegation that she had been beating her child. The mother, as a result, suffered nervous shock. Denning's statement was *obiter* only, since the point the Court of Appeal was asked to decide was whether the NSPCC should be obliged to disclose the name of its informant. Causing nervous shock need not, of course, occur through a statement only; physical action designed to scare will suffice. Nervous shock is also dealt with below in section 8.7.

7.6   Trespass to land and goods

LAND

Trespass to land is any unlawful entry upon or physical interference with the land or buildings in the possession of another. Any trespass is actionable *per se* and trespass to land is no exception to this rule. This, of course, means that it is not necessary to prove damage; an action can be brought against a trespasser even though he has not harmed the land in any way. Obviously, though, the court would take this into consideration when assessing the damages the defendant should pay and may award nominal damages only, and naturally the prospect of nominal damages is often sufficient to deter potentially frivolous proceedings.

The person alleging the trespass must have possession of the land, that is the right to exclude others from it. Possession does not merely signify physical control; it includes any situation where the possessor has the right to prevent others entering on to the land. A clear example is that a person who owns a holiday home in some remote part of the country in which he lives for only two weeks each year, retains the right to prevent any other person from entering the property even during the 50 weeks of the year in which he is not present. Where land is leased the lessee has possession for the purposes of bringing an action for trespass and may even be able to sue the owner (the lessor) if the owner enters the land without the lessee's permission and without any lawful right: the lessee has the right to sue where a third party trespasses and the owner can only sue if his reversionary right is damaged in some way.

Possession should be lawfully recognised, it should be by right, that is *de jure*; the possessor should have a proper title to the property, either as owner or tenant. A person who has no proper title, such as a squatter, enjoys only *de facto* possession. But even a *de facto* possessor may enjoy limited rights in law. Providing a squatter has exclusive control over the property, his possession is protected against any subsequent intruders. Under the Limitation Act 1980 a squatter who remains on property for 12 years becomes a *de jure* possessor; the title of the previous owner is extinguished. The period may be much longer where the land is leasehold rather than freehold. It does not have to be one squatter over twelve years; a period of *continuous* occupation by several adverse occupiers will suffice. However, under the Criminal Law Act 1977 it is a criminal offence to remain on residential premises once a request to leave has been made.

Trespass can be committed in a number of different ways, for example, by a person walking or riding or driving across land. These are probably the most obvious ways of trespassing but it is also a trespass to sit on a person's fence, to throw objects on to their land, to allow one's animals to go on the land or even to bore a tunnel under the land (*Cox* v. *Glue* (1848)). There can be a trespass where an object interferes with the airspace immediately over the plaintiff's land even though it does not actually touch the land. This point appears to be settled now, although early cases did not take this line. In the more recent case of *Kelsen* v. *Imperial Tobacco Co. Ltd* (1957), however, it was held that an advertising sign which projected over the plaintiff's land was a trespass and the plaintiff obtained an injunction for its removal. Also, in *Woollerton and Wilson Ltd* v. *Richard Costain Ltd* (1970) a crane which swung over another person's land was held to constitute a trespass. It has already been seen in Chapter 7 that the Criminal Justice and Public Order Act 1994 introduced a criminal offence of aggravated trespass; an example of a s.68 offence could be seen in *Winder* v. *DPP* (1996).

Airspace

With the increase of aircraft there has also been argument as to how high into the atmosphere one's possession of the airspace above the land projects. In order to facilitate the passage of aircraft the Civil Aviation Act 1982 as amended by the Civil Aviation (Amendment) Act 1996 provides a defence to any such possible trespasses where a civil aircraft merely flies over land at a reasonable height. (Military aircraft are excluded from the Act; they have greater freedom in the skies.) In *Lord Bernstein of Leigh* v. *Skyviews and General Ltd* (1977) there was held to be no trespass to land where the defendant's aircraft flew a few hundred feet above the plaintiff's house and took a photograph of it, thus disproving the literal application of the maxim *cuius est solum eius est usque ad coelum*. The Civil Aviation Act, however, enforces strict liability for any damage caused by anything falling from an aircraft on to land below. Similarly, the airspace above a highway is not sacrosanct, as long as the public's use of the road is not limited. The user of the highway might become a trespasser against the owner of the subsoil if he uses the road for purposes other than travel, as was shown in *Harrison* v. *Duke of Rutland* (1893) (the intention there was to interfere with the shooting rights of the neighbouring occupier). However, it is not a trespass to rest on the highway during the course of a journey. In *Liddle* v. *Yorkshire (North Riding) County Council* (1934) it was observed that pausing on the highway in order to sketch the surrounding countryside might not constitute a trespass either.

Permission

A person may trespass from the moment he goes on to the land or may enter the land with permission and later become a trespasser if he goes beyond that permission. This was shown in *Hickman* v. *Maisey* (1900) where the plaintiff owned land and an adjoining highway. The defendant walked up and down the highway for two hours in order to observe the form of race-horses being trained on the plaintiff's land. It was held that this was not an ordinary use of the highway and the defendant was therefore a trespasser. Where a trespasser does exceed his authority he may be sued for trespass *ab initio* – in other words the trespass is deemed to have commenced from the moment of entry, rather than from the point at which the permission was broken; this doctrine may be of relevance to wrongs committed in respect of the National Parks and Access to the Countryside Act 1949.

A person might also enjoy rights of entry on account of a long-standing local custom, as illustrated in *Mercer* v. *Denne* (1905) which concerned the right to dry fishing nets near the beach at Walmer in Kent. Equally, the common law may recognise rights to enter property. In *Clissold* v. *Cratchley* (1910) a representative of the defendant's firm of solicitors entered the property of the plaintiff, a Gloucestershire farmer, in order to enforce the collection of a debt which arose from earlier litigation between the plaintiff and defendant. However, the farmer had already paid the debt, although the solicitor was not immediately aware of this. It was held that a trespass had nonetheless taken place. And, of course, various persons in authority enjoy a statutory right to enter property, for example, the police and gas and electricity company officials. In any case permission to enter is frequently implied, as in the case of postmen and traders. Special areas of the countryside also give members of the public rights of access, as under the National Parks and Access to the Countryside Act 1949 and the Countryside Act 1968. The Access to Neighbouring Land Act 1992 provides that a person who, for the purpose of carrying out works to any land, desires to enter upon any adjoining or adjacent land, and who needs, but does not have, the consent of some other person to that entry, may apply to the court for an access order against that other person. The court will not grant the order if there is unreasonable interference, that is if the neighbour would suffer serious disturbance or hardship, and the access order can only be made to preserve the applicant's land, providing the works are reasonably necessary.

Defences

There are three particular defences to trespass to land apart from general defences such as *volenti non fit injuria* and necessity. The particular defences are, firstly, that the entry is justified by law as where a court bailiff enters in order to seize goods or a police officer enters to conduct a search of the premises under the authority of a search warrant. The second type of defence is the rule in *Doe d. Carter* v. *Barnard* (1849) or *jus tertii*. This controversial defence means that where a plaintiff attempts to recover land, the defendant trespasser may argue that the land is owned by a third person or should be lawfully occupied by a third person, such as a tenant or lessee. However, it should be emphasised that the general rule is that *jus tertii* is no defence in an action for trespass to land. In particular a defendant trespasser cannot rely upon another's right to possess (*jus tertii*) as a defence, where the plaintiff is in actual possession, in fact if not in law. The last defence is that the defendant had a licence to use the land, for example, a hotel guest is a licensee for the period of his stay in a hotel, or a member of a theatre audience has a licence to be in the theatre for the performance of the play. Where, however, the licensee goes beyond the terms of the licence then he becomes a trespasser as where the member of the theatre audience does not leave at the end of the performance but stays in the theatre overnight.

Remedies

The general remedy of damages is, of course, available. Where there has been no injury to the land the court may award nominal damages, but in other cases it can award compensatory damages and where the use of the land has resulted in profits for the defendant the court can award exemplary damages. The plaintiff can also obtain an injunction in appropriate cases, for instance where there is an on-going trespass. Another more specific remedy which the court can order in a suitable case where the plaintiff has been wrongfully dispossessed of land is that the land be returned to the plaintiff. (An action for recovery of land used to be known as an action of ejectment.) If the defendant refused to comply with the order of the court the plaintiff can further apply to the court to direct the bailiffs to remove the defendant, by force if necessary. The plaintiff can also seek an order for 'mesne profits' where the trespass has prevented him from using the land and the court will assess the amount to be paid for the loss of use. This is the effect of the doctrine of trespass by relation: a person dispossessed of his property may sue for any trespass committed during the entire period of dispossession.

There are also methods of self-help available, although these must be used with caution. A person in possession of land may use such force as is reasonably necessary to eject a trespasser from the land. Where the occupier is dispossessed by the trespasser then, provided he uses peaceable means of re-entry, he may also eject the trespasser using reasonable force to do so. The occupier must not, however, effect a forcible entry since, unless he is a displaced residential occupier, this could be a criminal offence under the Criminal Law Act 1977. Finally, where livestock has strayed on to property, the occupier has a right under the Animals Act 1971 to detain the livestock, pending compensation for any damage caused by them. The occupier must, if deciding to exercise this right, take reasonable care of the animals and report their detention to the police within 48 hours.

GOODS

The law is covered partly by the Torts (Interference with Goods) Act 1977 and partly by the common law. The Act recognised two main categories of 'wrongful interference' – conversion and trespass to goods. The Act abolished the ancient tort of detinue which related to recovering borrowed goods in their original form and condition. Conversion and trespass are examined separately below, but first a common point to consider is that of 'possession'.

Normally it is in order for the plaintiff to sue if he enjoyed ownership of the goods (chattels) that have been interfered with or taken away, or indeed if he enjoyed mere possession (control) of them, or in the case of conversion even if he was about to enjoy possession (particularly in hire-purchase agreements). Quite clearly the plaintiff does not have to be the owner of the goods for an action to lie; he may have hired, found or borrowed them. For example, in *Armory* v. *Delamirie* (1722) a boy chimney-sweep found a jewel. He took this to a jeweller for valuation who subsequently refused to return the most valuable part of the jewel. The boy, although he was not the true owner, successfully sued the jeweller for conversion (trover as it was then called). Similarly, in *Bridges* v. *Hawkesworth* (1851) a person found some banknotes in a shop and he rather than the shopowner was found to be the rightful possessor. And in *The Winkfield* (1902) case the Postmaster General sued the person responsible for the sinking of a ship carrying mail, although the PMG, of course, was not the true owner. In *Parker* v. *British Airways Board* (1982) the plaintiff found a gold bracelet on the floor of the executive lounge in Terminal One at Heathrow Airport. He handed the bracelet to an airline official and it was subsequently sold by British Airways for £850, no one having claimed it. The plaintiff successfully sued for £850 and £50 interest.

Lord Justice Donaldson made an important statement of what he considered the rules were:

Rights and obligations of the finder

1. The finder of a chattel acquires no rights over it unless (*a*) it has been abandoned or lost and (*b*) he takes it into his care and control.

2. The finder of a chattel acquires very limited rights over it if he takes it into his care and control with dishonest intent or in the course of trespassing.

3. Subject to the foregoing and to point 4 below, a finder of a chattel, whilst not acquiring an absolute property or ownership in the chattel, acquires a right to keep it against all but the true owner or those in a position to claim through the true owner or one who can assert a prior right to keep the chattel which was subsisting at the time when the finder took the chattel into his care and control.

4. Unless otherwise agreed, any servant or agent who finds a chattel in the course of his employment or agency and not wholly incidentally or collaterally thereto and who takes it into his care and control does so on behalf of his employer or principal who acquires a finder's rights to the exclusion of those of the actual finder.

5. A person having a finder's rights has an obligation to take such measures as in all the circumstances are reasonable to acquaint the true owner of the finding and present whereabouts of the chattel and to care for it meanwhile.

Rights and liabilities of an occupier

1. An occupier of land has rights superior to those of a finder over chattels in or attached to that land and an occupier of a building has similar rights in respect of chattels attached to that building, whether in either case the occupier is aware of the presence of the chattel.

2. An occupier of a building has rights superior to those of a finder over chattels upon or in, but not attached to, that building if, but only if, before the chattel is found, he has manifested an intention to exercise control over the building and the things which may be upon it or in it.

3. An occupier who manifests an intention to exercise control over a building and the things which may be upon or in it so as to acquire rights superior to those of a finder is under an obligation to take such measures as in all the circumstances are reasonable to ensure that lost chattels are found and, upon their being found, whether by him or by a third party, to acquaint the true owner of the finding and to care for the chattels meanwhile. The manifestation of intention may be express or implied from the circumstances including, in particular, the circumstance that the occupier manifestly accepts or is obliged by law to accept liability for chattels lost upon his 'premises', eg an innkeeper or carrier's liability.

4. An 'occupier' of a chattel, eg a ship, motor car, caravan or aircraft, is to be treated as if he were the occupier of a building for the purposes of the foregoing rules.

Finally, here, a small point but an important one: perhaps it can already be seen from the foregoing that phrases like 'finding is keeping' or 'possession is nine points of the law' contain germs of truth but germs that are dangerous and positively misleading. In the *Parker* case Lord Justice Donaldson said,

On 15 November 1978 the plaintiff had a date with fate – and perhaps with legal immortality. He found himself in the international executive lounge at Terminal One, Heathrow Airport. And that was not all that he found. He also found a gold bracelet lying on the floor. We know very little about the plaintiff, and it would be nice to know more. He was lawfully in the lounge and, as events showed, he was an honest man. Clearly he had not forgotten the schoolboy maxim 'Finders keepers'. But equally clearly, he was well aware of the adult qualification 'unless the true owner claims the article'.

In *Bristol Airport plc* v. *Powdrill* (1990) it was said that the defendant is entitled to take a reasonable time to verify the title of the person who requires the goods to be handed over to him.

Interference with goods: conversion

A definition of conversion is by no means easy; however, we can say that the common law rules are recognised by the 1977 Act. Conversion concerns the wilful and legally unjustified interference with goods, in a manner that is not consistent with the rights of another and which deprives that person of the use and possession of those goods. But, say, scratching a car or even removing the vehicle a short distance would not amount to conversion although it might constitute trespass. Nor is it conversion if the defendant negligently allowed the goods to be destroyed or stolen, as seen in *Ashby* v. *Tolhurst* (1937) in respect of the theft of a car from a car park, although the 1977 Act, s.2(2), does now provide an exception if a bailee (minder of goods) has breached his duty of care towards the bailor (the owner or rightful possessor of the goods). The difference between conversion and trespass can best be illustrated by the case of *Fouldes* v. *Willoughby* (1841). The plaintiff wanted to take himself and his two horses by ferry to Liverpool. But the ferry operator removed the horses to the shore and the plaintiff crossed alone. The defendant's action was one of trespass, not conversion, for the plaintiff need not have crossed the river, although it should be pointed out that the plaintiff had paid for himself and the horses but he apparently misbehaved himself once aboard. Later, despite notification, the plaintiff did not collect the horses and they were sold.

The mere receipt of goods may amount to conversion, and in that way the 'innocent' defendant can be caught. (An 'involuntary bailee' is a different matter and is dealt with below under bailment.) In *R H Willis and Son* v. *British Car Auctions* (1978) a car auctioneer was successfully sued in conversion for the sale of a car on which there were outstanding hire-purchase debts; the hirer was made bankrupt and the successful bidder disappeared with the car.

Essentially conversion takes four forms:

1 Detaining goods: the plaintiff must show that the defendant intended to keep the goods – it was clear that the defendant took action which was *adverse* to the plaintiff's title. In contrast, conversion in the sense of the taking of goods but no more than that may merely mean interference with the owner's or possessor's *use* of the goods. But intending to detain the goods indefinitely, which might also be theft under criminal law, implies denial of title. Denial of title is not itself conversion; it may though constitute the tort of slander of title (misrepresentation). The wrongful retention of goods which carries with it denial of title is, however, conversion.

2 Conversion by wrongful delivery occurs where goods are delivered to a third person with the intention of those goods changing hands or indeed substance. In *Hollins* v. *Fowler* (1875) a rogue obtained cotton from F. by fraud and sold it to H. who sold it to X. who spun it into yarn. H. took his commission and handed the balance to the rogue who promptly disappeared. H. was held liable to F. in conversion. In *Moorgate Mercantile Co. Ltd* v. *Finch* (1962) the defendant was held liable for the conversion of a car when it was seized by customs officers on account of the fact that he was using another's vehicle for the smuggling of watches. In *Elvin and Powell Ltd* v. *Plummer Roddis Ltd* (1933) a rogue, X., ordered the plaintiffs (P.) to supply the defendants (D.) at their Brighton store with some £350 worth of coats. X. then sent a telegram to D., saying that the goods had been despatched in error and that a van would collect them. This was done by a brother crook of X. P. sued for conversion, as well as negligence (in bailment). The court held that there was not conversion (it found for contributory negligence) since D. had behaved reasonably in returning the goods in question.

3 Related to this category is the situation where a person unjustifiably deprives a person of his goods by giving a third party a lawful title to them, such as the passing of goods under a hire-purchase agreement. This is sometimes known as conversion by wrongful disposition.

4 Conversion may also take place by destruction. A person is liable if he wilfully destroys or consumes the goods belonging to another. But damage alone will not amount to conversion, only to trespass.

Two other matters should be noted about conversion. Firstly, there is the problem of co-owners. Under the common law a co-owner has always enjoyed the full benefits of joint possession. Another co-owner would only have a right of action against that person where he took, or attempted to take, sole use of the goods without the agreement of fellow co-owners. 'Use' could include destruction of the goods. The 1977 Act restates the common law and also extends it (as under (b) below) in relation to disposition:

> **Co-ownership is no defence . . . where the defendant without the authority of the co-owner (*a*) destroys the goods, or disposes of the goods in a way giving a good title to the entire property in the goods, or otherwise does anything equivalent to the destruction of the other's interest in the goods, or (*b*) purports to dispose of the goods in a way which would give a good title to the entire property in the goods if he was acting with the authority of all co-owners of the goods.**

Secondly, the 1977 Act does now allow the right of a third party (*jus tertii*) to be used as a defence. Formerly, it meant that the wrongdoer could face double liability. X., say, removes goods from the possession of T., although R. is in fact the lawful owner. Until 1978, when the Act came into force, X. could be sued by T. and then by R., twice over in other words. The 1977 Act, however, allows the defendant to argue that a third party has rights to the goods superior to the plaintiff's, if necessary by joining that third party to the proceedings under the rules of the court. And where only one claimant is involved he is still accountable to other possible claimants; indeed he may be required to reimburse the wrong doer. No one person must be enriched unjustly. Thus if T. sues X. for £50, being the value of the goods removed, and then R. subsequently sues X. too, T. must either financially satisfy R. or appropriately reimburse X.

Where the property of A. is mixed with the property of B., being of roughly the same quality, and cannot be reasonably separated, then ownership is owned in common in proportion to the relevant quantity, it was held in *Indian Oil Corporation* v. *Greenstone Shipping SA* (1988).

The rules concerning co-ownership and *jus tertii* also apply to trespass which is now considered below. Contributory negligence is no defence in conversion.

Intereference with goods: trespass

Trespass means the physical interference with goods: such interference may also result in damage. It is unlikely that trespass will amount to absolute removal since that would probably constitute conversion. Of course, trespass is actionable *per se* – there is no requirement that special (actual) damage has to be proved. If no actual damage has been caused then nominal damages will be awarded, although in trespass to goods the possibility of exemplary damages should not be ruled out.

Normally trespass involves direct physical contact with goods, although it need not always be so – for example, the driving away of cattle by shouting. Where damage results indirectly from the application of force and is unintended the action is more likely to be one of negligence or nuisance. It is, though, possible to justify trespass to goods on the grounds that the action was undertaken to defend life or property, or if it is done in order to exercise a legal right or obligation. In this context a number of cases have centred on the straying and worrying of livestock.

Mistake, however, is not a defence to either trespass or conversion. This point was very much underlined in *Hollins* v. *Fowler*. Also in *Kirk* v. *Gregory* (1876) the defendant, following a death in the house, removed some jewellery from the room in question and put it in a cupboard for safe keeping. The jewellery subsequently disappeared and the defendant was held liable for trespass. A general defence of necessity might be raised in respect of the removal of goods for safe keeping or for preservation in the case of perishable commodities, but this defence would be less likely to succeed in conversion than in trespass. Contributory negligence is not a defence to *intentional* trespass.

Remedies

As indicated under trespass nominal damages may often be the order of the day. Equally, substantial (special) damages cannot be ignored – for instance, a valuable vase might be returned with a crack in it. On the other hand if a defendant, believing that he has a good title to the goods, improves or repairs those goods then he may claim for a reduction in damages awarded against him. Normally the value of the goods is assessed at the time that interference takes place, but in modern times it does appear that inflation has to be taken into account (the case of *Brandeis Goldschmidt & Co. Ltd* v. *Western Transport Ltd* (1981) illustrated the problem – here the fall in the price of copper). *Brandeis Goldschmidt* was upheld by the Court of Appeal in *IBL Ltd* v. *Coussens* (1991).

Special damages may be awarded if the loss of goods results in the plaintiff's loss of earnings. This would particularly apply where a skilled worker is deprived of tools or specialist equipment.

Three other points must be briefly considered: redelivery, replevin and recaption. Under the 1977 Act the plaintiff may be granted interlocutory relief in the County Court or High Court whereby the defendant is ordered to deliver up the goods which are the subject of present or future proceedings; as, for example, in *Howard E Perry & Co. Ltd* v. *British Railways Board* (1980), where the defendants had refused to deliver steel because of a fear of the consequences of crossing picket lines. Similarly, under the County Courts Act 1984 the district judge will order goods to be restored to the plaintiff providing he gives an undertaking to bring a case before the County Court or High Court – such an action is known as replevin. A plaintiff who has been wrongfully deprived of goods at common law may use reasonable force to recover the goods (recaption).

In addition, the courts will take into account distress and inconvenience that has been caused.

BAILMENT

Bailment, not the easiest of topics in law, is rooted in both tort and contract and there have been many learned arguments as to which category it best belongs. Essentially it means the voluntary delivering up of goods by one (the bailor) to another (the bailee) – that can cover a free loan of a book, the hire of a car or the storage of furniture. You have to give your consent to be a bailee; as indicated below you cannot have goods, and therefore duties, forced upon you. As outlined above, 'involuntary bailment' is not the same as the 'mere receipt of goods', for in the latter case the goods are still taken on a voluntary basis and therefore liability in conversion or trespass might arise, as underlined in the *Willis* hire-purchase case. Involuntary bailment means that while it may be 'bailment' in fact, it is not so in law: P. has not consented to mind goods for Q., he has not agreed to take on board the particular contractual responsibilities that bailment involves.

The bailee may be a gratuitous bailee (no financial consideration is involved) or a bailee for reward (a payment is made). The bailment may be for a fixed period or for an indefinite period of time (determinable at will). In the latter case the bailor is said to be in continuous possession, in law if not in fact; this is known as simple bailment. In simple bailment the bailor may sue the wrongdoer but not his bailee for the wrongful interference with his goods. Moreover, the bailee also has a right to sue the wrongdoer. But where the bailment is for an agreed period of time, then the bailor may sue the bailee. In the Malaysian case of *Port Swettenham Authority* v. *T W Wu and Co.* (1978) the appellant (the bailee) was held to be negligent in respect of the disappearance of 64 cases of pharmaceutical goods under its custody. In *Mitchell* v. *Ealing London Borough Council* (1978) the defendants stored the furniture of an evicted squatter. Later the property was stolen. The court gave judgment for the plaintiff, since although the defendants were gratuitous bailees and had taken reasonable care in the storage of the goods, nonetheless they failed to deliver up the goods on a date agreed earlier with the plaintiff.

The question of the innocent bystander, in other words of the involuntary bailment or reception of goods, has posed problems for the courts over the years. However, it is clear that being an 'involuntary bailee' does not amount to conversion or trespass – for example, where a thief, knowing he is about to be caught, puts an article into a bystander's pocket. So what is the position in respect of material sent, for instance, through the mail? Parliament saw fit to come to the rescue on this point, for under the Unsolicited Goods and Services Act 1971 the person who receives totally unsolicited goods may treat them as gifts after six months have elapsed from the date of receipt, or 30 days if notice is sent to the sender.

A number of cases have illustrated the problem of the 'involuntary bailee'. In *Lethbridge* v. *Phillips* (1819) L., who was a famous portrait painter in miniature, loaned a picture to X. X. wanted the defendant, P., to see it. Without P.'s knowledge he arranged for the painting to be taken to P.'s house where it was left on a mantelpiece near a large stove. The picture was damaged by heat, but P. was not liable to L. for the loss. Similarly, as underlined by *Howard* v. *Harris* (1884) publishers and literary agents will not be liable for unsolicited manuscripts. Of course, that does not mean to say that a person may intentionally damage or destroy the goods. On the other hand he may make reasonable efforts to return the goods; if he does so he cannot be liable for unfortunate consequences, as noted in *Elvin and Powell Ltd* v. *Plummer Roddis Ltd* (1933).

Finally, it has now been established that an employer (master) may well be liable for the goods bailed to him if they are stolen by an employee (servant) in the course of employment. But the 'course of employment' will usually mean that the goods have been entrusted to the care of that particular employee. If that servant does not act negligently then the master will not be liable for the theft of the goods by another employee or an outsider. In the case of *Morris* v. *C W Martin and Sons Ltd* (1966) a firm of specialist cleaners to whom another firm had sent the plaintiff's fur garment was held responsible for the theft of that article by its employee whose job was to have it cleaned.

7.7   Negligence

Negligence can refer to a mental element in a tort or it may mean an independent tort. In this section we are considering negligence as an independent tort. Moreover, negligence may overlap with contract, as shown for example, in the case of *Batty* v. *Metropolitan Property Realisations Ltd* (1978). In this case it was held that the plaintiffs, the purchasers of a house built on a hill subject to landslips, were entitled to a judgment against the developers both in the tort of negligence and for breach of contract. Negligence may also be partly related to statutory provisions. For example, in *Haydon* v. *Kent County Council* (1978), the plaintiff argued that if the county council, as the highway authority, in not clearing snow and ice from a busy footpath, was not actually in breach of the duty to maintain the path under the Highways Act 1959, it was still negligent at common law in failing to exercise its powers of salting or gritting roads with reasonable care. Negligence in criminal law has, of course, already been examined.

Negligence derives from trespass by way of action on the case and, therefore, it is not actionable *per se* but only on proof of damage. The modern law of negligence has developed piecemeal since the early nineteenth century and for that reason it is difficult to give an exact definition. A general statement, however, is that negligence is the breach of a legal duty to take care which results in damage caused by the defendant to the plaintiff. There are three constituents, all of which must be proved in order for an action to be successful. Firstly, the defendant must owe a duty of care to the plaintiff and that duty must be recognised by the law; secondly, there must be a breach of that duty; and lastly, the plaintiff must suffer damage as a result of that breach. A number of recent cases illustrate the point.

So, in *Kirkham* v. *Chief Constable of the Greater Manchester Police* (1990), the Court of Appeal said that the police were under a duty to apprise the prison authorities of the deceased's suicidal tendencies and were in breach of that duty. On the balance of probabilities the plaintiff's claim that the breach of duty had caused her husband's death had been made out. In contrast in *Wentworth* v. *Wiltshire County Council* (1993) the plaintiff was a dairy farmer who required a good road for the Milk Marketing Board to collect his milk; the county council under the highways legislation did eventually repair the road, but the farmer had by then gone out of business; he claimed economic loss since the tanker lorries had stopped coming to his farm. The Court of Appeal did not allow his claim, since under the relevant legislation he could not show that there was a dangerous road and therefore there was not a breach of statutory duty.

The decision in *Pape* v. *Cumbria County Council* (1992) was less kind to the defendants: the county council should have warned a part-time cleaner who contracted acute dermatitis about the dangers of certain cleaning products. The duty of care had therefore been broken, no attempt to warn had been made at all.

Johnson v. *Coventry Churchill International Ltd* (1992) concerned a building site accident in Germany; there was no safe system of working, so therefore the duty of care had been broken. In *Knight* v. *Home Office* (1990), a negligence action failed in respect of a prisoner who committed suicide in the hospital wing of Brixton Prison; the regime was one where the prisoner was observed every 15 minutes rather than under constant supervision. The Home Office argued that there were limited available resources.

DUTY OF CARE AND REASONABLE FORESEEABILITY

The existence of a duty of care is a matter of law. The leading judgment is that of Lord Atkin in the case of *Donoghue* v. *Stevenson* (1932). The facts of that case were that the plaintiff was bought a bottle of ginger beer by a friend at the Wellmeadow Cafe in Paisley. After she had drunk part of it she discovered a decomposed snail in the bottle which was made of opaque glass, and as a result she suffered severe gastro-enteritis and nervous shock. She sued the manufacturers of the ginger beer in negligence. The novelty of the action was that the plaintiff was suing the manufacturer rather than the retailer (the café proprietor). The question of any contractual relationship between the defendant and the retailer did not arise; but it was clear that there was no such relationship between her and the manufacturer, so she sued in tort. Lord Macmillan said that the categories of negligence were never closed while Lord Atkin in his judgment said: 'You must take reasonable care to avoid acts or omissions which you can reasonably foresee would be likely to injure your neighbour'. He went on to define 'neighbour' as 'persons who are so closely and directly affected by my act that I ought reasonably to have them in contemplation as being so affected when I am directing my mind to the acts or omissions which are called in question'.

Although this was not the *ratio decidendi* of the case – the other judges declined to formulate a general principle – Lord Atkin's definitions have been followed in numerous cases. Examples include *Haseldine* v. *Daw and Son Ltd* (1941), where the repairers of a lift were held liable for injuries sustained by a visitor to a block of flats when the lift slipped due to negligent repair work, and *Grant* v. *Australian Knitting Mills Ltd* (1936), where cloth caused irritation to the plaintiff's skin (the so-called 'itchy pants' case). The woollen underwear contained an excess of sulphite; the plaintiff contracted dermatitis. The manufacturers unsuccessfully argued that the pants should have been washed first. Although the neighbour principle is now accepted as part of English law, there is still some uncertainty as to exactly how far it does extend, as illustrated in the cases of *Anns* v. *Merton London Borough* (1977), *East Suffolk Rivers Catchment Board* v. *Kent* (1941) and *Dutton* v. *Bognor Regis UDC* (1971), all of which were controversial cases involving defective building work. Indeed, foreseeability in itself does not necessarily point to a duty of care.

Building cases

In *Dutton* it was held that the local authority did owe a duty of care towards the purchaser of a house which had inadequate foundations; the builder was also liable, but the local authority too was liable in respect of its breach of a duty at common law to take reasonable care in any inspection to ensure that local by-laws (made under statutory authority) were complied with, an important consideration in view of the fact that builders not infrequently go bankrupt. In *Perry* v. *Sidney Phillips and Son* (1982) the plaintiff was awarded damages not only for the cost of repairing a house negligently surveyed (the plaintiff had employed the surveyors himself to make a report) but also for the distress and inconvenience suffered. In *Anns* (1977) it was held that the exercise of a statutory discretion did not negative a common law duty of care. Damages would be recoverable for personal injury and damage to property. The somewhat neglected Defective Premises Act 1972 imposes a statutory duty on all persons connected with the construction of private homes to ensure that the building is properly completed and fit for habitation.

In *Anns* Lord Wilberforce observed:

> **The question has to be approached in two stages. First, one has to ask whether, as between the alleged wrong-doer and the person who has suffered damage there is a sufficient relationship of proximity or neighbourhood such that, in the reasonable contemplation of the for-mer, carelessness on his part may be likely to cause damage to the lat-ter, in which a *prima facie* duty of care arises. Secondly, if the first question is answered affirmatively, it is necessary to consider whether there are any considerations which ought to negative, or to reduce or limit the scope of the duty or the class of person to whom it is owed or the damages to which a breach of it may give rise (see the *Dorset Yacht* case, *per* Lord Reid).**

After *Anns* came the decision by the House of Lords in *Governors of the Peabody Donation Fund* v. *Sir Lindsay Parkinson & Co. Ltd* (1984). In this case plans were submitted by architects acting for the plaintiffs and approved by the local authority, an inner London borough. The drainage system subsequently installed was of a rigid design, and not flexible as shown on the plans. The local authority drainage inspector learned of this departure during the installation period, but he took no action. In the circumstances, the Lords held, it was not reasonable or just to impose liability upon the authority – other parties, the architects, engineers and contractors, were responsible. Lord Justice Neill observed in *Jones* v. *Stroud District Council* (1986) that the obligations of the local authority and the builder were not co-terminous and in many cases an action could be brought only against the builder. The *Peabody* decision showed that the high water mark, in respect of local authorities' liability for defective premises, had been reached with *Anns*. 'The tide of authority which had been flowing against local authorities before *Peabody*, has now almost certainly been halted', was one comment in 1986. Moreover, in the Privy Council case of *Yuen Kun Yeu* v. *Attorney-General of Hong Kong* (1987) warning was given against overstating the significance of the two-stage 'test' in *Anns*.

In *Yuen* Lord Keith of Kinkel observed:

> **The second stage of Lord Wilberforce's test in *Anns* v. *Merton London Borough Council* is one which will rarely have to be applied. It can arise only in a limited category of cases where, notwithstanding that a case of negligence is made out on the proximity basis, public policy requires that there should be no liability . . . In view of the direction in which the law has since been developing, their Lordships consider that for the future it should be recognised that the two-stage test in *Anns* is not to be regarded as in all circumstances a suitable guide to the existence of a duty of care.**

In *Lonrho* v. *Tebbit* (1992), which involved a report by the Monopolies and Mergers Commission to Norman Tebbit, the Secretary of State for Trade and Industry, that a takeover of the House of Fraser by the Al-Fayed brothers might be expected to operate against the public interest, the Vice-Chancellor, Sir Nicolas Browne-Wilkinson, held that the issue (of the exercise of statutory powers) was justiciable, that, drawing on *Anns*, there was a difference between operational discretions and policy discretions. In marked contrast to *Murphy*, the judge found that it was arguable that there was a sufficiently proximate relationship which gave rise to a duty of care to prevent economic loss, and that duty was not owed to the public at large, but if at all, to Lonrho alone. The damage could only have been economic loss, which should have been foreseeable. The decision was affirmed by the Court of Appeal.

The view of Lord Keith in *Yuen* was reinforced the following year in another Privy Council case, that of *Rowling* v. *Takaro Properties Ltd* (1988), on appeal from New Zealand. A similar line was taken in *Curran* v. *Northern Ireland Co-ownership Housing Association Ltd* (1987) where the plaintiffs alleged that an extension to the house they had bought had been negligently constructed with the aid of an improvement grant from the Northern Ireland Housing Executive. Lord Bridge cited with approval Lord Keith's observations in *Peabody*; Lord Bridge stated that the House should be wary of extending the *Anns* principle whereby, although under no statutory duty, a statutory body may be held to owe a common law duty of care. Such a body must be shown to have exercised its power in a way that did not avoid the danger in question and the negligent exercise or non-exercise of the power must have created a latent defect which could not have been discovered and remedied before the damage occurred. In the instant case *Anns* could be distinguished on the grounds that the Housing Executive only had a power to withhold payment of the grant if the work appeared to have been completed unsatisfactorily.

The immense difficulties of 'foreseeability' and Lord Wilberforce's two-stage test came to the fore in the 'Yorkshire Ripper' case. Suzanne Bailey has written:

> **Policy and principle are the parents or executioners of liability. In *Hill* v. *Chief Constable of West Yorkshire* (1988) the mother of the Yorkshire Ripper's last victim, Jacqueline Hill, argued that the police owe a duty of care to individual members of the public to prevent them being harmed by criminals. She relied [unsuccessfully] on the two-stage test devised by Lord Wilberforce in *Anns* v. *Merton London Borough Council*. The police officers investigating the case had failed to apprehend Peter Sutcliffe in time to prevent Jacqueline Hill's murder, the plaintiff claimed damages on behalf of her daughter's estate for breach of that duty.**

Similarly, in *Ancell* v. *McDermott* (1993) the Court of Appeal held that where police from one force provided assistance at a road accident, and where officers from another force assisted but also did nothing about spilt oil on the road, there was still no cause of action in negligence when the plaintiff's wife was killed (and others were injured) as a result of a car skidding on the oil, on grounds of public policy, since the duty imposed would be of unlimited scope (*Hill* v. *Chief Constable of West Yorkshire*, 1988).

In *Hill* the House of Lords ruled that in this context the police owed no duty of care to an individual member of the public unless there was an exceptional risk to the public at large. As a matter of public policy the police were immune from actions for negligence in relation to the investigation of crime. As will be seen below, the two-stage test became so discredited that *Anns*, together with *Dutton*, was subsequently overruled by *Murphy* v. *Brentwood District Council* (1990).

It should be stressed that the immunity of the emergency services from actions in negligence, especially in respect of positive acts is not absolute, as seen in recent decisions concerning the police and two concerning the fire service, in one context taking a mid-way position between *Hill* v. *Chief Constable of West Yorkshire* and *Home Office* v. *Dorset Yacht Co. Ltd*: *Swinney* v. *Chief Constable of the Northumbria Police* (1996), *John Munroe Ltd* v. *London Fire and Civil Defence Authority* (1996), *Capital and Counties* v. *Hampshire County Council* (1997), the second case not giving rise to liability since the fire service had extinguished a fire but failed to realise it had spread to adjoining premises. In *Capital and Counties plc* v. *Hampshire County Council* (1997), a fire brigade was held liable for negligently turning off an entire sprinkler system, but aside of positive acts of negligence the fire services normally enjoy immunity like the police on grounds of public policy, as seen in *Church of Jesus Christ of Latter-Day Saints (Great Britain)* v. *Yorkshire Fire and Civil Defence Authority* (1996) and *John Munroe (Acrylics) Ltd* v. *London Fire and Defence Authority* (1996). But in *Swinney* the Court of Appeal did not grant the police immunity where confidential documents were stolen from an unattended police car in an area of high crime, with the result that the informant and her husband were threatened with arson and violence leading to psychiatric injury.

The *Jones* v. *Stroud District Council* case was concerned with the problems of the limitation period, as highlighted in *Pirelli General Cable Works Ltd* v. *Oscar Faber and Partners* (1983). In *Pirelli* the Lords held that an action was brought too late, it was statute-barred, in respect of a defective factory chimney in Southampton. The Lords recognised that since the Limitation Act 1963 (as consolidated under the Limitation Act 1980) Parliament had provided that in cases of personal injury the limitation period of three years might run from the date on which the damage was actually and reasonably discovered. However, the Lords felt that in practice a distinction should not be made in respect of discoverability between damage to a person and damage to an object such as a house, but that it was up to Parliament to make the necessary change in the law in overriding the normal limitation period of six years in respect of tortious wrongs other than personal injury.

The Latent Damage Act 1986

In *Pirelli* the plaintiffs had engaged the defendants in 1969 to build a factory chimney. Cracks developed in 1970 but were not discovered until 1977. The Lords, reluctantly, held the claim to be statute-barred and it was left to Parliament to come to the rescue and to clarify this aspect of the *Anns* case. The Act provides that the time limit for such building cases is six years from the date on which the cause of action accrued, commonly the date of damage, or three years from the starting date, whichever is the later, the starting date being the earliest time at which a reasonable person would consider the damage sufficiently serious as to justify instituting proceedings. Both of these latent damage periods are nonetheless subject to a long-stop of 15 years from the date of an act or omission which constitutes the alleged negligence and to which the damage is alleged to be attributable, that is from the time of the defendant's breach of duty. The 1986 Act also covers, therefore, negligent misrepresentation and advice, such as misleading surveying. In a High Court case, *Nitrigin Eireann Teoranta* v. *Inco Alloys Ltd* (1992), it was held the period for negligence ran from 1984 (so the case was not statute-barred) when a pipe again cracked and burst, causing an explosion which damaged the structure of the plant, whereas a crack in 1983 constituted pure economic loss and was not recoverable in negligence.

Preventive action

It is also an important factor to consider the cost of preventive action, even if something was reasonably foreseeable, as seen in *Haley* v. *London Electricity Board* (1965) where a blind man tripped over a hammer left on a pavement; the hammer had been meant to warn people of building operations – here the cost of alternative preventative action would not have been large, whereas the cost of closing a factory after a thunderstorm had made the floors slippery was judged to be too great in *Latimer* v. *AEC Ltd* (1953).

A landowner, who designed or builds a house or flat, is no more immune from personal responsibility for faults of construction than a building contractor, or from personal responsibility for faults of design than an architect, simply because he had disposed of his house or flat by selling or letting it. Here in *Rimmer* v. *Liverpool City Council* (1984), the plaintiff tripped over some toys belonging to his son and putting his left hand forward to save himself, smashed a glass panel and thus sustained injuries to his hand and wrist. The council, the Court of Appeal held, had a duty to take such care as was reasonable in all the circumstances to see that he was reasonably safe from personal injury caused by the glass panel. In *Targett* v. *Torfaen Borough Council* (1992) the defendant was a council tenant who had complained about unlit steps before; when he fell down he was 25 per cent contributorily negligent, the trial judge held, because he could have taken greater care, but the Court of Appeal held, following *Rimmer* v. *Liverpool City Council*, the plaintiff's knowledge of the danger did not negative the council's duty of care or break the chain of causation.

The *Wagon Mound* case

In respect of Lord Atkin's definition of the duty of care Lord Reid in the *Home Office* v. *Dorset Yacht Co.* (1970) said, 'The time has come when we can and should say that it ought to apply unless there is some justification or valid explanation for its exclusion'. However, this statement looks far too *Anns*-like to be legally comfortable nowadays. The case concerned escaping Borstal boys who caused damage to a yacht at Poole.

One way of looking at the duty of care is that taken by Lord Reid himself in *The Wagon Mound (No 2)* case (*Overseas Tankship (UK) Ltd* v. *Miller Steamship Co. Pty Ltd*) (1967) where he stated that a person must be regarded as negligent if he does not take steps to eliminate a risk which he knows or ought to know is a real risk and not a mere or remote possibility which would never influence the mind of a reasonable man (as for example in *Tremain* v. *Pike* (1969), where a farm labourer in east Devon suffered a very rare disease through contact with rat urine). From this one can see that the duty of care depends on two premises; firstly, that the defendant could reasonably foresee that the act or omission would cause loss or damage to his neighbour and secondly, that he did not take reasonable care to avoid such loss or damage. When considering whether the defendant could reasonably foresee loss or damage, the test is one of possibility not probability. It is also objective, based on the hypothetical reasonable man.

Possibility and probability

If the test were limited to probability and not possibility, then it would be a narrow one. Foreseeability means likelihood, not simply in the sense of probability but also in the sense of possibility, according to the circumstances. Yet possibility in this context cannot include mere chance; it does not embrace fantastic or highly remote possibilities. This point was well illustrated in *Fardon* v. *Harcourt-Rivington* (1932). Here a dog was left unattended in a car while its owners went shopping; it became restless and broke a window, a splinter of which flew into the eye of a pedestrian, blinding him. The defendant was held not liable. The leading case, however, is *Bolton* v. *Stone* (1951). The plaintiff while standing in a quiet suburban street was struck by a cricket ball from the defendant's ground. The evidence was that balls had landed in the street approximately six times in about 30 years and that the road was about 100 yards from the bat. There was also a 17 foot high fence between the ground and the road. The House of Lords in reversing the decision of the Court of Appeal held that the defendant was not negligent because it was improbable that the ball would be hit out of the ground or that it would cause personal injury if it were. It is possible to argue that the decision appears to be at variance with that a few years later in *Carmarthenshire County Council* v. *Lewis* (1955) described below.

In his judgment in *McLoughlin* v. *O'Brian* (1982) Lord Bridge of Harwich quoted an American definition of reasonable foreseeability:

> **Reasonable foreseeability does not turn on whether the particular plaintiff as an individual would have in actuality foreseen the exact accident and loss; it contemplates that courts, on a case-to-case basis, analysing all the circumstances, will decide what the ordinary man under such circumstances should reasonably have foreseen. The courts thus mark out the areas of liability, excluding the remote and unexpected.**

Instances where the courts have held that the defendant could have foreseen the likelihood of injury include *Buckland* v. *Guildford Gas Light and Coke Co.* (1948) where a 13 year-old girl climbed a tree and was electrocuted by touching an overhead wire close to its branches, and *Carmarthenshire County Council* v. *Lewis* (1955) where a lorry driver was killed when he swerved to avoid a small child who ran out of a playground; it was held that the council could have foreseen the possibility of a child running out and causing an accident. In *Charlton* v. *Forrest Printing Ink Co. Ltd* (1980) it was held that an employer was not liable for injuries received by an employee when he was attacked while collecting the weekly wages from a bank. On the same side of the line it has been held that there was no duty of care in the case of *Bourhill* v. *Young* (1943) in which a pregnant fishwife sustained nervous shock resulting in the still-birth of her child after she had heard, but not seen, a fatal accident to a motor-cyclist and had witnessed blood on the road following the accident. It was held that the motor-cyclist could not in the circumstances reasonably have foreseen the likelihood of injury and his estate was not liable for any damages. Similarly, in the case of *King* v. *Phillips* (1953), where a taxi driver in reversing caused slight injury to a child, it was held that the driver did not owe a duty of care to the child's mother who from 75 yards away saw the child's damaged cycle and suffered severe shock.

NERVOUS SHOCK

Nervous shock must mean some recognisable medical condition, whether physical or mental; it does not embrace simple distress of the mind or anguish, as seen in the leading case of *Hambrook* v. *Stokes Bros* (1925) (a runaway lorry rounded a corner where a pregnant mother, who died from physical injury consequent upon nervous shock, had left her children). These last two cases contrast with *Boardman* v. *Sanderson* (1964) in which the Court of Appeal held that the defendant did owe a duty of care to the plaintiff who suffered nervous shock as a result of hearing his son's screams when the child was run over by the defendant while negligently backing a car belonging to the plaintiff out of a garage. The differentiating factor appears to be that the defendant in the *Boardman* case knew that the plaintiff was within earshot in another part of the garage.

Nervous shock will be allowed where the defendant should reasonably have anticipated the consequences of his action, or where the plaintiff properly feared for his own physical safety, or that of relations or close friends, but not that of strangers, for that would carry the issue too far. In *McLoughlin* v. *O'Brian* (1982), where the plaintiff was taken to hospital to see her family seriously injured in a road accident several hours earlier, the Court of Appeal held that the duty of care in respect of nervous shock was limited to the vicinity of the accident and that it was up to Parliament and not the courts to extend the boundaries of liability. In the Court of Appeal Lord Justice Griffiths had said that as the tort of negligence had developed, judges had felt their way forward towards acceptable frontiers within which to confine liability. They had to strive to be fair, but also not to impose a crushing burden on those who, through a moment's inattention, set in train a disastrous sequence of events. But the Lords thought otherwise: nervous shock caused by the seeing or hearing of injuries to close relatives was reasonably foreseeable. And the plaintiff's going to the hospital as quickly as possible after the accident was to be expected in the circumstances; it fell within the immediate aftermath of the accident. The defendants were therefore liable for the nervous shock of the mother as well as for the negligence that had caused the death of her daughter and injuries to her husband and other children.

The immediate aftermath test has been applied in more recent nervous shock cases – *Ravenscroft* v. *Rederiaktie Bolaget Transatlantic* (1991) and *Hevican* v. *Ruane* (1991). But as one commentator wrote about *Alcock* in 1992, if a person who loses two brothers in circumstances as horrifying as those in the Hillsborough football disaster cannot recover, it is not easy to conceive of a situation where someone other than a parent or spouse, and certainly a mere bystander, can.

In *Alcock* v. *Chief Constable of the South Yorkshire Police* (1991) the House of Lords rejected the appeals of 10 people who claimed that they had suffered nervous shock resulting in psychiatric illness when their loved ones were killed in the Hillsborough football stadium disaster in 1989. Due to overcrowding through police mismanagement at a football match numerous spectators were crushed to death or injured. The incident could be seen live on television, but no pictures of suffering by recognisable individuals were broadcast. P1 and P2 were present in the football ground; P3–P10 saw the disaster on television. P2 lost a brother-in-law; P1 and P3–P6 brothers, P7 a grandson, P8 and P9 a son and P10 a fiancé. Although the class of persons who could sue should not be limited to particular relationships, such as husband and wife, nonetheless only P8, P9 and P10 had the requisite ties of love and affection so as to make the risk of psychiatric illness reasonably foreseeable. Such ties were to be presumed from the particular relationships. In contrast, in *Frost* v. *Chief Constable of the South Yorkshire Police* (1997), some of police officers who suffered nervous shock as a result of their involvement in the Hillsborough tragedy, were owed a duty of care, underlining the fact that a rescuer may become a primary victim.

In *McLoughlin*, it was said in *Alcock*, there were policy reasons for not allowing too many such claims – there would be encouragement of a cottage industry of lawyers and psychiatrists; there would be an unfair burden placed on defendants, insurers and eventually road users; difficulties of proof would exacerbate litigation; and further research was required into the area of nervous shock, which could mean it was a matter for legislation. Each of the 10 appellants had received news of deaths in different ways. The key questions were:

1 *proximity* of the plaintiffs in time and space to the scene of the tragedy;

2 the relationship between the victim of the accident and the plaintiff;

3 the method by which the shock was transmitted.

In this case those present at the football ground were too far away to see in detail the faces of those killed and could not have identified relatives or friends; similarly, those who watched on television could not be affected since broadcasting guidelines prevented close-up pictures of victims of the tragedy. One plaintiff had identified his brother-in-law some eight hours later in the mortuary, but this did not fall within the 'immediate aftermath' of the accident. The House of Lords considered the closeness of the relationship, this could include a son or fiancé, but brothers and brothers–in–law could not prove a 'close and intimate relationship' with those who had died.

In effect, this reasoning was a narrowing of proximity which had not been seen before in *McLoughlin*.

In respect of television, if the broadcasting rules were broken, then the television company would be liable, as there was a *novus actus interveniens*. But it could be that even within the rules a television broadcast could still give rise to liability (*per* Lord Ackner and Lord Oliver), as in the instance of the destruction of the *Challenger* (the US space shuttle) upon take off in 1986.

So, for nervous shock the test of reasonable foreseeability legally remains, and there must be a close relationship with the victim, plus the test of proximity in terms of time and geography should be satisfied. This means that persons at the scene of the accident may suffer nervous shock as well as personal injury, or those whose safety is threatened might still suffer nervous shock alone; these are actionable as will be those who suffer nervous shock in rescue situations (eg *Chadwick*). Otherwise close relatives (eg parents) and fiancé(e)s can claim damages for nervous shock where they witness injury to or death of a loved one, if the accident has been witnessed from close quarters, or if they see the loved one within a short time of the accident in a state of serious injury or death; or if they witness the events on simultaneous television broadcasts and see close-up pictures of their loved ones, but here the television company would be liable if they had broken the broadcasting guidelines, or there could be liability if a disaster were shown on live television and it was clear there were no survivors. Also, close relatives must show the intimacy of their relationship with the accident victim; distant relatives, friends or even work colleagues may still succeed but only if they can prove a special bond of affection. As can be seen, this approach is a complex one, and the decision of the Lords in *Alcock*, it can be argued creates more problems than answers. Indeed the most serious criticism of the judgment is its vagueness, for instance, for Lord Keith the issue was simply a matter of reasonable foresight; refusing to list the kind of relationships he was thinking of, he observed that these matters varied from case to case, that on the one hand fiancés might enjoy a closer relationship than married couples, but that on the other hand they may not. A simpler test would be to say that either no victim of nervous shock should recover or all those of reasonable fortitude should be able to recover.

It should be added that nervous shock need not relate solely to personal injury; psychiatric illness brought about as a result of a fire which extensively damaged the plaintiff's home, caused by the defendant's negligence, could suffice: *Attia* v. *British Gas plc* (1987).

In *McFarlane* v. *EE Caledonia* (1994) the High Court held that a worker who witnessed the 1988 Piper Alpha oil rig disaster from a rescue vessel was entitled to claim damages for the psychiatric injury he suffered, but the Court of Appeal disagreed, saying that a person of ordinary fortitude and phlegm would not have been shocked by the events; given the nature of the catastrophe this seems a questionable finding, since his previous history appears, here, irrelevant. The principle was that it was not reasonably foreseeable that the chain of events triggered by negligence would include the risk that someone of reasonable fortitude would suffer nervous shock (*McFarlane* v. *Wilkinson, Hegarty* v. *EE Caledonia Ltd* (1997)).

The House of Lords in *Page* v. *Smith (No 1)* (1995) emphasised that a driver of a car who negligently caused an accident was liable for psychiatric illness suffered by a victim of the accident, even if the victim suffered no physical injury since any driver should have reasonably foreseen that if he drove carelessly he would be liable to cause injury, either physical or psychiatric or both, to others involved in an accident.

It was very important to distinguish between primary and secondary victims in cases of nervous shock, the Lords said, although the decision was by a bare majority.

Here a Datsun was carelessly driven by S. and collided with a Volvo driven by P.; the Volvo was old and had to be written off. Shortly after the accident P. suffered a recurrence of a condition variously described as a chronic fatigue syndrome amongst other things, from which he had been suffering intermittently for 20 years. Thus the *King* v. *Phillips/Wagom Mound (No 1)* test of foreseeability of injury by shock, will apply only to a secondary victim of an accident – 'the passive and unwilling witness of injury caused to others', in Lord Oliver's words in *Alcock*. In respect of a primary victim, someone who was a participant in the accident, as here in *Page*, then the defendant must take his victim as he finds him – the 'egg-shell skull' rule (see below and *Smith* v. *Leech Brain*), even if a person of normal fortitude would not have reacted in that psychiatric way. *Page* v. *Smith* is the first case to got to the House of Lords in respect of psychiatric injury to primary victims, since *Bourhill, McLoughlin* and *Alcock* were all concerned with secondary victims. The distinction between primary and secondary categories is highly unsatisfactory.

Lord Lloyd thought the decision in *King* v. *Phillips* could no longer be supported on its facts. He suggested:

1 it was necessary to distinguish between primary and secondary plaintiffs in nervous shock cases;

2 a defendant would not be liable unless the psychiatric injury was foreseeable in a person of normal fortitude, in respect of secondary victims, but this did not apply in cases involving primary victims;

3 hindsight might be relevant in applying the test of reasonable foreseeability to secondary victims;

4 physical and psychiatric injuries were subject to the same test – could the defendant reasonably foresee his conduct would expose the plaintiff to a risk of personal injury?

5 the psychiatric illness must be a recognisable medical condition.

OBJECTIVE STANDARDS AND MEDICAL NEGLIGENCE

As already indicated the standard of care to be taken is an objective standard; it is that of the reasonable and ordinary man in the circumstances of the case, as illustrated in *Glasgow Corporation* v. *Muir* (1943) (the case involved the spilling of boiling tea in a cafe) and *Fardon* v. *Harcourt-Rivington* (1932). Lord Macmillan in *Glasgow Corporation* v. *Muir* had this to say about the reasonable man: 'The reasonable man is presumed to be free from both over-apprehension and from over-confidence', while Lord Justice Romer in *Hawkins* v. *Coulsdon and Purley UDC* (1954) pointed out that the reasonable man did not have 'the prophetic vision of a clairvoyant'. Expert knowledge which would have enabled an expert to foresee the consequence in question should not be attributed to the reasonable man unless it can be said that in the circumstances he ought to have possessed it (*imperitia culpae adnumeratur*).

An interesting case on this point is *Roe* v. *Minister of Health* (1954) in which an anaesthetist was found not to be negligent because he did not appreciate a risk unknown to the medical profession at the time. In that case 'invisible cracks' had occurred in glass ampoules of anaesthetic allowing the anaesthetic to become contaminated and causing the paralysis of a patient injected with it. The risk of invisible cracks was drawn to the attention of the medical profession at a later date but prior to the hearing of the case. Lord Justice Morris said: 'Care has to be exercised to ensure that conduct in 1947 is only judged in the light of knowledge which then was or ought reasonably to have been possessed', while Lord Justice Denning observed, 'We must not look at the 1947 accident with 1954 spectacles'. However, in a world of increasing expertise, anyone engaged in a matter in which he holds himself out as having professional or expert skill is expected by the law to show the average amount of competence associated with the proper discharge of that skill. This rule must be applied with care, however, to ensure that too high a degree of skill is not demanded.

In *Whitehouse* v. *Jordan* (1981) which involved the difficult delivery of a brain-damaged baby, Lord Justice Donaldson said that if a doctor failed to exercise the skill which he had or claimed to have, he was in breach of his duty of care. He was negligent. But if he exercised that skill to the full, but still took – with hindsight – the wrong course – he was not negligent and not liable to anyone. Lord Denning saw the issue in quite clear-cut terms: he felt that in a professional man an error of judgement was not negligence. But the House of Lords disagreed; while it upheld the Court of Appeal's decision on the facts of the case, it took the opportunity to say that it was not correct to say that an error of clinical judgement could not amount to negligence. Among other professional people barristers and solicitors enjoy a certain degree of immunity from an action in negligence, and this matter has already been examined above under negligent misstatement (misrepresentation).

Once the existence of a duty of care plus a breach of that duty have been shown, the last element that the plaintiff must prove is that he suffered damage as a result of the breach of the duty of care. This is a question of fact and must be decided on the circumstances of each case. An example where there was a breach of duty of care, but the damage suffered was not caused by it, is *Barnett* v. *Chelsea and Kensington Hospital Management Committee* (1969). In this case three men called at a hospital; they complained of feeling ill after drinking tea. The tea, it appeared, was poisoned with arsenic. Later that day one of the men, the plaintiff's husband, died. The duty nurse had telephoned a doctor, but the message was that the men should go home and consult their physicians, by which time it was, for one of them, too late. However, the evidence presented showed that even if the hospital doctor had treated the men at once, the deceased would still have died. A duty of care had been broken, but it was not the direct cause of death.

Thus in *Hills* v. *Potter* (1983) the plaintiff's claim against the defendant surgeon in negligence and assault and battery failed, since it was held that although the operation was dangerous (the plaintiff suffered paralysis from the neck downwards) the defendant, whilst not required to go into technical detail, had given his patient sufficient information to make an informed judgement (*volenti*).

In *Maynard* v. *West Midlands Regional Health Authority* (1984) consultants thought that the plaintiff's illness might be, amongst other things, Hodgkin's disease which would prove fatal unless treated immediately. A diagnostic operation was carried out, which, though properly performed, damaged the plaintiff. The plaintiff argued that the consultants should have waited for the results of other tests, which subsequently confirmed the patient was suffering from tuberculosis. Medical opinion was given on both sides – the trial judge found for the plaintiff, but the Court of Appeal, upheld by the House of Lords, reversed this decision. The Lords said that failure to exercise the ordinary skill of a doctor had to be established to prove negligence.

Moreover, inexperience (here in respect of a junior hospital doctor) is no defence to an action for medical negligence, *Wilsher* v. *Essex Area Health Authority* (1988).

A duty of care will not normally be owed where the plaintiff has voluntarily consented to engage in criminal activity which in itself gives rise to damage, as illustrated in *Ashton* v. *Turner* (1980) which concerned a car accident following a burglary. It is not public policy for a tortious action to be based upon criminal matters: *ex turpi causa non oritur actio*. Similarly, in *Marshall* v. *Osmond* (1982) a police officer pursuing by car a person rightly suspected of having committed an arrestable offence did not owe the same duty of care as he would to a lawful, innocent road user, the trial judge said, although the Court of Appeal felt the duty of care was the same, but that the police officer was not actually negligent.

In contrast, Mr Kirkham, the deceased husband of the plaintiff in *Kirkham* v. *Chief Constable of the Greater Manchester Police* (1990), was an alcoholic with a history of depression. On the day after his remand, he committed suicide by hanging himself in his cell. Mrs Kirkham claimed damages on behalf of his estate under the Law Reform (Miscellaneous Provisions) Act 1934 and on behalf of herself and other dependants under the Fatal Accidents Act 1976, arguing that her husband's death was caused by the negligence of the police. Her claim succeeded and the police appeal was dismissed. The public attitude to suicide was now one of sympathy rather than abhorrence, the court said, and the defence of *ex turpi causa* must therefore fail.

The courts will not, though, assist the plaintiff who has been guilty of illegal or immoral conduct, *per* Lord Justice Kerr in *Euro-Diam Ltd* v. *Bathurst* (1988), and similarly Lord Justice Beldam in *Pitts* v. *Hunt* (1991) where a passenger was denied compensation when he incited an unlicensed and uninsured driver to drive recklessly.

The strictness with which *volenti* is applied probably means that it has little value as a way of amending the applicable level of care, although where there is both consent and illegality the *ex turpi causa* doctrine is now more commonly applied than before.

REMOTENESS OF DAMAGE

Apart from the three elements of duty, breach and damage, it can be seen that equally important is the rather elastic question of remoteness of damage, since even if all the elements are proved the action will fail if the harm the plaintiff has suffered is too remote a consequence of the defendant's conduct. Usually each case must be decided on its merits, but there are some general principles which can be applied. In practice, however, it is not always easy to separate the concept of remoteness of damage from that of reasonable foreseeability; they are, conceptually, legal twins, the Charybdis and Scylla of actions in negligence. The concepts of duty of care and remoteness of damage are alternative methods of restricting liability in negligence.

An important case is *Overseas Tankship (UK) Ltd* v. *Morts Dock and Engineering Co. Ltd*, usually known as *The Wagon Mound (No 1)* case, but not easy to reconcile with *The Wagon Mound (No 2)*. The facts were that fuel oil had spilled on to the water from a ship and, having been set alight by welding operations on another ship, burnt a wharf. The court found that it was foreseeable that some damage would be caused to the wharf from the spillage of the oil and that as a fact damage of a foreseeable nature had been caused in that oil had reached the slipways and interfered with their use. However, it was unforeseeable that fuel oil spread on water would catch fire and damage the wharf in that way. The Judicial Committee of the Privy Council, on appeal from the Supreme Court of New South Wales, held that the defendants were not liable for the fire damage because it was not foreseeable and therefore too remote. In any case damage becomes too remote if an intervening event breaks the 'chain of causation', as we have seen earlier (*novus actus interveniens*). *The Wagon Mound* has been followed by the English courts although as a decision of the Privy Council it is not binding. (However, in *The Wagon Mound (No 2)* the owners of ships that were damaged by the same fire succeeded in their claim in negligence before the Judicial Committee, although this action was based on nuisance as well as negligence.) What it really decided was that the actual type of damage must be foreseeable, although the precise nature and extent of the damage need not be foreseen. In *Stewart* v. *West African Terminals Ltd* (1964) Lord Denning put it thus:

> **It is not necessary that the precise concatenation of circumstances should be envisaged. If the consequence was one which was within the general range which any reasonable person might foresee (and was not of an entirely different kind which no-one would anticipate) then it is within the rule that a person who has been guilty of negligence is liable for the consequences.**

In short, reasonable foreseeability is the acid test of remoteness of damage, although where clear intention to cause harm is present the application of the test is redundant. In *Bolton* v. *Stone*, as we have seen, it was held that a cricket ball hit in an extraordinary manner could not have been reasonably foreseen, the damage caused was too remote.

This principle was also clear in *Hughes* v. *Lord Advocate* (1963), although it was a more complicated case. In this instance Post Office workers left a manhole open, although they covered it with a canvas shelter. The usual paraffin warning lamps were also left. That evening an 8 year-old boy removed one of the lamps and went behind the canvas shelter. As a consequence of playing with it he knocked the lamp into the manhole. There was a loud explosion and the plaintiff received very serious burns, having himself fallen into the manhole. It was not foreseeable that the lamp would explode, but a duty of care had been broken inasmuch as the manhole was left open and unattended and it was foreseeable that boys might take a lamp into the shelter and that it might break and cause injury by burning. The defendants were held liable therefore, although the precise chain of events could not have been foreseen. In *Crossley* v. *Rawlinson* (1982) an AA patrolman went to the rescue of the defendant whose lorry had caught fire through his own negligence. The reasonable man, it was held, would expect the patrolman to take his fire extinguisher to a vehicle on fire close by, but equally it could not be reasonably foreseen that while running along a rough path he would catch his foot in a hole and trip over; the damage caused was too remote. But in *Paris* v. *Stepney Borough Council* (1951) it was held that goggles should have been provided for a man with one eye: it was reasonably foreseeable that the chances of total loss of eyesight following an accident were greater in his case than in that of a man with two good eyes.

In *Walker* v. *Mullen* (1984) Mr Justice Comyn said that he could think of no more praiseworthy or natural action by a father than to stay on in the United Kingdom through his son's illness – his son had been injured in a road accident. It was entirely reasonable and proper. Such examples of family life needed to be encouraged and his Lordship had accordingly strongly desired to award damages in respect of earnings which the plaintiff's father had lost by not returning to his job in Jordan at the end of his leave. But the judge reluctantly came to the conclusion that the law as it stood did not permit such a claim because it was too remote from, and not sufficiently attachable to, the accident.

The *Polemis* issue

The judgment in *The Wagon Mound (No 1)*, although of persuasive influence only, had the effect of superseding a decision of some 40 years earlier. In *Re Polemis* (1921) the test was that of 'direct consequence' (the case involved the negligent dropping of a plank which caused a ship to be destroyed by fire). While the defendant could foresee the distinct possibility of certain damage to the plaintiff, a breach of duty of care having occurred, he might not be able to anticipate all the consequences: under *Polemis* that second test did not matter; the question of that type of 'remoteness' did not arise. In other words, the test in *Polemis* was stricter than that in *Wagon Mound*. It did not mean, however, that negligence was a tort of strict liability, that the defendant was liable for all consequences irrespective of fault. A duty of care had to exist and it had to be shown that the duty was broken. Moreover, the defendant had to foresee his action as being likely to cause some damage. If those conditions were satisfied, then under *Polemis* the defendant was liable for virtually all the consequences; under *Wagon Mound* he was not if it appeared the consequences were too remote, if a reasonable man would not have foreseen them. In the case of *Roe* v. *Minister of Health*, referred to above, Lord Justice Denning noted:

It may be said that, by reason of the decision of this court in *Re Polemis* the hospital authorities are liable for all consequences of the initial carelessness of the nurse, even though the consequences could not reasonably have been foreseen. But the decision in *Re Polemis* is of very limited application. The reason is because there are two preliminary questions to be answered before it can come into play. The first question in every case is whether there was a duty of care owed to the plaintiff; and the test of duty depends, without doubt, on what you should foresee. There is no duty of care owed to a person when you could not reasonably foresee that he might be injured by your conduct (see *Bourhill* v. *Young* (1943)). The second question is whether the neglect of duty was a 'cause' of the injury in the proper sense of that term; and causation, as well as duty, often depends on what you should foresee. The chain of causation is broken when there is an intervening action which you could not reasonably be expected to foresee.

In the first *Wagon Mound* case Lord Denning's observations were taken up by Lord Simonds:

It does not seem consonant with current ideas of justice or morality that for an act of negligence, however slight or venial, which results in some trivial foreseeable damage the actor should be liable for all consequences however unforeseeable and however grave, so long as they can be said to be 'direct'. It is a principle of civil liability, subject only to qualifications which have no present relevance, that a man must be considered to be responsible for the probable consequences of his act. To demand more of him is too harsh a rule, to demand less is to ignore that civilised order requires the observance of a minimum standard of behaviour.

This concept applied to the slowly developing law of negligence has led to a great variety of expressions which can, as it appears to their Lordships, be harmonised with little difficulty with the single exception of the so-called rule in *Polemis*. For, if it is asked why a man should be responsible for the natural or necessary or probable consequences of his act (or any other similar description of them) the answer is that it is not because they are natural or necessary or probable, but because, since they have this quality, it is judged by the standard of the reasonable man that he ought to have foreseen them. Thus it is that over and over again it has happened that in different judgments in the same case, and sometimes in a single judgment, liability for a consequence has been imposed on the ground that it was reasonably foreseeable, or alternatively, on the ground that it was natural or necessary or probable. The two grounds have been treated as coterminous, and so they largely are. But, where they are not, the question arises to which the wrong answer was given in *Polemis*. For, if some limitation must be imposed upon the consequences for which the negligent actor is to be held responsible – and all are agreed that some limitation there must be – why should that test (reasonable foreseeability) be rejected which, since he is judged by what the reasonable man ought to foresee, corresponds with the common conscience of mankind, and a test (the 'direct' consequence) be substituted which leads to nowhere but the never-ending and insoluble problems of causation. 'The lawyer,' said Sir Frederick Pollock, 'cannot afford to adventure himself with philosophers in the logical and metaphysical controversies that beset the idea of cause.' Yet this is just what he has most unfortunately done and must continue to do if the rule in *Polemis* is to prevail. A conspicuous example occurs when the actor seeks to escape liability on the ground that the 'chain of causation' is broken by a *nova causa* or *novus actus interveniens*.

As we have seen, the issue arose again a few years later in *The Wagon Mound (No 2)*. The facts were almost identical, that is that the charterers of the SS *Wagon Mound*, which was taking on bunkering oil at a wharf in Sydney Harbour, had via their servants carelessly caused some oil to be spilt on water. A concentration built up near a wharf, and the wharf's workmen were using oxyacetylene equipment to repair two other ships. The oil caught fire when molten metal had fallen from the wharf and set fire to some cotton waste or rag floating in the oil. The wharf caught fire and was damaged and the ships being repaired were also damaged, one very seriously. The ships' owners now sued, the wharf owners having failed in the first case.

Lord Reid noted:

In the present case the evidence led was substantially different from the evidence led in *Wagon Mound (No 1)* and the findings of Walsh J, are significantly different. That is not due to there having been any failure by the plaintiffs in *Wagon Mound (No 1)* in preparing and presenting their case. The plaintiffs there were no doubt embarrassed by a difficulty which does not affect the present plaintiffs. The outbreak of the fire was consequent on the act of the manager of the plaintiffs in *Wagon Mound (No 1)* in resuming oxyacetylene welding and cutting while the wharf was surrounded by this oil. So if the plaintiffs in the former case had set out to prove that it was foreseeable by the engineers of the *Wagon Mound* that this oil could be set alight, they might have had difficulty in parrying the reply that then this must also have been foreseeable by their manager. Then there would have been contributory negligence and at that time contributory negligence was a complete defence in New South Wales.

The crucial finding of Walsh J., in this case is in finding (v): that the damage was 'not reasonably foreseeable by those for whose acts the defendant would be responsible'. That is not a primary finding of fact but an inference from the other findings, and it is clear from the learned judge's judgment that in drawing this inference he was to a large extent influenced by his view of the law. The vital parts of the findings of fact which have already been set out in full are (i) that the officers of the *Wagon Mound* 'would regard furnace oil as very difficult to ignite on water' – not that they would regard this as impossible, (ii) that their experience would probably have been 'that this had very rarely happened' – not that they would never have heard of a case where it had happened, and (iii) that they would have regarded it as a 'possibility, but one which could become an actuality only in very exceptional circumstances' – not, as in *Wagon Mound (No 1)*, that they could not reasonably be expected to have known that this oil was capable of being set afire when spread on water. The question which must now be determined is whether these differences between the findings in the two cases do or do not lead to different results in law.

However, it has been argued that The *Wagon Mound (No 2)* and other cases have, since the mid 1960s, whittled down the differences between the tests of direct consequence and reasonable foreseeability for all practical purposes. Lord Denning said in *Lamb* v. *Camden London Borough Council* (1981): 'Duty, remoteness and causation . . . are all devices by which the courts limit the range of liability for negligence or nuisance'. The case concerned damage caused by squatters occupying a property vacated on account of damage caused by the local council.

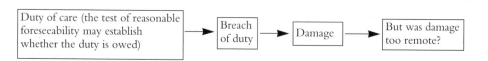

Damage is not too remote if:
1. the general type of damage caused by the defendant's careless action/omission is foreseeable (in respect of the plaintiff), although the precise details do not have to be foreseen   (*Wagon Mound* test)
2. the defendant is at fault (no damage in respect of the plaintiff need be foreseen)   (the wide interpretation of *Polemis*)
3. some, but not necessarily the actual type of, damage caused by the defendant's careless action/omission is foreseeable in respect of the plaintiff (the narrow and more usual interpretation of *Polemis* as used in the text above)

} direct consequence

1. is now regarded as the true test; 2. and 3. are inappropriate.
A break in the chain of causation (*novus actus interveniens*) will invariably indicate remoteness of damage; similarly, where the defence of *volenti non fit injuria* is successfully raised.

FIG. 3 *The 'range of damage' test*

The way in which the concept of 'reasonable foreseeability' can become intermeshed with that of 'remoteness of damage' was noted in a commentary on the *Lamb* case by Michael Jones:

What is plain from *Lamb* is that reasonable foresight is being asked to do too much in the realm of remoteness of damage. The problem arises from the positive formulation of the test of reasonable foresight, namely that a defendant is liable for any damage he can reasonably foresee as a consequence of the breach of duty. It has been argued that *The Wagon Mound* is authority only for the negative proposition that a defendant is *not* liable for *unforeseeable* damage. He *may* be liable for foreseeable damage, but in some circumstances further tests can exclude liability. *Perl* demonstrates that at times reasonable foresight is also being asked to do too much in the realm of duty of care. The plaintiffs' argument rested upon an undiscriminating application of Lord Atkin's neighbour principle – if the damage sustained was a foreseeable consequence of the defendant's act or omission, he is liable.

Here, in *P Perl (Exporters) Ltd* v. *Camden Borough Council* (1984), the defendant council had let business premises to the plaintiff. The council also owned an adjoining basement flat which was empty and unlocked. Complaints had been made to the council about lack of security, but nothing was done. Over a weekend thieves knocked a hole through the common wall and stole 700 garments belonging to the plaintiffs. The Court of Appeal, reversing the High Court, found the defendants not liable, despite 'very considerable carelessness'. Lord Justice Oliver said: 'I think that the question of the existence of a duty and that of whether the damage brought about by the act of a third party is too remote are simply two facets of the same problem.'

In *Brice* v. *Brown* (1984) the plaintiff, aged 42, who suffered since childhood from a personality disorder, was, with her daughter, a passenger in a taxi. A collision with a bus resulted on account of the defendant's negligence. Although the plaintiff was uninjured her daughter was not, with the consequence that on account of the alarm caused the mother's mental state deteriorated – she attempted suicide and had to be admitted to a mental hospital several times. The defendant was held liable – the nervous shock was a natural and probable result of the negligent action. The defendant was liable for something reasonably foreseeable and such of its direct consequences as were not dissimilar in type or kind, whether initially foreseeable or not.

Issues of causation were seen in the nervous shock case of *Page* v. *Smith (No 2)* (1996), where the plaintiff had suffered from myalegic encephalomyelitis (ME) for about 20 years. As seen above, a car accident made the ME worse and permanent; the Court of Appeal, applying *McGhee* and *Wilsher*, although the cases were not consistent, held the accident had on the balance of probabilities materially increased the symptoms of ME, and therefore liability had been established. The immense problems of drawing up satisfactory rules for nervous shock, as seen in *Page* v. *Smith (No 1)*, were further illustrated in *Vernon* v. *Bosley (No 1)* (1997) and *Vernon* v. *Bosley (No 2)* (1997), where a nanny drove into a swiftly flowing river, causing the plaintiff's two daughters to drown. The plaintiff arrived on the scene to witness the attempts to pull the car out of the river, but mere grief was not the same as nervous shock.

The House of Lords wrestled with the concepts of duty of care and reasonable foreseeability in *Smith* v. *Littlewoods Organisation Ltd* (1987), where the defendants bought a cinema, intending to demolish it. Teenagers trespassed in the building and burnt it down; the fire damaged neighbouring properties. Lord Goff noted, somewhat obscurely, that liability in negligence for harm caused by the deliberate wrongdoing of others could not be founded simply upon foreseeability that the plaintiff would suffer loss or damage by reason of such wrongdoing. The reason behind the principle was that there were circumstances where conditions of practical justice 'impel us to reject a general imposition of liability for foreseeable damage'.

ABNORMAL PLAINTIFFS

Where damage occurs only because of some abnormality in the person or property of the plaintiff which the defendant neither knew about nor could reasonably have foreseen, then no action will lie. Where, however, damage is foreseeable but is more severe than one would expect due to the abnormality of the plaintiff, the defendant is liable. In these circumstances the rule is that one must take one's victim as one finds him (*Smith* v. *Leech Brain* (1962)). For example, the fact that a person injured in a road traffic accident (one of the more common forms of negligence) has an 'egg-shell' skull and suffers more severe injuries than another person would, does not prevent the defendant from being liable for those severe injuries. Similarly, the fact that the injured person earns high wages does not mean that the defendant can argue that he should only pay compensation at the level of the national average wage. Does the 'egg-shell skull' rule apply to psychiatric or mental conditions? In theory the answer seems to be 'yes', as suggested by the decision in *Brice* v. *Brown*, but that does not entirely accord with the 1994 decision of the Court of Appeal in *McFarlane* v. *EE Caledonia* noted above.

ECONOMIC LOSS

The tort of negligence has been widened to bring economic loss within its scope, but only in certain circumstances, as already indicated earlier under consideration of certain building cases. Firstly, economic loss is recoverable where that loss is 'immediately consequential upon injury to the plaintiff's person or property' (*Cattle* v. *Stockton Waterworks* (1875)). The line drawn by this was clearly shown by the case of *Spartan Steel & Alloys Ltd* v. *Martin & Co.* (1973). The defendants negligently cut a cable carrying electric power to the plaintiff's factory, thus interrupting power supplies for 14 hours. It was held that the plaintiffs were entitled to damages for physical damage to the molten metal in their furnaces and also for the loss of profit on the sale of that metal. They could not recover the loss of profit on other work that they could have carried out during the 14-hour period as such loss of profit was not directly consequential upon any damage to the plaintiff's property. The Court of Appeal recognised that the rule concerning economic loss arising from physical damage was not particularly based upon any logical rule or legal principle, but rather upon policy.

However, liability for purely economic loss arising from a negligent *act* was considerably widened in 1982 by the judgment of the House of Lords in the Scottish case of *Junior Books Ltd* v. *Veitchi Co. Ltd*. Here the defendants were sub-contractors, nominated as such in a building contract between the plaintiffs and the principal contractors. The defendants' task was to lay floors in the plaintiffs' new factory. The floors proved to be defective. The plaintiffs decided to sue the sub-contractors in tort; they were not in a contractual relationship with the defendants, only with the main contractors whom the plaintiffs for some reason decided not to sue, either in contract or tort. Under English law the doctrine of privity of contract means that a person who is not a party to a contract cannot be sued for breach of contract, however close in practice he may be to the object of the contract. But the effect of the judgment in this case was, by means of tort, to deal another blow to the doctrine of privity.

There had been neither danger to health or property nor economic loss arising from any threat of damage to persons or property. Nonetheless the plaintiffs claimed substantial damages – £50,000 for replacing the cracked composition flooring and £150,000 for financial (economic) loss. The latter included loss of profit occasioned by a stoppage of work at the factory. The majority of the House of Lords seemed undeterred by the 'floodgates' argument, that a decision in favour of the plaintiffs would open up the way to a host of similar actions. Lord Roskill thought that the degree of proximity between the parties was as close as it could be short of actual privity of contract. Lord Roskill and two of his fellow Law Lords (Lord Fraser of Tullybelton and Lord Russell of Killowen) felt that a duty of care existed to avoid causing purely economic loss that was foreseeable and consequential on defective workmanship. Lord Keith of Kinkel did not go quite as far, but nonetheless he held that the plaintiffs were entitled to recover, not on the grounds that they had simply acquired a bad floor instead of a good one, but for the reason that manufacturing operations had become less profitable on account of the fact that maintenance costs had risen, including, presumably, the problem of moving machinery while the floor was repaired. The *Junior Books* decision thus travelled beyond that in *Anns* v. *Merton London Borough Council* (1977) which concerned the duty to avoid financial loss where the loss was incurred by money spent in order to avert physical damage.

In respect of the 'floodgates' argument it could be argued that the decision in the *Junior Books* case was in marked contrast to that in *Weller and Co.* v. *Foot and Mouth Disease Research Institute* (1966). In this case a virus escaped from a research establishment and killed nearby cattle. This in consequence affected a local cattle auction – the auctioneers had no cattle to sell and therefore suffered economic loss. Mr Justice Widgery noted that the world of commerce would come to a halt and ordinary life would become intolerable if the law imposed a duty on all persons at all times to refrain from any conduct which might foreseeably cause detriment to another. Dairymen, transport contractors, sellers of cattle feed and many others would all too have claims. In *Henderson* v. *Merrett Syndicates Ltd* (1994)

Lord Goff acknowledged that 'some difficulty' had been created by the decision in *Junior Books*.

In *Leigh and Sillivan Ltd* v. *Aliakmon Shipping Co. Ltd* (1986), a somewhat complex maritime case involving damage to goods caused by bad stowage, Lord Justice Oliver, in the Court of Appeal, whose decision was upheld by the House of Lords, after reviewing the authorities, noted that in *Margarine Union GmbH* v. *Cambay Prince Steamship Co. Ltd (The Wear Breeze)* (1969) Mr Justice Roskill in a classic judgment held that shipowners owed no duty of care in the carriage of goods to persons other than one who owned the goods or had an immediate right to possession of them. Lord Justice Oliver said that the development of the law of tort of negligence over the past 20 years had been such that the question was one upon which it was now very difficult to extract any clear guidance from authority. The starting point seemed to be the decision of the House of Lords in *Simpson* v. *Thomson* (1877), an authoritative exposition of the policy of the law then as to the limits of recoverability of damages for unintentionally caused loss – see the dissenting judgment of Lord Simonds in *The Greystoke Castle* (1947).

His Lordship respectfully questioned whether it was necessarily the right approach to every alleged case of tortious liability in negligence to assume first that a duty of care necessarily arose towards every person who could foreseeably suffer loss and then to qualify that assumed duty only if some 'policy' consideration (in the sense of some pressing commercial or social justification) could be found to justify its qualification. It seemed a misreading of Lord Wilberforce's formulation in *Anns* to treat it as laying down a general principle that in all cases a duty of care was the necessary consequence of the fact of foreseeability of damage and that once it was found the court had to give effect to the concomitant duty unless it could discern some policy consideration which appeared to afford a valid ground for restricting it.

Lord Justice Robert Goff, who took a different line over *The Wear Breeze*, said that the effect of the authorities was that:

1 There was a greater readiness to examine cases of economic loss in order to ascertain whether there should be liability in negligence.

2 There had been a reaffirmation of the widely accepted view that there could not be a general right of recovery for economic loss on the simple basis of proximity as in the case of damage to persons or property.

3 There had been a gradual recognition of a right of recovery in purely economic loss in certain specific cases.

In the *Muirhead* case (the House of Lords declined to hear an appeal) the Court of Appeal drew the boundaries of economic loss tightly. The plaintiff was a wholesale fish merchant who had arranged with D1 for the installation of a tank for the storage of lobsters. D2 and D3 supplied the pumps, but these were not converted from French to UK voltage range, with the result that the oxygen supply was cut off and the entire stock was lost. The plaintiff sued D1, D2 and D3. D2 was held not liable at trial, being protected by an exclusion clause; D1 and D3 were held liable, but the former had gone into liquidation. D3, the French manufacturer, appealed. The Court of Appeal held D3 liable for the death of the lobster stock and lost profit, since this was reasonably foreseeable physical damage, but not for purely economic loss, that is the cost of a replacement motor and profits in the meantime (see *Spartan Steel*). The relationship between the plaintiff and D3 was insufficiently proximate and could be distinguished from the special circumstances of *Junior Books* (*Muirhead* v. *Industrial Tank Specialists* (1985)).

So, in *Simaan General Contracting Co.* v. *Pilkington Glass Ltd (No 2)* (1988) the Court of Appeal said that the proper route for the claim was via contract. The plaintiffs should have sued the subcontractors who in turn had a right of action against the defendants, on the basis of the contracts and exclusion clauses that subsisted. Here the plaintiffs were the principal contractors for a building in Dubai, and the supply and erection of walling materials had been subcontracted. Glass units were to be supplied by the defendants, but they turned out not to be of uniform colour and the building owner as a result withheld payment from the plaintiffs who sued the defendants, the glass suppliers, for economic loss. Lord Justice Dillon remarked that the speeches in *Junior Books* had been the subject of so much analysis and discussion with differing explanations of the basis of the case that it could not now be regarded as a useful pointer to any development of the law – indeed, it was difficult, he said, to see that future citation from it could serve any useful purpose.

A similar point was made in *Greater Nottingham Co-operative Society* v. *Cementation Piling and Foundation Ltd* (1988) where Lord Justice Woolf said that he would not extend the exception to the general principle that economic loss was not recoverable in the absence of physical damage; in this case the defendants, who had a collateral agreement with the Society, were being sued for economic loss on account of negligent pile driving operations and the pure delay that ensued.

In the 1988 case of *D & F Estates Ltd* v. *Church Commissioners for England* the House of Lords dismissed a claim in negligence by the plaintiffs, occupiers of a block of flats built by the third defendants on land owned by the first defendants, the Church Commissioners, for faulty plastering which had been sub-contracted. The first plaintiffs, D & F Estates, took out a lease on one of the flats and allowed occupation of this flat by a Mr and Mrs Tillman, the second and third plaintiffs, who also were directors of D & F Estates. After moving in, the plaintiffs noticed cracks appearing in the plaster work, which had been carried out by an independent firm of plastering contractors employed by the (third) defendants. The (first) plaintiffs sued the (third) defendants for the cost of remedial work to the plaster, the cost of cleaning carpets, loss of rent whilst the work was carried out, and damages for disturbance to the second and third plaintiffs. (The second defendants, Hyde Park Property Development, were now in liquidation.) Lord Bridge observed that it was trite law that the employer of an independent contractor was not liable for the negligence committed by the contractor, subject to certain exceptions, and he added, as if finally laying the short-lived *Junior Books* to rest, that the majority decision in *Junior Books* v. *Veitchi* (1983) was so dependent on the unique relationship between the parties that the decision could not be regarded as laying down any principle of general application in the law of tort.

The *D & F Estates* case in 1988 was an important decision in a clutch of parallel cases dealing with economic loss, especially as it came from the House of Lords and addressed questions raised in both *Junior Books* and *Anns*. Of course, an important factual distinction was that *Junior Books* was concerned with a sizeable commercial operation, whereas *D & F* centred around a more limited but still substantial claim for faulty domestic plastering.

Lord Bridge went on to observe that the authorities, it seemed, spoke with such an uncertain voice on the question of whether the cost of making good the defective plaster was irrecoverable that, no matter how searching the analysis to which they were subjected, they yielded no clear and conclusive answer. It was more profitable to examine the issue in the light of first principles.

If a hidden defect, he said, in a chattel was the cause of personal injury or damage to property other than the chattel itself, the manufacturer was liable under the *Donoghue* v. *Stevenson* principle of duty of care to one's neighbour. If, however, the hidden defect was discovered before any such damage was caused, there was no longer any room for the application of that principle. The chattel was now defective in quality, but it was no longer dangerous. It might be valueless or capable of economic repair. In either case, the economic loss was recoverable in contract by a buyer or hirer entitled to the benefit of a relevant warranty of quality but was not recoverable in tort by a remote buyer or hirer.

If the same principle, Lord Bridge continued, applied in the field of real property to the liability of the builder of a permanent structure that was dangerously defective, that liability could only arise if the defect remained hidden until the defective structure caused personal injury or damage to property other than the structure itself. If the defect was discovered before any damage had been done, the loss sustained by the owner of the structure, who had to repair or demolish it to avoid a potential source of danger to third parties, would seem to be purely economic. In the instant case, the only hidden defect had been in the plaster. The only item pleaded by the plaintiffs as damage to other property had been 'cost of cleaning carpets and other possessions damaged or dirtied by falling plaster, £50'. Once it had appeared that the plaster was loose, any danger of personal injury or of further injury to other property could have been simply avoided by its timely removal. The cost of replacing it, either in 1980 or subsequently, had not been an item for which Wates could possibly be made liable in negligence under the principle in *Donoghue* v. *Stevenson* or any legitimate development of that principle, Lord Bridge concluded.

As noted earlier, in *Nitrigin Eireann Teoranta* v. *Inco Alloys Ltd* (1992), it was said that a cause of action in negligence does not accrue when a defect in a chattel occurs if the loss sustained is the pure economic loss of repairing the chattel. However, if the defect subsequently causes physical damage to other property, the loss is not economic loss and a cause of action then accrues. In this instance on 27 June 1984 a pipe cracked again and burst, causing an explosion and damage to the plant. The plaintiffs issued a writ on 21 June 1990 alleging negligence against the defendant. The defendant's argument, relying on *D & F Estates* and *Murphy*, was that a latent defect which caused personal injury or damage to other property gave rise to a cause of action but once the defect was no longer latent, the law did not provide a cause of action in negligence. However, the cases relied on supposed that the defect was discovered before any damage was done. The cost of so doing was then irrecoverable economic loss. But here physical damage to other property did occur, for the plaintiffs had not diagnosed the cause of cracking and had not therefore sufficiently repaired the pipe to avoid the physical damage caused by the explosion.

In the *D & F Estates* case Lord Oliver said that the underlying logical basis for, and the boundaries of, the doctrine emerging from *Anns* v. *Merton London Borough Council* were not entirely clear to him. It at least seemed clear that, in so far as the case was authority for the proposition that a builder responsible for the construction of a building was liable in tort at common law for damage occurring through his negligence to the very thing that he had constructed, such liability was limited directly to cases where the defect threatened the health or safety of occupants or third parties and, possibly, other property. In such a case, however, the damages recoverable were limited to expenses necessarily incurred in averting that danger. *Anns* could not properly be adapted to support the recovery of damages for pure economic loss going beyond that, and such loss was not recoverable in tort unless the case could be brought within the principle of reliance established by *Hedley Byrne* v. *Heller and Partners*.

It is clear therefore that one of the major implications of the House of Lords' decision in *D & F Estates* v. *Church Commissioners* was that the appellate courts were now worried that the floodgates were about to burst on claims for purely financial loss. Indeed this concern had largely been presaged in the *Peabody* case in 1984.

The judicial dicta in a number of cases in 1988 therefore pointed towards confining *Anns* to its particular facts as *Junior Books* already had been. And *Anns*, of course, was largely concerned with the difference between the powers and duties of public authorities under statutory law, and the relationship between such powers/duties and the common law duty of care. In the *Simaan* case the Court of Appeal decided that a builder could not sue his sub-contractor's supplier because no contract subsisted between them, and in the case of *Greater Nottingham Co-operative Society Ltd* v. *Cementation Piling and Foundation Ltd* (1988), just a few months later, a differently constituted Court of Appeal held that although a collateral contract did exist between the parties, the building owner could nonetheless not sue a sub-contractor since the contract did not provide for liability for that type of negligence. The *D & F Estates* case showed that a defect in a building causing personal injury will give rise to a claim for negligence, but if the defect is discovered before any injury or damage occurs the builder is not liable for the cost of repairs. In other words, outside of contract, the cost of repair amounting to purely economic loss is not recoverable. The House of Lords in *D & F Estates* also noted at some length how the Defective Premises Act 1972 and the NHBC scheme in relation to the Act had overtaken events considered in *Dutton* and like cases. In the *Greater Nottingham* case, Lord Justice Woolf bluntly observed:

> To apply *Junior Books* to the facts of this case would involve extending the exception to the general principle that economic loss is not recoverable in the absence of actual or apprehended physical damage beyond what is strictly required by authority binding on this court and as is now apparent the courts, for the time being at any rate, are clearly against any such extension.

Thus, in *Andrews* v. *Schooling* (1991), the economic loss concerned did come within the protection of the Defective Premises Act 1972, here failure to deal with penetrating damp in a cellar purchased on a 199-year lease. But the critical case was *Murphy* v. *Brentwood District Council* (1990). In the House of Lords Lord Keith said that it was difficult to draw a distinction in principle between an article that was useless or valueless and one that suffered from a defect that would render it dangerous in use but that was discovered by the purchaser in time to avert any possibility of injury. The purchaser might incur expense in putting right the defect or, more probably, discard the article. In either case the loss was purely economic. It had now to be recognised that, although the damage in *Anns* had been characterised as physical damage by Lord Wilberforce, it had been purely economic loss. That being so, the next point for examination was whether the avoidance of loss of that nature had fallen within the scope of any duty of care owed to the plaintiffs (in *Anns*) by the local authority. On the basis of the law as it had stood at the time of the decision the answer had to be 'No'.

The right to recover for pure economic loss, not flowing from physical injury, had not then extended beyond the situation where the loss had been sustained through reliance on negligent misstatements, as in *Hedley Byrne & Co.* v. *Heller & Partners*. The duty under *Anns* would open up an exceedingly wide field of claims, involving the introduction of something in the nature of a transmissible warranty of quality. Liability under *Anns* was postulated upon the existence of a present or imminent danger to health or safety. But considering that the loss involved in incurring expenditure to avert the danger was pure economic loss, there would seem to be no logic in confining the remedy to cases where such danger existed. It was clear that *Anns* had not proceeded on any basis of established principle but had introduced a new species of liability governed by a principle indeterminate in character but having the potentiality of covering a wide range of situations, involving chattels as well as real property, in which it had never hitherto been thought that the law of negligence had any proper place. There was much to be said for the view that in what was essentially a consumer protection field, as Lord Bridge had adverted in *D & F Estates*, the precise extent and limits of the liabilities that in the public interest should be imposed on builders and local authorities were best left to the legislature.

In *Murphy* the plaintiff had bought a new house which had been constructed on an infilled site. The foundations were made up of a special concrete raft designed specifically to prevent damage from any settlement that might occur. The local authority approved of the raft design and the house had passed the necessary building regulations. Ten years later serious cracks developed in the plasterwork, and the concrete raft was shown to be defective. The plaintiff was forced to sell the property for £35,000 below its market value. His insurance company backed him to bring a claim of negligence against the local council so as to recover the loss, alleging that the plaintiff and his family had been put in imminent danger because the settlement had fractured gas and soil pipes.

The Law Lords (unusually seven sat in this instance) accepted that his arguments were strong, but still held that he was not entitled to compensation. Lord Keith said: 'I think it must now be recognised that *Anns* [the homeowner suing Merton] did not proceed on any basis of principle at all, but constituted a remarkable example of judicial legislation'. Lord Bridge said:

> If the defect becomes apparent before any injury or damage has been caused, the loss sustained by the building owner is purely economic. If the defect can be repaired at economic cost, that is the measure of the loss. If the building cannot be repaired, it may have to be abandoned as unfit for occupation and therefore valueless. These economic losses are recoverable if they flow from breach of a relevant contractual duty, but, here again in the absence of a special relationship of proximity they are not recoverable in tort. The only qualification I would make to this is that, if a building stands so close to the boundary of the building owner's land that after discovery of the dangerous defect it remains a potential source of injury to persons or property on neighbouring land or on the highway, the building owner ought, in principle, to be entitled to recover in tort from the negligent builder the cost of obviating the danger, whether by repair or by demolition, so far as that cost is necessarily incurred in order to protect himself from potential liability to third parties.

Lord Oliver added:

> I frankly doubt whether . . . the categorisation of the damage as 'material', 'physical', 'pecuniary' or 'economic' provides a particularly useful contribution. Where it does, I think, serve a useful purpose is in identifying those cases in which it is necessary to search for and find something more than the mere reasonable foreseeability of damage which has occurred as providing the degree of 'proximity' necessary to support the action.

Lord Jauncey observed:

> Parliament imposed a liability on builders by the Defective Premises Act 1972 – a liability which falls far short of that which would be imposed upon them by *Anns*. There can therefore be no policy reason for imposing a higher common law duty on builders, from which it follows that there is equally no policy reason for imposing such a high duty on local authorities. Parliament is far better equipped than the courts to take policy decisions in the field of consumer protection.

Lady Wilcox, chairman of the National Consumer Council, said that the decision meant 'that for the first time this century, legal rights have been taken away from consumers'. She added: 'Parliament has legislated to give consumers greater protection from faulty and dangerous products in the 1987 Consumer Protection Act. It is high time that it also protected people who through no fault of their own find that their houses are faulty and dangerous.'

Richardson v. *West Lindsey District Council* (1990) was similar to *Murphy* and here the Court of Appeal decided that it was not normally just or reasonable to impose on the local authority a duty of care owed to the building owner himself to ensure that he had complied with the regulations, regardless of whether the loss suffered was physical or economic.

Essentially what *Murphy* and *Caparo* showed was that in order to claim for damages for economic loss in tort for negligence it is essential to bring the claim within the principles of *Hedley Byrne* v. *Heller*. Under *Anns* the categorisation of the resulting cracks to the building and threat to the occupants as property damage was always conceptually exceptionally difficult to follow. But the house-owner in *Anns* v. *Merton* had suffered essentially only economic loss; in other words he was out of pocket because he paid too much for the house, too much by the amount it would cost him to put right the defects, or move elsewhere. Even when injuries result it is only where the defect remains latent that the builder or local authority inspector can be liable. Once the defect has been discovered so that the occupant knows the full extent of the risk he will no longer be able to recover for personal injury. Any injuries that he suffers from staying on in the building will then be his own personal fault.

The builder (like the manufacturer) cannot now be liable to a subsequent purchaser of the building for defects due to careless construction except where those defects cause personal injury or damage to other property. But the defect must have remained latent until such damage was caused. He cannot therefore be liable for the pure economic loss suffered by a purchaser who having discovered the defect is forced to spend money in making the building safe and suitable for its intended use. This was also made quite clear by the House of Lords in *Department of the Environment* v. *Thomas Bates* (1990), where the design defects presented no immediate danger to those occupying the building, but even if they had it was apparent from the judgments in *Murphy* that the claim would still have been rejected. And if the occupier does not vacate he will be responsible for any injuries that result (with perhaps a right to contribution from the builders) but the repair bills will remain irrecoverable as economic loss. But where, as we have seen from Lord Bridge's comments above, a building is built close to the boundary of the owner's land and threatens injury to neighbours or those using the highway, then the owner should have the right to recover from the negligent builders the cost of removing the danger, that is demolishing or repairing the building. Both builder and occupier have jointly caused a nuisance which they can be compelled to remove, by the neighbour or local authority (private nuisance as far as the neighbour is concerned, public nuisance in relation to the highway).

In *D & F Estates* it was suggested that a 'complex structure' like a building could consist of separate items of property so that for example the foundations might damage the rest of the building built on top of them. The House of Lords in *Murphy* emphatically rejected this idea so that if the builder builds the entire building he has in fact built one item of property only. But under *Donoghue* v. *Stevenson* a subcontractor or manufacturer of materials installed in the building might be liable for causing damage to the building structure (eg defective equipment such as central heating boilers). And also negligent advice will fall under *Hedley Byrne*, as seen in *Pirelli*, which was originally decided under *Anns*, where consultant engineers negligently advised a factory owner as to the construction of a factory chimney. Even *Junior Books* v. *Veitchi*, is now seen as a *Hedley Byrne* case, where the factory owner acted on the negligent advice from subcontractors that the floor would be suitable.

In *Anns* Lord Wilberforce had characterised structural manifestations caused by an underlying defect in the foundations as 'material, physical damage'. In *Murphy*, the House held that this was incorrect. The damage suffered in this case was simply damage to the building itself. This was not damage that would ordinarily come within the type of damage recoverable as a result of *Donoghue* v. *Stevenson*. The relevant property for the purposes of recovery under *Donoughue* v. *Stevenson* is, as Lord Keith pointed out, property other than the very property which gave rise to the danger of physical damage concerned. What the plaintiffs were really complaining about was that, as a result of the defendants' negligence, their house had diminished in value (by some £35,000). This was pre-eminently economic loss, period.

To emphasise the point again, in reaching the decision that the loss was economic, the House of Lords rejected two 'escape routes' which the courts had used in previous cases to avoid such a characterisation, as the *All England Law Reports Annual Review* of 1990 put it. First, in *D & F Estates*, Lords Bridge and Oliver had postulated the notion of a 'complex structure', as outlined above, in order to explain *Anns*. 'The application of the 'complex structure' argument allowed the court to fit the claim in a case like *Murphy* within the conventional analysis of *Donoghue* v. *Stevenson*.' Essentially, the House of Lords rejected this argument.

> **Both Lords Bridge and Oliver in *Murphy* condemned the argument's artificiality and said that this was not an argument they had advanced with any enthusiasm in *D & F Estates*. Instead, they had advanced it as the only 'logically possible' explanation of *Anns*. Reconsidering the argument as a matter of principle, the House held that it was untenable and should not be used in the future. The House was clearly correct in identifying the fictional nature of the argument. This has always been clear. The attraction of the argument was that it enabled the courts to permit recovery in circumstances where the loss was economic without labelling it as such.**

Richard O'Dair commented in 1991:

> **The concept of a complex structure was mooted by Lords Bridge and Oliver in the *D & F Estates* case as a way of relocating *Anns* within the**

orthodox categories of the law of negligence. The theory involved viewing a piece of property such as a building in terms of its constituent parts. In *Murphy* whilst it was made clear that the theory could have no application to cases involving defective foundations, only Lord Oliver could bring himself to reject it altogether. Lords Bridge, Keith and Jauncey each gave examples of exceptional instances where the complex structure theory might be applicable. None of them, however, gave any coherent explanation of why these instances were exceptional. Lord Jauncey stated that a subcontractor who negligently incorporates into a building a steel frame which fails to give the required support to and thus damages the floors and walls may still owe a duty of care to the occupier. If so the complex structure theory would fulfil exactly the same function as the *Anns* doctrine. Then there is the question of the status and significance of *Junior Books* v. *Veitchi*. In *D & F Estates*, Lord Bridge said that the case involved a unique albeit non-contractual relationship but laid down no general principle of the law of tort. At this point one might have thought it reasonable to consign the case to legal history. In *Murphy*, however, Lord Keith's attitude is altogether different. His Lordship seems to regard the decision as within the well established principle of reliance-based liability exemplified by *Hedley Byrne*. Does this mean that upon proof of some as yet unspecified degree of reliance owners of property may still be able to sue the builders and architects in tort on the basis of *Junior Books*? If so, how does this affect the position of the local authority? If so, has not *Murphy* shut in the faces of litigants the door marked 'Anns' only to reopen that marked 'Junior Books'?

The second 'escape route', derived from the case of *Anns* itself, was that where the defective building or product threatens imminent danger to the health or safety of persons occupying it, damages were recoverable to put the building (or product) into a state where it was no longer a danger . . . The purchaser is left with something of less value than he originally acquired. The plaintiff's loss is thus economic.

A similar line of reasoning was taken in a different context, that of *Caparo*. As we have seen earlier, in *Caparo* (which held existing shares in Fidelity but wanted to purchase more to effect a take-over, and where Touche Ross had audited the accounts to reveal a pre-tax profit of £1.3 million, but in fact it was a loss of £400,000) the trial judge said no duty of care was owed, but the Court of Appeal said there was a duty to existing shareholders. The House of Lords upheld the trial judge. Lord Oliver referred to the danger of creating 'a liability wholly indefinite in area, duration and amount which opens up, a limitless vista of uninsurable risks for the professional man', a matter which was probably at the heart of this unsatisfactory judgment. What hope is there for the small investor? It might be argued that declining to hold auditors liable entails the partial abandonment of tort law as a deterrent to inducing auditors to maintain professionally acceptable standards. In reality, different policy arguments are being weighed against respective strengths.

The rationale in *Murphy,* therefore, is that to permit the building owner or occupier to recover his economic loss would logically lead to an unacceptably wide category of claims in respect of buildings or chattels which were defective in quality and would, in effect, introduce product liability and transmissible warranties of quality into the law of tort by means of judicial legislation.

Marianne Giles has noted:

> **The House of Lords decided that the liability of a local authority should not be greater than that of the primary tortfeasor, the builder. The House of Lords, taking an equally direct view of the damage and categorising it as pure economic loss, held that there was no special proximity between the local authority and the purchaser of a property in this kind of case which was sufficient to establish liability for economic loss in tort. This ruling effectively prevents claims for economic loss resulting from defective buildings, even the kind of claim which is based upon preventing danger to health and safety which had been the starting point of such claims in *Anns*.**

So in effect proximity is now the key word, although probably it unbolts few doors. In that regard Lord Oliver said in *Murphy* that *Anns* was irrational because although the claim was for the economic loss due to the defect, the claim lay only if the defect rendered the structure dangerous. David Howarth has remarked: 'All we are offered in the place of the two-stage test is a three-stage test that inserts between Lord Wilberforce's two stages a third stage called "proximity", something that even the judges admit is too vague to define.' 'Proximity' was 'merely a description of circumstances from which, pragmatically, the courts conclude that a duty of care exists', Lord Oliver said in *Caparo* v. *Dickman.*

It should be noted, however, that in the case of *Marc Rich & Co. AG* v. *Bishop Rock Marine Co. Ltd* (1995) (involving a loss of a cargo aboard a ship which sank on a voyage from Peru and Chile to Italy and the USSR in 1986) Lord Lloyd, dissenting, remarked that there was a risk that the law of negligence would disintegrate into a series of isolated decisions without any coherent principle at all and the retreat from *Anns* would turn into a rout. The Court of Appeal stressed that the test for whether or not a duty of care existed in respect of both physical damage and pure economic loss was the three stage test first outlined in *Yuen Kun-Yeu* v. *Attorney-General of Hong Kong*, that is:

1 Was the damage reasonably foreseeable?

2 Was there a proximate relationship between the plaintiff and the defendant?

3 Would it be just, fair and reasonable to hold the defendant liable to the plaintiff?

Negligent misstatement

Secondly, economic loss caused by a negligent misstatement can in some instances be recovered, as indicated earlier. This was laid down by the case of *Hedley Byrne and Co. Ltd* v. *Heller and Partners Ltd* (1964) in which the House of Lords unanimously decided that a duty to take care in making statements existed whenever there was a special relationship between the parties and the defendant had not disclaimed responsibility for the correctness of the statement. The decision of the House in respect of negligent misstatement was, in fact, *obiter* since the defendants had disclaimed responsibility at the head of their reply and the plaintiff's action failed for that reason. The circumstances in which a duty of care will arise when a person makes a statement was expressed by Lord Morris as follows:

> **If, in a sphere in which a person is so placed that others could reasonably rely on his judgment or skill or on his ability to make careful enquiry, a person takes it on himself to give information or advice to, or allows his information or advice to be passed on to another person who, as he knows or should know, will place reliance on it, then a duty of care will arise.**

This dictum was followed in the case of *Esso Petroleum Co. Ltd* v. *Mardon* (1976) in which a tenant was held entitled to recover loss caused when he was persuaded to take a lease on a petrol station by a negligent representation that its sales would be 200,000 gallons annually. The re-routing of a highway had, in fact, caused sales to drop considerably and the tenant suffered financial loss as a result.

In *Spring* v. *Guardian Assurance plc* (1994) the plaintiff worked for the Corinium companies and these were sold to GRE (Guardian Royal Exchange); he was dismissed. He then sold the products of Scottish Amicable and GRE supplied a reference to the latter, which was the 'kiss of death'. Spring was a fool but not dishonest, it was said. Scottish Amicable therefore did not take on Spring; the trial judge, dismissing the claims for malicious falsehood, and relying on *Lawton* v. *BOC Transhield Ltd* (1987) held the defendants had been negligent in preparing the reference. But the Court of Appeal overruled *Lawton* and followed the decision of the New Zealand Court of Appeal in *Bell-Booth Group Ltd* v. *Attorney General* (1989) – the duty of the provider of a reference was governed by the tort of defamation not by the tort of negligence, and the defence of qualified privilege would only be destroyed if malice were present. So, it would appear, accountants carrying out an audit in normal circumstances are now effectively free from all possible liabilities in tort and can only be liable for negligence to the company (ie in contract), *Caparo Industries* v. *Dickman* (1990) and *Mariola Marine Co.* v. *Lloyds Register (The Morning Watch)* (1990) where a surveyor could not be sued because the vessel was unseaworthy, because of a speculative investment in respect of an entry in the Lloyds register, since such an entry was only concerned with seaworthiness; a plaintiff who uses information provided for one purpose for a completely different purpose cannot make use of the *Hedley Byrne* liability.

But the House of Lords overruled the Court of Appeal in *Spring*, although the speeches do not have a great deal of analysis to them. Lord Woolf said the primary source of any liability was contractual rather than tortious, and Lord Slynn implied a term into the contract. Lord Goff said that the vast majority of employers would continue to provide careful references, but those who failed to achieve that standard would have to compensate their employees or former employees who suffered damage in consequence; justice required that that should be done and his Lordship could not see any reason in policy why that justice should be denied, but Lord Keith dissented on public policy grounds.

CONTRIBUTORY NEGLIGLENCE

At common law the rule was that a plaintiff who was in any part the cause of his own injury could not recover any damages at all. The Law Reform (Contributory Negligence) Act 1945 altered this aspect of the law. The Act provided that where a plaintiff suffered injury 'as the result partly of his own fault and partly of the fault of any other person', then he could recover damages, but the damages must be reduced 'to such an extent as the court thinks just and equitable having regard to the claimant's share in the responsibility for the damage'. This can affect the damages not only where the plaintiff is negligent and to some degree causes the accident, for example, where a road accident occurs due to the bad driving of both parties, but also where the plaintiff has failed to take reasonable care for his own safety and has thereby contributed to his injuries although he has in no way caused the accident. This second leg of contributory negligence is illustrated by the following two cases: *Froom* v. *Butcher* (1976) where the plaintiff who was thrown through the windscreen of a car in a collision was found to have contributed to his injuries by failing to wear a seat-belt, and *Owens* v. *Brimmell* (1976) where it was held that a person is liable to be found guilty of contributory negligence if he travels as a passenger in a car with a driver he knows to be drunk. Contributory negligence is not easy to assess and at best the court can only arrive at a rough approximation of the share of the blame. It is a highly discretionary concept. In the Scottish case of *Mackay* v. *Borthwick* (1982) the court held that failure to wear a seat-belt, in the case of a driver or front-seat passenger, would probably amount to contributory negligence, except perhaps on short journeys. Normally in English cases a 25 per cent reduction in damages has been made if it can be shown that no injuries would have resulted had a seat-belt been worn, and 15 per cent where some injuries would still have resulted (20 per cent not 15 per cent in *Salmon* v. *Newland* (1983)). But since early 1983 it has been a criminal offence for most people not to wear a seat-belt, and this has increased the contributory liability factor substantially since that time, to at least 50 per cent in most cases.

Froom v. *Butcher* was followed in *Capps* v. *Miller* (1989) where the Court of Appeal held that a reduction of 10 per cent should be made in the plaintiff's damages, rather than the 15 per cent usually applied where there is a failure to wear a crash helmet (or seat belt in a car), since here the helmet was worn but insecurely fastened.

In the Australian case of *Azzopardi* v. *State Transport Authority* (1982) the plaintiff boarded a bus owned and operated by the defendant authority and commenced to walk down the aisle of the bus towards a seat in the centre of the vehicle. The bus started off suddenly and the passenger fell to the floor and was injured. The defendant was found 80 per cent liable for starting off with a sudden jerk, but the plaintiff was 20 per cent liable for failing to grip firmly a handhold. In *Barrett* v. *Ministry of Defence* (1993) an airman, on duty in Norway, and who was a heavy drinker, was held 25 per cent liable for his own death at a birthday party where he had been left unconscious by his fellow airmen.

Perverse as the logic might seem the courts have found for 100% contributory negligence. This was illustrated in the Court of Appeal decision in *Jayes* v. *IMI (Kynoch) Ltd* (1984), a case of breach of statutory duty under the Factories Act 1961. Lord Justice Goff said that the plaintiff was a very experienced man. Trouble had been experienced with a power press machine, fitters had been called in to deal with the lubrication problem and the guard was removed from the moving part of the machine. The machine had to be started to see if that assisted the work. The plaintiff pointed out that grease was getting on to the belt and got hold of a rag to wipe the grease off. The plaintiff put the rag where the grease was spreading. The rag got caught up. He tried to pull the rag out but the machine pulled his finger in and he lost the tip of it. The plaintiff was a man of complete frankness and openness. He knew that what he did was a very foolish and crazy thing to do. However, in *Pitts* v. *Hunt* (1990) it was clearly held by the Court of Appeal that to hold the claimant 100 per cent responsible was not to hold that he shared in the responsibility for the damage and was logically unsupportable. This was a question of *volenti* and *ex turpi causa* – the plaintiff as a pillion passenger encouraged a motor cyclist to drive recklessly and dangerously after both had been drinking together, but s.148(3) of the Road Traffic Act 1972 had precluded the defence of *volenti non fit injuria*.

In *Fitzgerald* v. *Lane* (1988), a serious road accident case, the Court of Appeal, upheld by the House of Lords, overruled the trial judge, since if the plaintiff and two car drivers were equally to blame, the correct assessment of damages was 50:50 (50:25 + 25), not one-third each, as between plaintiff and defendants.

It should also be noted that contributory negligence is no defence at common law to a claim in contract, *Basildon District Council* v. *J E Lesser (Properties)* (1984) and *A B Marintrans* v. *Comet Shipping* (1985), unless the defendant's liability in contract is the same as his liability in the tort of negligence independently of the existence of any contract (*Forsikringsaktieselskapet Vesta* v. *Butcher* (1989)). Contributory negligence must not be confused with issues of probability or causation, as seen in *Hotson* v. *East Berkshire Area Health Authority* (1987). Here a 13 year-old boy fell from a tree and fractured his hip. The hospital was slow to diagnose correctly and liability was admiited for five days of pain and suffering. The boy was left with a permanent disability, but there was a 75 per cent chance that this would have still occurred, even if prompt treatment had been given. The House of Lords refused to award damages for the permanent disability, since once liability is established on the balance of probabilities, a plaintiff's loss is payable in full. The Lords therefore overruled the trial judge, who, upheld by the Court of Appeal, had awarded 25 per cent damages (that is the 100 less 75 per cent probability). The question of contributory negligence and contractual obligations arose again in *Barclays Bank plc* v. *Fairclough Building Ltd* (1994).

REMEDIES

The principal remedy for negligence is an award of monetary damages. The amount can in some clases be calculated exactly, for instance, where a car is damaged the cost of repairing it can be readily assessed. The main difficulties in assessing monetary awards arise when the courts are dealing with personal injury cases. In these instances the court is endeavouring to compensate the injured person for some physical or mental harm, and it is often difficult to place a cash value on the loss of a limb, blindness or any other serious disability. In cases where a person is unable to follow his chosen career as the result of his injuries, the court will award not only a sum of money for the actual injuries received, but also a sum for estimated future loss of earnings. This again is difficult to assess, particularly in times of inflation and rapidly rising wages. One of the main problems of lump sum awards is that once the award is made and the time for appealing over, little can be done at a later date to alter it if the circumstances should change. This can create apparent injustice on either side, for example, the plaintiff may make a miraculous recovery and be able to resume a normal life, or on the other hand some unsuspected complication might arise, aggravating the plaintiff's condition and causing him great hardship in the future. The case of *Lim Poh Choo* v. *Camden and Islington Area Health Authority* (1979) is particularly notable here. As we have seen earlier the facts, briefly, were these: the plaintiff was a young Malaysian doctor employed by the National Health Service. As a result of negligence in a minor operation she suffered irremediable brain damage; her life was now a total wreck. The House of Lords, after hearing fresh evidence, reduced the total damages awarded from £243,309 to £229,298. The court held that only in exceptional circumstances could the risk of inflation be taken into account in respect of the assessment of damages for future loss. In *Croke* v. *Wiseman* (1982) the Court of Appeal reaffirmed the urgent need to reform the law of damages for personal injuries. In this case the infant plaintiff had suffered cardio-respiratory arrest while under examination in a hospital. The health authority admitted vicarious liability for negligence and the trial judge awarded £269,698 damages. The courts have frequently called for the legislative rationalisation of the award of damages (for example, in *Gammell* v. *Wilson* (1981)).

However, the Administration of Justice Act 1982, especially s.6, has been of some help here, having enacted a little of the Pearson Report, together with the Damages Act 1996 (in respect of the awarding of provisional damages and structured settlements).

With many large sums being awarded by the courts today, and the £1 million mark having been passed, insurance has become increasingly important. Insurance against third party claims for road accidents is, of course, compulsory for all drivers. In this way the State tries to prevent the situation arising whereby a person obtains judgment for a large sum of money by way of compensation, but is unable to enforce that judgment because the defendant is 'a man of straw', and thus receives none of the money to which the courts have said he is entitled.

SUB-AGENTS

In the bizarre case of *Balsamo* v. *Medici* (1984) it was held that there was no direct action in tort against a sub-agent. Here the plaintiff, an Italian, arranged for his vintage car to be taken by his friend, the first defendant, and acting ostensibly as his agent, to London for auction and for the proceeds of the sale to be collected by the plaintiff's mother-in-law. But the defendant arranged for a friend, one Morris, the second defendant, to hand over the money. Morris lost a vital telephone number and through his negligence the monies fell into a stranger's hands. The receipt of money by a sub-agent was the same as receipt by the agent himself – Medici was therefore liable for damages for breach of contract. Mr Justice Walton acknowledged that in the light of the *Junior Books* case the principle of liability, whatever it might be, had been extended beyond bailment to negligent work done by a sub-contractor, but was it possible to extend it without limit? His Lordship thought not. Otherwise, he said, the principle would come perilously close to abrogating completely the concept of privity of contract.

RES IPSA LOQUITUR

One final point should be noted under negligence and that is the doctrine of *res ipsa loquitur* (the thing speaks for itself). The normal rule is that it is up to the plaintiff to establish that negligence has occurred. Yet it not infrequently happens in negligence that the plaintiff is able to point to his injuries – they are self-evident – but he cannot show how the defendant supposedly caused the damage done. In such a situation the court may still be prepared to recognise the justness of the plaintiff's claim and thus to ask the defendant to disprove that claim, the *res ipsa loquitur* since on the facts the plaintiff has shown that there is a *prima facie* case for the defendant to answer. It is then up to the defendant to rebut those charges. In short, the court assists the plaintiff by inferring negligence on the part of the defendant if the injured party has made out a case of *prima facie* carelessness.

However, *res ipsa loquitur* has caused both the courts and legal commentators considerable confusion and there are conflicting definitions. In *McGhee* v. *National Coal Board* (1973) it appeared that the dermatitis contracted was due to the lack of washing facilities at the brick kilns the plaintiff was emptying, although it could not with certainty be claimed that this would have totally prevented the complaint. The Lords allowed the plaintiff's claim, a breach of duty having been admitted by the employers. In *Houghland* v. *R R Low (Luxury Coaches) Ltd* (1962) the court inferred negligence on the part of the defendant, although again *res ipsa loquitur* was not raised as such, on account of the fact that the plaintiff's suitcase having been stowed in the coach at the point of departure was missing at the plaintiff's destination. And in *Jones* v. *Great Western Railway Company* (1930) the court felt it reasonable to infer that the defendant company's employee had been negligent in his failure to warn a man crossing a railway line, who as a result was crushed to death.

Res ipsa loquitur – essentially a rule of evidence – owes its origins to the cases of *Byrne* v. *Boadle* (1863) and *Scott* v. *London and St Katherine Docks Co.* (1865). In the first case the plaintiff was struck by a bag of flour falling from a shop window. In the second a warehouse crane dropped bags of sugar. It was suggested in the *Scott* case that for *res ipsa* to operate the thing that caused the damage must be shown to have been under the control or management of the defendant. Most cases have followed this *dictum* but a few have simply turned upon *res ipsa* as being a principle of self-evident negligence. The issue of control was illustrated in a more recent case, that of *Ward* v. *Tesco Stores Ltd* (1976) (in this case the plaintiff slipped on spilled yoghurt). The court held that it was for the defendants to show that on the balance of probabilities the plaintiff would still have slipped on the yoghurt despite any system that was designed to give reasonable protection to customers against such spillage. But some difficulty has arisen in respect of those instances where specialist skills are required (as in medical cases, such as *Roe* v. *Minister of Health* (1954), referred to above, *Cassidy* v. *Ministry of Health* (1951), which involved poor post-operative care, and *Mahon* v. *Osborne* (1939), which concerned a swab left in the patient's body).

The doctrine of *res ipsa loquitur* is not without other difficulties. Passage of time is one such problem. In one railway case, *Gee* v. *Metropolitan Railway* (1873), the defendants were held liable for the plaintiff's falling out of a train on account of an improperly closed door since the train had only just left the station. Had it been a case of a long distance train stopping infrequently, thus giving the passengers themselves ample opportunity to tamper with the doors, the outcome would have been different, as in *Easson* v. *London and North Eastern Railway* (1944).

The burden of proof

Moreover, as indicated above if the evidence becomes involved and the defendant is able to cast some doubt on the plaintiff's *res ipsa* argument then, of course, what is in effect the burden of proof will pass back to the plaintiff and he must start again, arguing general principles of negligence and adducing evidence on that basis. This is what happened in *Barkway* v. *South Wales Transport Co. Ltd* (1950) where a passenger on a bus was killed, the bus having fallen down an embankment on account of a defective tyre. The House of Lords held *res ipsa* did not apply since on the facts the bus company's system of tyre inspection was negligent. However, in the Privy Council case of *Ng Chun Pui* v. *Lee* (1988) it was denied that the burden of proof actually shifts. On the other hand the defendant may find it difficult, if not impossible, to explain the cause at all, in which case *res ipsa* may have a better chance of succeeding, as illustrated by the cases of *Piening* v. *Wanless* (1968) and *Ludgate* v. *Lovett* (1969) (both cases involved vehicle steering difficulties) and *Henderson* v. *Henry E Jenkins and Sons* (1970). The latter was a more complicated case involving a lorry which ran out of control down a steep hill and killed a person in its path. The lorry had been serviced at regular intervals, but nevertheless a hole had appeared in the brake pipe, perhaps on account of some latent defect. The plaintiff's plea of *res ipsa* succeeded, or at least so it appears, for the phrase itself was not mentioned in the Law Lords' judgments.

In *Piening* v. *Wanless* (1968), an Australian case, W. was a passenger in P.'s vehicle, an old car, which was being driven at a moderate speed along an open country road whose surface was good. The car suddenly swerved from one side of the road to the other and having left the road overturned. W. sued P., his brother-in-law, for the severe injuries received. The court held that the failure of the steering mechanism did not of itself afford evidence of negligence. Mr Justice Windeyer said:

> The owner, or other person having the care of a motor vehicle, might well be held to be negligent if he failed to take reasonable care that it was roadworthy and safe to drive before allowing anyone to take it upon the road. But to say that is very far from saying that whenever the steering mechanism of a motor vehicle fails and nothing more than that is proved, the thing speaks for itself and that a jury, or a judge of fact, could find that the driver was negligent. I do not think that common experience supports such an inference.

However, in *Ludgate* v. *Lovett* (1969) a van being driven on the M1 at about 60 mph late in the evening, suddenly swerved to the right. In correcting the swerve the driver made the van go to the left and the vehicle turned over and hit the verge. The defendant, the driver, was severely injured. The van owner sued the defendant for failure to take care of the van, which had been damaged in the accident. The defendant counterclaimed for personal injury, which the trial judge disallowed. The Court of Appeal, to whom the plaintiff appealed, held that in the circumstances there was insufficient evidence to rebut the inference of negligence as raised by the maxim *res ipsa loquitur* and the plaintiff's claim would be allowed. Lord Justice Harman observed:

> So it follows that, in a *res ipsa loquitur* case, even though you, the defendant, cannot explain why or how the accident happened, it is open to you to satisfy the [court] that you took all reasonable precautions, or did not, in other words, act in any negligent manner at all.

In the *Barkway* case Lord Porter said:

> The doctrine is dependent on the absence of explanation, and, although it is the duty of the defendants, if they desire to protect themselves, to give an adequate explanation of the cause of the accident, yet, if the facts are sufficiently known, the question ceases to be one where the facts speak for themselves, and the solution is to be found by determining whether, on the facts as established, negligence is to be inferred or not.

In *Lloyde* v. *West Midlands Gas Board* (1971) Lord Justice Megaw remarked:

> I doubt whether it is right to describe *res ipsa loquitur* as a 'doctrine'. I think it is no more than an exotic, though convenient, phrase to

describe what is in essence no more than a commonsense approach, not limited by technical rules, to the assessment of the effect of evidence in certain circumstances. It means that a plaintiff *prima facie* establishes negligence where: (i) it is not possible for him to prove precisely what was the relevant act or omission which set in train the events leading to the accident; but (ii) on the evidence as it stands at the relevant time it is more likely than not that the effective cause of the accident was *some* act or omission of the defendant or of someone for whom the defendant is responsible, which act or omission constitutes a failure to take proper care for the plaintiff's safety.

CONSUMER PROTECTION ACT 1987

The Consumer Protection Act 1961 had made provision for statutory control of the sale of various commodities, such as firearms, food for human consumption, coal and scrap metal. The Consumer Safety Act 1978 provided for regulation of the composition, design and safety of goods. However, these provisions had proved inadequate for the protection of persons injured by defective products, and were even grossly inadequate by comparison with the position in the USA, as seen in the claims for compensation from the use of the arthritis drug Opren. The deterrent of legal costs was all the more effective in the UK as until 1991 legal aid was not allowed for 'class actions', used in the USA to dispose in single proceedings of a large number of related claims. However pressure from the EC Commission finally pushed the United Kingdom into bringing in the Consumer Protection Act 1987.

Part I of the Act was enacted following an EC Directive of 1985 which required all the member States to enact similar legislation and made producers liable for death, personal injury or reasonably foreseeable contractual loss or damage caused by defective products. The Act provided that the 'producer' shall be strictly liable for the damage caused, unless one of certain limited defences was available, notably the 'state of the art' defence; that is 'the state of scientific and technical knowledge at the relevant time was not such that a producer . . . might be expected to have discovered the defect'. The definition of a Producer is widely drawn under s.1(2), to include manufacturers, processors, 'own branders' and importers into the EC. 'Product', however, is somewhat curiously defined as 'any goods or electricity'.

Part II relates to Consumer Safety, amending and consolidating the Consumer Safety Act 1978 and the Consumer Safety (Amendment) Act 1986. Part III of the Act provides for the offence of Misleading Price Indications (the 1979 Order under the Prices Act 1974), and includes references to the provision of services, facilities and accommodation as well as goods.

The Act clearly marks a substantial addition to consumer protection legislation and undoubtedly has far-reaching consequences. It is specifically provided that the producers' liability is to be treated as a tortious liability, a further instance of the trend towards amalgamation of the laws of contract and tort. Exclusion of liability under the Act, whether by notice, contractual term or in any other manner is prohibited (s.7). But to avoid a multiplicity of small claims, there is a minimum damages limit of £275 to any claim to *property* under s.5(4); if the claim comes to more than £275 then the entire sum may be recovered. Economic loss does not appear to be included. By s.5(1) 'damage' means 'death or personal injury or any loss or damage to property (including land)', but it excludes by s.5(2) damage to the product itself. Under s.5(3) where property damage is claimed the property in question must be of a type ordinarily intended for private use, occupation or consumption and so intended by the person suffering the loss or damage.

Under s.2(1) where any damage is caused wholly or partly by a defect in a product then there will be liability, and under s.2(2) the liability will fall upon the producer, 'own-marker' (ie someone who puts their own label upon someone else's manufactures), or an importer into the EC in the course of business; under s.2(3) the supplier may become liable if he cannot identify the source of the product. Section 3(1) says that the meaning of defect is where the safety of the product is not such as persons generally are entitled to expect. Section 3(2) outlines circumstances to be taken into account, including the manner in which the product has been marketed and what the product might reasonably be used for. The plaintiff has to prove on the balance of probabilities that the product contained a defect, that he suffered damage caused by the defect, and that the defendant fell within s.2(2). The most controversial defence is under s.4(1)(e), the state of the art defence mentioned above. Such a defence is not available in France, Belgium or Luxembourg, for instance, or in Germany for pharmaceutical products, since the whole point of the Act was to overcome the problems raised by the thalidomide tragedy. But other defences under 4(1) include: (*a*) compliance with a statute or Community obligation; (*b*) the defendant did not at any time supply the goods to another; (*c*) the supply was not in the course of business and s.2(2) does not apply; (*d*) the defect did not exist in the goods at the relevant time; and (*f*) the defect was in a product into which the product in question had been comprised (ie used as a component part). The limitation period is three years under Schedule 1 of the Act, inserting s.11A to the Limitation Act 1980; there is an overall long-stop period of ten years for discoverability, but the court's discretion under s.33 of the 1980 Act is strictly not allowed for claims under the 1987 Act. Contributory negligence is allowed as a partial defence under s.6 of the 1987 Act.

However, whilst many have applauded the introduction of strict product liability in Britain, and Europe generally, it is interesting to note that there is a discernible trend in the USA to a return to a fault-based standard because of the loss of competitiveness due to the stringent product liability in the USA.

7.8   Nuisance

PUBLIC NUISANCE

There are two categories of nuisance, public and private. Neither is really actionable *per se*, although in private nuisance damage may be inferred and on rare occasions the wrong may be classed as actionable *per se*, as seen in *Nicholls* v. *Ely Beet
Sugar Factory Ltd* (1936), where effluent from a sugar beet factory found its way
into fisheries along the same river. A public nuisance is a crime as well as a tort,
and for any action to lie it must interfere with the use or enjoyment of property
by the public in general or by a sufficiently large number of the public. Whether
the number of persons affected is large enough to constitute a public, as opposed
to a private, nuisance is a question of fact and it was suggested by Lord Justice
Romer in *Attorney-General* v. *PYA Quarries Ltd* (1957) that an appropriate test was
to enquire whether the nuisance was 'so widespread in its range, or indiscriminate
in its effects that it would not be reasonable to expect one person to take steps to
put a stop to it'. For instance, in *Jacobs* v. *London County Council* (1950) the plaintiff failed in his action concerning injury sustained by a stop-cock slightly protrud-
ing above pavement level (the stop-cock was on a private forecourt between a
shop and the highway). In *R* v. *Shorrock* (1993) the appellant let a field on his farm
for £2,000 for a weekend and went away. It was used for an 'acid house' party,
attended by up to 5,000 people, who had paid £15 each, lasting 15 hours. There
were 275 complaints of nuisance, some from people four miles away. S. was rightly convicted of public nuisance, the Court of Appeal saying that it was enough
that he ought to have known of the consequences of his action.

Typical examples of public nuisance include obstructing a highway or a waterway
used by the public. Where there is a public nuisance the Attorney-General, acting
on behalf of the public, can sue in the civil courts for an injunction to prevent the
continuance of the nuisance. He can do this in his own name or on the relation of
(that is joined with) an individual (a 'relator' action). A local authoritiy may sue
under the Local Government Act 1972, or with the permission of the Attorney-
General. However, in the light of the authorities, including *Gillingham Borough
Council* v. *Medway (Chatham) Dock Co. Ltd* (1992), it is questionable whether
actions for public nuisance need be retained. In the *Gillingham* case planning consent had been given to develop a commercial port; this entailed lorries (some 750
each day) passing through a residential area. Does this mean that planning permission, political acts, can always render lawful what might otherwise constitute public nuisance? In contrast to the *Gillingham* case planning permission had not
allowed a change in the character of the neighbourhood, and so did not amount
to a defence, in *Wheeler* v. *J J Saunders* (1995), which concerned strong smells from
two pig houses near the plaintiffs' property.

A private individual can only bring an action when he has suffered damage over and above that suffered by the public at large. This rule exists to prevent a multiplicity of actions. An example of a case in which an individual was able to sue is *Rose* v. *Miles* (1815) where the defendant obstructed a waterway causing inconvenience to the public. The plaintiff was able to bring an action because he relied on access by the waterway for delivering his goods and incurred additional expense for delivering by land.

In *Halsey* v. *Esso Petroleum Co. Ltd* (1961), smuts from the defendant's refinery blew on to the plaintiff's property; the plaintiff recovered under private nuisance for the damage done to washing hanging in his garden and under public nuisance for the damaged paintwork of his car parked in the road. In *Campbell* v. *Paddington Corporation* (1911) the Corporation had committed a public nuisance by obstructing the highway with a temporary grandstand built for viewing a procession. The plaintiff had suffered additional damage in that she was unable to let her windows for the same purpose of viewing the procession and it was held that she was entitled to damages.

Not all obstructions are necessarily nuisances. A highway may be partially blocked for the purpose of repairing it or for working on gas mains or sewers under the road and, provided that the amount of obstruction and the time for which it lasts are reasonable, it may not constitute a public nuisance. The amount of obstruction is relevant when considering whether a public nuisance has been caused and whether the offender is liable. In *British Road Services Ltd* v. *Slater* (1964) a tree that projected two feet into the roadway at a height of 16 feet above the road was held to constitute a nuisance, but as the owner of the land on which the tree was growing did not know nor could be reasonably expected to know that it was a nuisance, he was not liable for damage caused to the plaintiff's lorry. Apart from actions under the common law, many public nuisances are forbidden or restricted by statute, for example under the Environmental Protection Act 1990 as amended by the Clean Air Act 1993.

PRIVATE NUISANCE

This can be defined as unlawful and continuing interference with a person's use or enjoyment of land and, possibly, physical damage to that property. The type of things which have been held to be private nuisances by the courts include smoke, fumes, smells, noise, vibrations, heat, germs, polluted water and branches and roots of trees. Repetition of action is an important feature in nuisance. In *Bolton* v. *Stone* (1951) it was a matter of balls being hit occasionally over the boundary fence and it therefore did not constitute a nuisance. But in *Castle* v. *St Augustine's Links* (1922) golf balls were continually hit into the road because of the proximity of the green. In the latter case, a taxi driver lost an eye and recovered under public nuisance, it being doubtful whether personal injuries can found an action for private nuisance. In order to be able to bring an action for private nuisance the plaintiff generally must have a proprietary interest in the land affected, that is he must either own the land or have some interest in it such as a lease or a tenancy. A person may, however, sue where he has some incorporeal right such as the right to light or the right to the use of a stream.

In *The Wagon Mound (No 2)* case it was held that the loss of two ships by fire was foreseeable. The case illustrated the close, and sometimes confusing, relationship between nuisance and negligence, and underlined the uncertainty of whether fore-seeability is a prerequisite to a claim in nuisance. It might be suggested that liability in nuisance falls somewhere between reasonable foreseeability and strict liability. In *Hunter* v. *Canary Wharf Ltd* (1997) the Lords held interference with television reception was not actionable if the plaintiff was a mere occupier.

In order to constitute a nuisance the interference must be 'unlawful' and it will normally only be unlawful if it is in itself unreasonable (reasonable *foreseeability* is a somewhat different issue). This can be a difficult matter to decide for, as Lord Wright said in *Sedleigh-Denfield* v. *O'Callaghan* (1940), 'a balance must be main-tained between the right of the occupier to do what he likes with his own and the right of his neighbour not to be interfered with'. The reasonableness or otherwise of the defendant's act is a question of fact which has to be decided taking into account all the circumstances including time, place, duration, manner of commis-sion and the effect upon the plaintiff. These matters have to be considered since 'that may be a nuisance in Grosvenor Square which would be none in Smithfield Market', *per* Pollock CB in *Bamford* v. *Turnley* (1862). Where the interference has caused actual damage the courts will normally rule it to be unreasonable and therefore a nuisance, as seen in *St Helens Smelting Co.* v. *Tipping* (1865) in which physical damage had been caused to property by the emission of fumes. Damage to property poses less of a problem than interference with personal comfort. Most cases of private nuisance have involved interference with the plaintiff's enjoyment of land over a period of time, for example, *Leeman* v. *Montagu* (1936) where cocks kept in a residential area crowed for several weeks. However, a nuisance can be of short duration, even momentary in its effect as in *Midwood* v. *Mayor of Manchester* (1905) where as a result of the defendant corporation allowing gas to accumulate an explosion was caused which interfered with the plaintiff's property.

Malice

The reasonableness of the defendant's act may be negatived by his intention, for an act which is not otherwise a nuisance may become one if it is done *maliciously* with the intention of annoying the plaintiff, as in *Christie* v. *Davey* (1893) where the defendant deliberately created a noise whenever the plaintiff, who was his neighbour, gave music lessons. Also, in *Hollywood Silver Fox Farm Ltd* v. *Emmett* (1936) the defendant was held liable in nuisance when out of spite he fired guns on his own land, but near the fox farm, and thereby caused damage to some breeding vixens. The decision was in contrast to that in *Bradford Corporation* v. *Pickles* (1895) where because of a disagreement with the council the defendant reduced the water supply reaching the plaintiff. In this instance the defendant did not act out of malice, in the sense of ill-will or an improper motive; on the con-trary he was merely seeking to bring commercial pressure to bear upon the local authority. However, it should be added that the *Bradford* case represented 'an extreme concern for an occupier's freedom to do what he likes with his own, which may have suited the Victorians, but looks very out of place in a country as overcrowded as modern England'. Judges have nowadays limited that concept of freedom, as seen in *Tutton* v. *Walker* (1986) where it was held that an occupier was not free to spray his crops with insecticide with total disregard of his neighbour's bee-keeping activities, and in *Home Brewery Co. Ltd* v. *William Davis & Co. (Leicester) Ltd* (1987) where an occupier was held liable (in part) in respect of altering the drainage of water to an osier-bed, now to be used for development, causing dampness in a neighbouring public house.

Where the plaintiff suffers only because of some special or abnormal sensitivity, the defendant's act does not automatically become unreasonable. In *Robinson* v. *Kilvert* (1889) the plaintiff failed to establish nuisance where heat had risen from the defendant's cellar and caused damage to brown paper stored in the room above. The evidence in the case showed that the paper was abnormally sensitive to heat and that the temperature was such that would not have caused harm to ordinary paper. Although abnormal sensitivity is not taken into account in deciding whether or not a nuisance exists, a plaintiff can claim damages and seek an injunction for interference with delicate items once the nuisance has been established on other grounds.

The plaintiff will usually proceed against the occupier of the land from which the nuisance emanates, but he may also sue the creator of the nuisance even though this is not the same person as the occupier, and in some instances an action can be brought against the landlord of a property, although he is not in occupation. Thus the occupier may in certain circumstances be liable even though he has not created the nuisance: the occupier is responsible for any nuisance arising from the acts of servants or agents, or from acts by anyone under his control such as his family and guests or any person who is allowed on the premises. An example of this is *Matania* v. *National Provincial Bank Ltd* (1936) where the bank was held liable for a nuisance created by their independent contractors who were carrying on building operations on the bank's premises. Normally, however, there will, as in negligence, be no liability for the actions of contractors. An occupier can even be liable for the acts of a trespasser where he knows or ought reasonably to have known of the nuisance and takes no steps to abate it as in *Sedleigh-Denfield* v. *O'Callaghan* (1940) where the Middlesex County Council trespassed on the defendant's land and without his consent put a 15-inch pipe into a ditch on his land. When the pipe became blocked causing water to overflow on to the plaintiff's land the House of Lords held the defendant liable in nuisance because he knew or should have known of the nuisance. Normally, though, an occupier is not liable if it is reasonable to suppose that he would have no knowledge of the defect which caused the nuisance except as in *Wringe* v. *Cohen* (1940), where premises collapse on to an adjoining highway and cause injury, a rule of near strict liability.

Where premises are occupied by a tenant, he, as occupier, may be liable in nuisance, but in some circumstances the landlord may be liable as well. The main occasions when a landlord are liable are first, where the nuisance existed at the start of the tenancy and he knew or ought to have known of it, and secondly where he, as landlord, has retained the right to enter and inspect premises.

DEFENCES

It is, of course, a defence to rebut the allegation of nuisance, that is to prove that the activity complained of is not an unreasonable interference with the use or enjoyment of land. The law recognises that in life generally there must be some element of 'give and take', for example, noise caused by the undertaking of repairs. But repairs carried out in the middle of the night might not be reasonable. It is also a defence to show that the plaintiff consented to the nuisance, provided the defendant has not been negligent. It is more difficult to apply consent (*volenti non fit injuria*) to public nuisance, however. Apart from these general defences there are special defences available in actions for nuisance. A private nuisance can be legalised by continuance for a period of 20 years; this is known as *prescription*. The period does not start to run, however, until the plaintiff is aware of the nuisance. In *Sturges* v. *Bridgman* (1879) the defendant had caused noise and vibration for more than 20 years without any complaint for his neighbour, who was a physician. Then the physician built a consulting room at the end of his garden and found that the noise and vibration materially affected his practice. He therefore sued the defendant in nuisance and succeeded in his action. The defendant's claim to have a prescriptive right failed because the interference had not been an actionable nuisance until the consulting room was built. It is also a defence to show that the nuisance was caused by the act of a stranger provided that the defendant had no knowledge of it and was not negligent in not knowing of it. In *Cushing* v. *Peter Walker & Son Ltd* (1941), where bombing had loosened a slate but this was not apparent to anyone on reasonable inspection, it was held that the occupier was not liable.

Similarly, a secret and unobservable process of nature may afford a defence. In *Leakey* v. *National Trust for Places of Historic Interest or Natural Beauty* (1980) soil gradually fell over some 30 years on to neighbouring property near Bridgwater on account of natural weathering. The Court of Appeal held that the defendants were liable in nuisance (although it added that here the practical distinction between nuisance and negligence was not important) for they owed a general duty of care to their neighbours in respect of hazards on their land both natural and man-made, even if those neighbours were aware of the hazard and took or ought to have taken, protective steps to minimise the damage caused. So, natural causes may not always afford an excuse. In *Goldman* v. *Hargrave* (1967) the defendant failed to extinguish properly a burning tree which had been struck by lightning. As a result fire spread to the plaintiff's property. This case was one of negligence as much as nuisance, for it was reasonably foreseeable that the tree would continue to smoulder. Similarly, although the nuisance may have existed before the occupier took over the property, through the predecessor in title, if it can be shown that the new occupier knew or ought reasonably to have known of the nuisance then liability will arise, as underlined in *St Anne's Well Brewery Co.* v. *Roberts* (1929) which was concerned with the collapse of part of the old city wall in Exeter which in this case could not have been foreseen.

Another defence is that the 'nuisance' was authorized by statute – as in *Allen* v. *Gulf Oil Refining Ltd* (1981) where under the Gulf Oil Refinery Act 1965

Parliament had allowed a refinery to be constructed in West Wales on land compulsorily acquired. Similarly, under the Highways Act 1980 it is a defence to show that the local authority had sufficiently maintained the highway, given all the circumstances, for the use of the 'average' driver.

REMEDIES

Apart from the general remedies of damages and injunction, the plaintiff has the remedy of abatement available. This is a remedy of self-help which consists of the plaintiff terminating the nuisance without recourse to the courts. The law does not favour this since as Sir Matthew Hale said, 'This many times occasions tumults and disorders'. It is therefore subject to restrictions in that unless the nuisance can be abated without entering on to the defendant's land, or unless life or property are in immediate danger, notice must be given to the defendant and permission to enter the land obtained. Abatement should only be used in simple or emergency cases, it was said in *Burton* v. *Winters* (1993). The most usual use of the remedy of abatement is where a neighbour saws off branches of a tree which project over his land. He must not appropriate what he removes. If a person chooses to abate a nuisance he cannot then take any court action in respect of it.

The most often sought remedy is an injunction to prevent the nuisance from continuing. However, even where a nuisance is proved it does not automatically follow that an injunction will be made, especially where the nuisance is clearly temporary. In some cases damages may be awarded in lieu of an injunction, although on the whole the courts are unwilling to allow the defendant, in effect, to purchase a licence to continue tortious activity. The conditions under which damages will be awarded instead of granting an injunction were laid down in *Shelfer* v. *City of London Electric Lighting Co.* (1895); they are firstly that the injury to the plaintiff's legal rights is small, secondly that it is possible to estimate the injury in monetary terms and lastly that it would be oppressive to the defendant to grant an injunction. In *Miller* v. *Jackson* (1977) the Court of Appeal refused to grant an injunction against a cricket club whose activities were held to amount to a nuisance because balls landed in the plaintiff's garden. Lord Denning said that public interests should prevail over private interests and that the public hardship of losing cricket outweighed the private interests of not being able to use the garden while cricket games were in progress. The decision was disapproved of in *Kennaway* v. *Thompson* (1980) where the Court of Appeal granted an injunction to the plaintiff to prevent nuisance caused to her by the noise of racing activities of a motor-boat club. The court held that the plaintiff's rights should not be overridden by the interests of the club or of the public attending racing events organised by the club; the court made the point that in instances of continuing actionable nuisance damages should rarely be awarded; it was in the public's interest that the nuisance should be stopped by injunction.

7.9   Other forms of liability

STRICT LIABILITY

In the various torts examined above, we have seen different facets of the defendant's liability. We have also seen how that liability can, on occasion, seem onerous: in negligence, for example, we noted that before *Wagon Mound* a defendant might well be liable for his actions, even if the results of those acts had not been reasonably foreseeable.

Strict liability means, in essence, absolute liability. It is a tort in its own right and is frequently known as the Rule in *Rylands* v. *Fletcher*, which dates from the middle of the nineteenth century.

The facts of *Ryland* v. *Fletcher* (1868) were, briefly, these: Fletcher employed a contractor to build a reservoir upon his land. During the construction work the contractors came across some old mine shafts. These were now blocked up but were connected to Rylands' land. The contractor left the shafts as he found them. Once the reservoir, however, had been filled with water, the pressure on the shafts became too much to bear. The water broke through and on to the adjoining land, causing considerable damage.

Rylands sued Fletcher and the court held that an occupier of land or property is, irrespective of his state of knowledge or ignorance, responsible for things that may *escape* from his land, providing they cannot be regarded as natural things to have on the land (that is they are out of keeping with its normal use) and providing they can be regarded as potential dangers to others. Things that are 'non-natural' can include the storing of water under pressurised systems, the storage of electricity in bulk, the keeping of cars with petrol in their tanks, filth, stenches and beasts.

The *Rylands* v. *Fletcher* rule, it can be argued, is a mixture of other torts – nuisance, negligence and trespass. However, the essential element in nuisance is *recurrence* of the wrongful action in question and in trespass, of which the courts have in the past held *Rylands* v. *Fletcher* to be a subdivision, the injury is direct as opposed to indirect or consequential. Indeed, as we have seen, trespass is actionable *per se* – there may be no damage. If a case is submitted under the *Rylands* v. *Fletcher* rule, the defendant is responsible for any harm caused by the escape, irrespective of the absence of fault or any kind of foreseeability on his part, whereas if the plaintiff stated the case in negligence generally, the burden of proof would be that much greater (*res ipsa loquitur* apart). Above all else it is necessary to show that there has been an escape – it is not sufficient to show that land contains potentially dangerous things which could possibly escape.

In *Read* v. *J Lyons and Co. Ltd* (1947) the appellant was injured in the defendant's munitions factory, but she neither proved negligence nor was able to show that the explosion had actually escaped from the factory premises. As already stated, once it has been shown that an escape has occurred, it is also necessary to establish the dangerous nature of that object.

In *Crowhurst* v. *Amersham Burial Board* (1878) a poisonous tree was planted and its branches came to overhang the adjoining land. A horse was pastured on the land next door; it ate the poisonous leaves and died. It was held that it was not a natural use of the land to plant such trees.

In *E Hobbs (Farms) Ltd* v. *Baxenden Chemical Company Ltd* (1992), where farm buildings had been sprayed with 'self-extinguishing' foam and an employee who was undertaking grinding work caused a spark to fall onto debris which then spread fire at great speed through a barn, it was held an action could lie in both negligence and under *Rylands* v. *Fletcher*. Also, the duty of care had not been discharged by placing advertisements in *Farmers' Weekly* warning customers of the dangers of polyurethane foam.

Injuries and loss

One difficulty in the application of strict liability is the question whether the plaintiff can sue for personal injury, in addition to suing for damage caused to land or property. The law is not totally clear on this point. Nowadays, however, the answer appears to be 'yes', as *Hobbs* appears to suggest; indeed it has long been clear that the non-occupier can sue for personal injury (*Perry* v. *Kendricks Transport Ltd* (1956)).

Secondly, can the aggrieved party sue for financial (pecuniary) loss – that is loss of earnings – in addition to personal injury and/or damage done to property? Nowadays it can be assumed that courts would take a more liberal view of awarding damages for financial loss, as seen in the *Junior Books* case which was examined above under negligence proper, although *Junior Books* now has to be seen on its own special facts, that is, the owner of a building may sue in negligence a nominated subcontractor for loss of profits and other economic loss caused by the need to take the building out of use to repair it, even though there is no imminent danger to health and safety. Provided the plaintiff suffers injury due to 'an escape', it would seem likely that the plaintiff can sue for loss of earnings due to his injuries, as well as for pain and suffering. The point is not absolutely clear at present, however. Financial loss will clearly be taken into account where a strict duty is one imposed by statute. For example, under the Mines and Quarries Act 1954 a strict duty falls upon coal mine owners to ensure that all its relevant employees receive adequate instruction and training in order to work unsupervised (*Thompson* v. *National Coal Board* (1982)). It should be stressed that the former importance of *Rylands* v. *Fletcher* has been whittled away by the expansion of the principles of ordinary negligence and nuisance; the judgment of the House of Lords in the *Cambridge Water* case (see below) is critical in this context, the Lords ruling that foreseeability of damage of the relevant type is a prerequisite of liability.

Defences

1 Consent and common benefit

Inevitably there are instances when the rule of *volenti non fit injuria* must apply, where in other words the plaintiff consents to run the risk of escape on account of overriding social benefits. Consent may, of course, be given for a variety of reasons – for the individual's own benefit or for that of the defendant or third party. Where the benefit is for one or perhaps a few individuals, then the consent will probably have to be explicit. But where the hazard is for the benefit of the public, then the assumption of risk is implied. So, escapes from power stations can fall under this heading, for the provision of energy is for the public as a whole. In *Midwood* v. *Mayor of Manchester* (1905) inflammable gas escaped and the resultant fire damaged the plaintiff's nearby home. A defective electric cable had fused, thus causing the fire, but the defendants claimed that the cable had been laid for the public benefit. However, the court held that the defendants were nonetheless liable for the defective state of the cable, since apart from any question of negligence, the defendant's methods constituted a public nuisance. In *British Celanese Ltd* v. *A H Hunt* (1969) the defendants were manufacturers whose land had stored on it strips of metal foil. The foil was blown across to neighbouring land. The court held, that though the defendants were not strictly liable since the goods had been stored for the common benefit, they were nonetheless ordinarily liable in negligence (economic loss) and in nuisance.

In *Cambridge Water Co.* v. *Eastern Counties Leather plc* (1994) the allegation was that chemicals had escaped and polluted the water supply. At first instance, it was decided *Rylands* v. *Fletcher* did not apply and that the storage of the chemicals generally benefited the community by creating employment but the Court of Appeal did hold the defendants liable in nuisance. But the House of Lords took the opposite view, emphasising the link between nuisance and the *Rylands* rule, and the importance of the foreseeability test, irrespective of whatever reasonable care the defendant had taken.

2 Act of a stranger

If the escape is brought about by the actions of a stranger – and is completely unforeseeable – the defendant will not be liable for the consequences. In *Rickards* v. *Lothian* (1913) a stranger in a block of flats blocked up the lavatory pipes. The blockage took place on the fourth floor, but the effect was to flood the second floor. The court held that the occupier was not liable for the act of a stranger that was done deliberately. This point was illustrated more recently in *King* v. *Liverpool City Council* (1986) where, although the *Rylands* rule was not in issue, the Court of Appeal, applying the decision in *Perl* (1984), held that where vandals broke into an empty flat and damaged water pipes allowing water to escape into the flat below occupied by the plaintiff as a council tenant, in the absence of a special relationship between the defendant and the third party, the defendant council was not liable in negligence. In *Northwestern Utilities Ltd* v. *London Guarantee and Accident Co. Ltd* (1936) a hotel owned and insured by the respondents was burned down.

This was caused by gas escaping into the basement from the appellants' pressure main which had been damaged as the result of construction work by a third party (a stranger). The court held that the appellants, although not strictly liable under the *Rylands* rule, were liable in terms of general negligence; the consequence was reasonably foreseeable. In this respect the distinction between *Rylands* and negligence generally becomes an academic one, as seen in the *Cambridge Water* case.

It is not totally clear as to who in this context constitutes a 'stranger'. Certainly a trespasser will normally be a stranger. The key test is whether the defendant had control over the third party – for example, another member of the defendant's family or an employee acting within the course of employment; here the defendant will usually be vicariously liable for the acts of an independent contractor. Thus where control is deemed to be exercised, the third party will not be a stranger for the purposes of the *Rylands* rule.

3 Act of God

Any extraordinary act which causes an escape will amount to a defence, in other words acts which cannot be reasonably predicted, such as heavy rainfall and earthquakes. The case of *Greenock Corporation* v. *Caledonian Railway* (1917) illustrates the problem. The local council had constructed a paddling pool for children out of the bed of a stream, but in order to do this the council had had to alter the normal course of the stream. An extraordinary amount of rainfall caused flooding from the pool. However, the court held that the Corporation was still liable as the original course of the stream would have coped adequately with the rainfall, heavy as it was.

4 Default of the plaintiff

If the damage caused by the escape is, though, brought about through the action or omission of the plaintiff, then the defendant may not be liable. In *Ponting* v. *Noakes* (1894) it was held that the plaintiff could not succeed since the death of his horse was due to the fact that the horse itself had intruded on to the defendant's land and had eaten poisonous vegetation of its own volition (contrast the *Crowhurst* case). The defence of contributory negligence, therefore, may be applied to strict liability.

In *Eastern and South African Telegraph Co. Ltd* v. *Cape Town Tramways Companies Ltd* (1902) electricity used on the defendants' premises interfered with the plaintiff's telegraphed messages. But the court held that the action could not succeed since the plaintiff's abnormally sensitive equipment had clearly not been damaged, and in any case the amounts of escaping electricity were minute.

In contrast, in *Hoare and Co.* v. *McAlpine* (1923) the plaintiff did succeed. Although his hotel was old, he was making natural use of the premises; the defendant was therefore liable for the effects of vibrations from pile-driving on adjoining land.

5 Statutory authority

The rule of strict liability may be excluded by statute, for little can argue with an Act of Parliament. The leading case is that of *Green* v. *Chelsea Waterworks Co.* (1894). The defendant company had statutory authority to lay water pipes. During the course of this work a water-main burst and flooded the plaintiff's premises. The court held that as the water authority was under a duty to lay the pipes, they could not be liable for the escape. The company could not be shown to have acted negligently.

The Reservoirs Act 1975 imposes a strict liability upon those who construct and maintain reservoirs. (Legislation was originally passed in 1930 following a Welsh dam disaster.) Other Acts impose similar forms of strict liability upon public authorities (for example, the Environmental Protection Act 1990 and the Nuclear Installations Act 1965).

In *Merlin* v. *British Nuclear Fuels plc* (1990) there was a claim for breach of statutory duty under s.7 of the Nuclear Installations Act 1965, which provided for strict liability for 'property damage' or personal injury. The plaintiff's house had, it appears, become contaminated by radioactive particles. The house was reduced from £65,000 and sold for £35,000. Mr Justice Gatehouse held that property in s.7, as at common law, meant physical damage to tangible property and not damage to incorporeal property or property rights. But the judge suggested that s.7 could cover claims for contaminated livestock or other animals; perhaps this meant the Merlin family's pets were glowing with radiation.

Fire

As indicated in cases above fire is an area of tortious life that is considered under the rules of strict liability. There has long been recognition at common law that a person keeps a fire at his peril. Thus a fire which has become out of control through negligent action or omission will incur liability. Even if a fire does not get out of control the defendant may be liable under nuisance.

If a fire has been started deliberately or intentionally, then the defendant is strictly liable for the damage caused by its escape. General responsibility has been qualified by the Fires Prevention (Metropolis) Act 1774 which provided no liability for fires that had been started accidentally. The meaning of 'accidentally' may be different from 'negligently' or 'carelessly', and indeed it has posed problems of interpretation for the courts. In *Collingwood* v. *Home and Colonial Stores Ltd* (1936) a defective cable was responsible for an outbreak of fire. But the defendants had taken reasonable care to keep their equipment in proper order – there was no act of negligence on their part. The rule of strict liability in this instance was held not to apply: such electric wires were common enough household hazards.

On the other hand an unreasonable failure by the defendant to prevent a fire – even if accidental in origin – from spreading or escaping further, will render him liable to the plaintiff for damage caused. In that context liability is most certainly strict.

However a fire is started – intentionally or accidentally – an occupier is not liable for the actions of trespassers (strangers), nor is he liable for Acts of God, except in so far as he might stand idly by and allow the fire to escape unnecessarily – in other words make no reasonable effort to abate it, or make an inadequate attempt at extinguishing it as seen in *Goldman* v. *Hargrave* (1967). Liability does, though, extend to the actions of lawful visitors, independent contractors and employees, as illustrated by the case of *Musgrove* v. *Pandelis* (1919). In that instance a slow-witted chauffeur was responsible for not checking what was a small, containable fire. When he switched on the engine of the car the petrol in the carburettor – through no fault of his own – caught fire. Instead of switching off the petrol-tap, he allowed the fire to escape and thus damage the plaintiff's premises.

Animals

The usual torts apply to the control of the behaviour of animals – for example, it may well constitute a trespass to ride a horse over another person's land. If an excitable dog, for instance, gets out of control among neighbours or in a crowd, that may result in an action for nuisance or negligence. Conversely, it may be a trespass to beat another's animal.

But the position does not rest simply with the common law, for there are important rules of liability under the Animals Act 1971. The Act recognises two main groups of animals – dangerous species and non-dangerous species. Dangerous species animals, under s.2(1), fall under a rule of strict liability: any harm (including to property) they cause will be its keeper's fault, since the owner is presumed to know that the animal is dangerous. Dangerous species animals are defined by the Act in s.6(2)(a) as those which are 'not commonly domesticated in the British Isles'. Such a definition clearly includes foreign species but also wild animals that are indigenous to the United Kingdom and Ireland. Under the Dangerous Wild Animals Act 1976 certain dangerous wild animals can be kept only under licence. The Dangerous Dogs Act 1991 added other controls in this area. Further, dangerous species animals are those fully grown and which, if not adequately controlled, have such characteristics that they are likely to cause severe damage. Responsibility for the acts of animals can come early in life: an animal's keeper is its owner or anyone who has possession of it, but if that person is under 16, then it will be the head of the household in which he lives.

Section 2 of the Act is badly worded and it is difficult to make out its true intent. Under s.2(2) where damage is done by a non-dangerous species animal there will only be liability if the keeper had some knowledge of the animal's abnormal characteristics, and the damage caused by the animal was likely to be severe. This was seen in *Curtis* v. *Betts* (1990) in the context of an 11 year-old boy who was bitten by a bull mastiff weighing nearly 10 stone. In fact, the families concerned were well known to each other, and the young boy regularly loaded the dog into a Land Rover to take him for a walk. On the day in question, the boy pedalled up to the vehicle and shouted the dog's name; the dog leapt up and bit the boy on the chin. At the end of the day, the Court of Appeal upheld the trial judge's decision that the owners were liable for the personal injury caused.

The Act allows three possible defences to damage caused by dangerous species animals: consent (*volens*) (s.5(2)), that is the plaintiff accepted the risk of suffering injury; fault (s.5(1)), that is the plaintiff provoked the animal to act dangerously; and trespass – in other words the plaintiff was an unlawful visitor to the premises concerned, but if the animal in question has been kept there for the protection of the property or its occupier, then that purpose under s.5(3) must be 'not unreasonable'. Contributory negligence is also a defence, in part.

Of course, liability may occur in the general law of nuisance or negligence, as stated earlier. The case of *Ellis* v. *Johnstone* (1963) well illustrates the point – it involved a dog that rushed out of its owner's drive. It appeared that the dog often wandered across the busy road to the common opposite. In this case it was knocked down by a car and killed. The driver sued for damage caused to his vehicle. It was held that the owner of the dog was under no special duty of care, but Lord Justice Donovan said that if it had been established that the dog frequently bounded out of the gate, so that momentarily it became more like a missile than a dog, then there would have been special circumstances which would have taken the case beyond the normal rule that there was no duty on the owner or keeper of a dog to prevent it straying from land on to the highway.

However, as indicated above, the 1971 Act does impose liability in respect of non-dangerous species animals if the damage caused is a result of the unusual characteristics of the animal concerned, that is behaviour not normally associated with that particular species; in other words such animals are still 'dangerous'. The defences that may be raised are then the same as those for dangerous species animals already outlined, and in both instances liability embraces the acts of a keeper's servant, and to emphasise the point again, the keeper must have some knowledge of the animal's unusual tendencies. Thus in *Wallace* v. *Newton* (1982) the plaintiff succeeded on account of the fact that the horse was known to be of nervous and unpredictable temperament. Whilst the plaintiff, a groom employed by the defendant, was loading the horse on to a trailer, the animal leaped forward and crushed her arm against a breast bar.

In addition the Act (s.3) lays down certain rules in respect of dogs and livestock. The keeper of a dog may well be strictly liable under the 1971 Act if that dog causes damage by injuring or killing livestock. Moreover, the owner or person in charge of the livestock may take preventive action against the molesting dog by injuring or killing it, providing he notifies a police station within 48 hours of such action (s.9).

The keeper of the molesting dog will, of course, have a defence if the plaintiff has consented to run the risk of the dog being in the vicinity of the livestock or if the plaintiff had caused the trouble through personal foolish action or if the livestock had strayed on to the dog-keeper's land.

Indeed under the Act (s.4) the liability for damage caused by straying livestock is strict. An occupier may detain the straying livestock, but must adequately protect and care for them, and cannot detain them for longer than 48 hours unless he notifies (s.7) both the police and the owner of the livestock, if the occupier knows who that owner is. Of course, the plaintiff will have no claim if it can be shown that he provoked the livestock to stray in the first place; the Act does not mention *volens* in this context.

It should also be noted that under criminal law the Guard Dogs Act 1975 provides that a guard dog shall not be employed unless a competent handler is present and unless warning notices are displayed at entrances to the relevant business premises. Under the Animal Health Act 1981 the minister may make orders controlling stray dogs, in particular in order to stop the worrying of animals, including horses, at night.

Livestock

There is a general duty to fence in livestock and the 1971 Act also lays down a duty that the person in charge of livestock should take reasonable care to prevent those animals from straying on to the highway (s.8). That duty will not arise where the land in question is traditionally unfenced, for example, National Parks or common land. Secondly, the Act allows livestock to be driven along the highway from one field or farm to another; should the livestock stray on to private land during that process it is most unlikely that the occupier of the land will have grounds for action, unless he can clearly prove negligence on the part of the person driving the livestock along the road. In *Tillett* v. *Ward* (1882) the defendant was not held liable for an ox that wandered into a shop. Livestock does not, of course, include domestic pets such as dogs and cats.

Negligence

Actions under trespass and negligence for the acts of non-dangerous animals are extremely difficult in comparison with those for dangerous and wild animals. The most all-embracing area for action against non-dangerous animals is under nuisance. For example, in *Aldred's Case* (1610) the stench of pigs was held to constitute a nuisance; so too were noisy greyhounds in *Morrissey* v. *Galer* (1955). In *Leeman* v. *Montagu* (1936) the problem was the crowing of hundreds of cockerels in the small hours. Here the plaintiff bought a house in a largely residential but also partly rural area. A poultry farm adjoined the plaintiff's home, and about a hundred yards from the house there was an orchard in which the cockerels resided. At the plaintiff's request the birds were removed but before long they reappeared. It was argued that the plaintiff and his wife were forced to sleep with cotton wool in their ears and the windows closed. A witness gave evidence that he went to the house to record the noise which he likened to three cornets, two of which were out of tune. The plaintiff was granted his injunction. In *Pitcher* v. *Martin* (1937) a dog on a loose lead some 50 inches in length chased a cat. In so doing it caused the plaintiff, a woman of 73, to be thrown and to receive injuries as a result. It was held that a nuisance existed and that the woman exercising the dog was also liable in negligence.

OCCUPIERS' LIABILITY

An occupier's liability for land and structures – that is premises – is, under English law, split between common law principles and two Acts of Parliament, 1957 and 1984, a not untypical British approach.

The term 'premises' can cover a wide range of appropriate objects, besides houses and other similar buildings. Such things as ladders, lifts, aeroplanes, electricity pylons and sports stadiums fall within the legal meaning of 'premises' – in other words the term is not solely restricted to immovable objects. The 'occupier' can be anyone who is in *possession* of an object whose state or activity results in harm to others. He does not have to be the owner of the property in question.

The Occupiers' Liability Act 1957 largely came about as a result of a number of decisions by the House of Lords in the 1950s which clearly demonstrated the need for a clarification of the old common law principles. The Act, which effectively abolished the categories of 'licensees' and 'invitees', distinguished between two basic types of visitors – lawful and unlawful, in other words between those invited and trespassers. Lawful visitors, but not trespassers, are owed a common duty of care by the occupier, s.2(1) and s.2(2).

If an occupier of premises gives express permission to the entrant to stay on the premises, then usually the occupier's liability for damage caused by a structure is clear enough. But if the visitor arrives on those premises only by implied permission then all kinds of legal wrangles may ensue. Moreover, a lawful visitor can always turn himself into a trespasser; but if the circumstances are of an innocent nature – for example, a visitor getting lost in a very large building – then the court is bound to take a lenient view. As for damage caused by the faulty structure to a lawful visitor, this will cover not just compensation for physical injury but also for inconvenience caused, for loss of enjoyment of the visit and damage to property, subject, of course, to the rule that the damage alleged must not be too remote. The 1957 Act did not exclude the defence of contributory negligence under the Law Reform (Contributory Negligence) Act 1945. Until recently, however, occupiers' responsibilities under the 1957 Act could be avoided by contract. But in respect of business premises the Unfair Contract Terms Act 1977 under s.2 now prevents such exclusion clauses where the effect of the agreement might result in injury or death to the visitor, and in the case of other loss or damage a contractual term or a notice displayed must satisfy a test of 'reasonableness'. Generally speaking, under the 1957 Act it is difficult to exclude a duty of care by a contractual term in respect of strangers (third parties). For example, a landlord's obligations to the visitor of a residential tenant could probably not be excluded.

'Lawful visitors' under the 1957 Act will also include those who are given a right to enter such public places as pubs, churches, libraries, parks, and so on. Again, occupiers of such premises owe a common duty of care. Moreover, the Act recognises that anyone fulfilling a statutory duty, for example a postman, a fire officer or meter-reader, must be deemed as having implied permission to enter the relevant premises. That category also includes factory and health inspectors under the Factories Act 1961 and the Health and Safety at Work etc Act 1974.

In *Cunningham* v. *Reading Football Club* (1991) a football club which failed to maintain the concrete structure of its ground when it knew or ought to have known of the probability that visiting hooligans would, if they could, break off pieces of the concrete to use as missiles, could be held liable in negligence and under the Occupiers' Liability Act 1957 for injuries caused by such missiles to other visitors, such as policemen controlling the crowd. The common duty of care under s.2(1) of the Act is a duty to take such care as in all the circumstances of the case is reasonable to see that the visitor will be reasonably safe in using the premises for the purpose for which he is permitted or invited to be there.

Similarly, in *Salmon* v. *Seafarer Restaurants Ltd* (1983) where the defendants negligently caused a fire in their fish and chip shop and the plaintiff, a fireman, was injured in a gas explosion caused by the fire, it was held that it was reasonably foreseeable that a fireman would suffer injury as the result of such an injury and therefore a duty of care existed which had been breached. The decision was approved by the House of Lords in *Ogwo* v. *Taylor* (1987), where it was held that professional firemen should not be put at a disadvantage to the layman; in this case the occupier of a terraced house used a blow lamp to burn off some paint from the fascia boards beneath the eaves of his house, and in the ensuing fire a fireman who had entered a narrow hatch into the roof space suffered from serious burns. The Lords referred to the earlier case of *Hartley* v. *British Railways Board* (1981) where it was held that a duty of care was owed to a fireman who had been misled into thinking that a person was trapped inside a burning railway station and who sustained injuries as a result of his search. Strictly these cases fall under common law negligence, irrespective of occupiers' liability.

Knowledge of the danger

Even though the plaintiff may be aware of the danger of the structural or other condition of the premises, the occupier may not necessarily be excused from liability. For example, the warning notices displayed by an occupier on or near premises may prove to be insufficient, especially where such notices have been ignored by 'trespassers' over a long period of time. In such a situation a warning notice may have become virtually redundant, and those who would have formerly passed for trespassers have become lawful visitors by implied permission. This was well illustrated as long ago as 1911 in the case of *Lowery* v. *Walker* where for 35 years the public had used a farmer's field as a short-cut area and it was held that insufficient notice had been given by the farmer concerned when he moved a savage horse into the field. In *Staples* v. *West Dorset District Council* (1995) the Court of Appeal held that where the plaintiff saw the algae before the accident then there was no breach of the duty of care under s.2(2) of the Occupiers' Liability Act 1957.

In addition, certain people will be judged as being technically more competent than others to deal with any defects on an occupier's premises, in which case the occupier will not owe a duty of care towards that particular lawful visitor for he is deemed to have a relevant professional skill. This point was underlined by *Indermaur* v. *Dames* in 1866. Further, an occupier is not liable for damage caused by a third party's action if he could not reasonably foresee that particular danger arising, nor is he liable if he employs an independent contractor whose technical skill would make him, the contractor, liable rather than the occupier. In *Haseldine* v. *Daw* (1941) the plaintiff unsuccessfully sued the owner of a block of flats when injured as a result of a lift in the building falling to the bottom of its shaft, since the owner had engaged a firm of lift contractors to maintain the lifts and it was they, not the occupier, who had the technical expertise; it was they who were held liable therefore. A similar issue arose in *Ferguson* v. *Welsh* (1987), where the House of Lords held that the plaintiff, who had been engaged in demolition work carried out in a dangerous manner and had suffered partial paralysis as a result, had no claim against the district council either under the Occupiers' Liability Act 1957 or at common law since the council had tendered the work to an independent contractor.

Of course, the courts will not take a favourable view of visitors behaving in a manner inconsistent with the nature of the premises. As a judge once said – in 1927 – a staircase is not properly used if a person slides down the bannister. Thus in *Hillen* v. *ICI (Alkali) Ltd* (1936) a stevedore received no remedy for injuries received since he had been loading the ship in a proscribed way. In *Roles* v. *Nathan* (1963) two chimney sweeps acted carelessly in attempting to block up a dangerously fumed chimney; therefore the owner of the building was not liable for their deaths.

Highways

The general duty of care owed by occupiers to lawful visitors does not extend to highways in the same way as it does to premises. If a person possesses a public or private right of way across or along a road and injuries result from the condition of that highway, then the plaintiff may still not succeed if all he can show is that the surface of the highway has merely deteriorated in condition as opposed to having substantially altered in character. However, under the Highways Act 1980 the local authority does have a statutory obligation to maintain a public highway to a minimum respectable standard. Furthermore, Lord Denning said, *obiter*, in *Greenhalgh* v. *British Railways Board* (1969) that a lawful visitor did not include a person who crossed land in pursuance of a public or private right of way. In *Holden* v. *White* (1982) a milkman was unsuccessful in his claim for injuries to his foot caused by tripping over a defective manhole cover, for the cover was situated on a private right of way. It is clear therefore there is no liability to members of the public in respect of the owner of the land over which a public right of way passes (*McGeown* v. *Northern Ireland Housing Executive* (1994)).

Trespassers and children

The Occupiers' Liability Act 1957 circumvented the problem of trespassers; in essence it extends only to lawful visitors. The very definition of 'trespasser' has posed problems. Certain statutes, such as the Theft Act 1968 and the Animals Act 1971, give a reasonably wide interpretation of the word. The leading case has been that of *Addie* v. *Dumbreck* (1929): a boy of four was killed when playing with a machine on the defendant's land. The land, however, was surrounded by a hedge and from time to time the defendant's agents had chased children away from the area. The defendant therefore owed no duty of care to the boy who was a trespasser.

But an important principle was laid down in the *Addie* case, for it was conceded that if a trespasser was injured because the occupier deliberately intended to harm the trespasser or because the occupier carried on with the action with reckless disregard of his presence, then there would be a case to answer. Thus in a very old case, *Bird* v. *Holbrook* (1828), the defendant was liable to a boy who was injured by the spring-gun the defendant had laid in his garden as a trap when he went there to retrieve a bird.

In *Videan* v. *British Transport Commission* (1963), over three decades after the *Addie* case, the Court of Appeal modified the 1929 doctrine by applying a foreseeability test in respect of the industrial and commercial activities of premises, as opposed to a building's static condition. But this appears to have been rejected, and *Addie* restated, in *Commissioner for Railways* v. *Quinlan* (1964) – an Australian appeal case involving a vehicle traversing a level-crossing with inadequate notices and late warnings by an approaching train.

Of course, many cases of trespass have involved children, and it is notable that the 1957 Act under s.2(3) places a very particular duty of care upon occupiers towards children who are lawful visitors. Thus in certain situations children may be impliedly treated as lawful visitors where in similar circumstances adults would be regarded as trespassers, since the Act states that an occupier must allow for the fact that children are less careful than adults.

A number of cases have graphically illustrated the problem of premises acting as an allurement or dangerous trap to children. In *Phipps* v. *Rochester Corporation* (1955) a 5 year-old boy broke a leg, while accompanied by his sister aged seven, by falling down a hole on an uncompleted housing estate. The defendant was held not liable since wandering children were the preserve of parents. In this case the court treated the child as an impliedly lawful visitor. But in *Moloney* v. *Lambeth Borough Council* (1966) the defendants were held liable for injuries to a 4 year-old child resulting from a defective common staircase. As the child lived in the same premises he was obviously a lawful visitor.

Similarly, the plaintiff was successful in *Buckland* v. *Guildford Gas Light and Coke Co.* (1948) in respect of the death of a 13 year-old girl who while climbing a tree touched overhead electric cables concealed in the foliage. The girl was clearly a trespasser on the farmer's land and therefore in respect of the tree she climbed. But she was not a trespasser, the court held, in relation to the non-occupier, that is the defendant company. In *Glasgow Corporation* v. *Taylor* (1922) the appellants were found liable for the death of a child who had eaten poisonous berries – the berries had not been fenced off, nor were there warning notices. The child was in a public park and therefore was a lawful visitor, although he was probably as much a trespasser in relation to the bush and the berries as the girl was to the farmer's tree.

Lastly, in *Dyer* v. *Ilfracombe Urban District Council* (1956) a child injured on a playground slide had no remedy since the chute, although in one sense an allurement, was not of an essentially dangerous nature, it was not a concealed trap. In the Ilfracombe case a boy of four and a half fell from the platform of a chute in a public recreation area. The chute was 12 feet high, and the boy broke his arm.

Lord Justice Singleton said:

> A question of law arises which has been discussed in the courts frequently. It is agreed on both sides that the boy who was hurt was a licensee [a lawful visitor] and that he had all the rights of one who was permitted by the defendants to go on their recreation ground. The duty towards a licensee is that the occupier (the defendants in this case) must warn him of any concealed danger or trap of which the occupier knows. One question for consideration is: is there a distinction for this purpose between the case of a grown licensee and one who is quite young? May there be a danger which is not a concealed danger in the ordinary sense, but which ought to be regarded as a concealed danger if the licensee is of tender years? I see no distinction in principle between the case of the chute in the recreation ground and an artificial lake or water in a recreation ground. Neither can properly be regarded as a concealed danger to a boy four and a half years old.

Lord Justice Parker said:

> The duty of an occupier of land to a licensee applies equally to children as to adults, and the occupier will not be liable for the consequences of dangers, in the case of adults obvious to the adults and . . . in the case of children, obvious to the children. But the scope of the duty in the case of children is wider because what may be not an unusual danger or trap to an adult may be one to a child. And, again, a warning of the danger in question may be insufficient if the child were too young to take advantage of the warning. But this wider duty exists only when there is something on the premises, or in the present case in the implement provided, which amounts to a hidden danger or a trap, or where the implement is an allurement in the sense in which that word is used. Quite clearly, this implement – this chute – was an allurement in the sense that it was attractive to children and indeed was there for the use of children. But the fact that a child using it might injure itself does not make it an allurement in the sense in which that word is used. A child may hurt itself on anything . . . I cannot persuade myself that this chute was an allurement in the sense that it was inherently dangerous . . . It may well be that the reasonably prudent parent would insist on the child being accompanied by an adult, not because there was an concealed danger, not because the danger was not obvious, but because the danger though obvious was not such as the child was old enough to protect himself against.

None of the cases described above, from *Phipps* to *Dyer*, affected the *Addie* principles, although as has been seen the courts on occasion have treated *prima facie* child trespassers as impliedly lawful visitors. But since 1972 the law with regard to trespassers, and child trespassers in particular, has developed significantly. The turning-point came in the case of *British Railways Board* v. *Herrington* (1972). In a throw-back to, and an extension of, the *Videan* case the House of Lords developed a 'humanity' test. This particular case involved a 6 year-old boy, who, having crawled through a hole in a protective fence, was electrocuted by a 'live' railway line. The case was a difficult one since the five Law Lords each put forward a somewhat different *ratio decidendi*. However, they agreed that the test of humanity, following Australian decisions, basically meant that local authorities, nationalised and private industry and the like, given the extent of their resources and wealth, should owe a higher duty of care than the ordinary householder towards the trespasser. The judgments in the *Herrington* case were of sufficient import for the Lord Chancellor to refer the whole matter to the Law Commission for consideration.

In *McGinlay (or Titchener)* v. *British Railways Board* (1983), where the appellant, aged 15, was struck by a train and seriously injured whilst crossing a line between two suburban stations in Glasgow, it was held, by the Lords, *obiter*, that the existence and extent of the duty of a railway authority to fence depended on the circumstances of the case, including the age and intelligence of the particular person entering upon the premises; the duty would tend to be higher in respect of a very young or very old person compared with a normally active and intelligent adult or adolescent. The nature and obviousness or otherwise of the railway might also be relevant. Lord Hailsham added that the Board could not assume that it would have been immune from liability for the state of the fence from a different claimant had another and different accident occurred. But it was the decision in the *Herrington* case that led to further reform.

The 1984 Act

The Law Commission reported in 1976 and this eventually led to legislation in 1984, although the logic of having two different duties (to lawful visitors and non-visitors) is not easy to follow, and does not operate in Scotland. Section 1 of the Act substitutes statutory rules for those of the common law. Premises are defined in the same terms as under the 1957 Act, to include fixed or movable structures. Like the 1957 Act, the 1984 Act appears to say that an act or omission on the premises not in itself affecting visitors' or strangers' safety must be dealt with in accordance with the common law principles of negligence, as would the position of an independent contractor as opposed to 'occupier'.

Under s.1 the occupier owes a duty to 'persons other than his visitors'. This would include trespassers and those with an access agreement under the National Parks and Access to the Countryside Act 1949. Section 1 does not apply to those on the public highway, thus preserving the *Greenhalgh* decision; again common law principles apply. But the category of non-visitor is sufficiently wide to include persons exercising a private right of way – thus reversing *Holden* v. *White* (1982) in part.

The occupier owes the statutory duty under s.1(3) if he is aware of the danger or has reasonable grounds to believe that it exists, and similarly knows that the non-visitor is in the vicinity, and the risk is one against which in all the circumstances of the case, he may reasonably be expected to offer the non-visitor some protection. The duty, s.1(4), is one to take such precautions as are reasonable in all the circumstances to see that they do not suffer injury. Does this duty go beyond the old common law duty after all?

In *Revill v. Newbery* (1996) a burglar injured by shot from a gun recklessly discharged by a householder sued him for damages. Was the claim barred by *ex turpi causa non oritur actio*? If it was not what was the basis of the defendant's duty? If the duty was breached, could damages be reduced under the principle of contributory negligence? Nonetheless, the Court of Appeal held that the Occupiers' Liability Act 1984 did not apply, and the criminal quality of the plaintiff's conduct was ignored.

In *White v. St Albans City and District Council* (1990) the plaintiff fell into a 12 foot trench whilst walking across fenced-off council property to take a short cut to a car park. The fence was insufficient to stop all but the elderly and disabled from entering the land. However, there was no evidence that people tended to use the land as a short cut to the car park.

Whilst the duty under the 1984 Act is to see that the entrant does not suffer injury (this does not include damage to property), it may be discharged by warning of the danger or discouraging persons from taking the risk. But warning notices will often remain inadequate for children. The defence of *volens* is expressly preserved, s.1(6). A criminal trespasser (a burglar or thief) might be owed the duty – it is not excluded from the Act, but on the other hand the defence of *ex turpi* might be raised.

Section 2 of the Act seeks to promote greater public access to the countryside – it has amended s.1 of the Unfair Contract Terms Act 1977 by providing that admission to premises for recreational or educational purposes does not constitute a 'business liability', so that the occupier is free to exclude or restrict his liability. Thus free visits to a ruined castle, or pot-holing, would be covered by s.2, but it is doubtful if the section has actually increased access.

Lastly, it should also be mentioned that the Defective Premises Act 1972 imposed upon builders and constructors a duty to erect buildings properly – thus liability will arise for injuries resulting from dangerous structures. The Act also clarified the responsibilities of the landlord towards visitors, who might even include those passing by on the highway outside the premises that belonged to the landlord. In *McAuley v. Bristol City Council* (1991) the plaintiff was a council tenant who occupied her property under a weekly tenancy. She fell from an unstable step in her back garden and was injured. The plaintiff sued Bristol Council under s.4(4) of the Defective Premises Act 1972, arguing that the council was in breach of the duty of care which arose under the Act because it had an implied right to enter the plaintiff's property to do repairs to the garden.

DISCUSSION POINTS

1 Examine whether the extracts from Lord Simonds' speech are illuminating about the concepts of reasonable foreseeability and remoteness of damage.

2 Are there different tests for negligence and nuisance?

3 Is the idea of strict liability in tort at all useful?

E i g h t

CIVIL LAW:

CONTRACT

8.1

Obligations and

consideration

The law of contract is the law relating to agreements, and the consequences of breaking, or breach, of the agreements. To create a valid and enforceable contract, there must be two or more separate parties, who come to a mutual agreement, that is there must be a consensus *ad idem* and there must be an intention that the promises made shall be binding and enforceable.

A contract may be defined as an agreement to purchase goods or services where one party has made an offer which has been accepted by the other party for a consideration and where both parties intended to enter into a contractual relationship. The concept of bargain or consideration is fundamental to the English law of contract. Unlike certain continental systems, no question of moral obligation amounts to consideration for the purposes of enforcing a contractual agreement.

Even where there is consideration, not all agreements are covered by the law of contract. There are innumerable cases of informal agreements, particularly in domestic or friendship situations where an agreement to do something, whether or not for consideration, is unenforceable at law. 'David, will you mow the lawn for me after lunch? £5. Very well.' Implied terms, such as the area of lawn, free provision of petrol and mower in reasonable working order by the parent, together with assistance in case of stoppage and edging, could no doubt be obtained from evidence of previous transactions. Such a contract, however, would not be enforceable at law, quite apart from any question of David's age, for the reason that the parties would be held not to have intended to create legal relations. It would be quite otherwise if the parent had made an agreement for the cutting of the lawn with a gardening contractor.

In many cases the terms of a contract are not agreed in detail, but provided the main terms, for example, which lawn, how often, what price, are clear, then the courts will seek to give effect to the contract, provided that there was an intention to create legal relations, but in this context there will be many borderline cases.

Alternatively, the contract may be unenforceable because something in the agreement vitiates the contract, for instance, a mistake as to a main term ('it was not that lawn at all that I was contracting to cut') or illegality in the agreement, such as an agreement to perform a crime. Similarly, the courts will not enforce for one party a contract where it was induced fraudulently, or if undue influence was used by that party, but such contracts are voidable, rather than void as in the case of mistake or illegality.

Certain classes of people were traditionally 'protected' from the common law concept of contract. So 'lunatics' and 'infants' were only liable for contracts for 'necessaries', and married women were for long not capable of being sued in contract. Companies, which at law have an existence independent of their directors or shareholders, were liable only if and to the extent that the articles of association establishing the company provided that the contract was not *ultra vires* the company. Bankrupts, alien enemies and drunkards are further examples of persons having only a limited power to contract. While minors are still protected to some extent, lunatics are now treated as mental health patients and liable unless shown to have been incapable of appreciating what they were contracting to do. Happily, the final disabilities have been removed from married women and the doctrine of *ultra vires* for trading companies has been severely curtailed.

Apart from persons regarded as under a disability, the courts generally tried to uphold the strict terms of contractual agreements, treating individuals as fully entitled to make any lawful contract. The principle of sanctity of a contract was not to be questioned merely because one party or the other had made an improvident bargain; provided the terms were defined or capable of being implied, the contract would be upheld. As a result, the courts would not enter into any question of consideration, as to whether or not it was adequate for the contract: it was left to individuals, the parties, to agree their terms and provided there was consideration then its amount was relevant but not any question of adequacy. This concept of the sanctity of the law of contract developed particularly in the nineteenth century, reflecting the prevailing liberal political and economic beliefs and was regarded as a cornerstone of the liberty of the individual. 'Public policy requires,' stated Sir George Jessel, Master of the Rolls, in 1875, 'that men of full age and competent understanding shall have the utmost liberty in contracting and . . . contracts when entered into freely and voluntarily, shall be held sacred and . . . enforced by Courts of Justice.'

PROTECTING THE CONSUMER

In the latter half of the twentieth century, we have seen the 'sanctity of the contract' progressively reduced as the courts have moved to protect individuals from the harsher provisions of their contracts. The courts at first imported the doctrine of the 'implied terms' of the contract, which Lord Denning in *The Discipline of Law* has traced in origin to the case of *Gardiner* v. *Gray* (1815), where Lord Ellenborough found implied a warranty in a contract for sale of waste silk, that the goods actually delivered should be of 'a good and merchantable quality'. This expression was subsequently incorporated in the Sale of Goods Act 1893, a great piece of consumer protection legislation. Despite the efforts of the courts to develop the doctrine of implied terms, or presumed intent, of a contract, many organisations, particularly those in a monopoly situation, tended increasingly to limit their liabilities by exclusion clauses, frequently in small print or in situations where there was no real agreement by one party to the contract; provisions such as exemption clauses in transport undertakings and even by commercial firms in sales of goods to the public had become so widespread and unacceptable that by 1962 the final report of the Committee on Consumer Protection (the Molony Report) condemned the widespread practice of commercial organisations contracting out of their implied obligations as sellers of goods. The matter became a priority for the Law Commission when it was established in 1965. Recommendations for consumer protection in the matter of exclusion clauses were made by the Law Commission in 1969 and subsequently the Supply of Goods (Implied Terms) Act 1973 was brought into force, which made void exclusion clauses in consumer sales and hire-purchase agreements, and required such clauses to be 'fair and reasonable' even in non-consumer sales. The 1973 Act having amended the Sale of Goods Act 1893 and hire-purchase law in the matter of exclusion clauses, the Law Commission next turned to the question of exclusion clauses in other kinds of contract, and a second report followed in 1975 and the statutory result was the Unfair Contract Terms Act of 1977. The Act, which also applies to negligence and occupiers' liability, makes exclusion of liability in contract a matter of control as to its reasonableness, and makes specific provision for applying the test of reasonableness.

The Sale of Goods Act 1979 was a purely consolidating measure, incorporating the by now numerous amendments to the Sale of Goods Act 1893, which apart from one minor section was repealed. The Law Commission in 1979 recommended that the obligations of a supplier of goods in contracts analagous to sale should also be codified in a form similar to the 1979 Act and the Supply of Goods and Services Act 1982 was the next step. Part I of the 1982 Act dealt with contracts for the supply of goods, whether contracts of hire or contracts for the transfer of goods. A contract for transfer of goods was defined by the Act as 'a contract under which one person transfers or agrees to transfer to another the property in goods'. Such contracts may be of exchange, or barter or for the supply of work and materials. Certain contracts were specifically excepted as already covered by statutory provision; for instance, the sale of goods under the Sale of Goods Act 1979, hire-purchase under the Supply of Goods (Implied Terms) Act 1973, the transfer of goods for trading stamps under the Trading Stamps Act 1964, and a number of other minor cases.

Part II of the Act similarly codified contracts for supply of services; in certain respects it went beyond the recommendations of the Law Commission. Section 13 imported into contracts for the supply of services terms that suppliers will use reasonable care and skill. The Act provides for the Secretary of State to make exemptions of certain service industries from the obligations.

The development of the concept of consumer protection continues apace. It is clear that one problem is the excessive charges made by certain licensed moneylenders. Indeed it was held by the Court of Appeal in *Earl of Aylesford* v. *Morris* as long ago as 1873 that the Court could substitute an excessive rate of interest on a loan with an appropriate rate, reduced in this instance from 60 per cent to 5 per cent. Meanwhile, Parliament has now enacted, at the behest of the EC, legislation to make producers liable for death, personal injury and even certain specified property damage resulting from the manufacture of unsafe products. Part I of the Consumer Protection Act 1987, was enacted as the UK's response to the product liability directive of the Council of the EC (85/374). The Act, as has already been seen, makes the producer liable for injuries sustained from product defect without proof of negligence and even where there is no direct contractual relationship. In addition to the actual producer, generally the manufacturer, anyone holding himself out as a producer, eg 'own brand' retailers, or anyone adding a trade-mark or 'logo' to the product, is liable as a producer. Further, for articles produced outside the EC, the importer into the EC is liable 'as a producer'. In addition, the supplier of a product who fails to identify the manufacturer, processor, 'own brand' retailer or importer, become liable 'as a producer'.

FORMATION OF THE CONTRACT

An enforceable agreement, or contract, is formed when there is an offer, incorporating ascertainable terms, which may be manifest or implied, which receives unqualified acceptance by the person to whom the offer was made. There must be a mutual understanding of the terms, a *consensus ad idem*, with an intention to create legal relations and, unless the contract is under seal, it must be supported by consideration. An agreement must not be too vague, in other words there must be certainty of terms; if there is not, however much the court may sympathise such an agreement will not be held to be legally enforceable. This issue was well illustrated in *Sudbrook Trading Estate* v. *Eggleton* (1982). Here a lease gave the lessee an option to purchase the reversion, the price to be agreed by two valuers, one to be nominated by each side. The valuers would appoint an arbitrator in the event of their failure to agree. However, the lessor refused to appoint a valuer; the Court of Appeal held that there was no binding contract because the agreement had not provided for the effect of the failure to nominate such a valuer. But the Lords overruled the Court of Appeal; it took the view that the appointment of the valuers was a means to an end and that the court could if necessary intervene to replace what was in effect a defective piece of legal machinery.

Offer

The offer must be clear and unequivocal and may be made to a person, or persons or the general public. In the famous case of *Carlill* v. *Carbolic Smoke Ball Co.* (1893) the Court of Appeal rejected the defence that the offer to pay £100 to anyone who contracted influenza after using one of their smoke balls in a specified manner, was made to all the world and so was not capable of acceptance by any one individual. 'The offer is made to the world, the contract is made with that section of the public who . . . perform the condition on the faith of the advertisement.'

An offer must be distinguished from an invitation to treat. It is not always easy to decide what constitutes an offer in contractual terms, and what is merely an invitation to negotiate towards contractual relations. It has been held in a series of decided cases that goods displayed in a shop, or in a catalogue, or at an auction are not 'offered' so that a buyer can insist on a purchase. The display is an invitation to treat; the offer is made by the buyer tendering the money or making a bid which may then be accepted by the seller or auctioneer. The general position was confirmed in the case of *Pharmaceutical Society of Great Britain* v. *Boots Cash Chemists (Southern) Ltd* (1952) where goods displayed in a supermarket were held not to have been offered for sale, the 'offer' being the tender of money at the cash till.

In *Harvela Investments Ltd* v. *Royal Trust Co. of Canada (CI) Ltd* (1985) the plaintiff and the second defendant had been invited to bid for a controlling shareholding in a private company held by the first defendant. The invitation required the bids to be submitted by a sealed bid or confidential telex as a 'single offer' and bound themselves to accept the highest offer. The plaintiff made the higher bid, but the second defendant had also offered C$101,000 in excess of any other offer, as an alternative bid. The first defendant accepted the alternative bid. The House of Lords, unanimously reversing the Court of Appeal, upheld the plaintiff's claim that a bid by reference to another bid was invalid for a sale by fixed bidding where, as in this instance, the invitation to bid was an offer, not merely an invitation to treat.

Acceptance

As the offer of an agreement must be clear, so the intended acceptance must accord with the terms of the offer and be unequivocal. Like the offer, the acceptance may be oral, written or inferred by conduct, unless special requirements are specified in the offer. In *Taylor* v. *Allon* (1966) the appellant had been convicted of driving whilst uninsured; although he had received a 15-day cover note after the expiry of his insurance from his old insurers, the evidence was clear that he had decided to change insurers and had submitted a proposal to other insurers. Evidence from the old insurers was given that they would have considered themselves liable, but the justices ruled that the 15-day cover note had been an offer to continue insurance which had not been accepted, and further that the 15-day note was not supported by any consideration and so was unenforceable. The appeal to the Divisional Court was rejected, Lord Chief Justice Parker saying that 'a valid insurance . . . must arise from an enforceable contract and must arise by offer and acceptance.'

The acceptance must not be conditional, or seek to impose additional or amended terms. A conditional acceptance constitutes a new offer, which it is then open to the original offeror to accept or decline. An 'acceptance' that amends the offer in fact revokes the offer, so that the offeror is not bound if the offeree subsequently seeks to accept the original offer. However, a mere request for information does not revoke the original offer. The difference can be slight, and difficult to ascertain.

Similarly, a conditional acceptance does not constitute an agreement, hence the standard expression 'subject to contract' is particularly used in preliminary negotiations for the purchase of land. However, a provisional agreement 'until a fully legalised agreement is drawn up' was held in the case of *Branca* v. *Cobarro* (1947) to have been a binding agreement from the outset. And in *Pitt* v. *PHH Asset Management Ltd* (1993) a potential purchaser of property who, in order to protect himself against being 'gazumped', made a collateral agreement by which the vendor gave a negative undertaking he would not deal with any other purchaser for a clear specified period was entitled to enforce the agreement and claim damages for breach of the agreement when the vendor broke it. But in *Gibson* v. *Manchester City Council* (1979), which involved the sale of a council house to its sitting tenant, the House of Lords overturned the decisions of the Court of Appeal and the trial judge. Here the political control of the council changed after the local government elections of that year, 1971. As a result the corporation resolved not to sell council houses to tenants, except where legally binding contracts have been concluded. In the *Gibson* case the Lords could not accept that the relevant documents constituted an offer by the corporation, acceptance of which by the respondent, G., amounted to a legally enforceable contract for the sale of the house. Rather, it was simply a step in the negotiations for a contract, negotiations which never actually reached fruition.

So, in *Butler Machine Tool Co. Ltd* v. *Ex-Cell-O Corporation Ltd* (1979) the sellers offered to sell a machine tool for £75,535, delivery in two months' time, on its standard terms including a price review clause and a provision that the terms should prevail over any terms and conditions in the buyers' order. The buyers replied on their standard purchase printed form, which made no provision for price variation, and had a tear-off slip for acknowledgement and receipt of the order 'on the terms and conditions stated thereon' which the sellers completed. On delivery the sellers claimed a price increase of £2,892, which the buyers refused to pay. At first instance it was held that the price variation clause was a clear term and prevailed over the whole dealing, but the Court of Appeal unanimously held that the contract was on the buyers' counter offer terms.

Communication

The acceptance of an offer must be made to the offeror and unless the offeror defines the methods of acceptance it may be made in any normal manner, that is verbally or in writing, by telephone, telex or facsimile.

If the acceptance is posted, the agreement is made from the time of posting, even if the letter is delayed or lost in the post, unless there is an express stipulation, such as 'by notice in writing to the vendor', as in *Holwell Securities* v. *Hughes* (1974) where an acceptance was posted but never arrived; it was held that there was no contract for the sale of land. It should be noted that the contract is concluded when the offer is accepted unequivocally. If the acceptance is oral, either personally or by telephone, then the contract is effected at the offeror's address. If the acceptance is by letter or telegraph, it is deemed to be concluded on posting or telegraphing the acceptance, whether or not it is ever received; the contract is formed at the acceptor's point of posting.

The House of Lords has confirmed that acceptance by telex is to be treated as instantaneous and accepted at the offeror's office, as the offeror will be deemed to have control of internal office arrangements. In *Brinkibon* v. *Stahag Stahl* (1982) the Law Lords affirmed the Court of Appeal's decision in *Entores* v. *Miles Far East Corporation* (1955); in *Brinkibon* the defendant company in Vienna had telexed a counter offer which was accepted by the plaintiff's telex the next day from London.

However, for withdrawal of an offer the revocation must be actually communicated to the offeree prior to acceptance, and is not effective until communicated (*Byrne* v. *Van Tienhoven* (1880)). Acceptance of either an offer or counter-offer may be inferred by conduct of the offeree, provided that it is solely in respect of a clear offer. In the case of *Anglia Television* v. *Cayton* (1989), all the independent television companies made telex and oral offers to secure exclusive rights to televise a heavyweight boxing match, and paid for rights to three other contests on agreed terms. The plaintiffs sought injunctions to prevent interference with their alleged rights to the heavyweight contest, but the court held that the companies had relied on two different offers, neither of which was accepted, and that the payments for the other matches did not amount to acceptance by conduct of the fourth fight as an overall deal. As acceptance can be inferred by conduct, the question arises as to whether the offeror can claim that silence will be deemed to be acceptance. In the old case of *Felthouse* v. *Bindley* (1862), the plaintiff after some negotiations, wrote to his nephew saying, 'if I hear no more about him, I consider the horse mine at £30 15s', but the horse was included inadvertently in an auction sale with the nephew's other horses. The plaintiff's claim against the auctioneer failed, as there was no evidence of a concluded contract.

So, the person making the offer may prescribe any method for communicating the acceptance, but may not impose any implication of acceptance by, for instance, providing that silence, or non-refusal of an offer, shall be deemed to constitute acceptance.

Termination

The offer remains open, unless a time limit is prescribed, until either accepted or withdrawn, or by lapse after a reasonable time has expired. The timing of the acceptance is important as, until the offer is accepted, it may be withdrawn. A promise 'to keep the offer open' is not binding on the offeror unless consideration has been paid for the option. So in *Routledge* v. *Grant* (1828), where the defendant had offered to buy the plaintiff's house for a certain sum, 'a definite answer to be given within six weeks', it was held that the defendant could withdraw the offer at any time before acceptance; a similar issue arose in *Dickinson* v. *Dodds* (1876).

However, in *Walford* v. *Miles* (1992) the plaintiffs were negotiating to buy the defendants' business and submitted a subject to contract offer. The defendants' solicitor set out the terms for a sale of the business, the plaintiff spoke to the first defendant and undertook to obtain a 'comfort letter' from his bank and not to withdraw from the negotiations, and the first defendant agreed to break off negotiations with any other party. In fact, the defendants did not break off other negotiations and sold the business to a rival bidder. It was held by the court that there had been an enforceable collateral contract, that the plaintiffs had relied on the representation and were entitled to damages for the loss of the opportunity to buy the business. This decision was reversed on appeal to the Court of Appeal (by a majority of 2 to 1) which held that there had been no separate concluded and enforceable agreement to continue to negotiate with the plaintiffs, and this decision was upheld by the House of Lords, Lord Ackner stating that 'there is no reason in contract law why A. for good consideration should not agree with B. that he should not for a specified period negotiate with any other party. However, that is negative and while binding B. not to negotiate with another, it does not bind him to negotiate with A.'.

The effect of the words 'subject to contract' depends very much on the intention of the parties, as illustrated in *Tiverton Estates Ltd* v. *Wearwell Ltd* (1975).

The offer lapses on the death of the offeree; but on the death of the offeror, the offer lapses when the offeree has actual notice, unless there is an element of a personal nature in the offer, for example, to write a book or perform at a concert. In *Bradbury* v. *Morgan* (1862), where X. had guaranteed a loan by the plaintiff to Y., and the plaintiff in ignorance of X.'s death continued credit to Y., X.'s executors were held liable on the guarantee.

Meaningless phrases in a contract may be struck out, but the contract is still good. So, in *Nicolene Ltd* v. *Simmonds* (1953) an agreement was made to purchase steel, subject to 'the usual conditions of acceptance'. The court said the reference could be ignored. However, if the whole 'contract' is uncertain, then no legal agreement can exist. In *Harvey* v. *Facey* (1893) the plaintiffs telegraphed to the defendants, 'Will you sell us Bumper Hall Pen? Telegraph lowest cash price'. The reply was: 'Lowest price for Bumper Hall Pen, £900'. The plaintiffs agreed, by telegraph, to buy the land and asked for the title-deeds, but it was held that the second telegram was only an indication of a minimum price the defendants had in mind if a sale were to be arranged in the future.

INTENTION TO CREATE LEGAL RELATIONS AND CONSIDERATION

Contracts under seal

The word 'contract' derives from the Latin word for a bargain. However, although Roman Law recognised a promise made without consideration, and in Scotland there is a distinction between gratuitous and onerous promises, in England the courts in the Middle Ages required strict conformity with certain formal requirements to supply conclusive evidence of the intentions of the parties.

It seemed obvious to the medieval mind that if two parties embodied an agreement in a formal deed, then the courts should uphold and give effect to the contents of the deed. The corollary was equally simplistic – if two parties to an agreement could not be bothered to incorporate their agreement into a deed, then their informal agreements were not such as to be recognised by the King's courts.

Provided that the deeds were drawn in strict conformity with certain formal requirements, the courts accepted the deeds as conclusive evidence of the intentions of the parties. Furthermore, where there was a contract under seal, the courts accepted that the parties intended to import legal relations to their agreements and as such that the courts were bound to accept and enforce the contractual agreement.

Hence in the case of these formal, or specialty, contracts, the courts would examine the form to ensure compliance with the requirements, but were not concerned with any considerations other than those disclosed in the document. Seals provided the evidence of the participation of the parties. Originally elaborate and valuable objects, they were made for royalty and all great officers of state, religion or commerce, and the provisions of sealed agreements are enforceable at law, whether or not there is consideration.

It was customary for the person executing a deed to sign the document and then (when personal seals carried on a fob chain were no longer standard for gentlemen of business) to place the index finger on the seal and state 'I deliver this my act and deed'. In 1989 the requirements of sealing and delivery were removed, by s.1 of the Law of Property (Miscellaneous Provisions) Act 1989, and the formal requirements are now shortened to 'Signed as a Deed' followed by the signature, attested by an independent witness. Deeds may only be prepared by solicitors and notaries, but also licensed conveyancers are permitted to prepare conveyances or transfers of registered land, by virtue of s.11 of the Administration of Justice Act 1985.

Certain instruments are statutorily required to be effected by deed, such as the conveyance or transfer of a legal estate in land, which by the Law of Property Act 1925 must be effected by deed. It is immaterial to the effectiveness of the transfer whether it is for valuable consideration or by way of gift. Another example is that of covenants for gratuitous payments to a charity for a four-year period, when the charity can recover the income tax paid by the donor in addition to the sum covenanted.

Until the Corporate Bodies' Contracts Act 1960, corporations aggregate, mainly limited liability companies, could only be bound by contracts made under the company seal. However, this requirement was generally ignored and the courts had found a number of exceptions to the rule. Since 1960 corporations aggregate have been able to enter into contracts as informally as individual persons. Sometimes, however, certain contracts are made under seal, to give them particular solemnity, even when there is no legal requirement to do so. International commercial contracts are now affected by the Contracts (Applicable Law) Act 1990 which enacted the Rome Convention.

Intention to create legal relations

At the outset of this chapter, it is stated that an essential element in the formation of a contract is that both parties should have an intention to create a binding and enforceable agreement, that is that they intended to create a legal relationship. This is the accepted rule in English law, but it must be stated that a contrary view has been expressed in America, namely that it is not an essential element of the common law. Nevertheless, in cases of commercial agreements, the courts will infer an intention to create legal relations and seek to give effect to the agreement; but the converse will be implied in social and domestic situations, that no formal contract was intended. This general rule may be expressly negatived by the parties. For instance, in commercial agreements there may be an express disclaimer, particularly by the expression 'subject to formal contract' or some such phrase by one or other of the parties to the negotiations, or by incorporation of an 'honour' clause as is customary in football pools. In *Orion Insurance* v. *Sphere Drake Insurance* (1992) the Court of Appeal emphasised a goodwill agreement was not an intention to create legal relations and parol evidence was admissible.

However, the burden of proving there was no intention to create legal relations is on the party so asserting and in commercial transactions is very heavy. In the case of *Kleinwort Benson Ltd* v. *Malaysian Mining Corporation Berhad* (1989), the defendant company had provided the plaintiff with a 'comfort letter' in 1984 to assist one of its subsidiary companies to obtain a loan facility from the plaintiffs of £5 million. The comfort letter included a paragraph stating, 'It is our policy to ensure that the business of MMC Metals Ltd [the wholly owned subsidiary company of the defendants] is at all times in a position to meet its liabilities to you . . .' The maximum loan facility was subsequently raised to £10 million after a second comfort letter. The subsidiary company went into liquidation after the collapse of the tin market, and the case was one of many arising from the failure of the International Tin Council in 1985. The Court held that there was clear evidence that Kleinwort relied on the assurance of the defendants and that the presumption was reinforced that legal relations were intended. The defendants' repudiation of the liability of the subsidiary was a breach of contract. As the *Financial Times* said,

> **Comfort letters . . . are a soft alternative to a guarantee. They are given by a parent company to the creditor of its subsidiary for a variety of reasons: sometimes the parent does not want a guarantee to show on its balance sheet, it may wish to save on tax, or simply to avoid a legal obligation.**

A guarantee will normally be clear and enforceable by summary judgment proceedings in the case of default. The *Financial Times* continued:

> **Comfort letters are a species of those ambiguous declarations which negotiators often use to save a deal threatened by lack of agreement on an important point. They accept a formulation which allows each of the**

> **parties to believe it did not give up any ground. It is a lawyer's cover-up of a disagreement. The lawyer keeps his fingers crossed and prays that there may never be litigation over the meaning of his handiwork.**

However, the Court of Appeal reversed the decision; the case did not reach the House of Lords. It stated that the comfort letter had amounted to no more than a 'statement of present fact'; it was not a promise as to future conduct, and it gave rise to 'no more than a moral responsibility on the part of the defendants to meet the debt'. 'The consequences of the decision of the defendants to repudiate their moral responsibility are not matters for the court', said Lord Justice Ralph Gibson. The decision is in line with the House of Lords' finding in *Walford* v. *Miles* (1992), and confirms that comfort letters are not enforceable promises for contractual purposes and that the intention to create legal relations must be clear and unambiguous and cannot be presumed to have resulted in contractual agreements whilst only representing active negotiations towards an agreement; clearly, the distinction can be very fine.

An important statutory exception is that of collective agreements negotiated between employers and workers which are conclusively presumed not to be enforceable at law, unless the agreement incorporated a specific provision, however expressed, that the parties intend to be bound legally and the agreement was in writing, as provided under the Trade Union and Labour Relations Act 1974 which reversed the previous position under the Industrial Relations Act 1971. Section 18 of the 1974 Act (now ss.179,180 of the Trade Union and Labour Relations (Consolidation) Act 1992) reversed s.34 of the 1971 Act, but s.34 of the 1971 Act had itself been enacted to reverse the decision in *Ford Motor Co.* v. *Amalgamated Union of Engineering Workers* (1969). In that case it was indicated that collective agreements of the employers with the national joint negotiating committee of the AUEW were not, despite the wording of the 'agreements', legally enforceable contracts but 'statements of optimistic aspirations, presenting grave practical problems of enforcement – without clear and express provisions making them amenable to legal action'. In *Monterosso Shipping Co.* v. *International Transport Workers' Federation* (1982), the Court of Appeal, construing s.18 of the 1974 Act, said that a written collective agreement which did not contain any provision that the parties intended the agreement to be legally enforceable was not a contract at all. It had been argued that the effect of the section was not to negative the existence of the contract, but merely to make it unenforceable. However, Lord Denning said that s.18 drew a distinction between an 'agreement' and a 'legally enforceable contract'. 'The essence of a contract is that it is legally enforceable, whereas a mere agreement is not,' he observed.

Sometimes in social and domestic agreements the question of whether legal relations are intended is difficult to determine, and may depend on the particular facts; for instance, there have been conflicting decisions in cases where one person has given up a home to live with another, on the promise of being left the other's home. Again, the courts have been reluctant to construe any intention to create legal relations where car lifts are given in return for a contribution to expenses

(*Coward* v. *Motor Insurers' Bureau* (1962)). In *Connell* v. *Motor Insurers' Bureau* (1962) Lord Denning considered *obiter* that a contract was to be inferred in such a case. In the case of *Simpkins* v. *Pays* (1955) a paying boarder who took part with the family in a Sunday newspaper competition was held entitled to a share in the prize money of £750, because she had *regularly* contributed to the joint expenses of postage and so on.

Consideration

Many writers claim that the flexible development of the English law of contract derived from its origin as an action in tort, as a claim for the wrong of non-performance of a bargain, rather than an action for breach of a promise as is common in Roman Law systems, and which requires limitation of the kinds of promise that are legally enforceable.

In the fourteenth and fifteenth centuries, the only actions in contract available were for breach of covenant, in a contract under seal, for debt, for a liquidated sum and for the return of specific goods. No action lay for breach of an executory agreement. However, the remedy lay in a development of the action for trespass; trespass to the person lay for injuries, while trespass on the case lay for damage due to a wrongful act. At first the action lay for failure to perform a contract properly, and not for total non-performance, but this anomaly was overcome in the sixteenth century. From that time, the action of trespass on the case, or *assumpsit*, developed not as a breach of promise but as breach of bargain. Consideration became of primary importance in this context, as supplying the mutuality requisite for an enforceable bargain. Consideration is the 'price' paid by the plaintiff for the defendant's promise: the price may be a money payment, an act, or a counter-promise or any combination of them, provided it is for value.

During the eighteenth century doubt was cast on the necessity for consideration in commercial transactions, as in cases where there was a moral obligation and a promise to pay. In the case of *Pillans* v. *Van Mierop* (1765) Lord Mansfield held the defendant liable on a written bill of exchange, which conformed with the requirements of the Statute of Frauds 1677, and questioned whether there was any necessity for consideration in such a case. The moral obligation to pay a debt, itself not legally binding, was sufficient to found an action on a subsequent promise to pay, it was held in *Lee* v. *Muggeridge* (1813). However, the position was finally settled in the case of *Eastwood* v. *Kenyon* (1840) where the 'moral obligation' to pay a past debt was held to be insufficient, Lord Denman condemning the whole principle of moral obligation as opposed to the requirement of consideration.

Valuable consideration was defined in *Currie* v. *Misa* (1875) as 'some right, interest, profit or benefit accruing to one party or some forbearance, detriment, loss or responsibility given, suffered or undertaken by the other'. Such consideration may be 'executory', a promise for a promise, or 'executed', a promise for performance of an act. But consideration must not be 'past', for a promise subsequent to a transaction is a gratuitous promise, and so is not 'of value', as was held in the case of *Re McArdle* (1951).

In general, it is only the party that pays the price as part of the bargain that may sue on the breach of the agreement. Further, the promisee must be a party to the bargain. It is said that consideration 'must move from the promisee'. The doctrine of privity, which is discussed below, has been criticised judicially and academically, and the Law Revision Committee recommended its abolition, but that was as long ago as 1937.

A statutory exception to the general rule was introduced by the Bills of Exchange Act 1882, whereby payment of a debt by a bill or cheque, whether for a past debt or to a third party, was enforceable as being based on longstanding commercial custom. In such cases the payee may sue on the cheque without proof of consideration, or of contractual relations relations. However, in a recent case an employee of the plaintiff company did work for a customer and was paid by the customer's daughter by cheque. The defendant then being dissatisfied with the work, stopped her cheque, and the plaintiff company sued. The judge at first instance dismissed the claim on the ground that there was no consideration. On appeal, the Court of Appeal held, by a majority, that the defendant was not a party to the contract, that the employee did not have express or implied authority to accept a cheque from a third party and to exonerate the defendant's father from his obligation to pay, and so the defendant was a 'volunteer' who was entitled to stop the cheque before its presentation, *AEG (UK) Ltd* v. *Lewis* (1992).

Sufficiency of consideration

The courts from an early time declined to entertain argument as to the adequacy of the amount of consideration, on the principle that people must be free to negotiate their own bargains with complete commercial freedom of action.

This principle has been claimed as upholding the right of individuals to enter into bargains freely. It is more probably derived from the desire of the courts not to interfere in commercial transactions unnecessarily. If the price has been agreed, and neither fraud nor duress nor mistake is alleged, it is better for the courts to uphold the agreement.

Consideration must consist of something, whether money, work or a promise to do or refrain from doing, which is a 'benefit' to the promisor or 'detriment' to the promisee. The benefit or detriment must not be nominal only, but even if for one party the benefit is considerable and correspondingly the detriment to the other party is large, the agreement will be enforceable. So, if a farmer contracts to sell an acre of land to a neighbour, at agricultural value thinking that he wants it for a larger garden, and the buyer obtains planning consent for houses before completion, then the land would perhaps be worth substantially more, but the contract price was not 'nominal' and the agreement is enforceable. It is immaterial that the seller did not realise the true value of the object to be sold, provided there was no fraud or deception on the part of the buyer. In *Chappell & Co.* v. *Nestlé Co.* (1960) the House of Lords held that chocolate wrappers, although worthless in themselves, were part of a valid consideration where in a promotional scheme the price of a music record was lowered from 33p to 8p.

Nevertheless, whilst consideration need not be adequate, it must be of some value. As a result, past consideration is not of value. It may be true that one good turn deserves another, but that cannot be legally binding grounds for enforcement. A promise to do an act which is obviously impossible, at the time of the promise, is not of value. But if the act becomes much more expensive than anticipated, or even impossible subsequently, that is too bad for the promisor, as many experienced solicitors have discovered when they have given an undertaking carelessly.

In general in a series of cases in the last century very little consideration has been held as sufficient. So the abandonment of a claim, although subsequently thought to be worthless, was held to be sufficient in *Callisher* v. *Bischoffsheim* (1870), where the claim was reasonable, and at the time of its surrender was believed to have a reasonable chance of success. In *Williams* v. *Roffey Bros & Nicholls (Contractors) Ltd* (1990) the plaintiff was promised an extra £10,300 if he completed work on a block of flats, since the defendants were liable to pay liquidated damages in the main contract if they did not complete the refurbishment on time. The Court of Appeal held that in the absence of economic duress or fraud, a promise by one contracting party to pay money to the other in order to ensure continued performance by the other of his contractual obligations is binding, even though the other does no more than he was originally contractually bound to do. The *Williams* case underlines Sir Frederick Pollock's definition of consideration as 'the price for which the promise of the other is bought'. The plaintiff had been sub-contracted the carpentry work on the block of flats, but having received £16,200 on account of the £20,000 agreed (a low figure), found he was in financial difficulties, hence the extra inducement by the defendants, the main contractors. The difficulties thrown up by the *Williams* decision were further illustrated in *Ferguson* v. *Davies* (1997).

In the case of *Thomas* v. *Thomas* (1842) Mrs Thomas claimed to be entitled to occupy a house under the terms of her husband's will, provided that she kept the house in repair and paid a small ground rent of £1 per annum. The court held that the testator's wish was only a motive and did not, as a moral obligation on the part of the executor, constitute consideration, but that the widow's promise to pay the £1 a year was sufficient consideration.

On the other hand the courts have held as insufficient contracts where the act promised was in any case a duty imposed by statute, or where there was an existing contractual duty, or an agreement to accept a lesser sum in satisfaction of a debt, the so-called rule in *Pinnel's Case* (1602), unless there was some further consideration, such as the mode or time of payment. However, compositions by a debtor with his creditors are an exception to this rule.

8.2   Promissory estoppel

The rule that payment of a lesser sum cannot discharge a larger debt, without some other variation of terms, as lacking consideration, has been criticised but is still upheld (the rule in *Pinnel's Case*). However, if one party to a contract modifies the liabilities of the other party, then he may be estopped from enforcing the original contract if that would entail repudiating a promise which was intended to be acted upon and was acted upon by the other party, even if there was no consideration for the modification.

The rule can be stated as:

> **if a promise is given by one party to a contract, without consideration, not to insist upon his legal rights, then if that party breaks his promise and sues on the original contract, the promisee has a good defence; provided that it had been intended to create or affect the legal relations between the parties and that the promisee should act on the promise and that he did so act.**

This was the decision of Mr Justice Denning in *Central London Property Trust* v. *High Trees House* (1947). In that case a block of flats in London was let in 1937 at an annual ground rent of £2,500. During the Second World War many of the flats had been left empty because of bombing, and the landlords agreed to accept half rent only. After the War the receiver for the debenture holders of the landlords was held entitled to recover the full rent again, after reasonable notice, but would have been estopped by the promise from claiming the full rent for the war years. Lord Denning traced his authority from the decision of Lord Chancellor Cairns in *Hughes* v. *Metropolitan Railway Company* (1877), where in his judgment he had stated:

> **It is the first principle of Equity that if parties who have entered into definite and distinct terms involving certain legal results – certain penalties or legal forfeiture – afterwards by their own act or with their own consent enter upon a course of negotiation which has the effect of leading one of the parties to suppose that the strict rights arising under the contract will not be enforced, or will be kept in suspense, or held in abeyance, the person who otherwise might have enforced those rights will not be allowed to enforce them where it would be inequitable [to do so].**

In the later case of *Birmingham and District Land Co.* v. *London and North Western Railway Co.* (1888) Lord Justice Bowen stated that the principle was not confined to penalties and forfeitures, but extended to 'all cases of contractual rights'. However, despite this broad statement of principle, the courts had generally ignored the line of reasoning until the decision by Lord Denning in the *High Trees* case in 1946, only five months after his appointment as a judge. Lord Denning's comments on this case in his book, *The Discipline of Law*, emphasise that the parol agreement could even override the provisions of an agreement under seal, which the leases had been, despite the common law rule which had always held that an agreement under seal could only be varied by another deed. Lord Denning distinguished promissory estoppels from other estoppels, stating, 'they are not cases of estoppel in the true sense, they are really promises intended to be binding and acted upon – and in fact acted upon'.

Clearly, the party seeking to establish the defence of promissory estoppel will have to satisfy the court that it is inequitable for the promisor to sue. In the case of *Combe* v. *Combe* (1951) it was held that this will normally be established by proof that the promisee did act on the promise. However, Viscount Simonds in *Tool Metal Manufacturing Co.* v. *Tungsten Electric Co.* (1955) considered that the principle had been altogether too widely stated in *Combe* and that frequently it could be inferred that the promise was intended only to suspend and not to abrogate the full legal rights of the original contract, and then the promisor could give reasonable notice of resumption of his full rights under the original contract.

Lord Denning concluded his section on the *High Trees* case with the assertion that the effect has been to abolish the doctrine of consideration 'in all but a handful of cases'. However, even in the case of *Combe* it was stated that 'consideration is essential to the formation of a contract, but not to [its] modification or discharge'.

In 1937 the Law Revision Committee had recommended that 'an agreement should be enforceable if either the promise was in writing or if it was supported by valuable consideration *past* or present' – effectively the reinstatement of the moral obligation theory of Lord Mansfield in *Pillans* v. *Van Mierop* (1765). The amendment has never been made by statute, so still the argument goes on, and students will have to tread the wary path of their predecessors.

However, the old rule that *agreement* to accept payment of a lesser sum in full satisfaction of a larger debt due, lacked consideration and was unenforceable, is clearly amended by the *High Trees* principle and the defence of estoppel can be pleaded by the debtor if, but only if, he has paid the smaller sum on the new terms agreed between the parties.

One further point should be made concerning the doctrine of promissory estoppel. It is clear that the doctrine is founded on the equitable principle that the plaintiff should not be able to assert a right or benefit which by his own conduct or inactivity he has given the defendant cause to believe would not be asserted, that is it may be a defence but it cannot give rise to a cause of action in itself. It has been described as a shield, not a sword. In the case of *Amalgamated Investment and Property Co. (in Liquidation)* v. *Texas Commerce International Bank* (1981) Mr Justice Goff, affirmed by the Court of Appeal, in a full review of estoppels has shown that some can give rise to a cause of action, but not promissory estoppel. The distinction between estoppels is marginal, however (*Crabb* v. *Arun District Council* (1975)). In the *Texas* case the facts were that the plaintiffs wished to loan money to ANPP, a subsidiary company and signed a written guarantee of all the monies due to the defendants from ANPP. On account of exchange control regulations, the money was loaned by Portsoken, a subsidiary of the defendants. ANPP later failed to pay the money. Lord Denning said in the Court of Appeal:

> **When the parties to a transaction proceed on the basis of an underlying assumption – either of fact or of law – on which they have conducted the dealings between them – neither of them will be allowed to go back on that assumption when it would be unfair or unjust to allow him to do so. If one of them does seek to go back on it, the courts will give the other such remedy as the equity of the case demands.**

8.3   Forms and terms of
the contract

FORMS

A contract is in essence a legally binding agreement. English law recognises two kinds of contract, namely the specialty or contract under seal, and the simple contract. Contracts, as we have seen, may be formal and comprised in deeds, or written agreements or purely parol. Frequently the agreements are part written and partly verbal. The terms of the contractual agreement may sometimes be understood, being customary in the trade, or resulting from previous agreements between the parties.

Deeds

Certain agreements have to be effected by deed, particularly agreements for the sale or transfer of so-called real property, that is land and permanent structures attached to the land, or interests in land. A deed must be in writing; it takes a specific form and usually has to be prepared by a solicitor or notary. Conveyances or transfers of land may now also be prepared by licensed conveyancers. The document, formerly drawn on parchment, has to be signed as a deed. Most deeds have to be produced for stamping with the appropriate duty, unless covered by a statutory exemption.

Written contracts

In addition to specialty contracts, certain simple contracts are required by statute to be in *writing* to be enforceable. Contracts that are required to be in writing include bills of sale, bills of exchange and promissory notes, marine insurance and, most notably, all agreements covered by the Consumer Credit Act 1974, particularly hire-purchase and consumer credit agreements made by a person (or partnership) for hire or purchase of goods for sums of £50 to £25,000.

There are exemptions for credit card agencies (for example, Access and Barclaycard) and for the provision of mortgages by local authorities and building societies. The 1974 Act has copious regulations but in general provides for the agreements to be in a form prescribed by the Secretary of State, to be signed by both parties, and for cancellation of the agreement within a defined period, if only at the prospective stage or if arising from oral representations by the party giving credit. A notable feature is that the supplier of credit, a finance house, which must be licensed to deal in regulated credit or hire transactions, is generally made liable by the Act for any failure of the supplier of the goods, the creditor having a right of indemnity against the supplier.

Contracts of guarantee

Contracts of guarantee, where one person promises to answer for the 'debt, default or miscarriage' of another, are distinguished by the courts from contracts of indemnity. In the former the guarantor promises to pay 'if the principal debtor fails to do so'; in the latter the guarantor indemnifies the creditor directly. The distinction was formerly important where minors were concerned.

Thus if two friends, B. and G., go to a shop, B. having forgotten his wallet, G. says to the shop-keeper, 'I will pay you if B. doesn't', then that is a guarantee, but if he says, 'Let B. have it, I will see you are paid', then it is an indemnity. Such subtle distinctions are unfortunate in commercial circumstances and do not commend themselves to the general public. However, both contracts of surety and of indemnity come under the regulatory provisions of the Consumer Credit Act 1974, and require to be in writing in the form provided. In *Elpis Maritime Co. Ltd v. Marti Chartering Co. Inc, The Maria D.* (1991) the House of Lords held that s.4 of the Statute of Frauds 1677 can be satisfied either by a written agreement signed by the guarantor or by a note or memorandum of the agreement signed by the guarantor or his agent.

In contract a performance bond, granted by a subcontractor jointly with a surety, amounted to a guarantee it was held by the House of Lords in *Trafalgar House Construction (Regions) Ltd v. General Surety and Guarantee Co. Ltd* (1995).

Contracts for sale of land

It is generally known that agreements for sales and purchases of houses are not binding until a written document has been signed. Formal contracts used to attract a small amount of stamp duty and so were signed over a 6d (2½p) postage stamp affixed to the contract. Many people thought that the stamp authenticated the contract and sometimes a party signed an 'open' contract, believing that he would not be bound as there was no stamp.

The relevant statutory provision used to be s.40 of the Law of Property Act 1925 amending the old s.4 of the Statute of Frauds and provided that 'no action lies for the sale or other disposition of land or of any interest in land unless the agreement or a memorandum of it is in writing, signed by or on behalf of the party to be sued'. So an agreement for the sale of a house, building or any interest in land, or for a lease of three years or more, had to be *evidenced* in writing, and the actual conveyance or lease must be drawn as a deed. However, s.2 of the Law of Property (Miscellaneous Provisions) Act 1989 requires all contracts for the sales of interests in land to be *made* in writing. Section 2(1) states: 'A contract for the sale or other disposition of an interest in land can only be made in writing and only by incorporating all the terms which the parties have expressly agreed in one document or, where contracts are exchanged, in each'.

Simple contract

The vast majority of contracts are not required to be incorporated in deeds nor to be in writing to be effective. Such agreements may be purely verbal or comprised in an agreed document, or as frequently is the position, may be partly in writing and partly verbal.

People in their daily lives are constantly entering into enforceable contractual agreements. In contracts for the purchase of goods, for example, food, groceries and clothing; for services, for example, by a plumber, builder or doctor; for employment and so on; the phenomena of 'offer', 'acceptance' and 'consideration' are all present, although there may be no thought of legal relations.

Nevertheless an intention to create legal relations will be presumed in all such circumstances and the consequences follow the intentions, that the goods sold will, for instance, match the description and be of satisfactory quality, or that services will be completely performed. It is clearly unnecessary to include in such informal agreements any express words that the parties intend to be bound or any such phrase. It is an accepted implied term of the contract.

TERMS

As it is superfluous to state expressly that an intention to create legal relations is incorporated in the agreement, so it is frequently the case that other terms may be presumed or inferred. Moreover, the parties themselves may not have considered all the terms and the fact that the terms are neither readily apparent nor expressly incorporated into a formal agreement is not a ground for assuming that the contract is unenforceable, except as we have seen in the particular case of contracts for a sale of an interest in land. In all other cases, the courts will enquire into the background to the agreement and will try wherever possible to ascertain just what are the terms of the contract.

Agreements are frequently entered into after a course of negotiations, some of which may have been in writing, often against a background of customary or commercial arrangements that are 'understood'; indeed the written agreements may have been supplemented, or varied, verbally.

In the course of the negotiations, there may well have been statements or assurances by one party intended to encourage the other party to enter into the contract. Such a statement or assurance may have been incorporated as a term of the contract, or it may have been regarded as a 'mere representation' which induced the formation of, but was not fundamental to the contract. The statement may have been merely some flattering description or 'puff' which did not amount even to a representation. It is often not easy to decide into which category the statement falls, but the consequences of failure to comply with a term, a representation or a 'puff' are quite different, at any rate in theory. If there is a breach of a term incorporated as a condition of the contract, then the party not in breach is entitled to rescind the contract; but if the statement had only been an innocent misrepresentation, then the injured party's recourse is in damages, not a complete abrogation of the agreement it was held in *Oscar Chess* v. *Williams* (1957). If the statement had been just a 'puff', then there is no redress.

Taking the last point first, it is very true that in all contractual relations, the buyer or party obtaining a service should as a general rule satisfy himself as to what he is acquiring. The old rule was expressed in Latin (not just to annoy students) as *caveat emptor* – let the buyer beware! 'A beautiful cottage' may very well have a leaking roof and, if there is no specific warranty or guarantee as to condition, the buyer is presumed to have made his own enquiry or examination and the word 'beautiful' has probably not amounted to a representation but is purely a 'puff'. In an age of consumer protection, it is still important to remember this primary rule, before turning to examine what terms have been expressly or impliedly incorporated in a particular contract.

Express terms

Obviously the more formal the contract, the more likely that the terms would have been included in a written agreement. In that case, the general rule was, understandably, that oral evidence would not be admitted to disprove the express documents, in which the agreement was comprised.

The interpretation of exactly what is meant by the written documents was a matter exclusively for the court to determine, but evidence could not generally be brought to 'add to, vary or contradict' clear terms of a written agreement. However, the courts would allow oral evidence of certain matters, notably:

1 *Custom*, particularly in commercial agreements where there is evidence of terms that are understood as customary in the trade. Such matters are allowed to add to, but not to contradict, clear written terms (*Les Affréteurs Réunis* v. *Walford* (1919)).

2 *Postponed* operation of the contract may be adduced from a prior oral agreement; that is the written contract is shown to have been subject to an oral condition precedent, a specific verbal term made before the written contract (*Pym* v. *Campbell* (1856)). *Graham* v. *Pitkin* (1992) showed that a conditional

acceptance is not true acceptance, but that is different from a condition precedent. The Privy Council said it was up to the purchaser to decide whether to buy land for cash or on a now much delayed mortgage; the purchaser had not indicated repudiation of the contract and it was not in order for the vendor to rescind the agreement.

3 *Omitted* terms: parol evidence is acceptable if it is clear that the written agreement lacks some terms, as seen in *Walker Property Investments (Brighton) Ltd v. Walker* (1947), where evidence was allowed that the oral agreement for a lease of a flat had been made provided that the use of a basement and garden were allowed, which was not included in the written terms.

4 Exceptionally, extrinsic evidence may be allowed to remedy uncertainty in a contract and wherever the written agreement is not expressed to cover the whole of the contract such evidence, including *prior* oral agreement, may be allowed to contradict the clear terms of a written agreement, as in the case of the *SS Ardennes (Cargo Owners)* v. *Ardennes (Owners)* (1951) where a bill of lading of a shipment of oranges from Spain provided for 'any route, whether directly or indirectly to London' and the ship sailed via Antwerp missing the best market in London; evidence was allowed of a prior oral agreement that the ship would sail direct. It was held that the bill of lading was evidence of a contract for the carriage but was not exclusive of other terms and that the oral agreement was collateral to the contract.

But, rather surprisingly, in 1986 the Law Commission said that this rule, the so-called Parol Evidence Rule, was not a rule after all, and oral evidence could be admitted at will, and an Act was not required: 'a process of re-education . . . is a more satisfactory means of achieving justice than any attempt to legislate'.

We shall see shortly that individuals have certain protection now from unfair bargains, particularly where there is inequality of bargaining power. In commercial contracts, however, where the parties are not of unequal bargaining power and where the risks are normally borne by insurance in any case, then the judges prefer the concepts of 'freedom to and sanctity of contract'. This was the unanimous decision of the Law Lords in *Photo Production Ltd* v. *Securicor Transport Ltd* (1980), overruling the equally unanimous decision of the Court of Appeal. We shall return to this case later, but it is worth noting that Lord Salmon went so far as to state, succinctly, 'Any persons capable of making a contract are free to enter into any contract they may choose; and providing the contract is not illegal or voidable, it is binding on them'.

As a result of this decision, it has been postulated that there are now two laws of contract, one for the consumer and the other for the commercial sector. We shall examine the matter further under exclusion clauses, but it is sufficient here to emphasise the paramount importance in contract of express terms, for as Lord Diplock commented in the *Photo Production* case, 'If the parties wish to reject or modify primary obligations . . . they are fully at liberty to do so by express words'.

Implied terms

The general rule is that the terms of an agreement must be ascertainable with reasonable certainty; so a sale of goods at a price which might be increased if the horse sold was 'lucky', was held in *Guthing* v. *Lynn* (1831) to be too uncertain. However, the courts will always tend towards finding the terms of an enforceable contract, rather than deciding that the terms were too uncertain for a concluded agreement to be ascertained; particularly this is so in the case of commercial contracts, even if the terms incorporated in a printed form had been described almost two hundred years previously as 'absurd and incoherent', see *Brough* v. *Whitmore* (1791), cited in the Court of Appeal case of *Schiffshypothekenbank zu Luebeck AG* v. *Compton (The Alexion Hope)* (1988), a marine insurance case where Lord Justice Lloyd commented that 'the task of construing the contract . . . was not made easy by the combination of a medieval English form with a translation from modern Swedish'. In the Scottish case of *Neilson* v. *Stewart* (1991), the seller of a 50 per cent shareholding in a company's shares assisted the buyer with a loan to help the purchase, the loan being secured on the company's assets. Repayment was deferred for a year and was then to be negotiated to the parties' mutual agreement. The buyer failed to complete and in the seller's action for damages the buyer contended that the terms of repayment were too uncertain. It was held by the House of Lords, affirming the Court of Session, that the principal agreement for the sale of shares was clear and enforceable, the terms of the loan repayment were ancillary and severable, and would be implied even if the loan infringed the prohibition on a company providing finance for the acquisition of its shares.

There has been academic debate as to whether the courts are restricted in implying terms of the contract to those which can be *logically* implied. The position is that terms can be implied, even if they cannot be logically inferred from the words of the agreement, if the court holds that the terms would have been included if the parties had considered them at the time, or if they had considered the question or if they had foreseen the difficulty that had in fact arisen. In addition, the courts will readily imply terms where there is shown to be a custom or statute. Exceptionally, the courts may imply a term to give business efficiency also. In *Behzadi* v. *Shaftesbury Hotels Ltd* (1991) the Court of Appeal held that the innocent party could serve a notice making time of the essence as soon as there was any delay by the other party; so an innocent party can act promptly by calling on the defaulting party to act within a reasonable time, and thus terminate the contract. Implied contractual terms as to fitness for purpose arose in *Saphena Computing Ltd* v. *Allied Collection Agencies Ltd* (1995).

Custom
From earliest times, the common law courts accepted that local custom could be construed as incorporated in a contract where it would have been reasonable to suppose that the parties would have so intended. Early examples of such cases were frequently as between landlord and tenant, where local custom could be used to amplify the terms of an agricultural tenancy. 'Local custom' was defined (in the *Tanistry Case* in 1608) and in particular the custom must have existed from

'time immemorial', it should not be confused with general custom, which is the basis of common law anyway, or with local usage which need not have existed from immemorial time. Trade usage on the other hand merely needs to be well known in the trade (*British Crane Hire Corporation* v. *Ipswich Plant Hire* (1975)).

Normal commercial usage in a particular trade or business can supply additional terms on the same basis. The courts justify the incorporation of such implied terms as representing the presumed intention of the parties (*Hutton* v. *Warren* (1836)). This is, however, a specious reason as the courts will import custom or usage into a contract whether the parties were aware of the custom or not (*Hardwick Game Farm* v. *Suffolk Agricultural and Poultry Producers Association Ltd* (1969)).

However, a custom or usage of the trade may be excluded either expressly or impliedly; so in *Les Affréteurs Réunis* v. *Walford* (1919) it was shown that it was customary for a ship broker to be paid out of hire that was earned, but the contract provided for commission to be paid on 'signing this charter', ie irrespective of whether hire was earned or not.

Statute
When a custom or usage has become well-established, it is frequently incorporated in all contracts by implication, unless specifically excluded. The pressure of commercial convenience is then often sufficient for Parliament to adopt the custom and incorporate the terms in specific legislation. This development was followed particularly in contracts for the sale of goods.

At first the common law position was that the buyer of goods was not entitled to any implied warranty, it was up to the buyer to require express guarantees if he needed them; otherwise the buyer should rely on his own inspection. The general position was gradually modified as three major exceptions to the general rule of *caveat emptor* developed, namely:

1 where the buyer had made plain to the seller the purpose for which the goods were required *and* that he relied on the seller's skill and judgement;

2 where goods were sold by description, then they must not only be in accordance with the description, but must also be of a *merchantable quality*; and

3 where goods were sold by sample, then the bulk must correspond with the sample and the buyer should have reasonable opportunity of examining the bulk and comparing with the sample.

These terms were incorporated in the Sale of Goods Act 1893, which was substantially a codification of the common law, as Sir Mackenzie Chalmers the draftsman of the Bill, saw it. In particular, s.12 incorporated an implied *condition* in sales of goods, that the seller had the title and right to sell the goods, and an implied *warranty* for the buyer to have quiet possession free from any charge or incumbrance in favour of any third party; s.13 implied a condition that goods sold by description will correspond thereto; s.14 implied a condition of fitness for a purpose if stated by the buyer and of merchantable quality where goods are sold in the course of a business; and s.15 provided that in a contract for sale by sample there is an implied condition that the bulk will correspond with the sample in quality and that the buyer should have a reasonable opportunity to compare the bulk with the sample.

The Act stood the test of time reasonably for some eighty years, but was then amended by the Supply of Goods (Implied Terms) Act 1973, the Consumer Credit Act 1974, the Unfair Contract Terms Act 1977 and was finally repealed (except for s.26 which deals with the effect of writs of execution) and re-enacted with all the amendments by the Sale of Goods Act 1979.

It will have been noted that the sections of the 1893 Act differentiated between implied conditions, the breach of which gives a right of repudiation as well as damages, and implied warranties which give a right to damages only. The 1979 Act preserves the distinction between conditions and warranties, and provides, under s.11, that whether a stipulation in a contract is a condition or a warranty 'depends in each case on the construction of the contract', which is not particularly helpful to either business-people or their advisers. The rush of amending legislation, however, has not ceased. The Supply of Goods and Services Act 1982, which makes provision for terms to be implied in contracts for the transfer or hire of goods (Part I) and for the supply of services (Part II), gave effect to the Law Commission's recommendations as to implied terms in contracts for the supply of goods and the recommendations of the National Consumer Council in their report, *Service Please*, published in 1981.

Sections 1 and 6 of the 1982 Act define contracts for the transfer of property and hire of goods respectively, and ss.2–5 and 7–10 have made provision for implied terms as to title, description, quality or fitness and sample in broadly similar terms to those in ss.12–15 of the Sale of Goods Act 1979 as amended by the Sale and Supply of Goods Act 1994.

Part II of the Act, by s.12, defines a contract for the supply of a service, and, by s.13, provides an implied term that the service will be carried out with reasonable care and skill; by s.14, within a reasonable time and, by s.15, if no price is included in the agreement, that there will be paid a reasonable charge for the service.

Sections 11 and 16 provide that the implied terms may be expressly excluded or varied by the contract, or the course of dealings or usage binding both parties. The Secretary of State, moreover, may provide by Order in Council that one or more of the s.13–15, implied terms, should not apply to a particular service.

It appears that the lawyers and company directors were nodding when the Bill was passed in Parliament, as an exclusion order was subsequently passed providing that the implied terms should not apply to:

1 the services of an advocate in court, or before any tribunal inquiry or arbitrator, and in carrying out preliminary work directly affecting the conduct of the hearing; and

2 the services rendered to a company by a director of the company in his capacity
as such.

The exclusion orders were made after representation that the Act, which was
intended to codify existing implied terms, appeared to extend or create substantial
new obligations contrary to the intentions of the Act's sponsors and in particular
to solicitor/advocates (barristers were already immune on the grounds of public
policy) and non-executive directors of companies.

Courts (The Moorcock Doctrine)

Where the general ambit of the contract made by the parties is clear, but the
document drawn up is inadequate, the courts will seek to give 'business efficacy'
to the agreement, by implying any necessary term. This is the doctrine of *The
Moorcock* (1889).

In that case, the defendant wharfingers contracted with the plaintiff shipowners for
their vessel to discharge at the defendant's jetty on the tide-way in the Thames.
Both parties must have known that the vessel would ground at low water. The
ship settled on a hard ridge in the mud and was damaged. The defendants had not
warranted the safety of the berth, and did not own the bed of the river (which was
vested in the Thames Conservancy). The Court of Appeal implied an undertaking
by the defendants that 'the river bottom was, so far as reasonable care could
provide, in such a condition as not to endanger the vessel'.

The doctrine has been circumscribed by the courts and it has been held that a
term can only be read into the contract if it would have been clear that both
parties would have so confirmed at the time of the contract; it must have been 'so
obvious that it goes without saying', declared Lord Justice MacKinnon in *Shirlaw*
v. *Southern Foundries* (1939). The mere fact that the contract as drawn is *impossible*
to perform is not sufficient reason for the court to intervene. In the case of *Eurico
SpA* v. *Phillips Bros* (1987) where there was a contract for delivery of a cargo to a
'main Italian port' to be nominated by the buyers, and the port nominated,
Ravenna, had insufficient depth for the draft of the ship, the Court of Appeal held
that there could be no implied provision that the port would meet the ship's
requirements.

Similarly, in the case of *Stubbes* v. *Trower Still and Keeling* (1987), where a student
had been offered articles but then failed his examination and the firm withdrew
the offer of articles, the Court of Appeal held the student was entitled to damages
for the breach of contract. No term could be implied that the offer of articles was
dependent upon success in the examination.

The courts have been reluctant to extend the doctrine to conveyances or leases of
land. In the case of *Liverpool City Council* v. *Irwin* (1976) the House of Lords held
that there was an implied covenant on the part of the council, landlords of a
tower-block of flats, to maintain to a 'necessary' standard the common parts, such
as stairs, lifts and rubbish chutes, but no more than necessary to give 'business
efficacy' to the contracts for letting. However, in the case of *Wettern Electric Ltd* v.
Welsh Development Agency (1983) where the defendant agency had granted a

licence (to avoid security of tenure) to the plaintiff company of factory premises, the judge at first instance held that there should be implied in the agreement a term that the building was of sound construction and suitable for the licensee's purpose, and that this term was required 'to make the contract workable', on the *Moorcock* principle.

In general, however, the courts will be reluctant to imply any term unless it can be shown that the parties would have imported that term if the point had arisen in negotiation, provided that no bad faith in negotiation is disclosed. It is not enough to claim that it would make the contract more convenient, it must be a term that is necessary to make the contract workable, or one such that, as commented in *Shirlaw*, if an officious bystander had suggested it, the parties would have replied 'of course'.

Unfair terms

As we have seen, the law of contract was developed on the basis that agreements freely negotiated between competent parties should be strictly upheld, provided that the contracts had not been improperly induced. However, the Victorian age of railway and steamship travel ushered in the twentieth century of monopoly undertakings, where the concept of freely negotiated agreements has given way to the present day norm of single suppliers of many, if not most, of people's daily needs. Supplies of basic necessities such as electricity, water, gas, transport and drainage, of key services such as posts and telephones, and for very many such important matters as housing, education and medicine, are provided by monopoly organisations, or at best the individual has a limited degree of choice or negotiation.

Parallel with the growth of limited choice there developed the device of the 'standard form contract', where in reality there was no free negotiation, but a situation only of 'take it or leave it'. Passengers on railways or the buses, consumers of gas and electricity, users of posts, had in practice no alternative but to accept the goods or services subject to the conditions and terms of the monopoly suppliers; frequently, in standard form agreements, the terms were purely by reference to notices promulgated by the supplier. Such contracts were useful for saving time, and politically often highly desirable, but they clearly did not accord with the concept of free bargaining between equals. When standard form contracts began to include sweeping exclusion of liability clauses, it was time for the courts to intervene.

At first the courts were very reluctant to revoke the freedom of individuals to enter into any contract, however one-sided, but as early as 1877 the movement was apparent in a decision that if conditions were incorporated by reference in a document, then the contracting party was only bound if reasonable notice was given of the existence of the conditions (*Parker* v. *South-Eastern Railway Co.* (1877)). This was a small step to protect the individual, but the courts had reverted by the 1930s, contenting themselves with mutterings about 'regrettably small print', as seen in *L'Estrange* v. *Graucob* (1934) and in *Thompson* v. *LMS Railway*

Co. (1930) holding that a party was bound even if he did not, or could not have, read the conditions. Provided the conditions had been reduced to writing, and there had been no inducement by misrepresentation, a point illustrated in *Curtis* v. *Chemical Cleaning Co.* (1951), the courts still felt bound to uphold the strict terms of the contract. However, those seeking to enforce the contract, where there had been incorporated one-sided clauses, increasingly found that the courts would seek to assist the individual if the exclusion clause had, for instance, been badly drafted and was unclear or uncertain. The onus shifted somewhat from the party bound by the terms having to avoid the contract, to the party enforcing the term to assert the agreement and the incorporation of the exclusion clause. This is known as the *contra proferentem* rule, so that the party seeking to enforce an exclusion clause had to show that it was clearly incorporated as a term of the contract, and any ambiguity would be construed against that party. It was a short step then for the courts to start a line of reasoning that required proof that the exclusion terms were reasonable in the circumstances. However, as soon as the courts disapproved of a clause, the draftsmen of standard exclusion clauses produced ever better and more sweeping exclusion clauses, and something further was required.

Not surprisingly, there have been a considerable number of 'ticket' or 'notice' cases. In *Chapelton* v. *Barry UDC* (1940) the plaintiff hired two deckchairs and collected his tickets (for inspection, as a notice said). One of the deckchairs collapsed and caused him injury. The ticket, on its reverse side, had an exemption clause, excusing the council from liability for any accident or damage arising from the hire of the chair. The Court of Appeal took the view that most reasonable people would have taken the ticket simply as a receipt, and therefore the defendants were liable. The 'notice' had therefore arrived too late, as, too, in *Olley* v. *Marlborough Court Ltd* (1949) (a notice on a wall of a hotel room excluding liability for loss of guests' property) and *Thornton* v. *Shoe Lane Parking* (1971) (a ticket from an automatic barrier to a car park). All these cases, however, would now have to be read in the light of the 1977 legislation, as outlined below.

The doctrine of the fundamental breach

It is clear that if a buyer purchases a cow, and a pig is delivered, the contract is not performed. How far can the principle apply, however? If a buyer purchases a second-hand car, does it have to be in good working order, or just able to be driven, or is it a car if all the parts are there but the vehicle is a wreck? Is it an enforceable contract if the seller excludes all implied warranties and guarantees, and leaves it to the buyer entirely to check the condition of the vehicle? It was an enforceable contract, where the buyer did not reject the vehicle promptly, said the Court of Appeal in *Charterhouse Credit* v. *Tolly* (1963); it was not, said the same court in the earlier case of *Karsales (Harrow) Ltd* v. *Wallis* (1956) where the plaintiff had objected promptly.

The case of *Karsales* v. *Wallis* has been taken as the starting point of the doctrine of fundamental breach. Lord Denning had previously suggested that the courts might delete 'a wholly unreasonable term' from a contract (*John Lee and Son (Grantham) Ltd* v. *Railway Executive* (1949)). But the House of Lords would have none of it and restored the sanctity of the clear terms of a contract in the case of *British Movietonews Ltd* v. *London and District Cinemas Ltd* (1952), declaring that 'no court has an absolving power'. Nevertheless, the Lords in that case enunciated the terms of the doctrine that would be acceptable as:

> **If a consideration of the terms of a contract in the light of the circumstances when it was made, shows that the parties never agreed to be bound in a fundamentally different situation which has unexpectedly emerged, then the contract ceases to bind at that point – not because the court thinks it just and reasonable to qualify the terms of the contract, but because on the true construction it does not apply in that situation.**

This is the doctrine of 'presumed intent'.

The controversy between the Court of Appeal and the House of Lords had only just started. For 20 years and more the Court of Appeal developed and expanded the doctrine of 'presumed intent' into a rule of law, that where one party to a contract 'was guilty of a breach which went to the very root of the contract, sometimes called a "fundamental breach", or at other times a "total failure" of its obligations, then it could not rely on the printed clause to exempt itself from liability', *per* Lord Denning in *George Mitchell (Chesterhall) Ltd* v. *Finney Lock Seeds Ltd* (1985). By contrast, the House of Lords regularly queried, limited and finally rejected the whole doctrine, but not without a valedictory small cheer: 'The doctrine of "fundamental breach" in spite of its imperfections and doubtful parentage has served a useful purpose. There were a large number of problems, productive of injustice, in which it was worse then unsatisfactory to leave exception clauses to operate', stated Lord Wilberforce in *Photo Production* v. *Securicor Transport Ltd* (1980).

The extent of the problem was set out with clarity and simplicity by Lord Denning in the *Finney Lock Seeds* case, the last decision of the former Master of the Rolls before his retirement. Referring to the courts' problems in a review of the rise and fall of the doctrine, he stated, as to exemption clauses:

> **They were printed in small print on the back of tickets and order forms and invoices. They were contained in catalogues and timetables. They were held to be binding on any person who took them without objection. No one ever did object. He never read them or knew what was in them. No matter how unreasonable they were, he was bound. All this was done in the name of 'freedom of contract'. But the freedom was all on the side of the big concern which had the use of the printing press. No freedom for the little man who took the ticket or order form or invoice. The big concern said, 'Take it or leave it'. The little man had no option but to take it. The big concern could and did exempt itself from liability in its own interest without regard to the little man. It got away with it time after time . . . Faced**

with this abuse of power, by the strong against the weak, by the use of the small print of the conditions, the judges did what they could to put a curb on it.

If the doctrine had such an eminently reasonable basis, how is it that the doctrine was rejected in the Lords? The answer appears to be that there are now two laws of contract, one for 'consumers' who are protected by statute and the other for the commercial sector, where the parties are considered to be of equal bargaining power, and are generally both covered by insurance. In commercial cases the courts will follow the precepts of 'freedom and sanctity of the contract'. As Lord Scarman succinctly put it, in the *Photo Production* case, 'In a commercial dispute between parties well able to look after themselves . . . what the parties agreed (expressly or impliedly) is what matters; and the duty of the courts is to construe their contract according to its tenor'.

Before examining the statutory provisions, we must note that although fundamental breach has been discarded, and the case of *Charterhouse Credit* v. *Tolly* (1963) was specifically mentioned as overruled by the House of Lords in the *Photo Production* case, it was nevertheless noted that the same result might have been reached on 'construction of the contract'. The test was no longer breach of a fundamental term but whether the exclusion clause relied on was 'reasonable in all the circumstances'. In the Scottish case of *Ailsa Craig Fishing Co.* v. *Malvern Fishing Co.* (1983) the House of Lords made a distinction between clauses which excluded liability altogether and those which sought to limit liability; the first are inherently more likely to be unreasonable, and their clauses would be construed *contra proferentem* – against the party incorporating the clause.

The wording of exclusion clauses are interpreted strictly, as seen in *Middleton* v. *Wiggins* (1995), where the word 'disposal' did not cover an accident that did not actually occur in the process of disposing of waste.

So, the fundamental breach was banished – but the unreasonable exclusion clause admitted. In the *Finney Lock* case Lord Denning observed that a new concept was heralded, not only in the specific categories of the Unfair Contract Terms Act, but in all contracts, that exclusion clauses may have to meet a new test of reasonableness, depending for their effectiveness 'on the construction of the condition in the context of the contract as a whole'.

The decision of the Court of Appeal was upheld by the House of Lords. The Lords observed that an appellate court reviewing on appeal the application of a statutory provision requiring determination of the question whether a term in a contract was 'fair and reasonable' should treat the original decision with the utmost respect and refrain from interference with it, unless satisfied that it proceeded upon some erroneous principle or was plainly and obviously wrong.

So, similarly, even in a non-consumer case it was held that where one or more of a set of printed conditions is particularly onerous or unusual, the party seeking to enforce it must show that it had been brought to the notice of the other party, otherwise the condition would not be upheld. In *Interfoto Picture Library* v. *Stiletto*

Visual Programmes (1988), the Court of Appeal rejected one of nine conditions set out in four columns of print on a contract for hire of photographic transparencies, but which provided for unusually punitive charges for retention of the transparencies for more than 14 days.

Statutory unfair terms

The concept of reasonableness in relation to exclusion or limitation of liability, and in particular the emphasis that a clause restricting liability is more likely to be reasonable than one excluding liability altogether, appears to have derived directly from statute, and in particular from the Unfair Contract Terms Act 1977. Based largely on the second report of the Law Commission on exemption clauses, the Act, despite its name, was primarily concerned with exemption clauses both in contract and in tort.

As previously noted, the first major step by the legislature to control the use of exemption clauses followed the publication of the Molony Report in 1962. In that year, also, s.43 of the Transport Act 1962 had provided that railway authorities could neither restrict nor exclude liability for death or bodily injury to passengers. The Law Commissions were established in 1965 and one of their most urgent priorities was the practice of commercial organisations avoiding the obligations of a seller under the Sale of Goods Act 1893, which had been condemned by the Molony Report. The first report on exemption clauses was published in 1969, and in due course this led to the Supply of Goods (Implied Terms) Act 1973. The 1973 Act limited the exclusion of the rights in ss.12-15 of the Sale of Goods Act 1893, making 'void' any avoidance of the stipulation as to title to goods (s12) and making void in *consumer* sales the provisions in ss.13–15, that is merchantable quality, fitness for purpose and correspondence with description or sample, as now amended by the Sale and Supply of Goods Act 1994. A consumer sale, was defined as 'any sale of goods, other than by auction or competitive tender, when a seller in the course of a business sells goods ordinarily sold for private use or consumption and sold to a person who is not buying in the course of a business'. In non-consumer sales, the Act provided a more limited exclusion in relation to ss.13–15, namely that the terms should not be enforceable to the extent that it would not be 'fair or reasonable'. Guidelines as to what is fair and reasonable were provided in the Act. The Act also made similar provisions, prohibiting or limiting exclusion clauses, in contracts of hire-purchase.

The Unfair Contract Terms Act 1977 incorporated and developed the safeguards of the 1973 Act. The concept of a consumer sale was replaced by the notion of a buyer dealing 'as consumer', but the difference was small. The 1977 Act further extended the protection of the consumer to contracts other than sale and hire-purchase for the supply of goods, such as contracts for barter or hire, or contracts for work and materials. Also, in contracts not for the supply of goods, but for, say, bookings for travel or holidays, supply of correspondence courses or services such as maintenance of appliances, the consumer had rights granted to challenge exclusion clauses. In *Phillips Products Ltd* v. *Hyland* (1984) it was held that the defendants had not discharged the burden upon them of showing that an incorporated condition in the contract satisfied the requirement of reasonableness in the context of the particular contract of hire. In this instance the plaintiffs, steel stockholders, were carrying out an extension to their factory. A builder, Pritchard, was engaged to undertake the work, although Phillips were to be responsible for buying materials and providing plant, but Pritchard was given permission to hire a JCB excavator on behalf of Phillips. The driver of the machine, Hyland, made it clear to Pritchard that it was up to him the way he operated the machine. He subsequently drove it into the factory causing £3,000 damage. Phillips sued the machine's owners (Hamstead) and the plant operator (Hyland), Hamstead's employee. Condition 8 of the contract said that the plant operator would be under the direction of the hirer (here Phillips) and would be regarded as their servant for these purposes. The Court of Appeal held that on the evidence and in the context of the contract as a whole, the condition did not satisfy the requirement of reasonableness. Under s. 11(1) and (5) of the Unfair Contract Terms Act 1977 Hamstead had failed to show that the condition was so satisfied and that it was a fair and reasonable one to be included, having regard to the circumstances 'which were, or ought reasonably to have been, known to or in contemplation of the parties when the contract was made'.

Certain contracts were excluded from the provisions of both the 1973 and 1977 Acts, notably contracts of international sales, that is generally where the parties habitually reside in different countries, contracts of insurance, and contracts relating to the creation or transfer or termination of an interest in land.

By the mid-1980s it was fair to say that Parliament and the courts had combined to rescue individuals as consumers from the worst effects of exclusion clauses. The Law Commission reports had shown convincingly that the courts should only enforce terms and conditions unilaterally imposed in contracts 'if they were fair and reasonable in themselves and it was fair and reasonable to allow the big concern to rely on them', as Lord Denning had put it in the *Finney Lock Seeds* case.

In addition to the provision under s.6 of the 1977 Act, restricting the ability of a seller of goods to exempt himself from liability for breach of the stipulations implied in contracts of sale by ss.12–15 of the Sale of Goods Act 1979, as amended by the Sale and Supply of Goods Act 1994, other legislation has provided in many areas regulations governing the production and sale of certain goods, most notably the Consumer Protection Act 1987 which has been referred to in the previous chapter. It should also be noted that in 1993 the EC Council of Ministers adopted a Directive (93/13) on unfair terms in consumer contracts, which were implemented by British regulations in 1994.

Finally, it is a matter of public policy that compromises of civil actions are to be encouraged. In the case of *Tudor Grange Holdings Ltd* v. *Citibank NA* (1991) the plaintiff had released the defendant banks from 'claims, demands and causes of action' by a deed of release; subsequently the plaintiff started proceedings, and the defendants claimed the protection of s10 of the Unfair Contract Terms Act 1977, which provided that a person is not bound by any term purporting to exclude his rights in connection with another contract. The Vice-Chancellor held that the section did not apply to compromises, but only to exclusions of contractual rights.

8.4

Incapacity and Illegality

It is frequently easier to know what is a contract than to particularise when asked. However, certain guidelines such as offer and acceptance, consideration and intention to create legal relations, and so on, have been established and a number of legal concepts, such as presumption of agreement, implied terms and conditions, are imported to fill out the gaps left by the parties in their contractual negotiations. It is often clear that a business arrangement has been entered into and, with the guidelines that we have examined, the form and terms of the agreement may be discovered and so the details of the contract established. Nonetheless, there are many pitfalls that can invalidate a contract. We can classify these faults, or vitiating factors, as incapacity and illegality; mistake and misrepresentation; duress and undue influence, and these factors are now examined in this and the two ensuing sections.

INCAPACITY

The general position is that any person may enter into a valid contract. Certain classes of persons are not competent, however, or only to a limited extent. There are special provisions for bankrupts, drunkards, minors, persons of unsound mind and corporations, and a few other exceptional 'persons', for instance, alien enemies in time of war.

The old provisions of the common law that married women were not competent to contract, except perhaps as to necessities were progressively removed in the last century, although the final restraints were not abolished until the Married Women (Restraint upon Anticipation) Act 1949. However, the position as to minors, mental patients and corporations needs some further consideration.

Minors

The term 'infant' was often peculiarly inappropriate to large teenagers and 20 year-olds, particularly after two world wars and when many young men and women had spent some years in uniform and attained ranks and positions of authority. Nevertheless, it was not until the Family Law Reform Act 1969 that the age of majority was reduced from 21 to 18 years, and that the expression 'minor' was introduced as an alternative to infant. Prior to that Act there had developed a considerable body of law in relation to infants' contracts. The rules were still applicable to minors, many of the rules having been incorporated into statute in Victorian times. Many of these provisions, however, were repealed by the Minors' Contracts Act 1987.

At common law the general rule was that a contract made by an infant was voidable at his option, that is the infant could repudiate a contract made during infancy, or for a short time afterwards. There were two main exceptions to the rule – contracts for 'necessaries' and beneficial contracts for services.

By the Infants Relief Act 1874, three kinds of contract were declared to be 'absolutely void', namely, contracts of loan, contracts for goods other than necessaries and accounts stated, that is admissions of amounts due. As these contracts were void, they could not be sued upon after majority even if they had been ratified and the Act made void any fresh promise to pay a debt incurred or to ratify any promise made in infancy.

However, although such contracts were declared to be void, they were not without effect completely. It seems that although a minor could not be sued, he could himself sue, he could pass a good title to goods purchased, but he could not recover money paid unless there had been a total failure of consideration. Also, while a guarantee of a loan to an infant was unenforceable as the loan was void, an indemnity by an adult was enforceable as in that case the promise to pay would have been that of the adult as well as the minor – see respectively the cases of *Coutts and Co.* v. *Browne-Lecky* (1946) and *Yeoman Credit* v. *Latter* (1961). Section 1 of the 1987 Act removed the restrictions of the 1874 Act on the three types of contract, and s.2 provided that guarantees of loans to minors were enforceable against the guarantor and the decision in *Coutts* v. *Browne-Lecky* no longer applied, even if the loan itself was unenforceable against the minor or had been repudiated by him.

Contracts for necessaries, were enforceable against infants at common law and whilst the intention of the 1987 Act was to remove restrictions imposed by statute on the enforceability of contracts entered into by minors, it appears that the effect has been to re-establish the common law rules and in particular a minor is now be able to ratify a contract, other than one for necessaries or services, made during his minority or shortly after attaining the age of majority. Section 3 of the Sale of Goods Act 1979, defines necessaries as 'goods suitable to the condition in life of the minor or other person concerned and to his actual requirements at the time of the sale and delivery'. Further, the section provides that a minor (or a person mentally incapable or drunk) must pay a reasonable price, not necessarily the contract price, for necessaries. The claim is thus in quasi-contract in reality.

The other general exception to the common law rule that an infant could not be bound in contract was that from very early times it was held that contracts of apprenticeship or service could be enforced as they were presumed to be to his advantage, ie to learn a trade or to be enabled to earn a livelihood. The contract as a whole had to be shown to be beneficial to the minor. In *De Francesco* v. *Barnum* (1890), where a young girl of 14 was apprenticed to a choreographer for seven years to learn stage dancing, the contract was held not to be beneficial as there was no general provision for payment to the infant. But the contract is not necessarily unenforceable because one or two of the terms of the contract are onerous.

However, a minor cannot be made liable just because a contract is likely to be beneficial to him. The contract must be one of service, not a trading contract for that would encourage a minor to risk capital. So in *Cowern* v. *Nield* (1912), the purchaser of a consignment of hay from an infant hay and straw dealer was unable to recover his money for failure to deliver the load, despite payment. Also, although minors are in general capable of being sued in tort, a plaintiff cannot make a minor indirectly liable in contract, by, for instance, suing the minor for fraudulently misrepresenting that he was of full age (*R Leslie Ltd* v. *Shiell* (1914)). The modern tendency of the courts, however, has been to limit the extent of the minor's protection. In *Ballett* v. *Mingay* (1943) a minor was successfully sued for non-return (detinue) of a hired microphone and amplifier unit, which he had given to a friend, as that was not 'in the contemplation of the parties to the contract of bailment'.

Where goods were obtained fraudulently by a minor, the courts would order their return, under the equitable doctrine of restitution. However, the doctrine was only applicable to restore the actual goods and the courts had no power to order payment in lieu for the goods unless the plaintiff was able to 'trace' the actual proceeds of sale whilst the monies were still in the possession of the minor and before they had been dissipated or credited to a general fund, such as a bank account. Section 3 of the 1987 Act empowers the court to order restitution where there has been no element of fraud, but does not extend to restitution of the price of goods sold, where the minor repudiates the contract or it is otherwise unenforceable, as that would amount to enforcement of a void contract.

Persons of unsound mind, drunkards and drug addicts

The position of persons suffering from mental disorder, formerly called lunatics but now mental patients, and of drunkards, is similar to that of minors. For obvious reasons the courts have held that if one party to a contract to the knowledge of the other party is suffering from such a degree of mental disability as to be incapable of understanding the nature of the contract, then the contract is voidable at the option of the patient or addict.

The burden of proof that the other party was aware of the mental unsoundness is upon the patient, but it seems that this burden is not onerous. Moreover, it must be almost inconceivable that such a state of drunkenness as to entitle avoidance of a contract would not be known to the other party. It would seem to be logical that a person incapacitated by drugs would be treated in the same manner as a drunkard by the courts, but there appears to be no authority on this point as yet.

A contract made by a mental patient in a lucid interval is binding upon him and a contract for necessaries is enforceable to the same extent as for a minor, in the case of persons either mentally incapable or drunk, ie he must pay a reasonable price (Sale of Goods Act 1979).

In the Privy Council Case of *Hart* v. *O'Connor* (1985) concerning a land contract, on appeal from the Court of Appeal of New Zealand, it was held that the same standards applied in determining the validity of a contract entered into by a person of unsound mind who was ostensibly sane as a contract by a sane person, and the insane person or his representatives were only entitled to avoid the contract for unfairness if it constituted equitable fraud which would have enabled them to have had the contract rescinded even if he had been sane.

Jurisdiction in respect of mentally disordered people is conferred by the Mental Health Act 1983 upon a judge of the Court of Protection. Certain Chancery judges are nominated but the work is carried out by the Master of the Court who has a small staff. The court exercises control over the property and interests of mental patients who are incapable of managing their own affairs. In practice, the Court of Protection normally delegates the actual management to a 'receiver', frequently a relative or friend of the patient. A receiver for a patient may contract for the patient and such a contract may be enforced by or against the patient. Certain powers, however, may be exercised only by the authority of the judge, such as power to make a will on behalf of the patient disposing of his property. Such wills are made in special form and are subject to special rules (Administration of Justice Act 1969). In all proceedings involving a mentally disordered person, he must be represented by a 'next friend' or guardian *ad litem*.

The Crown and corporations

The Crown
The 'Government' today enters into the field of contractual law in numerous ways and the Crown has always been able to enforce a contract against an individual. It was not, however, until the Crown Proceedings Act 1947 that a contract could be enforced against the Crown by an individual except by claiming, with the consent of the Crown, a Petition of Right. Since 1947, the Crown has been liable in contract almost as a private individual, subject to a few exceptions where for political reasons the Crown could not bind itself, generally in reality a successor government, or in times of war.

The monarch, as the Head of State, even in her private capacity, cannot be sued and this exception extends also to the diplomatic representatives of foreign heads of government. The extent of diplomatic immunity from contractual liability, contained in the Diplomatic Privileges Act 1964 and the State Immunity Act 1978, and even more the extension of the immunity to a multiplicity of junior officials in foreign embassies, consulates, trade and other semi-diplomatic offices, has been increasingly criticised, owing to abuse of the privileges. In *Intpro Properties* v. *Sauvel* (1983) a decision of the Court of Appeal redressed the balance slightly, where it was held that a foreign state could be impleaded in an action relating to property occupied by one of its diplomats where the premises were not used for the purposes of a diplomatic mission but as the private residence of a financial counsellor at the French Embassy, although certain social functions were carried on there as part of the counsellor's duties.

In *Alcom Ltd* v. *Republic of Columbia* (1984) where the plaintiff was suing for the price of goods sold and delivered, and sought a garnishee order against the embassy's London bank account, the Court of Appeal held the defendants liable since the embassy bank account was used to pay for goods and services and to facilitate other transactions. But the House of Lords took a different view – the money in the embassy's bank account was not used for commercial purposes, but for the day to day running of the embassy, and the position would have been the same even if the account had been partly used for commercial purposes.

Corporations
There are two main classes of corporations – corporations sole and corporations aggregate. Typical examples of corporation sole are 'the Vicar' or 'the Bishop', that is a person who holds an office for the time being, and that person's predecessors and successors in the office. Similarly, a body of people such as 'the Mayor and Corporation', constitute a corporation aggregate, but more important are the members of organisations established as corporations. Corporations may be:

1 established by Royal Charter, such as the old trading companies like the Hudson's Bay Company, or the Chartered Bank; or

2 established by a particular statute, the nationalised industries being typical examples; or

3 companies incorporated under the Companies Act 1985 which are the most numerous and include all public limited companies (plc) and all the privately owned limited companies, designated as Limited, or Ltd, in their names.

Companies incorporated by Royal Charter have all the powers and liabilities of an individual, although the charter may be revoked for good cause. In the case of companies incorporated under statutory provisions, however, their powers derive from the statute, or if incorporated under the Companies Acts, from the Memorandum and Articles of Association.

The former rule, of great antiquity, that no contract with a corporation was enforceable unless the contract had been sealed was abrogated by the Corporate Bodies' Contracts Act 1960, which provided that a corporation could in general contract informally, as an individual, by the authority of a proper officer of the corporation.

Similarly, the enforceability of contracts with corporations was formerly subject to the rule that a trading company could only contract to the extent and for the purposes provided in the company's memorandum of association. The rule was established in the *Ashbury Railway Carriage* case (1875) and was based on the important doctrine of *ultra vires*. The rule led to injustice in many instances, as few people dealing with a representative of a company would expect to enquire as to whether the memorandum actually entitled the company to carry on the particular activity envisaged. The doctrine had been much criticised, but was enforced until Britain joined the EC, when the provisions were limited by the European Communities Act 1972 in respect of a person dealing in good faith with a company, whereby it is to be presumed that 'any transaction decided upon by the directors' is within the capacity of the company. It should be noted that the *ultra vires* doctrine is not abolished; s.9, now incorporated in s.3 of the Companies Act 1985, does not entitle the company to enforce an *ultra vires* contract, but it remains uncertain as to whether decisions of non-director employees of a company will be assumed by the courts to be 'transactions decided upon by the directors'. It is clear that a junior employee will not be assumed to have ostensible authority of the directors (*British Bank of the Middle East* v. *Sun Life Assurance of Canada*, 1983)), but the position is probably very different for a senior executive who is not, however, a director.

ILLEGALITY

Contracts to commit a crime are clearly illegal in themselves and the courts, quite apart from any question of conspiracy or criminality, will not assist either party to such an agreement whether to recover monies paid or in any other manner. Similarly, the courts will not uphold a contract to commit a tort or fraud on a third party, or agreements for sexually immoral purposes or contracts regarded as contravening public policy. The courts will not enforce the contract in such cases even if the defendant does not raise the illegality as an objection and even if it is not pleaded in the defence, the House of Lords held in *North Western Salt Co.* v. *Electrolytic Alkali Co.* (1914).

As there are innumerable degrees of crime, so the courts have varied the strictness with which they have regarded such contractual relationships. It is therefore difficult to lay down hard and fast rules. Some contracts are obviously illegal from the outset. So, for instance, a 'contract' in the modern sense to commit murder or a serious assault is clearly illegal from the start; such an agreement is completely void and the courts will not assist any party. But if the contract is for a less serious offence, and the objectionable part of the agreement is not the principal part of the contract, the invalid promise may be severed and the remainder of the agreement enforced (*Goodinson* v. *Goodinson* (1954)). In *Carney* v. *Herbert* (1985) in an appeal from the Supreme Court of New South Wales, the Privy Council held that severance is possible where the offending parts are illegal unless there are public policy reasons for not permitting severance, where the main contract itself is lawful but some ancillary provision is illegal *and* exists for the exclusive benefit of the plaintiff.

Where an illegal agreement is either criminal or *contra bonos mores*, that is against the public welfare, the illegality will prevent either party from enforcing the terms of the agreement, the court washing its hands of the whole business. So, for example, money paid cannot be recovered and an executory agreement will not be enforceable by an order for specific performance. It was formerly held that where the contract was still executory, a party could withdraw from the illegality, but that the repentance must have been before there had been a substantial carrying out of the illegal act.

It is said, therefore, that if the parties are equally at fault − *in pari delicto* − then the defendant is in the better position, as the plaintiff will not be able to succeed in his claim, whether for recovery of money paid, or return of goods or whatever. However, if the parties are not equally culpable, then the one that is the more innocent may be able to succeed in his action. So, in the case of *Kiriri Cotton Co.*

v. *Dewani* (1960), where the company had granted the plaintiff a lease of a flat in Uganda at a premium, where payment of a premium was contrary to statute but neither party was aware of the statutory provision, the Uganda High Court (upheld by the East Africa Court of Appeal), ordered repayment of the premium as 'money had and received illegally'. On appeal to the Privy Council, it was argued that the parties were *in pari delicto* as both parties were innocent of the statutory restriction, and that Mr Dewani could not succeed. But the Privy Council rejected that argument, pointing out that the statute was intended to protect tenants, and so Mr Dewani was deemed to be not equally at fault and was entitled to recover the illegal premium.

Sometimes a contract may be perfectly valid as formed, for instance an agreement to let a house or rent a vehicle, but becomes illegal in its performance, as, for example, in the use of a house for immoral purposes. In the well-known case of *Pearce* v. *Brooks* (1866) the hirers of 'a pretty carriage' were unable to recover their hire charges from Miss Brooks as the jury found that the plaintiffs were aware that she intended to use the vehicle, described as a miniature brougham of an unusual design, 'as part of her display to attract men' for immoral purposes. In Victorian times the courts were much concerned with cases involving immorality. Times and attitudes have changed and, quite apart from the virtual disappearance of civil juries, conduct that would in the past have been condemned, such as an agreement to cohabit, would probably not be regarded today as tending to deprave. But it is interesting to note the case of *H.* v. *H.* (1983), where Mr Justice Ewbank declared that a wife-swapping agreement made between four spouses prior to their respective divorces, that each husband would assume financial responsibility for the other's former wife on remarriage, was unenforceable and such agreements ought not to be encouraged.

It would appear after the Court of Appeal's decision in *Armhouse Lee Ltd* v. *Chappell* (1996), dealing with the recovery of payments for sex line advertisements, that contracts promoting sexual immorality are no longer immoral – 'individual judges exercising a civil jurisdiction [should not] impose their own moral attitudes', in contrast to *Pearce* v. *Brooks*.

In *Euro Diam Ltd* v. *Bathurst* (1990) in order to satisfy the German buyers of diamonds, subsequently stolen, the true value had been understated so as to exclude the payment of German customs duties, but this did not affect the value of the diamonds themselves for insurance purposes, so the insurance contract was not illegal, there was no causal connection the Court of Appeal held.

In *Davitt* v. *Titcumb* (1989) the defendant and the deceased had bought a house for £16,900, secured by a mortgage of £14,950 with an endowment policy on their joint lives. The defendant, who had murdered the deceased, was held not to be entitled to any of the proceeds of the insurance policy; Mr Justice Scott expressed the view that Commercial Union was right to pay the policy money to the building society. In *Alghussein Establishment* v. *Eton College* (1991) the House of Lords upheld the courts' decisions that the college was right to repudiate an agreement where the appellants, who unsuccessfully sought specific performance, had for five years wilfully delayed the development of land which had been leased to them.

Public policy

A number of types of contract have been held to be unenforceable as contrary to public policy, and generally these are self-evident and can be classified under five heads:

1 Contracts prejudicial to public safety, notably contracts with alien enemies in time of war. Contracts affecting the conduct of the war, such as purchase or sale of munitions, are discharged on the outbreak of hostilities. But contracts not inimical to public safety, for instance an agreement to make payments to a former wife who has become an alien enemy, will be suspended rather than discharged (*Bevan* v. *Bevan* (1955)), as are also rights which have already accrued under the contract at the outbreak of hostilities (*Arab Bank Ltd* v. *Barclays Bank* (1954)).

2 Contracts prejudicial to the administration of justice, such as an agreement to stifle a criminal prosecution, or to oust the jurisdiction of the courts. In the case of *Keir* v. *Leeman* (1846) the plaintiff agreed not to proceed with a prosecution for riot and assault, on the defendants agreeing to pay the monies owed to the plaintiff with costs. The plaintiff did not give evidence and the defendants were acquitted on the charge, but did not pay up. On being sued, the defendants pleaded the illegality of their agreement and their plea was upheld. In *Fulham Football Club Ltd* v. *Cabra Estates plc* (1992) a development company and a local council applied for planning permission to redevelop land. The plaintiffs agreed, for a large fee, not to support the council's application; later they refused to support the development company's application saying the agreement was void by reason of illegality. Whilst false evidence was against public policy, a commercial agreement to refrain from giving evidence was valid, and on appeal the development company was successful. It is a general rule of common law that contracts to oust the jurisdiction of the courts is against public policy and therefore void – *West of England Shipowners Mutual Insurance Association (Luxembourg)* v. *CRISTAL Ltd, The Glacier Bay* (1996).

It should be noted that concealment of a crime for a consideration may constitute an offence under s.5 of the Criminal Law Act 1967, or alternatively may be an attempt to pervert the course of justice. The compromise of a civil suit, however, is to be encouraged even to the extent of agreeing to submit disputes to arbitration without the right of appeal to the courts. This was held to be valid in the House of Lords case of *Scott* v. *Avery* (1855). However, an appeal lay on a point of law, and such provisions, known as Scott Avery clauses, have become common in commercial contracts; and in fact even an appeal on a point of law may now be excluded under the provisions of the Arbitration Act 1979 and may be incorporated by reference to standard rules, such as those of the International Chamber of Commerce (see *Arab African Energy Corporation* v. *Olie Produkten Nederland BV* (1983)).

3 Contracts tending to corruption in public life. Agreements for the purchase of military commissions and of public offices were common in the eighteenth century, but were condemned in Victorian times. However, gifts of large sums

of money to charity in the hope of public reward are not unknown today. But there can be no enforceable agreement, for instance a knighthood in consideration of such a gift, it was held in the case of *Parkinson* v. *College of Ambulance Ltd* (1924) where the money paid was irrecoverable. The case was followed by the Honours (Prevention of Abuses) Act 1925, since when such a contract has constituted an offence.

4 Contracts to defraud the revenue. It is open to all citizens to arrange their financial affairs in the best manner possible to mitigate their liability to taxation; however, conduct that amounts to evasion is not tolerated. In the case of *Miller* v. *Karlinski* (1945) Miller was to receive a salary of £10 per week, and inflated 'expenses' to include any income tax liability. In an action to recover arrears of salary the fradulent arrangement was disclosed. As both parties were involved in the fraud, the court would not uphold the claim whatever. In *Tinsley* v. *Milligan* (1993) the House of Lords took a critical view of the Court of Appeal developing a 'public conscience' test, that is if the public conscience was not affronted an illegal contract could still be relied upon; *Tinsley* concerned putting a house into one person's name only to assist in a fraud against the DSS, although on the facts a majority of the Lords held that there was no reliance on an illegal contract, rather it was an action to enforce a property right by way of a trust.

5 Contracts prohibited by statute. It is important to distinguish the reason for the statutory provision. In some cases the statute is intended to prohibit a particular type of contract, in which case the intention of the legislation is clear and will be enforced. On the other hand the intention of the statute may not relate to the contract but have another intention. The cases of *Smith* v. *Mawhood* (1845) and *Re Mahmoud and Ispahani* (1921) illustrate the difference. In the first case an unlicensed tobacconist was held entitled to recover the price of tobacco delivered, 'as the object of the legislation was for the purposes of the Inland Revenue'. In the second case, an unlicensed purchaser of linseed oil could not be liable to accept delivery of oil ordered, as there was a wartime order preventing dealings without a licence.

Under the Insurance Companies Act 1981 it is provided that no person in Great Britain should carry on certain classes of insurance, including marine insurance, without the permission of the Secretary of State. Thus in *Bedford Insurance Co. Ltd* v. *Instituto de Resseguros do Brasil* (1984) it was held that where an insurance contract was prohibited by statute it was void, whether or not it was made by an agent acting beyond his authority or later ratified by the principal. The court noted what Lord Devlin had said in *Archbolds (Freightage) Ltd* v. *S Spanglett Ltd* (1961): one effect of illegality was 'to avoid the contract *ab initio* and that arises if the making of the contract is prohibited by statute or is otherwise contrary to public policy'.

But in *Stewart* v. *Oriental Fire and Marine Insurance Co. Ltd* (1984) a differently constituted court of the Queen's Bench Divison held that the *Bedford* case was wrongly decided. The wording of the Act only made the carrying on of the *business* of marine insurance without the necessary authorisation an offence. It did not render the making of individual contracts of insurance illegal. Thus the re-insurance contract was not void for illegality.

Two further points in respect of illegality should be mentioned. Firstly, any contract which restrains a person from marrying is void, as is any agreement which amounts to a marriage brokage contract, where one person in return for payment promises to procure the marriage of another. Equally, contracts which interfere with parental duties are void.

Secondly, the courts do not look with favour upon contracts in restraint of trade. Strictly speaking both this sort of contract and those just mentioned are merely void rather than illegal, but very often such agreements are classified under illegality. It was not until the end of the nineteenth century that the doctrine of economic freedom in this area of the law was limited. The case concerned was that of *Nordenfelt* v. *Maxim Nordenfelt Guns and Ammunition Co.* (1894). Here the appellant, who was an inventor and manufacturer of guns, sold his business to the respondents for £287,500. He agreed, in so doing, not to be involved in the gun and ammunition industry for the next 25 years in a way that would be liable to compete with the respondents' activities. A few years later Nordenfelt entered into an agreement with a rival concern. The House of Lords held that the original contract was valid, even though it restrained N. from becoming involved in such business virtually anywhere in the world.

The *Nordenfelt* case established that what is a reasonable restraint of trade is for the courts to decide, having regard to present and future circumstances and the object of the agreement. Regard must also be had to the relative strength of the parties' bargaining position. This point has been well illustrated by a number of recent cases which have shown how the economic world has grown ever more complex. Such cases are frequently concerned with '*solus*' agreements, where a party agrees to take all his deliveries from one supplier, as, for instance, in the relationship between the owners of a petrol station and an oil company. In *Esso Petroleum Co. Ltd* v. *Harper's Garage (Stourport) Ltd* (1968) it was held that an agreement which was to operate for a period of four years and five months in respect of one garage was reasonable in the circumstances even if *prima facie* void, but that a 21-year agreement in respect of a second garage was unreasonable. However, in *Alec Lobb Ltd* v. *Total Oil (GB) Ltd* (1985) the Court of Appeal upheld a 21-year restraint on a trade *solus* agreement where there were break clauses at 7 and 14 years. The original tenants, who had been in financial difficulties, had obtained a leaseback agreement by selling all their interest in the land, but, although there was inequality of bargaining power, there had been no 'extortionate, unconscionable, oppressive or coercive' behaviour on the part of the defendant.

Agreements which restrain ex-employees from taking up employment in a similar concern must also be reasonable, not least in terms of the geographical area to which the agreement applies, as illustrated by *Fitch* v. *Dewes* (1921) where it was held a restraint upon a solicitor's clerk in Tamworth was reasonable in so far as it was limited to a seven-mile radius. Similarly, in *Clarke* v. *Newland* (1991), in respect of a doctor's practice in London, there was a three-year restraint within the geographical area of the practice, and this was reasonable. In *Deacons (A Firm)* v. *Bridge* (1984) the defendant had worked for an old-established firm of solicitors in Hong Kong. When he became a partner there was a restriction within the agreement to the effect that when he ceased to be a partner he was not to act as a solicitor in Hong Kong for a period of five years for any client of the firm including any person who had been a client in the three years preceding his departure from the firm. The Privy Council held that the defendant, who had received a substantial sum upon departure, could be so restrained. There was a public interest in protecting a firm's goodwill, not least as it encouraged younger members of the profession to enter established firms.

In *Bull* v. *Pitney-Bowes Ltd* (1967) it was held that it was a restraint of trade where a former employee was deprived of his pension rights because he joined a commercial rival, notwithstanding the fact he had worked for the previous company for 26 years. The court took the view that it was not in the interests of the public for it to be deprived of the plaintiff's specialist skills.

In 1977 the European Commission issued a Directive (77/187) to protect the rights of employees on the transfer of employers on the take-over of a company, which was incorporated in the United Kingdom under the Transfer of Undertakings (Protection of Employment) Regulations 1981. In the case of *Morris Angel* v. *Hollande* (1993), Mr Hollande was appointed managing director of a company and given a three-year contract, with a restrictive covenant that he should not deal with the company's customers for one year after the termination of his employment; the company was taken over by the plaintiffs and Mr Hollande dismissed. The Court of Appeal, citing the Lords' decision in *Litster* v. *Forth Dry and Engineering Dock Co.* (1989), said that the intention of the Directive was to transfer the burdens as well as the benefits of employment contracts.

Any agreement, however, which merely purports to restrain a particular aspect of trade, but is in fact an open-ended arrangement to limit competition generally, is void. This point was illustrated in *Vancouver Malt and Sake Brewing Co. Ltd* v. *Vancouver Breweries Ltd* (1934). There the appellants held a licence to brew beer but they only brewed sake, a potent Japanese liquor made from rice. It was therefore unreasonable upon assignment of the brewer's licence to covenant not to brew beer for 15 years when no beer was manufactured in the first place.

It is also important to note that there are important statutory provisions in respect of agreements by both parties to restrain trade, such as price-fixing or cartel arrangements, which adversely affect the interests of consumers or other third parties. The legislation concerned is the Resale Prices Act 1976, the European Communities Act 1972, the Fair Trading Act 1973 and the Restrictive Trade Practices Act 1976 (as amended by the Companies Act 1985). Under the latter Act the Director General of Fair Trading may refer any apparently restrictive trade agreement or arrangement to the Restrictive Practices Court. Most restrictive trading agreements must in any case be registered with the Director General, and such agreements will be presumed void unless it can be shown that they are in the public interest by virtue of passing through one of eight 'gateways' provided in the Act.

Gaming and wagering contracts

At common law, gaming and wagering contracts were enforceable. However, legislation was introduced in the eighteenth century and by the Gaming Act 1738 games of dice, except backgammon, and games of chance such as roulette, were declared illegal. Further, by the Gaming Act 1845 it was provided that 'all contracts . . . by way of gaming or wagering, shall be null and void; and no suit shall be brought . . . for recovering any sum of money or valuable thing alleged to be won on a wager'. Note that gaming is illegal but wagering contracts are void. The definition of gaming, in the Gaming Act 1968 as amended by the Gaming (Amendment) Act 1990, is 'the playing of a game of chance for winnings in money or money's worth'. In general, games of chance such as roulette or bacccarat are illegal if any person stands to gain a benefit, but provision is made under the Act for gaming in premises licensed for the purpose. In *Lipkin Gorman* v. *Karpnale Ltd* (1991) the House of Lords decided to reject the Playboy Club's claim of *bona fide* purchase, where a solicitor had used considerable sums from his firm's account to gamble, the bets being contractually void by s.18 of the Gaming Act 1845.

A wagering contract was defined in *Carlill* v. *Carbolic Smoke Ball Co.* (1893) as a contract where 'two persons mutually agree that one shall win from the other money or other stake upon the determination of some [future] event, neither party having any interest in the contract other than the stake'. The definition was approved by the Court of Appeal in *Earl of Ellesmere* v. *Wallace* (1929), where Edgar Wallace was sued by the Jockey Club for £2, the fee for a non-starter horse entered for a race. Wallace's plea that the charge was a wager was dismissed, as the Jockey Club did not stand to gain or lose to Wallace, since their liability was to pay the prize of £200 to whomsoever was the owner of the winning horse.

It is clear that football pools, totalisator bets and sweepstakes do not come within the definition of a wager, provided the organisers only deduct expenses from the payments to the winners, but a bet with a 'bookie' is a wager.

There are difficulties in many cases in deciding just what is a wager. In the case of *Hyams* v. *Stuart King* (1908) two bookmakers had bets; one became indebted to the other and failed to pay. In consideration of the creditor not declaring the debtor to be a defaulter, he promised to pay. The Court of Appeal held that there was a contract subsequent to the wagers and held it to be valid as there was new consideration. This decision was subsequently reversed by the House of Lords by a majority of 4 to 3 in the later case of *Hill* v. *William Hill (Park Lane) Ltd* (1949), where it was pointed out that the reality of the new promise was for the old consideration of the wagering debt.

A contract of insurance is similar to a wagering contract, but the essential difference is that in a wager the parties have no interest in the outcome of an event other than the stake. So if A. insures the safe arrival of a ship and cargo in which he has no interest, then it is a wager. But an insurance on the life of a spouse or a business partner, or by one of the parties on the life of a judge hearing a lengthy commercial action, are all instances of a person having a valid insurable interest.

Similarly, Stock Exchange dealings may be genuine investment dealings, and are so regarded even where a broker accepts an order for the purchase of shares, knowing that the buyer intends to re-sell. Formerly where there was a contract for 'differences', that is a payment to a broker on a fall in the share price, and to the other party on a rise, then the agreement was a wager and unenforceable (*Universal Stock Exchange* v. *Strachan* (1896)). However, s.63 of the Financial Services Act 1986 introduced certain exceptions, provided the contracts for differences were 'by way of business'. In the case of *City Index* v. *Leslie* (1991) the Court of Appeal, upholding the decision at first instance, confirmed that such a contract fell within one of the exceptions provided by the 1986 Act to the 'blunt, all-encompassing prohibition of the gaming legislation' as applied by the House of Lords in the *Strachan* case.

It should be noted that a cheque or other security given in respect of a gaming debt cannot be enforced by the payee, or a subsequent holder, unless that 'holder in due course' can prove that he gave value for the cheque and without knowledge of its illegal origin. Security for a wagering debt can be enforced by a 'holder for value', that is a subsequent holder, and the burden of proof is then on the payee to prove that the holder was aware of the void transaction. It appears that the position has not changed since the Gaming Act 1968 and whether or not the cheque is marked 'not negotiable' (*Ladup* v. *Shaikh Nadeem* (1982)).

8.5   Mistake and misrepresentation

As vitiating factors mistake and misrepresentation are close relations in the law of contract. Moreover, what is outlined here must also be read in conjunction with performance and discharge, as discussed later.

MISTAKE

'Mistake' is used here in a restricted specific sense giving a right to relief, since in the wider, more ordinary meaning of the word mistake embraces misrepresentation. Secondly, mistake may be interpreted differently according to common law or equity.

Mistake has been frequently taken to mean that the contract is fundamentally wrong in some way, to the extent that the agreement is void, and indeed void from the very beginning (*ab initio*). That being so, the parties by and large cannot come before the courts and seek to enforce rights against each other, for the courts will refuse to recognise competing claims arising from what is to be regarded as a nullity. But matters are never that simple and both the common law and in particular equity may be relied upon to provide some form of relief, if only by refusing to recognise that the contract was actually void *ab initio*. There is a historical reason as to why the common law was, and to some extent still is, reluctant to recognise claims arising out of mistake; once again it was a matter of the nineteenth century philosophy of the market place – each party enters into an agreement freely and voluntarily and the buyer should thus be wary (*caveat emptor*). In this modern age of consumer protection, it is a principle that is worth emphasising for it is still the most important concept that a bargain freely entered into should be upheld. It is up to the buyer to check in advance as to what he is buying, not, as a general rule, for the seller to do more than avoid a misdescription. In *Rover International Ltd* v. *Cannon Film Sales Ltd (No 3)* (1989), a case concerning film distribution in Italy and a subsequent takeover of Thorn-EMI by Cannon, monies paid in respect of consideration which had totally failed were recoverable, and also on the basis the monies were paid under a mistake of fact, for no binding contract had existed in the first place, since Rover had been incorporated after the date of the agreement.

Types of mistake

There are several different types of mistake at law. One is often referred to as mutual mistake. Mutual mistake is sometimes known as common mistake but it may be argued that common mistake is a category in its own right.

In mutual mistake the parties have become muddled: each is talking or writing about something different from what the other is communicating. They are, in short, at cross-purposes before or at the time the agreement was made, there is no *consensus ad idem*. In common mistake both sides have misunderstood some basic fact which goes to the root of the agreement. Where, however, only one of the parties makes a mistake this is known as unilateral mistake. There are a number of important cases illustrating these different types of mistake.

In equity, mistake gives rise to relief in a wider range of cases than at law. Further, as the contract need not be void, but merely voidable, third parties, who cannot obtain title under a void contract, may acquire rights. Contracts between parties where one has a duty to disclose all material facts and fails to do so, may be set aside on the ground of mistake also, as we shall see later under contracts *uberrimae fidei* and of fiduciary relationships.

One leading case was that of *Couturier* v. *Hastie* (1856). Here an agreement was made for the sale of corn which was en route from Salonica to the United Kingdom. But unknown to either party the ship's master had sold the cargo at Tunis on account of the fact that it had become overheated and had fermented. The House of Lords in effect held the contract void since its subject matter was no longer in existence (*res extincta*) at the time when the contract was made. The purchaser was therefore not liable for the price of the corn. It was a case of common mistake, although the word 'mistake' was not used in the judgments. But had the purchaser already paid the price he could have recovered the money, because it would not be fair or reasonable to expect a person to pay something for nothing, a point illustrated in *Hitchcock* v. *Giddings* (1817) which involved the purchase of a remainder of an entailed estate, when in fact the estate tail had already been barred, so that no remainder was in existence. In these instances there has been a total failure of consideration, irrespective of whether the contract was void or valid.

However, a somewhat different approach to a common mistake was taken in the Australian case of *McRae* v. *Commonwealth Disposals Commission* (1951). The defendants invited tenders for the purchase of a wrecked oil tanker off the New Guinea coast at Jourmaund Reef. There was no tanker in the vicinity, nor was there any such reef. The High Court of Australia allowed the plaintiff's claim for damages for the loss in undertaking an abortive salvage operation. Yet was not the contract void from the start, since there never was any ship? The trial judge felt bound to follow *Couturier* v. *Hastie* in the sense that the contract was void and therefore no claim for damages for breach could be entertained. But at least in *Couturier* the subject matter was in existence to start with. Indeed the High Court, having examined *Couturier*, took the view that it did not decide the contract was void for initial impossibility. Accordingly, it awarded damages on the ground that the Commission had by implication guaranteed the tanker's existence, notwithstanding the fact that s.6 of the Sale of Goods Act 1893 provided that where there was a contract for the sale of specific goods and the goods without the knowledge of the seller had perished at the time the contract was made, the contract was void. In this case, though, the tanker can hardly be said to have perished – it never existed in the first place. It is to be noted that in *McRae* the trial judge did uphold the plaintiff's claim in deceit. Since then the Misrepresentation Act 1967 and the effect of the decision in *Hedley Byrne* have opened further legal avenues to a plaintiff in a position such as that of McRae.

In the case of *Associated Japanese Bank* v. *Credit du Nord SA* (1988), Jack Bennett, an engineer dealing in precision equipment, arranged a 'sale and lease-back' for four packaging machines with the Japanese Bank (AJB), the lessee's obligations being guaranteed by the French Bank (CdN). Mr Bennett received over £1 million for the sale, but did not pay. In fact the machines did not exist and the lease-back was a fraud. AJB sued Bennett who became bankrupt and then sued CdN on the guarantee. Mr Justice Steyn held that the stringent test of mistake at common law was satisfied; the contract was void *ab initio* as was also the guarantee. The claim of AJB failed.

Another illustration of common mistake was *Bell* v. *Lever Bros Ltd* (1932). Here both parties made a mistake as to the nature of an employment contract. The case is a highly controversial one and the House of Lords came to its decision by a bare majority. The facts were that the respondents, Lever Brothers, had agreed to pay Bell £8,000 per year as chairman of the Niger Company for a five-year period. But after three years Bell was made redundant because the Niger Company, in which Lever had a controlling interest, was merged with another company. Bell was paid £30,000 compensation. Later Lever Bros discovered that Bell had already broken his contract of employment in such a way as to have entitled them to dismiss him without compensation. The respondents sought to rescind the agreement to compensate on grounds of mistake. On the other hand the appellant had not, it appeared, fully appreciated the consequences of his earlier breaches of duty. The Lords took the view that the contract was nonetheless valid.

The effect of the decision in *Bell* seems to have been to narrow the grounds on which a common mistake, even if fundamental, nullifies a contract. Indeed, *Bell* seems to be irreconcilable with *Solle* v. *Butcher* and the principles of *caveat emptor*. *Bell* was distinguished by the Court of Appeal in *Sybron Corporation* v. *Rochem Ltd* (1983) – the employer on account of a mistake of fact was entitled to repayment of monies since the employee, who had overseen his employer's European operations and had taken early retirement, had failed to disclose breaches of duty on the part of other employees, for he had been party to a conspiracy in a large commercial fraud on the employer: but *Bell* was followed in *Solle* v. *Butcher* (1950) where the parties mistakenly thought that the rent paid for a flat was not a controlled one within the statutory meaning.

Lord Justice Denning observed:

> **Let me first consider mistakes which render a contract a nullity. All previous decisions on this subject must now be read in the light of *Bell* v. *Lever Bros*. The correct interpretation of that case, to my mind, is that, once a contract has been made, that is to say, once the parties, whatever their inmost states of mind, have to all outward appearances agreed with sufficient certainty in the same terms on the same subject–matter, then the contract is good unless and until it is set aside for failure of some condition on which the existence of the contract depends, or for fraud, or on some equitable ground. Neither party can rely on his own mistake to say it was a nullity from the beginning, no matter that it was a mistake which to his mind was fundamental, and no matter that the other party knew that he was under a mistake. *A fortiori*, if the other party did not know of the mistake, but shared it. The cases where goods have perished at the time of sale, or belong to the buyer, are really contracts which are not void for mistake but are void by reason of an implied condition precedent, because the contract proceeded on the basic assumption that it was possible of performance.**

He then added, more controversially:

> **Let me next consider mistakes which render a contract voidable, that is, liable to be set aside on some equitable ground. Whilst presupposing that a contract was good at law, or at any rate not void, the court of equity would often relieve a party from the consequences of his own mistake, so long as it could do so without injustice to third parties. The court, it was said, had power to set aside the contract whenever it was of opinion that it was unconscientious for the other party to avail himself of the legal advantage which he had obtained (*Torrance* v. *Bolton* (1872)).**

> The court had, of course, to define what it considered to be unconscientious but in this respect equity has shown a progressive development. It is now clear that a contract will be set aside if the mistake of the one party has been induced by a material misrepresentation of the other, even though it was not fraudulent or fundamental; or if one party, knowing that the other is mistaken about the terms of an offer, or the identity of the person by whom it is made, lets him remain under his delusion and concludes a contract on the mistaken terms instead of pointing out the mistake.

Rectification of mistake in contract, as an equitable remedy, where one party gave false and misleading statements to the other intending thereby to cause a mistake, was illustrated in *Commission for the New Towns* v. *Cooper (Great Britain) Ltd* (1995).

In *Leaf* v. *International Galleries* (1950) both parties mistakenly believed a picture had been painted by Constable, it was not. The plaintiff argued his case on misrepresentation, but the Court of Appeal held that although the mistake was fundamental, the contract was not avoided and refused to grant rescission. Nor was the contract held to be void in *Frederick E Rose (London) Ltd* v. *William H Pim Junior & Co. Ltd* (1953) where 'horsebeans' were mistaken for 'feveroles'. In this case, as in *Leaf* and *Solle*, and in a rather different manner in *Bell*, the subject matter was in existence. In *McRae* it never was (in the locality described) and in *Couturier* it no longer was. Thus mistake as to quality is not in general a sufficient ground to avoid a contract, neither is a mistake as to price. In *Kaur* v. *Chief Constable of Hampshire* (1981) the defendant had selected a pair of shoes from a rack in a supermarket marked at £6.99. One shoe was marked £6.99, the other £4.99. The cashier demanded £4.99. The defendant was convicted of theft by the Southampton Justices, who held that the cashier had no authority to accept an offer of £4.99, which the defendant knew was an incorrect price, so the contract was void and as ownership had not passed the defendant had appropriated the property of the store. On appeal, it was held per Lord Chief Justice Lane that it was the cashier's mistake, that the mistake was not so fundamental as to render the contract void, only voidable, and as the contract had not been avoided, ownership has passed. However, *Kaur* was doubted in *R.* v. *Morris* (1983) by the House of Lords, where the defendant substituted different price labels for articles in a self-service store, as seen earlier.

Where an agreement has been made for the sale of a specific thing and agreement for its purchase is concluded, it is immaterial if the buyer had hoped for some other result than he obtained; the purpose of the contract is then irrelevant unless it has been specifically indicated to the seller and become a term of the contract. So if a buyer acquires a horse *hoping* it will win races, or purchases land *believing* it has valuable minerals or buys a cargo of commodities in the *expectation* of a profit, he cannot avoid the contract on the grounds of his own mistaken belief, provided that it was not induced by the seller.

In *Aiken* v. *Short* (1856) it was stated that 'in order to recover back money paid under a mistake of fact, the mistake must be as to a fact which if true would make the person paying liable to pay the money; not where if true it would merely make it desirable that he should pay the money.' This strict rule has been approved and, although it was criticised by Lord Greene in *Morgan* v. *Ashcroft* (1937), generally followed. In *Larner* v. *London County Council* (1949) moreover, the Court of Appeal held that the council were entitled to recover an over-payment of wages, intended to make up the difference for their employees who joined the forces during the war, where the employee had not disclosed his increased service emoluments as he should have done. The money was paid under a mistake of fact, although clearly the payment was not enforceable, but voluntary. It is not easy to discern just where the courts will draw the line, but in general it is the rule that 'money paid voluntarily under a mistake of fact as to a fundamental matter may be recovered, but that money paid voluntarily with full knowledge of the facts is irrecoverable'. The money may be recoverable even if the payment is for good consideration, such as the discharge of a debt, if the payer pays under a mistake of fact (*Barclays Bank* v. *Simms* (1979)).

Mutual mistake

As for mutual mistake – in order for the contract to be declared void, the plaintiff must show that what he had in mind at the time the agreement was made now turns out to be entirely different from what the defendant contemplated; there must be some kind of fundamental misunderstanding that strikes at the root of the contract. Such a mistake may be in relation to the subject matter of the contract, or to its quality or, for example, in respect of the identity of the other party. One of the leading cases in this area of mistake is that of *Raffles* v. *Wichelhaus* (1864). Here the parties contracted for a cargo of 125 bales of cotton. The cotton was to arrive on a ship called the *Peerless* from Bombay. In fact there were two ships called the *Peerless* sailing from Bombay, one two months after the other. There was no contract in effect, although for procedural reasons the court did not decide this point; the buyer was not liable for refusing to accept the cotton arriving on the later ship. There was no *consensus ad idem*. Similarly, in *Scriven Bros & Co.* v. *Hindley & Co.* (1913) there was confusion over shipping marks; the plaintiff through an auctioneer offered for sale what was understood to be bales of hemp and tow from Russia. Not unreasonably the defendants inferred from the catalogue that all the bales were hemp. It was held that the contract was void *ab initio*: there was no original agreement and accordingly the plaintiff was unable to sue for the price.

Mistake as to identity

There have been a number of cases illustrating a mistake made in respect of the identity of the other party; this form of mistake is invariably unilateral rather than mutual. In *King's Norton Metal Co. Ltd* v. *Edridge, Merrett & Co. Ltd* (1897) the plaintiffs were metal manufacturers. They received an order purporting to come from the firm of Hallam and Co. for metal wire. In fact the firm was the invention of a fraudulent man named Wallis. The plaintiffs unsuccessfully contended that the contract was void for mistake, for the court took the view that they had nonetheless intended to contract with the writer of the letter. The contract might well be voidable on grounds of deceit (fraud). But as the contract was not void the defendants, who had purchased from W., retained a good title to the goods. In *Boulton* v. *Jones* (1857) the plaintiff had acquired a business from one Brocklehurst. The defendant sent an order to the shop, but he was unaware of the change. The key point was that the goods supplied were intended by J. to be set off against a debt owed by Brocklehurst to J. Accordingly he refused to pay Boulton for the price and Boulton unsuccessfully sued J; the court held the contract to be void. In *Cundy* v. *Lindsay* (1878) the plaintiffs received an order for handkerchiefs from a fraudulent person named Blenkarn. He signed the letter in a way that made it seem the order came from Blenkiron & Co., a reputable firm based in the same street as Blenkarn, who resold the goods to the defendants. The plaintiffs sued the defendants for conversion. The House of Lords held that the contract was void *ab initio*; there was no contract between the plaintiffs and Blenkarn.

In *Phillips* v. *Brooks Ltd* (1919) a man called North visited the plaintiff's shop and bought pearls and a ring for £3,000. He paid for the goods by cheque and represented himself to be Sir George Bullough. The plaintiff checked the name and address given and allowed N. to take the ring which was then pledged to the defendant for £350. The plaintiff sued the defendant for the return of the ring. But in this case the court held the contract was not void but only voidable for fraud, and therefore a good title had passed to the defendant. The plaintiff was keen to do business with the customer, whether he was Sir George Bullough or not; although he had checked the name and address, his investigations were comparatively superficial.

Deciding whether a contract is void for mistake in this context is not an easy matter as the courts have found. In *Ingram* v. *Little* (1961) the three plaintiffs sold a car to a rogue called Hutchinson. H. had told them that he was a businessman, one P. G. Hutchinson, living in Caterham, Surrey. One of the plaintiffs consulted a telephone directory and found that there was such a name with a Caterham address. The defendant acquired the car in good faith from H. who paid the Ingrams with a worthless cheque. The Court of Appeal held that the contract was void and therefore the car was still the property of the plaintiffs. In contrast, in *Lewis* v. *Averay* (1972) a rogue passed himself off as Richard Greene, a well-known actor. He signed a cheque for £450 for a car in the name of R. A. Green. The rogue resold the car to the defendant who was now sued for conversion by the plaintiff. The Court of Appeal preferred to follow *Phillips* rather than *Ingram*; it took the view that the contract was not void for mistake but merely voidable for fraud. In *Citibank NA* v. *Brown Shipley & Co. Ltd* (1991), it was held that fraudulent transactions involving mistaken identity do not necessarily make the transaction ineffective, since here the plaintiff bank wanted to transfer the money to the defendant bank.

Equitable relief

At common law, mistake was a ground for relief to a plaintiff in an action to recover monies paid under a mistake of fact or to a defendant in an action where the mistake was such that the contract was void. A mistake of law was no ground for avoiding the contract, as a general rule, but a mistake as to foreign law was held by the House of Lords to be a mistake of fact in *Lazard Bros & Co.* v. *Midland Bank Ltd* (1933). Equitable relief, which may be for rectification of a contract, rescission or other relief is available, however, in a wide range of cases, if the court deems it just to grant dispensation to a party, especially where the other party has in some measure wrongfully induced an unfair contract.

As indicated in *Solle* v. *Butcher* (1950) above, equity is more flexible, in that the contract is not treated as void *ab initio*, but as voidable.

Hence, mistake as to the terms of a contract may be a ground for the court to refuse to grant specific performance. Alternatively, rescission may be ordered, where there has been a common mistake of both parties; or rectification of a written contract, if it is clear that the document did not fully express the contractual intentions of both parties. In other words, rectification applies to contractual words that have been badly or unnecessarily expressed and which are capable of misunderstanding, but which do not alter the common intention of the parties to the agreement. A pre-contractual written agreement, in other words an antecedent agreement, is also capable of rectification, as seen in *Joscelyne* v. *Nissen* (1970), where the final agreement had omitted mention of the daughter's payments of gas and electricity bills.

The party that seeks rectification must, it is said, show convincing evidence that the words in question do not properly reflect the parties' common intention. In addition, in equity the judge may use his discretion to refuse an order for specific performance, particularly, for instance, if the plaintiff does not come before the court with 'clean hands'. Thus in *Agip SpA* v. *Navigione Alta Italia SpA* (1984) the Court of Appeal held that where a person signs a contract but, due to his own carelessness and without the other's party knowledge, fails to notice that a provision differs from that which he thought had been agreed, he is not entitled to rectification of the contract in the absence of misrepresentation or 'sharp practice' by the other party. This contract concerned a charterparty agreement which contained an escalation clause covering increased costs of maintenance and repairs. At a later stage, the clause was expressed in US dollars, rather than Italian lire, and subsequently the lire fell against the dollar, to the plaintiff's loss. There was no question of common mistake; the plaintiffs, the charterers, had to rely on their own unilateral mistake.

Non est factum

There is one other important form of mistake which must be considered. Common law has long recognised that in cases of written agreements one of the parties may have signed the wrong document, often on account of the fraudulent representation of the other. This may be particularly so where the signatory is illiterate or short sighted; in practice he does not sign correctly, 'it is not his deed' (*non est factum*). The mistake must be a serious or fundamental one and it is no argument for the plaintiff to say that he did not have time to read the document properly, or left the other party to fill in the blank spaces (*United Dominions Trust* v. *Western* (1975)).

The leading case is *Saunders* v. *Anglia Building Society* (*Gallie* v. *Lee*) (1971). In this instance the plaintiff was a 78 year-old widow. She had given the deeds of her house to her nephew, P., in order that he might secure a loan. The condition was that she should be able to continue to live in the house for the rest of her life. P. used a friend, Lee, to raise money on the house since he feared that if he did so himself his separated wife would be able to claim maintenance money. L. was heavily in debt and he took a document to Mrs G. to sign. He told her it was a deed of gift to her nephew; as she had broken her glasses she signed without reading it. In fact the house was mortgaged to a building society. L. failed to pay money to the widow or the nephew or instalments to the society. The building society sought possession of the property. The widow sued both L. and the building society and argued the doctrine of *non est factum*, that the assignment was void. The House of Lords, while sympathetic to the plaintiff, did not accept the argument. It took the view that she intended to assign the property to the defendant in order that he might raise money for her nephew. It was her misfortune that both the defendant and the person who had prepared the document were dishonest. In *Norwich & Peterborough Building Society* v. *Steed* (1992) the Court of Appeal would not allow a plea of *non est factum* where the defendant had emigrated to the USA and had executed a power of attorney to enable his mother to sell the house; his sister and her husband used the house to obtain money and then payments fell into arrears. His mother's signature had been obtained by a trick or was a forgery, but *non est factum* did not apply since he had not explained to his mother the effects of a power of attorney.

MISREPRESENTATION

Another important vitiating factor is that of misrepresentation, which is where one party misleads the other by making false statements of fact which nevertheless have the effect of persuading that other party to enter into the agreement. The representation may not be intended by either party to be a contractual term, but nonetheless it plays an important part in influencing the mind of the injured party; such statements are sometimes known as 'mere representations'. 'Mere representations' must be distinguished from opinions made in the course of, for example, advertising; such are regarded as 'mere puffs', and the courts will always allow a degree of latitude in the marketing of a product. In *Bisset* v. *Wilkinson* (1927) the seller of land in New Zealand told the purchaser that in his opinion it would be good for carrying two thousand sheep. The land, it appeared, had not been used before as a sheep farm. The plaintiffs unsuccessfully claimed rescission of the contract on grounds of misrepresentation when the vendor claimed the rest of the purchase price. But, of course, separating fact from opinion is not easy. In this context, a true estoppel means that the representor can only be estopped from denying the 'truth' of a statement of fact already made.

The remedies for misrepresentation are complicated and depend upon the nature of the statement made, the rules of equity and common and statutory law and whether the statement is a mere representation or a contractual term. As a general rule it can be said that the contract is voidable at the option of the injured party; he may be entitled to rescission or damages or both, wherever the misrepresentation had been relied on.

There are three types of misrepresentation: fraudulent, negligent and innocent, and these, together with the different forms of remedy, are examined below. However, it should be added here that whatever category of misrepresentation the statement falls into, it should normally relate to a current or past fact, rather than to some future event or intention; it must also be concerned with fact rather than with a legal rule, although, again, separating fact and law is often easier said than done. Equity, to a limited degree, recognises liability for misrepresentation of the law. In *Edgington* v. *Fitzmaurice* (1885), although the statement related to the future, the defendants were held liable in deceit; the misrepresentation had clearly been made fraudulently, for the company did not intend to use directly the money raised to expand its future activities but rather to pay off existing debts. Lord Justice Bowen said:

> **The state of a man's mind is as much a fact as the state of his digestion. It is true that it is very difficult to prove what the state of a man's mind at a particular time is, but, if it can be ascertained, it is as much a fact as anything else. A misrepresentation as to the state of a man's mind is, therefore, a misstatement of fact.**

Where there is ambiguity in the statement, then the representor will be held liable if it was reasonable in all the circumstances for the representee to have understood a different meaning. Normally silence, as we have seen already in the tort of deceit, will not amount to misrepresentation, although where a special relationship exists, such as a fiduciary relationship, the position changes. This matter is also discussed later on. Partial non-disclosure may, however, give rise to liability, just as there is a general duty to correct a true statement which subsequently becomes false. And a nod or a smile does not constitute silence (*Walters* v. *Morgan* (1861)).

As already indicated above the plaintiff must show that the misrepresentation materially induced him to enter into the agreement; he will probably have no case if the statement had at best a marginal effect, or was not material to the reasonable man. Nonetheless he may still be entitled to relief where he did not avail himself of an opportunity of discovering the true facts. In the case of *Humming Bird Motors Ltd* v. *Hobbs* (1986) where the defendant had purchased a car with an odometer reading of 34,900 miles and resold it to the plaintiffs who sued for damages when they discovered the true reading was 80,000 miles, the judge at first instance found that the defendant had been negligent in making the incorrect declaration of mileage on re-sale. However, the Court of Appeal held that the declaration, which had been incorporated on the sale invoice, did not amount to a representation of fact, but merely of his belief as to the facts and that it was not therefore a term of the contract, or a collateral warranty.

Fraudulent misrepresentation

It is open to the party who has been induced to enter into the contract by a fraudulent misrepresentation, either to affirm the contract, and bring an action for damages for the deceit, or to repudiate the contract, claiming rescission or damages, or both. Indeed, in *Archer* v. *Brown* (1984) it was emphasised that damages plus rescission was always the entitlement in the case of a fraudulent misrepresentation. The question of granting rescission *ab initio* in the case of fraudulent misrepresentation was considered in the Australian case of *Vadasz* v. *Pioneer Concrete (SA) Pty Ltd* (1995).

So the usual rule is that where one party has induced another by means of deceit to enter into a contract, then the injured party may rescind (terminate) the contract and sue for damages in deceit. The leading case is *Derry* v. *Peek* (1889) which has already been examined earlier in tort. In that case Lord Herschell said that a deceitful misrepresentation meant one made knowingly or without belief in its truth or recklessly in the sense of not caring at all whether the statement was true or false. Recklessness here may also be akin to wilful blindness in criminal law. In short, there is some element of dishonesty in the way the plaintiff has made the statement. The action for damages in deceit (in tort) has as its object the restoration of the injured party to his earlier position, in this context to his pre-contractual position. That means that he will recover all monies paid, but it does not mean he may sue for 'loss of bargain' as he would in a normal action for breach of contract. Thus if X. buys from Y. a 'rare' Chinese vase for £2,000, which he believes is really worth £5,000, and it is in fact a fake worth £10, then he may sue for £1,990 but not for £4,990.

The fraudulent statement must be made by the representor, and must have been relied on by the party seeking redress. In the case of *Armstrong* v. *Strain* (1952), the vendor of a bungalow described by the agent as in 'very nice condition' had not told his agent that the foundations had been underpinned several times due to subsidence. The purchaser was unable to recover damages as the vendor had made no representation, and the agent was innocent, the Court of Appeal confirmed. In *East* v. *Maurer* (1991) the plaintiffs bought a hairdressing business in Bournemouth after the first defendant had fraudulently represented that he would no longer work in the same area. The Court of Appeal held that the loss of profits was recoverable as damages in the tort of deceit because lost profits are losses directly flowing from the fraud, but the *East* case may be seen on its own facts.

Negligent misrepresentation

Following the case of *Derry* v. *Peek*, the courts treated misrepresentation in contract as either fraudulent or non-fraudulent. The House of Lords' decision in *Hedley Byrne & Co. Ltd* v. *Heller & Partners Ltd* (1964) made it possible to bring a claim, in tort, for negligent statements that caused loss. Before that case it was assumed that fiduciary duties apart, the common law afforded no right to damages in respect of non-fraudulent (innocent) misrepresentations that caused purely economic loss, unless the representation was itself a term of the contract. In the contractual context the injured party would merely have the right to rescind. As we have seen, *Hedley Byrne*, building upon the liabilities for fiduciary relationships that were clearly set out in *Nocton* v. *Lord Ashburton* (1914), established that liability arose in tort where negligent misstatements were relied upon and which subsequently caused the plaintiff financial loss, providing a special relationship between the plaintiff and the defendant existed at the relevant time. In *Esso Petroleum Co. Ltd* v. *Mardon* (1976) it was held that there is a liability in tort for a pre-contractual misstatement where one party to the agreement relies upon the other party's skill or knowledge, and damages may be awarded; indeed in this context claims in both contract and tort are not mutually exclusive, as seen in *Midland Bank Trust Co. Ltd* v. *Hett, Stubbs and Kemp* (1978). The Misrepresentation Act 1967 confirmed the new category of negligent misrepresentation by s.2(1) and gave the courts a discretion by s.2(2) to award damages instead of rescission. Under s.2(1) the damages are as in tort, and include foreseeable consequential loss, but damages under s.2(2) do not include consequential loss (such as loss of profit), they are simply basic damages. In *Smith New Court Securities Ltd* v. *Scrimgeour Vickers (Asset Management) Ltd* (1996), the House of Lords applying *Doyle* v. *Olby (Ironmongers) Ltd* said the *Wagon Mound* test of remoteness of damage did not have to apply in respect of a contract induced by fraudulent misrepresentation; the measure of damages was reparation for all the loss directly caused, including consequential loss, but the plaintiff was under a duty to mitigate his loss once he became aware of the fraud.

The Act provides under s.2(1):

> **Where a person has entered into a contract after a misrepresentation has been made to him by another party thereto and as a result thereof he has suffered loss, then, if the person making the misrepresentation would be liable to damages in respect thereof had the misrepresentation been made fraudulently, that person shall be so liable notwithstanding that the misrepresentation was not made fraudulently, unless he proves that he had reasonable ground to believe and did believe up to the time the contract was made that the facts represented were true.**

The wording in s.2(1) does not contain the happiest of phrases and has led to various debates in the courts. In particular the phrase 'had the misrepresentation been made fraudulently' appears to be superfluous and it has led to the frequent comment that the Act has invented a 'fiction of fraud'. What is clear is that under the Act the representor must show that he was not negligent, unless he shows that there were reasonable grounds to believe that the facts represented were true throughout the whole of the pre-contractual period. The burden of proof is thus a heavy one, as illustrated in *Howard Marine and Dredging Co. Ltd* v. *A Ogden & Sons (Excavations) Ltd* (1978) where the defendants were unable to complete an excavation contract as quickly as envisaged on account of the fact the sea barges had a smaller payload than the plaintiffs had stated because of an error in Lloyds Register. The plaintiffs sued for the balance of the charter-hire and the defendants successfully counterclaimed for damages under the 1967 Act, since the plaintiffs' representative did not have reasonable grounds for believing the statement to be true, since the evidence available to him was contradictory.

An action for damages under the Act applies only where a contract has actually been entered into. Otherwise an action in tort for negligent misstatement might be more appropriate, and that also applies where either there is in effect no contract, that is the contract is void *ab initio* on grounds of mistake, or where the misrepresentation was made not by the other party to the contract but by a third party. An agent, acting under express or ostensible authority, will not be personally liable for the misrepresentation, as seen in *Resolute Maritime Inc* v. *Nippon Kaiji Kyokai (The Skopas)* (1983). In this case the thirteenth and fourteenth defendants were agents and shipbrokers, and Mr Justice Mustill held on a preliminary issue that they could not be liable in law under s.2 of the Act, a ruling that did not entirely accord with academic opinion.

In *Gran Gelato Ltd* v. *Richcliff (Group) Ltd* (1992) four Italians decided to set up a high-class ice-cream business in London, but the English weather did not assist them; when they attempted to sell, it became apparent in effect there were difficulties with the head-lease which the vendor's solicitors had omitted to reveal. The vendor, it was held, was liable to the plaintiffs at common law and under the Misrepresentation Act 1967, but the solicitors were not liable, for no cause of action lay under the 1967 Act against a negligent agent within the course of his authority.

In *Royscot Trust Ltd* v. *Rogerson* (1991) the plaintiff finance company was induced to enter into a hire purchase agreement with a customer (Rogerson) as a result of a misrepresentation by a car dealer (Maidenhead Honda). A second-hand car was sold by Honda to the plaintiff who hired it to Rogerson. Maidenhead Honda misrepresented the deposit; the plaintiff paid £6,400 to Honda; R. wrongfully sold the car to an innocent third party. The plaintiff brought an action for damages (for conversion) and for misrepresentation under s.2(1) of the Misrepresentation Act 1967 against Rogerson and Maidenhead Honda. The Court of Appeal allowed a claim of £6,400 less instalments already paid by R. (namely, £2,800). The measure of damages was tortious, not contractual, and the same as if the claim was for a fraudulent or negligent misrepresentation, even if the losses were unforeseeable. The decision was perhaps unfair, because, it is suggested, in principle it is wrong to put a fraudulent person on the same footing as a negligent or innocent one, and under *Hedley Byrne* an innocent misrepresentor would not be liable for all the consequences of his misrepresentation, but only for the reasonably foreseeable consequences: in any case under s.2(1) it is up to the defendant to prove that he had 'reasonable grounds to believe and did believe up to the time the contract was made that the facts represented were true'. The act of R. in selling the car was not a *novus actus*, the dealer should reasonably have foreseen the possibility that the customer might have wrongfully sold the car, and so the chain of causation was not broken. This case is considered further below.

When a person enters into a contract in reliance upon a negligent misstatement, the basic principle for the assessment of damages is that he should be put in the position he would have been in had the misrepresentation not been made. So, in *Hussey* v. *Eels* (1990) the land on which a bungalow suffering from subsidence which had been the subject of misrepresentation was sold for development purposes, and this extra profit was not taken into account, since it was inherent in the land. In *Naughton* v. *O'Callaghan* (1990) it was disregarded that the racehorse in question had been raced for two years, leading to a diminution in value; the pedigree of the horse had been misrepresented in the first place and the difference between what was paid and what it was worth after two years was successfully claimed; these were both Court of Appeal cases.

Of course, if the 'injured' party, the representee, after discovering the truth behind the erroneous statement, acts in a way that shows he is still treating the contract as operational, then any right to rescind may well be lost, as in *Kennard* v. *Ashman* (1894), where the tenant continued to pay rent under the lease.

Does, then, the award of damages under s.2(1) of the Misrepresentation Act 1967 relate to the tort of deceit, with liability for all losses flowing from the fraudulent misrepresentation, or to the tort of negligence where only foreseeable damages are recoverable? It was the former held the Court of Appeal in *Royscot Trust* v. *Rogerson* (1991). Lord Justice Balcombe said: 'the wording of the subsection is clear: the person making the innocent misrepresentation shall be "so liable", ie liable to damages as if the representation had been made fraudulently'. As already indicated, it can certainly be said that it is overly strict to apply a test designed for those guilty of fraud to those guilty of, at the very worst, negligence, but at least the Court of Appeal's decision is more consistent with the wording of the subsection and has the added merit of simplicity; in practice, moreover, the actual difference between the scale of damages in deceit and under negligent misrepresentation is often minimal. In this case a deposit for a car was misrepresented to be 20 per cent of the total price, whereas it was only 16 per cent. The hire-purchaser subsequently dishonestly sold the car on to a person who acquired a good title under the Hire-Purchase Act 1964 and he stopped his repayments. The finance company therefore claimed that the dealer was liable in damages for the difference between the sum which it had paid for the car and the amount repaid by the hire-purchaser. Did this loss flow from the misrepresentation by the dealer? This depended on whether the wrong sale of the car constituted a *novus actus interveniens* and so broke the chain of causation. As we have seen, the Court of Appeal held that, although there was no requirement that the loss should have been foreseeable, foreseeability was nevertheless a factor to be taken into account in deciding whether or not an event constitutes a *novus actus interveniens*. The finance company was entitled to the damages claimed, subject to giving credit for any sums which it might recover from the hire-purchaser. This decision, and that in *East* v. *Maurer* (1991), illustrate the growing recourse to claims for damages for misrepresentation in substitution for or in addition to damages for breach of contract. In *Harlingdon and Leinster Enterprises Ltd* v. *Christopher Hull Fine Art Ltd* (1990) the defendants sold some paintings to the plaintiff, which had been described in a previous catalogue as by a German painter. The plaintiff was told by the defendants that not much was known about the painting. The painting subsequently turned out to be a forgery. The plaintiff's claim for misrepresentation failed. The purchaser had relied upon his own inspection, and not on the description. The trial judge held that the painting was of merchantable quality, as it was capable of aesthetic appreciation, even if it was a forgery; this view, a rather strict and harsh one it is submitted, was upheld by a majority of the Court of Appeal.

Innocent misrepresentation

Before *Hedley Byrne* and the Misrepresentation Act 1967 all non-fraudulent misrepresentation was regarded as 'innocent'. However, it is now possible to see a category of innocent misrepresentation distinct from negligent misrepresentation. In other words there is no real carelessness on the part of the representor, there is no fault, but nonetheless he has made a false statement. In this instance the representee is entitled to rescind the contract but cannot obtain damages, whereas in cases of negligent or fraudulent misrepresentation this is possible. Instead he may be awarded an 'indemnity' to cover the essential expenses unnecessarily incurred as a result of relying upon the misstatement (*Whittington* v. *Seale-Hayne* (1900), a case of poisoned poultry). An indemnity is an equitable remedy, whereas damages are a common law remedy, and will be less than damages awarded in respect of fraudulent or negligent misstatements, even though, the damages so awarded are on an out of pocket basis, as opposed to damages for loss of bargain which are awarded for breach of contract where, for example, the misrepresentation itself has become a contractual term. However, in practice such distinctions are not always hard and fast, and s.2(2) of the Misrepresentation Act 1967, as already noted, gives the court a general power to grant damages in place of rescission, in respect of non-fraudulent misrepresentation.

Section 2(2) says:

> **Where a person has entered into a contract after a misrepresentation has been made to him otherwise than fraudulently, and he would be entitled by reason of the misrepresentation to rescind the contract, then, if it is claimed in any of the proceedings arising out of the contract that the contract ought to be or has been rescinded, the court or arbitrator may declare the contract subsisting and award damages in lieu of rescission, if of the opinion that it would be equitable to do so, having regard to the nature of the misrepresentation and the loss that would be caused by it if the contract were upheld, as well as to the loss that rescission would cause the other party.**

It is clear that whereas the general rule in contractual liability is and remains *caveat emptor*, in so far as representations are concerned the position is reversed. The seller must take care in his representations to ensure that they are truthful, to the best of his knowledge. Care must be taken to avoid giving ambiguous representations. If a representation can be intrepreted in one manner that is truthful, but the buyer takes the alternative meaning, the representor may be estopped from denying the interpretation acted upon by the representee *Low* v. *Bouverie* (1891). In *William Sindall plc* v. *Cambridgeshire County Council* (1994) which involved the purchase of playing fields from the education authority for over £5 million, at a time when property prices were falling dramatically, the Court of Appeal held that the discretion conferred by s.2(2) was a broad one. Lord Justice Hoffmann concluded that 'damages under s.2(2) should never exceed the sum which would have been awarded if the representation had been a warranty.' (see also *Witter (Thomas)* v. *TBP Industries Ltd* (1996)).

Misrepresentation as a term of the contract and rescission

As stated previously a misrepresentation may be of two types, where the misstatement is pre-contractual and induces the injured party to enter into the agreement (this is essentially what has been discussed so far), or where the misstatement is a term of the contract itself. Frequently it is difficult to categorise as such, and one thing inevitably leads to another. In *Oscar Chess Ltd* v. *Williams* (1957) the defendant, a private individual, innocently sold a 1939 car worth £175 as a 1948 model for £290. The Court of Appeal held the misstatement not to be a term of the contract.

Similarly, in the case of *Routledge* v. *McKay* (1954) the buyer of a 600cc motorcycle combination asked the seller its age and the seller stated late 1941 or 1942. The seller produced the registration book, pointing out that the capacity was incorrectly registered as 500cc and showing the registration book date of late 1941. In fact the machine had been made in 1930 and subsequently reconditioned and partly remade. The seller had not himself altered the registration document and there was no question of fraud. The buyer subsequently resold and the machine changed hands twice more, when the final buyer discovered the error in date of manufacture. He had bought for £100, and sued for £80 damages, the difference in value from the fourth seller, who claimed indemnity from the third, who claimed similarly from the second who also so claimed from the first seller. The County Court judge held that there had been a warranty, repeated by each seller, but the Court of Appeal, following the House of Lords decision in *Heilbut, Symons & Co.* v. *Buckleton* (1913), unanimously reversed the decision, 'albeit reluctantly as the entirely innocent second buyer was left to bear the whole burden of the case'. But in *Dick Bentley Productions Ltd* v. *Harold Smith (Motors) Ltd* (1965) a misstatement by a car dealer to the effect that a Bentley had covered only 20,000 miles whereas in fact it had covered 100,000 was held to be a term since a car dealer was held to possess special knowledge. In the *Humming Bird* case, Hobbs had been 'a wheeler and dealer' in cars, but not a car dealer as such.

In this respect the Misrepresentation Act 1967 (s.1) has provided some aid. It states, albeit obscurely, that in respect of such an incorporated misrepresentation the representee may still rescind the contract as well as bringing an action for damages for breach, whereas the normal rule is that setting aside the contract (rescission) excludes a claim for damages for breach. However, it must be stressed that 'rescission', although primarily an equitable remedy, is a term frequently used to mean a number of different things; the Act itself does not favour precise usage. In this context we may speak of rescission for breach or rescission for misrepresentation.

As already noted, the Misrepresentation Act 1967 contains a further important provision under s.2(2). The court may use its discretion to award damages in lieu of rescission for an innocent misrepresentation; this certainly applies to negligent misrepresentation, and it includes such incorporated misrepresentations, but as already indicated, the Act's language is not a model of clarity. Section 2(2) more likely applies to an executed as opposed to an executory contract. (Under s.2(2) rescission and damages are alternatives; but where the representee can sue for damages on account of fraud or negligence, he may sue for damages instead of rescinding, or elect to do both: damages and rescission are not in that context mutually exclusive.) Nor is it clear on what principle s.2(2) is based, for the damages here seem to be independent of fault (tort) or contractual intention, but it would appear that as damages are awarded in lieu of rescission for innocent misrepresentation, the effect of damages under s.2(2) should be that of rescission with an indemnity. Where damages under s.2(2) are awarded, s.2(3) requires the court to take such into account in the assessment of any other damages, for it would be inequitable for the plaintiff to be compensated twice over; so, it would be unlikely, that further damages would be awarded under s.2(1), for example.

Time and exclusion

Whenever the injured party elects to rescind the contract he must do so expeditiously. An unreasonable lapse of time will lose him this right, as illustrated in *Leaf* v. *International Galleries* (1950). Moreover, even if the person does act quickly he may not be able to notify the defaulting party, particularly where a fraudulent misrepresentation has occurred. The case of *Car and Universal Finance Co. Ltd* v. *Caldwell* (1965) illustrates this point. Here the defendant sold a car to N. After further resales the car was bought by the plaintiffs. Meanwhile N.'s cheque had been dishonoured and N. could not be traced, whereupon C. notified the AA and the police. It was held that C. had properly rescinded the contract and the plaintiffs had no title to the vehicle.

Rescission may not take place, however, if the representee has already affirmed the contract or where a significant part of the subject matter has, say, been destroyed. In respect of the latter the principle of rescission is *restitutio in integrum*; the parties must be satisfactorily returned to their precontractual position. Nor may rescission take place where third parties have already acquired interests in the subject matter for value, since it is clear that contracts in this sphere of the law are voidable rather than void. The essential point in the *Caldwell* case was that the defendant had acted immediately, even though he could not trace the rogue N. The Misrepresentation Act 1967 has, in effect, recognised these limits, but no more, to rescission.

Section 3 of the 1967 Act stated that misrepresentation could not be excluded by a contractual term. This was then replaced by s.8 of the Unfair Contract Terms Act 1977, another statutory provision which, it can be argued, was badly drafted. It reads:

> **If a contract contains a term which would exclude or restrict –**
>
> **(a) any liability to which a party to a contract may be subject by reason of any misrepresentation made by him before the contract was made; or**
>
> **(b) any remedy available to another party to the contract by reason of such a misrepresentation,**
>
> **that term shall be of no effect except in so far as it satisfies the requirement of reasonableness as stated in section 11(l) of the Unfair Contract Terms Act 1977; and it is for those claiming that the term satisfies that requirement to show that it does.**

In respect of the test of 'reasonableness' under s.11(1), the Act says regard must be had to the 'circumstances which were, or ought reasonably to have been, known to or in the contemplation of the parties when the contract was made'.

Section 8 of the 1977 Act (in contrast to s.3 of the 1967 Act) is limited to an incorporated representation, not a 'mere' misrepresentation, but as seen earlier it is often difficult to distinguish between the two.

It seems that the 1967 Act does not control the right of a party to limit the authority of an agent, so that a misrepresentation by an auctioneer where the sale catalogue included a specific disclaimer that the auctioneer had authority to make a representation on behalf of the vendor was held not to constitute an exemption clause at all in *Overbrooke Estates* v. *Glencombe Properties Ltd* (1974). But a similar disclaimer was held to be unreasonable, also at first instance, in the case of *South Western General Property Co. Ltd* v. *Marton* (1982) where the clause purported to exclude the liability of both auctioneer and the vendor.

In the case of *Goff* v. *Gauther* (1991) the defendants agreed to purchase a house, but had difficulty raising the purchase money; they were 'encouraged' to sign a contract by the plaintiff's solicitor who said that if they did not, the transaction would be terminated and the house sold to another party who had made a higher offer. The defendants exchanged but did not complete. The plaintiff sought to forfeit the deposit and claimed damages as he had to sell at a lower price. The defendants, who discovered that there had not been another offer, counterclaimed that the contract had been induced by the misrepresentation, as to which the plaintiff claimed that a clause in the contract excluded reliance 'on any warranty or representation . . . by or on behalf of the vendor other than the [plaintiff's solicitors'] written replies to inquiries raised'. The court held that there had been a material misrepresentation and that it would not be fair or reasonable for the plaintiff to rely on the clause in the contract to escape from liability for the misrepresentation.

Non-disclosure

It has been noted that non-disclosure does not amount to a warranty or representation and the 1967 Act did not change that general rule. Care, however, must be taken by the vendor not to cover up a defect as active concealment could amount to a misrepresentation, and in particular the vendor cannot imply, by, for instance, a shake of the head, or some such action in response to a query, that there is no known defect. There are, though, a number of exceptions to the general rule, where it is incumbent upon the vendor to make full disclosure and where failure to do so can give rise to a claim for misrepresentation.

1. Contracts uberrimae fidei

In certain instances the representor must disclose all relevant particulars and this is invariably required in contracts of insurance. Thus a person who fills in an application form for life insurance must disclose the fact that he is a physical wreck; he must show good faith (*uberimma fides*). Where the policyholder is guilty of fraud, the company can keep the premiums. In respect of marine insurance there is a statutory duty of disclosure (Marine Insurance Act 1906). Otherwise there is an implied term that full disclosure of all material facts has been communicated to the insurers by the proposer before the contract. The courts have interpreted these conditions strictly against proposers as in the case of *Locker Woolf Ltd* v. *Western Australian Inusrance Co. Ltd* (1936), where the insured in a proposal for fire insurance stated that no proposal had been declined by another company, when in fact another company had previously refused to issue a policy in respect of his motor vehicle.

The duty of disclosure is confined to facts, so that if a proposer to a life policy answers 'no' to a question of 'have you any disease?' and unknowingly has a disease, for example malignant cancer, then the policy is not necessarily invalidated. But many insurance companies provide in their 'small print' that replies are binding on the assured as to their accuracy, and the courts have generally upheld such conditions, even where they have been unfair to an innocent proposer. A similar rule operates in respect of contracts for family arrangements, such as for the settlement of property disputes.

The duty of disclosure may well overlap with the common law duty of care under negligence (in tort), as well illustrated in *Banque Keyser Ullmann SA* v. *Skandia (UK) Insurance Co. Ltd* (1989), where loan agreements totalling 80 million Swiss francs to a South American businessman were inadequately underwritten by insurance policies and gemstones on account of the deceit of a broker, deceit which became known to the senior underwriter. In *Reid* v. *Rush & Tompkins Group plc* (1990) the plaintiff was employed by the defendant as a quarry foreman in Ethiopia, where there was no compulsory third party insurance; he was injured by an untraceable driver. His employer was not liable in negligence for failing to insure him or give him advice, it did not fall into one of the rare categories of economic loss cases (*per* the *Banque Keyser* case), it was held; moreover, the Court of Appeal was unwilling to imply an appropriate term into the contract of employment.

However, although contracts of insurance are *uberrimae fidei*, that is they require utmost good faith of the insured party, the Court of Appeal held in *Banque Keyser,* now *Banque Financière de la Cité SA* v. *Westgate Insurance Co. Ltd* (1990), that the insurers have no such duty of good faith towards third parties, such as banks advancing monies to the insured on the strength of insurance policies; as indicated, the case involved dishonesty of an employee of the insurance brokers, but the Court held that the insurance company owed no duty of care to the bank and that no misrepresentation had been made, merely an omission by an employee of the insurance company, who was aware of the dishonesty of the broker, to disclose the fact to the bank. Lord Justice Slade, giving the judgment of the Court, deplored the fact that we lived in a world in which commercial dishonesty was rampant; however, the law could not police the fairness of every commercial contract by reference to moral principles, he stated. The House of Lords upheld the decision, but did not express an opinion on whether the insurers owed the banks a duty under the common law of negligence as they decided that the banks' loss did not flow from the breach of any such duty.

2. Companies

Under the Companies Act 1985 a company prospectus must make a full disclosure of matters specified in the Act. The Stock Exchange has control over public offerings of quoted companies.

3. Fiduciary relationships

As indicated under tort where a fiduciary relationship exists between two parties, that is a confidential relationship whereby one party is in a position of trust with regard to the other, then non-disclosure of a material fact will be actionable. Equity recognises that although no actual deceit is involved, an action for 'constructive fraud' may lie, for one party is in a position of dependence upon the other. The injured party will be indemnified accordingly. The relationship may well centre upon financial matters, as seen in the case of *Nocton* v. *Lord Ashburton* (1914) where a solicitor wrongly advised his client in respect of the release of a mortgage. Thus the relationships between principal and agent and trustee and beneficiary are fiduciary. But the relationship need not be a financial one; the confidentiality inherent in the relationship is the key factor, as, for instance, in that between parent or guardian and child.

4. Sale of land

Contracts for the sale of land, or an interest in land, have been likened to contracts *uberrimae fidei*, in that the vendor is frequently the only party in a position to know the facts concerning defects in the property. Such contracts indeed do not require positive disclosure, but the vendor must be very careful to disclose fully any replies to enquiries, or to substantiate any claims. So in the case of *Laurence* v. *Lexcourt Holdings Ltd* (1978), where a lease for 15 years of office premises was granted, but in fact the landlords had forgotten that there was a restriction of planning permission and use as offices was limited to two years only, the tenants were held entitled to resist an action for specific performance and to cross claim to rescind, and also to claim damages for their expenses in moving into the premises. It was held to be immaterial that the tenants could have made enquiry, because they had in fact relied on the misrepresentation. The judge further held that there had been a common mistake, and the tenants were entitled to rescind, quoting the dictum of Denning in *Solle* v. *Butcher* (1950): 'A contract is liable to be set aside if the parties were under a common misapprehension . . . provided that the misapprehension was fundamental and that the party seeking to set it aside was not himself at fault'. The description of the premises as offices was fundamental, and the failure of the tenants to make adequate searches, relying on the representation, was not a 'fault'.

8.6

Duress and undue influence

DURESS

Where it can be shown that one party to a contract has used unacceptable forms of pressure upon the other in order to obtain consent then that agreement is voidable. It is not entirely clear whether in common law, as opposed to equity, such contracts are void, the better view is that they are probably only voidable. It is also not entirely clear whether common law duress may be directed only against the person rather than to property or goods. It would seem that nowadays relief may be obtained where duress is so directed, although common law has long recognised that money paid could be recovered in quasi-contract. This point was illustrated to some degree in *Lloyds Bank Ltd* v. *Bundy* (1975) where the defendant guaranteed his son's debts by mortgaging his farm to the bank. Later the bank sought an additional charge to an amount greater than the market value of the farm. The Court of Appeal set aside the charge since the bank had not behaved fairly in giving the defendant independent advice. However, this particular case was more directly concerned with the question of fiduciary and other relationships in equity. It was held in *Skeate* v. *Beale* (1840), where a landlord had distrained on the tenant's goods for arrears of rent, that a threat against a person's goods, not the person himself, did not amount to duress. This decision has been criticised and perhaps can be ascribed to the special considerations that arise under distraint in landlord and tenant relationships. In *CTN Cash and Carry Ltd* v. *Callaher Ltd* (1994) the defendants' method of obtaining payment was unattractive, but it was not duress. Nonetheless the object of commercial law was fair dealing between the parties although the court could not recognise a concept of 'lawful act duress' on account of policy reasons.

Economic duress

Certainly blackmail would be one form of duress at common law; so, too, would threats of violence. However, economic coercion is too wide a concept to constitute duress in all instances. What is clear is that the duress must have constituted the major factor in inducing the injured party to enter into the agreement. Further, once the plaintiff has made out a *prima facie* case of duress, in terms of establishing duress as a fact, then the burden is upon the defendant to show that duress did not amount to a major consideration in the plaintiff's mind (*Barton* v. *Armstrong* (1976)). Two cases concerning duress are those of *Pao On* v. *Lau Yiu Long* (1979) and *North Ocean Shipping Co. Ltd* v. *Hyundai Construction Co. Ltd* (1979). The former concerned an agreement to indemnify on the threat of repudiation of a contract with a third party, and whether that agreement was contrary to public policy and whether economic duress vitiated consent. The defendants gave the guarantee to avoid adverse publicity, so there was no duress. In the latter the decline in the value of the American dollar led one party to the contract, the shipbuilders, to demand increased payments. The ship owners wanted the ship to be built as quickly as possible and therefore made the payment, but under protest. Eight months later the owners lodged a claim for refund of the 10 per cent excess, with interest. It was held by Mr Justice Mocatta in a careful judgment after review of the authorities here and notably in Australia, that the original contract had been varied by agreement, that the variation had been induced by 'economic duress' and was therefore voidable, but that the variation had in fact been affirmed by the shipping company making the final payment and by delaying for eight months in making any claim for refund. By contrast, in the case of *Atlas Express Ltd* v. *Kafco (Importers and Distributors) Ltd* (1989), the defendants were a small company importing basketware, the plaintiffs were transporters and contracted to carry the goods to the store of a large retailer at a price that proved uneconomic. The plaintiffs demanded an increased rate for the carriage for an 'updated' agreement, which the defendants could not refuse as they could not rearrange carriage urgently and would be liable for non–delivery of this consignment to the retailer. The defendants signed the new agreement, but in fact paid on the calculation of the original contract. The court dismissed the plaintiff's claim for the additional amount as having been obtained by economic duress.

Economic duress is also frequently brought to bear on employers by organised labour, sometimes in pursuance of a trade dispute and sometimes on wider grounds. Such action is by no means limited to the United Kingdom. The question of trade union immunity, furthermore, has been a political football for some time past, and may remain subject to legislative change in the future. The courts have found difficulty in determining the limits of the immunity. A good example is the case of *Universe Tankships Inc of Monrovia* v. *International Transport Workers' Federation* (1982) (the ITF) where the ship, the 'Universe Sentinel', was blacked whilst docked in Milford Haven by port employees on the instructions of the ITF, because of its policy to black ships sailing under flags of convenience and paying low wages. Agreement was reached with the owners that they would pay $80,000 to the ITF, mostly comprising back pay to the crew, and the balance of about $6,000, as a contribution to the ITF seamen's welfare fund. The owners paid up and signed new contracts with the crew incorporating ITF terms and the vessel was released. The owners subsequently sued to recover the monies paid. A compromise was effected as to about $50,000 of the claim and the company was held entitled to recover the $6,000 paid to the welfare fund and $25,000 paid in wages. The ITF appealed and the Court of Appeal, allowing the appeal in part, held that the $6,000 was not recoverable as although there was economic duress, the dispute was a trade dispute and the ITF had immunity. The owners appealed to the House of Lords, as to the $6000 only, and by a majority of 3 to 2 it was held the dispute was not a 'trade dispute' within the meaning of the Trade Union and Labour Relations Act 1974 and so there was no immunity and the money was repayable 'as money had and received' under duress. The difficulties of economic duress in relation to seamen's disputes were further illustrated in *Dimskal Shipping Co. SA* v. *International Transport Workers' Federation, The Evia Luck* (1992).

UNDUE INFLUENCE

A wider concept than duress has been developed by equity and that is the doctrine of undue influence (see *Banco Exterior Internacional SA* v. *Thomas* (1997)). If the parties to a transaction had a confidential relationship to one another at the time of negotiations leading to a contract, then the existence of undue influence will be presumed, and it will be for the party having the influence to disprove that it was used in an improper manner.

A confidential relationship is a wider concept than a fiduciary relationship, but is analogous to it and indeed almost all fiduciary relationships are confidential also, but not all confidential relationships necessarily entail a fiduciary status. Lord Selborne provided us with a useful definition of undue influence over a 100 years ago in *Earl of Aylesford* v. *Morris* (1873). He saw it as 'the unconscientious use by one person of power possessed by him over another in order to induce the other to enter into a contract'. It is enough in this context in equity for one party to dominate the other to such an extent that the other's will is overborne. But where a special or fiduciary relationship does exist then it is not necessary to show that the injured party's will has been overborne, rather that the position of trust has been abused. This may be in a fiduciary sense where a direct financial relationship exists, such as that between trustee and *cestui que trust*, or solicitor and client. Or it may be in a special or confidential sense, where the financial relationship is at best indirect, such as that between doctor and patient, teacher and student or vicar and church member.

A leading case here was that of *Tate* v. *Williamson* (1866). An Oxford undergraduate found himself in debt to about £1,000. He died from alcoholism a year later, but meanwhile had sold his estate to the defendant for £7,000. In fact the estate was worth much more on account of the presence of minerals, but the defendant did not disclose this fact. The executors successfully argued that the contract should be set aside. In such relationships it is up to the defendant to rebut the presumption of undue influence; that is where one party is in a fiduciary or confidential relationship to the other party, the existence of undue influence is *presumed* by the courts, and the onus is upon the party capable of exercising influence to disprove any coercion. There is no such presumption in the case of spouses, nor in the case of a companion, even if a trusted confidant, as seen in *Re Brocklehurst (deceased)* (1978).

In *O'Sullivan* v. *Management Agency Ltd* (1984) the plaintiff sought declarations that an employment contract, a publishing agreement and three recording agreements were void and unenforceable since they were an unreasonable restraint of trade and had been obtained by undue influence. The plaintiff was an unknown singer and songwriter in 1970 and as a result of entering into the arrangements he enjoyed considerable popular success. But by 1976 this success had begun to decline and he was unhappy with the contractual arrangements. In 1979 he commenced proceedings. As there was a fiduciary relationship with the plaintiff it was considered that there was evidence that the defendants had obtained their contracts through undue influence, and, said Lord Justice Dunn, such transactions may be set aside even though it is impossible to place the parties precisely in the position in which they were before, provided that the court can achieve practical justice between the parties by obliging the wrongdoer to give up his profits and advantages, while at the same time compensating him for any work that he has actually performed pursuant to the transaction – in this latter respect the Court of Appeal allowed the appeal in part by the defendants since they had promoted the performances of O'Sullivan and managed his business affairs.

Although there may be practical difficulties, it seems that there is no reason in principle why a confidential relationship should not be capable of existing between an individual plaintiff and an unincorporated association, as illustrated in *Roche* v. *Sherrington* (1982), the Opus Dei case.

Inequality of bargaining power

Where there is no special relationship between the parties, the burden of proof is on the party seeking to set aside the contract or to avoid a claim for specific performance. In the case of *Williams* v. *Bayley* (1866) a son gave the bank promissory notes with his father's signature forged. At a meeting of the father and son with the banker, the latter made it clear that the son would be prosecuted by making remarks such as 'we cannot be parties to compounding a felony', 'this is a serious matter, a case of transportation for life'. In despair the father agreed to grant the bank a mortgage in return for the promissory notes. As a threat of criminal prosecution for which there was sufficient grounds, it was not a case of duress, but the court held the agreement for a mortgage to be invalid, as undue pressure had been used. Of late, it would appear that the House of Lords has disapproved of the extension of the doctrine of the 'inequality of bargaining power', as illustrated in its setting aside the judgment in *National Westminster Bank* v. *Morgan* (1985) which concerned the repossession of a property near Taunton. The Lords held that the bank had not failed to prove it had fulfilled its fiduciary duty: in this instance the bank manager had visited the Morgans' home for about 15 minutes. He spent five minutes talking to Mrs Morgan at one end of a L-shaped room, while Mr Morgan was at the other end. (Mr Morgan was a civil engineer who fell into continual financial difficulties and had mortgaged his home in support of his business ventures.) The House of Lords held that the bank manager had never 'crossed the line' into the area of 'confidentiality' – in the circumstances it had no duty to ensure that she received independent advice; it had to be shown that the transaction was to the 'manifest disadvantage' of the person subjected to the 'dominating influence'. For Lord Scarman restrictions on freedom of contract were a matter for parliamentary legislation rather than judicial proclamation. Undue influence between the spouses will not be actionable if the bank is not put on notice, as seen in the House of Lords' decision in *CIBC Mortgages* v. *Pitt* (1993).

Apart from special relationships equity may also assist where it can be argued that there has been an unconscionable bargain, although such an action must be brought with great care, for notwithstanding the complexities of today's financial world educational standards have risen over the years. An unconscionable bargain means that a party in a position of considerable strength has taken unfair advantage of a poor or ignorant person or one, perhaps, who is weak-minded, especially on account of illness. Certain 'unfair bargains' are also covered by the Fair Trading Act 1973 and the Consumer Credit Act 1974.

In *Alec Lobb (Garages) Ltd* v. *Total Oil Great Britain Ltd* (1985) Lord Justice Dillon said that inequality of bargaining power must be a relative concept. It was seldom that bargaining powers were absolutely equal. The courts would only interfere in exceptional cases where as a matter of common fairness it was not right that the strong should be allowed to push the weak to the wall.

However, it is not in all cases that a person can set aside a bargain on the grounds of economic pressure or a failure to recommend the weaker party to seek independent advice, as was vividly illustrated in the case of *Moore* v. *Duport Furniture Products Ltd* (1982). In that case a deaf and dumb long-term employee of the defendant company which was in financial difficulties and reducing its workforce, was suspended without pay by the company on a spurious allegation of theft; an industrial relations officer from the Advisory Conciliation and Arbitration Service (ACAS) advised the company that to avoid a claim for unfair dismissal, the employee should be persuaded to resign on terms and that the agreement should be recorded by a conciliation officer of ACAS. The employee, who had a wife and young family, having been suspended, not dismissed, had been unable to obtain unemployment benefit for nearly three weeks and was in urgent need of funds, and he finally agreed to resign on payment of £300; the ACAS officer was then called into the room with the employee and employer and, in his changed role of conciliation officer, recorded the agreement. The Industrial Tribunal at Gloucester held, by a majority, that the conciliation officer had not 'taken action' as he was required to do 'to promote a settlement' between the parties, by merely recording this agreement, which was grossly unfair to the employee, and that the employee was not therefore prevented from making a claim of unfair dismissal. The decision was reversed on appeal and the House of Lords unanimously affirmed that the agreement was binding and that the conciliation officer was under no duty to caution the employee, despite his disabilities, to seek independent advice before entering into an improvident bargain, or indeed to give the employee any advice, Lord Russell stating that such a suggestion was 'absurd'.

If agreements are reached in litigation proceedings and embodied in a court order, they may be set aside if undue influence in obtaining the agreement can be shown. However, in the case of *Tommey* v. *Tommey* (1982) it was held that in divorce proceedings undue influence is not a ground for impeachment of consent orders, as the balance of advantage lies in encouraging finality in matrimonial proceedings, although such orders may be set aside on the grounds of fraud or mistake, or even material non-disclosure (*Robinson* v. *Robinson* (1982)). The doctrine of inequality of bargaining power (a harsh and unconscionable bargain) was acknowledged to exist, by the Court of Appeal, but only in very exceptional circumstances, in *Barclays Bank plc* v. *Schwartz* (1995).

The presumption of undue influence

It will be appreciated that contracts may be set aside and so are voidable, not void *ab initio*, on the grounds of undue influence. The equitable remedy of rescission, however, will not be granted if there has been affirmation, as in the case of duress, and further there must be no delay in bringing a claim once the party subjected to the pressure has been freed from its effects, as seen in *Allcard* v. *Skinner* (1887). Miss Allcard had entered a Protestant closed order and under the influence of her spiritual adviser, the confessor to the sisters, she gave substantial sums to the defendant. Six years after leaving the institution, Miss Allcard claimed to recover the money that had not been spent. Although the court held that, of all the special relationships raising a presumption of undue influence, that of religious adviser is the most dangerous and powerful, and that in principle the gifts could have been recoverable, the claim was nevertheless barred for 'laches' or delay in claiming her rights. In the similar case of *Morley* v. *Loughnan* (1893), however, where a wealthy man who suffered from epilepsy had a travelling companion, a member of the 'exclusive brethren', who acquired a substantial sum, £140,000, over a period of years having come to dominate the wealthy man's way of life, it was held that the money had been obtained by undue influence and must be refunded; there had been no delay in bringing the claim, as there had been continuing influence and the claim was lodged within six months of the donor's death. The question of undue influence was further illustrated in *Halifax Mortgage Services Ltd* v. *Stepsky* (1995).

In many cases the giving of substantial testamentary gifts to persons not related are the subject of claims of undue influence. Except in those cases where a presumption can be shown, the courts require the party seeking to set aside the gift to prove strictly the existence of the improper pressure. In the case of *Re Brocklehurst* (1978), where an eccentric, but strong-willed and wealthy landowner gave valuable gifts, substantially depreciating the value of the estate, to a person of inferior social status, having no call on his generosity, Lord Denning postulated a wider doctrine, that the courts would set aside such gifts, even where undue influence had not been proved, where a person's judgment had been impaired 'by reason of age or ignorance, eccentricity or infirmity, or even by a failure to know or appreciate the consequences . . . [if] the transaction is so exceptional and so unreasonable that it cannot stand'. The majority of the Court of Appeal would not accept such an extension of the doctrine, which Lord Denning likened to the courts' attitude to exemption clauses.

While Lord Denning may have attempted too great an extension, the need for some greater latitude for the courts lies in the great difficulty in proving strictly undue influence, particularly in the case of wealthy deceased testators, and in the cost of the necessarily lengthy hearings in such cases. If undue influence is pleaded, the unsuccessful relatives or other persons who are probably trying to establish a will executed when the deceased was less eccentric, will have to bear the enormous costs of several weeks hearing in the Chancery Divison, with probably expensive medical and psychiatric expert witnesses. If the validity of the eccentric will can be impugned on other grounds without an allegation of undue influence, the costs will at least normally be paid out of the estate of the deceased.

In general it may be said that this is still a developing area of the law. The authorities were reviewed in the case of *Midland Bank* v. *Shephard* (1988), when the Court of Appeal explained that the following four propositions appear to have been established: the relationship of husband and wife by itself does not give rise to any presumption; even if a relationship gives rise to a presumption, the party seeking to set aside the agreement must show 'manifest disadvantage', a point emphasised in *Bank of Credit and Commerce International SA* v. *Aboody* (1992). The court must examine all the facts to see if undue influence can be presumed and if so the extent of the disadvantage; in creditor actions, the court should check whether the creditor had entrusted the obtaining of consent to a person capable of exercising undue influence or of making fraudulent misrepresentations. It is not, however, necessary to show that the adviser has attained a *dominating* influence over the other person, it is sufficient if the person influenced had made 'a gift so large, or entered into a transaction so improvident as not to be accounted for on the basis of friendship, charity or the ordinary motives on which men acted', it was held by the Court of Appeal in *Goldsworthy* v. *Brickell* (1987).

In *Barclays Bank* v. *O'Brien* (1993), the husband wanted to increase the banking facility for his company and offered a personal guarantee which the bank required to be secured by a second charge on the matrimonial home. Mrs O'Brien signed the charge without taking separate advice, believing that it was limited to £60,000 whereas it was for £135,000. In the Court of Appeal Lord Justice Scott thought that protection should be extended to wives giving security for husbands' debts, or for instance elderly parents for adult children, where 'pressure' could be brought to bear, and the court held that the charge should be limited to £60,000 only. The decision does seem to accord with the judgment of Lord Selborne in *Earl of Aylesford* v. *Morris* (1873) referred to at the outset of this discussion of undue influence.

8.7

Privity, assignment
and agency

Privity

The general rule in English common law, although it should be said that it is not a rule that has found universal favour in the Commonwealth, is that only the parties to a contract can impose obligations upon each other, and conversely enjoy the benefits of their agreement. A. and B. cannot impose liabilities upon C., nor can C. derive a benefit from a contract between A. and B. There are exceptions to this rule, of course, which is known as the doctrine of privity of contract – there shall be no third party rights, no *jus quaesitum tertio*.

In *Darlington Borough Council* v. *Wiltshier Northern Ltd* (1994) the Court of Appeal said that a third party to a building contract, where it was the parties' expressed intention that the contract was for the benefit of the third party (who was assigned the contracting party's rights against the building contractor), was able to sue the building contractor for substantial damages for defects in the building work.

Logically, it is less easy to see why C. should not benefit from a contract made between A. and B. than to understand why C. should not have obligations imposed upon him by others. Moreover, the law does recognise unilateral contracts, that is where one party promises another, say, a sum of money if he undertakes or forbears to do some act. That other party, however, does not give a binding undertaking that he will do so; if he did the agreement would become the more usual bilateral contract. In other words A. makes B. an open-ended (but not gratuitous) promise, for example, where A. offers £100 to B. should he find his lost dog while he is out walking. Similarly, the law does recognise collateral contracts where there is a clearly established third party relationship and the principal contract is in effect dependent upon a secondary one. This was seen in *Shanklin Pier* v. *Detel Products Ltd* (1951), where the plaintiffs employed contractors to paint their pier in the Isle of Wight. The contractors were instructed to use the defendants' paint, which the defendants had assured the plaintiffs would be suitable for the purpose. In fact the paint lasted for three months instead of seven years and the plaintiffs successfully sued the defendants.

In the case of *Dunlop Pneumatic Tyre Co. Ltd* v. *Selfridge & Co. Ltd* (1915) Lord Haldane commented: 'In the law of England certain principles are fundamental. One is that only a person who is a party to a contract can sue on it. Our law knows nothing of a *jus quaesitum tertio* arising by way of contract.' But that remark was made some 70 years ago. Since then fundamental inroads into the doctrine have been made. In the first place, as previously mentioned, the Law Revision Committee in 1937 recommended its abolition. Then more recently the courts have sought to circumvent it in a variety of ways. For example, in *Jackson* v. *Horizon Holidays Ltd* (1975) Lord Denning appeared to suggest that a family as a whole had certain rights in so far as he regarded the £500 damages awarded by the trial judge to the plaintiff on account of the distress caused to him by a holiday that failed to meet the promised standards as excessive; but the court upheld the amount since the plaintiff's wife and children had also suffered. But in *Watts* v. *Morrow* (1991) where a second home that was purchased turned out to have major structural flaws, the trial judge awarded £1,500 for distress and inconvenience arising out of physical discomfort (eg from dust and repairs) and disappointment; the Court of Appeal could not agree with the latter and so halved the amount to £750. In *Beswick* v. *Beswick* (1968) Lord Denning was intent upon regarding the doctrine merely as a procedural rule. This case involved the transfer of a coal business from uncle to nephew. The nephew promised in return that he would pay £5 a week to the uncle's wife, upon the uncle's death. The nephew failed to fulfil his bargain. The widow brought an action against him and claimed specific performance. She was successful since the Lords held that she was the personal representative of the promisee, that is administratrix of her husband's estate.

More importantly, perhaps, is that in recent times the courts have had increasing doubts about the usefulness of the privity rule.

> **Clarion calls for law reform are not part of the everyday repertoire of the sound of forensic music made by the Law Lords. In *Woodar Investment Development* v. *Wimpey Construction UK* (1980), Lord Scarman sounded such a call. . . . He said: 'Certainly the crude proposition for which Wimpey contends, namely that the state of English law is such that neither C. for whom the benefit was intended nor A. who contracted for it can recover it if the contract is terminated by B.'s refusal to perform, calls for review, and now, not forty years on'**

was the comment of the *Financial Times* in 1980. The Law Commission took note some 12 years later and issued a Consultation Paper in early 1992 with the provisional recommendation that legislation should be enacted to enable third parties to enforce contractual provisions made in their favour which the parties to the contract intended to be enforceable by the third parties. In addition, the distinctions between tort and contract in this as in other areas are fading. The doctrine of privity may well be overcome by suing in negligence, providing a duty of care can be established. This was illustrated in *Ross* v. *Caunters* (1980), where a solicitor negligently allowed a will to be wrongly attested, and in the *Junior Books* case, involving defective flooring, which was discussed in the previous chapter. An interesting example has arisen in the case of *Law Debenture Trust Corporation plc* v. *Ural Caspian Oil Corporation Ltd* (1993). In 1917 following the Bolshevik revolution in Russia, the assets of the first four defendant companies, registered in England and carrying on business in Russia, were confiscated and the Bolsheviks refused claims for compensation. The plaintiff company acquired all the shares of the four companies but covenanted not to dispose of the shares without the transferee entering into similar covenants. In breach of the covenant the plaintiffs sold the shares to the fifth defendant who sold to the sixth, also without imposing the covenant. Due to improved relations with Russia in 1986 and 1990 some £13 million was paid to the companies in compensation but nothing was paid to the plaintiffs who started proceedings in contract and in tort. On a preliminary issue the claims in contract were struck out by Mr Justice Hoffmann in the Chancery Division, who held that the equitable principle that a party acquiring property with knowledge of a contractual covenant binding a predecessor could not use that property in a manner inconsistent with the covenant, did not provide a cause of action as there was no direct contract, but could only give rise to a negative injunction to prevent acts inconsistent with the covenant; on the facts the sixth defendant had acted in a manner which could lead to a claim in tort for procuring the violation of a right in contract, which had been established in *Lumley* v. *Gye* (1853) as grounding a cause of action.

Similarly, third parties do acquire rights and obligations under consumer law, in respect of retail prices (Resale Prices Act 1976), the provision of financial credit (Consumer Credit Act 1974) and, particularly now, under the Consumer Protection Act 1987.

Other exceptions are:

1 By s.56 of the Law of Property Act 1925, a person may take an interest in land or other property, or the benefit of any condition, covenant or agreement, although not named as a party to the conveyance or other instrument.

2 Insurance contracts are frequently made for the benefit of third parties. 'Third party risk' is now part of common parlance in respect of motoring, but it owes its statutory authority to the Road Traffic Act 1930 (now 1988)'. The Married Women's Property Act 1882 allows a husband to insure his life for the benefit of his wife and children. A wife may effect a similar contract under the Act.

3 Charterparties or maritime contracts modify the rule too, particularly in respect of exemption clauses and interference with contractual rights. Such matters have involved a series of complex and by no means clear-cut legal decisions: *Elder Dempster & Co.* v. *Paterson Zochinis & Co.* (1924), *Scruttons Ltd* v. *Midland Silicones Ltd* (1962), *Lord Strathcona SS Co.* v. *Dominion Coal Co.* (1926) and *Port Line Ltd* v. *Ben Line Steamers Ltd* (1958).

4 It can be argued that certain banking practices, particularly in an international context, have undermined the doctrine of privity. Bills of exchange are a statutory exception as, if a bill of exchange is dishonoured, the drawer, acceptor and indorsers are all liable to the holder in due course, under the Bills of Exchange Act 1882.

5 Equity has provided an exception in its concept of contractual trust, that is where one party holds property on behalf of another for a third party's benefit. This rule owes its origins to the case of *Tomlinson* v. *Gill* (1756) where the defendant promised a widow that he would pay her husband's debts, providing that he jointly administered her estate. Thus the creditors, it was held, could enforce the obligation or promise of the defendant. The principle was approved

by the Lords in *Les Affréteurs Réunis SA* v. *Leopold Walford (London) Ltd* (1919), a case of a promise to pay commission.

ASSIGNMENT

Assignment of 'choses in action' takes place when liabilities imposed or rights acquired under a contract between two parties are transferred to a third person, who was not a party to the original contract. Such an assignment may be made by the act of one of the parties; if A. sells goods worth £100 to B., and then assigns his right to the money to C., that is assignment of his chose in action, his right to sue at law for the money. Alternatively, the assignment may take effect by operation of law, for instance when one party dies or becomes bankrupt, his executor or trustee will succeed to his rights. As a general rule, the promisor cannot transfer his liability under a contract, without the consent of the other party to the contract. So, for instance, the tenant of property cannot normally assign his liabilities under a tenancy or lease, without the consent of the landlord; whereas the landlord may assign his rights to a third party without any consent of the tenant. Similarly, a creditor under an agreement may transfer his rights to sue the promisor or debtor to a third party, but is not normally bound to accept the debt or liability of a stranger, the assignee of the promisor. However, there are two exceptions to this general rule:

1 *Vicarious performance.* In certain instances it does not particularly matter who performs the work, as long as the degree of competence with which the task is completed is comparable. So, for instance in the case of *British Waggon Co.* v. *Lea* (1880) Chief Justice Cockburn declared that where personal performance is 'of the essence of the contract [it] cannot in its absence be enforced against an unwilling party'. But, he continued, 'much work is contracted for, which it is known can only be executed by means of sub-contracts [and] in these cases the maxim *qui facit per alium facit per se* applies'. The Court held that another wagon company, the original contractors with the defendant, could validly assign their rights; the repairs involved under the hire did not require specialist skills. However, the contracting party remains responsible for any breach of the contract, even if others have done the work. It is not therefore an instance of 'assignment' in the strict sense.

2 *Novation.* Again this is not strictly assignment. It is a contract between creditor, debtor and a third party that the debt shall be transferred to that third party. It is thus the substitution of a new contract for the old one, now rescinded.

Whilst common law courts did not recognise assignments of choses in action initially, exceptions had to be made for negotiable instruments at an early stage. Also the courts recognised assignments by and to the Crown, and also assignments under powers of attorney granted by an assignor. These exceptions were not sufficient, however, and equity and the legislature provided equitable and statutory rules governing assignments of contractual rights, in respect of both legal and equitable choses.

A legal chose was one which before 1875 could be actionable in a court of common law, and an equitable one in the Court of Chancery. Legal choses include a debt, a benefit or right in contract and an insurance policy. Equitable choses include interests in trust funds and wills. The distinction is less important since the fusion of common law and equity, although there remain certain procedural implications. Statute has provided for assignment in certain instances and particularly in the Law of Property Act 1925. Section 56 provides that a person may take an interest in land or other property, or the *benefit* of any condition, covenant or agreement respecting land or other property, although not named as a party to the conveyance or instrument. Further, whilst common law had treated rights and liabilities under contracts as unassignable under the doctrine of privity, equity had in many instances recognised even informal assignments, provided that there was consideration, or if assigned by way of gift then that the gift had been 'perfected', that is completed. By s.136 of the 1925 Act, which substantially re-enacted s.25 of the Supreme Court of Judicature Act 1873, it was provided that a legal or equitable chose can be assigned, without proof of consideration and the assignee can sue in his own name, provided that the assignor has given an absolute assignment 'of any debt or other legal thing in action' in writing, signed by the assignor, and notice of such has been given in writing to the debtor, trustee or other person concerned. 'Absolute' and 'not purporting to be by way of charge only' in the Act means that assignment must be unconditional as seen in *Durham Bros* v. *Robertson* (1898).

The phrase 'other legal thing in action' is not the most comfortable in terms of interpretation, but by and large it means a right which equity and the common law would recognise as an assignable chose in action. The question then arises as to whether an assignment can be enforced where the statutory provisions of s.136 have not been complied with, namely it was not absolute, or not in writing or not signed. The answer is that equity will recognise even an informal assignment, but if it was not absolute, then the assignor must be joined in the action and consideration must be proved. If it was an absolute assignment, consideration is not required but if it was a legal chose, the assignor must be joined; but that is not necessary for an equitable chose, which it will be recalled is an interest in a trust fund, or under a will or a similar interest.

In the case of a statutory assignment it is a requirement that a written notice is given to the debtor; it is desirable to give notice moreover for equitable assignments, firstly to bind the debtor (who may otherwise make payment to the assignor) and also to preserve the assignee's priority as against other creditors because of the rule in *Dearle* v. *Hall* (1823), that the priority of the creditors is not governed by the date of the assignment but by the date that the debtor receives notice of an assignment. In that case, A. assigned his interest in a trust fund to B., who then assigned it to C. who gave notice to the trustee before B. B. claimed that he was entitled to be paid in priority to C. as his equitable interest had been created first, but the court held that C. had priority, because the act of giving notice was going as far as was possible towards taking possession of the fund and the trustee had become a trustee for C.

Another point is that, irrespective of whether the assignment is of a legal or equitable chose, the assignee takes the matter 'subject to equities', that is subject to whatever claims there may be as against the assignor. He must take no more than the assignor may have taken, nor indeed be less liable than the assignor. The debtor's position must be protected, even if the assignee was not fully aware of the facts when the assignment took place. Any claim by the debtor must, however, arise out of the contract itself, as illustrated in *Stoddart* v. *Union Trust Ltd* (1912), which involved a fraudulent business transaction and where the right to rescind was apparently not relied upon by the defendants.

Finally, it should be re-emphasised that contracts providing for special knowledge or skills or other personal features, are not assignable either at law or in equity, and cannot be transferred by way of vicarious performance. So the house painter's contract can be vicariously performed by his assistant or sub-contractor, but not the contract with the portrait artist to portray a distinguished personage; the concert pianist's or other soloist's contract cannot be carried out by another, without the consent of the impressario, but that cannot apply to all the members of an orchestra. In general, it is an exceptional personal qualification, a star personality's attributes, that cannot be replaced, except by novation.

Negotiable instruments

As far as negotiable instruments are concerned, which were mentioned earlier on under this sub-section, the most recognisable form in everyday use is that of the cheque. Negotiable instruments are a particular form of chose in action which are transferable by one person to another, without notice in writing. So a cheque promises to pay a certain amount to the bearer, although if it is payable in respect of a named person (made to order) then the cheque can only be transferred if the person to whom it is payable endorses it by signing in the same form on the reverse of the cheque. The rule 'subject to equities' does not apply here. A bill of exchange, of which a cheque is a variation, is an order in writing from one to another. There are no conditions and the order can be in favour of the party issuing the order (the drawer) or a third party. The cheque is drawn on a banker (the drawee) payable on demand. A bill of exchange may be payable on demand or at a future date. A promissory note is an unconditional promise in writing that a person will be paid a sum of money, again either on demand or at a future date, and either to a named person or to the bearer. A £5 note is an example of a promissory note. Negotiable instruments are governed by the Bills of Exchange Act 1882, although the form and types of such instruments are perfectly capable of changing from time to time. Section 81 of the 1882 Act has been amended by the Cheques Act 1992: where a cheque is crossed and bears the phrase 'account payee' or 'a/c payee', with or without the word 'only', then that cheque is not transferable, but only valid between the parties named.

Parallel to negotiable instruments are bills of lading which concern the loading of goods on to ships, and nowadays aircraft and other forms of transport. A bill of lading is a record of the cargo and copies are kept by the master of the ship or the shipping agents, by the consignees, the person who will receive the goods, and the consignor, the person who despatches them. But the nature of assignment and endorsement has differed from negotiable instruments, since here an endorsement under the Bills of Lading Act 1855 conferred a remedy *in rem*, that is an action to claim particular goods, whereas a negotiable instrument is restricted to a remedy *in personam*, that is a particular person is entitled to certain money. Section 1 of the Act provided that not only the right to the goods, but also all rights and liabilities passed with the goods to the consignee or any endorsee 'as if the contract had been made with the holder of the bill'. The Carriage of Goods by Sea Act 1992 has replaced the 1855 Act and has tackled the problem of s.1 by breaking the link between the transfer of contractual rights and the transfer of property. The 1855 Act applied only to bills of lading. The new Act applies to bills of lading, sea waybills and some delivery orders. But it does not fully define a bill of lading.

AGENCY

An agent is a person, who has the authority to create legal relations, on behalf of his principal, with a third party. The principal (P.) agrees with the agent (A.) that A. may contract with B. on behalf of P. *Henderson* v. *Merrett Syndicates Ltd* (1994) underlined the close relationship between contract and tort in respect of the principal/agent relationship. Lord Goff observed: 'there is no sound basis for a rule which automatically restricts the claimant to either a tortious or a contractual remedy'.

The agency may be formed in a number of ways; by express arrangement, by apparent authority, by ratification, presumption, necessity or estoppel, or by operation of law. The usual position is that the agent is appointed by, and has express authority of the principal to enter into legal relations and to commit his principal to a contractual agreement. In general, a principal can authorise his agent to do anything which he is competent to do himself. The agent may normally be appointed quite informally, but if he is to execute a deed, for the purchase or sale of property, for instance, then he must be appointed by deed. Formerly, the deeds set out *in extenso* the powers and limitations of the agent, but the Powers of Attorney Act 1971 provided, by s.10, for a simple and short form of general power. In most cases, however, the agent may be appointed informally, even where the agent is to enter into a contract which might be in writing, as opposed to under seal; 'the authority of the agent may be by parol, though the agreement must be in writing' (*Mortlock* v. *Buller* (1804)).

Implied, ostensible and usual authority

In many cases, as an agent can be appointed informally, his authority can be implied from the agent's position or conduct or previous behaviour. It should be noted that, whilst an employee of the principal may be his agent, an agent as such is not a servant and, whilst bound to exercise his authority in accordance with his instructions, the agent is not subject to the direct control or supervision of the principal. This places a greater burden on the agent than a servant, in exercising his own judgment on behalf of his principal and yet not exceeding his authority. In the case of *Spiers* v. *Taylor* (1984), estate agents instructed by the principal agreed with a purchaser's agents for the sale of property at a lower price than the principal had instructed; the vendor and purchaser reached a compromise by splitting the difference and the sale was concluded. The agents claimed their commission on the sale, but the Court of Appeal held that they had failed to fulfil their agreement and that no commission was payable. Ostensible or apparent authority usually means A. believes he has P.'s actual authority, expressly or impliedly. A. may, however, be unable to contact P. to discuss the issue, but it nonetheless appears to him that he is acting within the general framework of P.'s authority. Thus where an organisation (here a trading bank in respect of a contract for the sale of 10,000 tonnes of Romanian cement) grants a manager (here a documentary credits manager) authority to handle a particular client's affairs, but gives no authority to sign alone on its behalf, it is nevertheless bound by his sole signature on an undertaking if the totality of its conduct led the client to understand that he had authority to sign alone, the Court of Appeal held in *Ebeed* v. *Soplex Wholesale Supplies Ltd* (1984).

Ostensible authority is a difficult concept and is, in effect, a variation of the estoppel principle. However, in order for C. to sue P., C. must not know or realise that A. had no real authority derived from P. Equally, C.'s right to sue will be vitiated where he did not avail himself of a clear opportunity of discovering that A. was not in fact P.'s agent. The circumstances in which ostensible authority may occur is where A. does have actual authority from P. but the contract concluded with C. appears to travel beyond the original brief. Such a problem will frequently occur in respect of commercial partners (Partnership Act 1890) and sub-contractors. On the other hand it may well be more appropriate for C. to sue A. in an independent capacity, particularly where P. unequivocally disowns the contract. And C. will not be able to sue P. where A. effected the contract through fraud, by, say, forging P.'s signature, the deceit being one of which P. had no knowledge. In *First Energy (UK) Ltd* v. *Hungarian International Bank Ltd* (1993) it was held that an agent who had no apparent authority to conclude a transaction might nevertheless have ostensible authority to make representations of fact concerning it, such as the fact that his principal had given the necessary approval for it.

A variation of ostensible authority is what is sometimes called 'usual authority'. This means an authority which is incidental to the business or operations of the principal; it occurs, in other words, mainly in commercial transactions. The leading but controversial case is that of *Watteau* v. *Fenwick* (1893). Here the owners of a pub, a brewery firm, were sued by the plaintiff for the unauthorised purchase of cigars. The defendants had bought the pub from H. whom they continued to employ as manager. He was instructed not to buy cigars on credit, which he did. The plaintiff thought H. to be the owner of the pub, but upon discovering the true facts sued the firm for the price of the cigars which H. had purchased in his own name. The defendants were held liable. Mr Justice Wills said: 'The principal is liable for all the acts of the agent which are within the authority usually confided to an agent of that character, notwithstanding limitations, as between the principal and the agent, put upon that authority'. In *Armagas Ltd* v. *Mundogas SA* (1986), a complex shipping case involving bribery and deceit, where the defendants unwittingly found themselves unable to meet a three year charter, the House of Lords, *per* Lord Keith of Kintel, observed that the essential feature for creating liability in the employer is that the party contracting with the fraudulent servant should have altered his position to his detriment in reliance on the belief that the servant's activities were part of his job.

Necessity and ratification

The law recognises that in crisis situations A. may act on behalf of P. and contract with C., but without P.'s permission. The courts are reluctant, though, to recognise the doctrine as operating within too many areas. A good example is salvage, as where a ship goes to the rescue of another in distress. Masters of ships also have the power to undertake reasonable actions in order to keep the ship and its voyage intact. The doctrine has a certain application in bailment, but this has been very limited since the passage of the Torts (Interference with Goods) Act 1977. Similarly, a deserted wife before the Matrimonial Proceedings and Property Act 1970 could enter into contracts for necessaries, such as food and clothing. However, where a married woman is still co-habiting with her husband then she has implied authority to order goods and services necessary for the maintenance of the household, although the husband may warn either his wife or the supplier that such goods or services should not be ordered or supplied, in which case implied authority is no longer presumed.

Unlike necessity where there is an element of urgency, ratification is frequently a matter of correcting the omission to obtain authority. Where the action of the agent is ratified, then it is the equivalent of prior authorisation and relates back to the time of the ostensibly unauthorised act or agreement. It was held in the Court of Appeal in *Bolton Partners* v. *Lambert* (1889), which involved the purchase of a sugar works, that the contract had been ratified even where the third party had given notice of repudiation. The decision has been criticised but it has not yet been overruled. However, there can be no ratification where other parties have acquired rights before ratification. Further, the agent must have purported to be acting as an agent, of an unnamed but identifiable principal, and so in *Brook* v. *Hook* (1871), where the agent had forged his principal's signature, there could be no ratification.

Types of agent

A factor has authority to sell goods with a discretion to raise the best possible price; the factor's powers are covered by the Factors Act 1889. An estate agent, however, is not really an agent at all. The main task is to sell property by way of introducing clients or prospective purchasers to the vendor. Estate agents may legitimately owe duties to numerous principals, many of whom would be in conflict with each other, but there should be no conflicts of interest, the House of Lords said in *Kelly* v. *Cooper* (1992).

The estate agent cannot effect a contract, unless directed to do so of course, which is unusual. On the other hand a well-known type of agency is that of the auctioneer, who acts as the agent for the vendor of the property. An insurance agent is the agent of a company with the object to persuade a third party to agree an insurance contract. An insurance broker acts as the agent of the person to be insured rather than of the company or underwriters. A barrister is not the agent of the solicitor, although a counsel's opinion should be sought usually via a solicitor. The solicitor may act as the client's agent, but a barrister is unlikely to be an agent of that client, except in respect of paperwork prior to trial.

Effects of agency

There is a three-way effect: between principal and agent; agent and third party; and third party and principal.

(i) Principal and agent
The agent must perform the task with the diligence and skill which would be commonly expected of members of his class of agents. This is particularly important where the agent performs the task for a remuneration or commission, compared with gratuitous action or a unilateral contract. The court will probably only recognise a right to remuneration or commission where there is reasonable certainty of terms in the contract between P. and A. (*Jaques* v. *Lloyd D George & Partners* (1968)). However, if A. as agent fails in his task, the principal may sue for damages for breach.

Moreover, since there is a fiduciary relationship between principal and agent, the latter must at all times act responsibly. Thus any profits from the transaction, over and above remuneration or commission, must be paid to the principal. Nor must he accept a bribe from the third party; in such a case the principal may also rescind the contract A. has effected between C. and P. And if P. does not claim the bribe he may, but only as an alternative, claim damages from the agent and the third party, jointly and severally, as illustrated in *T Mahesan s/o Thambiah* v. *Malaysia Government Officers' Co-operative Housing Society Ltd* (1978).

Also, an agent, as a general rule, should not appoint a sub-agent, unless expressly or impliedly authorised to do so. Even then no contract will exist between the sub-agent and the principal unless specifically provided for, although the sub-agent may be liable to the principal in tort or for breach of a fiduciary duty or 'constructive fraud' in equity.

(ii) Principal and third party
As indicated above a principal is liable to the third party for all the acts of the agent, providing those acts fall within the agent's actual or ostensible authority. Thus, by and large a principal is liable, in respect of the agent, for deceit and negligent misstatement; of course, the principal is also liable where he himself is the wrongdoer rather than his agent. Equally, as a general rule, where an agent disappears or becomes bankrupt, the principal's debt to the third party, or vice

versa, is not discharged, although if an agent has a clear authority to accept payment from the third party, then the third party's liability is so discharged.

(iii) Agent and third party
As the agent is merely the 'go-between', he normally has no rights or duties in relation to the third party. But there are exceptions.

1 The agreement between the principal and agent may provide that they will be jointly liable or the agent liable in certain respects only.

2 Where the principal is in fact non-existent, the agent will probably be liable at common law, and a similar statutory provision exists by virtue of the European Communities Act 1972 s.9(2), in respect of an unformed company.

3 The agent is liable for his own deceit or negligent misstatement. He may not, however, be liable if, acting within his express or ostensible authority he nevertheless makes an untrue statement without having reasonable grounds to believe it was true, as s.2(1) of the Misrepresentation Act 1967 applies to representations made between parties to a contract and not representations made on behalf of a party, it was held in *Resolute Maritime Inc* v. *Nippon Kaiji Kyokai (The Skopas)* (1983).

4 An agent may be liable personally on certain occasions where the name of the principal is undisclosed.

5 In respect of a contract under seal an agent who executes the deed in his own name is personally liable. It is possible that the Powers of Attorney Act 1971 has altered this rule.

The common law rules of the principal/agent relationship were further illustrated in the House of Lords' decision in *Boyter* v. *Thomson* (1995) and the Court of Appeal cases of *PCW Syndicates* v. *PCW Reinsurers* (1995) and *McCullagh* v. *Lane Fox and Partners Ltd* (1995). In the latter case it was held that an estate agent acting for the seller owed no duty of care to a purchaser in respect of negligent misstatement; a disclaimer negatived the effects of the proximity test under *Hedley Byrne*, notwithstanding the provisions of the Unfair Contract Terms Act 1977.

Termination of agency

Agency may be terminated by mutual agreement of the principal and agent, or, subject to any contrary provision in the agency agreement, by notice of revocation of either to the other. If the agency is formal, and is to secure an interest to the donee it will be irrevocable so long as the donee has the interest undischarged (Powers of Attorney Act 1971 (s.4) which codified the position at common law). The agency may also be terminated by the operation of law, where its continuance would be illegal. So, if that agent becomes an enemy alien, if war is declared between the principal's and agent's countries, the agency is terminated automatically. Similarly, the agency terminates if the principal's authority is deemed to have been withdrawn by reason of insanity of the principal. This proved to be a major disadvantage particularly of the simplified general power of attorney introduced by the Powers of Attorney Act 1971.

It is frequently convenient for an elderly person to entrust the management of his financial affairs to a close relative or friend, but owing to the doctrine that the principal can only authorise acts which he is competent to perform himself, at the very moment that the relative is most needed his authority in fact lapsed if the elderly person was deemed to be incapable of dealing with him, or frequently her, affairs. The Enduring Powers of Attorney Act 1985 provides, by s.1, that an enduring power is not revoked by the subsequent mental incapacity of the donor, and s.2 provides that the enduring power must be in a form prescribed by statutory instrument, which requires the execution by deed not only of the principal, the donor of the power, but also of the donee. Further requirements, for registration, are continued in s.4 and Schedule 1 to the Act.

Death of the agent automatically terminates his authority, which does not therefore pass to the agent's personal representative unless there is specific provision to the contrary. Death of the principal terminates the agent's authority only when knowledge of the death reaches the agent.

Bankruptcy of the principal terminates the agent's authority immediately. Bankruptcy of the agent will normally have the same effect, but the principal may ratify the agent's actions. The importance of bankruptcy to fiduciary relationships between principal and agent and bailor and bailee can be seen in the *Romalpa* case. In *Aluminium Industrie Vaasen* v. *Romalpa Aluminium Ltd* (1976) the defendant company went into liquidation and the plaintiffs were allowed a charge in respect of the debt owed to them of some £122,000 over some £35,000, being the proceeds of resold aluminium foil that the plaintiffs had originally supplied to the defendants. This case has given its name to 'Romalpa clauses', in commercial transactions, where sellers include clauses to retain the property in goods after delivery until payment in full has been completed, which is difficult where goods are intermixed, processed, manufactured or sold on to other parties, or where receivers, trustees in bankruptcy or liquidators have been appointed. In *Four Point Garage Ltd* v. *Carter* (1985) the High Court held that where a purchaser, acting in good faith, purchased goods from a buyer of those goods which were supplied subject to a 'Romalpa' clause, the purchaser established legal title to the goods since the clause did not prevent the buyer being entitled to resell the goods. The defendant, who wanted to purchase a new car, contacted Freeway (Cougar) Ltd, and the defendant paid them the sale price. Freeway arranged with the plaintiffs the purchase and delivery of the car, but the defendant was unaware of the plaintiffs' existence and the plaintiffs believed Freeway were not retailers but engaged in the hiring and leasing of cars. Freeway shortly afterwards went into liquidation. The 'Romalpa' clause here was insufficient as between commercial garages to preclude the implication of the buyer garage being entitled to resell if that was its ordinary course of business and being unaware that the seller garage believed otherwise.

But in the 'Romalpa clause' case of *Re Peachdart Ltd* (1983) it was held that when leather was appropriated to the manufacture of a handbag and the company began work on it, the leather ceased to be the exclusive property of the sellers. They did have a charge on the handbag, but the charge had not been registered and was void, although the conditions of sale between the seller and Peachdart had stated that a fiduciary relationship existed between the parties.

When the property had passed to sub-buyers the Romalpa chain was broken, it was seen in *Hendy Lennox (Industrial Engines) Ltd* v. *Grahame Puttick Ltd* (1984) where the sellers supplied diesel engines to buyers, who subsequently went into receivership, and the buyers incorporated them into a diesel generating set which were sold to sub-buyers.

8.8   Contractual Consequences

PERFORMANCE

The party to a contract who performs his side of the bargain is discharged from further responsibilities. However, the manner in which the party performs that part of the agreement must be precise. While the courts will allow minor deviations from contractual obligations, for the law does not concern itself with trifling matters, *de minimis non curat lex*, they will not look favourably upon other variations. Indeed such variations may mean that the innocent party can sue for breach of contract, or regard himself as thereby discharged from performance. Thus a contract was judged as not being adequately performed where packing cases which should each have contained 30 tins of canned fruit for the most part contained only 24 (*Re Moore and Co. and Landauer and Co.* (1921)).

Moreover, two 'wrongs' do not make a right. Thus where one party has only partly performed his part of the contract, he cannot sue for apparently incomplete performance by the other party. In the old case of *Cutter* v. *Powell* (1795) a seaman was employed as a mate for a journey from Jamaica to Liverpool, but he died on the way. His widow failed in her action to claim a proportion of his wages since her husband had not completed his contract for which he was to have been paid a lump sum. Today a different result would have been achieved on account of the Law Reform (Frustrated Contracts) Act 1943, quite apart from the improved terms of service for seamen nowadays (Merchant Shipping Act 1995). The Court of Appeal decided in *Howard* v. *Shirlstar Container Transport Ltd* (1990) that whilst the laws of Nigeria may have been broken in flying an aircraft out to the Ivory Coast, the plaintiff had performed his part of the contract and was escaping from danger and could recover the fee due under the contract.

On the other hand where in effect the terms of a contract are varied and one party accepts partial performance by the other, then that other party may bring an action for breach, if, for example, he is not paid. Essentially the party will be paid on a *quantum meruit* basis, that is a reasonable sum for the work completed. But acceptance of partial performance cannot be forced upon a reluctant party. So, in *Sumpter* v. *Hedges* (1898) where the plaintiff had failed to complete a building contract, he was unable to recover for the work done since the defendant had had to finish the job himself, although it was held reasonable for him to be able to recover for the value of the materials he had left on site which the defendant had used.

The rule of common law, that the party who has only partially performed the contract recovers nothing, neither under the contract, because it has not been performed, nor on a *quantum meruit*, because the implied promise to pay for part of the contract would be inconsistent with the express terms of the contract, can operate harshly, particularly in building and commercial contracts.

In building contracts, it is customary for an architect to be appointed who will act independently and to some extent as an arbitrator. The contract will frequently be in one of the standard forms prescribed by the Royal Institute of British Architects, which includes provision for regular payments to be made on the certificate of the architect that the work has been substantially completed to each stage.

In the construction of most domestic homes, the builders are registered with the National House Building Council, which provides the buyer with a certificate, guaranteeing the buyer against minor defects that may arise within two years, or major defects that arise within 10 years, of the construction of the house. The Council appoints its own inspectors to examine complaints and, where necessary, to enforce adequate remedial work by the builders. As most building societies require an NHBC certificate as a condition of a mortgage or a new house, there is considerable pressure on builders to register and they then have to comply with standards set by the Council.

In substantial commercial contracts, particularly those involving foreign trade, it is customary to appoint in the contract for disputes to be referred to arbitration. London has been pre-eminent as an international centre for such arbitration and it is a lucrative source of the country's 'invisible earnings'. A major feature of the London arbitration service is the body of experts available which usually enables a rapid resolution of disputes, which is essential for the smooth working of trade.

In *Berger & Co. Inc* v. *Gill & Duffus SA* (1984) by a contract of sale by sample the sellers sold to the buyers 500 tonnes of 'Argentine bolita beans' to be discharged at Le Havre. By error, 55 tonnes were over-carried to Rotterdam but the day after the sellers elected to rescind the contract, since the buyers had already rejected the cargo of 445 tonnes, the balance of 55 tonnes arrived back in Le Havre. Lord Diplock, in a single judgment for the House of Lords, said that the buyers' refusal to pay the contract price when the relevant shipping documents were presented, was a fundamental breach of contract. In this instance an arbitrator found in favour of the sellers, the Board of Appeal of GAFTA reversed that decision, the High Court found in favour of the buyers regarding the 55 tonnes and the sellers for the

445 tonnes, the Court of Appeal found in favour of the buyers in respect of the whole contract quantity of 500 tonnes, and the House of Lords held that once the sellers had elected to treat the buyers' refusal to pay as a repudiation of the agreement, the sellers' obligations ceased. The matter had taken nearly seven years to settle, which Lord Diplock called a 'disgrace to the judicial system'. The case did little to enhance London's reputation for arbitration.

Time

The general rule is that time, unless specifically made a term or precondition of the contract, will not require such precise compliance as the manner of performance. Where no time limit has been specified, then the contract must be performed within a period which is reasonable in the circumstances. In the case of *Staunton* v. *Wood* (1851), a contract for the delivery of goods forthwith to be paid for in 14 days, was held to allow delivery within 14 days.

Clearly if one party has shown by his conduct or express requirement that time is of the essence, then the court is likely to order specific performance and/or damages for delay. Contracts of a business nature, such as supply of machinery, or spare parts, or goods, are more likely to be upheld as inferring urgency, than contracts for sale of land and property where the general rule is that even if there is a date for completion of the sale, time is not of the essence unless specifically so provided. In such cases, the buyer will usually have paid a deposit, normally 10 per cent of the price, and the courts will not allow the seller to rescind the contract and forfeit the deposit without giving the buyer a chance to complete his financial arrangements. The seller must give notice to complete within a reasonable period of time, often 28 or 30 days in the case of dwelling houses. The seller may be compensated in damages, however, for any loss that he incurs because of the delayed completion.

Even if there has been unreasonable delay in completing a contract for the sale of land, it is safer for the seller to serve notice to complete, rather than to rescind the contract, the Privy Council held in the case of *Graham* v. *Pitkin* (1992).

Payment

In contrast to the presumption concerning time, there is no presumption that delay in payment for any period, whether 'reasonable' or not, is permissible. Payment is due on performance of the work, or delivery of the goods, or whatever the promisor has undertaken by the contract. Delayed payments, particularly by large corporations to smaller contractors or suppliers, has been a major cause of liquidity problems and insolvencies during recessionary times for small traders. There is no rule of law that allows payment to be deferred for one month, or to 28th of the month after delivery, or any other of the now standard practices of many large companies. The mercantile rule is that payment is 'on the nail'. This expression dates from the days when Bristol was a pre-eminent trading port, and the 'nails', flat-topped pedestals outside the Corn Exchange, stand to this day in mute protest at the deterioration of business standards. Further, the onus is on the debtor to seek his creditor and to make payment. Where payment is by cheque or some other negotiable instrument, then performance is not complete until the cheque is cleared, although the presumption is that the cheque is good and therefore in the meantime the plaintiff cannot sue. A receipt is not payment *per se*, but rather *prima facie* evidence that a debt has been honoured. In this context 'tender' may be taken as attempted performance, that is the debtor may have offered the creditor insufficient payment, or an unreasonably large sum – for instance, if X. offers Y. the equivalent of a £100 note of the Bank of China in satisfaction of a debt of 90p, this is unlikely to be acceptable to the court if it is unacceptable to the creditor. In essence, the debtor should pay the exact sum (*Robinson* v. *Cook* (1815)).

Vicarious performance

Performance may be vicarious, that is a third party may act on the debtor's behalf. If the creditor consents, then the legal position is relatively straightforward. So in *Hirachand Punamchand* v. *Temple* (1911) the father of an army officer paid part of his son's debts in agreed satisfaction of the whole amount. It was held that the creditors could not then sue the son for the balance. Where the creditor does not consent, he must show that payment by a third party makes a material difference to his own interests. Alternatively, the contract may have expressly provided for personal performance by the debtor. Vicarious performance, although outwardly similar, is not the same as assignment, for in the former liability is not transferred. Thus a sub-contractor may not be sued for faulty work, but rather the main contractor, as shown in *Stewart* v. *Reavell's Garage* (1952), a case of faulty brakes on a car. However, the sub-contractor may still be liable in negligence, a point underlined in the previous chapter.

Whether vicarious performance can fulfil the contract depends primarily on the nature of the promise. If an artist is commissioned to paint a portrait, his assistant cannot be given the work, but a builder can have part of his contractual work done by another. It is a question of whether personal skill is an essential element of the contract. If the person is unable to perform the contract whether by death, illness or other reason, and it is one where vicarious performance is not possible, then the contract is discharged.

The courts will, if it appears sensible, be prepared to imply a term that time is of the essence, where performance has not taken place within a reasonable period, especially where one party has unduly delayed. Regard must be had to the particular nature of the contract. In certain commercial, or mercantile, contracts time will be presumed to be of the essence, as for instance in the sale of a public house as a going concern (*Tadcaster Tower Brewery Co.* v. *Wilson* (1897)).

In *Johnson Matthey Bankers Ltd* v. *State Trading Corporation of India* (1984) it was held that where a seller fails to deliver goods on time the buyer is entitled to wait for delivery while the market price rises and then to treat the contract as at an end and claim higher damages for the breach, if the true purpose of his conduct, though not expressly or impliedly stated, was to encourage performance of the contract. In this instance the agreement, which contained a *force majeure* clause of limited effect, concerned the shipment and sale of silver bullion, which became subject to an export ban by the Government of India.

DISCHARGE

Discharge essentially concerns the premature termination of a contract. A contract may be discharged in one of three main ways: agreement, breach and frustration.

1 Agreement and rescission

In the first place where a contract is executory, that is both sides have yet to perform their side of the bargain, by mutual agreement the contract may be discharged. If the contract is executed in the sense that one party has performed his part, then generally such termination may only take place by a written agreement by deed, if there is no consideration for the release. Alternatively, there must have been 'accord and satisfaction', that is the defaulting party buys his way out of the contract, thereby avoiding an action in court. However, this route must be followed carefully, since in respect of debts in their pure sense the rule under *Pinnel's Case* is that payment of a lesser sum does not extinguish liability for the whole sum, equitable estoppel and the *High Trees* case notwithstanding, as discussed earlier.

Secondly, the original contract may, by mutual agreement, be rescinded, subject to its being replaced by a new contract; or certain of the terms may be completely changed. Indeed in this context a parol or simple contract may be substituted for a contract by deed.

However, where one party seeks rescission, the courts may be reluctant to agree if it appears that that party will be unjustly enriched by the failure of the other party to perform and that the 'injured' party is unwilling to return at least part of that benefit to the other side. It may well be that the injured party may prefer to opt for rescission (since he may be better off) than to continue to perform his side of the contract and then be left to sue the other party for damages for breach of contract. But a court will not look favourably upon one party attempting to rescind because he realises he has made a bad bargain, even if the other side has failed to perform. Moreover, the courts may face problems if the defaulting party has substantially performed his part of the contract: this may depend on whether his obligation was an 'entire' one, as in *Cutter* v. *Powell* (1795), or was in fact a series of related obligations.

Thirdly, the contract itself may provide for rescission. In short the agreement may contain 'conditions subsequent', whereby once facts become known in the future, knowledge which was not available to the parties at the time they made the agreement, then one or both parties may rescind the agreement.

Fourthly, any breach of a condition of a contract will give the other party a right to rescind. But where a breach of warranty is concerned the position is more complicated. Rescission for a breach of warranty arises in two particular instances: where there is some misrepresentation of fact (Misrepresentation Act 1967) and where there has been a clearly substantial failure in performance.

Fifthly, the parties may agree not to rescind but rather to vary some of the terms, although if most of the terms are varied the thin line between rescission and variation almost vanishes entirely. Until 1986, as seen earlier (the Parol Evidence Rule), a variation had to be in writing where by law the original contract had to be evidenced in writing.

Sixthly, if one party agrees to forgo part of the other's obligations, for example, a place of delivery or time limit, then he waives his rights. A waiver frequently occurs in commercial transactions, not least in relation to the sale of goods, and is binding upon the party making it. Historically, waiver was developed by the common law, but as Lord Denning noted in *Charles Rickards Ltd* v. *Oppenheim* (1950) it is a close relation of promissory estoppel. However, it will be recalled that the extent of this estoppel was doubted, *obiter*, by Viscount Simonds in the case of *Tool Metal Manufacturing Co. Ltd* v. *Tungsten Electric Co. Ltd* (1955), and that it probably operated to suspend rather than to abolish completely the rights of the party making the waiver, so that he could give reasonable notice to re-assert his full rights under the contract. In any case, for waiver to operate, the party granted the concession must have acted in reliance on the waiver.

2 Breach

A breach of contract is, quite simply, where one party fails to perform or performs unsatisfactorily. The other party may then sue for breach and damages is the usual remedy sought. However, unless the defaulter clearly repudiates the contract, by refusing to perform, this does not necessarily mean the contract has come to an end, it may still be operational. For example, A. may sue B. because of specific delay on B.'s part, something which broke a term of the agreement; nonetheless A. and B. agree that they should still carry out their bargain. In broad terms A. has the choice of treating the contract as discharged or not. It used to be said that if the breach by B. is a serious one, a fundamental breach, then A. will have no choice: the contract is discharged automatically. However, as seen earlier, the doctrine of fundamental breach was buried by the House of Lords in *Photo Production Ltd* v. *Securior Transport Ltd*; although the Lords had denied in 1966 in the *Suisse Atlantique* case that such a rule of law existed, the courts continued to apply it wherever convenient, the courts using the expression 'serious breach', rather than 'fundamental breach'.

The House of Lords, emphasising the finality of arbitration awards, overruled the Court of Appeal in *Vitol SA* v. *Norelf Ltd* (1996), by holding that a failure to perform a contract can sometimes amount to an acceptance of a wrongful repudiation. But such a decision must be conveyed by the aggrieved party clearly and unequivocally to the repudiating party.

'Force majeure'

The injured party may be assisted where the liability of the other is strict. For example, a builder must construct a house soundly; a serious breach will arise if the building shows signs of falling down. Similarly, liability is strict where a charterer agrees to supply a cargo, although here there is always the possibility of a *force majeure* clause, of which a good illustration is the *Rolimpex* case. In *C. Czarnikow Ltd* v. *Centrala Handlu Zagranicznego Rolimpex* (1978) the defendants, a Polish state enterprise, agreed to sell 200,000 tons of sugar to an English company. But owing to floods the 1974 crop was so poor that the Polish government required all of it for home consumption and prohibited the export of sugar. The Lords upheld Rolimpex's reliance on a *force majeure* clause, to the effect that they were released from their contractual liabilities by reason of government intervention beyond their control. The contract was void on breach, or rather upon declaration of *force majeure* by Rolimpex.

The example of the *force majeure* clause shows how discharge by rescission, breach and frustration all overlap. It may well be that the failure to perform by one party was due to a legitimate reason; it may have been frustrated by external factors, in which case the injured party will have the option to rescind or terminate the contract. In that sense a breach of contract may lead to rescission. But in most cases a breach of contract will lead to a claim for damages, or possibly an injunction or an order for specific performance, because the defaulting party simply refuses to perform his side of the bargain – in short, he wishes to avoid contractual responsibilities. And, indeed, a refusal to perform may take place before the actual time of performance, as where an employer changes his mind before the new employee is due to start work. This is known as an 'anticipatory breach', as seen in *Hochster* v. *De la Tour* (1853).

Similarly, if the 'defaulting' party has not actually refused to perform, by carelessness or design he may have made it impossible to do so, as underlined in *Universal Cargo Carriers Corporation* v. *Citati* (1957) where the defendants left themselves only three days in which to provide a cargo and arrange other matters for a chartered ship. The charter party was held entitled to rescind.

As indicated above in respect of rescission, where a condition is breached then usually the whole contract is discharged, but in the case of a warranty the contract will continue, notwithstanding a claim for damages, except where there occurs either a substantial failure of performance (as discussed in *Hong Kong Fir Shipping Co. Ltd* v. *Kawasaki Kisen Kaisha Ltd* (1962)) or a misrepresentation of fact. However, in respect of the latter under the Misrepresentation Act 1967 the court has the right to exercise its discretion and substitute damages in place of rescission, particularly where the operation of the contract is not adversely affected to any significant degree. But, of course, the courts frequently find it difficult to distinguish between a condition and a warranty, unless the contract itself is expressly clear on this point, or where a statute, such as the Sale of Goods Act 1979, so provides. It was this sort of problem that arose in *Bunge Corporation, New York* v. *Tradax Export SA, Panama* (1981) where buyers were two days late in giving notice to the sellers for the shipment of soya bean meal. The sellers declared the buyers in default and claimed damages for repudiation of the contract. The Lords declared that the term in respect of notice of delivery was a condition rather than a warranty; time was of the essence in mercantile contracts. Indeed, it is possible to view a third category of terms, that is intermediate or innominate terms as discussed in the *Hong Kong Fir* case where there was a judicial reluctance to adhere to a hard and fast divison between conditions and warranties; rather the approach was to retain a measure of flexibility by looking at the circumstances of the breach: what were the consequences, were the results a 'breach of a fundamental term', was the outcome serious? These points were returned to in the case of *Reardon Smith Line* v. *Hansen-Tangen* (1976) and more dramatically and more recently in *Union Eagle Ltd* v. *Golden Achievement Ltd* (1997). Where a contract is rescinded on account of a breach of a condition, a claim for damages may still be allowed in addition. Conditions, warranties and innominate terms were further examined by the Court of Appeal in *Barber* v. *NWS Bank plc* (1995).

3 Frustration

The phrase 'discharge by frustration' almost speaks for itself. It is where a contract becomes impossible to perform on account of subsequent events which may well have been unforeseeable by either party. A frustrating event defeats the common purpose or intention of both parties and thus the contract becomes void. Before the case of *Taylor* v. *Caldwell* in 1863 English law did not recognise a doctrine of frustration. Nowadays, however, contractual disputes before the courts often turn upon arguments of frustration. In *Taylor* v. *Caldwell* the defendants agreed to hire a music hall to the plaintiff for four days. On the day before the first concert the hall was burnt down. The defendant was held not liable for breach of contract, for advertising and incidental expenses, the plaintiff not actually claiming for loss of profits.

Subsequent cases have illustrated other aspects of frustration. For example, in *Krell* v. *Henry* (1903) the commercial object of the entire contract was obviated when the coronation processions of Edward VII were cancelled on account of the King's illness. The court took the view that the flat in question had been rented for the purpose of watching the processions and therefore the plaintiff could not recover the balance of money due. But in *Herne Bay Steamboat Co.* v. *Hutton* (1903), which again involved the King's coronation but this time a naval review, the decision went the other way. The court held that the defendant could still have viewed the fleet and he hired the boat at his own risk. Constant revisions of plans to construct an oil rig did not lead to frustration, it was held in *McAlpine, Humberoak Ltd* v. *McDermott International Inc* (1992).

The effects of frustration in contract (here a pop concert in an unsafe stadium in Spain) were considered in *Gamerco SA* v. *ICM/Fair Warning (Agency) Ltd* (1995).

Death or incapacity may frustrate a contract, as seen in *Robinson* v. *Davison* (1871) where a concert pianist fell seriously ill. Similarly, a change in the law may effect frustration. This has been illustrated in *Nile Co. for the Export of Agricultural Crops* v. *H and J M Bennett (Commodities) Ltd* (1986) where a contract for the sale of

Egyptian potatoes to English buyers provided for disputes to be referred to arbitration on strict terms; the buyers failed to comply with the arbitration procedures but rejected nine consignments alleging the potatoes were in poor condition. The parties reached a compromise: the sellers would continue further shipments, the buyers to pay cash on the bills of lading. The Egyptian government brought in new regulations requiring payments for agricultural exports to be made by irrevocable letters of credit. The court held that the change frustrated the compromise, so that the original claim was reviewed and the buyers were liable for the unpaid consignments. But the buyers were entitled to counterclaim for the lack of 'merchantable quality' of the potatoes.

War will often frustrate a contract, but even here the courts will not agree to the contract being discharged if the restrictions appear to be temporary, as in the case of the 99-year lease in *Cricklewood Property and Investment Trust Ltd* v. *Leighton's Investment Trust Ltd* (1945). The same line was taken in a number of cases brought in respect of the closure of the Suez Canal in 1956 and 1967, as illustrated in *Tsakiroglou and Co. Ltd* v. *Noblee Thorl GmbH* (1962), where the Lords held that the shipment of groundnuts was still possible via the Cape route although at great loss to the carriers. Similarly, the requisitioning of a ship in the First World War did not frustrate the contract (*F A Tamplin Steamship Co. Ltd* v. *Anglo-Mexican Petroleum Products Co. Ltd* (1916)).

The *Cricklewood* case showed that frustration could not apply to a contract where the contract was for a long period of time, here a lease. A similar point arose in *National Carriers Ltd* v. *Panalpina (Northern) Ltd* (1981). Here the plaintiffs leased a warehouse for 10 years to the defendants, but because the local council closed the only access road for about 20 months, the defendants did not pay the rent. The plaintiffs sought to recover the monies. The House of Lords held that the doctrine of frustration, although in principle applicable to leases, could only rarely be properly applied in such cases, and so the plaintiff succeeded (the lease was not frustrated).

A prison sentence may have the effect of frustrating a contract. In one case, employers engaged an apprentice plumber, who was convicted of an offence during the course of his apprenticeship and sentenced to borstal training. On his release, the employers refused to allow the apprentice to continue his training. The Court of Appeal, reversing the Employment Appeal Tribunal, held the contract was frustrated and that the apprentice could not plead his own criminal behaviour in order to claim compensation for the frustrating event: *F C Shepherd & Co. Ltd* v. *Jerrom* (1986).

Mere delays will not usually amount to frustration. It was so held in *Davis Contractors Ltd* v. *Fareham UDC* (1956) where a building project was completed some 14 months late owing to an unexpected shortage of labour and materials. However, frustration must not be self-induced, as illustrated in *Maritime National Fish Ltd* v. *Ocean Trawlers Ltd* (1935). Here the defendants obtained three licences, instead of the five they wanted, for operating ships with otter trawls. They had chartered two of the ships, including one from the plaintiffs. But the defendants allocated the three licences to their own ships and thereby claimed that their contract with the plaintiffs was frustrated.

The Law Reform (Frustrated Contracts) Act 1943 provides ground rules for returning the parties to such a contract to their original financial position, had they not entered into the agreement. But the Act also allows the court a discretion to award one party expenses that may have been incurred before frustration intervened, and to recoup this from the sums of money that would be due from the other party in the ordinary course of events. The Act excludes certain contracts from its ambit: contracts of insurance, maritime contracts, that is carriage of goods by sea or a charterparty, and contracts for the sale of perishable goods. An illustration of the award of a just sum under the 1943 Act was the protracted case of *BP Exploration Co. (Libya) Ltd* v. *Hunt (No 2)* (1982) which involved an oil prospecting contract which was frustrated by the Libyan government's expropriation of the concessions.

In *Finelvet AG* v. *Vinava Shipping Co. Ltd* (1983) it was held that it was not the declaration of war itself but acts done in furtherance of a war which would tend to frustrate the performance of a contract. Here an arbitrator had held the contract frustrated at the end of November 1980 (the event being the outbreak of war between Iraq and Iran in the Persian Gulf) but the charterers of the ship concerned unsuccessfully appealed to the High Court on the grounds that the charterparty had been frustrated during the previous month.

If the reader is himself feeling doubtful and frustrated by this section, let him take heart in the knowledge that this part of contract has been justly described as one of the most difficult to understand. J. E. Stannard has graphically observed: 'We have an avalanche of technical terms; frustration, frustrating breach, repudiation, termination, discharge. And even the ordinary words used are not clear; what is meant by 'fault' and when is frustration 'self-induced'?'

REMEDIES AND RESTITUTION

The main remedy for breach of contract is that of damages at common law, and this is considered first. However, there are also available *quantum meruit* and restitution, and the equitable remedies of injunctions and orders for specific performance.

Damages

Damages are usually described as compensatory. In other words an award must restore the plaintiff to his contractual position, in the sense that the gain that was due under the contract must be made good, as if, in short, the contract had been performed. It does not matter that it was profitable for the other party to break the contract, except in cases involving the sale of land, breach of confidence and agency. The rule, therefore, is that the plaintiff must not be unduly enriched – he must be no worse or no better off than if the other side had performed its side of the agreement. If the plaintiff has suffered a substantial 'loss of bargain', substantial damages may be given, although exemplary damages, designed to punish the wrongdoer, are not awarded in contract; they are, though, in tort, and they may be in contract if there is also a claim in tort. In *Surrey County Council* v. *Bredero Homes* (1993) where a developer built 77 bungalows and houses instead of 72 in breach of planning consent, the plaintiff councils were not allowed damages by the Court of Appeal since they had suffered no actual loss.

However, it may not always be practicable to award damages which do not place the plaintiff in a more advantageous position than but for the breach he would have been. For example, in *Harbutt's 'Plasticine' Ltd* v. *Wayne Tank and Pump Co. Ltd* (1970) there was no alternative to building a new factory since the old one had been destroyed by fire. In *Dominion Mosaics and Tile Co. Ltd* v. *Trafalgar Trucking Co. Ltd* (1990) *Harbutts' Plasticine* was applied, here in respect of rebuilding business premises badly damaged by fire which would have cost £570,000; the plaintiffs rightly claimed the cost of leasing alternative premises at £390,000 and the cost of 11 machines which had been destroyed (£65,000).

Where the plaintiff suffers no discernible loss from the breach of contract, where for instance the goods are in short supply and can easily be resold, then he will be awarded only nominal damages, say, £5. But the usual damages are the cost of repair, or replacement or reimbursement of whatever is missing or inadequate under the contract. In *Thornton* v. *Abbey National plc* the plaintiff, the Court of Appeal held, had suffered no discernible loss in respect of the late delivery of a replacement vehicle. The general measure of damages for breach of contract was seen in *Banque Bruxelles SA* v. *Eagle Star Insurance Co. Ltd* (1996); but a claim for special damages for trading losses was dismissed where the defendants wrongly dishonoured the plaintiff's cheque for £4,550.

Apart from measuring the loss of benefit or bargain under the contract, substantial damages may also include an award for sheer inconvenience or distress. An illustration of the former was *Hobbs* v. *London and South Western Railway Co.* (1875) where the plaintiff was forced to walk home through the rain on account of his being put on the wrong train. In respect of the latter the importance of the decision in *Jackson* v. *Horizon Holidays* (1975) has already been noted. Similarly, in *Jarvis* v. *Swans Tours Ltd* (1973) the plaintiff won his action for a holiday that failed to be as entertaining as the brochure had described. On the other hand damages do not usually include an amount for the loss of reputation, as laid down in *Addis* v. *Gramophone Co. Ltd* (1909) where the defendants' manager in Calcutta was dismissed without adequate notice. However, this general rule holds less true nowadays, especially in contracts of employment – the stigma of unfair dismissal has been taken more seriously of late by both Parliament and the courts. The same is true in commercial contracts, where a trader can point to his business reputation being adversely affected.

Reliance loss
As an alternative to substantial damages – although sometimes as an addition – the plaintiff may claim for those expenses incurred before moving into a contractual relationship. Such a claim restores him to the precontractual position and is virtually identical to *quantum meruit* discussed below. Thus in *Anglia Television Ltd* v. *Reed* (1972) the plaintiffs successfully claimed £2,750 costs incurred on the

preparation for a television play in which, in breach of contract, the defendant refused to take the leading part. Moreover, the plaintiff may be burdened by expenses after the contract has been agreed and perhaps partly performed. This, for example, could include the cost of hiring alternative machinery (as in *Dominion Mosaics* above). Such 'incidental loss' will normally be added to the claim for loss of bargain. But incidental losses have to be carefully pleaded, as seen in *Swingcastle Ltd* v. *Alistair Gibson (a firm)* (1991) where if a valuation had been carried out carefully the respondent would not have loaned the money, and could have earned interest, which the House of Lords assessed at 12 per cent, but not at 46.5 per cent the rate for falling into arrears under the mortgage.

Remoteness of damage

Assessing the amount of damages may not, therefore, be a straightforward matter. The market prices might be such that they fluctuate wildly from day to day. Or, for instance, the nature of the contract may be very specialised and any market value is therefore difficult to measure. In *Chaplin* v. *Hicks* (1911) a participant in a beauty contest was awarded substantial damages for being unfairly excluded from the later stages of the contest, even though there was no certainty that she would have won the competition. Also, in a world of complex international trade, judging in which currency the damages should be awarded may pose problems for the courts. In *Services Europe Atlantique Sud (SEAS) of Paris* v. *Stockholms Rederiaktiebolag Svea* (1978) the House of Lords held that unless the contract expressly or impliedly referred to a particular currency for such an award, damages should be paid in the currency which best expressed the plaintiff's loss. A similar rule was adopted in tort in its parallel judgment in *The Despina R* (1978).

One key principle in the assessment of damages is the rule in *Hadley* v. *Baxendale* (1854). The case involved the late delivery of a repaired crankshaft to the plaintiff's mill at Gloucester. The action was brought for loss of profits. It was held that the damages which the other party ought to receive should be

> **such as may fairly and reasonably be considered either arising naturally, ie according to the usual course of things, from such breach of contract itself, or such as may reasonably be supposed to have been in the contemplation of both parties at the time they made the contract as the probable result of the breach.**

In other words damage must not be too remote; if it is the defendant will not be liable. *Hadley* v. *Baxendale* was followed in *Victoria Laundry (Windsor) Ltd* v. *Newman Industries Ltd* (1949) which involved the late delivery of a boiler, where Lord Justice Asquith observed:

> 2. **In cases of breach of contract the aggrieved party is only entitled to recover such part of the loss actually resulting as was at the time of the contract reasonably foreseeable as liable to result from the breach.**

3. **What was at the time reasonably so foreseeable depends on the knowledge then possessed by the parties or, at all events, by the party who later commits the breach.**

4. **For this purpose, knowledge 'possessed' is of two kinds; one imputed, the other actual. Everyone, as a reasonable person, is taken to know the 'ordinary course of things' and consequently what loss is liable to result from a breach of contract in that ordinary course. 'This is the subject-matter of the 'first rule' in** Hadley **v.** Baxendale**. But to this knowledge, which a contract-breaker is assumed to possess whether he actually possesses it or not, there may have to be added in a particular case knowledge which he actually possesses, of special circumstances outside the 'ordinary course of things', of such a kind that a breach in those special circumstances would be liable to cause more loss. Such a case attracts the operation of the 'second rule' so as to make additional loss also recoverable.**

Asquith's remarks led to the view that there was little to distinguish between remoteness of damage in tort and in contract; the tests for each, 'reasonable foreseeability' and 'reasonable contemplation', were essentially the same – the differences were semantic, Lord Justice Scarman said in the more recent case of *H. Parsons (Livestock) Ltd* v. *Uttley Ingham & Co. Ltd* (1978). Here the action was in respect of the supply of a defective pig food hopper; the food became mouldy and led to the death of the pigs. However, in *The Heron II* case (*Koufos* v. *C. Czarnikow Ltd* (1969)), the House of Lords held in effect that the degree of probability must be of a higher standard in contract if the test of remoteness were to be fully satisfied. That loss would occur would have to amount to 'reasonable foreseeability' in tort, that is damage is of a kind, although unlikely, that would have been foreseen by the reasonable man; whereas in contract the possibility of damage would be strong, and not at all remote, it is a 'serious possibility' or even a 'real danger' – it would be within a specific range, that is the assessment of damages would turn upon the common knowledge and contemplation of the parties to the contract. But this issue, as might be gathered, has proved troublesome for the courts, and various judgments have been confused.

Other cases which illustrated the principle of *Hadley* v. *Baxendale* were *Horne* v. *Midland Railway* (1873) and *Simpson* v. *London and North Western Railway* (1876). In the former, the defendants delivered a batch of shoes a day late. The plaintiff was unable to recover the abnormally high price he would have received had the shoes, destined for France, been delivered on time. In the latter, specimens of the plaintiff's cattle-food arrived too late for display at an agricultural show in Newcastle. Here the company was held liable for the loss of profits, for through its agent it was aware of the commercial importance of meeting the delivery deadline. In *Seven Seas Properties Ltd* v. *Al-Essa (No 2)* (1993) the plaintiffs had deliberately withheld from the defendants that they intended to sell on; therefore the loss suffered by the plaintiff in respect of a contract for the resale of properties was not within the contemplation of the parties.

Mitigation

Another important aspect of the rules relating to damages is mitigation. It is well established that where the plaintiff has not taken reasonable steps to mitigate the loss arising from the breach, then the amount awarded him will be correspondingly reduced. What, of course, is 'reasonable' depends upon the facts. Where a case is complicated and involves a number of defendants, the court may find it just to order that one or more of the defendants should indemnify some or all of the remaining defendants. A case which in some measure illustrated this point was that of *Lambert* v. *Lewis* (1982). In this instance the plaintiffs were injured and the husband and son of the family were killed when the trailer behind a Land Rover detached itself and crashed into their car. An action was brought under the Fatal Accidents Acts 1846 to 1959 and the Law Reform (Miscellaneous Provisions) Act 1934. The first defendant (D1) was the owner of the Land Rover and trailer. The second defendant (D2) was the driver of the vehicle and an employee of D1. The third defendants (D3) were the manufacturers of the towing hitch for the trailer. The fourth defendants (D4) were the retailers for the towing attachment. In the action D1 brought third party proceedings against D4, claiming that the hitch was neither fit for the purpose supplied nor of merchantable quality under the Sale of Goods Act. D4 brought fourth party proceedings against D3 for negligent misrepresentation and breach of 'warranty' (or condition, as the court should have said). The trial judge found D1 25 per cent liable and D3 75 per cent. The Court of Appeal held that D4, the retailers, were liable to indemnify the owner, D1, since his conduct was neither so unreasonable as to be beyond the contemplation of D4 nor such as to break the chain of causation between 'warranty' and the accident: the damage was a natural consequence of the breach. But the House of Lords took a rather different view and upheld D4's appeal against the indemnity.

Liquidated damages

A contract may provide for damages in the event of breach. These are of two kinds: *penalties* and *liquidated damages*. The contract, though, may not be clear as to which type the clause relates to and the courts will be left to determine the issue; even if the words *penalty* or *liquidated damages* are used, the courts may not take them at face value (*Cellulose Acetate Silk Co. Ltd* v. *Widnes Foundry Ltd* (1925)). The distinction is an important one. A penalty clause means precisely that: if one party fails to perform in some way he must pay the other party a stipulated sum of money. A penalty is unenforceable at law and bears no relation to any award the court might make for breach. A penalty is the more easily identified where it is for an amount of money greater than the loss actually sustained by the injured party, and this is the usual form it takes. In other words it is a sum held *in terrorem* of the party that commits the breach, where as Lord Denedin said in *Dunlop Pneumatic Tyre Co. Ltd* v. *New Garage & Motor Co. Ltd* (1915) it is 'extravagant and unconscionable'. In *Clydebank Engineering & Shipbuilding Co.* v. *Don Jose Ramos*

Yzquierdo y Castaneda (1905), Lord Halsbury said in construing a penalty clause the court should look at the real nature of the transaction and the mere use of the words 'penalty' or 'damages' was not conclusive. It was impossible to lay down any abstract rule as to what might or might not be extravagant or unconscionable. Such points about penalty clauses were illustrated in *Ariston SRL* v. *Charly Records Ltd* (1990) and also in *Jobson* v. *Johnson* (1989), where it was said that the retransfer of football shares in the event of the default of payment of subsequent instalments was not a genuine pre-estimate but a penalty. In *J. F. Finnegan Ltd* v. *Community Housing Association Ltd* (1993) it was held that although the sum withheld by the defendant for the delay by the plaintiff in completing the building contract between them was not a penalty, the defendant had not followed the correct procedure under the JCT standard form building contract of 1980 for withholding the sum and was not entitled to make the deduction.

Conversely, where the sum is a genuine pre-estimate by the contracting parties of the loss arising from a possible future breach, it is to be regarded as liquidated damages. If, as often occurs, the sum falls short of the injured party's actual loss, then it is still operative – that is the maximum amount the plaintiff will receive. But where the estimate, even though it is not always easy to calculate scientifically and precisely, is an extravagant exaggeration of the actual loss then it is, of course, a penalty, and the parties are not bound. So, a sum significantly greater than the actual loss is invariably a penalty, and a smaller sum usually liquidated damages.

Assessment of damages were further considered by the House of Lords in *Ruxley Electronics and Construction Ltd* v. *Forsyth* (1995), a case of a swimming pool built to the wrong specifications. Lord Jauncey said: 'Damages are designed to compensate for an established loss and not to provide a gratuitous benefit to the aggrieved party'. In this instance the House of Lords allowed nominal damages, including the trial judge's award of £2,500 for loss of amenity, thus disallowing the Court of Appeal's award of £20,000 to meet the cost of reconstruction. The Lords' decision seems to be over-generous towards the sloppy construction work. The state of the market in times of recession is also relevant to the quantification of damages, *Western Web Offset Printers Ltd* v. *Independent Media Ltd* (1995) and *White Arrow Express Ltd* v. *Lamey's Distribution Ltd* (1995).

Action for an agreed sum
In many contracts a specific price or payment on the part of one party is named in return for some act or forbearance by the other. As an alternative to an action for damages it is possible at common law to sue for that particular sum. In this case the rules under *Hadley* v. *Baxendale* are not relevant, except where in certain instances an action for damages and an agreed sum is brought. An action for an agreed sum often pertains to those agreements covered by the Sale of Goods Act 1979.

Quantum meruit
Another alternative to damages is that of *quantum meruit*. It arises indirectly rather than directly from the contract and is a restitutory remedy. It may only operate

where the contract has come to an end; as we have seen earlier damages can be awarded for breach of warranty, yet the contract may still limp along even if it does not run entirely smoothly. The plaintiff must have chosen to determine the contract upon its being broken by the other party. And only the injured party may claim *quantum meruit*, even if the defaulting party has partly performed his side of the bargain. That being so, the plaintiff may claim for the work already done in fulfilling his side of the agreement. A *quantum meruit* returns the injured party to his pre-contractual position. The leading case is that of *Planché* v. *Colburn* (1831); here the plaintiff partially completed a book on ancient armour and costume when the defendants stopped publication: the plaintiff was awarded half the contract price as reasonable remuneration for the work he had done.

Specific performance

Specific performance and injunctions are equitable remedies. Specific performance is an order by the courts to the defaulting party that he will execute his side of the agreement fully, or at least in part. However, it is a discretionary remedy, even where it is incorporated into statute law, such as the Sale of Goods Act 1979, and the court will make such an order only where it is satisfied that an action for damages would not leave the plaintiff adequately compensated, or where the damages awarded can only be purely nominal (*Beswick* v. *Beswick* (1968)). This situation might arise in those instances where the subject matter of the contract is not easily obtainable elsewhere – say a Chün ware incense burner of the Sung dynasty. But the maxims of equity must also be taken into account – he, for example, who 'comes to Equity must come with clean hands.' Thus if the injured party had outrageously provoked the defendant to default, it is most unlikely he would be granted an order for specific performance. *Record* v. *Bell* (1991) concerned the sale of a residential property at £1.3 million; it was held that there was no reference in the contract of sale to the supplementary term relating to office copies of entries from the Land Registry and that accordingly the letters did not satisfy the requirements of s.2 of the Law of Property (Miscellaneous Provisions) Act 1989. However, the vendor's letter had created a collateral contract in respect of which specific performance could be ordered.

An order for specific performance is limited in other ways. Firstly, it was always assumed that if mutuality did not exist, then an order would not be made. In other words if the plaintiff in practice could not be ordered specifically to perform, neither could the defendant. This rule has now been amended as a result of the judgment in *Price* v. *Strange* (1978); an order may still be made against the defendant if it appears damages would be an adequate remedy in the event of any default by the plaintiff. Specific performance (here the question of the opening of a supermarket under the terms of a lease) was considered in *Cooperative Insurance Society Ltd* v. *Argyll Stores (Holdings) Ltd* (1996).

Secondly, it is usual that no order will be made where the contract is vague, where certainty of terms is lacking.

Thirdly, if for specific performance to be effective constant supervision is required by the courts, then the order may again be refused. However, in certain relatively recent cases, such as *C. H. Giles & Co. Ltd* v. *Morris* (1972) it has been shown that this is not necessarily a hard and fast rule. The court could refuse specific performance where hardship was suffered subsequent to the date of the contract. In *Patel* v. *Ali* (1984) the defendant became ill, resulting in the amputation of a leg, after she had agreed to sell her house. If the sale was completed, it meant that she would have to move to a strange neighbourhood and be deprived of her relatives' help. However, in this instance conditions were attached in the court's ruling. Indeed, an action for specific performance is more frequently suitable for land and property than for goods, as seen in *Seven Seas Properties* v. *Al-Essa (No 1)* (1989).

Fourthly, contracts that involve personal service, such as employment contracts, are not usually specifically enforceable. This was recognised by the Trade Union and Labour Relations Act 1974, although under the Employment Protection (Consolidation) Act 1992 an industrial tribunal has power to order the reinstatement of an employee rather than solely compensation, but in practice this power is seldom used, especially in the case of small companies. In *Warren* v. *Mendy* (1989) it was held that to grant an injunction would mean applying coercive force to a contract of personal service.

Injunctions

An injunction is again a discretionary remedy. In contract the granting of an injunction is usually only in the negative sense, that is it restrains one party from breaking the contract where he has promised under its terms not to undertake some act. The 'negative' terms in the contract must be express where contracts of personal service are concerned.

The court, in granting an injunction, will examine who is to blame; it does not need to concern itself with the 'balance of convenience' argument – in other words it does not have to consider whether the 'defaulting' party might be inconvenienced by the granting of an injunction. This is so where the errant party is about to commit a breach: the injunction is a prohibitory one. But where the defaulter has already committed a breach, then the court will need to address itself to the 'balance of convenience' argument before granting a mandatory injunction. Such an injunction will be granted only where the breach is serious, where the plaintiff's interests are severely prejudiced.

Furthermore, an injunction may not be granted if its effect would be to make an order of specific performance which would not otherwise have been decreed. This is particularly so in respect of contracts for personal service, although even here circuitous routes may be followed as shown in the controversial case of *Lumley* v. *Wagner* (1852). The defendant agreed to sing at the plaintiff's London theatre for three months and nowhere else except by permission. She then agreed to sing elsewhere and refused to perform in the plaintiff's theatre. The court did not order specific performance, but did grant an injunction which restrained her from singing in G.'s theatre.

Equitable remedies are not subject to the limitation periods. Under the Limitation Act 1980 an action in simple contract must be brought within six years of the actual breach, 12 years for a specialty contract. Nonetheless an application for specific performance or an injunction or a claim for rescission or for rectification of a mistake must be brought speedily. Equity will not be well disposed towards the plaintiff who delays, even for a short period; therefore the limitations of six and 12 years are not in themselves entirely relevant to equitable relief. However, in *Peco Arts Inc* v. *Hazlitt Gallery Ltd* (1983) the plaintiff in 1970 purchased what was believed to be an original drawing from a reputable art gallery. It was revalued in 1976, as an original. In 1981 it was revalued again, when it was discovered it was a reproduction. The plaintiff brought an action under mistake (recovery of the purchase price and interest as money paid under a mutual mistake of fact; or rescission of the contract in equity and return of the purchase price on the ground of a common or unilateral mistake of fact). The defendants argued the action was time-barred under the six-year rule of the Limitation Act 1980. The plaintiff argued the limitation period did not begin to run until the mistake was discovered or could with 'reasonable diligence' have been discovered. It was held the action was not time-barred.

Restitution and Quasi-contract

There is a general principle at common law, and also in equity, that a person must not receive money or a benefit which but for particular or abnormal circumstances he would not have enjoyed. Essentially this is the rule that there shall be no 'unjust enrichment', a matter referred to above. Restitution is not confined to contractual accidents or breakdowns, but in this context 'restitution' and 'quasi-contract' are one and the same thing.

The most obvious example of restitution is where one party to a contract may claim back his payment where there has been a total failure of consideration by the other party. Thus, if X. gives Y. £20 for a book, but Y. fails to deliver the book, then it is in order for X. to claim his £20.

Restitution also relates to those situations where there is no contract as such, but where there have taken place contractual negotiations in anticipation of the agreement becoming finalised or fully operative. But it never does, and it would be unjust for A. to be benefited unintentionally by B.

Where a contract is void money paid is recoverable, but not if so excluded by statute, nor usually where the contract is void by virtue of incapacity or illegality, as illustrated in *Reading* v. *Attorney-General* (1951).

Restitution may take the form of a claim for pre-contractual expenses or *quantum meruit* as discussed above. Moreover, the contract itself may expressly provide for the remuneration or *quantum meruit* of one party by the other where there is a subsequent breach or frustrating event, or where the contract itself becomes void or voidable in some other sense such as on account of a basic mistake of fact.

However, if the contract is void *ab initio* it may be difficult for the court to give effect to such a term. Where a frustrating event is concerned it is the Law Reform (Frustrated Contracts) Act 1943 which will assist, as seen earlier, but its provisions are essentially restitutionary in nature. In *British Steel Corporation* v. *Cleveland Bridge and Engineering Co. Ltd* (1984) BSC manufactured and delivered all but one of a number of steel nodes required by the defendants. BSC sued CBE for the value of the nodes and CBE counterclaimed for damages for breach of contract. The High Court held that BSC was entitled to the sums claimed in restitution (*quantum meruit*) since no actual contract (either executory or of the 'if' type) had come into existence. It is, however, important to remember that a plaintiff may only claim for reimbursement if he was under a lawful obligation to expend the money in question. A plaintiff who decides in his own interests to take a risk and voluntarily pay money in the hope of reclaiming it, should the other party be unwilling or unable to return it, is in a weak position before the courts, as seen in *Macclesfield Corporation* v. *Great Central Railway* (1911), where the plaintiffs repaired a canal bridge but were not obliged to; conversely, where the money has been paid under duress then it is recoverable.

Quasi-contract and restitution were further considered by the Privy Council in the New Zealand case of *Murray Stanley Goss* v. *Laurence George Chilcott* (1996). Also in *Kleinwort Benson* v. *Birmingham City Council* (1996), involving interest rate swap agreements, the Court of Appeal made it clear that a claim for restitution meant that the plaintiff had to prove that the defendant had been unjustly enriched at the plaintiff's expense (interest-rate swap agreements were also considered by the House of Lords in *Westdeutsche Landessbank Girozentrale* v. *Islington London Borough Council* (1996)).

The rules of restitution or quasi-contract will also apply where A. has paid C., a third party, money at the request of B. for a contractual liability. But the fact that B. may not have been *bound* to pay the money would not be sufficient grounds for A. to recover, for instance, the payment of an honour debt, a gambling wager or a statute-barred sum of money. The concept of restitution being ordered because the defendant would otherwise unjustly benefit was propounded by Lord Mansfield in *Moses* v. *Macferlan* as long ago as 1760 in a famous dictum that 'the defendant, upon the circumstances of the case, is obliged by the tier of natural justice and equity to refund the money'. The defendant should be required, it was held, to account for benefit gratuitously or improperly obtained, or paid by mistake or forcibly paid by wrongful authority or influence or for a consideration which had wholly failed. It is a concept which is wider and outside the normal rules of contract, and the principle has been questioned; in *Sinclair* v. *Brougham* (1914) Viscount Haldane advanced the concept that the claim must rest on an 'imputed promise' to pay, which has been called the implied contract theory. This view has been followed in a number of cases and has entailed the concept that the claim can only operate where there is some privity of contract, albeit implied perhaps, between the parties.

8.9   Sale and supply of goods

The buying and selling of goods are the most common forms of contractual agreements – the number and variety bear testimony to that statement. Many such transactions are simply oral in nature, or are very frequently of the standard printed form variety. The printed document may be limited to a mere receipt. It should be noted that the 1979 Act does not replace the common law in respect of goods – it is a 'fall-back' provision. In other words as everyday purchases of goods will have nothing more about them than the price and perhaps delivery, and even more complicated commercial transactions are often silent in respect of the consequences of the agreement, so the legislation fills in the gaps in the event of a dispute.

Caveat emptor

Until the nineteenth century virtually the only rule in commercial law was *caveat emptor* – 'let the buyer beware'. The courts were reluctant to interfere with a bargain once it had been struck, however unequal in terms of economic power the parties to the agreement actually were. The *caveat emptor* rule was limited by the Sale of Goods Act 1893 (today the Sale of Goods Act 1979). It was now recognised that the 'everyday customer' needed to be afforded additional legal protection over and above that afforded to the seller. Thus while the principle of *caveat emptor* remains all important, it has over the years been considerably qualified.

Price

Under the 1979 Act the transfer of goods is for a 'money consideration', that is a price. Contracts involving the supply of goods, however, are now also covered in broadly similar terms under the Supply of Goods and Services Act 1982. It is usual, therefore, for an order for goods to remain at the price originally agreed – even if before the delivery date the shop (retailer) has found that the manufacturer (wholesaler) has raised his own price. Such a sale would be absolute, but conditions precedent or subsequent under the general rules of contract law need not necessarily be excluded. If a price is not fixed at the outset, it must be a reasonable one. The problems of reasonableness were shown in *Foley* v. *Classique Coaches* (1934) (an agreement to buy petrol). A 'quotation' is usually a firm price; and 'estimate' does not strictly amount to a fixed price contract, especially where certain work, such as repairs, can only be completely valued once that work has been finished. Under s.49 of the 1979 Act the seller may claim the price of the goods from the buyer, but only if the property in the goods has passed, unless the price is payable irrespective of delivery. Late payment does not entitle the seller to repudiate the contract, unless it is an express condition of the contract. Under the Law Reform (Miscellaneous Provisions) Act 1934 the seller is allowed to claim interest for late payment.

Goods

'Goods', as defined by the 1979 Act, include most tangible things, 'all chattels personal'. That can cover virtually anything from food to works of art, from aeroplanes to pianos, from animals to furniture. It does not include contracts about purely money matters (for example, cheques, mortgages and shares) or contracts involving the sale of services. 'Services', which are now covered by the 1982 Act, include labour, work and skill; materials, for instance paint, used in the performance of that labour or skill cannot be treated separately as a contract of sale of goods. In *Philip Head* v. *Showfronts Ltd* (1969) the fitting of carpets (including their provision) was regarded as a contract of labour. In *Lockett* v. *Charles Ltd* (1983) on the other hand, a hotel meal was a contract of sale of goods.

The distinction between a sale of goods agreement and a contract for the provision of services or labour is less important nowadays. In a contract for services similar implied terms as to reasonable care and skill, performance within a reasonable time and for a reasonable price have been incorporated by the 1982 Act. However, it is true to say that as a general rule the equitable remedy of specific performance is applied more frequently to goods than services, where on occasion damages would prove insufficient, for example for the purchase of a work of art; in general it will not be ordered for a service, although restriction on the provision of certain services to a competitor can be upheld in certain cases. Further, in a contract of sale of goods the seller may be liable for 'product liability', that is he will be strictly liable for defects in the goods, where, for example, those defects cause injury. This is now particularly important in respect of Part I of the Consumer Protection Act 1987 where strict liability is implied in respect of defective products. Products are defined as goods (including substances, growing crops, things attached to land, ships, aircraft or vehicles) or electricity, which have been subject to an industrial process. A defect in a product is defined by the Act as where 'the safety of the product is not such as persons generally are entitled to expect'.

Destruction

If the goods have perished before the agreement is made, then the contract is void, under the normal contractual rules of mistake and frustration; consignment of food is an obvious example here. If the goods in question have never existed at all, as seen earlier in *McRae*, it may be possible to sue for negligent misstatement as formulated in the *Hedley Byrne* case as well as under the tort of deceit.

If goods perish after the agreement has been concluded, then the contract is voidable in certain instances. Otherwise the general contractual rules of frustration and impossibility apply.

Express terms

The categories of conditions and warranties that we have already come across under general contract law apply equally to the sale and supply of goods. And normally once a buyer has accepted the goods he is obliged to treat any breach of condition as a breach of warranty, unless there is a term, express or implied, to the contrary.

Delivery

Goods should normally be delivered within a reasonable time; time may be of the essence in a contract and therefore constitute a condition, as seen in *Charles Rickards* v. *Oppenheim* (1950) involving the late delivery of a car chassis. Equally, the buyer must accept the goods within a reasonable time, unless a time is stipulated.

Under s.51 of the Sale of Goods Act 1979, it is provided that any measure of damages (for the buyer) for failure to deliver at the right time should be based on the difference between the market price at time X. and the subsequent market price at time Y. If prices have fallen in the intervening period then no damages may be awarded. 'The right time' means the delivery date in the contract, or if no time was fixed, the time of refusal to deliver by the seller.

Section 53 lays down that in the case of breach of 'warranty of quality such loss is *prima facie* the difference between the value of the goods at the time of delivery and the value they would have had if they fulfilled the warranty'. Consequential loss will be included in damages where the goods are to be used personally, but not in respect of a straightforward resale.

Where delivery is refused by the buyer, s.48 gives the seller the right to resell the goods: he has a duty to mitigate his loss. If the goods are not perishable he must give the buyer notice of the intended resale.

Section 50 of the Act provides for damages in a similar vein to s.51, in respect of the buyer's failure to accept the goods. If the sale is a private sale, the seller will be indemnified against the loss, that is the difference between the value of the goods and the sale price on a certain date. If the seller is a dealer in the goods, then the court will, under s.50, look at the overall market position. So, in *W L Thompson Ltd* v. *Robinson (Gunmakers) Ltd* (1955) the plaintiffs were car dealers who managed to persuade the wholesalers to take back the car in question. The judge held that as the supply of the cars in question exceeded demand the dealers were still entitled to loss of profit. In contrast, in *Charter* v. *Sullivan* (1957) only nominal damages were awarded where demand exceeded supply.

But the buyer's principal remedy for any breach by the seller is simply to reject the goods. Essentially any such right of rejection must relate to a breach of a condition, or possibly a serious breach of an intermediate term. In *Vaswani* v. *Italian Motors Ltd* (1996) the sellers of a Ferrari car were entitled to keep the deposit and the car where the buyer had failed to pay the balance even though the sellers had increased the price by an incorrect amount.

Under s.34 of the Act the buyer must have a reasonable opportunity of acceptance, otherwise there will not be 'acceptance'. But if, under s.35, the buyer retains the goods for a 'reasonable time', then the 'acceptance' will be deemed to have taken place. In commercial matters, a reasonable time will usually be quite short, although the courts will never give precise guidance. The issue may become more complicated where the consumer attempts to claim under the manufacturer's guarantee; if this route proves unsatisfactory too much time may have elapsed for the buyer to reject the goods as against the seller. Under s.11 the buyer has a right to claim damages rather than reject the goods. In the *Rickards* case the buyer of a Rolls Royce chassis waived the original delivery date (in March). But by June he set down a new date in July. The chassis was delivered in October, and the court held the condition as to time had been breached.

Right to sale and title

The general principle is *nemo dat quod non habet* – a seller cannot confer a good title to goods which he does not possess. But the 1893 Act (as amended by the Supply of Goods (Implied Terms) Act 1973 and consolidated as the Sale of Goods Act 1979) recognised a number of exceptions. In the first place there is implied a condition in every contract of sale that the seller has a 'right to sell'. Section 12(2) of the 1979 Act states there is an implied warranty that 'the goods are free . . . from any charge or encumbrance . . . and the buyer will enjoy quiet possession of the goods . . .' Thus the purchaser may enjoy a legal right to sell goods, but that does not necessarily mean he has a good title. For example, where the seller has a voidable (as opposed to void) title on account of misrepresentation which in most cases turns out to be fraudulent, and where the contract has not been avoided at the time of sale, then the purchaser is given protection of possession, and therefore the right to sell, having thus received a good title. Usually, therefore, transfer of title and the slightly broader concept of the 'right to sell' run together. The purchaser may well have to return the goods to the original owner, but he will have a right to full damages, even though he has used – or even consumed – the goods in question. In *Mason* v. *Burningham* (1949) the plaintiff returned a stolen typewriter to its rightful owner, but successfully sued the seller for both the amount paid and the cost of subsequently repairing the machine. It is the wrongful seller rather than the purchaser who is most at risk in an action for conversion, under the Torts (Interference with Goods) Act 1977.

The problem of passing on a good title frequently occurs in stolen car cases, as seen in *Shaw* below. In a South Wales case, *National Employers' Mutual General Insurance Ltd* v. *Jones* (1988), a stolen car was resold a number of times until purchased in good faith by the defendant. The plaintiff insurance company, to whom the vehicle had been assigned by the owner from whom it had been stolen, demanded delivery or its value. The Court of Appeal (Sir Denys Buckley dissenting) upheld judgment for the plaintiff for the value of the car plus interest, rejecting the defendant's claim to a good title by virtue of s.9 of the Factors Act 1889 (and s.25 of the Sale of Goods Act 1979).

Secondly, under the Hire-Purchase Act 1964 the private purchaser of a car from a hirer who has not completed payments will receive a good title, providing the car was bought in good faith. The strange case of *Butterworth* v. *Kingsway Motors* (1954) underlined this point – the plaintiff sued for the full purchase price given on a hired car, although his own title was protected. Miss A. had sold the car to B.

who resold to C. who sold to Kingsway Motors who then sold to Butterworth who used the car for nearly a year. A few days after Butterworth informed the sellers of the problem and demanded the return of the purchase price, Miss A. completed the payments. But Butterworth's letter indicated that there had been a total failure of consideration and the car therefore returned to Kingsway Motors, although the plaintiff had had free use of the vehicle. Kingsway Motors, C. and B. obtained the appropriate damages from each respective seller. But the court's decision was questionable and this case occurred some years before the 1964 Act ever reached the statute book; the only statute that could be relied upon was the 1893 Act itself, together with any relevant common law principles. But the 1893 Act could hardly be conceived as covering hired car situations, hence the 1964 legislation.

Thirdly, under the Sale of Goods Act the seller is strictly liable for defects in title, for example, for failure to give quiet possession. Ignorance of such defects is no excuse. Alternatively, since the amending legislation of 1973 it has been possible for the seller to intend transfer of only limited title, but subject to implied warranties in the contract that all charges on the goods known to the seller have been made clear to the buyer and that the buyer will enjoy quiet possession. This rule gives less protection to the consumer, especially in standard form agreements, than where the seller impliedly intends to transfer 'full title'. If the vendor, however, purports to transfer full title he, as seller, will be clearly penalised in favour of the purchaser where that buyer's right either to sell or to own (or both) is breached.

Fourthly, the Sale of Goods Act recognises, in accordance with the principles of estoppel, that where the owner of the goods has negligently or fraudulently represented that the seller of the goods is entitled to sell those goods (and as a result of that misrepresentation the purchaser has been induced to buy) then the buyer receives a good title.

The problems of 'sale' and 'title' were recognised in *Shaw* v. *Commissioner of Police of the Metropolis* (1987). Here the plaintiffs agreed to buy a car for £11,500 to be paid by a banker's draft for £10,000 with the balance in cash, from one 'Jonathan London'. The bank refused to cash the draft and London disappeared. London had responded to an advertisement placed by the claimant, a Mr A.D.H. Natalegawa, an Indonesian student about to return home, offering his car for sale for £17,250. 'London' had called on the student, saying he was a car dealer, and the student let him have the car, a red Porsche.

The banker's draft was never cashed and the bank reimbursed the plaintiffs on the understanding if the draft should be presented the plaintiffs would indemnify the bank. The car had come into the possession of the police. The Court of Appeal held that it would be wrong for the plaintiffs (Shaw and Nidd Vale Motors) to obtain the car for nothing, indeed they had gained £1,500 in cash. The plaintiffs could not rely on s.25 of the Sale of Goods Act 1979 (a second purchaser will be protected if he buys in good faith and without notice of the previous sale) nor upon s.21 which provided that a buyer might acquire good title if the owner by his conduct was precluded from denying the seller's authority to sell. If the plaintiffs had bought the car the Court should have held that they had acquired good title against the claimant, and in practice all the world, by virtue of s.21, or alternatively, by virtue of common law estoppel by representation (if different at all). Transfer of possession was not enough: the plaintiffs had never been the lawful owners of the car; though the claimant had been exceptionally gullible, it would offend the Court's sense of justice if he were to lose the car.

Description and sample

Under the 1979 and 1982 Acts the goods must correspond with any description given – including packaging, labelling, photographs, quantities, shipment and, perhaps most important of all, samples. A sample (s.15) must correspond with the bulk of the goods. In contrast, s.13(2) of the 1979 Act states that if the sale is by sample as well as by description it is not sufficient that the bulk of the goods corresponds with the sample if the goods do not also correspond with the description. Section 15(2) states that the buyer must have a reasonable opportunity of comparing the bulk with the sample. Thus if you order ten BMW cars (on the basis of one seen in the showroom) and you receive nine BMW cars and one Datsun you may be entitled to repudiate the whole contract if the seller cannot supply the vital tenth BMW.

The decision in *Harlingdon* further blurs the distinction between sales by description under s.13, and misrepresentations of fact. The distinction is important in that a breach of s.13 will entitle a party (usually the buyer) to repudiate the contract and claim damages, whereas by merely establishing a misrepresentation of fact, the buyer may be limited to a claim for damages. By virtue of the Misrepresentation Act 1967, s.2(2), a court may award damages in lieu of rescission of the contract. Thus the court has a discretion whether or not to grant rescission. In *Harlingdon and Leinster Enterprises Ltd* v. *Christopher Hull Fine Art Ltd* (1990), it will be recalled that the Court of Appeal (Lord Justice Stuart-Smith dissenting) found that the buyers had not relied on the description of a forged painting to be one by Gabriele Munter, bringing the sale under s.13(1) of the Sale of Goods Act 1979 (sale by description), and they had failed to establish the painting was not of merchantable quality under ss.14(2) and 14(6) of the Act.

Merchantable quality, fitness of purpose

Where goods are sold in the course of *business*, but not by a private individual, the 1893 Act provided an important exception to the *caveat emptor* rule. Agents of private individuals are not necessarily excluded, however, although auction sales, like competitive tenders, cannot constitute consumer sales. It said that such goods must be of merchantable quality, unless either certain defects had been drawn to the buyer's attention before the sale took place or the buyer had made a reasonable examination of the goods before acceptance. 'Merchantable quality' was not defined until the 1973 amending Act, as now consolidated under the 1979 Act, s.14(6). The definition was not exhaustive. Merchantable quality would, however, be related to all the circumstances of the case – price, description and purpose for which the goods were bought. Generally speaking, we can say that merchantable quality meant sound quality, a suitable standard. Goods only needed to be fit for any one of their ordinary purposes for them to be of merchantable quality, as emphasised by the Court of Appeal in *Aswan Engineering Establishment Co.* v. *Lupdine Ltd* (1987), where plastic pails containing liquid waterproofing compound for export collapsed on account of the high temperature on the quayside at Kuwait, leading to the loss of the entire consignment. In considering whether a second-hand car was of merchantable quality for the purposes of the Sale of Goods Act 1979 the appropriate test was not to be limited to its state of roadworthiness but was to include the wider definition contained in s.14(6) of the Act that required all the circumstances to be taken into consideration, so stated the Court of Appeal in *Business Application Specialists Ltd* v. *Nationwide Credit Corporation Ltd* (1988).

Satisfactory quality

The 1979 Act also provided by s.14, that the goods must be fit for the purpose for which they were manufactured and sold, unless it can be shown that the buyer did not, or could not reasonably, rely on the seller's skill or judgement.

The Sale and Supply of Goods Act 1994 has changed the 1979 Act; s.1 of the 1994 Act has amended s.14 of the 1979 legislation which now reads in s.14(2): 'where goods are sold in the course of a business there is an implied term that goods are of satisfactory quality'. Satisfactory quality is defined as being of a standard that a reasonable person would regard as satisfactory having regard to description, price and all other relevant circumstances. But under s.14(2)(C) the implied terms will not apply if the defects had been drawn to the buyer's attention, or if the buyer examined the goods beforehand and the examination revealed or ought to have revealed such defects. The Sale of Goods (Amendment) Act 1994 abolished the rule relating to the sale of goods in market overt; the Sale of Goods (Amendment) Act 1995 amending the 1979 legislation dealt with the difficulties faced by an unsecured creditor in respect of the sale of goods out of a specified bulk.

Similarly, all food for sale must be fit for human consumption, and strict liability is imposed here under the Food Act 1984. Under the Food Safety Act 1990, which repealed part of the Food Act 1984, s.15(1) provides:

> **Any person who gives with any food sold by him, or displays with any food offered or exposed by him for sale or in his possession for the purpose of sale, a label, whether or not attached to or printed on the wrapper or container, which (*a*) falsely describes the food; or (*b*) is likely to mislead as to the nature or substance or quality of the food, shall be guilty of an offence.**

Section 15(2) says:

> **Any person who publishes, or is a party to the publication of, an advertisement (not being such a label given or displayed by him as mentioned (1) above) which (*a*) falsely describes any food; or (*b*) is likely to mislead as to the nature or substance or quality of any food, shall be guilty of an offence**

and, under s.15(3),

> **any person who sells, or offers or exposes for sale, or has in his possession for the purpose of sale, any food the presentation of which is likely to mislead as to the nature or substance or quality of the food shall be guilty of an offence.**

To return to s.14 of the 1979 Act, it certainly can be said that a car sold without an engine is hardly capable of displaying satisfactory quality. In *Shine* v. *General Guarantee Corporation* (1987) the Court of Appeal held that in considering whether a car was of merchantable quality it was necessary to look not only at the mechanical and other condition of the car, but to stand back and ask what the purchaser was entitled to think he was buying. The plaintiff bought a 'superb' Fiat X19 sports car, but was understandably ignorant of the fact the car had been submerged in water, and was a write-off for insurance purposes. A car was not just a means of transport; it was also a form of investment, although a deteriorating one, and, said Mr Justice Bush, every purchaser must have in mind its eventual saleability, and in the plaintiff's case, his pride in it as a specialist car for the enthusiast. So, 'the merest cosmetic blemish on a new Rolls Royce might render it unmerchantable, whereas it might not on a humbler car', said Mr Justice Rougier in *Bernstein* v. *Pamsons Motors (Golders Green) Ltd* (1987). A vehicle is not of merchantable quality simply because it can be driven from place to place since in relation to a passenger vehicle, regard must be had to the degree of comfort, ease of handling and reliability and the owner's pride in the vehicle's outward and interior appearance. In addition, the fact that the buyer is entitled to have the defects remedied under a warranty has no bearing on whether the vehicle is of merchantable quality or not at the time of delivery, *Rogers* v. *Parish (Scarborough) Ltd* (1987). The leading cases on merchantable quality are *Grant* v. *Australian Knitting Mills* (the itchy pants case – sulphite in wool causing dermatitis) and *Chaproniere* v. *Mason* (1905) (a stone in a bath bun). Contrast *Griffiths* v. *Peter Conway Ltd* (1939), where the plaintiff's failure to disclose the fact that her skin was very sensitive was material; the decision in Griffiths was approved and extended by the House of Lords in *Slater* v. *Finning Ltd* (1996), where an implied condition as to fitness for purpose did not require goods to cope with abnormal and undisclosed circumstances of their planned use (in this instance a repair to an engine in a fishing boat).

Second-hand goods (or 'seconds' in shops) must still be of merchantable quality and fit for their purpose. But satisfactory quality will only be for a reasonable length of time, and what constitutes a reasonable length of time in the case of second-hand goods is particularly open-ended. It should be noted here that in the case of new goods a manufacturer's guarantee, while of practical aid to the consumer, is of little legal relevance.

The consumer may be protected where goods are bought for a specific purpose that he, as buyer, has in mind. For example, if a customer buys a particular type of glue to mend bone china, he will have no redress if the retailer explained that the glue 'might not work'; if on the other hand the retailer had said, 'that will do the trick', then the buyer would be in a very different position. The buyer will not be protected, though, if it was understood that he would alter the goods in some way in order to meet particular requirements. In the same way emulsion paint bought to paint the outside of a house may be of merchantable quality, but not fit for that purpose.

Fitness of purpose carried with it strictness of liability on the part of the seller, that is, normally, the retailer. Like merchantable quality fitness of purpose was always an implied condition, unless there were exceptional circumstances where it would not be reasonable to rely upon the seller's skill or judgement (as in *Henry Kendall and Sons* v. *William Lillico and Sons Ltd* (1969), a matter of poisonous groundnut extract). It is no defence to show that no ordinary skill or reasonable care could have prevented the injury caused. Thus a tin of poisonous corned beef will lead to a claim for medical expenses, loss of wages and general compensation, notwithstanding the fact that the seller would have been required to open up every tin of corned beef in the shop to discover – possibly – the toxic matter. The implied terms as to merchantable quality or fitness of purpose were incorporated into contracts for the supply of goods by the 1982 Act, as amended.

A recent case neatly illustrating the 'merchantable quality' and 'fitness of purpose' concepts was *Wormell* v. *RHM Agriculture (East) Ltd* (1987): a farmer bought some £6,500 worth of weedkiller to deal with wild oats infesting wheat; this proved to be totally ineffective outside the recommended period. It was easier here to sue under the Sale of Goods Act 1979, independently of fault, rather than prove negligence against the manufacturers. However, the Court of Appeal, overturning the decision of the trial judge, said that the manufacturers had given a clear warning about the risks of late spraying, and therefore, the plaintiff could not claim the herbicide was not reasonably fit for its purpose.

Strictness of liability was invariably the retailer's not the manufacturer's. In *Frost* v. *Aylesbury Dairy Co. Ltd* (1905) it was accepted that no extra care would have enabled the dairy to detect that the milk from which Mrs Frost died was contaminated with typhoid germs. We should note here, however, that it was her husband who was the buyer. He successfully sued for the loss of his wife's 'services'. Had Mrs Frost lived she would have had no right to compensation from the seller, for the rule of privity of contract prevailed in English law as we have already seen. Moreover, actions for 'loss of services' were abolished by the

Administration of Justice Act 1982. Nonetheless it can be argued that in a few cases the rule of privity has been re-interpreted. For example, in *Jackson* v. *Horizon Holidays Ltd* (1975) damages were awarded on account of the distress that the plaintiff and his family suffered from a holiday that went badly wrong.

Of course, it may be that the retailer will in turn successfully sue the wholesaler or manufacturer, as illustrated by *Godley* v. *Perry* (1960) which involved a retailer, importer and manufacturer; a plastic catapult had caused injury to a boy's eye.

Liability

But what of the manufacturer's liability? Until recently to prove liability on the part of the manufacturer was much harder, for it was necessary to prove fault (negligence). Strict liability did not exist here, despite the recommendations of the Pearson Commission in 1978. And without working on the factory floor itself, the plaintiff may find fault difficult to prove. The titanic struggles in the thalidomide tragedy, against the Distillers Company, underline that point. The manufacturer's liability in tort, in respect of negligence, was, as we have seen earlier, widened in the famous case of *Donoghue* v. *Stevenson*. Now, however, the position has been substantially altered by the Consumer Protection Act 1987, which under Part I provides for strict product liability, in civil law, of manufacturers and all concerned in the chain of sales, in the course of business, as wholesalers and retailers, for defective products, but not the private producer (for example, of home-made jam at the local charity or Women's Institute). There is a limitation period of three years for claims from the time the plaintiff would reasonably have had knowledge of the damage, and no action may be brought after 10 years from the 'relevant time', that is from when the product was put into circulation, at which point the defect did not as such exist.

Further, not only the purchaser but members of the family or strangers are all owed a duty of care and are able to sue primary or substitute defendants. 'Damage' includes death or personal injury, or loss of or damage to any property (including land). 'Products' under the 1987 Act do not include agricultural produce unless it has been subjected to an industrial process; it has not been clear whether pasteurisation of milk in a dairy constitutes an industrial process, but logically the manufacture of powdered milk should be so treated. The exemption would cover such matters as fish affected by pollutants. The plaintiff does not have a claim if it appears he has grossly misused the product. Section 4 of the Act lists the various defences available in civil liability under Part I of the Act, including the defence that the state of scientific and technical knowledge at the time when the product was supplied was not such that a producer of products of the same description as the product in question might be expected to have discovered such a defect – the controversial so-called 'state of the art' defence. This is particularly important for drug companies, where side-effects of a new drug may not be discovered for some time. So it may be that liability in these cases remains based on negligence (tort), although effectively the burden of proof is reversed.

Strict liability had also been imposed upon a manufacturer under the Consumer Safety Act 1978 as extended by the Consumer Safety (Amendment) Act 1986. (In the USA strictness of manufacturer's liability has been more commonplace.) The Act empowered the Secretary of State to make regulations regarding the safety of manufactured goods and the supply of dangerous goods. Regulations have been issued covering domestic heating appliances, crayons, children's nightdresses, electric blankets, and other materials. If a trader fails to comply with a regulation or prohibition order or notice, the injured party has a civil remedy (which cannot be excluded) over and above general rights in contract and negligence. Part II of the 1987 Act consolidated the 1978 and 1986 legislation, and implemented a general safety requirement under s.10, primarily to be enforced by criminal sanctions. Goods are regarded as complying with the general safety requirement if they comply with any safety regulations, approved safety standards or relevant subordinate legislation.

It is also possible – but more remotely so – for a manufacturer who has made an express but general offer to be held liable, despite the rules under privity of contract. *Carlill* v. *Carbolic Smoke Ball Company* (1893), where the manufacturer promised a payment in the event of their medicine not curing anyone suffering from influenza, was an example of such liability (collateral contract).

Exclusion

1. Under the Unfair Contract Terms Act 1977 (s.6) it is not possible to exclude liability for implied conditions, such as those mentioned above regarding merchantable quality, fitness of goods, title (right to sell), description and sample. This applies where the sale is a 'consumer sale'. A consumer sale is defined as one made by the seller in the ordinary course of his business. The goods must be of the type usually supplied for private use or consumption and therefore not bought by another trader. A 'non-consumer' sale is one between two traders, that is where both parties act 'in the course of business'. The provisions apply, unless otherwise stated, to contracts for the sale, supply and hire-purchase of goods. Transactions between consumers (that is private individuals) are not therefore covered by the Act. Sale of goods falls under s.6, supply and so on under s.7.

2. In the case of non-consumer sales any attempt to exclude an implied condition as to title is absolutely void. But other implied conditions, such as quality, sample, description and fitness, may be excluded if it is reasonable to do so. The test of reasonableness is 'defined' in the Act: overall, under guidelines in s.11(2) (Schedule 2), the court must take into account such things as the strength of the parties' bargaining positions, having regard to the availability of alternative suppliers; where the term excludes or restricts any relevant liability if some condition is not complied with, whether it was reasonable at the time of the contract to expect that compliance with that condition would be practicable; the customer's awareness or ignorance of the exclusion clause, having regard to any custom of the trade and any previous course of dealing between the parties; the customer's special requirements in respect of the manufacture of the goods;

whether the customer received any inducement to agree to such a term. The question of insurance cover arises under s.11(4).

These guidelines in respect of 'reasonableness' strictly only relate to exclusion or the restriction of liability for the breach of implied obligations in contracts of sale of goods and hire-purchase and contracts of supply under ss.6 and 7. But the guidelines in practice are applied to other parts of the Act where the reasonableness requirement arises, as outlined under ss.11(1) and 11(3). The guidelines are not intended to be exhaustive. Under s.11(5) it is for those who claim that a contract term or notice satisfies the reasonableness requirement to show that it does. The test of reasonableness under s.3 was illustrated in *St Albans City and District Council* v. *International Computers Ltd* (1996), where the district council lost £3.1 million but owed £685,000 to Hertfordshire County Council as the result of defective computer software supplied by ICL, with liability being limited to £100,000.

Descriptions in both consumer and non-consumer sales must be reasonably clear, of course. In *Corfield* v. *Starr* (1981) an odometer in a car displayed a figure of 35,000, but its true figure was 55,000. A disclaimer read: 'With deep regret due to the Consumer's Protection Act we can no longer verify that the mileage shown on this vehicle is correct'. The court held that the disclaimer was not clear – it included a reference to a non-existent Act of Parliament. In *R.* v. *Southwood* (1987) the appellant was a dealer in second-hand motor cars and was convicted of applying a false trade description, under s.1(1a) of the Trade Descriptions Act 1968, by reducing the mileage on the odometer on 10 cars. The Court of Appeal held that a disclaimer could not be relied upon in this instance.

3. An exclusion clause in a contract with a consumer or on standard form terms is subject to the reasonableness test where it purports to exclude liability for breach of contract or failure of performance either totally or in the way originally contemplated by the parties (s.3).

4. The burden of proving that a party did not deal as a consumer rests firmly upon the party seeking to rely upon the exemption clause, s.12(3).

5. The Act also stipulates that liability for death or personal injury resulting from a party's negligence cannot be excluded by a contractual term or by notices on display, s.2(1). Other losses arising from negligence are subject to the reasonableness test, s.2(2). Negligence is defined under s.1, and includes a failure to exercise reasonable care and skill in the performance of a contract.

6. The 1977 Act (s.4) says that a *consumer* cannot under contract be made to indemnify another person for loss arising from breach of contract or negligence unless the contract term in question satisfies the reasonableness test. Similarly, loss or damage arising from negligent manufacture of consumer goods cannot be excluded or restricted in a manufacturer's warranty or guarantee, providing the manufacturer did not sell directly to the consumer (s.5).

7. The Act also under s.8 amended the Misrepresentation Act 1967 by stating that all exemption clauses which seek to exclude liability for general contractual

misrepresentation may not be relied upon, unless the 'reasonableness' test is satisfied. It is not necessary for one party to be a 'consumer'.

8. It should be noted that under Schedule 1 certain forms of contract are excluded wholly or partially from the Act's provisions – that is arbitration agreements, commercial charterparties and carriage of goods by sea, employment contracts, the creation or transfer of interests in land or securities, insurance contracts and the dissolution or formation of companies and partnerships.

9. Finally, the Act (s.7) extends to contracts of not only hire but also services and labour. Where a person deals as a consumer, liability cannot be excluded in respect of any term implied in relation to description/sample, satisfactory quality. Where he deals as a non-consumer then exclusion may operate if it satisfies the reasonableness test. Liability in respect of the transfer of ownership (implied terms as to title) or the assurance of quiet possession under such contracts is also subject to the reasonableness test. Under s.7(3A) liability cannot be excluded in respect of implied terms as to title etc. in contracts for the supply (transfer) of goods under s.2 of the 1982 Act. It should be noted that the courts have for long been prepared to imply into service contracts a condition that a professional person or craftsman must exercise skills reasonably and competently.

The EC Directive on unfair contract terms came into force in 1995. The Directive takes a broader approach than the provisions under the 1977 Act, in terms of a general standard of fairness. Article 3 says:

> **A contractual term which has not been individually negotiated shall be regarded as unfair if, contrary to the requirement of good faith, it causes a significant imbalance in the parties' rights and obligations arising under the contract, to the detriment of the consumer.**

By way of the Directive the Director General of Fair Trading has new powers to investigate offending terms.

The Defective Premises Act 1972 stipulates that building work must be done in a workmanlike manner and that completed dwellings must be suitably fit for habitation.

The relationship of 'fundamental breach' of contract to exclusion clauses and the importance of the *Photo Production* case have already been noted.

Misrepresentation

The essential elements of misrepresentation have been covered above in the main body of contract law and under tort.

DISCUSSION POINTS

1 Consider whether Lord Denning's observations are an accurate reflection of what is understood by contractual mistake,

2 How can a contract be frustrated?

3 How wide is the concept of duress in the law of contract?

TABLE OF CASES

TABLE OF STATUTES

ADDENDUM

Some additional cases may be taken note of, that were unable to be inserted into the main text at the time of writing:

1. In *O'Rourke* v. *Camden London Borough Council* [1997] 3 All ER 23 the House of Lords again highlighted the difficulties of drawing a distinction in housing cases between private and public law; there was some criticism of Lord Bridge's remarks in *Cocks* v. *Thanet District Council*.

2. *Smith and New Court Securities Ltd* v. *Citibank NA* [1997] AC 254 was a House of Lords' decision concerning the assessment of damages arising out of fraudulent misrepresentation.

3. With regard to the relationship between provocation and diminished responsibility in *R.* v. *Campbell (No. 2)* [1997] 1 Cr App Rep 199 the Court of Appeal refused to be bound by the Privy Council case of *Luc Thiet Thuan* v. *The Queen* (1996), but followed its own previous decisions.

4. The operation of precedent in the High Court arose in *R* v. *Governor of Brockhill Prison ex parte Evans* [1997] 1 All ER 439, where a previous decision was departed from.

5. In *R* v. *Powell and English* [1997] 3 WLR 959, two cases involving killings arising from drug-dealing or drug-taking, the House of Lords gave further consideration to the liability of secondary parties for murder and causing grievous bodily harm on the part of the primary party in the light of the principles of *Chan Wing-Su* (1995), and it was noted Parliament had not tackled the issue of law reform in homicide.

6. In *Bolitho* v. *City and Hackney Health Authority* [1997] 4 All ER 771 the House of Lords examined the duty of care again on the part of doctors in the light of the Bolam test.

7. Juries should be guided by the judge in assessing exemplary and aggravated damages for unlawful conduct by the police: *Thompson* v. *Commissioner of Police of the Metropolis* [1997] 2 All ER 762.

8. *R* v. *Parliamentary Commissioner for Standards ex parte Al Fayed* [1998] 1 WLR 669 illustrated the testing of the new office of Parliamentary Standards Commissioner.

9. Foreseeability of risk, here a playground accident, was underlined in *Mullin* v. *Richards* [1998] 1 WLR 1304.

10. *Hunter* v. *British Coal Corporation* [1998] 2 All ER 97 was a case again illustrating the judicial problems surrounding nervous shock.

11. *Economides* v. *Commercial Union Assurance plc.* [1997] 3 WLR 1066 concerned misrepresentation.

12. *Jolley* v. *London Borough of Sutton* [1998] 1 WLR 1546 – see *The Times*, 23 June – was an important decision on occupiers' liability.

An example of Parliament acting in almost undue haste was in September 1998 when both Houses were recalled to pass further anti-terrorist legislation in three days, in the wake of the Omagh bombing, being targeted largely at the Real IRA – the Criminal Justice (Terrorism and Conspiracy) Act 1998.

The Crime and Disorder Act 1998 provides for the offences of racially aggravated assaults under s.29 and and racially aggravated criminal damage under s.30; s.31 provides for racially aggravated public order offences (under ss.4, 4A and 5 of the Public Order Act 1986 as amended by the Criminal Justice and Public Order Act 1994), whilst s.32 amends the Protection from Harassment Act 1997 by establishing the offence of racially aggravated harassment.

The European Communities (Amendment) Act 1998 gives statutory recognition to the Treaty of Amsterdam.

At the time of completing the script in the summer of 1998, the Government was promising a major White Paper on legal services and the legal aid scheme. The Middleton Report (on the consequence of Woolf) in 1997 was critical of the civil justice system and stressed the need for both the criminal and civil legal aid schemes to be developed under contracts between the Legal Aid Board and approved suppliers, and there should be a greater emphasis on ADR. The Civil Justice Council should be strengthened, a Community Legal Service established and conditional fee arrangements should become available for all civil proceedings. The limits of fast-track and small claims should be raised.

The Bowman Report was published in 1997 on the organisation of the civil division of the Court of Appeal, a number of the recommendations being quite technical, but aimed at streamlining the procedures for dealing with applications for leave to appeal and to develop initiatives to clear the backlog of cases. Nonetheless, the Bowman report and the two consultation papers issued as a result by the Lord Chancellor in July 1998 are fundamental to the civil justice reforms and the appeal process, and although not acted upon at the time of completing this script in September 1998, deserve careful attention by students, as well as the White Paper Modernising Justice, and the Access to Justice Bill in December 1998.

The Glidewell Report in 1998 was very critical about the CPS in that it was too bureaucratic and over-centralised, and that there had to be a re-organisation and more co-operation with the police about which cases were prosecuted.

Derek Bentley was given a posthumous pardon – see *The Times*, 12 June 1998.

In the earlier part of 1998 the Government published proposals to reform the jury system in complex fraud trials, thus reviving the Roskill debate of 1986.

Also, the House of Lords' decision in *White (Frost) v. Chief Constable of South Yorkshire Police* [1998] 3 WLR 1509 (arising from the Hillsborough tragedy in respect of nervous shock) is critical, in December 1998; whilst at the same time the Pinochet rehearing was remarkable.

INDEX

BARRY COLLEGE
LRC

17 MAY 2020

WITHDRAWN
FROM STOCK